The speaker's resource book

an anthology, handbook, and glossary

CARROLL C. ARNOLD
The Pennsylvania State University

DOUGLAS EHNINGER
The University of Iowa

JOHN C. GERBER
The University of Iowa

SCOTT, FORESMAN AND COMPANY

Chicago ▪ *Atlanta* ▪ *Dallas* ▪ *Palo Alto* ▪ *Fair Lawn, N.J.*

L. C. Catalog Card #66-11092

Foreword

The beginning student of public speaking will find that advice on how to make a speech is plentiful—and sometimes inconsistent. But he can be reasonably sure that all reliable advisers will urge him to listen to good speakers, read many speeches carefully, and practice making speeches as often as possible. The second edition of *The Speaker's Resource Book*, like the first edition, is based on these principles. It combines the features of an anthology and a guidebook. It tries to serve college students of oral communication by making their study of speeches convenient and purposeful, and it points to ways of achieving challenging content in their own practice speeches.

The first edition of *The Speaker's Resource Book* was planned primarily for use either as a basic textbook or as an auxiliary work to accompany any good textbook on public speaking. The experience of teachers and students demonstrated, however, that the book was also a useful sourcebook for studies in rhetorical theory at both undergraduate and graduate levels. Accordingly, the editors have represented additional forms of discourse and have considerably enlarged the Glossary of Rhetorical Terms in this second edition. In so doing, their ambition has been to preserve all features that made the first edition useful in basic courses while enhancing the resources that are of chief value when the book is used for advanced studies.

In coverage and organization *The Speaker's Resource Book* continues to reflect the editors' conviction that whoever would learn the art of speaking must understand the social nature of speaking, must study models critically, and must carry content as well as method from his reading to his practice. The new edition, like the first, provides a consideration of speech as a subject for study and as a social force; a collection of over forty speeches that can be used as models, as objects for criticism, and as sources of ideas; guidance in analyzing speeches; suggestions on composing and delivering speeches; and information about the theory of communication.

The opening section, The Study of Speech, explores speech as an academic study and as a social art. Its four speeches and accompanying introductions and questions also serve to introduce the anthology proper—Speeches for Analysis and Ideas.

In choosing the selections in Speeches for Analysis and Ideas the editors first looked for materials likely to provoke discussion and suggest ideas for students' speeches. Their second criterion was: Does the complete collection of speeches exemplify the variety of rhetorical problems and situational demands the modern public speaker confronts? To provide revealing comparisons and contrasts this edition includes some classic addresses, three essays, six student speeches made in different settings, one example of a public discussion, and a controversial type of press conference. The selections are accompanied by (1) a brief introduction containing information about the speaker, the audience, and the occasion; (2) questions drawing attention to the compositional problems confronting the speaker and additional questions inviting the student speaker to probe the topic in search of new ideas for his own speeches; and (3) a reading list from which the student may begin to pursue the general subject further.

The last three sections summarize the leading principles of speech criticism, composition, and delivery. The section, Analyses of Three Speeches, illustrates alternative methods of studying and evaluating a speech. The Student's Handbook of Public Speaking recommends procedures to be followed in composing and delivering a speech. In the enlarged Glossary of Rhetorical Terms, only the most elemental concepts relating to delivery are included, but virtually all other rhetorical concepts consistently discussed in contemporary books on public speaking are now identified, defined, and, where possible, illustrated. To this extent the Glossary is a comprehensive inventory of the principal features of the theory of oral communication. Its main entries may profitably be used as the foci of classroom discussion when theory is at issue. When criticism of speeches is the subject of study, headnotes and questions appended to the speeches will direct the student's attention to appropriate sections of the Glossary for explanations of concepts necessary in making critical judgments. Wherever possible, cross-references to passages in the anthology have been supplied to provide illustrations of the concepts and practices defined in the Glossary.

Editorial responsibilities

The editors believe it is desirable to represent alternative approaches to the study of speeches, since no one mode of analysis is likely to reveal all the resources of an oral communication. Although they planned the book together, consulted frequently during its development, and read and criticized one another's materials, each editor took responsibility for specific parts of the volume and allowed his own approach to the problems of communication to be reflected in his work. In short, the editors have aimed at stimulating the reader through variety both in rhetorical materials and in editorial method.

Professors Arnold and Ehninger were responsible for The Study of Speech. In Speeches for Analysis and Ideas Professor Gerber was responsible for the sections on Education, The Arts, Science, and Ethics and Morals; Professor Ehninger for the section on Social Problems and for the new section on America and the World; Professor Arnold for the sections on The Media of Mass Communication and Politics. All three editors contributed definitions and illustrations for the Glossary, but Professors Ehninger and Arnold took major responsibility for its development and final form. The Student's Handbook contains the ideas and language of more than a dozen persons associated with the teaching of public speaking at Cornell University. The editors alone are responsible for the present form of this material, but they gratefully acknowledge their borrowings of thought and phrase. The analysis of Huxley's speech was prepared by Professor Walter Blair of the University of Chicago, General MacArthur's speech was analyzed by Professor Ehninger, and Jonathan Smith's speech by Professor Arnold.

Acknowledgments

For suggestions and advice, the editors are grateful to many persons. However, they wish to express their special appreciation to the speakers and publishers who very kindly granted permission to reprint their addresses in this book, and to the following people who contributed helpful suggestions for this second edition: Herman Cohen, Carl A. Dallinger, Ralph T. Eubanks, James W. Gibson, David Potter, William D. Smith, and John F. Wilson.

CCA
DE
JCG

Contents

6 / ETHICS AND MORALS

7 / POLITICS

8 / AMERICA AND THE WORLD

ANALYSES OF THREE SPEECHES

293 STUDENT'S HANDBOOK OF PUBLIC SPEAKING

Classification of the speeches according to purpose*

*Any classification of speeches according to purpose or intent is necessarily open to dispute. The precise balance of a speaker's intentions is not always obvious, the terms with which such intentions can be described are numerous, and few speeches exhibit a single, exclusive purpose throughout. Occasions for speechmaking, too, can be variously described. Therefore, the classifications that follow are suggestive only. For other possible systems of classification, see the Glossary entries *Ends of Speaking*, p. 307, and *Occasion*, p. 313.

Classification of the speeches according to occasion

The study of speech

Speech as a liberal study

CARROLL C. ARNOLD

The editors of *The Speaker's Resource Book* hope that those who read this volume will derive new insights into how speeches are formed and how composition helps to determine the effect of a speech. Some, we dare to hope, may even form a comprehensive view of that intricate occurrence, persuasion through oral discourse.

It is of practical importance to be able to compose a valid argument, to manage one's body while speaking, to make an acceptable "s" sound, and to acquire the many other specific skills that render one a competent communicator. But to learn such things as isolated skills without exploring the whole event of communication is to miss much that the study of speechmaking can reveal about mankind. There are large questions, as well as small ones, that need to be asked as one begins the study of speeches. What makes a speech different from other kinds of communication? Why do some speeches influence listeners and others fail? What are the differences among audiences, and how far do these differences control what speakers may or may not do with ideas? True, these are social and psychological questions, but they are intensely relevant to the study of speeches, for public speeches are always attempts at social control.

A speech may illustrate the devices of composition, but behind each choice of a compositional device there lies a bit of drama concerning the speaker's courtship of his reluctant listener. He pits his wish against the listener's inclination, chooses or fails to choose an action appropriate to the hearer's disposition, and thereby wins or loses much of his suit. Thus the scenes are played, the speaker's success hinging always upon the sureness of his adaptive skill and his understanding of his listener's nature. It is from observing such successes and failures that students of speaking begin to acquire the qualifications which Plato insisted the fully formed speaker must possess: "Such and such persons, he will say, are affected by this or that kind of speech in this or that way—and he will tell you why."

The selection "Speech as a Liberal Study" is placed at the head of this anthology of public addresses because it argues that all academic study of speech and drama should have as its ultimate goal the discovery of the kinds of effects speech may have—and why. This address was delivered to the General Speech Division of the Pennsylvania Speech Association, meeting in Philadelphia on October 17, 1959. It was the opening speech in a symposium-forum on the subject "Is Speech a Liberal Art?" Fred B. Millett,

professor emeritus of Wesleyan University (Connecticut), replied to Professor Arnold's remarks, contending that speaking and writing are remedial studies unfortunately necessary in American colleges but without any "liberal" content of their own. Following the formal presentations, the two speakers engaged in informal discussion and debate, with members of the audience participating. Those attending the program were chiefly teachers and students of speech.

When reading this address, it is important to remember that the audience was presumably biased in favor of Arnold's general position. For this reason he chose not to anticipate Millett's specific arguments even though he was fully acquainted with them before the program began. Arnold tried instead to prod his listeners toward a critical evaluation of their own objectives in teaching and studying speech. Whether his "defense" of a somewhat sociological approach to the study of speech could affect his hearers as he intended is the kind of question Plato believed a qualified student of public speaking should be able to answer.

Carroll C. Arnold was born at Lake Park, Iowa, in 1912. He received his B.A. from Sioux Falls College in 1933 and his M.A. in 1940 and Ph.D. in 1942 from the State University of Iowa. From 1946 to June 1963, he was on the faculty at Cornell University, where he was Professor and Chairman of the Department of Speech and Drama. He is presently Professor of Speech at The Pennsylvania State University. Throughout his professional career he has been chiefly interested in the theory and criticism of speech composition; he has also written and spoken on such subjects as group discussion and general speech education.

Arnold's speech is printed here from the manuscript he used in delivering the address, edited to represent as exactly as possible the changes introduced in the actual presentation.

Good morning. I thank you for inviting me to join you in your convention. I especially thank you and Professor Millett for the privilege of appearing here with so distinguished a visitor. /1

I wish I were as sure about the meaning of our basic terms this morning as I am sure that Professor Millett and I enter this discussion sharing a strong allegiance to the educational aspirations that are always connoted by those sometimes imprecise phrases "liberal education" and "liberal arts." My view is that the academic study called Speech is capable of making major contributions to an undergraduate's understanding of what *he* is like, how he may constructively direct a significant portion of his energies, and what constitutes the social environment in which he lives. I tend to think these things make Speech a "liberal study," even though I despair of finding a neat and precise definition of what a liberal study is. /2

Let me make one other preliminary observation. When I speak of "speech" this morning, I have always in mind the full range of Man's speech behavior—the act of utterance, the symbol system of spoken language, the integration of matter and manner in spoken discourse, and dramatic communication in which discourse among characters is a central means of furthering the dramatic action. /3

Now, let me pose two elementary questions to open an exploration of how significant it may be to understand Man's speech behavior. When Man vibrates his glottal closure and manipulates his nasopharyngeal cavities in order to signal someone else, have these events psychological and social implications of a fundamental sort? Or are they events of marginal significance, comparable to manipulating the oral cavity and glottal closure in order to swallow? Again, when Man plans and personally executes sustained symbolic utterance in combination with symbolic action for the purpose of influencing the human forces in his environment, are these events capable of revealing fundamental truths about the human mind and the nature of social behavior? Or are they marginally significant like the bookbinder's execution of a book cover design? /4

Speech behavior is significant for the same reason other universally expressive behaviors are significant. No matter what aspect of speech you examine, you are always examining Man in the process of making what is, for him, an important adjustment to his surroundings as he perceives them. *This* is what makes his writing, his music, his painting—and his speech—important objects of study if we are to understand the marvelous complexity and the potentiality of Man's nature. Sometimes, indeed, it may be more important to understand *speech* behavior than the other modes of expression just because it is less self-conscious and more rapidly adaptable and consequently furnishes a more precise, though sometimes not very ennobling, insight into human nature. /5

There is also another way in which Man's speaking is uniquely significant. Speech is a *universal* fact of social environment. Men have lived, and some still live, innocent of writing or serious art. But so far as we know, speech is always one of Man's modes of dealing with the world about him. Thus, to know the influences under which a man or a society exists, one needs to know the contents, the forms, and the manners of the oral discourse that was a pervasive part of that man's or that society's conditioning environment. *If* there was writing, it must be known too. *If* there is serious art, it must be known. But there *will* be speech; it behooves us to know how to understand it. /6

Post-Gutenberg generations have, perhaps, been too impressed by the permanence of print. Often they have forgotten what Plato and, especially, Aristotle emphatically knew: that though speech is fugitive, it is a unique mirror of Man responding to his surroundings and, at the same time, it is a pervasive force regulating behavior in the human part of every environment. "To discern the nature of the soul and discover the different modes of discourse which are adapted to different natures" is the necessary aim of any true rhetoric, said Plato at the end of his *Phaedrus.* He was thinking of the speech event more than of the written record. When Aristotle observed that rhetoric and public address are always associated with ethics and politics, he seized upon the social force of all speaking and some kinds of writing. And when he insisted that in dramatic production Thought is usually conveyed through rhetorical-behavioral reflections of each character's moral and intellectual choices, Aristotle reminded his time and ours of the social readings which speech behavior always permits. These Greeks, and others, knew truths that the study called Speech amplifies: that Man's speech displays his nature in unique ways, and that its *immediate* influence is a different kind of influence from that which the remains of speech will have, however permanently sealed in written form. /7

By now you see my thesis. It is that every event of speech is in some degree a fundamental and socially significant event for the speaker, the spoken-to, and perhaps for those who come after. Whatever study, under whatever academic flag, will erode our ignorance about events of this kind will be a liberal and liberating study. Perhaps this is why Western Man has tried for at least 2500 years to subject his power of speech to systematic study. /8

I cannot pause to trace the triumphs and the miscarriages, the strokes of insight and the lapses into pedantry that have marked the human explorations of human speech. We ourselves are less than two generations away from some of the more bizarre episodes in Man's search for ways of understanding the nature and arts of speech. I think this is the chief reason we are today discussing the "liberality" of Speech as a study. /9

Happily for liberal studies, wisdom displaces error. Modern science is fortunate that Ptolemaic theories of the universe were laid to rest almost four hundred years ago. Ptolemy's ghost haunts no laboratory. It has been the misfortune of Speech that those eccentric mixtures of science and mysticism, Delsartian doctrines and Elocution, still linger in the folklore of the thoughtless and the misinformed. It is the misfortune of Speech that utterly mechanistic views of speech behavior did not disappear when surgeons ceased to "cure" stuttering with the knife. The naïve may even today buy mouth-machinery for the "cure" of lisping, stuttering, and like behaviors. /10

Admittedly, the sum of all our knowledge about speech is still expressed by a small fraction. But in the fifty years or so since Speech began, once more, to be accepted as a possibly liberal study, the fraction has grown. At least mechanics and mysticism no longer govern most undergraduate instruction. The undergraduate may, once more, find in studying Speech some of his most fruitful opportunities to explore the relationships between the different natures of men and the different manners and modes of discourse. /11

It is scarcely possible today for anyone to explore his own speech behavior under sensible guidance from persons who know what is now knowable about speech without making significant, intimate discoveries about the nature of Man—his infirmities and his potentialities. For this reason properly conducted speech rehabilitation consultations, properly taught courses in general public speaking or argument or discussion or rhetorical literature, and properly directed dramatic rehearsals and productions become liberal education of a most meaningful sort. Only laboratory experience in science and in creative writing equal the speech clinic, the platform, and the stage in producing personalized understanding of the self and the realities of the external world. And in addition there are the commonly admitted values of accumulating factual knowledge about human speech and the literary remains of Man's significant speaking efforts. /12

But, "What is the *content* of Speech?" The central and unique "content" of Speech is the range and consequences of the choices Man may make in influencing others through speech. Speech explores the potentialities of a pervasive medium of human expression; its special peculiarity is that the "choices" and intentions of Man, when using this medium, are always in some degree more *social* than aesthetic. /13

What William E. Gladstone paused in a busy political career to write to himself about the "content" of public speaking, he might have written about the entire study we now call Speech:

"[T]he broad and essential difference between [the philosophical student] . . . and . . . the public speaker is this, that the latter is bound to have always alive in his mind as an original coordinate principle of his process, a regard to the mind of the hearer, its capabilities and its infirmities: how to avoid the aggravation of its defects by not giving them opportunity to work; how to secure encouragement . . . of its better tendencies by presenting them the . . . aid of opportunity."

"The mind of the hearer," the resources of Man's most personal mode of communication, and the methods of mediating between truth and Man Listening: these are the subjects central to all constructive study of speech and drama. /14

Speech can show to the youth bearing with him truths and aspirations derived from Philosophy and Literature and History and Science, the choices he must make if he would give his truths currency in a society that scrutinizes the spoken word confidently but often uninformedly. In the process of this showing, the youth will also learn much that he could not elsewhere discover about himself, his brothers, and their most basic form of public behavior. /15

Is this a liberal undertaking? Men have thought so, more often than not, perhaps for the good reason that few studies deal so fundamentally and directly with the vehicles of social experience. With or without the blessings of his academic proctors, Man has insisted upon exploring his speech as behavior and as a social force. Apparently, he has believed these studies could spur his judgment and imagination and enlarge his understanding. Perhaps then we ought to change our question and ask: "Will the college calling itself "liberal" organize and systematize the study of Speech, or will it have the subject studied piecemeal, narrowly, and anarchically in its porticoes?" This is about the only choice the liberal college has ever had since its conception. I think it is the only choice it has today. /16

For discussion

1. What is "speech"? Does it consist only of audible elements—word symbols, tones, and inflections produced by the voice—or are such visible elements as body movements, arm gestures, and facial expression also to be regarded as integral parts of "speech"?

2. If you decide to include visible elements in your definition of "speech," how would you classify talking done over the telephone or on the radio—in fact, in any situation where the speaker cannot be seen by the listener? Would you say that this sort of communication is not "speech"?

3. What is "good speech"—speech that meets certain predetermined standards of correctness and beauty, or speech that accomplishes its purpose by conveying the speaker's message clearly and convincingly?

4. To what extent do you believe a person's speech can be improved? What sort of training and practice are most useful for this purpose?

5. Distinguish between *self-expression* and *communication*? May a speaker express himself well and yet fail to communicate his ideas to another person? Conversely, may one communicate without expressing himself well? As a student of speech, which are you interested in: improving your ability to express yourself or improving your ability to communicate?

6. In what ways may a man's speech help us form a judgment concerning his personality, character, educational background, place of birth or residence, etc.?

7. Try to think of all the ways in which the speech of a national or cultural group may "mirror" the ethical, esthetic, and social standards by which that group is governed.

8. Arnold argues that the study of speech may properly be regarded as a "liberal" discipline because it helps a person understand (a) "what he [himself] is like," (b) "how he may constructively direct a significant portion of his energies," and (c) "what constitutes the social environment in which he lives." Would you agree that the study of speech, properly conceived and conducted, may indeed accomplish these ends? Why or why not?

9. If a man understands himself and his environment and if he habitually directs his energies toward constructive ends, would you regard him as "liberally" educated? What precisely does *liberal education* mean anyway?

10. On what grounds might it be argued that the study of speech is not a "liberal" discipline?

11. Cicero, the famous Roman orator, was in the habit of saying: The man who possesses knowledge and wisdom but does not know how to communicate them to his fellows is of little use in the world. On the other hand, the man who is a skilled and artful speaker but does not possess knowledge and wisdom is a danger to the state. Comment on this statement.

12. Justify Professor Arnold's assertion that speech is "a pervasive force regulating behavior in the human part of every environment." By what other forces is group behavior also regulated? Would you say that speech is more or less powerful and pervasive than these? Why?

13. What place do you think "liberal" studies should have in a college education? Which subjects would you classify as "liberal," and which would you exclude from this category? Why?

14. Explore the statement, ". . . the sum of all our knowledge about speech is still expressed by a small fraction." What are psychologists, speech pathologists, physicists, phoneticians, linguists, rhetoricians, anthropologists, etc., doing to extend this knowledge?

15. Arnold maintains that speech is one of the most important means man has for adjusting himself to his environment. What does he mean by this statement? In answering, give actual instances and examples.

Effective speech in a democracy

WILLIAM G. CARLETON

The cry that "oratory is a lost art" is often a hackneyed and thoughtless cry. Too often those who deplore the absence of Websterian and Lincolnian speaking think only of Webster's and Lincoln's memorable phrases and grieve that their like is not heard from contemporary politicians. Professor Carleton, on the other hand, offered a much more penetrating criticism of modern American public address when he spoke to the members of the Southern Speech Association in Gainesville, Florida, on April 5, 1951.

"Effective Speech in a Democracy" deserves close and thoughtful study for a variety of reasons. Among them is the fact that it diagnoses one of the chief causes of sterility in public address: the want of comprehensive, independent, adaptive mental activity. Carleton's proposition is that modern American speakers too often propound their conclusions without probing their subjects and fail to impose the stamps of their own minds on the discourses they compose and deliver. If this is right, the proof should be found

William G. Carleton, "Effective Speech in a Democracy," *Vital Speeches of the Day*, Vol. XVII, June 15, 1951, pp. 540-544. Reprinted by permission of the author.

in the addresses published in this volume and elsewhere. The speeches by Pericles (pp. 191-195), Emerson (pp. 39-47), Huxley (pp. 264-269), Theodore Roosevelt (pp. 102-106), Darrow (pp. 142-147), and Franklin D. Roosevelt (pp. 135-139) which appear here have achieved the status of classics in the literature of public address. To compare them with the less famous addresses on comparable subjects, also provided in *The Speaker's Resource Book*, should lend support or refutation to Carleton's characterization of public speaking today.

Equally important to students of public speaking is Carleton's emphasis on the speaker's unique opportunities to contribute original thought and independent influence in an industrial, metropolitan society. In such opportunities lie the special challenges for beginning and experienced speakers. The speaker's communication is uniquely his to control, as Carleton implies. From the first glimpse of his rhetorical purpose to the last phoneme of his final utterance, the speechmaker's speech is an intensely personal creation if he will make it so. Should it prove otherwise and the speech be imitative, timid, or bland, the mind and method of the speaker are at fault. He was not restrained from penetrating his subject nor from adapting his thoughts to the needs of his hearers. How highly society prizes such potential independence is shown by the fact that the speaker's right to speak the fresh results of his thought and the right of others to assemble peaceably to listen, are guaranteed by the first amendment to the Constitution of the United States.

Carleton's career as a student of political action in the United States gives him special authority when he discusses the political significance of popular discourse. He has been a member of the faculty of the University of Florida since 1927 and is now Professor of Political Science and Head of the Department of Social Sciences. He has studied and written much on American political parties and political activity in the nineteenth century. He was born at Evansville, Indiana, in 1903 and received his A.B. from Indiana University in 1926. He also received the degree of Doctor of Jurisprudence from the University of Florida in 1930 and an M.A. from Indiana University in 1934.

The audience that heard Professor Carleton in 1951 was composed largely of teachers and students of speech; however, the general appeal of the address was recognized by the editors of *Vital Speeches of the Day*, who published it soon after its delivery.

Clear and effective speech in our American democracy is more necessary today than at any time in our history. A larger number of people participate in community and government decisions than ever before. Mass democracy, numerical democracy, the phenomenon so dreaded and so hoped for by people in the eighteenth and early nineteenth centuries, is here all about us. Wider and wider popular participation in government requires that the issues of the time be carried to all types and conditions of men, men who every day are contributing to the making of community and government decisions. /1

Moreover, not only do a larger and larger number of people participate in our elections and decisions, but the problems which must be considered and upon which judgment must be passed are more intricate and complex than they once were. And they are growing in intricacy and complexity all the time. In addition, American leaders increasingly must speak to win not only the attention and the understanding of American citizens but also of citizens in lands beyond the seas. All of this makes it imperative that in our oral and written speech on public affairs we strive more and more to practice rigorous integrity, intellectual clarity, and a lucid style. /2

Modern technology has made the mechanical tasks of today's speaker much simpler. The loudspeaker makes it much easier for the orator; it saves tremendous energy; it allows an effectiveness almost impossible for the unfortunate orator appearing before large audiences in pre-microphone days. For one Webster or one Bryan who could be heard by a large audience, there were a hundred speakers who could not be heard beyond the first rows. Indeed, quite frequently in the old days a speaker rose to prominence not because of his gifts of mind and expression but solely because nature had endowed him with leather lungs and a stentorian sound box. The radio and television have also added immeasurably to the opportunities of the contemporary speaker. Today the speaker can extend his mind and his personality into every nook and cranny of the world. A speaker in New York can come about as close to his physically remote audience sitting in San Francisco as an orator in the Ecclesia in Athens or a protest speaker in a New England town meeting ever came to his small and immediate audience. Today a speaker can literally bestride the world like a Colossus, and he can become as big an influence in the world as he has the mind and personality (and the social forces and pressure groups) to become. /3

However, in spite of the imperative need for effective speech today and in spite of the multiplying of mechanical aids, in my opinion there has been a decline in able public speech, a decline in the number of first class speakers and orators. True, more people participate in public speaking, more people are doers—and this is all to the good—but there has been a deterioration in the intellectual content, in the literary style, and in the method of delivering speeches, even among those who by reputation stand in the first rank of contemporary oratory and speech. There are, of course, notable exceptions to this general indictment. But the general indictment, I think, should stand, even when all due allowances are made for the tendency of contemporary man, in any stage of history to look back on the past with rose-tinted glasses, to romanticize it, to glamorize it, to dream of it as the golden age of oratory or literature or liberty or virtue or happiness or wisdom. /4

There has been a decline in the art of delivering a speech. There is the failure to convey a feeling of deep earnestness. (There is seriousness, yes, a simulated and stereotyped seriousness, the seriousness of dullness, of banality.) There is a lack of animation, of passion, of fire; a lack of rhythm and of music. The speaker today rarely communicates to his hearers the electric tension of a nervous system and a brain working at high gear—under control, of course, and always held in leash by reasonable and intellectual restraints—a nervous system and a brain working under immediate pressure, under the stimulation of having to think rapidly and out loud, and responding with flexibility, spontaneity, imagination, verve, vividness, and punch. /5

The truth is that too many speakers today are afraid to concede anything to the immediate occasion and to the moment. They perhaps come too well prepared. I do not mean, of course, the preparation of a well stored mind, which is the preparation of a lifetime. Nor do I mean the preparation which thinks out ahead of time the reasoned organization of a speech, an analysis of the propositions and the alternatives, how one topic will flow logically from the preceding one, and even many of the striking and quotable phrases. There can never be too much of this kind of preparation. But I do mean that speakers nowadays often come too well prepared in meticulous detail; they leave nothing to chance, to the occasion; they ignore the possibilities of cutting here and expanding there while in action; they do not yield sufficiently to the delights of spontaneous asides and anecdotes, of vivid illustrations thought of on the spur of the moment. Too many speakers use too many notes; the notes are too copious; and worse still, more and more speakers read their speeches. Even when notes or even manuscripts are in order, often the speaker does not know when to interpolate new material, when to depart

from the too well prepared sheaf of papers he holds in his hand. /6

Much of this slavish dependence on notes and manuscripts is due to the radio. However, even when the speaker cannot be seen, his tell-tale manner lets the hearers know that the speech is being read and not delivered. A few speakers can read a speech *almost* as well as they deliver one—F. D. Roosevelt and Winston Churchill, for instance—but few are in the Roosevelt and Churchill class. /7

Most speakers—indeed, all speakers—need a little uncertainty to be at their best. There must be excitement, even actual stage fright, for a speaker to be stimulated to the point of brilliantly effective speech. Every great speech in history has been made under the impetus of stage fright. If the speaker or the actor does not experience stage fright—that last minute electrical charge of anxiety and challenge—there is something wrong. Speakers and actors know this. The story is told that Sir Robert Peel, for many years a leader in the British House of Commons, on important occasions was in the habit of letting a fellow member of the Commons take his pulse just before Peel was to rise in Commons to speak. Peel's racing pulses indicated that Peel was in good shape for a supreme forensic effort. /8

Even the most experienced speaker knows—indeed the more experienced he is the more deeply he is likely to know it—that there is always the possibility of failure in time of crisis. Who can forget the three or four awful minutes when Edmund Burke, with a long lifetime of superlative oratory behind him, faltered and failed when he faced a critical Scotch audience at the time of his inauguration as rector of the University of Glasgow? Yes, failure can come to the best and the greatest of them, and it is this possibility of failure which acts as a whiplash to the orator and the actor on critical occasions and produces the finest speaking and the finest acting in history. Present-day speakers rob themselves of this stimulus when they come to the loudspeaker too well prepared in details. /9

There has been a deterioration in the literary style of speeches. Politicians, lawyers, and ministers, the ranks from which most of our speakers are drawn, live in a busy and hurried age; they have less and less time for reading, reflection, and the maturing of their own literary styles; they do not read the masters and the classics as they once did. They are readers of newspapers and periodicals in an age when newspapers and periodicals are less literary and more journalistic. Practitioners of the art of public speaking today are apt to piece together a speech from newspaper clippings and current editorials. Or worse still, the busy public man, engrossed with a thousand and one duties and increasingly dependent upon experts in technical fields for the intellectual materials covering his job, calls upon numerous ghost writers to prepare his speeches. Paragraphs from many sources are then assembled and fitted together into a speech. /10

What is the result of all this? The result is the loss of honesty in style, even the disappearance of style altogether. The result is that too often our contemporary speeches are pallid, synthetic hodgepodges that might well be produced by public relations firms or advertising agencies, hodgepodges devoid of unity, philosophy, perspective, integrity, personality, or craftmanship. This results in productions without figures of speech and vivid illustrations, without cryptic phrases and terse aphorisms, without lights and shades, wit and humor, roll and rhythm. Even when speeches are not ghost-written, the ghost-written ones, representing as they do the speeches of our very highest politicians, are coming to set the pattern, and so today speeches that are not ghost-written are coming to sound ghost-written, synthetic, stereotyped. /11

There are exceptions, of course. A century which has produced a Jean Jaurès, an Aristide Briand, a Woodrow Wilson, and a Winston Churchill is not wholly devoid of oratory of the highest order. But the oratory of our run-of-the-mill politicians is not what it once was. One has but to read the Parliamentary Debates, the Congressional Globe, and the Congressional Record of the nineteenth century to be struck by the stylistic decline of much of the oratory and the public speaking of the twentieth century. /12

Now I realize, of course, that tastes in styles differ not only from individual to individual but from age to age. Much of the oratory and public speech of the nineteenth century would today sound pompous, florid, ornate. Even the sonorous, rolling, Romanesque style of Daniel Webster, so much admired in Webster's own day, often sounds to us today forced and artificial, and Stephen Vincent Benét, in his great American epic on John Brown, reveals how deeply a sensitive poet of our century can be offended by the Olympian periods of Webster. Even Webster was irritated by his many second-rate imitators, and he has recorded his own disgust at having to slay (that is, blue pencil) scores of Roman consuls and pro-consuls in editing the Latinesque inaugural address of President William Henry Harrison. And by

the time the 1880's had been reached, much of American oratory had become so sickeningly sentimental as positively to revolt twentieth century taste. For 1880's sentimental oratory at its worst, take a look at James G. Blaine's funeral oration at the bier of James A. Garfield. Yes, we of the twentieth century have different tastes, and we demand styles that are more simple and direct. But—and this is the point—side by side with the rococo public speech of the nineteenth century there was also a style characterized by plain, clear, lucid, Anglo-Saxon address; many public men of that century used it and used it well; no one in the twentieth century—certainly not Woodrow Wilson or Franklin Roosevelt—can rival John C. Calhoun and Abraham Lincoln in the classic use of a simple, vigorous, and chaste style. /13

Most important of all, in our time there has been serious deterioration in the content of public addresses, but content cannot be separated from style, for style and content go hand in hand and it is difficult to distinguish cause and effect. /14

American speeches today, even those by leading statesmen, for the most part have ceased seriously to examine fundamental policy, to discuss first principles, to isolate and analyze all the possibilities and alternative courses with respect to a given basic policy. For the most part American speeches today assume a given policy; they proclaim it rather than debate it; they enumerate the "points of a program" necessary to implement the assumed policy and to reach the assumed goal; they confirm the faith of their followers in the assumed policy and goal; they rally enthusiasm; they exhort to action. The result is that speeches today are rarely intellectually comprehensive or cogently analytical. The result of this tendency toward mere enumeration and exhortation is to render formal public address superficial and arid; speeches sound like advertising copy in which one takes pains not to mention competing products (that is, competing ideas, competing alternatives of policy) for fear that the public might become acquainted with competing products (that is, competing ideas, competing alternatives of policy). One simply ignores competing ideas and alternative policies—or dismisses them with an epithet—and repeats the virtues of his own idea or his own policy. But things in this world are relative, and a given candidate, idea, or policy makes intellectual sense only in relation to other candidates, ideas, and policies. The failure in a single speech to examine, analyze, discuss, and debate alternative points of view with respect to a given policy robs that speech of deep intellectual content and conviction, and is not even fair to the point of view held by the speaker. Intellectually, the speaker is selling short his own point of view when he fails to examine it fairly in relation to other points of view. /15

The development of mass democracy and the growing complexity of public problems seem to have combined to give American politicians and other public speakers the idea that issues must be flagrantly over-simplified to reach the intelligence of the average citizen. This is a mistaken attitude and in many cases a cynical and snobbish one. Where speakers fail, they usually fail because they underrate the intelligence and maturity of audiences, because they "speak down" to audiences. Every great speech in history has aimed high; every great speech in history has assumed a generous degree of virtue, intelligence, and maturity in those to whom it was addressed. /16

Let me illustrate what I mean when I say that I believe that today's speeches should be intellectually more comprehensive and analytical. For five months now, since the November elections of 1950, we have been witnessing "the great debate" on foreign policy. We have *claimed* that we have been debating the fundamental alternatives of American foreign policy. But how many speakers in this "great debate" actually examined all the points of view, all the possibilities, all the alternatives, in American foreign policy? Very few. Almost every speaker *assumed* the course he favored, and proceeded to confirm that point of view in terms of itself, to set up a "point program" to achieve it, and to exhort to action. /17

What are the various possibilities in American foreign policy? There is the globalism of world federalism, at present hardly a practical alternative. There is the globalism of the United Nations, where the United States, although taking the lead, makes no important moves without carrying the support of the United Nations. There is the globalism of American imperialism, in which the United States takes the lead in Europe and Asia against Communism, and carries out its policies even though it does not have the backing of a majority of the nations or even of a majority of the important nations in the United Nations. There is the partial globalism of a federal state of the democracies or a federal state of the Atlantic community. There is the return to American isolation, in which the United States would withdraw from the leadership of the anti-Communist forces in both Europe and Asia. There is a partial

American isolation, in which the United States would withdraw from leadership in Asia but not Europe, or from leadership in Europe but not Asia. There is the possibility of America's taking the lead to build up the social-democratic and democratic socialist forces in Europe and Asia to check the Communists. There is the possibility of breaking the current and dangerous polarization of power between the United States and the Soviet Union and returning to the old multiple balance-of-power system. Now it is quite possible that any given speaker will favor a combination of several of these possibilities, but by no stretch of the imagination could he favor all of them, for some of them are contradictory. To me, the intellectually convincing speech on American foreign policy would have to analyze and defend the course favored by the speaker, but it would also have to analyze fairly and combat the alternative courses the speaker opposed. /18

Will you permit me to illustrate my point by demonstrating for a moment how I would construct a speech on current American foreign policy? It so happens that I favor the following foreign policy: In the countries of Asia and Europe where the non-Communists are in control, I would, where conditions indicated, put the United States squarely behind a policy of social democracy or even democratic socialism as a way of combating Communism; and in the countries where the Communists are in control, I would play upon the nationalistic tendencies everywhere evident in Communist governments and Communist parties, to attempt to divide Communist countries from each other on national grounds and thereby contribute to the restoration of a multiple balancing-of-power system, a system which would prevent the Communists from acting together in a Communist front and threatening to upset the balance of power. For if we can remove the Communist threat to the balance of power we can remove the real cause of another great war. /19

In order to present effectively my point of view on the importance of playing wise social politics, it seems to me that I would have to show how and why conditions in Europe and Asia are converging to produce collectivist movements there and why laissez-faire capitalism there is not feasible; also I would have to show the difference between totalitarian socialism and democratic socialism and examine the reasons why I believe America's backing of social-democracy and even democratic socialism in Europe and Asia would check Communism and serve America's national interests. In order for me to present effectively my belief that nationalism within Communist countries and parties could be used to divide Communism and restore a multiple balance-of-power system, I would have to examine in some detail the degree to which Communist revolutions and movements are in fact nationalistic in aim, method, and development, and actually point out the specific grounds of possible national conflict between specific Communist countries. (In the main, Communism has spread not by international revolution but by a series of national revolutions; industrial revolutions are being built inside Communist countries on national patterns; potential national conflicts exist between Communist countries, as for example a possible future conflict between China and Russia over Manchuria.) /20

However, even when I had done all this my intellectual task would not be completed. I would have to point out why other courses in foreign policy would not serve America's national interests as well as the policy I favored. This would . involve my examining the reasons why political isolation would not work today; why a policy of mere military containment of Communism through the United Nations would not be enough and would not work permanently; why even if it worked it would be the hard way to do something that could be done with less possibility of war and fewer long-time sacrifices; why a policy of mere military containment of Communism by the United States alone—a policy of American imperialism—would be even less workable and less desirable than a policy of military containment through the United Nations. In short, in order to carry intellectual conviction on so large and controversial a question, it seems to me I would have to construct a speech that analyzed critically all courses —those I oppose as well as those I favor. /21

In domestic affairs, too, the great issues of our time have never been adequately debated in public address. There is no great oration or debate to which one can point and say, "There is the preeminently able presentation of the case for the welfare state, with all alternative solutions weighed and examined." Neither can one point to any such oration or debate in opposition to the welfare state. /22

In the past the great issues of the day frequently have been debated in able and definitive fashion. Take for example Burke's pleas for British reconciliation with the American colonies; or Fox's appeal in 1800 for a cessation of the war with Revolutionary France; or the debate on the Reform Bill of 1832; or the arguments of Bright and Cobden for the repeal of the Corn Laws; or Gladstone's arguments for free trade or for Irish Home Rule. In American history, take for example the great debate over the adoption and ratification of the Constitution; or Calhoun's speech on the Independent Treasury; or Lincoln's cool and logical discussion of slavery from 1858 through the Second Inaugural of 1865; or even the debate of 1919-1920 over the League of Nations. Read these and then ask yourselves whether the great issues of our time are being debated with equal vigor, insight, comprehensiveness, and analytical power. I think you will be forced to agree that the issues of today are not being debated with equal ability. /23

The truth is we are in somewhat of a crisis in the practice of human communication, both written and oral. Technical and specialized subjects of all kinds are effectively communicated to technicians and specialists in the technical, scholarly, and professional journals. But where can the average citizen go to get an intelligent approach to a question, an approach intellectually competent and related in a comprehensive way to the average citizen's needs and experiences? If our speeches have become more platitudinous and aridly categorical, our printed matter in editorials and articles has also suffered. /24

Current periodical literature in America suffers on many counts. Our magazines of large mass circulation, those upon which the average man relies, increasingly have shied away from serious articles and given more and more space to "human interest" material. The digest magazines, for instance, with their huge circulations, boast of reproducing articles of permanent and lasting interest, but most of their articles deal with peripheral, marginal, and miscellaneous topics, and only about one article in twenty deals seriously with an important political, economic, or social question. Even when serious and important questions are dealt with, they have tended to become more superficial, more platitudinous, more pat, and more "humanized." Today a "profile" or character sketch of some public figure is often published as a substitute for a more solid approach to a political campaign or a political question. Publicity is more and more centralized; the costs of production reach staggering sums; an eye must be kept constantly on circulation and advertising figures. Magazines are more and more inbred and staff-written; articles of intrinsic intellectual merit and sound originality are passed over because they do not fit the "editorial needs" or conform to the personal views of the editors. (Perhaps I should say here that personally I have no grievance with editors; they have been generous with me; but as a citizen I resent the increasingly slick and stereotyped material I am forced to read. A few days ago I chanced to see a British periodical of last summer which contained an article by Bertrand Russell. The editor explained that while he personally differed from Russell's conclusions, he was publishing the article for its intrinsic intellectual content; that the article was a vivid illustration of how a first class mind operated on important subject matter in a comprehensive way vital for the average reader. There is too little of this sort of thing, particularly in the United States.) /25

The chief enemy of clear thinking and communication is the development of a stereotyped public opinion. Our agencies of news and information are highly centralized. Our economic and social life has become closely interwoven and interdependent. A mass impression is made rapidly and stereotyped for short periods, and then the first mass impression is followed by a second. Intellectually, we have become the victims of the stereotype of the week or the stereotype of the month or the stereotype of the year. Publishers are fearful of going against mass opinion because circulation and advertising are involved, and circulation and advertising are more and more important as production costs go up. Editors are afraid to go contrary to the stereotypes, and as a result they demand intellectual conformity and discourage intellectual individuality. Thus stereotyped thinking produces the periodicals, and the periodicals reinforce stereotyped thinking. It is a vicious cycle. /26

We have come to think too exclusively of political and governmental centralization as the producer of conformity and the enemy of freedom. But our problem is much broader than this. Conformity is the result of political centralization, but it is also the result of economic centralization and social centralization and publishing centralization and literary centralization and artistic centralization and intellectual centralization. And all of these flow from the machine and modern technology and the growing interdependence of industrial and metropolitan civilization. (However, this should not be considered an indictment of the machine or of industrial or metropolitan civilization; the machine releases human energies as well as curbs them; and there are many forms of administrative and managerial and group-life decentralization possible and yet to be explored—forms of decentralization that are consistent with a machine and an industrial civilization—but that is not my topic today; that is another story, and I have dealt with it on other occasions.) /27

We practitioners of public speech can do much to break the trend toward stereotyped thinking. It is easier for us to be original and to depart from the current mode of thinking than it is for publications of mass circulation. We do not have a huge capital investment to consider or a large payroll to meet; we need not keep our eyes on the cash register. The public will listen to our views, all the more so if our views are original and fresh, if we come with something to say and say it well; if we avoid the methods of the smart aleck and the exhibitionist; if we speak out of knowledge, understanding and conviction; if we present our own and conflicting points of view with fairness and insight. /28

Let us do our part to prevent the world of complete conformity, the nightmare world of George Orwell, from coming to pass. Let us be broad, comprehensive, and pluralistic in our intellectual approach; let us avoid the dogmatic, the doctrinaire, and the absolute; let us keep alive in our speeches a large measure of respect for diversity, individuality, and originality—even when we ourselves happen to be on the popular and winning side of the day—for it is from these sources that flow the springs of human freedom. And let us all take a turn now and then at using freedom, at differing from the majority and from the stereotype of the time, for freedom withers and dies when it is not used. /29

For discussion

1. While modern means of mass communication may have greatly increased the size of the audience a public speaker can reach, as is frequently pointed out, such an enlarged audience also imposes upon a speaker many restraints and limitations unknown to the orators of a century ago. What are these restraints? How and why do they arise? What, if anything, may a speaker do to overcome them?

2. Describe in some detail the role which public speaking plays in the life of a democratic society. By what ethical and social standards should speech in a democracy be governed?

3. Why are public choices and decisions more difficult to make today than ever before? Why is it more important that as a nation we choose and decide wisely?

4. Admitting the validity of Carleton's criticisms of the read speech, can you think of any occasions on which it might still be preferable for a speaker to read from a manuscript rather than speak extemporaneously?

5. Consider the statement: "Most speakers—indeed, all speakers—need a little uncertainty to be at their best. There must be excitement, even actual stage fright, for a speaker to be stimulated to the point of brilliantly effective speech." Do you agree or disagree? Defend your answer.

6. How much conscious attention should the average public speaker pay to the language or "style" in which his ideas are expressed—to the choice and arrangement of words, the use of figures of speech, epithets, antitheses, alliteration, etc.? What are some of the dangers of giving too much or too little attention to certain aspects of style?

7. In your judgment, are there significant differences between good oral and written style? If so, what are they, and why are they important?

8. Are you willing to accept Professor Carleton's contention that contemporary speakers are less "comprehensive and analytical" than the speakers of earlier generations? Base your answer not upon opinion or guesswork but upon careful research into several of the speeches to be found in this and other collections of speeches.

9. What, as you see it, causes styles and tastes in oratory to change? In view of these changes, can we ever hope to determine the essential qualities of truly great speaking?

10. Reread paragraphs 10 and 11 of this speech, and then read Robert T. Oliver's defense of ghost writing, page 20. What do you think of the widespread current practice of ghost writing speeches? Must ghost writing necessarily contribute to such rhetorical faults as Carleton describes in paragraph 10? Under what circumstances could this be avoided? Are there ethical problems as well as rhetorical problems involved in the use of ghost writers? If so, what are they and how are they to be resolved?

11. Evaluate the recipe or formula that Carleton believes a speaker should follow in presenting his views on foreign policy. Would this formula make for a fair and rounded discussion of the subject? Would it make for a rhetorically effective speech? Can you think of any objections which might be raised against this recommended pattern?

12. Investigate some of the speeches given by the four modern speakers that Carleton regards as "great" (Jean Jaurès, Aristide Briand, Woodrow Wilson, and Winston Churchill). What dominant traits or characteristics do you find in their speaking? Would you agree that they deserve to be classified as "great"?

13. Who was the most effective public speaker you ever heard? Explain why he was effective.

14. Do you agree with Carleton's assertion that our present-day newspapers and periodicals foster "the development of a stereotyped public opinion"? What do you think about radio and television in regard to this statement?

15. What, specifically, can you as a student speaker do to help break "the trend toward stereotyped thinking"?

16. If, as Carleton maintains, the quality of contemporary speechmaking is low, what causes other than those outlined in his address do you think may be responsible? What conditions and motives must be present within a culture if great oratory is to result?

Four ways of looking at a speech

IRVING J. LEE

Irving J. Lee of Northwestern University delivered this address at the annual convention of the National Association of Teachers of Speech (now the Speech Association of America) on December 30, 1941. His discourse succinctly describes the chief ways of analyzing and evaluating the texts of speeches. Each method can reveal different facets of the speeches assembled in this volume. But, as Lee implies, one learns most by looking at speechmaking in several ways. The editors of The Speaker's Resource Book suggest that the speeches published here can be studied most profitably by raising the rhetorician's, the semanticist's, the logician's, and the general semanticist's questions in that order. To do so will bring successively to the mind the psychological and literary, the linguistic, the logical, and the sociological significance of these public addresses.

Lee's remarks are also worthy of study as an example of a "convention paper." Convention papers and their cousins, research reports, are not fundamentally different from lectures or other formal, expository speeches. Their uniqueness lies in the fact that they are discourses prepared for audiences of experts. Usually, too, they are presented at meetings to which the experts-as-listeners bring a special sense of professional responsibility. Such papers are usually

Irving J. Lee, "Four Ways of Looking at a Speech," Quarterly Journal of Speech, Vol. XXVIII, April 1942, pp. 148-155. Reprinted by permission of the Speech Association of America.

read, for precision is what such listeners demand of their reporters. But good convention papers and good research reports are not just "essays on their legs." Although the speakers may assume extraordinary knowledge and unusual powers of attention on the part of the audience, good papers of this kind still accommodate to listening man's limited span of attention, to his difficulties in remembering what he hears, to his gratefulness for topical allusions and touches of humor and human interest, and to his need for clear organization. That technical papers are written and delivered from manuscript makes it all the more important that learning by listening be made as easy and efficient as the subject will allow. Listeners do not become readers, with leisure to reflect and re-examine, just because a subject is difficult or a speaker decides to write out his speech.

"Four Ways of Looking at a Speech" was in many ways a model convention paper. It nowhere sacrificed the accuracy and precision that the subject and the audience of experts demanded; yet in composing it, Lee rendered the labor of analytical listening humanly possible—even pleasurable. The rhetorical means by which he did this can be discovered by reading the text carefully as Lee's rhetorician would read it. On December 30, 1941, in the Statler Hotel in Detroit, Michigan, these rhetorical designs turned into *events* as Lee began to read his address. They bound the speaker, his subject, and his listeners in a lively, human relationship as the subject unfolded; in that way they made a speech out of the paper Professor Lee had brought from Evanston, Illinois. To a lesser extent these same rhetorical procedures become events again as we read the printed version today. They still tell us we are reading a *speech*— not a soliloquy, or a thesis, or the typical sort of essay. Whoever would understand the art of public address must learn by what means speakers achieve or miss such effects. Lee and the other speakers whose addresses appear in this volume have furnished the laboratory materials for this kind of learning.

Irving J. Lee was born in New York City in 1909 and attended the public schools of Wharton, New Jersey. He received his B.A. from New York University in 1931 and his M.A. in 1935 and Ph.D. in 1938 from Northwestern University. From 1937 until his death on May 23, 1955, he was a member of the faculty of the School of Speech, Northwestern University. As a scholar and teacher he was especially interested in how meanings operate in public addresses; he published four books and numerous articles on this and related subjects. A considerable portion of his speaking, writing, and research was devoted to exploring the relevance of Alfred Korzybski's theories of general semantics to the study of public speaking. Lee also served a number of industrial corporations and governmental departments as a consultant on problems of communication.

The advance of any science becomes apparent first in a systematic refinement of its methods and then in the development and application of *new* methods. Thus, the history of internal medicine and psychiatry shows a steady movement from the rules of thumb of an earlier era to the specialized procedures of today. But unco-ordinated specialization can make for new confusion unless we are ever aware of relationships. /1

Something like this has been happening in the field of speech criticism in recent years. The development of new modes of analysis with varying terminology and apparatus has left some of us in need of reorientation. It is, perhaps, time to say with Lincoln, "If we could first know where we are, and whither we are tending, we could better judge what to do and how to do it." /2

Then, too, new methodologies are often introduced amidst attitudes of hostility and defensiveness. Students who have not been exposed to new doctrines seem inevitably to feel that their proponents come as legislators likely to repeal every last thing that is known. The unfamiliar procedures are looked upon as something antithetical, antagonistic, ready to replace the old and the presumably worn out. But new methodologies may well be not antithetical but complementary, not antagonistic, but additive. /3

Thus it is with some of the "new" ways in speech criticism. Students working entirely apart from each other have focused on perspectives which can throw light on particular areas in the speech process otherwise neglected by the others. It is my point that there are available today at least four different ways of looking at a speech which can be applied individually and co-operatively for knowledge about what goes on when someone speaks to someone else. My plan is to discuss in order the dominant concern of the rhetorician, the student of meanings or semanticist, the logician, and the general semanticist. In what way would each be interested in a public speech? What does each look for? What are the questions that each would ask? On what basis would each judge whether the speech was "good" or "bad"? /4

In this quest the analysis, if successful, could be used on the speech of any public figure, a radio commercial, a class assignment, this paper, or on any sort of connected discourse whatever. /5

Let me begin with the rhetorician. His first concern is the discovery of the effect of the speech. Did it make an impression? Was it accepted or rejected, approved or disapproved in varying degrees? Were audience attitudes solidified or changed? Modern techniques of direct polling, accompanied by tests of attitudes, make answers possible to these questions that are now more precise than ever before. But it is only after those findings are in that the rhetorician would get under way. His work would begin when he asked: What did the speaker do that got results? What did he say that influenced them? How did he say it? What strategies accounted for the acceptance of his argument? What peculiar tactics marked the method of his appeal? /6

Our rhetorician might be guided by the experience of students in the last 2,000 years. For observers of such processes have been all too numerous. They have noticed that minds were manipulated by an almost endless list of devices. We must be content here with a mere suggestion of the scope of the patterns of persuasion. The rhetorician would look for the attitudes of the speaker, the disguised or overt flatteries, the modes of insinuation, the sources of personal prestige. He would study the manifestations of voice, bodily movement, and gesture. He would analyze the progress and gradations of the attack, the lines of argument and the modes of support. He would be concerned with the specificity, the associational power, the interestingness, the varieties of suggestion, the spread or limitation of the *topoi*,* the sources of humor, the paths of action, the impressions of universality. He would listen carefully for the colloquiality, the impersonality, the special adaptations, the turns and figures, the memorable phrases, the maxims, and the subtle devices of stylistic ingratiation. /7

In short, the rhetorician tries to overlook nothing that a speaker did that might affect his control of his audience. If, by chance, the speaker alienated his hearers, that, too, should be explained. And if ours was the complete rhetorician, he might then go on to generalize, to show us that the rhetorical performance was or was not the inevitable one, for when rhetoric will have become a science, rather than an art, the student will "be able to tell under what circumstances what devices will get what effects."[1] /8

The student of meanings, that is, the semanticist, has, however, an interest in other matters. His concern centers on these questions: What does he mean? Do I understand the speaker? How can I find out whether he is saying what I think he is saying? What, in other words, is being said? /9

For the ordinary business of living, in the daily round of domestic affairs, when dealing with the butcher or the newsboy, such questions seem point-less. Without too much effort we manage to take in and presumably understand whatever we hear. But as soon as we leave the ordinarily mundane, for talk of life and love, of purpose and significance, of use and method, of needs and programs, the old sureness is no more. What seems simple can often take on new complexity when disturbed by a question. Momentary doubt is often enough to reveal the tenuousness of one's grasp on an argument, for what appears inordinately clear on first hearing may, on further scrutiny, be susceptible to many diverse interpretations. /10

It is common knowledge that many a speech turns out to be all things to all men. The task of the semanticist is the reduction of this possible multiplicity to simplicity, the discovery of the sources of ambiguity, and the provision of the means whereby the speaker's intent may be faithfully reflected. /11

In this quest the semanticist is guided by three fundamental facts about the working of our language. /12

1. He starts with the fact of *ambiguity*. He knows that metaphor is not merely a decorative device but a necessary manifestation of language in use, insofar as a relatively small vocabulary must serve an inexhaustible number of purposes. It is small cause for wonder, then, if even our simplest words are ever turned to new uses. We learn very early that such a phrase as "he pinched her" may, on occasion, be used in a situation betokening social familiarity, an arrest, or a kidnapping. And that such a word as "operation" is used with by "no means the same 'working' in the technical vocabularies of theology, surgery, mathematics, and strategics."[2] When Secretary Knox said that the naval establishment in the Pacific was not "on the alert," he was not using that phrase in the sense of watchfulness or sleepiness, but in the technical sense that "certain essential preparations" should have been but were not made.* I. A. Richards[3] called attention to the lament of the philosopher G. E. Moore, "Why we should use the same form of verbal expression to convey such different meanings is more than I can say. It seems to me very curious that language should have grown up as if it were expressly designed to mislead philosophers; and I do not know why it should have." The diversity of interpretations, so characteristically common in discussion, may be cause for lamentation, but it is the work

---

* From the Greek; meaning here, the speaker's topics. (Editor's note)
[1] See Harwood L. Childs, *An Introduction to Public Opinion* (1940), pp. 89-102.

[2] Louis H. Gray, *Foundations of Language* (1939), p. 257.
* The reference is to the Japanese attack on the naval base at Pearl Harbor, Hawaii, with which the United States' active involvement in World War II began. Frank Knox was U.S. Secretary of War from 1940-1944. (Editor's note)
[3] *The Philosophy of Rhetoric* (1936), p. 96.

of the semanticist to take such difficulties as his province, to reckon with them, and then to help us find a way around them.[4] /13

2. *Generality* is the second important factor. A very large portion of the key terms of any speech will show such largeness of coverage that it is not always easy to discover which particular areas of human concern are being referred to. In a recent speech Robert Maynard Hutchins said, "Education implies teaching. Teaching implies knowledge. Knowledge is truth. The truth is everywhere the same. Hence, education should be everywhere the same." The very breadth and scope of these terms must give one pause. So much is included under their tentlike expanse, that the semanticist must needs wind in and through them lest he assume particulars not otherwise intended. Generality is not something to be stigmatized, but, rather, to be realized and analyzed anew. (Incidentally, with the coming of the censors, we may expect many an example of that maddening and sterile double-talk as the characteristic trade mark of most official public pronouncements—especially if the practice of the last war prevails.)* /14

3. The third focus of his attention involves a ferreting out of the terms which stand for *fictitious entities*.[5] Teachers of grammar have instilled the notion that "a noun is the name of a person, place, or thing," so religiously that speakers very often go on to use "any" and "all" nouns as if they were talking of similarly observable and verifiable matters. Such words as Right, Power, Obligation, Justice, Beauty, Art, Service, etc., which the semanticist calls "fictions" are to be understood as "mental inventions and abstractions" and not as the names of "direct and specific sense-experiences." In the warmth and immersion of the speech situation it is not difficult for a speaker to hypostasize,[6] to reify these "big words," endowing them with form and substance as if they necessarily stood for phenomena whose existence is readily manifest. The student of meanings, however, seeks to locate these fictions, warn us of their character, and determine in any case how they are being used. /15

Guided by the facts of ambiguity, generality, and fiction-making, the semanticist's task is set out: He must, by a process of "equivalent statement" somehow bring to earth, pin down, and *fix* the specific areas of reference. He must try to translate what was said so that the speaker's words are closely approximated in terms which dissolve the sources of confusion. When faced with a speech in which the opportunities for vagueness are exploited to the full, the semanticist, bent on clarity, does not dismiss the speech as a stupid mess of blabs, but, ever mindful that understanding is not quickly won, he systematically moves to his probing. For this work a battery of highly sophisticated procedures has been devised. There is space here to mention but a few. /16

1. He will investigate the key terms in their setting and context as the ground of meaning.[7] (To study them out of such focus is much as if one were to sing a bass accompaniment as a solo.) /17

2. He will analyze each metaphor into its tenor and vehicle.[8] /18

3. He will list the modes of definition which were used in the speech and those which may be applied in further clarification and explanation.[9] /19

4. He will provide the fictions with *archetypes*, as a way of fixing "the reference of words to observed entities."[10] /20

5. He will make use of an *analytical paraphrase*, by which the original sentences are translated into the simple 850 word vocabulary of Basic English. This kind of translation provides "a gauge by which to judge the original; by comparison of the two we have more chance of discovering what the original almost said, or might have said, or does not quite make clear whether it is saying or not."[11] /21

In short, then, when the semanticist has made his study, we should presumably know what the speaker has said. The nature of the symbolic process, making difficult the verification of any interpretation, will, of course, impose limits on the semanticist's knowledge. Whether or not we agree with the speaker is here not relevant. At least we should be clear on this, that we seek to know *what* it is about which a judgment must be made. /22

But it may be useful to raise the questions that are irrelevant in the analysis of "meanings." *Should I agree with the speaker? Is what he said a sufficient*

---

[4] See I. A. Richards, *Interpretation in Teaching* (1938), pp. 23-170; also James MacKaye, *The Logic of Language* (Hanover, N. H.: Dartmouth College Publications), Ch. V.

* The United States had entered the second World War only twenty-two days before this speech was made. Wartime censorship was thus a very new experience for Americans. *(Editor's note)*

[5] Hugh R. Walpole, *Semantics* (1941), Ch. 8. See also C. K. Ogden, *Bentham's Theory of Fictions* (1932), pp. 7-105.

[6] James W. Woodard, *Intellectual Realism and Cultural Change* (Hanover, N. H.: The Sociological Press), 1935, Chs. II, III and V.

[7] I. A. Richards, *The Philosophy of Rhetoric*, Chs. II, III, and IV. See the Report of the Committee on the Function of English in General Education, *Language in General Education* (1940), pp. 89-155.

[8] *Ibid.*, Chs. V. and VI. See *Interpretation in Teaching*, pp. 115-144.

[9] Hugh R. Walpole, *Semantics*, Ch. 6.

[10] *Ibid.*, Ch. 8. C. K. Ogden, *Bentham's Theory of Fictions*, 86ff, 105ff, 138ff.

[11] *Ibid.*, 234. See C. K. Ogden, *The System of Basic English* (1934).

statement of the case? Does his statement satisfy the requirements of valid demonstration? Was his argument adequately "reasoned"? With these questions we come to the province of our third student—the logician. His way of looking at a speech has little to do with the persuasiveness, the meaningfulness, or the scientific basis of the utterance, but in the main, with the way that the factual sentences of the speech are related one to another. Logic as a discipline gives the logician no way of testing the accuracy of the speech; it gives him nothing more than a set of rules by which to test the various *relations* between sentences.[12] What is involved here will, perhaps, be evident as soon as we see what the logician looks for. /23

1. The first step in his criticism requires the careful distinction between two kinds of sentences.[13] He gets at it by asking two different questions: First, which sentences in this speech say something about people, places, happenings, relationships, etc.? Are these sentences true or false and to what extent? Second, which sentences tell us not about the *outside* world but about the feelings, fancies, wishes, and imaginings *inside* the speaker? With the statements revealing the states-of-mind of the speaker, the logician has nothing to do. /24

When a man asserts something about the world-outside, others can go look, examine, test, and check. But when we are told *how he feels* about things, there is no further searching possible. We may wish, perhaps, that he "felt" otherwise, but his speaking now is in the realm of the non-logical. The logician is not surprised (though often distressed) when he finds that many public speeches (because of inside manifestations) are, thus, outside his field of study, for the expressive function is revealed in all pictorial descriptions, commands, pleadings, reveries, longings, urgings, hopes, fears, doubts, etc. Of all these the logician says simply, "These forms of utterance belong to poetry, and there is nothing I can do with them." Others, however, may ask: Are they sufficiently poetic? Could the sentiments be put with more fervor, more aptness, more adornment? Have others said them better? But in any case, such materials are incapable of logical analysis. /25

This distinction between factual and expressive sentences is often obscured by the fact that both may have the same grammatical form. The reporter's verifiable story of a wrestling match may, on paper, be filled with the same sort of declarative sentences which grace the lyric poet's "Ode to Melancholy." But when it is not clear that the one describes what can be seen, whereas the other expresses an inner-mood, we are ready for vast confusion. The next time you read a speech of Hitler's, blue pencil the mood-lines. Only what remains may be discussed as variants of the true and the false. To argue about the validity or relevance of the verbal products of his inner perturbation is not to understand how the logical discipline works. /26

2. The logician then inquires into the *condition of consistency*.[14] He wants to find out whether the assertions or suppositions of the speaker are consistent with each other. Do the views in the early part of the speech square with those of the later? Do the sentences follow one from another? Are they compatible? /27

There is nothing in logic which says that certain statements are to be accepted or rejected. There is merely the simple demand that a speaker does not at the same time accept and also reject his assertions. /28

At first glance the task of inquiring into consistency may seem trivial and simple. And yet the great contribution of symbolic logic in the last 100 years, in the writings of Boole, Peirce, Frege, Whitehead, Russell, and others, was (and is) to build up "a vast treasure of validating forms, conditioning valid inferences" entirely unknown to the traditional Aristotelian logic.[15] Students who would overlook this "instrument for exhibiting the relations of consistency and deducibility"[16] must be left with blunter tools and duller insights. /29

3. The third focus of study for the logician is the *adequacy of the evidence*.[17] He proceeds to ask: Is there "sufficiently secure empirical foundation" for the theorems and conclusions of the speaker? How well established in prior knowledge are the predictions which he makes? How many instances in support of his assertions are confirmed by observation? How meager or how exhaustive is the data on which the conclusions are based? /30

The answers to these questions are of tremendous practical importance. The discovery of the empirical basis of a speech (or its inadequacy) may have far-reaching consequences. We may well be reminded here of some of the effects on social legislation and human relationships of the highly questionable as-

---

[12] Rudolf Carnap, "Logic," Factors Determining Human Behavior (Cambridge, Mass.: Harvard University Press), 1937, pp. 107-108. The following analysis of the work of the logician draws heavily on this paper.

[13] Ibid., pp. 108-112.

[14] Ibid., pp. 112-115.

[15] Ibid., p. 113. For further study see Willard Van Orman Quine, Elementary Logic (Boston, 1941).

[16] Ibid.

[17] Ibid., pp. 115-117.

sertions that grew out of data obtained in the First World War. /31

"For example, the statistics of intelligence tests upon men drafted for army service have been used to bolster up the view that most men are slaves by nature, and to support the prediction that the run of mankind is incapable of higher forms of civilization."[18] /32

One may also be excused the passing reflection that the public soothsayers and pseudo-pundits, so much with us these days, too often honor this requirement of adequacy of evidence with but a passing nod. /33

The task of the logician, then, is to look at a speech with his tests of sentence function, consistency, and evidentiary basis. These conditions he establishes not because they have some "absolute metaphysical validity" or because they rest "on the will of God"—but very simply on the fact "that unless they are satisfied, thought and knowledge cannot perform their function as instruments for arriving at successful decisions in practical matters."[19] /34

I come now to the fourth critic, the general semanticist. His questions pick up at the precise point where the student of meanings and the logician leave off. He proceeds to elaborate their findings by a methodology which reveals the unnoticed nuances and subtleties of inaccuracy and misevaluation. He asks very bluntly: Does it make sense? Does the speech properly evaluate whatever the words are intended to represent? How does what is said correspond to what can be found in life? Both the student of meanings and the logician focus on verbal matters so thoroughly that both they and we may tend to forget that there is also a non-verbal world to be accounted for. Indeed, there are many today who would say with Plato, "But there is no use of our disputing about (words) when we have (life-) realities of such importance to consider." To correct this neglect, the general semanticist[20] starts with and keeps constantly uppermost the connections between two levels: the verbal and the non-verbal, the worlds of the speakable and the un-speakable. He seeks to check the language at every point for the relationship it has to the discoverable facts of life. He would stress what most students seem not to have realized: that language has no other function than to serve as a form of representation of something else. Let me summarize the direction of his attack in the following set of analytical questions: /35

1. Is the speech marked by elementalistic terms so that the speaker splits verbally what cannot be found so split in life? /36

2. Does his analysis encourage the view that things are ever static, when life manifests progress everywhere? Does he assume that the permanence suggested by the structure of his language is to be found as well in the life-facts his talk represents?/37

3. Does he suggest in his argument a sense of the uniformities in situations where novelty and variety are readily discernible? Does he obliterate differences in his gross formulations? /38

4. Has he sought the final causes of happenings, asking unlimited questions to which only limited answers are possible? /39

5. Is there sharp awareness that statements of fact are not the same as his statements about them, that his inferences and high order abstractions are not directly descriptive of happenings? Or does he act as if there is no difference between them? (A heightened understanding of this principle might have made some of our ubiquitous "experts" and commentators aware that their inferences about the coming of Mr. Kurusu* were not first order descriptions. Public policy based on the one as if it were the other must too often leave us a prey to disillusionment and tragedy.) /40

6. Is he oriented by the verbal definitions of "things," so that he deals in averages and properties, thus obscuring the sense of existing individuals which only can be found in life? (Have you noticed how the attempts to define the differences between the Chinese and the Japanese in terms of similarity-marking characteristics so often end in humorous futility, because in life there are only unique individuals? Averages by emphasizing similarities may apply to all but they cover no one.) /41

7. Does he lead us to assume that his views exhaust the details of happenings? Is he aware that one may have convictions without being overcome by the lust for conclusiveness? Or, in his speaking, does he remind us of the question posed by Lytton Strachey in his essay on Macaulay, "How can one fail to miss a great deal if one persists in considering

[18] *Ibid.*, p. 116.
[19] *Ibid.*, p. 117.
[20] Alfred Korzybski, *Science and Sanity, an Introduction to Non-Aristotelian Systems and General Semantics* (Lancaster, Pa., The Science Press, second edition, 1941), v-xlix. The index of this book will indicate paginations for the suggested formulations.

* Saburo Kurusu was one of two special Japanese envoys who came to Washington in November 1941, ostensibly to confer with U.S. officials on ways of easing the threat of war in the Pacific. The Japanese attack on Pearl Harbor on December 7 occurred during their negotiations. Predictions that the conferences would prevent American involvement in the war were thus brought to naught. (*Editor's note*)

the world from one side or the other of the House of Commons?" /42

8. Is the speaking the sort that produces automatic, signal reactions, or does he seek to orient his audience to delay, deliberate, and investigate? /43

9. Does his argument boil down the infinitely-valued and varied facts of existence into but few values? /44

10. How aware is he in his definition-making that any definition of words by words must be based ultimately on undefined terms? /45

11. Is he at all conscious of his verbalizing as verbalizing, so that at any moment he might stop for a look at things and people, and with Paracelsus cry, "Let us forget words and manners, and treat our patients." Or, with magnificent unawareness, does he try "to adjust the empirical non-verbal facts to his verbal patterns"? Or is he one of those about whom Montaigne was properly ironical? "Through presumptions they make laws for nature and marvel at the way nature ignores these laws." /46

In short, the probings of the general semanticist lead us to an index of the intelligence, to the "good sense" of the speech, to the nicety with which the speaker discriminates, to the degree with which we can, with security, rely on his evaluations, to the awareness that any utterance must be dealt with as a mode of behavior, as a living issue. If his language use is cluttered up with identifications, objectifications, distortions, oversimplifications—then for our survival, those evidences of immaturity and unintelligence must be revealed. If he is oriented in the patterns of the primitive, we must be protected, lest we succumb to counsel that may lead to disaster. /47

By way of perspective and summary, it may be useful to list the four basic questions which lead to these four ways of looking at a speech.

For the rhetorician—How did he get his effects?

For the semanticist—What, in other words, did he say?

For the logician—Is what he said a sufficient and consistent statement of the case?

For the general semanticist—Does he make sense, properly evaluating what it is he talks about? /48

It should be clear, of course, that my four experts are "fictitious entities," that men of such carefully circumscribed interests are nowhere to be found. Nevertheless, the emphases embodied in each are readily available for study. The following four books should be enough as a starter:

1. *The Rhetoric of Aristotle*
2. *The Meaning of Meaning* by C. K. Ogden and I. A. Richards
3. *The Logical Syntax of Language* by Rudolf Carnap
4. *Science and Sanity* by Alfred Korzybski /49

It may, perhaps, not be amiss here to suggest that speech teachers have too long and, perhaps, too carefully given themselves over with unselfish devotion to the rhetorical perspective. But in a world torn with the heated bludgeonings of oversimplifications, distortions, and prejudices, speech teachers who would help to preserve freedom of expression might well, before it is too late, begin the search for that more precious freedom—expression buttressed with maturity, adequacy, and good sense. /50

For discussion

1. What are the four ways in which Lee suggests a speech may be examined?
2. Look up in an unabridged dictionary the words *rhetoric*, *semantics*, and *logic*. Consult one or more encyclopedias in order to gain a clearer notion of the arts or sciences which these terms name.
3. What is the "first concern" of the rhetorician in studying a speech? What basic questions does he ask about the speech, speaker, and audience?
4. To what additional and more specific matters does the rhetorician also direct his attention?
5. What is the central concern of the semanticist when he evaluates a speech?
6. Compare the questions the semanticist asks about a speech with those asked by the rhetorician. Is there any duplication or overlapping? Are the answers to the rhetorician's questions in any way dependent upon answers supplied by the semanticist?
7. What three fundamental facts about the working of language guide the semanticist's "quest"?
8. Explain in your own words the "highly sophisticated procedures" the semanticist employs in probing a speech.
9. What does Professor Lee mean when he says, "The nature of the symbolic process, making difficult the verification of any interpretation, will, of course, impose limits upon the semanticist's knowledge"?
10. State the central concern of the logician when he examines a speech. To what three subsidiary matters does he direct his attention? With what sort of "sentences" is he especially concerned?

11. Compare the central concern of the general semanticist with the concerns of the semanticist and the logician. In what way does the general semanticist supplement and extend their findings?

12. In your opinion, does the rhetorician, the semanticist, the logician, or the general semanticist ask the most significant questions concerning a speech? Or does good rhetorical criticism entail approaching an address from all four points of view?

13. Distinguish between the "verbal" and "non-verbal" levels—between "the worlds of the speakable and the un-speakable."

14. Select one of the speeches in this book and apply to it each of the four methods of criticism which Lee describes. Compare the results.

15. How do the aims of the critic of speaking, regardless of the approach he may use, differ fundamentally from the aims of the critic of literature, art, or music?

Culture and communication
ROBERT T. OLIVER

The historical records known to us place the beginnings of formal rhetorical studies in the fifth century B.C. at the Sicilian city-state of Syracuse. As Professor Oliver indicates in the address below, the circumstances of those beginnings are significant in themselves, because they show how democratic processes have been directly associated with our rhetorical traditions.

Following a period of democratic government, Syracuse fell under the rule of tyrants from 485 to 466 B.C. When democracy was re-established, the citizens had to appear in the courts to reclaim title to their properties lost under the tyranny. Since they were required to plead their own cases and since many felt inadequate to the task, they enlisted the aid of what we would today call ghost writers, who supplied them with persuasive speeches to deliver in the courts. Two of these ghost writers were Corax and Tisias, who, apparently, also

Robert T. Oliver, "Culture and Communication," *Vital Speeches of the Day*, Vol. XXIX, September 15, 1963, pp. 721-724. Reprinted by permission of the author.

wrote a manual on public speaking. With their book, now lost, the record of formal studies in speaking and rhetoric begins for the Western world. At Athens and Rome, in later times, it was again the citizens' need to exercise the responsibilities of democratic self-government that gave impetus to further and more penetrating explorations of how men influence others through speech.

Across the centuries, the study of practical rhetoric has been largely confined to societies culturally indebted to Greece and Rome. In consequence, perhaps, democratic and other Athenian and Roman values have never been completely lost from this body of theory and advice. The rhetorical writings of Aristotle (Greece), Cicero (Rome), St. Augustine (North Africa), Juan Luis Vives (Spain), Francis Bacon (England), François Fénelon (France), James A. Winans (United States), Chaim Perelman (Belgium)—to name a few distinguished rhetoricians from different lands and different eras—are all indebted to the tradition that originated at Syracuse and flowered at Athens. Moreover, as experimental inquiries into rhetoric have been conducted in America and Europe, far more of the ancient suppositions and practices in communication have been confirmed than refuted. But how far these durable rhetorical principles have practical applications in other than Western cultural systems has never been systematically investigated.

Professor Robert T. Oliver has unique qualifications to challenge the assumption that effective rhetoric is everywhere the same. He is student, teacher, historian, and active practitioner of the arts of speaking and writing. Moreover, he has successfully carried major responsibility for formulating messages—especially speeches—by means of which Oriental problems and ideas were made intelligible and persuasive to Occidental minds.

Since 1942, Professor Oliver has served in various consultative capacities to the Republic of Korea, especially as adviser to the Korean Delegation to the United Nations and as personal adviser to the late President Syngman Rhee. During the formative years of the modern Korean Republic, Dr. Oliver's task was to help Korean leaders express themselves meaningfully and persuasively to the peoples of Western societies and to their own people. In these and other connections, he has visited Asia frequently and has also traveled in Europe, the Middle East, and Latin America. His *Syngman Rhee: The Man Behind the Myth* (first published in 1954, revised in 1955, and republished in 1960) and *Why War Came in Korea* (1950) were cited among the "best non-fiction books" by the New York *Times*. In addition, he is author or coauthor of some twenty books on speech and speaking, two of the most recent being *Culture and Communication* (1962) and *The History of Public Speaking in America* (1965).

The address that follows was first delivered from manuscript at a speech convocation sponsored by the School of Speech at Kent State University (Ohio), April 3, 1963. Between 700 and 1000 persons overflowed an auditorium in the newly constructed Speech Building. Professor Oliver, the featured speaker, was introduced by Professor L. LeRoy Cowperthwaite, Chairman of the School of Speech. The meeting was open to the public, but special invitations had been issued to Kent State students and faculty members in speech, history, and the social sciences.

Professor Oliver delivered extemporaneously a version of this same speech to a seminar of graduate students and faculty members in speech and communications at the University of Denver on August 15, 1963. On September 15, 1963, the text of the speech as read at Kent State University was published in *Vital Speeches of the Day.*

Robert T. Oliver was born at Sweet Home, Oregon, July 7, 1909. He received the A.B. degree from Pacific University in 1932, the M.A. (English) from the University of Oregon in 1933, and the Ph.D. (Speech) from the University of Wisconsin in 1937. He has served as a faculty member at Bradley University, Bucknell University, and Syracuse University. Since 1949, he has been Professor and Head of the Department of Speech at Pennsylvania State University. He was President of the Speech Association of America in 1964 and Vice President of the Speech Association of the Eastern States in 1965.

The editors of this volume invited Professor Oliver to supply observations, addressed to students of speech, on the subject of ghost writing. He graciously agreed, and his statement follows:

"A ghost writer is an administrative assistant to the man for whom he writes: much more than a secretary, much less than a colleague or associate. In my own experience of more than twenty years in writing at least two hundred speeches and magazine articles, besides numerous formal statements, for President Syngman Rhee and other high officials of the Republic of Korea, what I chiefly learned is that a 'ghost' is of no value whatsoever unless or until he attains the ability to say what his principal wants to say in ways that he wants to say it.

"This does not mean that a ghost makes no substantial contribution to the nature of the final product. President Rhee, a very generous man, used to give me full credit for the work I did for him, introducing me in various groups as 'The man who helps me say what I want to say in ways that keep people from getting mad at me.'

"Some people have questioned the ethics of ghost writing. This questioning is on the basis that a public man should be evaluated by the public on his own merits, not misrepresented as possessing superior merits which are in fact those of some anonymous ghost. I know that in my own writing for President Rhee, I was never in the slightest doubt that he understood both the fundamentals and the nuances of international affairs far better than I. Before I could write for him successfully, he spent many hours, over a period of about two years, patiently explaining to me and illustrating what he believed and why. During all this time, he had considerably to revise the speeches I wrote for him. Finally, however, I did, through intimate companionship, become sufficiently acquainted with his purposes, methods, and personality so that I could write for him not what I wanted to say, but what *he* wanted to say. This is the essential condition for being a successful ghost.

"It seems strange to me that critics should object to ghost writing. The president of any nation has to issue a great many formal statements—supporting Milk Week, the Boy Scouts' anniversary, etc., etc. Surely it would be stupid for a chief executive to write such statements, stealing time from more important duties. Executives also need to give speeches supporting the programs of various departments under their supervision, explaining the soil-bank program, for example. It seems obvious that such talks should be written for them. And presidents must appear before numerous conventions of organizations, ranging from the Daughters of the American Revolution to the Steelworkers' Union; and they need to report from time to time to the Congress and to the public. In any and all of such speeches, what a president wants to say should be prepared in the way he wants to say it, but there is every reason why the actual composition should be by a ghost writer. 'The hand is the hand of Esau, but the voice is the voice of Jacob.'"

As a Professor of Speech I feel just a bit abashed to appear here before you with a manuscript in hand. But I do it for two reasons: first, because I was asked to do so, which surely is reason enough; and second, because, as the nature of the situation suggests, I have made a special effort to set forth some ideas in more definitive form than is likely to be accomplished extemporaneously. /1

Now, even if I do have a manuscript to read from, I want to assure you that I have written it myself. I know about ghost writers, as you do. I know about them with special cogency, because I am one myself

—and therein lies a point pertinent to the problem we are considering today. /2

It happens that some time ago I engaged over a span of months in a running discourse—you might even call it an argument—with a professor who was on our campus as a visitor from his native land of India. The subject of our discussion was the nature of certain qualities of the Oriental value system with which our own democratic heritage could most readily interlock. For months he kept insisting to me that I had the ideas almost but never quite right. Then I had occasion to ghost-write a speech for a distinguished Oriental statesman on this very theme; and in a short time it appeared in print. A day or so afterwards the Indian professor burst in to see me with the published speech in hand and said, "I want you to read this. Here is a statement by one of my fellow Orientals that says exactly what I have been trying to tell you and says it so clearly I don't think you can miss the point." Of course I never did tell him who the author was. /3

I tell this incident with a mingling of pride and frustration. It was pleasant, of course, to win my argument with the gentleman from India—even though I was trapped by circumstances and could not tell him I had won. But it was frustrating to be reminded so vividly and dramatically that no matter how hard I tried I could not communicate my ideas to him—at least not until they seemed to come not from me but from one of his own fellows. /4

The point, I am afraid, is all too clear. When we peoples of the world try to address one another across cultural gaps, we encounter two serious kinds of difficulties. The first is that we may not and probably usually do not understand one another's point of view. And the second is that even when we do, we speak to one another essentially as strangers, as foreigners, as spokesmen for and from differing and even competing ways of life. /5

This is my introduction to the topic I have chosen to discuss with you today. In a sense, it is an epitome of the whole speech. For, in essence, it contains the message I have in mind. What follows is chiefly elaboration, or interpretation or an effort to justify or to prove, together with an implied plea that we all work harder and more cooperatively than we have in the past to try to solve the problem I am trying to define. /6

Now, in these introductory comments, I have tried to accomplish two purposes: to indicate, first, that I shall have nothing either very new or very startling to say; and second, that there are some rather commonplace facts available to all of us that ought to be considered somewhat differently than they commonly are—and that if this is done we may become significantly more successful in our attempts at international and intercultural communication. It is, as you know, one of the strange characteristics of our minds that we find the obvious almost as elusive as the abstruse—so that, as it has been said, if water were unknown, fish would be the last creatures to discover it. /7

People are smarter than fish; but I think there are some facts about our world situation that are far too completely obvious to seem to most of us to be worthy of special attention. /8

What I chiefly have in mind is the truism that we now have become citizens of the world. This surely is one of the obvious facts. /9

This is a time in history in which it is difficult to be provincial. Technology has done wonders in compressing distance, so that our large world has become a small one. There are no strange places anymore. All roads lead to wherever one happens to live, whether it be in Teutopolis, Illinois, or in Tanganyika. Not only do we hear and read about the whole world, but we also go out into it. /10

Travel is supposed to be broadening; but in my observation, many times, for many people, it is actually narrowing. The farther they get away from Dubuque, the better Dubuque looks to them. When they are confronted with a delicious platter of steamed octopus, they long for a hamburger with catsup. We may go out into the world, but we never become a part of it as long as we take our own value systems, our own habits, our own expectations with us. I have known Americans who have lived for twenty years in the Orient without ever leaving home. On the other hand, there are receptive minds that know how to establish friendly contact with foreign cultures on the first meeting with them. /11

The point I want to make can be put into one single sentence, namely: We can communicate with people in another culture only in terms that make sense to them. Prime Minister Nehru,* on his visit to America in 1950, made the same point a bit more explicitly, and cogently enough to merit quotation. "If we seek to understand a people," he said, "we have to put ourselves, as far as we can, in that particular historical and cultural background. . . . One has to recognize that . . . countries and peoples differ in their approach and their ways, in their

---

*Jawaharlal Nehru (1889-1964), British-educated associate of Mohandas Gandhi in the movement for Indian independence, for which Nehru was the outstanding orator; first Prime Minister of India (1947-1964). (Editor's note)

approach to life and their ways of living and thinking. In order to understand them we have to understand their way of life and approach. If we wish to convince them, we have to use their language as far as we can, not language in the narrow sense of the word, but the language of the mind." /12

Now, the cultural anthropologists have gone a long way toward defining the special characteristics of differing societies. And the historians, and the political scientists, and the economists, and the sociologists also have gone a long way toward identifying the problems that must be solved to eliminate the clashes of interest between competing groups. We in the Speech profession have not as yet made comparable contributions toward developing rhetorical methods suitable to bridge the gaps between divergent culture groups that are now in contact but not yet in communication. /13

If we have lagged behind in confronting our own professional challenge, this fact should occasion no surprise. The divergencies in world cultures have always existed and have long been readily available for our professional colleagues to examine. But the critical need for cross-cultural understanding has come hurtling upon the world with both a speed and an urgency that were wholly unexpected. The world did not really become one community even in the thirties, with its introduction of trans-global radio, nor in the forties, with a genuinely worldwide war in progress. It is only in the past ten years or so that planes, and missiles, and space satellites and now even trans-oceanic television have made universal communication a necessity, rather than a luxury. It is only in very recent years that the peoples of every portion of the globe have come into direct confrontation—sometimes in open enmity, sometimes with a wistful effort to be friendly. /14

What we must not ignore is the desperate urgency of the need for undertaking a new approach to the problem of people-to-people communication. Not only in our Cold War struggle with communism, but also in our relations with such old and close friends as France and Canada, it is evident that the rhetoric of international communication has proved inadequate to the demands made upon it. No one, I think, will deny that the survival of our civilization, if not of the human race itself, may depend upon the speedy development of effective means of bridging culture-gaps. /15

It is a task of such importance that governmental agencies and private research foundations should be initiating, encouraging, and supporting widespread inquiries and programs directed toward its solution.

Yet nowhere in the world has there yet commenced a systematic and determined effort to devise means by which peoples of divergent value systems can come into close and cordial communication. Sir Winston Churchill has said that "Jaw, jaw, is better than war, war." Yet while we strive mightily to avoid falling behind in atomic weaponry, we don't as yet study the means of engaging in an effective global dialogue. /16

As you may well guess at this point, what I am trying to do is to ask questions rather than to answer them. The answering will take the work of a great many people, armed with tremendous resources. What is of most urgency now is that we should direct our attention to the right question. And in my judgment this question may be stated as follows: *Should we abandon our traditional concept of a unitary or generic rhetoric and develop the ability to deal with a complex series of divergent rhetorics?* /17

Perhaps the question sounds a bit anticlimactic! First we confront the possible apocalyptic destruction of the world—through an atomic war; then I ask you to seek salvation through an academic inquiry into the nature of rhetorical theory. Let me try rephrasing the solution we should seek: the peoples of the world need to start talking to one another in ways that make sense to the listeners. You could say that what we need is better audience analysis—but it's more than that. What we need is to learn how to hook into one another's modes of thinking. What we need is to learn how to bridge from one culture to another. /18

But this is precisely, it may be argued, what rhetoric always has intended to do. Rhetoric, in fact, has been defined as the art of using language in such a way as to produce a desired impression upon the hearer or reader. It is, then, a generic term, of universal application. Whatever the communicative barriers may be, we utilize our rhetorical tools in an effort to penetrate them. But this is not the case. We have failed to confront the essential problem. /19

Let me back away for the moment from rhetoric to look at its companion science, logic. For a great many centuries logic was also considered to be an indivisible generic term. As late as the middle of the nineteenth century, it was quite proper for the Deacon in Oliver Wendell Holmes's poem, "The Wonderful One Hoss Shay," to exclaim, "Logic is logic, that's all I say." Alcuin, Spinoza, Hobbes, Locke, Hume, and Mill could introduce amendments or refinements to Aristotle's logic; but after all, it was a cardinal characteristic of logic as a system that it was unescapable—indivisible—inevitable. The laws of connection or of relationship or of definition that it described were in fact, it was assumed, prescribed by internal necessity. To speak of conflicting systems of logic was an absurdity. /20

But, as we know, the situation today is vastly different. In addition to Aristotelianism and Korzybskian* or Bogoslovskyan** Anti-Aristotelianism, we have now a dozen or more divergent systems, including the Classical Symbolic, the Intuitionist, the Combinatory, the Modal, etc. Each of these logics operates within its own conceptual universe. To a considerable degree they do not so much as touch upon one another. They offer to the logician a wide range of choice of analytical and synthesizing tools for dealing with quite different types of problems. /21

This is what is happening today in the field of logic, with astonishingly productive results. Yet listen to how logic *per se*, logic as a generic term, has been and often still is defined: "Logic works by obedience to inevitable connections between objectively existent facts. Its principal test is internal coherence." From this generic conception of logic, however, it was easy to proceed to a liberating realization that any system of logic is justified if it produces valid conclusions by a consistent methodology. /22

To remain with logic for a few moments longer, let us examine an article by C. Wright Mills, entitled "Language, Logic, and Culture," which he published in 1939 in *The American Sociological Review,* and which has just been reprinted in a collection of his essays, under the title *Power, Politics, and People.* "Problems set by one logic are, with a change in interests, outgrown, not solved," Professor Mills wrote. "The rules of the game change with a shift in interests, and we must accept the dominant rules if we would make an impress upon the profile of thought. Our logical apparatus is formulated by the rebuffs and approvals received from the audiences of our thought." In the same essay he also says, "Arguments which in the discourse of one group or epoch are accepted as valid, in other times and conversations are not so received." /23

*Alfred H. S. Korzybski (1879-1950), Polish-American scientist and author who founded the psychological-philosophical school of thought called general semantics through his *Science and Sanity; an Introduction to Nonaristotelian Systems and General Semantics,* 2nd ed. (1941). See also Irving J. Lee, "Four Ways of Looking at a Speech," pp. 12-19 in this volume. (Editor's note)

**Boris B. Bogoslovsky, writer on education associated with the "progressive education" movement and author of *The Technique of Controversy; Principles of Dynamic Logic* (1928). (Editor's note)

Even so rigid a logician as John Stuart Mill once wrote that if the rules of geometry had not proved to be useful, mankind would have pronounced them to be false. Now, I shall leave it to the logicians whether or not they accept this doctrine. To me it seems antithetical to the conception that logic deals with immutable relationships that are immune from the accidents of time or place. But whatever the logicians may do with it, it seems to me that we rhetoricians should welcome the statements by both Mills and Mill as a description not of logic but of rhetoric. /24

Rhetoricians are not concerned with immutable relationships but with probabilities. Our problems are not objective but subjective. Of rhetoric it surely may be said that "the rules of the game change with a shift in interests" and that "we must accept the dominant rules if we would make an impress upon the profile of thought." /25

This may seem harmless enough and simple enough. Remember, I warned you at the outset that my purpose was to emphasize the obvious. But if we simply accept what we are saying here, a tremendous difference would be introduced into the scholarship of our field. And if our professional colleagues would go along with us, it may be that collectively we could solve some of the problems of impenetrable distance that prevent the flow of understanding from one culture to another. For what this "obvious" interpretation leads to is an abandonment of the term rhetoric, and a replacement of it with the plural, *rhetorics.* What we would then need to deal with is not rhetoric *per se,* but a Confucian rhetoric, a Taoist rhetoric, a Buddhist rhetoric, a Communist rhetoric, a Muslim rhetoric, indeed even a Swahili rhetoric, and a Congolese rhetoric. /26

At this point it may appear that I am dealing less with the obvious than with chaos. To insist upon a different rhetoric for every different cultural entity may appear the same thing as having no rhetoric at all. I would ask us to remind ourselves, however, that our brethren in Speech Therapy made comparatively little advance upon the problem of stuttering until they recognized that it is not one problem after all, but a cluster of problems—that instead of stuttering, they are confronted with stutterings. Then, upon this revolutionary change of approach, they began to develop differential diagnoses, which in turn led to individuation of proposed remedies. /27

The rhetoric we think of as generic was in fact devised for a specific kind of society, with its own view of the nature of human nature. It was designed for the use of free men who have the right to cast free ballots. It was developed for individuals who were considered to be essentially rational—beset by emotionalism, of course, but finally "available" to the prescriptive conclusions of fact and logic. Its field of concern was with probabilities, or with relativistic values—with propositions concerning which a choice had to be made by weighing considerations of greater or lesser, better or worse. The decision, finally, was intended to accord with the "greatest good for the greatest number" by the mechanism of a majority vote. /28

It is no accident that this rhetoric was invented by Corax in Syracuse when Syracuse adopted a democratic form of government, nor that it was elaborated and given its final structure by Aristotle for use by the self-governing minority in Athens.* For the relatively closed world of Europe and America, this rhetoric has, by and large, met the pragmatic test: it has worked, at least well enough to escape serious question. /29

However, we have all of us been propelled out into a world nowadays where no single one of the presumptions upon which this rhetoric works is universally true. /30

Freedom, for example, is a matter of degree, varying widely from one country to another. Some cultures flatly reject the notion that man is rational, lending their prestige, rather, to appeals and responses based upon intuitive insight. Relativism concerning ultimate values is in some cultures regarded as a sinful philosophy, with authoritarianism the court of final appeal. Still other cultures reject the idea that a majority vote is superior—or, as in communist states, control the voting to assure virtual unanimity. /31

It is obvious, also, that in different cultures people think about different subject matter. Industrialization, with its whole complex of problems and attitudes, means nothing to a Zulu. On the other hand, the very elaborate and all-embracing system of witchcraft of a Bushman dominates his thinking but scarcely so much as brushes against the edges of our minds. The Australian Aborigines, to cite another example, could not count beyond ten; hence their awareness of number was limited. Cultural anthropologists have multiplied such instances. /32

Beyond this, different peoples also think in different ways about the same or similar subject matter. For example, it is a matter of pride to an American boy to rise to a higher status than that of

---

*Citizens—those possessing full political rights and obligations—were usually a minority of the Athenian population. (Editor's note)

his parents. But for an Oriental it would be a cause of shame even to contemplate doing so. To us self-preservation is the first law of life. But to a Japanese who values the Shinto tradition, the state is of more consequence than the individual. Equality, individuality, and freedom of the will are valued in some cultures; whereas, subordination, conformity, and predestination are preferred in others. /33

As we all know, Benjamin Lee Whorf, following the cue of Edward Sapir, correlated some of these ideas with his study of language and formulated what has come to be known as the Sapir-Whorf Hypothesis—that language serves as a perceptual mold, shaping how people think and also influencing their choice of objects of attention or interest.* And we know, too, that Harry Hoijer and his associates have directed some very telling criticism at what appears to have been Whorf's exaggeration of the dominant power of linguistic forms.** Culture, these critics point out, influences language, as well as the reverse. However, both Whorf and his critics combine to direct our thinking toward the same point: namely, that language and culture together do either reflect or cause basic and significant group differences in modes of thinking. /34

We as rhetoricians can afford to be relatively indifferent to the question of whether the cultural characteristics or their linguistic expression come first. What we cannot be indifferent to is the very evident fact that every culture, by definition, constitutes a unique value system, with its own mode of thought. A Hindu cannot think as an American does; he cannot be similarly motivated; he cannot follow the same kind of mental processes. The two are unlikely to start from the same premises and even when they do they are unlikely to reach the same conclusions. /35

I don't see how anyone can doubt this interpretation. Indeed, it is less likely to be doubted than to be accepted with a shrug as being obviously true but relatively unimportant. To deny its truth would be to wipe out at one stroke the whole field of cultural anthropology and to deny to sociologists the validity of one of their key terms—culture. /36

But if it is true that every culture has its own typical mode of thinking, this fact must inevitably

---

*Edward Sapir (1884-1939) and Benjamin Lee Whorf (1897-1941). The view associated with these linguists was stated by Whorf: "We cut nature up, organize it into concepts, and ascribe significance as we do, largely because we are parties to . . . an agreement that holds through our speech community and is codified in the patterns of our language." Whorf, *Language, Thought, and Reality*, J. B. Carroll ed. (1956). (Editor's note)

**Harry Hoijer, anthropologist and linguist. Dr. Oliver is referring to Hoijer's *Language in Culture* (1954). (Editor's note)

demand a renunciation of the concept of rhetoric, in favor of the idea of a cluster of rhetorics. It must, that is, if we think of rhetoric as a mode of thinking, comparable, let us say, to dialectic, and logic, and the so-called scientific method. /37

Within the scope of this lecture, time does not permit me to develop the ideas I have so hastily sketched. For those who may wish to pursue them further, I can only suggest that they are spelled out in greater detail, with rather complete if far from exhaustive illustrations from the areas of rhetoric represented by Communism, Confucianism, Taoism, Shintoism, and the Hindu-Buddha idea system in my recent book, *Culture and Communication*, especially in Chapters VII through XII. /38

I shall conclude with a simple instance of changing the tone of an international dialogue by the use of an appropriate cultural rhetorical frame of reference. /39

I recall very well a scene of some years ago, just as daylight was breaking, on the island of Wake, in the mid-Pacific. The commercial passenger plane on which I was flying from Tokyo to San Francisco had put down to refuel, and we passengers were shepherded into the restaurant at the terminal building to have breakfast. All of us were sleepy, disheveled, and tired after a night-long flight. As a consequence, we did not feel particularly sociable. I took my seat at a small table along with two other American men, who appeared to be businessmen, and a middle-aged Japanese, who proved to be a college professor barely able to speak a few words of English. /40

None of us paid any attention to any of the others until I noticed that the Japanese was regarding his American companions with rather obvious distaste. Then I smiled at him, and handed him the salt cellar for his eggs, holding it toward him in my right hand, with the fingers of the left hand lightly touching the base of my right hand palm—a typical Japanese gesture of respect. For a moment he looked unbelievingly at the unexpected behavior of this strange foreigner. Then his face broke into a broad smile of sheer relief and I could almost hear him say to himself, "Perhaps they are not barbarians, after all." It was quite a lot to accomplish by so simple a device as knowing how to hold one's hands. /41

This, I think, is a good point at which to come to rest. The change in theory and in method for which I am asking is neither complex nor considerable. But if we should make the shift and learn how to operate upon the concept of multiple rhetorics, the change in effect might be as great as was the change in medicine when Pasteur said to his colleagues, "It is not vapour or dirt, gentlemen, that carries the disease, but germs." /42

For discussion

1. Can a great orator develop in an unfree society? Or does what we call "greatness" in a speaker depend on the atmosphere of freedom which only democracy provides?

2. Investigate the beginnings of the systematic study of speechmaking in Greece and Sicily during the fifth century B.C. (In this connection, see R. C. Jebb, *Attic Orators*, Vol. 1; Lester Thonssen and A. Craig Baird, *Speech Criticism*; George Kennedy, *The Art of Persuasion in Greece*; the article on "Rhetoric" in the *Encyclopaedia Britannica,* etc.)

3. Speeches have been ghost written for twenty-five centuries. What do you think are the unique problems of a ghost writer in composing a speech for another person? Must ghost written speeches have the superficial qualities Carleton (paragraph 11, p. 8) finds in so many speeches today? What moral issues, if any, do you think ghost writing presents to the writer? To the speaker?

4. After reading Vera Micheles Dean's speech (pp. 234-240) or Charles de Gaulle's press conference statements (pp. 248-254), hold an informal discussion on one of the following questions:
   a. How would an American speaker have to modify his ways of arguing and expressing ideas if he were to try to persuade a listener of De Gaulle's views that a strong NATO is more important than a "European Europe"?
   b. How would American discussants have to modify their topics and discussion methods in order to explain their purposes to representatives of such undeveloped countries as Mrs. Dean describes?

5. How would you answer Oliver's central question: "Should we abandon our traditional concept of a unitary or generic rhetoric and develop the ability to deal with a complex series of divergent rhetorics?"

6. At the close of his *Techniques of Persuasion* (Penguin Books, 1963), J. A. C. Brown says, " . . . it would appear that the main lesson to be drawn from our present study of propaganda is how very resistant people are to messages that fail to fit into their own picture of the world and their own objective circumstances, how they deliberately (if unconsciously) seek out only those views which agree with their own." Does Brown's finding imply that Oliver is right in insisting that to persuade we

must find out the special rhetoric of each culture, or does his finding imply that persuasion across cultures is scarcely possible?

7. If teachers of speech and writing adopted Oliver's suggestion that a "traditional concept of a unitary . . . rhetoric" be abandoned, how do you think they should change their speech, writing, and literature courses?

8. What does Oliver mean when, in paragraph 18, he distinguishes between "better audience analysis" and learning "how to hook into one another's modes of thinking"?

9. To what extent, if at all, do you think our American conception of "effective speaking" is determined by our belief that individual liberty, self-government, and rational behavior are among the highest goods man can attain?

10. Oliver seems to equate the manner of handling a saltcellar with "rhetoric" (paragraphs 40-41). What justification, if any, is there for his extension of the term "rhetoric" to apply to acts as well as to discourse?

11. Read Colin Legum's speech on "Pan-Africanism" (pp. 255-259). Do you find any evidence in this speech that Legum's experience of living in both Africa and England helps him make the Africans understandable to the English? Cite specific features of the speech to support your conclusion.

12. How would you explain the "fact" that a single rhetorical theory, with some variations and extensions to suit changing needs, has served the Western world for more than twenty centuries? Or is this the "fact"?

Speeches for analysis and ideas

The place and the price of excellence

JACQUES BARZUN

Jacques Barzun, author, scholar, lecturer, and editor, was born in Creteil, France, in 1907, but came to the United States in 1920. In 1923 he entered Columbia University, where he received his A.B. and Ph.D. degrees and later became a member of the faculty. He was appointed Professor of History in 1945 and is now Provost and Dean of Faculties at Columbia. Among his best known works are *Teacher in America* (1945), *Berlioz and the Romantic Century* (1950), *God's Country and Mine* (1954), *The House of Intellect* (1959), and *Classic, Romantic and Modern* (1961).

Barzun delivered the following address before the third convocation of the Graduate School of Cornell University in December, 1958. The convocation was held in the Alice Statler Auditorium on the Cornell campus, the audience consisting of between five and six hundred graduate students and members of the faculty. Barzun was introduced by the Dean of the Graduate School, John W. McConnell. The program consisted simply of the Dean's welcome to the new students and faculty and Barzun's address.

Published in pamphlet form by Cornell University, the speech was widely distributed on campus. The impact was remarkable. For example, the undergraduate organizers of the Cornell United Religious Organizations Program chose Barzun's speech as the basis of a panel discussion for incoming freshmen in the fall of 1960. One faculty member was so moved that he wrote: "I can think of no speech made here in the last half-dozen years that has received such continuing attention and restudy by the University community."

When asked about his training as a public speaker, Barzun replied, "I've been speaking since birth!" His philosophy of effective speaking rests on the notion that one should be heard and understood. He thinks a speech for a large audience should be written out but read as if it were impromptu. For smaller gatherings he thinks the speaker should carefully prepare the order of topics and memorize the opening and closing remarks word for word, but should speak without a script and without notes.

Although there are many subjects in which I am sure you take an interest comparable to mine, I have chosen one which (as I hope) is particularly suited to your present concerns and also to the times. You are students, presumably engaged in studying; you are graduate students, who may soon become teachers; you are parents or shortly to become parents; you are citizens, whose votes and whose taxes are being, or are going to be, solicited in the name of education. I am accordingly going to talk to you about education—or so it would seem. But as I have often said, talk about education bores me, so under guise of education I am going to talk to you about Intellect, and Intellect of the kind that is rarest and most excellent. I am going to use the facts and the follies of education to talk to you about intellectual excellence. /1

The word *excellence* has a pleasing sound. But it has been a long time since we in the United States have heard it from anybody but an advertiser. We associate excellence with the products of industry, not only because we are told they are excellent, not only because the price we pay and the effort we make to obtain these artifacts seem to justify our hope of their excellence, but also and, I think, chiefly, because we are very sure that, being artifacts, those which are declared excellent will not incur the resentment of the others. /2

If this is true, it means that we are still very much alive to the idea that underlies excellence—the idea of excelling, of raising oneself so as to be better or greater than, or superior to, another. We are alive to this idea at large, but we do not like to apply it to persons. We suppress it in our social life and even in our private thoughts, because it seems to run counter to another idea that we cherish more stubbornly—the idea of equality. We find it repugnant

By permission of Dr. Barzun. From a reprint of his address issued by Cornell University.

to our political professions and our democratic manners that anyone should be believed in any way better or greater than someone else, should know himself to be, or should act as if he were in any way superior. /3

Very recently, however, a public report on the state of education, prepared for the Rockefeller Brothers' Fund and drafted under the direction of Mr. John Gardner, the head of the Carnegie Corporation, was issued with the title: "The Pursuit of Excellence." In the light of our ancient prejudice about the word, the use of that phrase seems to me to mark a turning point in the national opinion. /4

The phrase did not, of course, provoke the change. Rather, it confirmed the fact that the change was taking place. For the change is not merely in education, any more than it is a rediscovery of excellence in living beings after a long siege of confinement in dead things. To talk of excellence in connection with education is much more momentous than appears on the surface. For what does excellence in education or learning really refer to? It refers to Intellect. To talk of excellence in education means to talk of the place of Intellect in the national life. And this is almost unheard of. Education with us has been for every good purpose, I will not say, *except* an intellectual purpose, but every good purpose *ahead* of an intellectual purpose. It has been for character, citizenship, health, social and individual adjustment, cultural assimilation, vocational aid, profitable friendships, marriage opportunities, and hobbies of distinction. The desire to raise the Intellect to new heights has not existed or been avowed. And we are still far from according Intellect a clear place; the Rockefeller Brothers' report seems to speak of it as if it were the same as creativity, which it is not; but even creativity they want to have thrive "in a context of concern for all." This is hedging: clearly we do not quite know what Intellect is, and what we do know we are afraid of. But we have at last come face to face with the fact that Intellect exists, and we mean somehow to come to terms with it. /5

The general public today probably thinks that the present agitation about education and the training of talents dates from the Russian success in launching rockets. But that is not so. The unrest and criticism came well before. Some of you will remember the reports of the President's Commission on Higher Education, the vogue of the book *Why Johnny Can't Read,* the mounting protest against so-called progressive methods, and the repeated exposures of folly and futility in our colleges and teachers' colleges. These and other like events show that the unassuming citizen has in the last few years been acquiring a new and well founded worry. /6

Still earlier, there had been a good deal of quiet self-scrutiny by professionals, usually encouraged by the foundations. The phrase "gifted child" emerged from these inquiries. The two most notable were perhaps the experiment in Portland, Oregon, which put the brightest children of all grades in speedier classes, and the advanced placement plan of acceleration devised by three colleges and three leading private schools in the East. The result of these pointed attentions that are paid to intellectual talent and have regard to the flight of time has been to make the American people recognize the inadequacy of their schools. The schools are inadequate because they culpably neglect the national resource of Intellect. /7

But this growing recognition, important as it is, does not bring us the remedy. Mere speed for the gifted is not enough. Larger doses of science and mathematics and American history will not change the strength and character of the instruction. If the diet is poor, undernourishment is not cured by larger amounts. Most important, inadequate arrangements cannot be bettered by people who have never found anything wrong with them. To put it more generally, the country is only beginning to perceive that its schools are not independent of the surrounding world: the world of parents, legislators, businessmen, journalists, and government officials. It is their ideas that have so far prevailed—ideas we need not scorn entirely, for they have made good up to a point the adventure of mass education. In 1900 no one believed that the free, public, and compulsory high school could work. Well, it does not work very much or very well, but it works. Enough to be imitated, right now, by most of the countries of Europe, which are cheerfully repeating our early mistakes: our colleges and universities are also semi-mass institutions, remedial institutions for high school deficiencies; and to this Europe has not yet attained. *We* are at the point of farthest advance, and we are dissatisfied. Looking back on half a century of improvisation, we begin to see that some of our deepest convictions will have to change if our various schemes of improvement are to make a difference. /8

For the admitted evil—the inadequacy of school and college, in particular the wastefulness of the high school—is not one that can be removed by once more tinkering at the curriculum and patting a few gifted youths on the head. The notion of the gifted is true and useful, but it stops short of the response to Intellect which we must make if, hand in hand with the Rockefeller Brothers, we are not only to pursue excellence but occasionally to catch up with it. /9

At the moment, the gifted child stands in the public mind as an agreeable freak of nature, hitherto undervalued but well worth cultivating, indeed, almost as interesting as the retarded child. The two types balance each other like a pair of exotic vases on a mantelpiece. Both types, we think, are given us plainly marked by nature, fated to be what they are. This may be true of the retarded; I am sure it is not true about the gifted. Their discovery, to themselves and by others, is not inevitable: it depends on the presence or absence of an intellectual atmosphere, on the awareness and acceptance of Intellect as a force. One of the most unexpected results of the Portland experiment was that, after a few months of the accelerated program, *those not in the program began to do better work*. Another startling result was that some notorious problem children, when given harder work to do, became good citizens. They had been bored, of course, and they had set fire to wastebaskets in order to have something to occupy their minds. Surely, in the light of such facts, we cannot consider the gifted child a natural species, which only requires the good treatment of a well-run zoo. We must on the contrary regard Intellect as potentially present in many individuals, and therefore as a power to be brought forth by making the school a place where intellectual effort and achievement are regarded as normal and necessary. /10

In the opposite outlook, which is still strong, I detect a secret desire to go on protecting equality, that is to say, to continue muffling excellence by showing, as is easy to do, that "Intellect isn't everything," that "to be smart isn't an unmixed blessing." Both propositions are true, but what have they to do with a school or university? As well argue in an opera house that "singing isn't all of life," and that Mozart's lot was not one of unmixed blessings. The equalitarian tradition, misapplied to our educational institutions, is still so powerful that even in our present anxiety about places for the new generations in school and college, there lurks a hope that the strict measures being advocated may be only temporary. When our own rockets are cutting figure eights around the Russians', we can go back to quietly neglecting all normal, healthy, unintellectual American boys, and to lavishing expensive care on our true favorite, the slow mind. /11

You will not, I am sure, suspect me of wanting to deprive unfortunate boys and girls of the least help which lovingkindness bestows upon them. I dwell on their situation because the country dwells on it, and in so doing creates the contrast I want to make clear. As regards the mind, the American school or college is, generally speaking, not an educational, but a *philanthropic* institution. It tries to reduce competition and abolish failure; it is interested in the sociable personality rather than the powers of Intellect; above all, it wants to preserve its own brand of happiness, in which everyone can—indeed must—participate. The worthy effort to make the handicapped feel that they are not outcasts but fully accepted members of the group—that effort is matched by another, directed at the gifted, superior, perhaps eccentric person, and intended to assimilate him—literally to make him similar, to rub down his natural contours till he, too, is spherical and smooth, fit to serve as an interchangeable part in the social machine. /12

The proof that this characteristic effort of our schools springs from philanthropic feeling and not from hostility to special talents is that our schools and colleges make a great point of self-development and the diversity of aptitudes. Teachers are instructed to watch for individual differences and to let each student develop at his own pace. That is why the idea of intellectual competition has nearly disappeared, why in many places numerical grades have been replaced by verbal accounts written like psychological novelettes, why courses once taken and credited are good forever, regardless of evaporation, and why the word and the fact of failure are forbidden as scandalous and destructive. The ideal modern school, as we all know, is one in which contentment reigns because the young person is steadily pleased both with what he does and with the fact that others are pleased with him. /13

Now if we step from this little utopia to the training quarters of a successful athletic team, we find a very different state of affairs. The boys being trained are indeed the same that we encounter in any of a thousand classrooms in the country; but on the field their view of life is suddenly and radically altered. To begin with, a special seriousness pervades the atmosphere; the boys are not contented but visibly anxious. One feels the concentration of many strong wills on one object. There is little aimless action. Everyone takes advantage of the intervals of free time to jump, swing, flex the muscles, to practice throwing, catching, running. The coach and his assistants are as much interested as the classroom instructor in individual development, and they are keen watchers of diverse aptitudes. But they clearly have in mind for each individual a fixed idea of what constitutes performance. Far from letting each set his own pace, they hold him to a standard of their own choosing. If he does not meet it, he fails. Let me make the point clear: if he fails, he fails. There may be reasons for the failure, but no excuse, and certainly no consolation prizes and no verbalized psychoapologies to the parents. On the contrary, I am told that the verbalizing of football coaches in moments of stress is far from apologetic. /14

The reason for this atmosphere of the training quarters is quite simple: the game is serious business. It engages the minds, hearts, and passions of all concerned, from coach to player to spectator. Training is therefore serious too. And when people are serious, no confusion is tolerated between performance and failure. No amount of desire to make up for the accidents of birth would induce anyone to give a slow-footed or slow-witted youth a place on a team. Our philanthropic, remedial impulses do not stretch quite so far. Indeed, we would consider any such tempering of the wind either corrupt or stupid, and we would sack the coach. When, on the contrary, one of his athletes is named to the All-American team, after the most solemn screening by the best official and unofficial judges in the country, all those interested are confident that they have witnessed from first to last the true way of discerning, developing, and rewarding excellence. /15

The comparison I have just drawn, obvious as it is, contains the lesson American parents and teachers must learn. They must not say: "Yes, yes, we know it." They must believe it and act on it; they must do this no matter how strange it feels to believe what you say when you speak about education. /16

What the lesson tells us in familiar, unmistakable steps is what the definition of excellence implies: excellence means excelling, which means exerting the will to improve on nature according to rule. To squeeze high performance out of native ability, stern demands must be made by the talented on themselves, but these demands must come ultimately from the world that desires and rewards the performance. /17

And yet, and yet . . . simple and persuasive as is this set of specifications, it is likely that something more has to be said before we are finally convinced. The contrast between classroom and playing field seems to accuse us too easily of being serious about games and frivolous about brains. Not all Americans are lifelong children enamored of sports. Not even all Europeans, whose sporting fever is by now worse than ours, have lost their senses. Why then do we hear of Europe's growing difficulty in maintaining intellectual standards—in their schools, universities, and professions? Since European attempts at mass education are much more recent than ours, we are forced to conclude that a connection exists between the neglect of intellectual excellence and the culture of a thoroughgoing democracy. /18

Ask anybody why it is right that tennis players should be weeded out by ruthless public competition and why it is also right that Johnny, who cannot spell, should merely be asked to try again a little harder. You will be told that the object of tennis championships is simply to discover winners, whereas democratic schools have complex goals, of which supremacy in spelling is not even one. Schools are to keep children out of mischief and out of the labor market; they are to give the young of the country a common experience and a sense of their opportunities. The most taxing business of the modern school is to take the native and the foreign, the poor and the well-to-do, and induct them into the maze of industrial life. The school's primary aims are thus social and vocational rather than intellectual. And properly so, because the home is no longer an educational institution. It is at school that children must learn about hygiene and safe driving, about the machinery of local government and the problems of adolescence. On top of this, the majority will want to learn shorthand and typewriting, home economics and the shop techniques known as industrial arts. What is now going on in the schools of Western Europe is a reminder of our own past, an explanation of the natural law that, under the pressure of numbers, public schools will turn from being seminaries of Intellect to being social centers for multiple "adjustments." /19

Since this is true and since what we learned of the nature and conditions of excellence is also true, we would seem to have reached a deadlock. Or rather, our present desire to exploit the national resources of Intellect has brought us to see that there is a need, there is a place, for two markedly different institutions under the one name School. I also include under it college and university. We cannot do without the type of school or college I have described as a social center for assimilation and vocational guidance, and it is a safe guess that we shall continue to have it. The question is whether we want the other kind, the intellectual institution, which must take for granted much that the first kind is meant to impart. In other words, Intellect is a special interest requiring a special apparatus, a special nursery, if you will, though one which, to be effective, must not look like an isolation ward. /20

There is in fact no reason why the two types of school should not exist side by side in the same building, or on the same campus; nor why boys and girls with an intellectual bent should not share certain classes with others and attend special ones of their own. According to the National Defense Education Act (Public Law 85-864), the country needs linguists. Now, good linguists start young, and learned ones need to know many languages, including Latin, which the sales manager and the agriculturist do not need. Why not, then, have the future linguists go to Latin class by themselves and join their friends, the farmer and businessman, in the government class? The way the president is elected and the principles of public hygiene are the same for all, whereas the concern with deponent verbs is not. /21

In theory and practice, then, the country's desire to see some of its young pursue intellectual excellence does not imply any new and invidious segregation. Such separation as must come is exactly like that required by the pursuit of athletic excellence. There is a training table reserved for the fit competitors and denied to the rest. No choice is imposed by force or privilege. Nature, taste, and sometimes family tradition dictate the path. /22

Fortunately for our intellectual renascence, separations on intellectual grounds already exist or survive in rudimentary form. Certain high schools are noted for their excellence in art or in science or in the academic program generally. They serve communities where these accomplishments are valued. Certain colleges are renowned for their faculty and for the atmosphere of Intellect and the tradition of excellence which they have sustained for generations, since a time before mass education. The position of these schools and colleges makes them the natural leaders and best models of the School as an institution designed to nurture Intellect. They are free from close legislative control, free to choose their staff and students, free from irrelevant demands by militant and misguided taxpayers. All they have to contend with is lack of money and interference by militant and misguided parents and alumni. And by and large, thanks to intelligent and courageous leadership, they have resisted these errors born of meddlesomeness out of cultural conformity. /23

But this ever-present threat from the naive champions of thoughtless social pressures brings us back to the central issue: what should the cultural temper be to foster excellence, what price must we pay—quite apart from fees and gifts to endowment—to provide the favoring conditions? /24

Please note that I speak of providing *the favoring conditions*. Excellence cannot be bought or even asked for. You cannot without absurdity tell the waiter to bring you "an excellent cup of coffee." You can only ask him for a cup and hope that when tasted it will prove to be excellent. Similarly, the desire for intellectual excellence must begin soberly with the simple desire to establish and maintain the conditions of good work. Well, up to a point there is no lack of that desire. Those in charge of education, and the public too, acknowledge the need for good equipment. Modern seats of learning can generally boast a superb physique. But this is evidently not enough, or we should not be at the critical juncture we are discussing here. No one has ever believed that the high quality of the training table was the sufficient cause of a winning team. /25

Nor in scholastic work is the cause exclusively good teachers. You can anticipate what I am about to say: the conditions that favor excellence cannot work singly. If we cannot have them all, we must at least have several, and these must be bound together by the atmosphere of concentrated effort and high seriousness which we saw in the training quarters, the discontent and the will to excel which we find wherever achievement is preferred to pious hopes. /26

Once established, that atmosphere is not difficult to sustain. What is hard is to begin. The world is still amazed at the remarkable outburst of great painters in the small towns of Renaissance Italy. A glance at the history shows that after a school had got under way, thanks to the coming together of two or three geniuses, talent sprang out of the ground and rushed to the masters' ateliers. The concentration of eager minds, the intensity of their rivalry, and the awareness of an enthusiastic public, raised otherwise ordinary gifts to a higher power, to excellence. Atmosphere did it. /27

If, therefore, I am to answer literally the question implied in my title, the place of excellence is wherever there is the least glimmer of consciousness about its nature and requirements. If we grant that the country's main discovery and training of Intellect—for science, art, and public life—can be carried on only in school and college, in certain dedicated schools and colleges, these places will be hampered and diminished if they are not surrounded by an atmosphere in which excellence is a familiar spirit. The home must, before all others, give it thought and room. How can a child or youth strive to excel in study, if his parents in their unguarded moments show their indifference to Intellect, books, ideas, science, art—in a word, to the mind of man? /28

In the second place, the school or college must be staffed by men who recognize intellect when they see it, in one another and in their students. There is nothing automatic about this. Many teachers respect industry, politeness, and even flattery, who would be quite taken aback by an encounter with Intellect. For the young Intellect who is laboring to excel is quite different from the grind and the apple polisher trying to impress or to please. The test of Intellect is that its interest is genuine. It is indeed often necessary for a student to pretend an interest he does not feel: he *has* to do twenty calculus problems or write a 3000-word essay. But if he is ever to be educated, there must come a time when the problems grip him like a detective story and when he chafes at the 3000-word limit because he has so much to say. /29

Intellect, in short, is a passion like any other. We who teach acknowledge this when we say of a student that he has at last caught fire. This is the very reason why the young Intellect must not be isolated. He must have others of his age similarly engrossed, or the fire will be that of the single stick—a spark, a bit of smoke, and then blackness. Nor is it enough for him to be encouraged at home and by the masters. The regular fellows, with palpable muscles and wearing the right kind of disreputable clothes, must also feel the nascent intellectual passions before any one youth—and by extension any school or college—can tread firmly and with characteristic zest on the path of excellence. /30

These being the geographical conditions, so to speak, what are the emotional costs? And first of all, do we, for the sake of Intellect have to give up, two centuries after Jefferson's *Declaration*, the doctrine of equality? A few weeks ago in *Time* magazine there appeared a report that a new college for science and engineering was being sponsored by a group of midwestern businessmen. Seeking excellence, they said in commenting on the new college, they were bound to confess their disbelief in equality. The doctrine was false and must be given up. /31

If correctly reported, the statement is a foolish one. Equality has nothing to do with merit, talent, or Intellect. Equality is a social and political assumption necessary to a certain form of government and congenial to the citizens of the United States. When we say that we are all equal, we mean precisely that the possession of wealth, or physical stature, or mental powers will make no difference in law and in manners. Equality in this sense is the result of a deliberate choice which requires self-control and aims at social simplicity. /32

Consequently, the discovery that men are not equal because one is tall and the other short, one stupid and the other bright, is irrelevant. Equality simply enjoins that these obvious differences shall make no difference in rights and privileges—it is the way a host treats his guests. You may say that Jefferson believed we were "created equal," not simply endowed with equal rights. True, but if by analogy with a parent we try to imagine the point of view of the Creator, we see at once that our individual differences of talent or merit simply do not matter. That, if anything, is the meaning of the Fatherhood of God—in essence, stripped of local attributes, we are equal, if only because any virtue or power we may boast of implies no other. And who can add up all our traits and reach a total to compare with others? We are therefore equal in being incommensurable. /33

By the same token, when society incurs expense to develop intellectual power in those capable of it, the cost does not include giving up the principle of equality. Even now, the physician's education costs perhaps ten times as much as anybody else's. We think, rightly, that he amply repays the social investment, and we know that his difference from the rest of us does not make him a member of a dangerous elite. /34

No, the emotional price we must pay for intellectual excellence is not the loss of social equality. It is a more personal and intimate loss, to which I alluded earlier in speaking of competition and in contrasting our present philanthropic schools with the educational ones we are beginning to desire. The price of excellence is the acceptance of pain, error, failure, even, I dare say, cruelty. This we are not used to. We love the young and want to see them happy and successful. We understand so well their confused feelings, their good intentions, their seemingly limitless possibilities of worth, that we instinctively avoid dwelling upon their shortcomings. When rules are set up to guide their development and the rule makes them stumble, we bend the rule. This is undoubtedly proper at their first entrance into the world of obligation and responsibility, but we carry it so far that the very idea of effort and the fundamental difference between doing and failing to do are lost, forgotten alike by the teacher and by the student and absolutely unsuspected by the parent. /35

The moral is plain. It is hard enough to say: you have not done what you should have done; you have wasted your many chances; we have both warned and aided you, and you have given nothing of yourself: therefore find you own way outside the path that leads to praise and glory, and perhaps to wealth and power. Still harder, and indeed cruel, is to say: you have tried your best, but you are not made for the life you have chosen. Nature denied you the eye, hand, and brain. /36

But I submit that there is a cruelty far greater than either of these, an easy, indolent, irresponsible cruelty, which is to see the young, with their bursting energies and hopes and ambitions, flounder for lack of that special encouragement which is called Difficulty; to see them grow up full of fresh intelligence but with an Intellect like a garden full of weeds; to see them so naively pleased with their own accomplishments that the first stern demand, too long postponed, must be a shattering blow; to see them so accustomed to their own pace that they do not suspect the deep layers of grit and mother-wit they hold within; to see them, finally, when well past college age, discover with shame and remorse what they might have been if, instead of being neglected like mongrels or incubated like sickly growths, they had been urged and pressed and compelled to perform to the limit of their talents. /37

It is therefore not for the sake of turning out more engineers than Russia, not to manufacture as many linguists as the State Department wants, not to provide the colleges with enough teachers, it is not even to enable the du Pont Company to hire more chemists and produce the ultimate plastic which shall be food, clothing, and shelter all in one—it is not for these imperative or alluring prospects that this country must radically change its attitude toward scholastic excellence: it is simply and solely to put an end to the cruel injustice of letting rot, through protracted cowardice masquerading as kindness, the unimaginable endowments of youth and the tradition of Intellect which is their birthright. /38

The speech

1. What is the central issue discussed in this speech? Where is it best stated?
2. What does Barzun mean by "excellence"? What specific passages make this meaning most clear? What method or methods of definition does Barzun use?
3. What relationship between himself and his audience does Barzun establish in the introduction? Show how it might be a useful relationship for his purpose.
4. Is the organization of this speech an example of the motivated sequence? Develop your answer by making a careful analysis of the pattern of the speech's organization.

5. Do you find Barzun's evidence too general to be convincing? Support your answer with specific references to the text.
6. Do you believe that the contrast between what happens in the classroom and what happens on the athletic field is a valid one? An appealing one? Give reasons for your answers.
7. Does Barzun weaken his attack on schools for being philanthropic organizations by admitting that under the pressure of numbers public schools will inevitably become "social centers for multiple 'adjustments' "? Explain.
8. Cite examples of irony, sarcasm, and analogy. What effect do these devices have upon the style of the speech?
9. What precisely would Barzun do with our educational system? Is it a weakness in the speech that he did not spell out a series of specific changes he would favor? Explain your answer.

For further study and discussion

1. How do you define excellence in education?
2. Is it undemocratic to put the superior students in special sections where they get more demanding assignments?
3. Was your high school more of a philanthropic institution than one devoted to the training of the intellect? In answering this question, cite particular courses and activities.
4. How much time were your teachers forced to spend upon matters not concerned with the training of the intellect? Be as exact and specific as you can.
5. Does your community look to the schools as sources for adult entertainment? If so, give examples.
6. To what extent would you say your college is a philanthropic institution as Barzun uses that term?
7. What courses are you now taking, if any, that offer only feeble training for the intellect? Do you believe they should be eliminated from the curriculum?
8. In your opinion does a strong program in athletics contribute to excellence in education?
9. What conditions do you think are essential to creating an atmosphere in which excellence in education is properly valued?
10. Do you agree that pain and failure are the inevitable price of the pursuit of excellence? Cite personal experience to support your answer.

Suggestions for further reading

Arthur E. Bestor, *The Restoration of Learning* (New York, 1955)
James B. Conant, *The Child, the Parent, and the State* (Cambridge, Mass., 1959)

—————, *The Revolutionary Transformation of the American High School* (Cambridge, Mass., 1959)

Benjamin Fine, *Democratic Education* (New York, 1945)

John W. Gardner, *Excellence* (New York, 1961)

Robert M. Hutchins, *The Conflict in Education in a Democratic Society* (New York, 1953)

Frederick Mayer, *Creative Universities* (New Haven, 1961)

Alonzo F. Myers, *Education in a Democracy* (New York, 1954)

H. G. Rickover, *Education and Freedom* (New York, 1959)

David Riesman, *Constraint and Variety in American Education* (Lincoln, Neb., 1956)

What every Yale freshman should know

EDMUND S. MORGAN

The following speech, delivered at Yale University before the entering freshman class in September 1959, is in effect the personal manifesto of a professional scholar. Edmund Sears Morgan (1916-   ) has spent virtually his entire life engaged in scholarly pursuits. He has taught at the University of Chicago and Brown University, and since 1955 has been a professor of history at Yale. He has published numerous articles and books on early American history, among them *The Puritan Family* (1944), *Virginians at Home* (1952), *The Stamp Act Crisis*, with Helen M. Morgan (1953), *The Birth of the Republic* (1956), *The Puritan Dilemma* (1958), and *Visible Saints* (1962). Presently he is a member of the editorial board of the *New England Quarterly*.

The students who heard this speech, like students at most of the better colleges and universities today, were from the top ranks of their high-school classes. While some of them were undoubtedly entering college for a good time and for the prestige involved, many more were there for serious scholarly purposes. Professor

Edmund S. Morgan, "What Every Yale Freshman Should Know," *Saturday Review*, January 23, 1960, pp. 13-14. Reprinted by permission of the *Saturday Review*.

Morgan, therefore, could count on a receptive audience for this speech. When he says that Yale expects students to be curious for the truth, he is uttering more than a pious hope. Given the competition to get into such schools, Yale and other universities *can* and *do* expect such curiosity, even of their entering freshmen.

The world does not much like curiosity. The world says that curiosity killed the cat. The world dismisses curiosity by calling it idle, or *mere* idle, curiosity —even though curious persons are seldom idle. Parents do their best to extinguish curiosity in their children, because it makes life difficult to be faced every day with a string of unanswerable questions about what makes fire hot or why grass grows, or to have to halt junior's investigations before they end in explosion and sudden death. Children whose curiosity survives parental discipline and who manage to grow up before they blow up are invited to join the Yale faculty. Within the university they go on asking their questions and trying to find the answers. In the eyes of a scholar, that is mainly what a university is for. It is a place where the world's hostility to curiosity can be defied. /1

Some of the questions that scholars ask seem to the world to be scarcely worth asking, let alone answering. They ask about the behavior of protons, the dating of a Roman coin, the structure of a poem. They ask questions too minute and specialized for you and me to understand without years of explanation. /2

If the world inquires of one of them why he wants to know the answer to a particular question, he may say, especially if he is a scientist, that the answer will in some obscure way make possible a new machine or weapon or gadget. He talks that way because he knows that the world understands and respects utility and that it does not understand much else. But to his colleagues and to you he will probably not speak this language. You are now part of the university, and he will expect you to understand that he wants to know the answer simply because he does not know it, the way a mountain climber wants to climb a mountain simply because it is there. /3

Similarly a historian, when asked by outsiders why he studies history, may come out with a line of talk that he has learned to repeat on such occasions, something about knowledge of the past making it possible to understand the present and mold the future. I am sure you have all heard it at one time or another. But if you really want to know why a historian studies the past, the answer is much simpler: he wants to know about it because it is there. Something happened, and he would like to know what. /4

All this does not mean that the answers which scholars find to their questions have no consequences. They may have enormous consequences; they may completely alter the character of human life. But the consequences seldom form the reason for asking the questions or pursuing the answers. It is true that scholars can be put to work answering questions for the sake of the consequences, as thousands are working now, for example, in search of a cure for cancer. But this is not the primary function of the scholar. For the scholar the consequences are usually incidental to the satisfaction of curiosity. Even for the medical scholar, the desire to stamp out a dreaded disease may be a less powerful motive than the desire to find out about the nature of living matter. Similarly Einstein did not wish to create an atomic bomb or to harness atomic energy. He simply wanted to find out about energy and matter. /5

I said that curiosity was a dangerous quality. It is dangerous not only because of incidental effects like the atomic bomb but also because it is really nothing more or less than a desire for truth. For some reason this phrase sounds less dangerous than curiosity. In fact, the desire for truth sounds rather respectable. Since so many respectable people assure us that they have found the truth, it does not sound like a dangerous thing to look for. But it is. The search for it has again and again overturned institutions and beliefs of long standing, in science, in religion, and in politics. It is easy enough to see today that these past revolutions brought great benefits to mankind. It was less easy to see the benefits while the revolutions were taking place, especially if you happened to be quite satisfied with the way things were before. Similarly it is not always easy today to see that the satisfaction of a scholar's curiosity is worth the disruption of society that may result from it. The search for truth is, and always has been, a subversive activity. And scholars have learned that they cannot engage in it without an occasional fight. /6

You may therefore find them rather belligerent toward any threat to the free pursuit of curiosity. They are wary of committing themselves to institutions or beliefs that might impose limitations on them or deliver ready-made answers to their questions. You will find them suspicious of loyalty oaths, religious creeds, or affiliations with political parties. In particular they will try to preserve their university as a sanctuary within whose walls *any* question can be asked. /7

This wariness of commitment can sometimes degenerate into a scholarly vice, a vice that paralyzes curiosity instead of preserving it. A scholar at his worst sometimes seems to be simply a man who cannot make up his mind. Every classroom from here to Melbourne has echoed with the feeble phrases of academic indecision: "There are two schools of thought on this question, and the truth probably lies halfway between them." When you hear this sentence repeated, or when you are tempted to repeat it yourself, remember that the truth may lie between two extremes, but it assuredly does not lie halfway between right and wrong. Don't short-circuit your curiosity by assuming you have found the answer when you have only made a tidy list of possible answers. /8

Dedication to curiosity should not end in indecision. It should, in fact, mean willingness to follow the mind into difficult decisions. /9

A second quality that makes a scholar has no apparent relation to the first and yet is inseparably connected to it. It is a compulsion to communicate. A scholar is driven by a force as strong as his curiosity, that compels him to tell the world the things he has learned. He cannot rest with learning something: he has to tell about it. Scholarship begins in curiosity, but it ends in communication. And though scholars may in a university take refuge from the world, they also acknowledge responsibility to the world, the responsibility to communicate freely and fully everything that they discover within the walls of their sanctuary. The search for truth needs no justification, and when a man thinks he has found any part of it, he cannot and ought not to be silent. The world may sometimes not care to listen, but the scholar must keep telling it until he has succeeded in communicating. /10

Now, there are only two methods of communication for scholars, writing and speaking. The scholar publishes his discoveries in books and articles and he teaches them in the classroom. Sometimes one or the other method will satisfy him, but most of us feel the need for both. The scholar who merely writes books falls into the habit of speaking only to the experts. If he works at his subject long enough, he reaches the position where there is no one else quite expert enough to understand him, and he winds up writing to himself. On the other hand, if he writes not at all, he may become so enamored of his own voice that he ceases to be a scholar and becomes a mere showman. /11

Communication is not merely the desire and the responsibility of the scholar; it is his discipline, the proving ground where he tests his findings against criticism. Without communication his pursuit of truth withers into eccentricity. He necessarily spends much of his time alone, in the library or the laboratory, looking for the answers to his questions. But he needs to be rubbing constantly against other minds. He needs to be tested, probed, and pushed around. He needs to be made to explain himself. Only when he has expressed himself, only when he has communicated his thoughts, can he be sure that he is thinking clearly. /12

The scholar, in other words, needs company to keep him making sense. And in particular he needs the company of fresh minds, to whom he must explain things from the beginning. He needs people who will challenge him at every step, who will take nothing for granted. He needs, in short, you. /13

You may have various purposes in coming here, and you may fulfill them: you may play football or tennis or the trombone; you may sing in the glee club, act in plays, and act up on college weekends. But what the faculty expects of you is four years of scholarship, and they will be satisfied with nothing less. For four years we expect you to join us in the pursuit of truth, and we will demand of you the same things we demand of ourselves: curiosity and communication. /14

Curiosity, of course, is not something you get simply by wishing for it. But it is surprisingly contagious. The curiosity we expect is more than a passing interest. We will not be satisfied by your ability to ask an occasional bright question, nor yet by your assimilation of a lot of predigested information. The accumulation of information is a necessary part of scholarship, and unfortunately the part most likely to be tested on examinations, especially those wretched ones called "objective examinations" where the truth is always supposed to lie in answer space A, B, C, D, or E, but never apparently in X, Y, or Z. But the curiosity we expect of you cannot be satisfied by passing examinations or by memorizing other people's answers to other people's questions. We do not wish to put you through a mere course of mental gymnastics. We want you to be content with nothing less than the whole truth about the subject that interests you. Which means that we want you to be forever discontent with how little you know about it

and with how little we know about it. We want you to back us into corners, show us up, make us confess we don't know. Does this sound formidable? It is not. We may tell you what we know with great assurance, but push us and you will find the gaps. /15

Follow your own minds into the gaps. Follow your minds where curiosity takes them. You will not get the whole truth, not about protons, not about the structure of a poem, not even about a Roman coin. Nobody does. But if you learn anything, it ought to change your minds, and hopefully it will change ours too. It will be a sign that we have both wasted four years if you leave here thinking pretty much the same way that you do now or if you leave us thinking the same way *we* do now. /16

We expect of you, then, that you will be curious for the truth. We also expect that you communicate whatever truth you find, and that you do it both in speech and in writing. Many people suppose that they know something if they can stammer out an approximation of what they mean in speech. They are mistaken. It is extremely unlikely that you have thought clearly if you cannot express yourself clearly, especially in writing. Writing is more than an instrument of communication. It is an instrument of thought. You should have acquired some competence in its use by now. I suspect from past experience that you have not. But even if you have, you have a great deal more to learn about it. And if you do not know much more about it four years from now, it will again be a sign that we have failed in part of our job, the job of making you communicate clearly. /17

Communication is a two-way process, and a university is a community of scholars, where questions are asked and the answers communicated, your answers to us, ours to you. For the next four years we will be engaged as scholars together in this community. After the four years are over, most of you will leave Yale, but if our community is a successful one, if we really do communicate with each other, I believe that you will continue to be in some sense scholars, asking new questions, looking for new answers, and communicating them to the world. /18

The speech

1. How would the fact that the speaker is a professor of history at Yale affect the audience's attitude toward this speech? Why is Professor Morgan wise in not resorting too explicitly to ethical proof?

2. How does Morgan define *curiosity*? *University*? Are there any other key terms that must be understood in order to follow the argument closely?

3. By what means does the speaker catch the audience's attention in his introduction? What means does he use throughout in an attempt to hold it?

4. How many main divisions are there in the speech, and where does each begin?

5. In what way does Morgan believe that communication is "inseparably connected" with curiosity?

6. In attacking indecision, is Morgan arguing that a scholar should not look at both sides of a question?

7. What precisely does Morgan want Yale freshmen to know? Besides knowing, is there anything he wants them to do? What for you seems to be the central idea of the speech? Where is it best stated?

8. Would you say that the style of the speech is conversational? Explain your answer.

For further study and discussion

1. How do you define a university? A scholar? A student?

2. How do you account for the nonscholar's preoccupation with practical results and his disdain for scholarship for its own sake?

3. Can any curiosity properly be called "idle curiosity"?

4. What in your experience tends most strongly to stifle curiosity? To encourage it?

5. How do writing and speaking contribute to the development of a scholar? Are there significant differences in what they contribute toward his development?

6. What is "wretched" about objective examinations? Are they really objective? What do they demand of the student, and what do they not demand?

7. Which is more likely to encourage the development of a lively curiosity, the discussion-type class or the lecture-type class? Give the reasons for your answer.

8. What means of satisfying his intellectual curiosity are readily available to the college undergraduate? In answering this, give examples to support your main points.

Suggestions for further reading

Margaret E. Bennett and Molly Lewin, *Getting the Most Out of College* (New York, 1957)

Otto Butz, ed., *The Unsilent Generation* (New York, 1958)

Roger H. Garrison, *The Adventure of Learning in College* (New York, 1957)

Philip E. Jacob, *Changing Values in College* (New York, 1957)

Burges Johnson, *Campus Versus Classroom* (New York, 1946)

Elton Trueblood, *The Idea of College* (New York, 1959)

F. Zweig, *The Student in the Age of Anxiety* (New York, 1963)

The American scholar
RALPH WALDO EMERSON

Ralph Waldo Emerson (1803-1882) was the leading figure in the Transcendentalist movement in America. Viewed as a religious demonstration, this movement was a revolt against the Unitarian Church and its teachings which rested on a fundamentally rational basis. In its liberalism the Unitarian Church had argued away hellfire and damnation; but it had also taken away much of the warmth and mysticism normally found in religion. What had started out as a rational alternative to the excesses of Calvinism ended up in the opinion of the Transcendentalists as a sterile formalism, which in turn encouraged a dangerous complacency. The chief contention of the Transcendentalists was that everything and everybody are part of a great unity which they variously called God, the Absolute, the Over-soul, and the First Cause. Man, they believed, had access to the Over-soul directly through this intuition (which Emerson called the Reason) and indirectly through nature, which was the great physical symbol of the Over-soul. Thus, instead of emphasizing the importance of the rational faculty, they emphasized the primacy of the intuition which provided those mystical contacts with the Over-soul.

Emerson came from a long line of Puritan and Unitarian clergymen. His father was the pastor of the First Unitarian Church of Boston. Emerson, in turn, also became a Unitarian minister; by 1829 he was sharing the pulpit of the Second Unitarian Church with Henry Ware, a dynamic preacher of the period. By 1832, just as he was beginning to be recognized as a success in the pulpit, he resigned from the ministry because he felt he could no longer conscientiously perform the sacrament of the Lord's Supper. He also claimed (at a later date) that "in order to be a good minister it was necessary to leave the ministry." The breach with the Unitarian Church became complete when in 1838 he said before the Harvard Divinity School that "the idioms of his [Jesus'] language and the figures of his rhetoric, have usurped the place of his truth; and churches are not built on his principles, but on his tropes. Christianity became a mythus, as the poetic teaching of Greece and of Egypt, before."

Because of his views he was labeled an infidel by Professor Andrews Norton of the Divinity School. More calumny was to follow. It was only years later that the epithets ceased as people realized his teaching lent itself to virtue rather than to vice. Also, younger clergymen, more favorable to his views, had ascended to many of the pulpits in Boston. In short, the revolt was in time assimilated.

The Transcendental movement was not confined solely to religion. With its insistence on self-reliance, it inevitably concerned itself with other matters as well. The literary and scholarly aspects of American life especially came under close scrutiny. Emerson's sharpest criticism of American failings in these areas came in the following speech entitled "The American Scholar," which was delivered before the Phi Beta Kappa Society at Cambridge on August 31, 1837.

The speech was hastily composed because Emerson had been called on to substitute for the Reverend Dr. Wainwright. In spite of the short notice, the speech is well developed because Emerson had been thinking about its theme for a number of years and was greatly concerned about the lack of literary output in America.

The audience consisted of 215 members of Phi Beta Kappa as well as invited guests, who gathered in the meeting house near Harvard Yard. The rest of the program consisted of a poem read by the Reverend William Parsons Lunt, a few selections by a band, and a prayer. Emerson took one hour and fifteen minutes to read his oration.

The reception was mixed. Ralph L. Rusk, Emerson's biographer, reports that John Pierce listened impatiently. He was struck by Emerson's "misty, dreamy, unintelligible style" and credited it to "Swedenborg, Coleridge, and Carlyle." Long afterwards, James Russell Lowell summarized the conflicting moods of the listeners by saying, "What crowded and breathless aisles, what windows clustering with eager heads, what enthusiasm of approval, what grim silence of foregone dissent!" He also called the address "our Yankee version of a lecture by Abélard." Oliver Wendell Holmes didn't care for the esoteric passages but later referred to the speech as "our intellectual Declaration of Independence."[1]

Mr. President and Gentlemen, I greet you on the recommencement of our literary year. Our anniversary is one of hope, and, perhaps, not enough of labor. We do not meet for games of strength or skill, for the recitation of histories, tragedies, and odes, like the ancient Greeks; for parliaments of love and poesy, like the Troubadours; nor for the advancement of science, like our contemporaries in the British and European capitals. Thus far, our holiday has been simply a friendly sign of the survival of the love of letters amongst a people too busy to give to letters any more. As such it is precious as the sign of an indestructible instinct. Perhaps the time is already come when it ought to be, and will be, something

else; when the sluggard intellect of this continent will look from under its iron lids and fill the postponed expectation of the world with something better than the exertions of mechanical skill. Our day of independence, our long apprenticeship to the learning of other lands, draws to a close. The millions that around us are rushing into life, cannot always be fed on the sere remains of foreign harvests. Events, actions arise, that must be sung, that will sing themselves. Who can doubt that poetry will revive and lead in a new age, as the star in the constellation Harp, which now flames in our zenith, astronomers announce, shall one day be the pole-star for a thousand years? /1

In this hope I accept the topic which not only usage but the nature of our association seem to prescribe to this day,—the AMERICAN SCHOLAR. Year by year we come up hither to read one more chapter of his biography. Let us inquire what light new days and events have thrown on his character and his hopes. /2

It is one of those fables which out of an unknown antiquity convey an unlooked-for wisdom, that the gods, in the beginning, divided Man into men, that he might be more helpful to himself; just as the hand was divided into fingers, the better to answer its end. /3

The old fable covers a doctrine ever new and sublime; that there is One Man,—present to all particular men only partially, or through one faculty; and that you must take the whole society to find the whole man. Man is not a farmer, or a professor, or an engineer, but he is all. Man is priest, and scholar, and statesman, and producer, and soldier. In the *divided* or social state these functions are parcelled out to individuals, each of whom aims to do his stint of the joint work, whilst each other performs his. The fable implies that the individual, to possess himself, must sometimes return from his own labor to embrace all the other laborers. But, unfortunately, this original unit, this fountain of power, has been so distributed to multitudes, has been so minutely subdivided and peddled out, that it is spilled into drops, and cannot be gathered. The state of society is one in which the members have suffered amputation from the trunk, and strut about so many walking monsters,—a good finger, a neck, a stomach, an elbow, but never a man. /4

Man is thus metamorphosed into a thing, into many things. The planter, who is Man sent out into the field to gather food, is seldom cheered by any idea of the true dignity of his ministry. He sees his bushel and his cart, and nothing beyond, and sinks

[1] Ralph L. Rusk, *The Life of Ralph Waldo Emerson* (New York, 1949), pp. 262-266.

into the farmer, instead of Man on the farm. The tradesman scarcely ever gives an ideal worth to his work, but is ridden by the routine of his craft, and the soul is subject to dollars. The priest becomes a form; the attorney a statute-book; the mechanic a machine; the sailor a rope of the ship. /5

In this distribution of functions the scholar is the delegated intellect. In the right state he is *Man Thinking*. In the degenerate state, when the victim of society, he tends to become a mere thinker, or still worse, the parrot of other men's thinking. /6

In this view of him, as Man Thinking, the theory of his office is contained. Him Nature solicits with all her placid, all her monitory pictures; him the past instructs; him the future invites. Is not indeed every man a student, and do not all things exist for the student's behoof? And, finally, is not the true scholar the only true master? But the old oracle said, "All things have two handles: beware of the wrong one." In life, too often, the scholar errs with mankind and forfeits his privilege. Let us see him in his school, and consider him in reference to the main influences he receives. /7

I. The first in time and the first in importance of the influences upon the mind is that of nature. Every day, the sun; and, after the sunset, Night and her stars. Ever the winds blow; ever the grass grows. Every day, men and women, conversing, beholding and beholden. The scholar is he of all men whom this spectacle most engages. He must settle its value in his mind. What is nature to him? There is never a beginning, there is never an end, to the inexplicable continuity of this web of God, but always circular power returning into itself. Therein it resembles his own spirit, whose beginning, whose ending, he never can find,—so entire, so boundless. Far too as her splendors shine, system on system shooting like rays, upward, downward without centre, without circumference—in the mass and in the particle, Nature hastens to render account of herself to the mind. Classification begins. To the young mind every thing is individual, stands by itself. By and by, it finds how to join two things and see in them one nature; then three, then three thousand; and so, tyrannized over by its own unifying instinct, it goes on tying things together, diminishing anomalies, discovering roots running under ground whereby contrary and remote things cohere and flower out from one stem. It presently learns that since the dawn of history there has been a constant accumulation and classifying of facts. But what is classification but the perceiving that these objects are not chaotic, and are not foreign, but have a law which is also a law of the hu-

man mind? The astronomer discovers that geometry, a pure abstraction of the human mind, is the measure of planetary motion. The chemist finds proportions and intelligible method throughout matter; and science is nothing but the finding of analogy, identity, in the most remote parts. The ambitious soul sits down before each refractory fact; one after another reduces all strange constitutions, all new powers, to their class and their law, and goes on forever to animate the last fibre of organization, the outskirts of nature, by insight. /8

Thus to him, to this schoolboy under the bending dome of day, is suggested that he and it proceed from one root; one is leaf and one is flower; relation, sympathy, stirring in every vein. And what is that root? Is not that the soul of his soul? A thought too bold; a dream too wild. Yet when this spiritual light shall have revealed the law of more earthly natures, —when he has learned to worship the soul, and to see that the natural philosophy that now is, is only the first gropings of its gigantic hand, he shall look forward to an ever expanding knowledge as to a becoming creator. He shall see that nature is the opposite of the soul, answering to it part for part. One is seal and one is print. Its beauty is the beauty of his own mind. Its laws are the laws of his own mind. Nature then becomes to him the measure of his attainments. So much of nature as he is ignorant of, so much of his own mind does he not yet possess. And, in fine, the ancient precept, "Know thyself," and the modern precept, "Study nature," become at last one maxim. /9

II. The next great influence into the spirit of the scholar is the mind of the Past,—in whatever form, whether of literature, of art, of institutions, that mind is inscribed. Books are the best type of the influence of the past, and perhaps we shall get at the truth, —learn the amount of this influence more conveniently,—by considering their value alone. /10

The theory of books is noble. The scholar of the first age received into him the world around; brooded thereon; gave it the new arrangement of his own mind, and uttered it again. It came into him life; it went out from him truth. It came to him short-lived actions; it went out from him immortal thoughts. It came to him business; it went from him poetry. It was dead fact; now, it is quick thought. It can stand, and it can go. It now endures, it now flies, it now inspires. Precisely in proportion to the depth of mind from which it issued, so high does it soar, so long does it sing. /11

Or, I might say, it depends on how far the process had gone, of transmuting life into truth. In proportion to the completeness of the distillation, so will the purity and imperishableness of the product be. But none is quite perfect. As no air-pump can by any means make a perfect vacuum, so neither can any artist entirely exclude the conventional, the local, the perishable from his book, or write a book of pure thought, that shall be as efficient, in all respects, to a remote posterity, as to contemporaries, or rather to the second age. Each age, it is found, must write its own books; or rather, each generation for the next succeeding. The books of an older period will not fit this. /12

Yet hence arises a grave mischief. The sacredness which attaches to the act of creation, the act of thought, is transferred to the record. The poet chanting was felt to be a divine man: henceforth the chant is divine also. The writer was a just and wise spirit: henceforward it is settled the book is perfect; as love of the hero corrupts into worship of his statue. Instantly the book becomes noxious: the guide is a tyrant. The sluggish and perverted mind of the multitude, slow to open to the incursions of Reason, having once so opened, having once received this book, stands upon it, and makes an outcry if it is disparaged. Colleges are built on it. Books are written on it by thinkers, not by Man Thinking; by men of talent, that is, who start wrong, who set out from accepted dogmas, not from their own sight of principles. Meek young men grow up in libraries, believing it their duty to accept the views which Cicero, which Locke, which Bacon, have given; forgetful that Cicero, Locke, and Bacon were only young men in libraries when they wrote these books. /13

Hence, instead of Man Thinking, we have the bookworm. Hence the book-learned class, who value books, as such; not as related to nature and the human constitution, but as making a sort of Third Estate with the world and the soul. Hence the restorers of readings, the emendators, the bibliomaniacs of all degrees. /14

Books are the best of things, well used; abused, among the worst. What is the right use? What is the one end which all means go to effect? They are for nothing but to inspire. I had better never see a book than to be warped by its attraction clean out of my own orbit, and made a satellite instead of a system. The one thing in the world, of value, is the active soul. This every man is entitled to; this every man contains within him, although in almost all men obstructed, and as yet unborn. The soul active sees absolute truth and utters truth, or creates. In this action it is genius; not the privilege of here and there a favorite, but the sound estate of every man. In its

essence it is progressive. The book, the college, the school of art, the institution of any kind, stop with some past utterance of genius. This is good, say they, —let us hold by this. They pin me down. They look backward and not forward. But genius looks forward: the eyes of man are set in his forehead, not in his hindhead: man hopes: genius creates. Whatever talents may be, if the man create not, the pure efflux of the Deity is not his;—cinders and smoke there may be, but not yet flame. There are creative manners, there are creative actions, and creative words; manners, actions, words, that is, indicative of no custom or authority, but springing spontaneous from the mind's own sense of good and fair. /15

On the other part, instead of being its own seer, let it receive from another mind its truth, though it were in torrents of light, without periods of solitude, inquest, and self-recovery, and a fatal disservice is done. Genius is always sufficiently the enemy of genius by over-influence. The literature of every nation bears me witness. The English dramatic poets have Shakespearized now for two hundred years. /16

Undoubtedly there is a right way of reading, so it be sternly subordinated. Man Thinking must not be subdued by his instruments. Books are for the scholar's idle times. When he can read God directly, the hour is too precious to be wasted in other men's transcripts of their readings. But when the intervals of darkness come, as come they must,—when the sun is hid and the stars withdraw their shining,— we repair to the lamps which were kindled by their ray, to guide our steps to the East again, where the dawn is. We hear, that we may speak. The Arabian proverb says, "A fig tree, looking on a fig tree, becometh fruitful." /17

It is remarkable, the character of the pleasure we derive from the best books. They impress us with the conviction that one nature wrote and the same reads. We read the verses of one of the great English poets, of Chaucer, of Marvell, of Dryden, with the most modern joy,—with a pleasure, I mean, which is in great part caused by the abstraction of all *time* from their verses. There is some awe mixed with the joy of our surprise, when this poet, who lived in some past world, two or three hundred years ago, says that which lies close to my own soul, that which I also had well-nigh thought and said. But for the evidence thence afforded to the philosophical doctrine of the identity of all minds, we should suppose some pre-established harmony, some foresight of souls that were to be, and some preparation of stores for their future wants, like the fact observed in insects, who lay up food before death for the young grub they shall never see. /18

I would not be hurried by any love of system, by any exaggeration of instincts, to underrate the Book. We all know, that as the human body can be nourished on any food, though it were boiled grass and the broth of shoes, so the human mind can be fed by any knowledge. And great and heroic men have existed who had almost no other information than by the printed page. I only would say that it needs a strong head to bear that diet. One must be an inventor to read well. As the proverb says, "He that would bring home the wealth of the Indies, must carry out the wealth of the Indies." There is then creative reading as well as creative writing. When the mind is braced by labor and inventions, the page of whatever book we read becomes luminous with manifold allusion. Every sentence is doubly significant, and the sense of our author is as broad as the world. We then see, what is always true, that as the seer's hour of vision is short and rare among heavy days and months, so is its record, perchance, the least part of his volume. The discerning will read, in his Plato or Shakespeare, only that least part,—only the authentic utterances of the oracle;—all the rest he rejects, were it never so many times Plato's and Shakespeare's. /19

Of course there is a portion of reading quite indispensable to a wise man. History and exact science he must learn by laborious reading. Colleges, in like manner, have their indispensable office,—to teach elements. But they can only highly serve us when they aim not to drill, but to create; when they gather from far every ray of various genius to their hospitable halls, and by the concentrated fires, set the hearts of their youth on flame. Thought and knowledge are natures in which apparatus and pretension avail nothing. Gowns and pecuniary foundations, though of towns of gold, can never countervail the least sentence or syllable of wit. Forget this, and our American colleges will recede in their public importance, whilst they grow richer every year. /20

III. There goes in the world a notion that the scholar should be a recluse, a valetudinarian,—as unfit for any handiwork, or public labor as a penknife for an axe. The so-called "practical men" sneer at speculative men, as if, because they speculate or *see*, they could do nothing. I have heard it said that the clergy,—who are always, more universally than any other class, the scholars of their day,—are addressed as women; that the rough, spontaneous conversation of men they do not hear, but only a mincing and diluted speech. They are often virtually disfran-

chised; and indeed there are advocates for their celibacy. As far as this is true of the studious classes, it is not just and wise. Action is with the scholar subordinate, but it is essential. Without it he is not yet man. Without it thought can never ripen into truth. Whilst the world hangs before the eye as a cloud of beauty, we cannot even see its beauty. Inaction is cowardice, but there can be no scholar without the heroic mind. The preamble of thought, the transition through which it passes from the unconscious to the conscious, is action. Only so much do I know, as I have lived. Instantly we know whose words are loaded with life, and whose not. /21

The world,—this shadow of the soul, or *other me*,—lies wide around. Its attractions are the keys which unlock my thoughts and make me acquainted with myself. I run eagerly into this resounding tumult. I grasp the hands of those next me, and take my place in the ring to suffer and to work, taught by an instinct that so shall the dumb abyss be vocal with speech. I pierce its order; I dissipate its fear; I dispose of it within the circuit of my expanding life. So much only of life as I know by experience, so much of the wilderness have I vanquished and planted, or so far have I extended my being, my dominion. I do not see how any man can afford, for the sake of his nerves and his nap, to spare any action in which he can partake. It is pearls and rubies to his discourse. Drudgery, calamity, exasperation, want, are instructors in eloquence and wisdom. The true scholar grudges every opportunity of action past by, as a loss of power. It is the raw material out of which the intellect moulds her splendid products. A strange process too, this by which experience is converted into thought, as a mulberry leaf is converted into satin. The manufacture goes forward at all hours. /22

The actions and events of our childhood and youth are now matters of calmest observation. They lie like fair pictures in the air. Not so with our recent actions,—with the business which we now have in hand. On this we are quite unable to speculate. Our affections as yet circulate through it. We no more feel or know it than we feel the feet, or the hand, or the brain of our body. The new deed is yet a part of life,—remains for a time immersed in our unconscious life. In some contemplative hour it detaches itself from the life like a ripe fruit, to become a thought of the mind. Instantly it is raised, transfigured; the corruptible has put on incorruption. Henceforth it is an object of beauty, however base its origin and neighborhood. Observe too the impossibility of antedating this act. In its grub state, it cannot fly, it cannot shine, it is a dull grub. But suddenly, without observation, the self-same thing unfurls beautiful wings, and is an angel of wisdom. So is there no fact, no event, in our private history, which shall not, sooner or later, lose its adhesive, inert form, and astonish us by soaring from our body into the empyrean. Cradle and infancy, school and playground, the fear of boys, and dogs, and ferules, the love of little maids and berries, and many another fact that once filled the whole sky, are gone already; friend and relative, profession and party, town and country, nation and world, must also soar and sing. /23

Of course, he who has put forth his total strength in fit actions has the richest return of wisdom. I will not shut myself out of this globe of action, and transplant an oak into a flower-pot, there to hunger and pine; nor trust the revenue of some single faculty, and exhaust one vein of thought, much like those Savoyards, who, getting their livelihood by carving shepherds, shepherdesses, and smoking Dutchmen, for all Europe, went out one day to the mountain to find stock, and discovered that they had whittled up the last of their pine trees. Authors we have, in numbers, who have written out their vein, and who, moved by a commendable prudence, sail for Greece or Palestine, follow the trapper into the prairie, or ramble round Algiers to replenish their merchantable stock. /24

If it were only for a vocabulary, the scholar would be covetous of action. Life is our dictionary. Years are well spent in country labors; in town; in the insight into trades and manufactures; in frank intercourse with many men and women; in science; in art; to the one end of mastering in all their facts a language by which to illustrate and embody our perceptions. I learn immediately from any speaker how much he has already lived, through the poverty or the splendor of his speech. Life lies behind us as the quarry from whence we get tiles and copestones for the masonry of to-day. This is the way to learn grammar. Colleges and books only copy the language which the field and the work-yard made. /25

But the final value of action, like that of books, and better than books, is that it is a resource. The great principle of Undulation in nature, that shows itself in the inspiring and expiring of the breath; in desire and satiety; in the ebb and flow of the sea; in day and night; in heat and cold; and, as yet more deeply ingrained in every atom and every fluid, is known to us under the name of Polarity,—these "fits of easy transmission and reflection," as Newton called them, are the law of nature because they are the law of spirit. /26

The mind now thinks, now acts, and each fit reproduces the other. When the artist has exhausted his materials, when the fancy no longer paints, when thoughts are no longer apprehended and books are a weariness,—he has always the resource *to live*. Character is higher than intellect. Thinking is the function. Living is the functionary. The stream retreats to its source. A great soul will be strong to live, as well as strong to think. Does he lack organ or medium to impart his truth? He can still fall back on this elemental force of living them. This is a total act. Thinking is a partial act. Let the grandeur of justice shine in his affairs. Let the beauty of affection cheer his lowly roof. Those "far from fame," who dwell and act with him, will feel the force of his constitution in the doings and passages of the day better than it can be measured by any public and designed display. Time shall teach him that the scholar loses no hour which the man lives. Herein he unfolds the sacred germ of his instinct, screened from influence. What is lost in seemliness is gained in strength. Not out of those on whom systems of education have exhausted their culture, comes the helpful giant to destroy the old or to build the new, but out of unhandselled savage nature; out of terrible Druids and Berserkers come at last Alfred and Shakespeare. /27

I hear therefore with joy whatever is beginning to be said of the dignity and necessity of labor to every citizen. There is virtue yet in the hoe and the spade, for learned as well as for unlearned hands. And labor is everywhere welcome; always we are invited to work; only be this limitation observed, that a man shall not for the sake of wider activity sacrifice any opinion to the popular judgments and modes of action. /28

I have now spoken of the education of the scholar by nature, by books, and by action. It remains to say somewhat of his duties. /29

They are such as become Man Thinking. They may all be comprised in self-trust. The office of the scholar is to cheer, to raise, and to guide men by showing them facts amidst appearances. He plies the slow, unhonored, and unpaid task of observation. Flamsteed and Herschel, in their glazed observatories, may catalogue the stars with the praise of all men, and the results being splendid and useful, honor is sure. But he, in his private observatory, cataloguing obscure and nebulous stars of the human mind, which as yet no man has thought of as such,—watching days and months sometimes for a few facts; correcting still his old records;—must relinquish display and immediate fame. In the long period of his preparation he must betray often an ignorance and shiftlessness in popular arts, incurring the disdain of the able who shoulder him aside. Long he must stammer in his speech; often forego the living for the dead. Worse yet, he must accept—how often!—poverty and solitude. For the ease and pleasure of treading the old road, accepting the fashions, the education, the religion of society, he takes the cross of making his own, and, of course, the self-accusation, the faint heart, the frequent uncertainty and loss of time, which are the nettles and tangling vines in the way of the self-relying and self-directed; and the state of virtual hostility in which he seems to stand to society, and especially to educated society. For all this loss and scorn, what offset? He is to find consolation in exercising the highest functions of human nature. He is one who raises himself from private considerations and breathes and lives on public and illustrious thoughts. He is the world's eye. He is the world's heart. He is to resist the vulgar prosperity that retrogrades ever to barbarism, by preserving and communicating heroic sentiments, noble biographies, melodious verse, and the conclusions of history. Whatsoever oracles the human heart, in all emergencies, in all solemn hours, has uttered as its commentary on the world of actions,—these he shall receive and impart. And whatsoever new verdict Reason from her inviolable seat pronounces on the passing men and events of to-day,—this he shall hear and promulgate. /30

These being his functions, it becomes him to feel all confidence in himself, and to defer never to the popular cry. He and he only knows the world. The world of any moment is the merest appearance. Some great decorum, some fetish of a government, some ephemeral trade, or war, or man, is cried up by half mankind and cried down by the other half, as if all depended on this particular up or down. The odds are that the whole question is not worth the poorest thought which the scholar has lost in listening to the controversy. Let him not quit his belief that a popgun is a popgun, though the ancient and honorable of the earth affirm it to be the crack of doom. In silence, in steadiness, in severe abstraction, let him hold by himself; add observation to observation, patient of neglect, patient of reproach, and bide his own time,—happy enough if he can satisfy himself alone that this day he has seen something truly. Success treads on every right step. For the instinct is sure, that prompts him to tell his brother what he thinks. He then learns that in going down into the secrets of his own mind he has descended into the secrets of all minds. He learns that he who has mastered any law in his private thoughts, is mas-

ter to that extent of all men whose language he speaks, and of all into whose language his own can be translated. The poet, in utter solitude remembering his spontaneous thoughts and recording them, is found to have recorded that which men in crowded cities find true for them also. The orator distrusts at first the fitness of his frank confessions, his want of knowledge of the persons he addresses, until he finds that he is the complement of his hearers;—that they drink his words because he fulfils for them their own nature; the deeper he dives into his privatest, secretest presentiment, to his wonder he finds this is the most acceptable, most public, and universally true. The people delight in it; the better part of every man feels, This is my music; this is myself. /31

In self-trust all the virtues are comprehended. Free should the scholar be,—free and brave. Free even to the definition of freedom, "without any hindrance that does not arise out of his own constitution." Brave; for fear is a thing which a scholar by his very function puts behind him. Fear always springs from ignorance. It is a shame to him if his tranquility, amid dangerous times, arise from the presumption that like children and women his is a protected class; or if he seek a temporary peace by the diversion of his thoughts from politics or vexed questions, hiding his head like an ostrich in the flowering bushes, peeping into microscopes, and turning rhymes, as a boy whistles to keep his courage up. So is the danger a danger still; so is the fear worse. Manlike let him turn and face it. Let him look into its eye and search its nature, inspect its origin,—see the whelping of this lion,—which lies no great way back; he will then find in himself a perfect comprehension of its nature and extent; he will have made his hands meet on the other side, and can henceforth defy it and pass on superior. The world is his who can see through its pretension. What deafness, what stone-blind custom, what overgrown error you behold is there only by sufferance,—by your sufferance. See it to be a lie, and you have already dealt it its mortal blow. /32

Yes, we are the cowed,—we the trustless. It is a mischievous notion that we are come late into nature; that the world was finished a long time ago. As the world was plastic and fluid in the hands of God, so it is ever to so much of his attributes as we bring to it. To ignorance and sin, it is flint. They adapt themselves to it as they may; but in proportion as a man has any thing in him divine, the firmament flows before him and takes his signet and form. Not he is great who can alter matter, but he who can alter my state of mind. They are the kings of the world who give the color of their present thought to all nature and all art, and persuade men by the cheerful serenity of their carrying the matter, that this thing which they do is the apple which the ages have desired to pluck, now at last ripe, and inviting nations to the harvest. The great man makes the great thing. Wherever Macdonald sits, there is the head of the table. Linnæus makes botany the most alluring of studies, and wins it from the farmer and the herb-woman; Davy, chemistry; and Cuvier, fossils. The day is always his who works in it with serenity and great aims. The unstable estimates of men crowd to him whose mind is filled with a truth, as the heaped waves of the Atlantic follow the moon. /33

For this self-trust, the reason is deeper than can be fathomed,—darker than can be enlightened. I might not carry with me the feeling of my audience in stating my own belief. But I have already shown the ground of my hope, in adverting to the doctrine that man is one. I believe man has been wronged; he has wronged himself. He has almost lost the light that can lead him back to his prerogatives. Men are become of no account. Men in history, men in the world of to-day, are bugs, are spawn, and are called "the mass" and "the herd." In a century, in a millennium, one or two men; that is to say, one or two approximations to the right state of every man. All the rest behold in the hero or the poet their own green and crude being,—ripened; yes, and are content to be less, so *that* may attain to its full stature. What a testimony, full of grandeur, full of pity, is borne to the demands of his own nature, by the poor clansman, the poor partisan, who rejoices in the glory of his chief. The poor and the low find some amends to their immense moral capacity, for their acquiescence in a political and social inferiority. They are content to be brushed like flies from the path of a great person, so that justice shall be done by him to that common nature which it is the dearest desire of all to see enlarged and glorified. They sun themselves in the great man's light, and feel it to be their own element. They cast the dignity of man from their downtrod selves upon the shoulders of a hero, and will perish to add one drop of blood to make that great heart beat, those giant sinews combat and conquer. He lives for us, and we live in him. /34

Men such as they are, very naturally seek money or power; and power because it is as good as money,— the "spoils," so called, "of office." And why not? for they aspire to the highest, and this, in their sleep-walking, they dream is highest. Wake them and they shall quit the false good and leap to the true, and leave governments to clerks and desks. This revolu-tion is to be wrought by the gradual domestication of the idea of Culture. The main enterprise of the world for splendor, for extent, is the upbuilding of a man. Here are the materials strewn along the ground. The private life of one man shall be a more illustrious monarchy, more formidable to its enemy, more sweet and serene in its influence to its friend, than any kingdom in history. For a man, rightly viewed, comprehendeth the particular natures of all men. Each philosopher, each bard, each actor has only done for me, as by a delegate, what one day I can do for myself. The books which once we valued more than the apple of the eye, we have quite exhausted. What is that but saying that we have come up with the point of view which the universal mind took through the eyes of one scribe; we have been that man, and have passed on. First, one, then another, we drain all cisterns, and waxing greater by all these supplies, we crave a better and more abundant food. The man has never lived that can feed us ever. The human mind cannot be enshrined in a person who shall set a barrier on any one side to this unbounded, unbound-able empire. It is one central fire, which, flaming now out of the lips of Etna, lightens the capes of Sicily, and now out of the throat of Vesuvius, illuminates the towers and vineyards of Naples. It is one light which beams out of a thousand stars. It is one soul which animates all men. /35

But I have dwelt perhaps tediously upon this ab-straction of the Scholar. I ought not to delay longer to add what I have to say of nearer reference to the time and to this country. /36

Historically, there is thought to be a difference in the ideas which predominate over successive epochs, and there are data for marking the genius of the Classic, of the Romantic, and now of the Reflective or Philosophical age. With the views I have intimated of the oneness or the identity of the mind through all individuals, I do not much dwell on these differ-ences. In fact, I believe each individual passes through all three. The boy is a Greek; the youth, ro-mantic; the adult, reflective. I deny not, however, that a revolution in the leading idea may be distinct-ly enough traced. /37

Our age is bewailed as the age of Introversion. Must that needs be evil? We, it seems, are critical; we are embarrassed with second thoughts; we can-not enjoy any thing for hankering to know whereof the pleasure consists; we are lined with eyes; we see with our feet; the time is infected with Hamlet's un-happiness,—

"Sicklied o'er with the pale cast of thought."

It is so bad then? Sight is the last thing to be pitied. Would we be blind? Do we fear lest we should outsee nature and God, and drink truth dry? I look upon the discontent of the literary class as a mere announcement of the fact that they find themselves not in the state of mind of their fathers, and regret the coming state as untried; as a boy dreads the water before he has learned that he can swim. If there is any period one would desire to be born in, is it not the age of Revolution; when the old and the new stand side by side and admit of being compared; when the energies of all men are searched by fear, and by hope; when the historic glories of the old can be compensated by the rich possibilities of the new era? This time, like all times, is a very good one, if we but know what to do with it. /38

I read with some joy of the auspicious signs of the coming days, as they glimmer already through poetry and art, through philosophy and science, through church and state. /39

One of these signs is the fact that the same movement which effected the elevation of what was called the lowest class in the state, assumed in literature a very marked and as benign an aspect. Instead of the sublime and beautiful, the near, the low, the common, was explored and poetized. That which had been negligently trodden under foot by those who were harnessing and provisioning themselves for long journeys into far countries, is suddenly found to be richer than all foreign parts. The literature of the poor, the feelings of the child, the philosophy of the street, the meaning of household life, are the topics of the time. It is a great stride. It is a sign— is it not?—of new vigor when the extremities are made active, when currents of warm life run into the hands and the feet. I ask not for the great, the remote, the romantic; what is doing in Italy or Arabia; what is Greek art, or Provençal minstrelsy; I embrace the common, I explore and sit at the feet of the familiar, the low. Give me insight into to-day, and you may have the antique and future worlds. What would we really know the meaning of? The meal in the firkin; the milk in the pan; the ballad in the street; the news of the boat; the glance of the eye; the form and the gait of the body;—show me the ultimate reason of these matters; show me the sublime presence of the highest spiritual cause lurking, as always it does lurk, in these suburbs and extremities of nature; let me see every trifle bristling with the polarity that ranges it instantly on an eternal law; and the shop, the plough, and the ledger referred to the like cause by which light undulates and poets sing; —and the world lies no longer a dull miscellany and lumber room, but has form and order; there is no trifle, there is no puzzle, but one design unites and animates the farthest pinnacle and the lowest trench. /40

This idea has inspired the genius of Goldsmith, Burns, Cowper, and in a newer time, of Goethe, Wordsworth, and Carlyle. This idea they have differently followed and with various success. In contrast with their writing, the style of Pope, of Johnson, of Gibbon, looks cold and pedantic. This writing is blood-warm. Man is surprised to find that things near are not less beautiful and wondrous than things remote. The near explains the far. The drop is a small ocean. A man is related to all nature. This perception of the worth of the vulgar is fruitful in discoveries, Goethe, in this very thing the most modern of the moderns, has shown us, as none ever did, the genius of the ancients. /41

There is one man of genius who has done much for this philosophy of life, whose literary value has never yet been rightly estimated;—I mean Emanuel Swedenborg. The most imaginative of men, yet writing with the precision of a mathematician, he endeavored to engraft a purely philosophical Ethics on the popular Christianity of his time. Such an attempt of course must have difficulty which no genius could surmount. But he saw and showed the connection between nature and the affections of the soul. He pierced the emblematic or spiritual character of the visible, audible, tangible world. Especially did his shade-loving muse hover over and interpret the lower parts of nature; he showed the mysterious bond that allies moral evil to the foul material forms, and has given in epical parables a theory of insanity, of beasts, of unclean and fearful things. /42

Another sign of our times, also marked by an analogous political movement, is the new importance given to the single person. Every thing that tends to insulate the individual,—to surround him with barriers of natural respect, so that each man shall feel the world is his, and man shall treat with man as a sovereign state with a sovereign state,—tends to true union as well as greatness. "I learned," said the melancholy Pestalozzi, "that no man in God's wide earth is either willing or able to help any other man." Help must come from the bosom alone. The scholar is that man who must take up into himself all the ability of the time, all the contributions of the past, all the hopes of the future. He must be an university of knowledges. If there be one lesson more than another which should pierce his ear, it is, The world is nothing, the man is all; in yourself is the law of all nature, and you know not yet how a globule of sap ascends; in yourself slumbers the whole of Reason; it is for you to know all; it is for you to dare all. Mr. President and Gentlemen, this confidence in the unsearched might of man belongs, by all motives, by all prophecy, by all preparation, to the American Scholar. We have listened too long to the courtly muses of Europe. The spirit of the American freeman is already suspected to be timid, imitative, tame. Public and private avarice make the air we breathe thick and fat. The scholar is decent, indolent, complaisant. See already the tragic consequence. The mind of this country, taught to aim at low objects, eats upon itself. There is no work for any but the decorous and the complaisant. Young men of the fairest promise, who begin life upon our shores, inflated by the mountain winds, shined upon by all the stars of God, find the earth below not in unison with these, but are hindered from action by the disgust which the principles on which business is managed inspire, and turn drudges, or die of disgust, some of them suicides. What is the remedy? They did not yet see, and thousands of young men as hopeful now crowding to the barriers for the career do not yet see, that if the single man plant himself indomitably on his instincts, and there abide, the huge world will come round to him. Patience,—patience; with the shades of all the good and great for company; and for solace the perspective of your own infinite life; and for work the study and the communication of principles, the making those instincts prevalent, the conversion of the world. Is it not the chief disgrace in the world, not to be an unit;—not to be reckoned one character;—not to yield that peculiar fruit which man was created to bear, but to be reckoned in the gross, in the hundred, or the thousand, of the party, the section, to which we belong; and our opinion predicted geographically, as the north, or the south? Not so, brothers and friends,—please God, ours shall not be so. We will walk on our own feet; we will work with our own hands; we will speak our own minds. The study of letters shall be no longer a name for pity, for doubt, and for sensual indulgence. The dread of man and the love of man shall be a wall of defence and a wreath of joy around all. A nation of men will for the first time exist, because each believes himself inspired by the Divine Soul which also inspires all men. /43

The speech

1. What is the essential difference for Emerson between the thinker and Man Thinking?
2. What are the three important influences on the scholar? Would you say that Emerson discusses them in what

for him is an ascending order? Give the reasons for your answer.

3. Explicate the statement: "In self-trust all the virtues are comprehended." What for Emerson is one really trusting when one trusts the "self"? Show how the whole argument depends upon the assumption that the source of man's power lies within the self.
4. What does Emerson find auspicious about the signs of the times? How do these auspicious circumstances reflect what Emerson believes to be a growing trust in the individual self?
5. Emerson has often been accused of delivering provocative but disorganized lectures. Is this one disorganized? If not, show what its organization is. If so, suggest a more coherent organization.
6. It is said that in his lectures Emerson seldom argued but only asserted his position. Is this true of "The American Scholar"? Find illustrations to support your answer.
7. What kind of proof or amplification is Emerson using in paragraph 13 to support the conclusions he draws in paragraph 14? Is this proof by reasoning? Suggestion?
8. By many Emerson was thought to speak at an inordinately high level of abstraction. Do you find this to be true of "The American Scholar"? Select two or three typical paragraphs and analyze them for their level of abstractness—or concreteness.
9. Emerson felt that we should not listen or read for systematized ideas but for isolated ideas that excite us to fresh vision. Show how he accommodates his own style to this theory.
10. In paragraph 31 Emerson describes what he believes to be the difference between the way a poet serves humankind and the way a public speaker serves them. Why do you agree or disagree with his description? It has been said that the passage of this paragraph beginning "The orator distrusts. . ." and ending "This is my music; this is myself" is a description of Emerson's personal experience when he lectured to audiences across the country. Can you find evidence that he may have had this kind of feeling when he delivered this lecture?

For further study and discussion

1. Define Transcendentalism, and tell how much of a Transcendentalist you are.
2. How do you account for the rise of Transcendentalism in this country? For its decline?
3. What do you believe is valuable in the study of history? To what extent can it help us to handle the present and to prepare for the future?
4. How do books serve you? Classify them according to their function in your intellectual development.

5. Do you consider yourself a student or a man studying? Develop your answer with examples.

6. David Riesman has said that whereas ours is an other-directed society, Emerson's was an inner-directed one (i.e., we get our values from listening to others; he got his values from reflection and contemplation). What are the advantages and disadvantages of each process? Which of the two is in your opinion superior?

7. To what extent do you find among your classmates the kind of scholar Emerson describes? Among the faculty?

8. What do you consider to be the chief functions of scholars in our modern society? Do you find that many of them fail to perform these functions adequately? If so, wherein does the fault lie?

Suggestions for further reading

A. Whitney Griswold, *In the University Tradition* (New Haven, 1957)

Karl Jaspers, *The Idea of the University* (Boston, 1959)

Jose Ortega y Gasset, *Mission of the University* (Princeton, 1944)

Howard Mumford Jones, *The Scholar as American* (Cambridge, Mass., 1961)

Mark Van Doren, *Liberal Education* (New York, 1943)

Alfred North Whitehead, *The Aims of Education and Other Essays* (New York, 1929)

Excellence in teaching

BEN EUWEMA

The dean of a college in a large university has in what many ways is a thankless and impossible task. On the one hand, he must be a loyal subordinate to the president and provost, and, on the other hand, he must be a bold and imaginative leader of the faculty. A middle man, he must interpret the views of the president to the faculty, and must fight for his faculty before the president and other deans. Ben Euwema was extraordinarily successful in this difficult role. When he requested in 1964 that he be relieved of his duties as dean to return to the classroom as professor of English, not only the president but the faculty acceded to his request only with great reluctance. An awareness of this rapport between Euwema and his faculty is necessary to keep in mind if his speech is to be read perceptively.

Reprinted by permission of Ben Euwema

Euwema was born in Chicago in 1904, earned his B.A. at Calvin College, his M.A. at Michigan, and his Ph.D. at Chicago. He taught at Westminster College (Pennsylvania), at Kent State, and at Michigan State before going to Pennsylvania State University (then Pennsylvania State College) in 1939. There he successively became Professor and Head of the Department of English, the Director of the Division of Language and Literature, and, finally, Dean of the Liberal Arts College in 1946. He is a specialist in nineteenth-century English literature; probably his best known work is on George Eliot. Additionally, he is editor of the *Journal of General Education.*

The speech that follows was an address of welcome to the members of the faculty of the College of Liberal Arts at Pennsylvania State University. It was delivered on September 23, 1963, at the resumption of classes for the new academic year. The setting was a breakfast meeting in a large hotel dining room on the campus of the university. As is his custom in almost all formal speaking situations, Dean Euwema read his address, and the text below follows the manuscript he used. The speaker read expertly; the papers before him in no way hindered his rapport with his audience or diminished the personal warmth and liveliness his listeners had learned to expect from him.

Let me begin by thanking you for being here this morning. I very much appreciate your attendance. I should especially like to welcome the new members of the faculty. We are proud and happy to have you associated with us, and we promise to do whatever we can to make your first year at Penn State memorable, happy, and effective. /1

This breakfast convocation is concerned with teaching in general and one of our most important and most neglected teaching duties—advising—in particular. I shall address myself specifically to teaching; those who follow me will deal more specifically with advising. /2

If what I shall say about teaching sounds familiar to some of you, it is simply because I have said most of what I am about to say on many earlier occasions —and none of it was new then. I shall, therefore, as always depend upon your native kindliness and poor memories. /3

I shall begin by mentioning two enemies of sound academic work in American higher education: /4

1. *Quantification.* (I am not absolutely sure that there is such a word; but if there isn't, let's pretend there is.) I mean by it the assumption that one

subject is as valuable as any other, and one assignment as beneficial educationally as any other. (This idea has really become vicious when used in the secondary schools.) In other words, it is the belief that a teacher is doing his full duty if, somehow or other, his students are kept busy at no matter what. I grant the importance of industry, but only if it is directed upon a carefully selected corpus of data and towards carefully predetermined ends. You can keep young people busy at sorting pebbles and a good deal of so-called "applied" education is of that sort; but education should have higher aims, objectives, and purposes. In the social sciences, for example, you could devote your students' full time to a careful counting of random opinions picked up on campus or on the street—but you might approach only very obliquely, if at all, the basic objectives of a liberal education. /5

What we should really like our students to learn is the reality that lies behind and beyond appearances. Perhaps only God can do this in any absolute sense; we should at least try to do the best we can. We should get our students to search for fundamentals and not to be satisfied with a sort of "how-to-do" attitude: how to be cultured, how to order a meal in French, how to make friends, how to be happy, how to sell insurance, how to make religion work—and so on. The really literate person must learn to see beneath the surface appearance to the fundamental realities of human personality and human society. /6

2. *Experience.* This second enemy is an enemy only under special conditions. It is trite to say that "experience is the best teacher," but actually it is often the very worst. All of us are tempted, in dealing with educational matters, to fall back upon our own experience. This would be helpful—if somewhat unimaginative—if we were all perfectly educated ourselves; but, on the contrary, as we grow older we arrive at the serious conviction that we were all very badly educated indeed. /7

It is not enough to fall back upon the habits, practices, and idiosyncracies of our own teachers. Many of *them* merely served as faded carbon copies of *their* teachers. Teaching is not a trick that can be taught or a set of habits that can be imitated. It results from deliberate, purposive thought as to the objectives of the course, the resources of the subject matter, and the character of the students. No two groups can properly be taught in precisely the same way, nor need they necessarily be taught precisely the same things. The effective teacher builds the course, a step at a time, giving constant thought to the development of the students' grasp of the subject matter. And, without lessening his demands upon the students, he selects and arranges the subject matter in such a way as to make the quest of knowledge exciting and rewarding. /8

In this process, of course, his own experience as a student will be helpful, but not if it is looked upon as a kind of academic ultimate, above criticism and perfect by definition. /9

And now, let's be more positive and mention three characteristics of good undergraduate teaching: /10

1. A very significant aspect of good teaching is *simplicity.* And simplicity, as we all learn sooner or later, is not something that comes as a matter of course; it must be laboriously sought and conscientiously acquired. When we begin to teach we are so full of erudition and learning that we ourselves are overwhelmed and confused by it. It is only later that the seeming complexity of the subject becomes a real simplicity—or, is it more correct to say that the real complexity becomes an apparent simplicity? In any case, great teaching is simple. /11

All good teachers—even as you and I, in our better moments—are aware of this. Some morning while he is shaving, or walking to the campus, or lecturing to a class, or merely looking out of the classroom window, the hitherto disparate and disunited elements of the subject fall into a pattern. He now has his formula for simplification and, like Newton, he is unaware of the apple striking his pate. /12

Because this is true and highly desirable, it is almost impossible to over-emphasize the importance of sound and broad scholarship. For the kind of insight I am mentioning here is vouchsafed only to the man who can see all sides of a problem and who is aware of all of its ramifications. It is good to learn *how* to teach; but it is as true today as it was in the days of Confucius, that the best way to learn *how* to teach is to learn *what* to teach. /13

A lifetime is not nearly long enough to learn one subject thoroughly, and to see it so clearly and in such relationship with other subjects that it appears to be and *is* simple. I think we all learn, sooner or later, that we should really teach fewer *things* and more *principles,* fewer statistics and more interpretations. The older and more expert we become as teachers, the more we desire to teach our students how to think about the subject, how to learn, and how to simplify. /14

There is nothing more admirable in academic life than to see a teacher who is so thoroughly on top of his subject that he can make the abstruse simple and the complex clear. /15

I recall now, as you will too, a few of my own teachers who did this rare but beautiful thing. A philosophy professor who could teach the history of philosophy by the Socratic method and somehow relate the monads of Leibniz to last night's basketball game. A teacher of musicology and musical theory, who could take the most complex and esoteric musical composition and lead his students through it as unerringly as though they were following him from the dormitory to the classroom. A professor of history, whose specialty was the antebellum South and who could, without affectation, refer to Henry Clay as "Henry" and to all the worthies of the time as though they were his contemporaries. A teacher of composition, who could draw out of a student his precise intention in writing a paper and then help him to say exactly what he meant to say—something almost impossibly difficult for anyone, even for a professional writer. /16

2. Another quality is humor, I do not mean wit—although no one has higher regard for wit than I—but the kind of sensibility we call humor. For it is humor which, in the last analysis, can change the very nature of our thoughts, and hardly anything else can change it more. It is the ability to see the incongruous, the inconsistent, the pompous, the inflated, the unnatural, the unnecessarily complex, the long-winded, the asinine qualities of men and women. It is, for the most part, a rather gentle thing. It is generally sympathetic and warm; its barbs are directed not so much at people as at ideas, postures, and attitudes. /17

Its objective is, of course, a life of reason. Like so many other things, it really aims at its own destruction; for in a perfectly sane and reasonable society, humor would hardly find anything to feed on. This eventuality is, fortunately or not, rather remote; and there is no danger that as long as human beings inhabit the planet, humor will not have its place. /18

And one important place for it is the classroom. I don't mean that—heaven forbid!—we should all set out to act like Bob Hope! I am not pleading for wisecracks or jokes, although I have nothing against them either. I *am* pleading for a warm, sympathetic, and decorously playful attitude towards the subjects under discussion. /19

Learning should be fun. It is, at its very best, a form of play. History is a good detective story—all the better for being true. All of the arts and the humanities are based upon the instinct of play.

Philosophy is Socrates disputing with the young men in the public forum—not to earn money, or fame, or position, but for fun, for the sheer joy of following an idea to its logical conclusion. Mathematics is, of course, sheer make-believe—"nothing intricately drawn nowhere in shapes of shifting lineage." And language, while it has its practical aspects, is basically two monkeys chattering in a tree. /20

Perhaps I am overstating the case. However, I do want to emphasize the fact that a sense of humor is a basic requirement in teaching the arts and sciences. I am sure you will agree that saying this does not constitute a disparagement of the arts and sciences. We all recognize that man is never more rightfully himself than when he is balanced, sane, and able to see things in their proper perspective. To call humor a basic ingredient of any approach to the arts and sciences is, actually, to pay the arts and sciences the highest possible compliment. For, as we know but usually keep to ourselves, a good deal of so-called "applied education" is, in its very essence, too pompous or inflated or pretentious to survive a humorous attitude towards it. /21

In his ideal nature, man is the laughing animal; and he is never more distinctively human than when he laughs. /22

3. The third and finest quality in a teacher is (quite simply) intellectual honesty. This is so closely allied with a sense of humor that it is hard to imagine one without the other. It is only by being completely honest with the student in exploring the subject, in assessing its possibilities and limitations, in evaluating the work of other scholars, and in every other phase of the work that the teacher can bring his students to grips with the subject. /23

This, of course, is not easy either. Honesty is every bit as difficult to achieve as simplicity. /24

By honesty in teaching I do not mean merely that the teacher should not lie to his students. I mean much more. He should tell the students as much of the truth as he himself knows, without distortion (if possible); he should attempt to assign to the various aspects of the course their proper value; he should explain clearly not only what the various assignments are but also what they are *for;* he should assess the student's work objectively and fairly. But more than all this, he should attempt to develop in the classroom an atmosphere of intellectual honesty. It is only in this way that he and the student can seriously attack their mutual problems, and it is only in this way that the student can be inspired to independent thought. To me it is clear that, in the classroom, honesty means a much more studied effort to deal with primary sources than is common with many of us. Let us try to stop distilling books from books, lectures from lectures, and concepts from concepts. Let's try to get back, as often as we can, to the primary sources—which, in the liberal arts, are the great intellectual and artistic monuments of our tradition. /25

As usual, we have our work cut out for us in 1963-64. /26

The speech

1. Since faculty members were obligated to attend the meeting at which Euwema spoke, why should he begin by thanking them for coming?
2. What emotional appeals has Euwema built into the first three paragraphs? Since his audience would be reasonably sophisticated about speech techniques, would you guess that the appeals would be effective? Explain your answer.
3. Describe in your own words the opposition that the speaker establishes in the section on quantification.
4. Is Euwema denying the usefulness of experience? If not, what is he attacking?
5. What does the speaker mean by simplicity in teaching? How valuable are his illustrations in making the concept clear (e.g., the professor who called Henry Clay "Henry")?
6. Why does Euwema reject wit but accept humor as a quality necessary for the good teacher? What type of definition does he use in defining humor? (See *Definition* in Glossary.)
7. Evaluate the order of the main points: simplicity, humor, and honesty. Is there any danger that listeners might get this list of items confused with the preceding two items, quantification and experience? Has the speaker done enough to keep them separate?
8. Compare what Euwema has to say in his last long paragraph with what Emerson has to say about books in paragraphs 10-20, pp. 40-42. To what extent do the two speakers agree?
9. What precisely is Euwema trying to accomplish with this speech? How would you classify it? (See *Ends of Speaking* in Glossary.)
10. The ideas in this speech seem so simple and obvious that one wonders how it could have made much of an impression upon a college faculty. What kind of speaker and what kind of relation between speaker and audience would have had to exist for this speech to be effective? Could an outsider giving the same speech have been equally effective?

For further study and discussion

1. Would you agree that quantification has become vicious in our secondary education? Can the same thing be said of college education? Elaborate upon your answer.
2. Comment on the old saying that "experience is the best teacher." Why do you suppose the adage has been so popular? In what ways is it true? In what ways, false? How much formal education is presently based upon it?
3. Given Euwema's principles, how important is a course in practice teaching? Do not answer this until you reflect upon it.
4. Is learning really play? Define the terms *learning* and *play*, and indicate the circumstances under which learning can be play. Does learning cease when it ceases to be play? Is all play learning?
5. Do you agree that it is hard to imagine intellectual honesty unaccompanied by a sense of humor? Compare Euwema's belief in this regard with Mark Twain's statement that there is no laughter in heaven (i.e., that there is nothing humorous about truth).
6. Why should simplicity be hard to achieve? Is simplicity possible in this age of specialization?
7. Distinguish between simplicity as Euwema uses the term and simple-mindedness. How are they alike and how are they different?
8. To what extent do your college instructors possess the qualities listed by Euwema? In which characteristic are they strongest? Weakest?
9. List the qualities you think necessary for a good college teacher. Do you find any omitted by Euwema that you think indispensable?
10. What are the most important characteristics, do you suppose, of a good dean? Do they differ in any regard from the characteristics necessary for a good teacher?

Suggestions for further reading

Willard Abraham, *A Time for Teaching* (New York, 1964)

Jacques Barzun, *Teacher in America* (Boston, 1945)

Richard Hofstadter and Walter P. Metzger, *The Development of Academic Freedom in the United States* (New York, 1955)

Sidney Hook, *Education for Modern Man, A New Perspective* (New York, 1963)

Bliss Perry, *And Gladly Teach* (Boston, 1935)

William Lyon Phelps, *The Excitement of Teaching* (New York, 1931)

Ordway Tead, *The Climate of Learning* (New York, 1958)

The writer's duty

WILLIAM FAULKNER

William Faulkner, in this speech read in Stockholm, in 1950, at the time he received the Nobel prize for literature, underlines the theme that gives his work its remarkable universality: man's endurance despite the enormous odds against him. For such an occasion, it is an unusual statement because it ignores all of the amenities of the situation, but in this instance it is the stronger for doing so.

Faulkner lived almost all his life in Mississippi. He was born there, on September 25, 1897. He grew up there and, after a short period as an aviator in World War I, he returned there to attend the University of Mississippi and to settle down in Oxford. He died in Oxford in 1962.

After *Soldier's Pay* (1926) and *Mosquitoes* (1927), Faulkner began, with *Sartoris* (1929), the series of works that were to make the fictional Yoknapatawpha County, Mississippi, the best known county in the United States. Following *Sartoris*, came, among others, *The Sound and the Fury* (1929), *As I Lay Dying* (1930), *Sanctuary* (1931), *Light in August* (1932), *Absalom, Absalom!* (1936), *The Hamlet* (1940), and *Intruder in the Dust* (1948). His best known story, "The Bear," appeared in its most complete form in *Go Down, Moses* (1942). Taken as a whole, these works form a gigantic and penetrating study of the disintegration of Southern white society. Apart from the Yoknapatawpha saga, Faulkner's most notable work is *A Fable* (1954), an involved allegorical novel, which won him the 1955 Pulitzer Prize.

On the occasion of his receiving the Nobel prize, Faulkner appeared before a microphone and TV cameras for the first time in his life. Among other dignitaries, the audience included Swedish royalty and fellow prize-winners Bertrand Russell (philosophy and mathematics), Cecil Frank Powell (physics), and Otto Diels and Kurt Adler (chemistry). Faulkner had been cited in the presentation "for his powerful and artistically independent contribution to the new American novel." In his re-

sponse, reprinted here, he reminded his hearers of the high calling of writers, especially in a time of crisis. The point was relevant since it *was* a time of crisis. The date was December 10, 1950. Five months before, President Truman had ordered American forces to the support of South Korea. By November, American and other United Nations forces had reached the Yalu River. But just a few days before this speech there had been a serious United Nations defeat. Furthermore, there were rumblings that Red China was about to unleash an attack. All of these events, together with the still fresh memories of the bombings of Hiroshima and Nagasaki five years before, created the larger context in which the speech was heard and in which it must be read.

I feel that this award was not made to me as a man but to my work—a life's work in the agony and sweat of the human spirit, not for glory and least of all for profit, but to create out of the materials of the human spirit something which did not exist before. So this award is only mine in trust. It will not be difficult to find a dedication for the money part of it commensurate with the purpose and significance of its origin. But I would like to do the same with the acclaim too, by using this moment as a pinnacle from which I might be listened to by the young men and women already dedicated to the same anguish and travail, among whom is already that one who will someday stand here where I am standing. /1

Our tragedy today is a general and universal physical fear so long sustained by now that we can even bear it. There are no longer problems of the spirit. There is only the question: When will I be blown up? Because of this, the young man or woman writing today has forgotten the problems of the human heart in conflict with itself which alone can make good writing because only that is worth writing about, worth the agony and the sweat. /2

He must learn them again. He must teach himself that the basest of all things is to be afraid; and, teaching himself that, forget it forever, leaving no room in his workshop for anything but the old verities and truths of the heart, the old universal truths lacking which any story is ephemeral and doomed—love and honor and pity and pride and compassion and sacrifice. Until he does so he labors under a curse. He writes not of love but of lust, of defeats in which nobody loses anything of value, of victories without hope and worst of all without pity or compassion. His griefs grieve on no universal bones, leaving no scars. He writes not of the heart but of the glands. /3

Until he relearns these things he will write as though he stood among and watched the end of man. I decline to accept the end of man. It is easy enough to say that man is immortal simply because he will endure; that when the last ding-dong of doom has clanged and faded from the last worthless rock hanging tideless in the last red and dying evening, that even then there will still be one more sound: that of his puny inexhaustible voice, still talking. I refuse to accept this. I believe that man will not merely endure: he will prevail. He is immortal, not because he alone among creatures has an inexhaustible voice, but because he has a soul, a spirit capable of compassion and sacrifice and endurance. The poet's, the writer's, duty is to write about these things. It is his privilege to help man endure by lifting his heart, by reminding him of the courage and honor and hope and pride and compassion and pity and sacrifice which have been the glory of his past. The poet's voice need not merely be the record of man, it can be one of the props, the pillars to help him endure and prevail. /4

The speech

1. What, apparently, was Faulkner's major purpose in this speech?
2. To what audience does the speech seem to be addressed? In your answer refer to the speech.
3. Develop in your own words Faulkner's argument for the immortality of man.
4. For Faulkner what are the true responsibilities of the writer? (Note that he uses the term "poet" in an older sense to mean any writer.) Do Faulkner's beliefs and Buchan's (pp. 54-61) complement or contradict each other? Explain your answer.
5. What characteristics of the speech would make it a moving one to listen to? Consider content and style.
6. Are there ways of telling that this speech was written to be delivered orally?

For further study and discussion

1. Think of the works by Faulkner that you have read.

Do you find in them the theme that man will not only endure but prevail? If so, what characteristics make this possible?
2. To what extent can Faulkner's be called a Christian faith?
3. Define existentialism, and indicate to what extent Faulkner can be called an existentialist.
4. Has the social context changed enough since 1950 to make the major points of the speech outdated? To be more specific, do you feel that the only question in your life is: When will I be blown up? What aspects of your thought and behavior are colored by the possibility of sudden annihilation?
5. What current writers might be said to be creating the "pillars" to help man "endure and prevail"?

Suggestions for further reading

David Daiches, *A Study of Literature* (Ithaca, 1948)
James T. Farrell, *Literature and Morality* (New York, 1947)
Gilbert Highet, *Talents and Geniuses* (New York, 1957)
William D. Howells, *Literature and Life* (New York, 1902)
Robert Maynard Hutchins, *Great Books, the Foundation of Liberal Education* (New York, 1955)
Herbert E. Read, *The Nature of Literature* (New York, 1956)
Rene Wellek and Austin Warren, *Theory of Literature* (New York, 1949)

The novel and the fairy tale

JOHN BUCHAN

By most Americans who have heard of him, John Buchan, the first Baron Tweedsmuir, is probably best remembered as the author of The Thirty-nine Steps, the classic detective story later made into a motion picture. Actually, Buchan was preëminent in many fields.

Born at Perth, in 1875, he grew up in Glasgow, attended Oxford, practiced law in the Middle Temple, and for two years was a minor diplomat in South Africa. In 1907, he joined the publishing firm of T. A. Nelson as "literary adviser" and as a limited partner. Ill at the outbreak of World War I, he recovered in time to be-

---

From *English Association Pamphlets*, 1931, No. 79: 3-16. Reprinted by permission of The English Association.

come a staff member of the *Times* at the front in 1915, and to join the army as a major in the Intelligence Corps, in which he served with Sir Douglas Haig. In 1917, he was recalled to London to be one of the heads of the new Department of Information.

After the war Buchan divided his time between writing and politics, serving in Parliament from 1927 to 1935, when he was elevated to the peerage and sent to Canada as Governor-General. No Governor-General before or since has been so enormously popular, not only with those of English descent but with the French Canadians as well. His friendship with President Franklin Roosevelt brought new vitality and cordiality to the relations between Canada and the United States. His death at Montreal, on February 11, 1940, was a loss the world could ill afford at such a crucial time.

Buchan's writings include the adventure novels such as *Greenmantle* (1916), *Mr. Standfast* (1919), and *John McNab* (1925); the histories such as *The History of the Great War*, written over a period of years, and *The History of the Royal Scots Fusiliers* (1925); the biographies such as *Sir Walter Scott* (1932) and *Cromwell* (1934); and the autobiography *Pilgrim's Way* (1940). In addition, he wrote essays, poetry, travel sketches, law treatises, and literary criticism, not to mention news reports and government documents in which he had a hand.

The following Presidential Address was given to the Glasgow branch of the English Association on November 22, 1930. It illuminated Buchan's attitude toward literature, which was characterized by balance, common sense, and historical perspective.

I propose this afternoon to amuse myself—and, I hope, to interest you—with something which rarely comes my way—an informal gossip about literature. It is now a good many years since I first became interested in books. But all my life I have also been interested, professionally interested, in other things, so that I have no title to speak on literature as a man of letters for whom the written word has been the working instrument of his career. The result of this imperfect absorption in the subject has been to make my views on many literary subjects highly unorthodox. I do not seem to have the right standard of values—at least I have not quite the same standard as the authoritative critics. /1

For example, I am of the opinion that *Middlemarch* is one of the half-dozen greatest novels ever written, but I do not find many people to-day who have a good word for George Eliot. Again, I think that the best modern English prose has not been written by professed stylists, but by people like Huxley and Newman, whose one aim was to say clearly what they had to say and to have done with it—a creed which would be regarded, I fear, as a sort of black-legging by most men of letters. Again, I think that, among English poets since Keats, probably a larger proportion of Matthew Arnold's work will endure than that of any other; but I fancy that there are not many who share that opinion. /2

But my chief heterodoxy—heterodox, I mean, as regards the professional critics, not as regards the ordinary reader, who, I suspect, often shares these views—my chief heterodoxy has to do with the English novel. It has always been my secret view that the English novelists of the eighteenth century were a little overpraised—even Defoe and Fielding. But I think that the nineteenth-century novel in England is one of the main achievements in our literature, comparable with the Elizabethan drama. I should rank without hesitation Sir Walter Scott and Charles Dickens among the greatest of the world's novelists, and I should class at least two novels of Thackeray, one of George Eliot's, and three of Thomas Hardy's, among the world's greatest works of fiction. /3

I apologize for these egotistical confessions, but they have brought us to our starting-point—the Victorian novel. It is hard to say what is the special gift of our people in literature. Sometimes I think it is for a kind of lyric; sometimes I think it lies in the writing of history; but on the whole I believe it is for fiction. The Victorian novel is the most typical product of our national genius. Now that, I fear, is an unfashionable opinion. The novel, we are told to-day, has progressed far beyond such jejune methods. To-day it is weighted with a psychological profundity of which the Victorian innocents never dreamed. They, poor souls, believed that black was black and white was white; we now know that there are no clean colours, but that everything is a muddy yellow. They thought it their business to tell a story, but to tell a story is to shape existence into an arbitrary pattern for which there is no warrant. The true artistry of the novel, we are told, should be a thing of infinite delicacy and precision, which can catch and register the faintest whispers of the sub-conscious. It should take the whole complex of life for its province, neglecting nothing as common or unclean, and finding its unity not in any pattern super-imposed, but in what the subject matter itself presents, if viewed with complete detachment and sincerity. /4

Now, I am not going to argue against that doctrine, but I would suggest that for the sake of clearness we should get a new name for the work which it has inspired. These contemporary palimpsests of sensations and emotions and passions may have their scientific value, they have undoubtedly their literary value, but obviously they belong to an entirely different class from the books which we have been accustomed to call novels. There is no common denominator which enables us to compare *David Copperfield* with the fiction of certain modern French, English, American, and German writers. Let us confine the word novel, for our present purposes, to the kind of book which the great Victorians produced, and disregard the question as to whether it is inferior as a literary kind to that which is produced by the new iconoclasts. It is enough for us that it is different. A novel, in the sense in which I use the word, is *The Heart of Midlothian* and *Our Mutual Friend* and *Vanity Fair* and *Middlemarch* and *Tess of the D'Urbervilles*. /5

There is a passage in Coleridge's *Biographia Literaria* which I think puts very well the general purpose of this kind of novel. He is speaking of Wordsworth's poetry, and his words apply to any great work of art, and especially, it seems to me, to prose fiction as the Victorians conceived it. Its purpose, he says, is:

'To give the charm of novelty to things of every day, and to excite a feeling analogous to the supernatural by awakening the mind's attention from the lethargy of custom, and directing it to the wonders of the world before us; an inexhaustible treasury, but one for which, in consequence of the film of familiarity and selfish solicitude, we have eyes that see not, ears that hear not, and hearts that neither feel nor understand.' /6

From that sentence of Coleridge it would be easy to develop a whole philosophy of the art of fiction. Fiction deals with ordinary life; but, without ever losing touch with the ground, it must somehow lift it into the skies. It must give it for us an air of novelty and strangeness and wonder, by showing beauty in unlikely places, courage where one would not have looked for it, the jewel in the pig's snout, the flower on the dunghill. A poet like Milton or Dante brings cosmic sublimities within hail of our common life; a great novelist makes our common life itself cosmic and sublime. /7

But we must go farther than the general purpose. If it is to be attained, certain rules must be observed. Take first the method by which life is to be presented. Certain modern critics of the Victorian novel complain of its lack of realism. It sentimentalizes life for us, they say, and fails to tell the whole truth about it. Life, we are told, should be allowed to speak for itself, and not be selected and winnowed by the arbitrary will of the novelist. The novelist should be merely the medium through which the real world speaks in all its crudeness and confusion. Well, I would remark that on that principle you will get an inventory, not a work of art. The business of art is to present life, the real point of life, and for that selection is necessary, since a great deal of life is off the point. It must clear away the surplusage of the irrelevant, the inessential, the inorganic. It must provide the only true kind of picture, which is an interpretation. /8

The real objection of these critics is, I think, that the Victorians were not ugly enough. They did not believe that the pathological was the most important thing in the world, and that the most characteristic thing about a house was the adjacent dust-heap. They were too deeply interested in humanity to be obsessed by that side which humanity shares with the brute creation. They were too interested in the human soul to give all their time to its perversities and vagaries. They had a cleaner palate and a robuster philosophy than their critics, and if they are blamed on this score, then they must share the blame with all the greatest literature of the world since Homer. /9

Again, they were not clever people, like those who decry them, and in this they were akin to the ordinary man, who is nearly as suspicious of mere cleverness as Mr. Baldwin. The trouble about cleverness is that it is so rarely greatness. The clever person is much more interested in himself than in anything else, and in whatever he does he is always looking at his own face in the mirror. It is a curious fact that since the War, which meant for all the world such a noble renunciation of self, most of our poetry and fiction should be so egocentric. The writers are perpetually wrestling with their own moods and tinkering with their own emotions, and they rarely rise to the self-forgetfulness of the greater art. The Victorian novelist was sublimely unconscious. He was absorbed with life and lived fiercely in his characters. He was not a showman exhibiting a set of puppets, boring his audience by telling it constantly what he felt about it all. /10

Now it is a futile business to compare incomparables, and the work of many of our recent novelists, who are in strong revolt against the great Victorian novels, is not comparable with them. It is based on a different theory of art, on a different conception of the novel. Brilliant and valuable as much of their work is, I do not think that they succeed in what I regard as the central and dominant type of fiction, of which the Victorians have given us the greatest examples in our own or in any language. /11

But I want to invite you to-night to a different and, I think, more fruitful kind of inquiry; and all I ask of you is that you fling your mind back to the literature of your childhood. We have always had story-tellers and makers of fiction since the days of the cave-man. There is an eternal impulse in human nature to enliven the actual working life by the invention of tales of another kind of life, recognizable by its likeness to ordinary life, but so arranged that things happen more dramatically and pleasingly—which indeed is the familiar world in a glorified and idealized form. /12

That is the origin of what we call the folk tale or the fairy tale—we need not for our present purpose make any distinction between them. These tales come out of the most distant deeps of human experience and human fancy. They belong to the people themselves, not to a specially gifted or privileged class, and they are full of traces of their homely origin. They deal with simple and enduring things, birth and marriage and death, hunger and thirst, natural sorrows and natural joys. They sprang from a society where life was hard, when a man was never quite certain of his next meal, when he never knew when he arose in the morning whether he would be alive in the evening, when adventure was not the exception in life, but the rule. It was a dangerous world and a cruel world, and therefore those who dwelt in it endeavoured in their tales to escape from it. They pictured weakness winning against might, gentleness and courtesy against brutality, brains as against mere animal strength, the one chance in a hundred succeeding. Such things do sometimes happen, and the society where the folk tales were born clung fiercely to this possibility, because on it depended their hope of a better time. Like Malvolio, they 'thought nobly of the soul.' The true hero in all the folk tales and fairy tales is not the younger son, or the younger daughter, or the stolen princess, or the ugly duckling, but the soul of man. It was a world where a great deal of discomfort and sorrow had to be borne, and where the most useful virtue was the passive virtue of fortitude; but in the folk tales it is not this passive virtue that is exalted, but daring, boldness, originality, brains—because the people who made them realized that the hope of humanity lay not in passivity but in action. /13

The appeal of such stories has not been lessened by time. In one form or other they have delighted youth for a thousand years and more. Poets and artists have borrowed from them and made elaborate artistic creations out of their simplicities. Their appeal is to every class and age; indeed they form a kind of *corpus* of popular philosophy. But the particular point I want to make is this: in a sophisticated society something more is wanted than the simple folk tale, and that something is the novel. My argument is that only in so far as the novel is a development of and akin to the folk and fairy tale does it fully succeed, and that it is in this kinship that the virtue of the great Victorian novels especially lies. /14

I observe about these novels that in the first place they tell a good story—something which grips and enthrals the reader, with true drama and wonder in it. In the second place they are full of characters recognizable as real types, and they pass judgements on these characters; that is, the story-teller regards some as definitely good and some as definitely bad. In the third place, their method of reproducing reality is not that of an inventory of details, but of a judicious selection. In the fourth place, the story-teller is primarily interested in the events he has to tell of, and not in what the jargon of to-day calls his 'reactions' to them. He does not stop to obtrude his own moods. Lastly, he has a dominant purpose, a lesson, if you like, to teach, a creed to suggest, the nature of which we shall consider later. /15

Now all these things the great Victorians had. Most of these things their critics lack. All these things the folk tales possess. Let us look a little farther into them. /16

First for the story. I believe that there are only a very limited number of good plots in the world, though you have endless variations of them. That was more or less the idea of the Greek dramatists; it seems to have been more or less the idea of Shakespeare; and it is more or less the idea of the great novelists. It is curious, if you consider the classic novels, how limited is the number of motives. Moreover, I think you will find them all already in the folk tales. Let us make a short list of them. /17

There is first of all what we may call the picaresque motive, the story based on extension in space, on the fact that the world is very wide, and that there are a great many odd things in it. A young man sets out to seek his fortune; an ill-treated child runs away from its stepmother; a pretty girl is driven into the forest. There are endless variations on the subject. The hero may be the pure adventurer in the void, waiting to see what turns up; or he may have a serious quest to find something or somebody that is lost, to unravel a mystery, to marry a lady the fame of whose beauty has reached him. And the thing may be done seriously or in a spirit of comedy. It may stick close to earth or adventure into the clouds. The road may be a pleasant and bustling highway running past windmills and gardens and farms and little towns, or a mysterious path through enchanted forests. The one thing common to them all is the conviction that the world is full of surprising things and that anything may happen to the adventurer. /18

Open Grimm, or Perrault, or any of the great folk tale collections, and you will find a multitude of examples in this class. 'Little Brother and Little Sister,' 'Hop o' My Thumb,' 'The Little Tailor,' 'The Two Brothers,' 'Puss in Boots,' 'The Sleeping Beauty' are a few of the most familiar. In fiction we have *Don Quixote* and *Gil Blas*; we have *Tom Jones* and *The Cloister and the Hearth*. When D'Artagnan rides to the sea he is doing what the people in folk tales did. So is Mr. Polly when he sets out on his travels, and so is Mr. Pickwick when he mounts the Rochester coach. /19

Next there is the motive which Aristotle said was one of the chief things in drama, and which he called *Peripeteia,* or Reversal of Fortune. It is the commonest subject of the folk tales. We can picture the peasant in the Middle Ages, groaning under the exactions of kings and nobles and churchmen and accustomed to see proud cavalcades drive him off the road into the ditch, consoling himself with tales which told how the mighty were brought low, and grace was given to the humble. And we can imagine the peasant's son, full of young ambitions which he sees no way to attain, being cheered by the tales of swineherds who became kings, and goose-girls who became princesses, and the plain fighting man who married the Sophy of Egypt's daughter. It is a very old motive and a very modern one. You will find it in the Bible, in the stories of Ruth and Saul and David, and of Nebuchadnezzar the King; you can find it in the latest trashy feuilleton, in which the beautiful kitchen-maid becomes a duchess. Very closely connected with it is another theme which Aristotle made the second staple of tragedy, and which he called *Anagnorisis* or Recognition. That is, so to speak, the proper climax of Reversal of Fortune, and you find it alike in the greatest and crudest of tales. Its crude form is the child changed at nurse, the missing heir with the strawberry mark on his arm,

and all the business which concludes with 'You are my long lost brother!' The mere fact that you find it in the most elementary literature which possesses any popular appeal seems to suggest that it is rooted in something very deep in human nature. The reason is obvious. It is the most dramatic form of happy ending. One look is given, one word is spoken, and the prince who has been a swine-herd is a prince again, while the usurper is cast out upon the world. /20

The folk tales based on Reversal of Fortune are among the best. At the top I should put one which is not a folk tale at all, but the invention of a modern writer, Hans Andersen's 'Ugly Duckling.' It is modern, but it is in the true folk tradition. Among the old stories I would cite 'The Hut in the Forest,' 'The Goose Girl,' and 'Cinderella.' If you want parallels from the great Victorians I would suggest *Guy Mannering* and *The Antiquary*, and *Ivanhoe* from the beginning of the era, and Thomas Hardy's *The Mayor of Casterbridge* from the close. Mr. Hardy is always very near the soil and the traditions of the soil, and the ascent of Donald Farfrae and the descent of Michael Henchard are in the true folk spirit. /21

The third theme is what I venture to call the Survival of the Unfittest, the victory against odds of the unlikeliest people. That is based upon the incurable optimism of human nature. The men who made the folk tales had no notion how it happened, so they were forced to bring in enchantments of all sorts to make it possible—fairy godmothers, benevolent old women, magic rings and swords and shoes and cloaks. But they had an unshakable conviction that it would happen and that it could happen, and they believed in happily fated people who had more luck than others, more courage, and more dexterity, who were somehow blessed by the gods, and were able to perform feats impossible for others. The popularity of certain film stars is a proof that human nature has not outgrown this belief. /22

The theme takes various forms. There is courage against impossible odds, as in the stories of the conquests of dragons and giants. 'Jack the Giant-Killer' and 'Jack and the Beanstalk' are familiar examples. Dumas is full of the same story, as in the deeds of D'Artagnan and the Three Musketeers, and the death of Bussy d'Amboise. Again, there is escape against all reasonable odds, as in 'Blue Beard' and 'Snowdrop' and 'Rumpelstiltskin' and 'Hansel and Gretel.' Enchantments are unhappily denied to the modern novelist; he is not allowed to bring in fairies to help him out; but you will find the same situation when Dugald Dalgetty escapes from the dungeon at Inverary, and young Waverley is delivered from the hands of the Gifted Gilfillan by the Highlanders, and in Jeanie Deans's journey to London to see the King. The scale must be weighted against the hero in the folk tale; he must be the youngest son with no patrimony, the poor boy with no friends. His task must be made as difficult as possible, for how otherwise can we get the full drama—how otherwise can ordinary folk be persuaded that life has colour in it and a wide horizon? /23

One of the commonest varieties of this type is the story of the uncouth lover who at first sight has nothing to recommend him. You get it in 'Bear-Skin,' you get it in 'The Frog Prince,' in 'Snow White and Rose Red,' and in 'Beauty and the Beast.' The handsome swashbuckling gallant is all very well, but the folk mind did not think too highly of him. It suspected the obviously heroic and preferred to look deeper for quality. In this respect the folk tale has been followed in some of the greatest Victorian novels. What is the plot of *Vanity Fair*? It is the contest of two suitors for the hand of a very tiresome young woman—the dashing George Osborne and the cumbrous Dobbin, and the book is a record of the struggle of the homely worth of Dobbin against the glamour of his rival both in life and death, until at long last it is duly rewarded. In George Meredith's *Diana of the Crossways* it is Tom Redworth who wins the glittering lady, not Percy Dacier; and in Mr. Hardy's *Far from the Madding Crowd* Shepherd Oak, after many ups and downs, eventually is the accepted lover of Bathsheba Everdene. Truly the folk tale has august descendants. /24

So much for the plot and the theme of the story. The next thing to be noted about the great Victorian novelists is their handling of character. Now, in the folk tale there is never any mistake about the people. The characters are human beings, and represent humanity in its central region, and not in its remote suburbs. The old story-teller was not interested in freaks. He understood a great villain and a great hero, but above all things he understood ordinary men, and he makes them reveal their character in their deeds, and does not make any pother about describing it. 'If you cannot get hold of my people,' he seems to say to the reader, 'by seeing the kind of thing they do, then you are past praying for.' Now this seems to me to be the very essence of good fiction. I have read novels by able men and women in which the characters could not get started to do anything because of the meshes of analytic psychology with which their feet were clogged. Pages of torturous analysis had to be waded through before the hero could kiss his wife or eat his breakfast. The trick of dissecting a character before a reader's eyes seems to me abominably bad craftsmanship. The business of the novelist is to make men and women reveal themselves in speech and action, to play the showman as little as possible, to present the finished product, and not to print the jottings of his laboratory. /25

Another point. The makers of the folk tales were not afraid to pass judgement upon their characters. A man was brave or he was not; he was kind or he was cruel; he was foolish or he was wise. There is a school of fiction to-day which objects to passing moral judgements on anything or anybody. It derives principally from a really great man, the Russian Dostoievsky, and people have praised his divine humanity which finds surpassing virtues in the worst of rogues. Now, I have nothing to say against this impartiality, though I think it may as easily have its roots in moral apathy and intellectual slovenliness as in divine wisdom. Philosophically, it may have its justification, but I suggest that since fallible men must have their standards and stick to them, such detachment is rather for their Maker than for themselves. In any case it is no virtue in a novelist who can only get drama by strong contrasts. The moral molluscs of certain fiction of to-day, who spend their time, if I may borrow a phrase of the late D. H. Lawrence, in sinning their way to sanctity, would have puzzled the makers of folk tales, as they puzzle any ordinary man. The great Victorian novelists have the same clearness of moral outline. They realize that all of us are a compost of good and bad, but that the orientation of certain men and women is as clearly towards evil as that of others is towards good, and they do not scruple to say so. /26

One last word on the question of character. The folk tale is not afraid of greatness. It believes that humanity is not a drab collection of mediocrities, but that nearly everybody has some poetry in him, and that it can flower at times into something which leaves the earth altogether and strikes the stars. Because it believed in human nature it believed that human nature could transcend itself and become god-like. Its heroes are so full of vitality that no giant or dragon or wicked stepmother manages to hamper them in the long run. They go their appointed course with a divine carelessness. They are immortal until they have fulfilled their purpose. /27

Such a creed springs from optimism about human nature, and I do not think that any great imaginative writer has been without it. The power of creating a figure which, while completely human, seems to soar beyond humanity, is the most certain proof of genius. In such cases the creator seems to be dominated by his creation. It takes charge of him and has an independent life of its own over which he has no control. /28

There are two characters which seem to me to have taken charge of Shakespeare—Cleopatra and Falstaff. Whenever Cleopatra appears she dominates the scene, and the author is only a curtain raiser in the wings. She and Antony both die, but speaking for myself, while I believe in Antony's death, I do not believe in Cleopatra's. As for Falstaff, it is a platitude to say that he got completely out of Shakespeare's control. The time came in the beginning of *Henry V*, when Shakespeare wished to dismiss him to make room for his reformed hero, and in order to wean the reader's affections from him it was necessary to degrade him. But Falstaff obstinately refuses to go, and all Shakespeare's art cannot degrade him. As Professor Bradley says, 'Shakespeare created so extraordinary a being and fixed him so firmly on his intellectual throne that when he sought to dethrone him, he could not. A moment comes when we are to look at Falstaff in a serious light, and the comic hero is to figure as a baffled schemer, but we cannot make the required change either in our attitude or our sympathies. We wish Henry a glorious reign and much joy of his hypocritical politicians, lay and clerical; but our hearts go with Falstaff to the Fleet, or if necessary to Arthur's bosom, or wheresomever he is.' /29

Let me offer you one or two other instances. There is Becky Sharp. Becky is too much for Thackeray. She is a little green-eyed, false, cold-hearted wretch, but vitality has nothing to do with morals. She keeps the stage to the end of the book and holds our sympathies even when she is deservedly punished; while Amelia Sedley, though her creator may sentimentalize as much as he pleases about her sweetness, remains a doll stuffed with sawdust. /30

Take Andrew Fairservice in *Rob Roy*. No sooner had Scott created him than he obviously began to dislike him, and he depicts him in all kinds of meannesses and cruelties. But our interest in the worthless Andrew does not ebb. He has only to appear on the stage and he blankets everybody else, even Bailie Nicol Jarvie and Rob Roy himself. Or take Trollope's Mrs. Proudie. You remember that in the *Last Chronicle of Barset* she suddenly dies. A friend once told me that he remembered the publication of the novel. One man would go up to another in the club and say, 'They tell me that Mrs. Proudie is dead. I don't believe a word of it.' /31

So, too, with two at least of Dickens's characters, Mr. Pickwick and Sairey Gamp. Mr. Pickwick, as Mr. Chesterton has pointed out, is simply the fairy prince, unconquerable, immortal, stumbling into troubles only to soar above them. Happily Dickens never tried to kill Mr. Pickwick, for he would have found it impossible. We could have believed in most things which he chose to tell us, but never in Mr. Pickwick's death. But a greater instance is Sairey Gamp. Actually she is a dreadful being, drunken, fraudulent, avaricious; but she is clearly immortal. Her quarrel with Betsey Prig is the only scene in literature which ranks beside the scenes into which Shakespeare introduces Falstaff. Imagine how the ordinary conscientious realist of to-day would have managed Sairey. He would have made her squalid and revolting: he would have blinked no sordid detail of her life; he would have turned her poor old rag bag of a mind inside out; and all the while she would have been as dead as Queen Anne. As it is, nothing can kill her. She goes her wheezy, alcoholic way, a certain immortal. We are not told what became of her, and we do not need to be told, for she is as assured of continuance as the Solar System. /32

I will pass lightly over the other two characteristics of the great Victorian novels which I have cited, and in each of which they show their kinship with the folk tale. Both represent a world in which the selective power of art has been at work. The Victorian novel is often prolix but it is never confused. The main lines of development are always crystal clear. Scott, for example, is fond of pouring the contents of an antiquarian's memory into his pages, but when things begin to happen there is no prolixity. He selects infallibly the details which print a great scene eternally on the memory. So, too, with the folk tales. They never fumble. The right details are unerringly selected. A proof is their enduring power over the child's mind. Young people are gluttons for details and have an acute sense of what is fit and proper in that respect. They know that Robinson Crusoe found just the right number and kind of things at the wreck to satisfy the imagination, while they remember that that fearsome household, the Swiss Family Robinson, found so much that every scrap of interest goes out of the tale. And for generations youth has accepted the folk tale as never blundering in this vital matter. /33

Again, both the folk tale and the Victorian novel have the merit of being unselfconscious. The great Victorians did not lay bare their souls, apart from the souls of their characters. They were not concerned to preach a new metaphysic or a new morality. What they had to give in that respect must be implied. Their view of the universe is to be deduced from the drama unfolded; it is never given in set terms. Thackeray, indeed, has sometimes the air of a coy and sentimental showman, as in the last paragraphs of *Vanity Fair;* but this is a mere trick of his. His real views on the problems of life must be looked for in the fortunes of Becky Sharp and Dobbin and Pendennis and Colonel Newcome, and not in any irrelevant interpolations. The Victorian novelist at his best was as objective as Shakespeare, and as the anonymous folk tale. /34

I come lastly to the greatest of the links between the two—the fact that they have a dominant purpose and the same purpose. The Victorian novels and the folk tales are not mere transcripts of life— they are interpretations of life, and they are interpretations of life in a hopeful spirit. In the folk tale the plain man comforted himself in his difficulties by showing that the weak things of the earth can confound the strong; that nothing is impossible to the courageous and single-hearted; that the unfittest in the worldly sense can survive if he is the fittest in more important respects. They are a glorification of the soul of man, an epic of the resurgence of the divine in human nature. They make the world a happier place because they show it interpenetrated by hope and opportunity. /35

The great novelists do the same thing by subtler methods. With them it is not the good fairy that solves the problem, but something unconquerable in the human spirit. They make the world more solemn, for they show the darkest places in it. They show the capacities for evil in man's breast, the cruelty and callousness of life, the undeserved suffering of the good, and the undeserved fortune of the evil; they show the transience of human glory and the fragility of human hopes. But if they make life more solemn they also make it brighter. They enlarge our vision, light up dark corners, break down foolish barriers, and make the world more sunlit and more spacious. If they do not preach any single philosophy they, in Shelley's words, 'repeal large codes of fraud and woe.' They revive hope in humanity by revealing its forgotten graces and depths. They are optimists in the largest sense, for without optimism there can be no vitality. Thackeray, indeed, indulges often in a kind of gentle melan-

choly, but it is not to be taken too seriously. His gusto, his delight in his personages, gives the lie to his occasional pessimistic meditations, which indeed are only bits of self-humiliation designed to propitiate the gods. /36

The optimism of such novels and of the folk tale is a profound thing, for it is based upon a very clear and candid view of life. The folk tale knows only too well the stubborn brutality of things; and, knowing this, it is still prepared to hope. Such optimism is far more merciless than any pessimism. Also it is far closer to reality. A tale which describes any aspect of life and makes of it nothing but a pathological study in meanness and vice is more fantastic than any fairy tale. You remember Stevenson's fable of the *Lantern-Bearers,* where he pictures a camp of small urchins who carry their smelly tin lanterns buttoned under their overcoats, and reflects what asses such a group, sheltering in the cold sand on a bleak sea-shore on a dark autumn night, must have seemed to the spectator who could not understand their recondite pleasures. And from the picture he draws a profound moral. /37

'To miss the joy,' he says, 'is to miss all. . . . Hence the haunting and truly spectral unreality of realistic books. Hence, when we read the English realists, the incredulous wonder with which we observe the hero's constancy under the submerging tide of dulness, and how he bears up with his jibbing sweetheart, and endures the chatter of idiot girls, and stands by his whole unfeatured wilderness of an existence, instead of seeking relief in drink or foreign travel. Hence in the French, in that meat-market of middle-aged sensuality, the disgusted surprise with which we see the hero drift side-long, and practically quite untempted, into every description of misconduct and dishonour. In each, we miss the personal poetry, the enchanted atmosphere, that rainbow of fancy that clothes what is naked and seems to ennoble what is base; in each, life falls dead like dough, instead of soaring away like a balloon into the colours of the sunset; each is true, each inconceivable; for no man lives in the external truth, among salts and acids, but in the warm, phantasmagoric chamber of his brain, with the painted windows and the storied walls.' /38

You have the same moral in a verse of Francis Thompson's:

'The Angels keep their ancient places—
    Turn but a stone, you start a wing!
'Tis ye, 'tis your estranged faces,
    That miss the many splendoured thing.'

and in some delightful doggerel lines of Mr. Masefield:

'I have seen flowers come in stony places,
And kindness done by men with ugly faces,
And the Gold Cup won by the worst horse at the races,
So I trust, too.' /39

The folk tale belongs to no one country or age. Many go back to the ancientry of our race. They are part of the common stock of humanity and are closer to mankind than any written word. They are the delight of our childhood and they are part of our unconscious thought. I have a notion that things so long descended and prepotent are not likely to be forgotten. I have a notion, too, that any form of literature related to them, inspired by the same creed, close to the earth and yet kin to the upper air, will have the same immortality. Today we are sometimes told that Scott and Thackeray and Dickens, and even Thomas Hardy, are back numbers, that they practised a superseded form of art, that the novel of the future will be a far more recondite thing, tremulous with meaning, profoundly 'aware,' surcharged with subtle psychology, and that the old crude business of story and character and moral preference and a cheerful philosophy is only for the amusement of children. I take leave to doubt that forecast. The other day I took up a book of essays on the 'Eighteen-seventies,' and I found these words by one of the truest of our living poets—Mr. Walter de la Mare:

'The distant rumour that thrills the air is not only the sound of Time's dark waters, but is mingled with the roar of our own busy printing presses. "As we are, so you shall be!" The very years that we now so actively occupy will soon be packed up in an old satchel, and labelled "The Twenties"; and our little hot, cold, violent, affected, brand-new, exquisite, fresh little habits of mind, manners, hobbies, fashions, ideals, will have thinned and vanished away, will steadily have evaporated, leaving only a frigid deposit of history; a few decaying buildings, a few pictures, some music, some machine-made voices, an immense quantity of print—most of it never to be disturbed again. In the midst of the battle maybe it is indiscreet to muse on the tranquil, moonlit indifference of the night that will follow.' /40

It is a salutary thing to remind oneself that the judgements of posterity may be different from our own. But it is permissible, I think, to claim endurance for things which have the qualities that hitherto have endured—things that are close to the taproot of humanity. I believe that so long as youth ascends the beanstalk with Jack, and rides in the glass coach with Cinderella, and sets off with the youngest son to seek his fortunes—that so long all ages will continue to dance with Becky at the Waterloo Ball, and take the heather with Rob Roy, and mount the Rochester diligence with Mr Pickwick. /41

The speech

1. What is gained by the low-keyed introduction?
2. What does Buchan consider to be the chief differences between himself and the literary critics?
3. What kind of fiction is Buchan ruling out in paragraphs 4-5?
4. What characteristics of his audience is he presumably appealing to in paragraphs 8-10? Are these the ones that he appeals to in the speech as a whole?
5. How does identifying the Victorian novel with the fairy tale strengthen his case against the critics?
6. The fiction Buchan likes was thought to be second-rate by the literary critics because it was unrealistic. How does he manipulate the term *realism* to his advantage and to the disadvantage of the critics?
7. Describe the kinds of plots Buchan finds in both fairy tales and the novel. What do they all have in common? Why might they not be valued highly by the literary critics?
8. What does he admire about the handling of characters in the Victorian novel? Why does he dislike the amorality of the naturalistic novel?
9. Does Buchan feel that optimism is of chief importance in fiction?
10. What devices does Buchan employ to make the ending moving and memorable?
11. Has Buchan convinced you that the Victorian novel is greater than the modern realistic or naturalistic novel? Indicate what arguments you found especially convincing, what ones especially unconvincing.
12. List all of the techniques Buchan uses to help listeners follow and remember what he has to say.

For further study and discussion

1. Define *romanticism, realism, naturalism,* and *Freudianism* as these terms apply to literature.
2. *Point of view* in fiction has been defined as "the angle of vision," the position from which the author and hence the reader observe the action. The two basic points of view are the point of view of a character and the point of view of an omniscient observer. Refer to recent novels and short stories

you have read, and describe the advantages and disadvantages of the point of view each employs.

3. Discuss the importance of plot or action in fiction. Why should modern authors seem less concerned with plot than did Victorian authors? Do you agree that fiction becomes second-rate when the plot is the author's major concern?

4. Characterization ordinarily develops from some conflict, either outer (between characters or between a character and his environment) or inner (within a character). Why do modern writers seem far more concerned with inner conflicts than with outer conflicts?

5. Tone results from the author's attitude toward his material. It can be serious, flippant, compassionate, sarcastic, or whatever. What tones seem to characterize the last contemporary fiction you have read? Do you find that these fictional tones accurately represent the attitudes we have toward life today?

6. Realism has been described as holding a mirror up to life. But can fiction really do this (i.e., report everything)? Why must an author be selective, and what are the common criteria authors use in selecting their material?

7. Naturalism is sometimes said to be amoral in its reporting of life (i.e., unconcerned with moral considerations). Why can fiction never be completely amoral? Give instances of considerations that *are* amoral (e.g., the multiplication tables) and show the differences between them and fiction.

8. In talking about the fairy tale characters as he does, is Buchan really talking about Jungian archetypes? Do you agree that the presence of archetypal characters in a narrative (e.g., a Prometheus-like figure, a Christlike figure) gives power to the writing?

9. There are various ways of evaluating fiction. What would you especially look for in using each of the following critical approaches: analytic, biographical, psychological, sociological, moral, and mythical?

10. Who are the leading critics today? As a group do they seem to hold the same attitudes that Buchan attributed to the critics of his time?

Suggestions for further reading

Eugene Current-Garcia and Walton R. Patrick, **Realism and Romanticism in Fiction** (Chicago, 1962)

Northrop Frye, **Anatomy of Criticism** (New York, 1957)

Nathaniel Hawthorne, Preface to **The House of the Seven Gables**

Daniel Hoffman, **Form and Fable in American Fiction** (New York, 1965)

Henry James, Preface to **The Ambassadors,** reprinted in **The Art of the Novel** (New York, 1934)

Percy Lubbock, **The Craft of Fiction** (New York, 1957)

Mark Schorer, Josephine Miles, and Gordon McKenzie, **Criticism** (New York, 1958)

In defense of abstract art

HERBERT READ

Sir Herbert Read (1893-   ), who has been described as "one of the most important of living critics," comes from a long line of Yorkshire farmers. He was educated at a boarding school and at the University of Leeds. During World War I he was captain of the Yorkshire Regiment and received the Distinguished Service Order and the Military Cross.

From 1922 to 1931 he was an Assistant Keeper at the Victoria and Albert Museum and from 1931 to 1933 a professor of fine arts at the University of Edinburgh. He has been a director of Routledge and Kegan Paul, Ltd., Publishers, President of the Institute of Contemporary Arts, London, and of the Society for Education in Art. In 1953-1954 he was Charles Eliot Norton Professor of Poetry at Harvard University and in 1954 A. W. Mellon Lecturer in Fine Arts, Washington, D.C. His extensive publications include: *English Prose Style* (1928), *The Meaning of Art* (1931), *Art and Society* (1937), *The Philosophy of Modern Art* (1952), *The True Voice of Feeling* (1953), *Icon and Idea* (1955), *The Art of Sculpture* (1956), *The Tenth Muse* (1957), *Forms of Things Unknown* (1960), *To Hell with Culture* (1963), and *The Contrary Experience* (1963).

Sir Herbert, who has shown particular interest in the theory and practice of his contemporaries, is a vigorous defender of the theoretical foundation of modern art. His views have been the source of controversy, particularly his belief that the arts can be "progressive." It is his opinion, as he says in the last sentence of this essay, that "Abstract art is perhaps more distant than any art of the past; it is perhaps also more beautiful."

In addition to the three paintings reproduced here, the following works were included in the original publication of this essay: "Night, Day and Transformation," by Wojciech Dlugosz; "Narcissus," by Jan Kotik; "Suprematist Composition," by Kasimir Malevich; "Spiral Theme," by Naum Gabo; "Composition," by Joan Miro.

Although this work was originally an essay, it is included here partly because it is a provocative discussion of abstract art and partly because it provides material for an interesting review of the likenesses and differences between speeches and essays.

Herbert Read, "In Defense of Abstract Art," *New York Times Magazine,* April 17, 1960, pp. 32, 40, 45, 48. By permission of the author.

It is exactly half a century since Wassily Kandinsky painted the first abstract picture. During that time the abstract movement has continued to grow, until now non-abstract, or representational, painters are the ones in a minority—at least, among painters of the younger generation. And yet the abstract artists (we must remember that sculptors as well as painters are involved) have not carried a majority of the public with them. /1

Perhaps the gap between the *avant-garde* and the main body of educated taste is always wide, but surely never before has it been as wide as it is today. In spite of the high esteem which abstract art enjoys among collectors, and the fantastic prices paid for it in the salesrooms, the man in the street remains bewildered, sometimes angry, often indifferent. He has an obstinate feeling that his leg is being pulled, that the abstract artist cannot really expect to be taken seriously, that the whole business is a racket of some kind. /2

What are the main charges brought against the abstract movement? Five are set out below, and I shall do my best to answer them one by one. /3

(1) *It fails to communicate any meaning, representing only the artist talking to himself. As Francis Henry Taylor has said, "unless participation is allowed the spectator [a painting] becomes a hopeless riddle and ceases to be a work of art at all."* /4

C. K. Ogden and I. A. Richards wrote a famous book called "The Meaning of Meaning," dealing with problems of language and logic. A similar problem exists in the plastic arts. What is the "meaning" of a painting or a piece of sculpture? /5

Only the most simple people would suggest that the meaning of the picture is the story it tells—that a work of art should be the description of a scene or the narration of an event. Tolstoy, who was not a simple person, asserted that the value of the work of art lies in its truth, and Ruskin, though he had a different conception of the truth, argued in much the same way. /6

The Socialist realists of Russia today adopt this same argument. Art for them, as for Tolstoy and Ruskin, is a means of communicating a message of some kind—about social conditions, about natural phenomena, about human relations—and, as Francis

Jackson Pollock—"Number 1," 1948. (Collection, The Museum of Modern Art, New York.)

Henry Taylor implied in his statement, what should be communicated by the work of art is understanding. /7

At this point we encounter a philosophical problem. Is understanding a rational process, the kind of discourse that should be confined to logical statements; or is it possibly an irrational process, the kind of discourse we can carry on only by the use of symbols? /8

The defender of abstract art believes that art is a form of symbolic discourse, and that, even when it is representational, its message is conveyed by form and color rather than by the imitation of the things we see. He points out that other arts, such as music and architecture, do not necessarily imitate anything in nature, but communicate by abstract arrangements of sounds, intervals, proportions and rhythms. There is no reason why the arrangements of lines and colors on a canvas, or of mass and volume in a piece of sculpture, should not be abstract in the same way. /9

It is merely a convention, of limited historical significance, to maintain that the visual arts should communicate their meaning by imitating the arbitrary forms that nature has evolved. Music might just as logically be confined to the imitation of bird songs or thunder; architecture, to the imitation of caves and mountains. /10

The abstract work of art may be a riddle, but it is not hopeless nor is it meaningless: it is a symbol which may stand for the artist's deepest emotions and intuitions, and in which the spectator may find his own emotions and intuitions defined and illuminated. /11

(2) *There are no standards of imagery or technique. Anyone—even a child—can paint an abstract painting. Mere doodling may be offered as abstract art. Thus, it becomes impossible to tell a good abstract painting from a bad one.* /12

What is a standard of imagery? Presumably, the visual images given in our perception of the external world. Again a philosophical problem is involved, for there is no standard image of the external world. /13

The image of the external world which we have at any moment is a convention, and varies from age to age. This is evident enough from the history of art—each period has its own method of constructing an image of the external world; there is little in common between an image of the Byzantine period and an image of the classical Renaissance. /14

The image of man, as the recent exhibition at the Museum of Modern Art showed, varies not only

Wassily Kandinsky—"Improvisation 29," 1912. (Courtesy of Philadelphia Museum of Art, The Louise and Walter Arensberg Collection.)

from age to age but also from artist to artist. What is a standard image of man? The Chinese have one image; the Greeks had another. Some religions create an image of the ideal man; others, such as the Mohammedan, forbid the representation of such an ideal (for only God is perfect, and it would be pre-

Piet Mondrian—"Composition in White, Black and Red," 1936. (Collection, The Museum of Modern Art, New York.)

sumptuous of man to consider himself capable of representing such perfection). /15

One kind of abstract artist, like the Islamic artist, believes there is an ideal of perfection, but that it is impersonal: that is to say, a question of quantitative harmony—the rhythmical succession of lines, the balance of areas, the harmonious unity of colors, the organic articulation of space. Another kind of abstract artist seeks an image that may, or may not, have such concrete quantities, but is essentially expressive of emotion, or has some inexplicable magical quality. /16

There are shapes that appeal to us for no rational reason—the graining of wood, the eroded pebbles in a stream, cloud formations, sunsets, blots of ink, flotsam from the sea. The Chinese and Japanese take great, irregular pieces of rock and erect them in their gardens because they have a strange animistic power or charm. Form is as mysterious as life itself. The artist is a man who reveals the mystery of form. /17

Even the child as it scribbles can do this. An American teacher, Rhoda Kellogg of the Golden Gate Nursery School in San Francisco, has classified children's scribbles and revealed their symbolic significance. A comparison of abstract art with children's scribbles does not make abstract art ridiculous; on the contrary, it connects it organically with the beginnings of all visual symbols. /18

As for technique, much as this may baffle the critic of abstract art, I would say that the standard is the same as in representational art. It is a question of the artist's skill in using his tools and his materials to their best advantage. There are badly painted abstract pictures just as there are badly painted representational pictures; and there are well painted pictures of each kind. Even spontaneity, which is characteristic of abstract expressionist art, is also found in representational art—in Tiepolo or Magnasco, in the impressionists and the expressionists. /19

In abstract art and in representational art, the standards are the same. There is only good art and bad art. /20

Coherent composition, sensibility to color harmonies, rhythmic movement and significant imagery —abstract art possesses all the essentially esthetic qualities that have been present in the art of the past. David Jones, an English painter who is not abstract, has made this point in his book "Epoch and Artist": /21

"Those of us whose work no one, I imagine, would call 'abstract' know, nevertheless, that it is an abstract quality, however hidden or devious, which determines the real worth of any work." /22

(3) *It represents novelty for novelty's sake. There is a primary concern with being "different" that leads to mere sensationalism. There is a difference between a movement and a cult.* /23

It is true that modern art of all kinds, including poetry and music, has been deliberately concerned to "make it new." At the most general and perhaps profoundest level, this is a reflection of our historical situation. We live in a revolutionary period, and the changes in art are but a reflection of the changes in society. But the position is more paradoxical than this generalization implies, for often the most revolutionary societies—those of Russia and China—have been the most conservative in their arts. /24

This, I believe, has been due to the fact that a revolutionary dictatorship has little understanding of the conditions in which art flourishes. As a result, many of the best artists in these countries (Stravinsky, Kandinsky, Chagall), escaped to become leaders of the modern movement elsewhere. /25

More direct causes for the novelty of modern art are to be found in the scientific and technical discoveries of our time. The invention of photography and the moving picture had a profound effect on the art of painting. So did technical advances in speed, the new dimensions of space given by the airplane, the new world of form revealed by the microscope. Form itself was established as a guiding principle in nature, in the universe, and form inevitably (and perhaps unconsciously) became the preoccupation of the artist. /26

It would be absurd to complain of novelty for novelty's sake in science; it is equally absurd to complain of it in art. Art has merely kept in step with a changing world, and the more art has changed the more it has remained the same thing: the symbolic representation of reality. /27

The suggestion that such an activity constitutes a "cult" is far from the truth. There have been cults in the past—the Pre-Raphaelite Brotherhood was one—and in our own time the surrealist movement had some of the characteristics of a cult—rigid rules, manifestoes of aims, organs of propaganda, etc. /28

Abstract art, by contrast, is one of the most nearly universal movements in the history of art. It is practiced in every country in the world apart from Russia and China (even Communist countries like Poland, Czechoslovakia and Yugoslavia have active movements). Abstract art can accommodate all varieties of human temperament and expression, from the severe classicism of Mondrian to the wild romanticism of a de Kooning. /29

(4) *It is mere decoration, no more profound than a pattern for wallpaper or draperies. Does not the abstract artist work first toward the effect of his canvas on a museum wall (witness the enormous size of abstract-expressionist canvases) rather than toward the intensification of experience?* /30

Ruskin once said that all great art was essentially decorative. The great compositions of Titian, Michelangelo and Rubens are "decorative." In the same manner, the paintings of Kandinsky, Mondrian, Nicholson or Pollock are decorative. If the abstract artist "works first toward the effect of his canvas on the wall," he is doing exactly what Titian, Michelangelo and Rubens did. /31

What are exceptional in the history of painting are the small "cabinet" pictures which are popular with bourgeois collectors. The modern painter wishes to be emancipated from this convention of the past century or two, and to return to the "grand manner" of the great painters of the past. He may not be wise to limit his market in this way, but he is demanding the full scale of his medium. We do not expect architects to restrict themselves to the building of cottages, or musicians to the composition of songs. /32

It is true that some abstract compositions are empty, but that is because they are poor compositions, not because they are abstract. "Intensification of experience" is not a question of size, but of the effectiveness of the symbols used. Any Gothic cathedral will serve as an illustration of intense grandeur; and, in its over-all effect, of abstract spatial expression. /33

(5) *It is devoid of human emotion. It has no philosophical foundation, no concern with basic and permanent values, as great art has always had.* /34

No art could have deeper philosophical foundations. Books like Worringer's "Abstraction and Empathy," Kandinsky's "Art of Spiritual Harmony," Mondrian's "Plastic Art," the writings of Gabo, Malevich, Klee—all these constitute a wealth of speculation on the principles of art without rival in history. All these writings are concerned with "basic and permanent values," and such values are human values. /35

Nevertheless, the charge that abstract art is "devoid of human emotion" has some force if by human emotion is meant the day-to-day feelings of joy and sorrow, hope and despair, which are our normal experiences. If the purpose of art were to "express" such feelings, to embody them in realistic pictures, in music or in drama, then art would be identical with life: a transcript, a report, a reflection. If the artist did no more than this he might be a good journalist or a good photographer, but he would not be venerated as we venerate Michelangelo or Rembrandt. /36

The purpose of the artist is not to represent emotion, but to transcend it. There are two aphorisms of Georges Braque's which describe the true function of emotion in art: "Emotion is neither added nor imitated: it is the seed, and art is the blossom." And "I love the rule that corrects emotion; I love the emotion that corrects the rule." /37

Art is a dialectical process: the resolution of contradictions and ambiguities. A work of art is removed from mundane strife; it is an object of disinterested contemplation. /38

"Distance," said Simone Weil, "is the soul of the beautiful: beauty, a fruit which we look at without trying to seize it." Abstract art is perhaps more distant than any art of the past; it is perhaps also more beautiful. /39

The essay

1. What is Read's purpose in answering what he calls the main charges against modern art? What is gained by this negative approach? Would his position have been stronger had he simply ignored the criticisms of modern art?

2. What methods does he use in answering the charges?

3. Is the analogy with music and architecture in paragraphs 9 and 10 a sound one in your opinion? A convincing one? Why not an analogy with poetry?

4. What are the criteria for measuring the modern artist's excellence? Are these criteria essentially different from those used to establish the excellence of conventional art? Develop your answers with examples.

5. What according to Read are the historical causes for abstract art? Do you agree with Read that it is not a cult? Explain your answer.

6. What does Read mean when he says that abstract art is "perhaps more distant than any art of the past"? Why does he consider this a good thing?

7. Could this article be delivered as a speech to your class just as it is? If not, what changes would you make? Explain them in detail. Especially explain what pictures or slides you might want and how you would use them.

8. How would you handle this material in a speech presented to your public speaking class if you were to ignore the charges against modern art and simply argue positively for it. What material might you want to add? Outline such a speech.

9. How would you handle this material if you were using it in an introductory lecture on abstract art in a required college course on art? In an elective course on modern art? In a graduate course on abstract painting?

For further study and discussion

1. How do you define abstract art? Name three artists whose works fit your definition and indicate what they have in common and how they differ.

2. What do you consider to be the basic appeals of abstract art? How do these appeals differ from those of conventional or representational art?

3. In what sense is abstract art properly decoration? Why, then, is it being attacked for being decoration?

4. What do you think abstract painting has in common with architecture? With sculpture? With music? With poetry? With rug and drapery design? How does it differ in function and effect from each of these?

5. What aspects of our age are clearly represented in abstract art? What aspects are not so clearly represented?

6. What philosophy or philosophies of life might logically give rise to abstract art?

7. How would you defend art against the charge that it is not practical?

8. What is the ultimate function, as you see it, of art?

Suggestions for further reading

George Biddle, **The Yes and No of Contemporary Art** (Cambridge, Mass., 1957)

Rudi Blesh, **Modern Art USA** (New York, 1956)

Katherine S. Dreier, Naum Gabo, and James J. Sweeney, **Three Lectures on Modern Art** (New York, 1950)

Paul Klee, **On Modern Art** (London, 1948)

Wyndham Lewis, **The Demon of Progress in the Arts** (Chicago, 1955)

Pieter C. Mondriaan, **Plastic Art and Pure Plastic Art and Other Essays** (New York, 1945)

Edward Wind, **Art and Anarchy** (London, 1963)

Wilhelm Worringer, **Abstraction and Empathy** (New York, 1953)

The world of jazz
LEONARD BERNSTEIN

It is difficult to classify Leonard Bernstein (1918-   ), for to label him as pre-eminent in one field would be to of-

From *The Joy of Music*, copyright © 1959 by Leonard Bernstein. Reprinted by permission of Simon and Schuster, Inc.

fend those who revere him for his performance in others. He has been conductor, composer, pianist, teacher, author, and television lecturer. Serious students of music are acquainted with him through his compositions in the classical mode. Devotees of the musical stage know him as the man who wrote the scores for such Broadway hits as *On the Town, Wonderful Town, Candide,* and *West Side Story.* For some time Bernstein has been well known as a conductor, both here and abroad, but in his latest role as television performer he has gained even greater fame. Perhaps it would be simplest and most descriptive to call him "New York's Mr. Music."

In his book, *The Joy of Music* (1959), Leonard Bernstein has published several of the *Omnibus* scripts which endeared him to his viewers. In "The World of Jazz," which was first presented October 16, 1955, readers can see something of the vivacity of the man who has educated and entertained huge television audiences. Bernstein's performances are full of vitality and abundant nervous energy. No matter what subject he is dealing with, he has never lost the ability to be both engrossed in the work and yet naïvely amazed at its composition.

The following speech ably demonstrates Bernstein's ability to explain a difficult topic by reducing it to terms that can be readily grasped even by the uninitiated. In its unity, organization, movement, use of examples, language, and good humor, this speech bears study as a masterpiece of exposition.

JAZZ BAND:

LEONARD BERNSTEIN:

Now, anyone hearing this music, anyone on any civilized part of this earth, east or west, pole to pole, would immediately say: That is jazz. We are going to try to investigate jazz, not through the usual historical approach which has become all too familiar, but through approaching the music itself. We are going to examine the musical "innards" of jazz to find out once and for all what it is that sets it apart from all other music. /1

Jazz is a very big word; it covers a multitude of sounds, all the way from the earliest Blues to Dixieland bands, to Charleston bands, to Swing bands, to Boogie-Woogie, to crazy Bop, to cool Bop, to Mambo—and much more.[1] It is all jazz, and I love it because it is an original kind of emotional expression, in that it is never wholly sad or wholly happy. Even the Blues has a robustness and hard-boiled quality that never lets it become sticky-sentimental, no matter how self-pitying the words are. /2

BLUES SINGER:

"EMPTY BED BLUES"[2]
by J. C. Johnson

And, on the other hand, the gayest, wildest jazz always seems to have some hint of pain in it. Listen to this trumpet, and see what I mean:

TRUMPET:

"OLE MISS"[3]
by W. C. Handy

That is what intrigues me about jazz; it is unique, a form of expression all its own. /3

I love it also for its humor. It really plays with notes. We always speak of "playing" music: we play Brahms or we play Bach—a term perhaps more properly applied to tennis. But jazz is real play. It "fools around" with notes, so to speak, and has fun with them. It is, therefore, entertainment in the truest sense. /4

But I find I have to defend jazz to those who say it is low-class. As a matter of fact, all music has low-class origins, since it comes from folk music, which is necessarily earthy. After all, Haydn minuets are only a refinement of simple, rustic German dances, and so are Beethoven scherzos. An aria from a Verdi opera can often be traced back to the simplest Neapolitan fisherman. Besides, there has always been a certain shadow of indignity around music, particularly around the players of music. /5

I suppose it is due to the fact that historically *players* of music seem to lack the dignity of *composers* of music. But this is especially true of jazz, which is almost completely a player's art, depending as it does on improvisation rather than on composition. But this also means that the player of jazz is

---

[1] For those who wish to follow examples of the foregoing terms, these recordings are recommended:

Leadbelly: "Good Morning Blues," in *Take This Hammer*, Vol. 1, 10" Folkways, FA 2004

King Oliver, Jelly-Roll Morton, etc.: "Back o' Town," 12" Riverside 12-130

Red Nichols, Dorsey Bros.: "Charleston," in *Jazz of the Roaring Twenties*, 12" Riverside 12-801

Benny Goodman: 1938 *Carnegie Hall Jazz Concert*, 2 12" Col. OSL-160

Meade Lux Lewis, Albert Ammons, etc.: *Giants of Boogie-Woogie*, 12" Riverside 12-106

Charlie Parker: *The Immortal Charlie Parker*, 12" Savoy 12001

Lee Konitz: *Lee Konitz with Warne Marsh*, 12" Atlantic 1217

Perez Prado: *Mambo Mania*, 12" Victor LPM-1075

himself the real composer, which gives him a creative, and therefore *more* dignified, status. /6

Then there are those who argue that jazz is loud. But so are Sousa marches, and we don't hear complaints about them. Besides, it's not always loud. It is very often extremely delicate, in fact. Perhaps this objection stems from the irremediable situation of what is after all a kind of brass band playing in a room too small for it. But that is not the fault of jazz itself. /7

However, the main argument against jazz has always been that it is not art. I think it *is* art, and a very special art. And before we can argue about whether it is or not, we must know *what* it is; and so I propose to share with you some of the things I know and love about jazz. /8

Let's take that Blues we heard before and find out what it's made of:

JAZZ BAND:

Now what are the elements that make that jazz? /9

First of all there is the element of melody. Western music in general is based, melodically speaking, on scales, like the major scale you all practiced as kids:

L. B. PLAYS PIANO:

But there is a special one for jazz, which is a variation of that regular major scale. /10

In jazz, this scale gets modified three different times. The third note gets lowered from this:

to this:

The fifth from this:

to this:

And the seventh from this:

to this:

Those three changed notes are called "blue notes."[4]

So instead of a phrase which would ordinarily go something like this:

which is not particularly jazzy—we would get, using blue notes, this phrase:

—which begins to show a jazz quality. /11

But this so-called "jazz scale" is used only melodically. In the harmony underneath we still use our old unflatted notes, and that causes dissonances to happen between that tune and the chords:

L. B. PLAYS PIANO:

---

[4] Actually, these blue notes are most commonly used in terms of the descending scale:

Leonard Bernstein. (© Roy Stevens.)

But these very dissonances have a true jazz sound. For example, jazz pianists are always using these two dissonant notes together:

—and there is a reason for it. They are really searching for a note that isn't there at all, but one which lies somewhere between the two notes—between this:

and this:

—and the note is called a quarter-tone. /12

The quarter-tone comes straight from Africa, which is the cradle of jazz and where quarter-tones are everyday stuff. We can produce one on a wind instrument or a stringed instrument or with the voice, but on the piano we have to approximate it by playing together the two notes on each side of it:

The real note is somewhere in there, in that crack between them. /13

Let's see if I can sing you that quarter-tone, if you will forgive my horrid voice. Here is an African Swahili tune I once heard. The last note of it is a quarter-tone:

L. B. SINGS:

Sounds as if I'm singing terribly out of tune, but actually I am singing a real note in another musical language. In jazz it is right at home. /14

L. B. PLAYS PIANO:

Now, just to show you how important these so-called "blue notes" are to jazz, let's hear that same Blues played without them, using only the plain white notes of the scale:

CLARINET:

There is something missing, isn't there? It just isn't jazz. /15

But even more important than melody in jazz is the element of rhythm. Rhythm is the first thing you associate with the word *jazz*, after all. There are two aspects to this point. The first is the beat. This is what you hear when the drummer's foot is beating the drum:

or when the bass player is plucking his bass:

or even when the pianist is kicking the pedal with his foot:

All this is elementary. The beats go on from beginning to end of a number, two or four of them to a measure, never changing in tempo or in meter. This is the heartbeat, so to speak, of jazz. /16

But more involved, and more interesting, is the rhythm going on *over* the beat—rhythmic figures which depend on something called "syncopation," a word you have certainly heard but maybe were never quite sure of. A good way to understand syncopation might be to think of a heartbeat that goes along steadily and, at a moment of shock, misses a beat. It is that much of a physical reaction. /17

Technically, syncopation means either the removal of an accent where you expect one, or the placing of an accent where you least expect one. In either case, there is the element of surprise and shock. The body responds to this shock, either by compensating for the missing accent or by reacting to the unexpected one. /18

Now where do we expect accents? Always on the first beat of a bar, on the downbeat. If there are two beats in a bar, *one* is going to be strong, *two* is going to be weak—exactly as in marching: *right,* left, *right,* left. Even if there are four beats in a bar, it is still like marching. Although we all have only two legs, the sergeant still counts out in four: *hup,* 2, 3, 4, *hup,* 2, 3, 4. There is always that natural accent on *one.* Take it away, and there is a simple syncopation:

L. B. GASPS DURING MISSING FIRST BEAT:

(*!*) 2, 3, 4   (*!*) 2, 3, 4 etc.

You see that that missing accent on the first beat evokes a body response. /19

Now, the other way to make syncopation is exactly the reverse: put an accent on a weak beat, the second or the fourth, where it doesn't belong. Like this:

One, *TWO,* three, *FOUR*
One, *TWO,* three, *FOUR*

This is what we all do, listening to jazz, when we clap our hands or snap our fingers on the offbeat. /20

Those are the basic facts of syncopation; and now we can understand its subtler aspects. Between one beat and another there lie shorter and even weaker beats; and when these get accents the shock is correspondingly greater, since the weaker the beat you accentuate, the greater the surprise. Let's take eight of those fast beats in a bar: 1 2 3 4 5 6 7 8. The normal accents would fall on one and five: 1! 2 3 4 5! 6 7 8. Now, instead, let's put a big accent on a real weak one, the fourth:

1 2 3 4! 5 6 7 8

(*Drum takes up from count, then claves, trumpet, etc.*)

As you see, we get a pure rhumba rhythm. /21

Of course, the strongest syncopation of all would obviously be obtained by doing both things at once:

putting an accent on a weak beat and taking away the accent from the strong. So now we will do this double operation: put a wallop on the weak fourth, and remove the strong fifth beat entirely; and we get:

1 2 3 4!   − 6 7 8

(*Various percussion instruments take it up*)
It begins to sound like the Congo, doesn't it? /22
TRUMPET ADDS MELODY:

Now that you've heard what syncopation is like, let's see what that same Blues we heard before would sound like without it. I think you'll miss that essential element, the very life of jazz:
PLAYED "SQUARE" BY SAX, NO VIBRATO:

Sounds "square," doesn't it? /23

Well, that takes care of two very important elements: melody and rhythm. But jazz could not be jazz without its special tonal colors, the actual sound values you hear. These colors are many, but they mostly stem from the quality of the Negro singing voice. For instance, when Louis Armstrong plays his trumpet, he is only doing another version of his own voice. Listen to an Armstrong record, like "I Can't Give You Anything but Love," and compare the trumpet solo with the vocal solo. You can't miss the fact that they're by the same fellow.[5] But the Negro voice has engendered other imitations. The saxophone is in itself a kind of imitation of it—breathy, a little hoarse, with a vibrato, or tremor, in it. /24
(*Here a saxophone plays a passage first with and then without vibrato*)
Then there are all the different growls and rasps we get by putting mutes on the horns. Here, for example, is a trumpet with a cup mute:
(*The sounds of these instruments are heard while they are being shown*)

[5] Louis Armstrong: "I Can't Give You Anything but Love," Armstrong Favorites, Columbia.

and a wah-wah mute:

And a trombone with a plunger mute:

There are other tonal colors that derive from Afro-Cuban sources: Bongo drums:

maracas:

the Cuban cowbell:

and all the others. /25

Then there are the colors that have an Oriental flavor: the vibraphone:

the various cymbals:

and so on. /26

These special colorations make their contribution to the total quality of jazz. You have certainly all heard jazz tunes played "straight" by non-jazz orchestras and wondered what was missing. There certainly is something missing—the coloration. /27

There is one more jazz element which may surprise some of you who think jazz is not an art. I refer to form. Did you know, for example, that the Blues is a classical form? Most people use the word *Blues* to mean any song that is "blue" or torchy or lowdown or breast-beating—like "Stormy Weather," for example. But "Stormy Weather" is not a Blues, and neither is "Moanin' Low," nor "The Man I Love," or even "The Birth of the Blues." They are all popular songs. /28

The Blues is basically a strict poetic form combined with music. It is based on a rhymed couplet, with the first line repeated. For example, Billie Holiday sings:

"My man don't love me, treats me awful mean;[6]
Oh, he's the lowest man I've ever seen."

But when she sings it, she repeats the first line—so it goes:

"My man don't love me, treats me awful mean;
I said, my man don't love me, treats me awful
*   mean;*
Oh, he's the lowest man I've ever seen."

That is one stanza of Blues. A full Blues is nothing more than a succession of such stanzas for as long as the singer wishes. /29

Did you notice that the Blues couplet is, of all things, in iambic pentameter?

"My man/don't love/me, treats/me aw/ful mean"

This is about as classic as one can get. It means that you can take any rhymed couplet in iambic pentameter—from Shakespeare, for example—and make a perfect *Macbeth* Blues:

---

6 "Fine and Mellow" by Billie Holiday.

"I will not be afraid of death and bane,
Till Birnam forest come to Dunsinane."

It makes a lovely Blues:

L. B. SINGS:

Now if you've noticed, each of these three lines got four bars apiece, making it all a twelve-bar stanza. But the voice itself sang only about half of each four-bar line, and the rest is supposed to be filled up by the accompaniment. This filling-up is called a "break." And here in the break we have the origin of the instrument imitating the voice, the very soil in which jazz grows. Perhaps the essential sound of jazz is Louis Armstrong improvising the breaks in a Blues sung by Bessie Smith. From this kind of voice imitation all instrumental improvising has since developed.[7] /30

Did you notice the instrument that has been accompanying our singers today? It is a harmonium, that wheezy little excuse for an organ which we all associate with hymn tunes. But far from being out of place in the Blues, this instrument is especially appropriate, since the chords in the Blues must always be exactly the same three chords we all know from hymn tunes:

L. B. PLAYS ON HARMONIUM:

These chords must always remain in a strict classical pattern, pure and simple. Try to vary them, and the Blues quality flies out the window. /31

Well, there you have it: melody, rhythm, tone color, form, harmony. In each department there are special features that make *jazz*, instead of just music. Let's now put them all together, and hear a full-blown, all-out happy Blues. Oh, did you know that Blues could be happy? Just listen.
(Jazz Band plays a Blues arrangement of "King Porter Stomp," Dixieland style)

[7] Bessie Smith and Louis Armstrong: "Reckless Blues," *The Bessie Smith Story*, Vol. I, Columbia LP ML 4807.

By this time I've probably given you the impression that jazz is nothing but Blues. Not at all. I've used the Blues to investigate jazz only because it embodies the various elements of jazz in so clear and pure a way. But the rest of jazz is concerned with applying these same elements to something called the popular song. The popular song, too, is a form; and it has certain strict patterns. Popular songs are in either two-part or three-part form. By far the most numerous are in the three-part. You all know this form, of course, from hearing it so much. It is as simple as pie. Anyone can write one. /32

Take "Sweet Sue," for instance. All you need is the first eight bars, really—which in the trade are called the front strain:

L. B. PLAYS PIANO:

Now the song is practically written, since the whole thing will be only thirty-two bars long—four groups of eight bars apiece. The second eight is the same exactly as the first:

Sixteen bars, and we're already half finished. Now the next eight bars, which are called the release, or bridge, or just simply "the middle part," must be different music. But it doesn't matter if it's very good or not, since most people don't remember it too well anyway:

And then the same old front strain all over again:

and it's finished. Thirty-two bars, and a classic forever. Easy, isn't it? /33

But "Sweet Sue" is still not jazz. A popular song doesn't become jazz until it is improvised on, and there you have the real core of all jazz: improvisation. Remember, I said that jazz was a player's art rather than a composer's. Well, this is the key to the whole problem. It is the player who, by improvising, makes jazz. He uses the popular song as a kind of dummy to hang his notes on. He dresses it up in his own way, and it comes out an original. So the pop tune, in acquiring a new dress, changes its personality completely, like many people who behave one way in blue jeans and a wholly different way in dinner clothes. Some of you may object to this dressing-up. You say, "Let me hear the melody, not all this embroidery." But until you accept this principal of improvisation, you will never accept or understand jazz itself. /34

What does improvising mean? It means that you take a tune, keep it in mind with its harmony and all, and then, as they used to say, just "go to town," or make it up as you go along. You go to town by adding ornaments and figurations, or by making real old-fashioned variations just as Mozart and Beethoven did. Let me show you a little of how Mozart did it, and then you may understand how Erroll Garner does it. Mozart took a well-known nursery rhyme, which he knew as "*Ah, Vous Dirai-je Maman,*" and which we know as "Twinkle, Twinkle Little Star" or as a way of singing the alphabet:

L. B. PLAYS PIANO AND SINGS:

Now Mozart makes a series of variations. One of them begins:

Then another:

Another:

And another:

They are all different pieces, yet they are all in one way or another that same original tune. /35

The jazz musician does exactly the same thing. There are infinite possible versions of "Sweet Sue," for example. The clarinet might improvise one chorus of it this way:

CLARINET:

Now he could have done that in any number of ways; and if I asked him to do it again tomorrow morning, it would come out a whole other piece. But it would still be "Sweet Sue," and it would still be jazz. /36

Now we come to the most exciting part of jazz, for me at any rate: simultaneous improvising. This happens when two or more musicians improvise on the same tune at the same time. Neither one knows exactly what the other is going to do; but they listen to each other, and pick up phrases from each other, and sort of talk together. What ties them together is the chords, the harmony, of "Sweet Sue." Over this harmony, they play two different melodic lines at the same time, which, in musical terms, makes a kind of accidental counterpoint. This is the germ of what is called the "jam session." Now the trumpet is going to join with the clarinet in a double improvisation on "Sweet Sue." See if you can distinguish the two melodic lines:

TRUMPET AND CLARINET:

You see how exciting this can be? This business of improvising together gave rise to the style called Dixieland, which is constantly having a big revival. One of the most exhilarating sounds in all music is that of a Dixieland band blaring out its final chorus, all stops out, with everyone improvising together.[8] /37

But jazz is not all improvisation, not by a long shot. Much of it gets written down, and then it is called an arrangement. The great days of the arrangements were the Thirties, when big, startling swing arrangements were showing off the virtuosity of the great bands—like Casa Loma, Benny Goodman, Artie Shaw, the Dorsey brothers, and so on. Now jazz is hard to write down. There is no way of notating exactly those quarter-tones we talked about, nor the various smears and growls and subtle intonations. Even the rhythms can only be approximated in notation, so that much of the jazz quality is left to the instincts of the player who is reading the music. Still, it does work, because the instincts of these players are so deep and genuine. /38

Let's listen to a good, solid swing arrangement of a chorus of "Sweet Sue" as we might have heard it back in 1938.[9] /39

Now remember, this arrangement was for dancing. In 1938 we were all dancing; and that brings up the most important point of all. Nobody seems to dance to jazz very much any more, except for mambo lovers, and they are limited to those who are athletic enough to do it. What has happened to dancing? We used to have a new dance practically every month: the Lindy Hop, the Shag, the Peabody, the Big Apple, Boogie, Susie-Q. Now we have only dances you have to take lessons to do. /40

What does this mean? Simply that the emphasis is on listening, these days, instead of on singing and dancing. This change had to happen. For one thing, the tremendous development of the recording industry has taught us to listen in a way we never did before. But even more significant, with the advent of more complicated swing and jazz like Boogie-Woogie and Bop, our interest has shifted to the music itself and to the virtuosity of its performance. That is, we are interested in what notes are being played, how well, how fast, and with what originality. You can't listen to Bop intelligently and dance too, murmuring sweet nothings into your partner's ear. You have to listen as hard as you can to hear what's happening. /41

So in a way, jazz has begun to be a kind of chamber music, an advanced sophisticated art mainly for listening, full of influences of Bartók and Stravinsky, and very, very serious. Let's listen for a moment to this kind of arrangement of our old friend "Sweet Sue."

L. B. PLAYS VERY COOL ARRANGEMENT OF "SWEET SUE":[10]

---

[8] Bix Beiderbecke: "Sweet Sue," *The Bix Beiderbecke Story,* Vol. 3, Columbia LP ML 4813.
[9] Benny Goodman: "Sweet Sue," *This Is Benny Goodman,* Victor LP M 1239.

[10] Arrangement by Danny Hurd; reproduced by special permission.

Whether you call this kind of weird piece "cool" or "crazy" or "futuristic" or "modernistic" or whatever the fact is that it is bordering on serious concert music. The arrangement begins to be a *composition*. Take away the beat, and you might not even know it's jazz at all. It would be just a concert piece. And why is it jazz? Because it is played by jazz men, on jazz instruments, and because it has its roots in the soil of jazz and not of Bach. /42

I think the key word to all this is the word *cool*. It means what it implies. Jazz used to advertise itself as "hot"; now the heat is off. The jazz player has become a highly serious person. He may even be an intellectual. He tends to wear Ivy League clothes, have a crew cut, or wear horn-rimmed glasses. He may have studied music at a conservatory or a university. This was unthinkable in the old days. Our new jazz man plays more quietly, with greater concentration on musical values, on tone quality, technique. He knows Bartók and Stravinsky, and his music shows it. He tends to avoid big, flashy endings. The music just stops when it is over. /43

As he has become cool, so have his listeners. They don't dance; they listen respectfully, as if to chamber music, and applaud politely at the end. At jazz night clubs all over the world you find audiences who do not necessarily have a drink in their hands and who do not beat out the rhythm and carry on as we did when I was a boy. It is all rather cool and surprisingly controlled, considering that jazz is essentially an emotional experience. /44

Where does this lead us in our investigation? To some pretty startling conclusions. There are those who conclude from all this that here, in the new jazz, is the real beginning of serious American music, that at last the American composer has his own expression. Of course when they say this they are intimating that all American symphonic works up to now are nothing but personalized imitations of the European symphonic tradition from Mozart to Mahler. Sometimes, I must say, I think they have a point. At any rate, we can be sure of one thing: that the line between serious music and jazz grows less and less clear. We have serious composers writing in the jazz idiom, and we have jazz musicians becoming serious composers. Perhaps we've stumbled on a theory. /45

But theory or no theory, jazz goes on finding new paths, sometimes reviving old styles, but, in either case, looking for freshness. In any art that is really vital and searching, splits are bound to develop; arguments arise and factions form. Just as in painting the non-objectivists are at sword's point with the representationalists, and in poetry the imagists declaim against the surrealists, so in jazz music we have a major battle between the traditionalists and the progressives. /46

These latter are the ones who are trying hardest to get away from the patterns of half a century, experimenting with new sonorities, using note relationships that are not common to the old jazz, and, in general, trying to keep jazz alive and interesting by broadening its scope. Jazz is a fresh, vital art in the present tense, with a solid past and an exciting future. /47

The telecast

1. What is Bernstein's specific purpose in this telecast? Quote the sentence that best states it. Does everything in the telecast relate directly to this central purpose?
2. What is gained by enumerating at the beginning several of the charges against jazz? Does Bernstein successfully refute all of these charges in the course of the talk? Which does he refute most successfully? Why?
3. What according to Bernstein are the main elements of jazz? In your own words describe each element.
4. What is the distinguishing difference between popular music and jazz? How is jazz like chamber music?
5. What are Bernstein's main conclusions about jazz? Is each successfully prepared for in the telecast itself? If so, show how.
6. Clearly this is an expository speech. Indicate what the essentials of such a speech are and how they are exemplified here.
7. What terms does he define in the course of the talk? Discuss his methods of definition.
8. Discuss Bernstein's use of musical passages in detail. What would the telecast lose if they were deleted? How does he get variety in them? Are there any points without musical illustration that you think should have them?
9. Comment on Bernstein's style: lengths and kinds of sentences, choice of words, use of technical talk, concreteness, humor, and so on. Would you call the style colloquial?
10. Thousands of viewers have come to believe that Bernstein has been the clearest expositor of music to appear on radio or television. How do you account for this high reputation he enjoys?

For further study and discussion

1. What briefly are the origins of jazz?
2. What varieties of jazz do you know? Define each and illustrate it with a recording.

3. Why should jazz have become respectable in the last twenty years?

4. Do you consider listening to jazz more of an intellectual experience than an emotional one? Develop your answer in detail. If possible, use recordings to support your points.

5. How can jazz be at once sad and humorous? Illustrate your points with recordings.

6. What do you consider to be essential in the training of a good jazz player?

7. Imitate Bernstein's explanation of "Sweet Sue" but use another song.

8. Draw as many comparisons as you can between jazz and chamber music, jazz and sonatas, jazz and symphonies.

9. In what respects do you consider jazz an expression of our age?

10. Do you agree that jazz is the only really original American contribution to music? To all the arts? Explain your answer in detail.

Suggestions for further reading

Louis Armstrong, *Satchmo* (New York, 1954)

Rudi Blesh, *Shining Trumpets* (New York, 1958)

Dave Dexter, *The Jazz Story, from the '90's to the '60's* (Englewood Cliffs, N.J., 1964)

Leonard G. Feather, *The Book of Jazz* (New York, 1957)

W. C. Handy, *Father of the Blues* (New York, 1941)

LeRoi Jones, *Blues People; Negro Music in White America* (New York, 1963)

Nat Shapiro and Nat Hentoff, eds., *Hear Me Talkin' to Ya* (New York, 1955)

Marshall Stearns, *The Story of Jazz* (New York, 1956)

3/SCIENCE

Science and society
HAROLD C. UREY

Harold C. Urey's speech on the intellectual aspects of science was delivered at the 100th Anniversary Academic Convocation of The Cooper Union for the Advancement of Science and Art in New York City on November 2, 1959.

Urey, a Nobel Prize winner in 1934 (for discovery of deuterium, or heavy hydrogen), and a professor of chemistry at the University of California, La Jolla, chose an appropriate subject for a speech to be delivered at the Cooper Union. Edwin S. Burdell, director of the Cooper Union, has said in the *Encyclopedia Americana* that the institution is devoted to "instruction in the application of Science and Art to the practical business of life," and that the guiding policy of the institution is "the educational philosophy of Scientific Humanism, a curricular synthesis of science, art, and the humanities."

Of the difficulties of talking to a general audience on a specialized subject, Urey has written: "In order to make a good scientific speech it is necessary to speak loud enough so the person in the back row can hear, and not do as some people do—talk to a little group in the front row. It is necessary to remember that if the subject is complicated and intricate, the complicated and intricate details are known to specialists in the field, in which case they do not need to hear them again; if these details are unknown to others, then they cannot possibly learn them in a few minutes. Hence, again it is useless to include such things. Beyond this, it is always necessary to speak slowly and clearly, and have something to say in which one has interested one's self and which may be of interest to the audience."[1] In making scientific information accessible to a wide audience, Urey is pursuing the basic purpose of the Cooper Union. It is with the crucial problem of applying the complexities of modern scientific investigation to social needs that Urey is concerned.

One approach to understanding and evaluating this speech will be to investigate how extensively Urey's views

---

Harold C. Urey, "Science and Society," *Vital Speeches of the Day*, Vol. XXVI, December 15, 1959, pp. 141-144. By permission of the author and The Cooper Union for the Advancement of Science and Art.
[1] Letter to the editors, June 15, 1960.

are compatible with the scientific humanism of the Cooper Union and its desires to promote a "synthesis of science, art and the humanities" and to sponsor instruction in "the application of Science" to "the practical business of life."

During the years of this century and particularly since the end of World War II, it has become evident to the people of civilized countries that the practical applications of scientific knowledge are of immense importance in our modern society. To those of us who have been interested as professionals in science and engineering, this fact has been recognized even earlier than it has by the non-specialist in these fields. In fact, these practical applications of science come close to dominating all considerations of government and economics of our own country and those of Europe and Asia. Also, the purely intellectual aspects of science are beginning to dominate our ideas in philosophical and religious matters. /1

It may be well to recall to ourselves certain immense developments of this century particularly. At the turn of the century, the steam engine, the railroad, telegraph and telephone represented the outstanding technical achievements of the nineteenth century, and they were very great achievements indeed. In all countries of the world where these developments occurred, one of the most ancient and disgraceful institutions disappeared never to return, namely, that of slavery. It is well to remember that these developments, and particularly that of inanimate power, abolished this hard labor of unfortunate human beings which had supported all the luxury of the ancient and medieval civilizations. But the closing years of the old century or the beginning years of the new witnessed the beginnings of the development of the internal combustion engine, wireless telegraphy, the aeroplane, and the discovery of radioactivity which led inevitably to the development of atomic energy. These developments have given the modern technical countries a degree of luxury beyond the most fanciful dreams of the preceding centuries. The steady developments of biology and their application to agriculture have produced such an abundance of food that in this country this abundance has produced economic embarrassment. /2

The most effective way of illustrating these general statements is by means of the statistics relating to the use of mechanical power and the use of steel, since these are general measures of activities of the kind being considered. /3

The use of fossil fuels in this country increased by a factor of 8 between 1900 and 1955. Coal was the principal source of energy in 1900. In 1955, petroleum and natural gas contributed 67% of the total energy, while coal supplied only 30%. Electrical power increased from negligible amounts in 1900 to about 500 watts per person. This is not large but nevertheless about 6 per cent of our total energy is in this flexible form, enabling us to do such neat and convenient things as light our houses, run the many small convenient machines, operate our communication systems, etc. This growth of the use of power emphasizes the physical basis of our industrial transformations. The increased use of steel and other metals and of many other substitutes emphasizes the same point in another way. /4

Such statistics may be necessary as a means of impressing the younger generation present in this room but are quite unnecessary for those of my age. I remember easily events and conditions of the last 60 years. These years span the time between the horse and buggy age and that of 55,000,000 private automobiles; also, the time between Marconi's primitive experiments and television in the many homes of the U.S.; also the time when the 20th Century Limited was the magnificent train through the local town of my boyhood and its virtual discontinuance because of the competition of aeroplanes. I have some nostalgia for the old days. What could be so thrilling as a ride with grandfather in a sleigh behind a matched team of blacks on a clear night with stars above and white snow around, with me and grandpa nestled warm and cozy beneath a buffalo robe? My own children have never known this luxury at all. Today we read about these things or see them in the Currier and Ives prints. /5

The great changes in our everyday mode of life that have resulted from these developments have been so rapid that it is difficult to visualize them. Sixty years ago, people were often born in a house and lived in that house as children, took over the place from their parents, and were taken care of by their children in their old age and died in that same house. Various deviations from this situation existed, of course, since the population of this country has increased rapidly, but during the course of one generation a very cohesive family development existed and this has been even more true of some other countries. Since 1900, the situation has changed markedly. At the present time, my own children and those of my near relatives and of my friends and acquaintances live far from their parents and scattered over the entire United States and sometimes abroad as well. This fundamental change has come about because of the rapid means of transportation and communication and our dependence on modern industrial developments for our livelihood. /6

Also, our mutual dependence on other sections of the community has greatly increased. Today even farmers do not grow their own food or even essential parts of it, and this was definitely not the case 60 years ago. We do not do any of our own carpentry or other building. Our plumbing facilities and electrical requirements are beyond our capacities to install or repair. I studied in grade and high school by the light of a kerosene lamp and the only place which uses these at the present time so far as my experience goes is Sequoia National Park. /7

What was once a society of rather small, closely knit communities in the rural and small town regions of the United States has been replaced by a roving population where blood relatives know each other only slightly and see each other only a few times a year in many cases. This has come about because of the rapid means of transport and the demands of industrial employment, or because of wanderlust made easy by these means. These few simple illustrations point up a very great social change in our country and other parts of the world within two generations. These changes could not have occurred without the help of applied sciences. /8

The methods of making war have changed greatly in these 60 years. In 1900, General Bacterium and his hordes probably claimed more lives of soldiers than did the weapons of human enemies. Today this is not true, but the expense of preparation for war and the stupendously greater expense of actual war have both greatly increased during these years. Wars and the curious psychology of politicians have produced a fantastic national debt in the United States. The physical cost in machines and weapons was met during the war by greater effort on the part of the populations of the world and by reduced standards of living. Only the paper value as debts plagues us since then. However, all these things are finally the result of the applications of science to another phase of human activity. /9

These activities have had profound effects upon government activities and undoubtedly we have not learned how to adjust our governments to them. A few illustrations show how these industrial developments have increased government activities. Not only have government budgets increased because of the decreasing value of the dollar, but they have increased in proportion to the total income of countries. /10

Automobiles require vast expenditures for roads and police. Aeroplanes require airfields, air navigation facilities and government regulation. Radio and television must be regulated by the community. In my opinion, this is done better in the United Kingdom than in the U.S.A. (Parenthetically, I do not like advertising.) Electric power requires public regulations and the practical requirement of monopoly leads to price control. (Again, more control is needed in order to do something about those ugly power poles which have not been improved in the last 60 years. Odd, isn't it, that street lighting can be supplied from underground, but private power cannot? I speak feelingly. The view of the Pacific Ocean from my house is through a maze of power lines.) Railroads long ago required public regulation in the U.S. or public ownership in Europe. Large manufacturing facilities and the necessary large labor organizations require government control because of the great financial interests of the public. The mobility of the population leads to additional social security needs and additional police problems. This feature affects our moral and religious problems. Large and effective weapons have completely changed our international problems in the last 60 years. /11

I wish to state as my firm belief that the enormous growth of government activities since 1900 is due in large measure to the importance of applied science in this age, and to predict that this growth will continue to a very substantial degree in the future. Probably all of us deplore this situation, but only a return to the general conditions of 1900 or possibly 1859 by us and the rest of the world could correct the trend. In a certain sense, applied science is forcing various phases of socialism upon the modern world in the sense that its successful activities require more community interference in our activities. /12

Those who discuss these problems often mention the exponential character of the increase in all these things, i.e., the factor by which they have increased since 1900 is about the same as that by which they increased between 1840 and 1900. But there is a difference. Somewhere in this century some saturation must occur. There are only so many waking hours in which to use gadgets, to listen to radios, to drive cars or space machines, etc. Also, surely we have now reached the limit of our use of war in human disputes. This country has in some ways marked certain approximate limits with respect to some of these activities. /13

To those of us who spend our lives working on scientific problems, science is a great intellectual adventure of such interest that nothing else we ever do can compare with it. We are attempting to understand the order of a physical universe, vast in extent in space and time, and most complicated and beautiful in its details. In this vast universe we find living things of which we ourselves are a part and these living things, constituting in bulk only a minute fraction of the whole, are yet some of the most amazing and most fascinating parts of the whole. The ideas developed in these studies are changing the entire philosophy of men, their entire view as to their place in this universe. The applications of science are purely incidental to these intellectual studies and we believe that these purely intellectual aspects will modify the lives of man more than will all the applications of science to the material welfare of men. /14

It is well to mention some of the more important intellectual developments of the past centuries: /15

1) The structure of the solar system as developed by Copernicus was one of the first intellectual achievements that modified men's ideas profoundly. The earth was no longer the center of the universe and established institutions at the time realized this and attempted to extinguish this idea. The victory has gone to science without question. /16

2) The proposal of biological evolution, a century old this year, again modified the ideas of men regarding themselves and their place in nature. This idea was again opposed by established institutions. The victory has gone to scientific thought overwhelmingly. /17

3) Geology has established the history of the earth and today we know much about its age, namely some 3 billion years for the oldest rocks and about 4.5 billion years for the meteorites. These facts have greatly increased our concepts of time and the intricate details of the history of the earth and universe. /18

4) The nineteenth century witnessed the discovery and development of our ideas regarding electricity, magnetism, the properties of light and the fundamental laws of thermodynamics. These ideas laid the basis for much of our exact knowledge in

physics and chemistry, and their application to practical affairs has given us our important sources of energy during this century. /19

5) During this century we have learned much in regard to the structure of the universe, its extent to vast distances, its possible origin and details of evolution, its possible age. These ideas have not been opposed and this signifies an acceptance by a large section of the community. /20

6) Other scientific ideas have not been so controversial because they did not contradict established thought, as they were not capable of being observed without the aid of complex apparatus. Today after two centuries we know much about the chemical and physical properties and structure of matter. This is of great intellectual success. It has resulted from the work of many minds of varying capacities. This knowledge made a very important contribution to man's physical existence and also to his effectiveness in waging war. /21

7) During this century we have learned much about the mechanisms of living things. Among these one of the most fascinating has been the problem of heredity. Today the actual details of these mechanisms are being elucidated so that we begin to understand the actual punch card system by which hereditary characteristics are carried from one generation to the next. /22

8) At the close of the nineteenth century and the beginning of the twentieth century, the quantum theory and the relativity theory were discovered. They have profoundly influenced all physical thought during the years since. They deal with concepts not easily observed and they are the result of most careful and penetrating analysis. With their aid we have come to understand much about the structure of matter. In fact, we understand the origin of all chemical phenomena in principle from these developments even though the immense detailed complexity largely can be described only by direct observation. /23

9) During the years of this century and especially during the last 20 years, we have learned much in regard to the nuclei of atoms. This is one of the most magnificent intellectual accomplishments of all history. It leads to an understanding of the evolution of stars, the origin of the elements and the vast supplies of energy required for these processes. It influences our lives mostly through its practical applications. Its revolutionary conclusions on the intellectual side are accepted today without question. One wonders how they would have been received a century ago! /24

10) During recent years another great intellectual scientific advance is in the making. Out of the rockets which bombarded England, that stubborn stalwart of freedom, and the possibility of launching atomic bombs from great distances has come the possibility and, indeed, the fact of space exploration. Radiation belts about the earth have been explored and we now know that the moon has no magnetic field and that it has a "peculiarly low" level of radioactivity in its surface. Why do we investigate these things? The great fundamental driving force of the human intellect is curiosity, but it is a very sophisticated curiosity that drives us to investigate these things. Thus the radiation belts are due to the high energy particles moving in the neighborhood of the earth as they are trapped by the earth's magnetic field, and we are interested in these very energetic particles, where they originate, and how they acquired their high energies. Also, a study of the moon's surface tells us much about its past history, and thus of the history of the earth and solar system, and thus of the development of the stars generally. During the coming years, space exploration will proceed at an increased pace. Eventually we may prove that life does exist or has existed on Mars and Venus. /25

These ideas and many others have fascinated active scientists during all the time which they have been developed. But they are modifying the most fundamental ideas of people also. /26

By religion most scientists are sceptics, that is, they do not subscribe to the dogmas of Christianity, Judaism, or any other religion. They mostly regard the supernatural aspects of these religions in the same light as they do those of the religions of ancient Egypt, Greece and Rome. On the moral side, they are mostly close followers of the precepts of Christianity and Judaism. It seems to me that these attitudes have resulted from their scientific studies. This is true of myself. It is my opinion that these attitudes have already spread to the general population to some extent and that this will occur to an even greater degree in the future. To many, these are unpleasant statements, but I believe they are facts and progress is not made by sweeping facts under the rug. /27

Science is not a substitute for religion. It very often imposes a condition represented by the word "must." We cannot do things which do not conform to the requirements of natural laws and facts. But science never imposes a condition represented by the word "ought." There is no requirement imposed by science that certain types of human behavior are morally right and others are morally wrong. Scientists live by the morals taught to them directly or indirectly by the great religions practiced in the countries where they reside. /28

Also, science gives us no purpose in living beyond having a pleasant existence in one way or another. Scientists themselves are inspired by the magnificent things which they study. But science does not give the ordinary man whose daily life is often drab and anything but sublime any objective that gives him a feeling of dignity. Such feelings are so necessary if he is to rise above the disappointments and temptations of life and if he is to do the best of which he is capable. One of the great needs of this age is a great prophet who can accept the facts of science and at the same time can give inspiration to fill this great void. I do not believe that current evangelists so popular from time to time have made any contribution to this fundamental problem. /29

It may be that the view expressed here is unduly pessimistic. Probably at all times in the past some fraction of the population was frankly sceptical, another most thoughtfully devout, and the great mass mostly unconcerned and mostly uncritically thoughtless and conforming and possibly this will continue into the future. Certainly, certain situations relative to these problems have been anything but ideal at certain historical periods of the past. But may it not be that the rapid rise of juvenile delinquency in recent years is due to the lack of the feeling given by the word "ought" imposed by the community, by parents, or by teachers, and may it not be that this in turn is due to its absence from science which is coming to dominate the thinking of this age? /30

These things could all become much simpler if the clock were turned back one century. This cannot be done and most of us do not wish for this at all. What some people desire is that it be turned back on some phases and not on others. We wish for low cost government, but wish for new roads for that new Detroit monstrosity and a new airport able to handle those new jets. We wish for a decreased state budget in California, but also demand a new irrigation ditch. We wish for a lower military appropriation, but at the same time worry about falling behind in the missile race. We wish for a return to the old philosophical security, but are fascinated by the new ideas brought forth by science. /31

We cannot turn the clock back. We must face our social, philosophical, and governmental problems in each age. They present a great challenge to us and surely we will solve our problems again in this scientific age. I hope that the solutions may be better than were some such solutions of past problems. /32

The speech

1. What is the central idea of this speech? Basically, is the speech expository or argumentative? Defend your answer.
2. In what ways does the speaker establish his authority to speak on the subject? Quote specific passages where he does this.
3. Since Urey's main interest here is obviously in the intellectual aspects of science, what is the purpose of the first part of the speech where he discusses the practical applications of science?
4. What are the chief effects on society of the practical application of science? Of the intellectual developments in science? Compare the two sets of results in their implications for human happiness.
5. Do you believe that the speech supports the conclusion that "surely we will solve our problems again in this scientific age"? Give the reasons for your answer.
6. Since Urey's audience at the Cooper Union would know all of the ten "important intellectual developments of the past centuries," what is gained by listing them?
7. How completely do you feel the speaker has covered the relation between science and society? Can you think of any major effects science has had upon our society that are not mentioned here?
8. What different kinds of support does Urey employ? Which kind do you think is most effectively used? Why?
9. What devices does he use to keep the attention of the audience?
10. Characterize the style in detail. Especially, show why it is or is not appropriate to the subject and audience.

For further study and discussion

1. In what ways did technical achievements help to eliminate slavery?
2. Are they likely to help us eliminate our present racial discord?
3. Do you feel that your family is less cohesive than your father's family was? Than his father's was?
4. How does our mutual dependence liberate us? In what ways does it make living more precarious?
5. Show by a careful cause and effect sequence how applied science can result in big government.
6. Do you think we have reached the saturation point in gadgets and luxury items? Explain your answer.
7. Which intellectual developments of the past century do you consider the most influential in shaping man's thought and life?
8. How do you account for man's "sophisticated curiosity"?

9. Is it progress to discard the dogmas of religion? Develop your answer in considerable detail.

10. What do you believe are the chief limitations of science?

11. What do you think would be the nature of the teaching of a prophet who bases his arguments and exhortations upon scientific truth?

12. How can science serve to improve our moral conduct?

Suggestions for further reading

Lyman Bryson, *Science and Freedom* (New York, 1947)
Vannevar Bush, *Endless Horizons* (Washington, D. C. 1946)
I. Bernard Cohen, *Science, Servant of Man* (Boston, 1948)
Albert Einstein, *The World As I See It* (New York, 1949)
Aldous Huxley, *Science, Liberty, and Peace* (New York, 1946)
Julian Huxley, *The Human Crisis* (Seattle, 1963)
William L. Laurence, *Men and Atoms* (New York, 1959)
Bertrand Russell, *The Scientific Outlook* (New York, 1931)
C. P. Snow, *The Two Cultures: And a Second Look* (Cambridge, Eng., 1964)
Edward Teller and Albert L. Latter, *Our Nuclear Future* (New York, 1958)
George P. Thompson, *The Foreseeable Future* (Cambridge, Eng., 1955)

Science, technology, and world development

HARRISON BROWN

This speech by Harrison Brown, professor of geochemistry at the California Institute of Technology, was delivered in Austria in 1958 at the third Pugwash conference, which was attended by some eighty scientists, including twenty from the United States and ten from the U.S.S.R.

The Pugwash conferences resulted "from a spontaneous movement among scientists of different countries, seeking international exchange of ideas on problems arising from the impact of science on human affairs."[1] They were originally undertaken to examine the perils resulting from the development of weapons of mass destruction, but the third conference was more extensive in scope than the earlier meetings. In addition to the dangers posed by modern weapons, the scientists discussed political problems of the arms race; science, technology, and education in the scientific age; international exchange and cooperation in science; and the responsibility of the scientists.

The public statement (called the Vienna Declaration) which was issued at the end of the conference "calls upon scientists not merely to serve willingly as experts for their governments, but to assume on their own initiative a pioneering role in the education of public opinion and political leadership to the facts of the atomic age. . . ."[2]

It is, of course, in the context of this international meeting of scientists, with its broad concern for the relationship between science and the improvement of man's condition, that Brown's speech must be read. Additional information and the official statement of the Pugwash conference may be found in *Science*, 128:1071-73, in the *Bulletin of the Atomic Scientists*, 14:338-44, and in F. L. Wormald's *The Pugwash Experiment; an Essay in Liberal Education* (Washington, D.C.: Association of American Colleges, 1958).

The most obvious threat to the survival of civilization today is nuclear war between the present world powers. This is also the most immediate threat, but in the long run it is not necessarily the most serious one. In the decades ahead we are going to be faced by a sequence of problems of great complexity, all of which will demand solution and which must be anticipated if they are to be solved. Most of the problems are directly related to the changes which are taking place in the world as a result of the upsurge of science and technology. Solution of the problems will necessitate the concerted and intensive application of science and technology on an unprecedented scale. /1

Most of the difficulties confronting us today stem from the fact that we are living in the middle of an enormous revolution which is characterized primarily by rapid technological change. Never before in history has society changed as rapidly as it is changing today. The closest parallel to our modern situation occurred about 7,000 years ago when our primitive food-gathering ancestors learned that they could cultivate edible plants and that they could domesticate animals. With the emergence of these new techniques more than 500 persons could be supported in areas where previously only one could be supported. /2

Harrison Brown, "Science, Technology, and World Development," *Bulletin of the Atomic Scientists*, December 14, 1958, pp. 409-412. Reprinted by permission of the *Bulletin of the Atomic Scientists*.
[1] *Bulletin of the Atomic Scientists*, XIV (November 1958), p. 338.

[2] Ibid., p. 340.

During the past 300 years, man has attained a remarkable degree of control over his environment. Through the achievement of a partial understanding of how nature operates, he has learned how to grow more crops on a given piece of land; he has learned a great deal about disease and how to control it; he has learned how to harness the energy of fossil fuels; he has learned how to transport himself, his ideas, and his goods rapidly. /3

One result of these innovations has been to accelerate the spread of agriculture over the world. A second result has been to shift man in many parts of the world from a predominantly rural existence within the framework of an agricultural economy to a predominantly urban existence within the framework of an industrial economy. A third result has been to stimulate increasing individual demands for material possessions. A fourth result has been to stimulate an unprecedented rate of increase of human population. /4

During the last three centuries, we have seen the emergence of industrial-scientific civilization in England, and we have seen it spread throughout Western Europe. In the last 150 years, we have seen industrialization cross the Atlantic and spread over North America. In the last sixty years, we have seen industrialization cross the Pacific to Japan. In the last thirty-five years, we have seen it spread to the USSR. Today, we can observe it spreading to Australia and to parts of Africa. We can hear rumblings of impending industrialization in India, China, southeast Asia, and South America. /5

In the absence of a world catastrophe, this spread of industrialization to the rest of the world is inevitable, in the same sense that the spread of agriculture throughout the world was inevitable, once agriculture was invented. It seems unlikely that industrialized and unindustrialized nations can coexist indefinitely any more than the agricultural and food-gathering cultures of the past were able to coexist indefinitely. /6

In addition, it seems clear that the further spread of industrialization necessarily must take place within a framework that differs considerably from the framework within which industrialization has thus far spread throughout the Western world. One of the primary reasons for this is that the ratios of people to available land, and of people to readily available resources, are much larger now than they were then. /7

Industrial civilization consists today of a vast interlocking network of mines, factories, and transportation systems. It feeds on huge quantities of raw materials such as ores of iron, copper, and aluminum, phosphate rock, sulfur, and water. Huge quantities of energy in the form of fuels such as coal, natural gas, and petroleum are necessary for its functioning. /8

As per capita demands for goods continue to grow, as population increases, and as industrialization spreads to other regions of the world, the demands for raw materials will surge upwards. Each decade we must produce more metals than were produced the decade before, we must produce more fertilizers, insecticides, machines, and medicines. Correspondingly, we must consume more ores, more coal, more petroleum, and we must tap new sources of energy. /9

In terms of the changes which are being brought about by the spread of industrial civilization, we are much closer to the beginning of the revolution in which we now find ourselves than we are to its end. The problems which will confront us will increase in complexity as time goes by. /10

Today we are confronted by diminishing grades of raw materials in many areas of industrial activity. For example, only a few decades ago copper ores were being mined that contained 5 per cent copper. Today our average copper ore contains only 0.6 per cent of the metal. Undoubtedly in the years ahead we shall be mining ores that contain even smaller concentrations of the element. From the point of view of technology, this is something well within the realm of technological feasibility—but at a price. In order to extract copper from ores of still lower grade, we must pour more technology into the system; we must move and process larger quantities of ore per unit of production; we must use more machines and consume more energy. In short, extraction of metals from lower grades of ore requires using more steel and other metals, and consuming more energy. /11

No matter how we look at the situation, we must conclude that consumption of energy and raw materials, even in the presently industrialized societies, must continue to increase with time. When we couple this with the fact that per capita demands for goods are still increasing, population is increasing, and industrialization is spreading, it seems inevitable that world-wide demands for raw materials in the years ahead will pale those of today into insignificance. /12

As the changes take place it will be necessary for nations to obtain their raw materials from progressively leaner ores. In order to do this, it will be necessary to put more technology into the system, and to consume larger quantities of energy per unit of production. /13

So long as there is an ample supply of energy, we shall be able to process extremely low-grade substances in order to obtain the raw materials we need. As grades move downward, increasing emphasis will be placed on the isolation of by-products and co-products, and eventually we may reach the time when as many as twenty to thirty products are obtained from the single operation of "mining" ordinary rock. As grade goes down, energy costs per unit of output will of course go up, but given adequate energy, industry can be fed for a very long time from the leanest of substances. /14

Fortunately, nature has placed at our disposal huge reservoirs of energy. We know that, if necessary, the sun's rays can be harnessed directly to produce mechanical power. We know that useful power can be produced from uranium and thorium, and we know that sufficient quantities of these substances are available in the earth's minerals and rocks to keep a world civilization operating at a high level of productivity for many millennia. We know that it is possible to generate eventually thermonuclear power in almost infinite quantities. We know that in some regions of the world there are large quantities of coal and petroleum that have not yet been tapped. It seems clear that given the trained manpower, imagination, and the collaborative research, man has at his disposal ample supplies of energy. /15

In the years ahead we can expect that competition between nations for the earth's resources will become increasingly keen. But resource depletion will eventually become the great leveler of nations, and most of the major industrial areas of the world will eventually find it easier to gain their sustenance by applying science and technology to the task of processing domestic, low-grade substances than to look abroad. /16

The depletion of resources will make it more and more difficult for the less developed areas of the world to obtain the materials they need for their own industrialization. Increasing difficulty of importation will necessitate the application of an ever greater amount of technology to their own industrialization problems. Indeed, it seems likely that we are approaching the interesting situation in which the less developed and more impoverished an area is, the higher is the level of technology required to achieve and maintain an adequate standard of living. For these reasons, the industrialization of the unindustrialized part of the world will become more difficult with each passing year. /17

The industrial-scientific revolution has had profound effects upon human populations. World population jumped from about 500 million persons in 1650 to about 2,700 million persons in 1958. Even more significant is the fact that the *rate* of increase of population is increasing rapidly as well. /18

Some of the reasons for this accelerating population growth are clear. Scientific methods of agriculture make it possible to obtain higher crop yields. Modern transportation systems have virtually eliminated large-scale famine in most regions of the world by making it possible to transport food quickly from one region to another. Techniques of immunization and sanitation have eliminated a variety of epidemic and endemic diseases. Widespread use of insecticides such as DDT have greatly decreased the incidence of malaria in many regions and have eliminated a variety of other insect-borne diseases. Infant mortality and childhood diseases have been greatly decreased so that increasing numbers of persons survive to reproduce. /19

How far will this upsurge in population carry us? It is, of course, impossible to predict but we can obtain some idea by examining past patterns of behavior. /20

Throughout the greater part of human history human numbers have tended to increase up to the limits imposed by the food supply. There is little reason to suppose that this situation is not true today. /21

The availability of techniques of contraception has, of course, resulted in a lowering of birth rates in the industrial world, and the birth rates themselves are now sensitive to fluctuating economic conditions. But although we see about us these variations in rates of growth, the number of human beings inhabiting the earth appears to be moving inexorably upward. It is obvious that this increase cannot continue indefinitely. But at what point will population cease to grow? /22

In the absence of a major catastrophe there does not appear to be the slightest possibility that world population will level off much below 7 billion persons. As industrialization spreads throughout the world and if our ability to produce food is indeed the population-determining factor, the number of human beings might eventually exceed even that high figure. Ten billion persons could be supported but with extreme crowding and using the most elaborate of technologies. A much greater number is difficult to imagine. /23

It is clear that at some point in time population growth must stop. When growth ceases, it will either be within the framework of high birth rates balanced by equally high death rates, or by low death rates balanced by equally low birth rates. The outcome will be determined by the efforts which are placed upon these problems in the years which lie immediately ahead. /24

The slow rate at which food production can be increased within the framework of our existing abilities aggravates the situation still further. It is possible to grow enough food on the earth's surface to support the growing population of the world for the next fifty years—and this merely by doing more intensively things we already know how to do. In principle, too, it is possible, through extending our agriculture by procedures which we now regard as uneconomical, to produce sufficient food to support the growing population through perhaps the next century. But, unfortunately, although there is no barrier in principle to feeding a far larger number of persons than now exist in the world, the fact remains that it is difficult to increase the amount of food produced each year as rapidly as the number of people is likely to increase. Thus, unless it is possible in some way to slow down birth rates or to speed up production rates, we are faced with the prospect of watching industrialization spread to areas where people are hungry today and will remain hungry for a long time. /25

One important aspect of the dangers which confront us is concerned with the understandable impatience of people to improve their lot. The process of industrialization is a slow one when viewed in terms of the length of a human lifetime. A doubling time of between five and ten years for industrial production represents a very rapid rate of growth. Yet even under conditions of such rapid development a considerable span of time is required for the average individual to notice much improvement in his life. One reason for this is that the products of industry at first must be diverted largely to the creation of new industry. Machines must be built which can be used to produce other machines. In economic terms, there must be "savings," the creation of capital, with the result that the consumer's lot is not rapidly improved. The delay in the arrival of visible economic benefits to the average person can lead, particularly in the growing cities, to discontent and violence. /26

Thus, it seems likely that, in the absence of our bringing something new into the picture, the process of industrialization in the underdeveloped areas of the world will be characterized more by increasing numbers of people, by poverty and deprivation, than by a rapid improvement in the standards of living. /27

The vast network of mines, factories, and communication systems, upon which the industrialized part of the world has become dependent, is extremely sensitive to disruption. So interdependent are the components of the network that the sudden failure of but a relatively small section of it could result in a breakdown of the entire system. It is for this reason that machine civilization is probably far more vulnerable to disruption from nuclear attack than most persons suspect. For example, not many well-placed hydrogen bombs would be required to destroy the productive capacities of the larger world powers. Indeed it is quite possible that far more persons would die in the chaotic aftermath of a nuclear war as a result of the breakdown of the industrial network than would be killed directly by explosions. /28

As industrialization spreads, the world as a whole will become more vulnerable in this respect. At the same time as the years pass by, increasing numbers of nations will find themselves in a position to wage large-scale nuclear war. Hand in hand with industrialization goes the power of manufacturing the tools of war, including nuclear armaments. Thus, it would appear that the likelihood of disruption will increase steadily in the future—at least in the absence of some semblance of international order. /29

If industrial civilization were destroyed on a world-wide basis, there would be a very real question as to whether it could ever be started again. Our own civilization was made possible by an abundance of ores and other resources which could be easily tapped. As we have seen, these resources are disappearing and will one day vanish. As long as we maintain a high level of technology and an intact industrial network we can keep going for an indefinitely long period of time. But if there were a catastrophe, the technological requirements of getting started again might prove to be impossible to surmount. We are indeed approaching a "point of no return"—a point in time beyond which the machines of the world must continue to function, or industrial civilization will perish, possibly never to reappear. /30

The problems which face us in the years ahead are indeed both numerous and grave, but, theoretically at least, it seems likely that they can be solved by the proper application of our intelligence. For example, some of the dangers which confront us can be relieved by strengthening the international institutions which are designed to prevent war, such as the United Nations and its subsidiary organizations. Others can be minimized by concerted effort on the part of the present industrialized countries to enable the inevitable industrial transition of the underdeveloped areas to be made with minimum difficulty. This can be done in part by the transfer of machines and goods and in part by technical assistance. It can be promoted also by the development of new techniques in industry, agriculture, education, and birth control—techniques which have thus far not yet been developed in the industrialized areas because they have not been needed, but which would be of great value to developing countries. /31

It is in these areas that scientists and engineers can make contributions of considerable importance, first by creating an awareness among the world's people concerning the gravity of the dangers which lie ahead, and second by establishing collaborative programs aimed at anticipating and solving the problems we must face. /32

There are a number of approaches which might be used to encourage this collaboration. I believe that one of the more useful approaches would be establishing an International Institute of World Development, which would be staffed by physical, biological, and social scientists, and engineers. The Institute would be financed jointly by the participating nations and its services would be made available to all nations which are faced by development problems. /33

One can conceive of a variety of problems which might be studied profitably in such an institute. Generally speaking, these would be problems which are not at present receiving adequate attention in those areas of the world which are already industrialized, because they are not critical problems in those areas and, similarly, although these problems are of the greatest importance to the unindustrialized areas, they are receiving insufficient attention there because of the lack of adequate technical manpower and facilities. /34

A part of the effort in such an institute might be devoted to devising techniques of fertility control which might be applicable in specific unindustrialized areas, and studies of ways and means of spreading knowledge of these techniques. New methods of producing and preserving food might be devised. Other efforts might be placed on problems of solar energy utilization, the application of nuclear energy, the development of pumps and engines for special purposes, the reclamation of sea water, and special mining and metallurgical operations. Attention could be given to speeding up education in unindustrialized areas. Techniques of construc-

tion, transportation, and communication might be studied. /35

I believe that given a broad international base, such an institute could aid materially in world development, and although its operations would be expensive, the cost would be trivial when compared with the gains to be achieved. And, perhaps even more important, it could provide a precedent for broad international technological collaboration on a large scale in which science and technology are mobilized for constructive uses. /36

The speech

1. What is Brown's specific purpose here? Would you label it expository or argumentative? Defend your choice.
2. What pattern of organization do you find in the speech? Show each of the main divisions of the organization. Is the organization especially well suited to the speaker's purpose?
3. Brown does not suggest to his audience how the proposal for an International Institute of World Development can be implemented. Is this a weakness in the speech? Explain your answer.
4. Plot on paper the cause and result sequence that emerges from this speech.
5. Brown does not resort to anecdotes, humor, novelty, or other such devices to gain and keep the attention of his audience. Do you feel that he should have done so?
6. In what sense can it be said that there is an emotional appeal in this speech?
7. This is a rather short speech for treating so vast a problem. Is there too little support for the main propositions? In answering this, keep the audience in mind.
8. Tell how you would deliver a speech such as this.
9. Analyze the style, giving special attention to transitions, sentence structure, and diction. For what kinds of subjects would a style like this not be appropriate? Compare Brown's style with that of Urey.
10. Does Brown's description of the problem lead you to believe that his proposed solutions will be adequate?
11. In what way can it be said that Brown's speech is an extension of one aspect of Urey's?

For further study and discussion

1. In what ways do we have firm control over our physical environment? In what respects do we still lack control?
2. Why should the spread of industrialization to Asia and Africa seem inevitable?
3. Has the United States already seriously depleted one or more of its resources? Support your answer with as many facts as you have time to pull together.

4. Will the depletion of resources encourage or discourage war? Explain your view on this in detail.
5. What differences has the population explosion already made in the United States?
6. What new means of feeding the world's growing population could conceivably be developed in the next one hundred years?
7. Do you agree that industrial civilization as we know it could not be re-established if the present one were wiped out?
8. What obvious difficulties will face any organization attempting to work out and put into effect a plan for world development?
9. Do you feel that the future of our civilization rests primarily in the hands of the scientists and engineers? Explain your answer.
10. Discover what you can about the theories of Thomas R. Malthus (1766-1834), and compare them with the ideas of Harrison Brown.

Suggestions for further reading

John D. Bernal, *The Social Function of Science* (London, 1939)

Farrington Daniels and T. M. Smith, *The Challenge of Our Times* (Minneapolis, 1953)

Julian Huxley, *Science and Social Needs* (New York, 1935)

Frank Pirone, *Thinking Ahead of Communism* (Brentwood, N. Y., 1954)

Reflections on Our Age (New York, 1949). Lectures given at the opening session of UNESCO at the Sorbonne University of Paris.

Don K. Price, *Government and Science* (New York, 1954)

Glenn T. Seaborg, *Education and the Atom* (New York, 1964)

James Stockley, *Science Remakes Our World* (New York, 1946)

Science and spiritual values

JAMES B. CONANT

James B. Conant's recent study of high schools in the United States is known to all those who are interested in modern education. His career in education includes teaching chemistry at Harvard University, being chairman of Harvard's department of chemistry, and finally, serving as president of Harvard from 1933 to 1953.

From *Modern Science and Modern Man* by James B. Conant. Copyright 1952 by Columbia University Press.

After retiring from Harvard, Conant served as United States High Commissioner to Germany (1953-1955) and Ambassador Extraordinary and Plenipotentiary to the Federal Republic of Germany (1955-1957). His study of United States high schools was made in 1957-1958, under a grant from the Carnegie Foundation.

In addition to specialized studies in chemistry, Conant's published works include: *On Understanding Science* (1947), *Science and Common Sense* (1951), *The Citadel of Learning* (1956), *The American High School Today* (1959), *The Child, the Parent, and the State* (1959), *Slums and Suburbs* (1961). His work as scientist, writer and lecturer, educator, and public servant shows the scope of his achievement.

This lecture, given to a Columbia University audience in 1952, concluded a series of four lectures, the title of which was "Modern Science and Modern Man." Conant's explanation at the beginning of the first lecture indicates the general context of the series:

"When I was honored by the invitation to be the Bampton lecturer for 1952, President Eisenhower, then of Columbia, expressed on behalf of the committee the hope that I would undertake to provide some understanding of the significance of recent developments in the physical sciences.' On my inquiring as to the nature of the audience, I was assured that professional philosophers and scientists would be conspicuous by their absence. My exposition, if not aimed at the proverbial man-on-the-street, was to be directed to the equally proverbial college graduate—the hypothetical individual whom college presidents welcome each commencement to the fellowship of educated men. Being thus assured that I was not expected either to give an appraisal of the impact of physics on metaphysics or a technical account of the inner workings of the atom, I gratefully accepted the privilege of being a guest lecturer at Columbia University."

Conant offered the following statement of purpose for the four lectures:

"I propose to examine the cultural significance of what has been going on in science since, say, 1935. And by cultural' I have in mind the whole social pattern of Western civilization. I have in mind far more than the modes of production, distribution, and communication; I wish to include in my survey the impact of modern science on the philosophic presuppositions of the average enlightened citizen of a modern democracy—on his ambitions, his hopes, his fears, his outlook on the world. So in a sense I shall relate physics to philosophy, but only by handling both subjects in a general fashion and viewing each from the point of view of a deeply troubled modern man."[1]

[1] Quotations are from the published lectures: *Modern Science and Modern Man* (New York, 1952), pp. 3-5.

In my last lecture I explored the false antithesis between science and value judgments. Let me continue this exploration by examining the impact of science on one type of conduct that is associated with a moral judgment shared in common by many different cultural groups. A recurring phenomenon in history is the attempt of individuals to mitigate the physical suffering of others. In the Judaic-Christian tradition such attempts have been given a high status; they have been portrayed as examples of a conduct to be emulated. So much so that out of a hundred people picked at random here in New York, I would wager at least ninety would assert that helping the sick and suffering was "good" and that indifference or cruelty was "bad." Furthermore, a large majority would have demonstrated by their actions their adherence to this value judgment. The reasons for the judgment would cover a wide range, but whether expressed in dogmatic religious terms or related only to broad philosophic ideas, almost all of these come within the scope of what I am going to call "the realm of spiritual values." In one way or another it is implied or explicitly stated that an unselfish act is a good act; that quite apart from the social consequences to the individual performing the act, lending a hand to a sufferer is something a person ought to do. /1

Whatever may be the basis for our belief in the imperative, "Help the suffering," this precept can be an effective guide for conduct only insofar as one has power to alleviate such suffering. It need hardly be pointed out that the advance of the medical sciences has made possible the mitigation of many types of human misery to a degree undreamt of a few centuries ago. The present status of medicine and public health is the result of the efforts of thousands of scientists over the last three hundred years. Admittedly, many of these men were not motivated in the least by their concern with suffering humanity. Indeed, some were totally unaware of the fact that their work would throw light on the problems of the physician. On the other hand, in the last hundred years a great many investigators have been prompted by their desire to improve the ancient art of healing; not only physicians but chemists and biologists as well. /2

A conscious effort on the part of many investigators to control disease, to prolong life, and to alleviate pain has yielded results of a most dramatic nature. I should like to point out that the conduct of almost every individual who participated in this advance of science and progress in the art of healing was determined by a set of value judgments. These judgments were closely connected with the exhortation, "One ought to help the suffering." The conduct of doctors, we all know, is regulated by a set of ethical principles which in themselves are based on value judgments. What I am here emphasizing is the degree to which a judgment of value has determined the investigation of scientists or those seeking by empirical means to improve an art. Once again I make the point that those who say that science and value judgments are in separate compartments have failed to examine the nature of scientific undertakings and the motivation of many scientists. /3

Considering how much is now published about technical achievements in the way of atomic bombs, poison gas, even the possibility of bacteriological and radiological warfare, it is well to stop a moment and recognize what an army of men and women is now employed in helping sufferers by means of tools provided by modern science. This is something quite different from providing additional creature comforts, raising the standard of living, increasing the pleasures of either the mind or the flesh. Much of what our modern industrial civilization produces for the consumer can be branded as materialistic—the invention of the devil, some ascetic Christian fundamentalists would say. But strengthening the hand of the Good Samaritan is an entirely different matter. This consequence of science needs to be underlined. If loving your neighbor as yourself is the epitome of a religious outlook, it can only have meaning as a policy to the extent that one is able to help the neighbor when he or she is in pain or trouble. /4

As to relieving physical pain, there can be no doubt of the effectiveness of the advance of science. Whether a hundred years from now a similar statement will be possible about emotional and mental suffering, no one can say. The hope that this may be the case is surely one of the factors spurring on the efforts of those who study the behavior of human beings. Once again a value judgment is seen at work. /5

The whole idea that the practical arts can be improved by other than empirical procedures is relatively new, as I pointed out in my first lecture. As a firm conviction on the part of a number of influential citizens, this idea is a product of the seventeenth century. That the arts thus improved included the healing arts was inherent in the dreams of the proponents of the new experimental philosophy of that time; making these dreams come true has taken much longer than many of them imagined. On the other hand, all sorts of powers have been made available for transforming nature, for transportation, and for communication that could not have been imagined three hundred years ago. From the Renaissance on, there was an increasing stream of opinion in Christian countries to the effect that some of the sufferings of the human race could be relieved by human action. Utopias were depicted where not only did milk and honey flow, but disease was cured, pain removed. That the alleviation of physical distress would be not only desirable but also in the spirit of the Christian religion, only a few doubted. Those who did would be likely to turn to the Book of Job. /6

The problem of evil as set forth in the Book of Job is not the problem of evil conduct on the part of humans but the problem of why good men suffer grievous calamities. The problem is recurring; what one of us has not felt its bruising impact within the year? Of the answers given by Job's comforters, none suggested that some evils of the flesh could be overcome by human action. Yet this in essence seems to me the eighteenth century's rationalistic answer to Job's laments. It was an answer that ever since has been echoed by ardent supporters of the work of scientists. Forty years ago it was widely accepted by what are now called "liberal" Christians; in the last twenty years, doubts as to its validity have been expressed by certain Protestant leaders as well as Catholics. The liberal tradition, it is constantly asserted today, has been forced "by the wry advance of world events to adjust its large principles to the hard reality of things as they are." Of the world events, Hitler, Stalin, and the explosion of the atomic bomb are usually cited as examples. /7

If I read the Book of Job correctly, its lesson is a denial of the assumption that the universe is explicable in human terms; it is a corrective to the presumption of human beings in applying their standards of value to the cosmos. The Lord rebukes Job's three comforters for their attempt to persuade the sufferer that he must have sinned by arguing that otherwise he would not have been afflicted. The universe is not constructed along the lines of an automatic machine distributing rewards and punishments—at least not in this world of mortals. As to a future life, the Book of Job reflects the Judaic as contrasted to the Christian position; the New Testament answer to the problem of evil is largely absent in the Old Testament. And as to the exact meaning of that answer, Christians have been debating for nearly two thousand years. /8

Salvation by good works as opposed to salvation by faith, I shall not discuss. Rather I wish to stay within the setting of the Book of Job. The writer presents two answers, it seems to me, to the question of why men and women of the purest character may suffer the most hideous afflictions. The first is essentially that the universe is inexplicable. With almost a stoic resignation, Job accepts this fact and ceases to lament. This is the philosophic answer; the other is the spiritual one; it may be expressed in Job's own words. After the Lord had answered him out of the whirlwind, Job said, "I have heard of thee by the hearing of the ear; but now mine eye seeth thee. Wherefore I abhor myself, and repent in dust and ashes." /9

Taken literally, this passage means something very specific in theological terms to an orthodox Jew or fundamentalist Christian. Taken symbolically, it has deep spiritual meaning for those who interpret broadly the Judaic-Christian literature. I shall so regard it. Indeed, to those who ask, "What do you mean by the term 'spiritual values'?" I would reply by reference to this episode in the Book of Job. /10

To explain further what I have in mind, let me give one example of an evaluation that seems to me significant. People have undergone a spiritual enrichment as a consequence of their sufferings, I would say, if they have become less rebellious in their attitude towards the universe, less frightened of the future, more sympathetic towards other people; on the other hand, those who have become more embittered, more apprehensive, more hostile have suffered a spiritual deterioration. Such changes are only partially indicated by the verbal formulations of the individual in question; the state of a person's spirit is indicated far more by actions than by formal statements of a philosophy of life. Judgments of the type I have just mentioned seem to me to have meaning and to be concerned with a value we may well call spiritual. /11

The twofold answer of the Book of Job stands in sharp contradiction to the belligerent optimism of a typical nineteenth-century materialist. For such a person there was only one explanation of Job's afflictions—ignorance. Disease could be conquered if scientists kept at work and people were sensible enough to follow their advice; so, many an intelligent person maintained as early as the 1800's. And as a bit of prophecy, I submit, fewer statements by optimists have ever been more right. This needs to be emphasized in these days when prophets of gloom are so readily listened to on all sides. We have been triumphantly successful in our efforts to right the scales of apparent injustice in this vale of tears, at least as regards the ills of the flesh; and it was this type of affliction—Satan's touching "his bone and his flesh"—which finally moved Job to question God's justice. /12

But it is one thing to make great progress in curing or preventing disease and another to say that *all* the afflictions of man can be overcome by human intelligence. Yet this almost became the creed of those who, throughout the nineteenth century and well into this, proclaimed the coming salvation of man on this earth by the good works known as science! This outlook on the world has become embodied—one might almost say enshrined—in the set of doctrines known as dialectical materialism. One version of these doctrines is the official philosophy of the Kremlin and all those who obey its injunctions and slavishly follow its moods. Another version is, I believe, the accepted philosophy of the Communists of Yugoslavia; in less belligerent and doctrinaire form, the Russian version is accepted by some non-Communist Marxists in English-speaking countries. But in all its forms, it breathes that spirit of the mid-nineteenth century, which was carrying forward the rationalistic optimism of the eighteenth. /13

To the doctrinaire dialectical materialist, the Book of Job is worse than nonsense—it is an opiate of the people. His answer to the problem of all evil, to calamities of all sorts, is essentially as follows: Through science all evils may be overcome. By "science" he means science based on the doctrine of dialectical materialism, the laws that govern not only inanimate nature but the development of society as well. Of these laws, the recognition of the triad—thesis, antithesis, synthesis—as illustrated by the equation, heat plus ice equals water, is usually given prominence in popular expositions. /14

I do not propose to discuss the grim political consequences of accepting the Soviet interpretation of dialectical materialism. Philosophically the whole doctrine seems to me utter nonsense. It presents in the most dogmatic and extravagant form the optimism of those scientists who are interested in translating their discoveries into practical effects. It is a creed suited in a crude way to the scientist turned inventor, for it glorifies his role; more than that, it denies that the scientist ever was anything more than an inventor or ever could be. Indeed, this point of view has been widely publicized by some non-Marxists who to my mind have unwittingly swallowed a bit of the Communist bait! /15

I have purposely placed before you a false dichotomy—the Book of Job taken literally or dialectical materialism. I have already suggested, I hope, my own predilection; I would not repudiate the nineteenth-century optimism about the continued improvement, with the aid of science, of all the practical arts (including the art of human relations). I would not, however, subscribe to any "in principle" argument about what science can accomplish. I would be certain that for the next century, under the best conditions, the areas of uncertainty and empiricism[1] would remain enormous. As to the Book of Job, I would subscribe to the answer that the universe is essentially inexplicable and I would interpret Job's vision symbolically, using this as one entrance to the whole area of inquiry that can be designated as the universe of spiritual values. /16

Before proceeding further with an exposition of my own ideas about the relation of the realm of spiritual values to the universes of inquiry wherein, as practical men and scientists, human beings daily operate, let me remind you that many scientists interpret modern physics in a different light. To them, not only does the universe have a structure of which modern physical theory provides at least an approximate picture (though a very difficult one to explain, they must admit), but the history of this universe is also of significance. Here there is a cleavage among those who take seriously the map-maker analogy of my previous lectures. Some would adhere to a naturalistic evolutionary philosophy not too unlike that of certain nineteenth-century materialists. Others see in the new physics, and above all in the most recent cosmology, evidence for some form of theism quite compatible with the Judaic-Christian tradition. /17

I quote two recent authors to illustrate the latter trend in modern thought. Sir Edmund Whittaker in his *Space and Spirit*, written in 1946, expresses the opinion that "the achievement of mathematical physics is precisely this, that it has constructed a scheme of the universe which is trustworthy (that is, predictions based on it are always verified by experience), and which can be carried backward . . . to a time before the emergence of any sentient creature." After stating that "the line of descent of the modern physicist is to be traced not from the humanists of the Renaissance, but from the schoolmen of the

---

[1] The philosophically minded reader is reminded that I am using the word "empiricism" as defined on p. 23; see also p. 26. [On page 23, Conant says: "(And I am giving this quotation to define my use of the word 'empirical.') 'By this is meant the observation of facts apart from the principles which explain them, and which give the mind an intelligent mastery over them.'" On page 26, Conant states: "What is often defined as the scientific method is nothing more or less than an approximate description of a well-ordered, systematized empirical inquiry. Now, systematized or well-ordered, empirical inquiries are one element in the advance of science; the other element is the use of new concepts, new conceptual schemes that serve as working hypotheses on a grand scale."—[Editor's note]

twelfth and thirteenth centuries," he concludes his review of the theories of the universe and the arguments for the existence of God as follows: /18

"It cannot be denied, however, that natural theology is not an altogether straightforward matter to the inquirer who has been trained in the ways of modern science. The aim of the present work has been to indicate—for the consideration of theologians who are not men of science—what the obstacles are, and to show—for the consideration of the scientific inquirer—that they are less formidable than has sometimes been supposed, and moreover, that the deeper understanding of the nature of the material universe . . . has opened up new prospects and possibilities to the advocate of belief in God."[2] /19

Pascual Jordan in his *Physics of the Twentieth Century,* published in 1944, gives a clear exposition of those new ideas to which I referred briefly in my second lecture. He does not seek to escape the difficulties inherent in the altered picture; for example, he writes, "From a really modern standpoint the older idea of the atom must be regarded as just as much disproven as confirmed, since the corpuscular concept considers only one side of the picture, neglecting the other complementary side. If the quantum theory strips the atom of its clear tangible qualities and leaves only a framework of mathematical formulae for its characterization, our theory of knowledge attitude is confirmed again—physical research aims not to disclose a 'real existence' of things from 'behind' the appearance world, but rather to develop thought systems for the control of the appearance world." In spite of this and similar expressions which seem to place Jordan on the side of those who regard scientific theories as policies rather than creeds, his account of the modern ideas of cosmology is as definite as that of a geographer about a thoroughly explored island, for he writes: "It might well have been expected that the great sun were a much older inhabitant of the universe than the small earth expelled from it; but as we see, that is not the case at all. [He is referring to the data from radioactivity as to the age of the earth.] No less remarkable are the result of age determinations on meteors which likewise become possible through radioactivity investigations. . . . If we summarize our knowledge up to the present, we must say that we have found no body the age of which was shown to be higher than ten billion years. . . . Let us look back into the past; the world diameter, growing with the velocity of light, was formerly smaller than it is now; if we mentally pursue the development of the universe farther and farther back, we come to a point where everything is at an end, or rather, everything is at the beginning . . . ten billion years ago . . . the initially small universe arose from an original explosion." He concludes his book as follows: /20

"It is remarkable that modern natural research gives rise to knowledge and ideas which drive our feelings in such different directions from those of natural research from the times of Lamettrie to Haeckel. It is doubtless very justifiable for the author of a modern book on the mathematical theories of relativity and cosmology to pronounce at the conclusion that our scientific research on the future and past of the universe need not be influenced by human desires and hopes or by theological theories of creation. It is also characteristic that the state of development of our science suddenly makes such warnings necessary again. /21

"But when we pay just recognition to this warning, when we don't allow any motivation for our scientific research other than the inexorable striving after the knowledge of truth, who would hinder us *afterwards* from once dreaming about the results achieved? /22

"And certainly this picture of the universe as exploding fireworks which went off ten billion years ago invites us to consider the remarkable question of Miguel de Unamuno, whether the whole world—and we with it—be not possibly only a dream of God; whether prayer and ritual perhaps be nothing but attempts to make HIM more drowsy, so that HE does not awaken and stop our dreaming."[3] /23

I have referred to these two writers in order to do justice to one significant trend in the recent interpretations of the relation of modern science to the predicament of modern man. Time does not permit me to review the neo-Thomistic approach to the same subject; nor consider to what extent a faith in the ability of modern science to give a clear description of the structure and history of the universe will conflict with faith in the evidence presented in the New Testament, which, if taken literally, requires belief in lapses in the validity of the laws of the conservation of mass and energy. I have seen no attempt by fundamentalists, who might welcome the new cosmological theories as evidence for a creation and a creator, to handle the problem of the empty tomb in terms of any scientific conceptual scheme. /24

---

[2] *Space and Spirit* (Chicago: Henry Regnery Co., copyright 1948), pp. 128-29. Reprinted with permission of the publishers.

[3] Pascual Jordan, *Physics of the Twentieth Century* (New York: Philosophical Library, Inc., 1944). Reprinted with permission of the publishers.

My own inclinations lie in a totally different direction. Scientific theories are guides to the action of scientists which gradually become part of our common-sense ideas about the material universe. They have little or no bearing on the age-old problem of good and evil. I would attach meaning to Job's vision, but a symbolic meaning. Inquiries into the nature of this meaning would be inquiries about what I have called spiritual values. /25

The dialectical materialists and also some agnostics would question whether the universe of inquiry I have just postulated is more than a name for a mythology. They would relate all ethical behavior to the welfare of society or to an individual's adaptation to human relationships. Some sort of materialistic World Hypothesis would provide a unifying principle; there would be no place for any theistic interpretation. Almost certainly these people would maintain that advances in the social and biological sciences could eventually result in the final substitution of value judgments based on science for those now accepted as part of our Judaic-Christian tradition, that it would be possible some day for psychiatry, social psychology, biology, and anthropology to occupy this whole area of inquiry. Yet they would hardly challenge the statement that a vast number of value judgments today contain elements that have no connection with science. The question then appears to come down to this: Can those value judgments that do not now involve scientific concepts be replaced in principle by those that have originated in scientific investigations? /26

I have referred more than once in these lectures to this "in principle" argument and expressed my suspicion of it. To me, its use indicates an attempt by someone who is constructing a new hypothesis to overreach himself. I doubt if the employment of this type of argument has advanced the physical sciences, though it has often inflated the ego of some scientists. I doubt its applicability to the wider topic that I am attempting to explore; there is nothing to be gained by asserting that in principle all our common-sense ideas about the universe and human behavior, all our ethical principles, and our moral convictions could be replaced by "concepts growing out of experiment and observation." Even in the restricted area of the physical sciences there are huge spots where empiricism alone is the guide for the conduct of scientists as scientists. One can argue that for the sake of his morale a scientific investigator must believe that in principle all these spots can be eliminated. Possibly this may be true, but I doubt it. All that an ardent scientist has to believe is that

the lowering of the degree of empiricism can go on indefinitely, not infinitely; as a cautious investigator he should be wary of unnecessary and unwise extrapolations. /27

As to the unifying, materialistic World Hypothesis, my doubt stems from its manifest inadequacy. As a conceptual scheme attempting to account for everything in the whole universe, it seems to me unsatisfactory because it is incomplete. It fails to provide for the altruistic and idealistic side of human nature. It fails to accommodate what I regard as highly significant facts, not facts of science but facts of human history. These are the unselfish ways in which human beings often act with compassion, love, friendliness, self-sacrifice, the desire to mitigate human suffering. In short, it is the problem of "good," not "evil," that requires some other formulation of human personality than that provided by the usual naturalistic moralist. On the other hand, the formulations that attempt to include spiritual values, modern physics, biology, and cosmology within one total consistent scheme attempt, to my mind, far too much. Whether the unifying principle can be a dualism of matter and spirit, mechanism, formism, or some form of idealism, the whole attempt seems to me to be in the wrong direction. My preference would be for more adequate exploration of special limited areas of experience; one of these would include those experiences which can be ordered in terms of a system of spiritual values. /28

Each of these restricted areas of exploration I venture to designate a universe of inquiry. I do so only to underline my objection to those who insist on using the "in principle" argument to relate concepts in one set of inquiries to those used in another. Such insistence is, of course, almost second nature for those who regard a scientific theory as a creed or a map of at least a portion of the universe. But for those who regard scientific concepts and conceptual schemes as policies and guides for action, the need for an "in principle" consistency between inquiries in different areas disappears. If two policies in two areas (universes of inquiry, to use my phrase) can actually be brought into conflict as guides to action, then an observational or experimental test between them becomes possible. The conflict generates, so to speak, a series of limited working hypotheses, a chain of reasoning that finally eventuates in a hypothesis so restricted that a fairly clean-cut yes or no answer can be obtained. But if attempts to bring the two policies into conflict fail, as in the case of the corpuscular and wave theories of light, then one may say that the two theories are so dissimilar as to constitute incompatible universes of inquiry. In the case of physics, the possibility of this dissimilarity was denied for years by those who clung to the "in principle" type of argumentation. /29

How many universes of inquiry can be conveniently recognized today I would not care to state. For practical purposes two or more may be telescoped and treated as one by means of suitable postulates and sets of rules. In a sense, a unitary theory can be constructed to handle the dissimilarities of two universes of inquiry. This is what has occurred in modern physics, according to my reading of recent scientific history. When the highly limited working hypotheses in each area can be formulated quantitatively, then, by the use of mathematical reasoning, the unitary theory can be so stated as to be a very useful policy—so useful, in fact, that if its origins are not carefully traced, one can easily be deceived into thinking it represents a consistent map of one section of the universe. /30

Within the general field of the natural sciences, I suggest that those inquiries that involve the assumption of the uniformity of nature over long periods of time constitute a special universe of inquiry (or perhaps a group of such universes). To what degree the concepts used in paleontology, for example, must be in principle entirely consistent or compatible with those employed in biochemistry is for me an open question. Such questions arise, for example, whenever cosmologists, biologists, and chemists discuss the origin of life. Many of the so-called theories of the origin of life are not scientific theories at all in the sense of being guides to action. They are merely speculative ideas which no one now knows how to connect with new experiments or observations. On this point, by the way, the general public is apt to be much confused. People fail to distinguish between a new theory about the origin of life (or the origin of granite or of petroleum), which is merely one more speculative idea, and a theory from which flow new consequences that can be tested. Speculation in the field of cosmogony is not to be disparaged, but the wide publicity given to each new flight of fancy tends to confuse the general public and encourage credulity. /31

The point of view I have presented regards scientific theories as restricted policies, not parts of a unified cosmic creed. I am well aware that it can be attacked in the name of man as a rational being. It can be labeled defeatist, obscurantist,[4] or just a lazy man's way out of embarrassing difficulties. The adherents of a religious creed which sets forth in detail the origin, nature and destiny of man are almost sure to repudiate any view of the universe that is as provisional and fragmentary as the one I am suggesting. Materialistic atheists, interestingly enough, react in much the same fashion. Indeed, as witnesses for my defense I might call representative proponents of various unitary systems, including systems expressed in theological terms, and by cross-questioning show the diversity of their arguments. There would be no agreement among them, that much is clear. Another witness might be, of course, a modern physicist confronted with the ghost of his professional grandfather. On the consequences of such a confrontation I need not elaborate, for I have already pointed out that as regards particles and waves, the present picture would be regarded by the nineteenth-century physicists as the juxtaposition of two theories so dissimilar as to be in principle incompatible. /32

A view of the universe that rejects the necessity for a unified World Hypothesis consistent in principle throughout is not defeatist as regards the advance of science. For if one regards scientific theories as guides to investigations, each theory is continuously open to testing by experiment and observation. Such a view leads to suspicion of all assumptions carried over from one area of investigation to another. It represents a skeptical approach to all arguments divorced from actual observation or experimentation. It places the burden of proof on those who claim that *all* of a given set of concepts are, in practice as well as in principle, in the same universe of inquiry. There is nothing in such an outlook to discourage attempts to bring different scientific theories into close relation. On the contrary, since the compatibility of two theories can only be determined by the consequences of an apparent conflict and never can be assumed, the emphasis is on observation and experiment rather than on speculative thinking or abstract reasoning. /33

"The man of action has to believe, the inquirer has to doubt; the scientific investigator is both." This statement of Charles S. Peirce will serve to direct attention to the two fold purpose that many of our general ideas must fulfill. At least some of the concepts and conceptual schemes with which we as scientific investigators work must have a provisional status.

---

4 I doubt if believers in astrology, bizarre interpretations of astronomy, or modern necromancy will find any comfort in these lectures. A basically skeptical outlook, even if it denies the ability of science to provide a map of the structure of the universe, can hardly provide a platform for the superstitious. The extension of common-sense ideas by domesticated scientific concepts provides the framework of the modern world. The burden of proof is heavy on one who claims to have found a new effect contradicting accumulated practical experience.

They are working hypotheses on a grand scale, to use the terminology of a previous lecture. On the other hand, even in scientific investigations, some of the ideas that originated in the early advance of science must be regarded as having a more durable status. They must, that is, if progress is to be made. If a scientist attempted, every time he entered his laboratory, to retrace the steps in the development of the scientific theories he takes for granted, he would go mad. /34

When the scientist steps out of his laboratory and takes part in activities other than research, as a man of action he has to believe. The philosopher, whose profession it is to doubt, is under the same compulsion. All of us as sane individuals accept without a flicker of doubt a mass of concepts whose origin is obscure because they have been part of each of us as long as we can remember. As children, at least, we never doubted the reality of a three-dimensional world or the existence of other people. In other words, our degree of attachment to a certain set of ideas is so high as to constitute a belief. The reality of other people, of a solid world with a past and future, and of the partial uniformity of nature are thus matters of common-sense faith. Our degree of conviction as to the correctness of this faith is so great that I do not think anyone can question it in the sense that one questions the existence of a neutrino or even the germ theory of disease. To entertain the solipsist doctrine is not possible in the sense that it is possible for a beginner to consider the pros and cons of the caloric theory of heat. /35

Scientists have a degree of attachment to some scientific theories almost as great as that which all of us have for the concepts of a real world of rocks and trees and people. There is obviously no clear-cut line. Faith in the validity of the principles of physics and chemistry over billions of years and in the reality of a cosmic history is essential for an astronomer, a geologist, or a paleontologist. This is completely unnecessary and often lacking in a microbiologist or a nuclear physicist, to choose only two examples of scientists who are investigating immediate occurrences. An organic chemist's belief in the reality of atoms arranged in three-dimensional patterns in a molecule is usually almost as great as his belief in the existence of other people. But his predecessors of the nineteenth century held the same views to be highly provisional, it may be noted. And lest any one be tempted to generalize from this instance and say that the history of all science has been from provisional belief to faith, I would remind you of the discarded theories of phlogiston, the caloric fluid, the luminiferous ether, and the idea that the electron could be exactly located within a molecule. /36

As a man of action, each of us must not only manipulate a world of inanimate nature full of all sorts of plants and animals (including pathogenic bacteria), but also accommodate ourselves to other people. We must have not only common-sense concepts about a real world, but also some general principles about those entities we believe to be other personalities. We must deal as best we can with what William James has called "the whole paradoxical physico-moral-spiritual Fatness." Only as an inquirer, philosophical or scientific, can a man "single out some skinny fragment" of this Fatness. /37

For many people in the Western world the concepts that are particularly relevant to human intercourse are religious doctrines. For some, these are provisional beliefs; for others, ideas to which the degree of attachment is extremely high. This is particularly true for those who have grown up in an orthodox form of Christianity or have undergone a conversion of the type described by William James in his *Varieties of Religious Experience.* The parallel with the common-sense belief that other people exist and with the geologists' belief in a geologic past can hardly be denied. Therefore, I am not inclined to quarrel with those who say that a faith in the reality of the God of Calvin, or the God of Catholicism, or the Jehovah of Orthodox Judaism is the same sort of faith as faith in a real external world. But I would question the correctness of considering a belief in God which carries no consequences for the believer as parallel to a belief in the reality of other people which clearly carries some meaning for everyone, except perhaps the sole inhabitant of a desert isle. /38

Those people who have a high degree of attachment to the beliefs that are orthodox within a certain religion may well be said to have a firm conviction that their theology is not only right but also real. Others may have different degrees of faith in regard to various parts of the total doctrine. But in general, all those who adhere even loosely to a formal religious creed will wish to substitute the word "religious" for "spiritual" wherever I have used the term in this lecture. They would probably not agree that there is any separate universe of inquiry embracing religious values, for their theology would involve a unitary World Hypothesis; but as to the reality of what I have called the realm of spiritual values, they would have no doubt. /39

My concluding remarks will be addressed not to those whose theology is so certain as to be comparable with a belief in the reality of an external world. Nor will they be addressed to those whose picture of the universe leaves no room for spiritual values. Neither the Christian who interprets the Bible literally rather than symbolically nor the materialist will find any sense in what follows. But for the others I should like to suggest that in regard to many phenomena, we require, as men of action, at least provisional beliefs. These phenomena are open to scientific investigation, but until the degree of empiricism has been greatly lowered, we must operate with rules of conduct that are *not* based on science. This being so, I doubt if we can escape some attempt to put these rules into a conceptual scheme, however hazy. The evidence for the scheme is not affected one way or another by findings of the scientist, whether he be a physical scientist or social scientist. The evidence is based on personal experience and its prolongation by history. It is in the category of naive common-sense assumptions about a world of objects and persons. In the background of most people's thoughts there appears to be a World Hypothesis to portions of which, at least, they have a high degree of attachment. Just as I doubt our ability to think ourselves into the state of solipsism, so too I doubt the ability of most people to escape from some elements of a conceptual scheme which is keyed to human conduct, to moral principles or ethical rules, and to value judgments. Statements by an individual to the contrary are of little value as evidence against my generalization. We all know that actions speak far louder than words, and modern psychiatry has drawn attention to the number of mentally sick persons who seem to have difficulty in making decisions because of a conflict between their guides to action. /40

Among the common-sense ideas from which we cannot escape, even if we would, is our belief in the reality of other people. This conviction is the starting point for one set of ideas that are involved in making moral value judgments. We are convinced that except for minor differences, our close relatives are essentially like ourselves; they seem close duplicates in regard to what we call physical actions, thoughts, and feelings. We step both literally and figuratively on other people's toes; we hurt their feelings. This we know, because we have toes on which we can ourselves step and feelings that can be hurt. The attachment to this conviction about the close relation of ourselves to others is for most people extremely high and in origin similar to the other common-sense beliefs. It may be modified by sophistication, weakened by some types of argumentation, strengthened by some experiences. A test of the degree of attachment is suggested by the behavior of the Indian guide I mentioned in my last lecture. He vomited when he saw someone else do something that would have caused him to vomit himself. The phenomenon of nausea at the sight of human suffering is by no means rare. Such physical behavior is real testimony to the strength of the attachment of an individual to a point of view. The pain and distress of other people become to some degree our pain and distress. And except for mentally sick people, avoidance of personal pain and distress is as basic a postulate as acceptance of a three-dimensional world. /41

What are the minimal commitments required by a modern man to construct his philosophy of life if he be neither a religious dogmatist nor a materialistic atheist? What is the minimum number of postulates required to bring into some system the deeply imbedded assumptions about human conduct? These are questions which can hardly be answered except in terms of each individual's total experience. For if I am right, each person will have a different degree of attachment to those ideas which have been part of the Judaic-Christian tradition for generations. His rational construction of a conceptual scheme involving human beings will attempt to accommodate the presuppositions on which he really acts. Of these, his assumption of his close relation to other people, his almost physical identification with them, seems likely to be so basic as to be an essential element in a concordant scheme. For him to act as though cruelty were good in itself is no less difficult than to act as though cannibalism were good. If this be so, then a number of consequences follow that seem to lead back to the realm of spiritual values to which I have so often referred in this lecture. Time permits me to name but two. /42

The postulation of a sharp cleavage between animal behavior and human conduct seems essential in order to give meaning to the ideas expressed in terms of any system of spiritual evaluations. A further assumption following close on the first is that, as a minimum, the possibility may exist that our intentions and our overt actions have a relation to some large pattern of events. These would seem the minimal commitments for a modern man in the Judaic-Christian tradition who seeks to develop a philosophy of life without "jumping the fence" into the materialistic camp. /43

I am concerned here with the minimal commitments we seem to be driven to accept as practical men, not scientists. I am suggesting that these are imbedded in a man's total personality, much as are his beliefs in a real world, and that there is a minimal content of his ideas about what one ought and ought not to do not dissimilar to his ideas about what one ought or ought not to eat. This search is by definition a highly individual undertaking, and the results are not as uniform as those gained in the search for premises in the common-sense world of objects and other people. The results are more like the ingrained dietary beliefs to which I have already referred in these lectures. However, for people with a common cultural background, I think the basic postulates are more uniform in motivation than a verbal analysis might reveal. At all events, it seems to me worth while to attempt to formulate the minimal assumptions along the lines I have just suggested. That they represent far too small a commitment to satisfy most believing Christians, I readily admit. Yet the assumptions necessary to give meaning to the words "a universe of spiritual values" can be regarded as a common denominator among all religious faiths. /44

In this search for the minimal commitments, modern science can be of little or no service to modern man. Nevertheless, the benefits that flow from scientific investigations are by no means all material. Quite apart from what has been done to strengthen the hand of the Good Samaritan, science creates an atmosphere that encourages those who believe that man is not merely a social animal. The history of the last three hundred years is a record of accomplishment in the manipulation of ideas; it is a story of the flowering of the creative powers of the human mind. In the present period of reaction, in the shadow of fusion and fission bombs, we do well to stress this aspect of modern times. To have constructed a great fabric of new concepts and conceptual schemes arising from experiment and observation and fruitful beyond measure of new experiments is no small achievement. Like the Parthenon and the cathedrals of the Middle Ages, the scientific theories of the nineteenth and twentieth centuries stand as witnesses to what the human spirit can accomplish. With humility we recognize the vast oceans of our ignorance where empiricism alone can be our guide; yet we can set no limits to the future expansion of the "empire of the mind." A continued reduction in the degree of empiricism in our undertakings is both possible and of deep significance—this, in a few words, is the message that modern science brings to modern man. /45

The speech

1. What is the specific purpose of this lecture?
2. What does Conant mean by the terms *science* and *spiritual values*? How does he make his meaning clear? How does he feel each depends upon the other?
3. What two extreme interpretations of the Book of Job does Conant describe? Show how his own position lies between these two extremes. Comment upon the effectiveness of this kind of exposition. Does it result in argument that is largely implicit but nevertheless effective?
4. What does Conant mean by "World Hypothesis"? By "in principle" type of argumentation? What is his attitude toward each?
5. With examples of your own choosing, build up Conant's argument that the scientist must be both a believer and a doubter.
6. Trace the argument of the speech carefully. If possible, work it out graphically showing extreme and mean positions.
7. Does the conclusion involve what properly can be called an *action step*? (See Glossary.) If so, what action is called for? If not, what does the conclusion involve?
8. Characterize Conant's style.

For further study and discussion

1. Do you find that the scientists you know or have read are profoundly interested in spiritual values?
2. How do the dialectical materialists make use of science? Evaluate their use of it.
3. Has science given support to Christian beliefs and doctrines? If so, how?
4. Would you say that most modern scientists believe in God? In immortality? Cite examples to prove your point.
5. Why cannot Conant be called a religious dogmatist? A materialistic atheist? What label, if any, does seem appropriate for him? If you cannot think of an appropriate label, describe his religious position.
6. What do you find most provocative about the lecture for your own thinking? Give reasons for your choice.
7. How do you label yourself: an orthodox Christian? An orthodox Jew? A materialist? A skeptic? What? Justify the label you choose. If no label fits, tell why.
8. What conditions must obtain for personal immortality to be a reality?
9. Read the Book of Job. How do *you* interpret the story?
10. Read Archibald MacLeish's *JB*, a play based on the story of Job. What is MacLeish's interpretation of Job's suffering? Which of the interpretations put forth by Conant does MacLeish's most closely resemble?

11. Do you feel that science will ultimately, assuming that the race persists, fill in all the gaps in our information and understanding? Why or why not?

12. What minimum commitments have you made in constructing your philosophy of life? Explain each of them.

Suggestions for further reading

Jacques Barzun, *Science: the Glorious Entertainment* (New York, 1964)

P. W. Bridgman, *The Way Things Are* (Cambridge, Mass., 1959)

Arthur H. Compton, *The Human Meaning of Science* (Chapel Hill, N.C., 1940)

Julian Huxley, *Religion Without Revelation* (New York, 1957)

Pascual Jordan, *Physics in the Twentieth Century* (New York, 1944)

Charles E. Raven, *Science and the Christian Man* (London, 1952)

——————, *Science, Medicine, and Morals* (New York, 1959)

Bertrand Russell, *The Will to Doubt* (New York, 1958)

Edmund Whittaker, *Space and Spirit* (Chicago, 1948)

Mingled blood

RALPH ZIMMERMANN

"Mingled Blood" was composed and delivered by Ralph Zimmermann when he was a senior at Wisconsin State College, Eau Claire, Wisconsin. He presented the speech in the 1955 annual contests of the Interstate Oratorical Association, winning first place in the men's final contest. The following year, in March 1956, Zimmermann then a student at the School of Law, University of Wisconsin, died. The oration was published by the Interstate Oratorical Association, and the 1956 edition of *Winning Orations of the Interstate Oratorical Association* was dedicated to Mr. Zimmermann's memory.

The oration was also printed by The National Hemophilia Foundation, 175 Fifth Avenue, New York City. A prefatory note to this pamphlet states: "Ralph Zimmermann was one of the hemophiliacs who joined the Foundation in its earliest stages. The Foundation was able to furnish him with some help at the time he needed his first braces. We take pride in the fact that one of 'our boys' overcame so many obstacles to prove himself a credit to his family, his college and the Foundation. The oration speaks for itself and is, as many will recognize, a typical personal experience."

Reprinted by permission of the Interstate Oratorical Association.

A concluding note in the pamphlet says: "The author wishes to express his gratitude to Miss Grace Walsh, Chairman of the Forensic Department at Wisconsin State College at Eau Claire. Her understanding of the problem and her aid and encouragement were primary factors in making this oration a reality."

I am a hemophiliac. To many of you, that word signifies little or nothing. A few may pause a moment and then remember that it has something to do with bleeding. Probably none of you can appreciate the gigantic impact of what those words mean to me. /1

What is this thing called hemophilia? Webster defines it as "a tendency, usually hereditary, to profuse bleeding even from slight wounds." Dr. Armand J. Quick, Professor of Biochemistry at Marquette University and recognized world authority on this topic, defines it as "a prothrombin consumption time of 8 to 13 seconds." Normal time is 15 seconds. Now do you know what hemophilia is? /2

It is by no means a 20th century phenomenon. Ancient writings reveal the Jewish rabbis upon the death of first born sons from bleeding after circumcision, allowed the parents to dispense with this ceremony for any more sons. Family laws of ancient Egypt did not permit a woman to bear any more children if the first born should die of severe bleeding from a minor wound. How odd it seems to link the pyramids of the 4th dynasty with prothrombin consumption of 1955. /3

Hemophilia has had significant influence on the pages of history. Victoria, the queen of an empire on which the sun never set, was a transmitter of this dread ailment. Through her daughter, Alice, it was passed to the Russian royal family and Czarevitch Alexis, heir apparent to the throne of Nicholas II. Alexis, the hemophilic heir apparent, was so crippled by his ailment that the Bolshevik revolters had to carry him bodily to the cellar to execute him. And through Victoria's daughter, Beatrice, it was carried to the sons of the Spanish monarch, Alfonso XIII. While this good queen ruled her empire with an iron hand and unknowingly transmitted this mysterious affliction, my forebears, peasants of southern Germany, worked their fields, gave birth to their children, and buried their dead sons. Hemophilia shows no respect for class lines. It cares not whether your blood be red or blue. /4

For hemophilia is a hereditary disease. It afflicts only males, but paradoxically is transmitted only by females. The sons of a victim are not hemophiliacs, and do not pass it on. However, all of the daughters are transmitters. Of the transmitter daughter's children, half of the girls may be transmitters like their mother, and half of the sons may be hemophiliacs. Thus the net spreads out and on. Theoretically, it follows strict Mendelian principles. But because it is a recessive characteristic, it may lie dormant for generation after generation. As far back as my ancestral line can be traced, there is no evidence of hemophilia until my older brother Herbert and me. The same is true of 50 per cent of America's bleeders. /5

And there are many of us. Medical authorities estimate that there are some 20,000-40,000 hemophiliacs of all types in the United States. Clinically we divide into three groups: classic hemophilia AHG, and two other less common types of hemophilia, PTC and PTA. I am a classic hemophiliac—the real McCoy. /6

What does it really mean to be a hemophiliac? The first indication comes in early childhood when a small scratch may bleed for hours. By the time the hemophiliac reaches school age, he begins to suffer from internal bleeding into muscles, joints, the stomach, the kidneys. This latter type is far more serious, for external wounds can usually be stopped in minutes with topical thromboplastin or a pressure bandage. But internal bleeding can be checked only by changes in the blood by means of transfusion or plasma injections. If internal bleeding into a muscle or joint goes unchecked repeatedly, muscle contraction and bone deformity inevitably result. My crooked left arm, the built-up heel on my right shoe, and the full length brace on my left leg offer mute but undeniable testimony to that fact. Vocal evidence you hear; weak tongue muscles are likely to produce defective L and R sounds. /7

Childhood and early adolescence are the danger periods of a hemophiliac's life. As recently as November, 1950, *The Science Digest* reported that 85 per cent of all hemophiliacs die during that period. While the figure is exaggerated, it tends to indicate this salient point: if society can keep a hemophiliac alive until after adolescence, society has saved a member. During those years, society is given a responsibility it too often refuses to accept. /8

You might ask—but what can I do? What do you expect of me? The answer lies in the title of this oration: mingled blood. For all that boy needs is blood, blood, and more blood. Blood for transfusions, blood for fresh frozen plasma, blood for serum fractions. Not Red Cross Bank Blood, for stored blood loses its clot-producing factors. But fresh blood directly from you to him in a matter of hours. Your blood, dark and thick, rich with all the complex protein fractions that make for coagulation—mingled with the thin, weak, and deficient liquid that flows in his veins. Blood directly from you to the medical researcher for transformation into fresh frozen plasma or antihemophilic globulin. During those years, his very life is flowing in your veins. No synthetic substitute has been found—only fresh blood and its derivatives. /9

Because medical science had not advanced far enough, and fresh blood not given often enough, my memories of childhood and adolescence are memories of pain and heartbreak. I remember missing school for weeks and months at a stretch—of being very proud because I attended school once for four whole weeks without missing a single day. I remember the three long years when I couldn't even walk because repeated hemorrhages had twisted my ankles and knees to pretzel-like forms. I remember being pulled to school in a wagon while other boys rode their bikes, and being pushed to my table. I remember sitting in the dark empty classroom by myself during recess while the others went out in the sun to run and to play. And I remember the first terrible day at the big high school when I came on crutches and built-up shoes carrying my books in a sack around my neck. /10

But what I remember most of all is the pain. Medical authorities agree that a hemophilic joint hemorrhage is one of the most excruciating pains known to mankind. To concentrate a large amount of blood into a small compact area causes a pressure that words can never hope to describe. And how well I remember the endless pounding, squeezing pain. When you seemingly drown in your own perspiration, when your teeth ache from incessant clenching, when your tongue floats in your mouth and bombs explode back of your eyeballs; when darkness and light fuse into one hue of gray; when day becomes night and night becomes day—time stands still—and all that matters is that ugly pain. The scars of pain are not easily erased. /11

Once a hemophiliac successfully passes through the dangerous period, his need for blood steadily decreases and his health improves. The nightmare of youth is gradually hidden behind a protective curtain of objectivity that is seldom raised. In contrast to my childhood days, I can look back on more than three years of college with joy and a sense of achievement. I've had some good breaks. I've been in debate and forensics for four years and had a variety of satisfying experiences. I've been lucky in politics. My constituents, the student body at our college, elected me President of Student Government. Like so many other American youths, I've worked my way through college as a clerk in a hardware store. On warm weekends, while not a Ben Hogan at golf, I have shot an 82. And back home, a girl wears my wedding band. /12

For today, except for periodic transfusions, my life is as normal as anyone else's, and my aims and ambitions are the same as anyone else's. But now, a different type of social relationship needs to be found. Because a hemophiliac is so totally dependent on society during his early years and because his very existence is sometimes then precarious, society now tends to lag in recognizing the change. It sometimes fails to realize that this hemophiliac's life is no longer in serious question and that now his right to aspire to any new height should not be frowned on by a society still vividly remembering the past. Now, he seeks neither pity nor privilege. He wishes to be regarded not as a hemophiliac but rather a human being to be evaluated like any human being. /13

I cannot change that part of my life which is past. I cannot change my hemophilia. Therefore, I must ask you to help those hemophiliacs that need help. For I remember too well my older brother Herbert, so shattered in adolescence by hemophilia, that his tombstone reads like a blessing: "May 10, 1927–April 6, 1950, Thy Will be Done." And I ask you to help hemophiliacs because one day my grandson may need your blood. But I also must ask you to recognize a hemophiliac for what he is today; to realize that past is prologue, that weakness some-times begets strength; that man sometimes conquers. And so I pray: /14

"God give me the courage to accept the things that I cannot change; the power to change the things which I can; and the wisdom always to know the difference between the two." /15

For discussion

1. How does Zimmermann catch his listeners' attention immediately? And by what means does he hold it throughout?

2. Outline the speech, and characterize its pattern of organization.

3. What is gained by the historical sketch?

4. Note the careful transitions between paragraphs. Make a list of the various transitional devices used.

5. What senses are appealed to here? Describe carefully the effect that sensory or concrete details have that generalizations do not have, and account for this difference in effect.

6. What part of the speech is most moving for you, and why?

7. Describe carefully the nature of the proof used here. How does it differ, if it does, from the proof employed in most of the other speeches you have read in this volume?

8. Assuming that it was well delivered, why would a speech like this be even more moving when heard than when read? Tell in detail how you think it should be delivered.

9. Compare the style of this speech with the style of your own speeches. Is there anything you can learn from a style like this?

The man with the muck-rake
THEODORE ROOSEVELT

Theodore Roosevelt, twenty-sixth President of the United States, was born in New York City in 1858, graduated from Harvard College in 1880, and began a remarkably vigorous public life by winning election to the New York State Assembly in 1882. His rise in the councils of the Republican party was at first slow, for he associated himself with the reform wing of the organization. The Spanish-American War gave him opportunity to attract truly national attention, first as Assistant Secretary of the Navy and then as lieutenant colonel and leader of the famous cavalry group known as "Roosevelt's Rough Riders." Nomination and election to major public offices quickly followed. In November 1898 he was elected governor of New York; in 1900 he was nominated and elected Vice President of the United States on the Republican ticket headed by William McKinley. Upon McKinley's death in September 1901, Roosevelt succeeded to the Presidency. He was elected to the same office in 1904, retired in 1909, but re-entered politics in 1912 to seek the Presidency again, this time as the candidate of the Progressive party. The Democratic candidate, Woodrow Wilson, won the election of 1912, and Theodore Roosevelt withdrew from active public life. He died in 1919. During his busy political career he had also found time to engage in ranching, to establish some reputation as a naturalist, and to write extensively.

On the speaker's platform as elsewhere Roosevelt was energetic and enthusiastic. He "incessantly extolled some gospel, and in a manner distinctly homiletical."[1] "The Man with the Muck-Rake," of all his many addresses, was the speech "most attuned to the times and having the greatest impact on the culture of the period."[2] Its subject was an important one in 1906, and the address was eagerly awaited for several reasons. In March 1906 Roosevelt had given an informal, unreported speech on journalistic responsibility to the Washington Gridiron Club, an associa-

tion of newspaper men. The press understood that the President would later make a formal address on the same subject. When his son-in-law, Nicholas Longworth, told a Chicago audience on April 5 that journalistic attacks on public men had reached hysterical proportions, the public assumed Roosevelt's own attack on the press would be strong indeed. At least some journalists were uneasy. The editor of *Collier's Weekly*, one of the leading "muckraking" magazines, was moved to defend himself and his profession in advance of Roosevelt's speech. "Slight and necessary exaggerations" were inevitable "when any good work like this goes on," he told the Phillips Exeter alumni in New York on April 10.

The so-called muckrakers were journalists and publishers who had discovered that detailed exposures of malpractice in government and business sometimes contributed to reform and almost always built newspaper and magazine circulation. Some who made exposure their chief occupation aimed at producing legitimate historical studies: Ida Tarbell had bared the monopolistic and exploitive practices of the Standard Oil Trust with this hope in view. Some muckrakers were lifelong social and political reformers: Lincoln Steffens, Gustavus Meyers, Upton Sinclair. Others were simply sensationalists who had found a market for cynicism and innuendo. "What was new in muckraking . . . was neither its ideas nor its existence, but its reach—its nationwide character and its capacity to draw nationwide attention, the presence of mass muckraking media with national circulation and huge resources for research that went into exposure."[3] It was not the fact of muckraking but its intensity and pervasiveness that caused President Roosevelt to make it the subject of a major address.

Roosevelt chose as the occasion for his speech the ceremony at which the cornerstone was laid for a new House of Representatives Office Building in Washington. Here, on April 14, 1906, he undertook to define the responsibilities of critics using a mass medium of communication. Whether by accident or design, he incidentally dropped the hint that he favored federal income and inheritance taxes, and this small portion of the speech received more public attention than what he said about journalism. Whether he intended this immediate effect, we do not know. Four days after the speech the great San Francisco

From Maurice G. Fulton, ed., *Roosevelt's Writings*. Copyright 1920 by The Macmillan Company and used with their permission.

[1] Richard Murphy, "Theodore Roosevelt," in Marie K. Hochmuth, ed., *History and Criticism of American Public Address* (New York, 1955), Vol. III, p. 347.

[2] Ibid., p. 359.

[3] Richard Hofstader, *The Age of Reform* (New York, 1956), p. 186.

earthquake drove discussion of muckraking and income taxes from the press of the country; hence the immediate results of the speech are almost impossible to assess. Sensational muckraking did decline somewhat in the months that followed the speech, and the address has been read and reread in the years since its delivery. At least Roosevelt brought the dignity of his office to bear in behalf of fairness in the management of the media of mass communication. Because he dealt with a persistent problem of free societies, most of what he said is as relevant to our day as to his own.

Over a century ago Washington laid the corner-stone of the Capitol in what was then little more than a tract of wooded wilderness here beside the Potomac. We now find it necessary to provide by great additional buildings for the business of the Government. This growth in the need for the housing of the Government is but a proof and example of the way in which the Nation has grown and the sphere of action of the National Government has grown. We now administer the affairs of a Nation in which the extraordinary growth of population has been outstripped by the growth of wealth and the growth in complex interests. The natural problems that face us to-day are not such as they were in Washington's time, but the underlying facts of human nature are the same now as they were then. Under altered external form we war with the same tendencies toward evil that were evident in Washington's time, and are helped by the same tendencies for good. It is about some of these that I wish to say a word to-day. /1

In Bunyan's "Pilgrim's Progress" you may recall the description of the Man with the Muck-rake, the man who could look no way but downward, with the muck-rake in his hand; who was offered a celestial crown for his muck-rake, but who would neither look up nor regard the crown he was offered, but continued to rake to himself the filth of the floor.* /2

In "Pilgrim's Progress" the Man with the Muck-rake is set forth as the example of him whose vision is fixed on carnal instead of on spiritual things. Yet he also typifies the man who in this life consistently refuses to see aught that is lofty, and fixes his eyes with solemn intentness only on that which is vile and debasing. Now, it is very necessary that we

should not flinch from seeing what is vile and debasing. There is filth on the floor, and it must be scraped up with the muck-rake; and there are times and places where this service is the most needed of all the services that can be performed. But the man who never does anything else, who never thinks or speaks or writes save of his feats with the muck-rake, speedily becomes, not a help to society, not an incitement to good, but one of the most potent forces for evil. /3

There are, in the body politic, economic, and social, many and grave evils, and there is urgent necessity for the sternest war upon them. There should be relentless exposure of and attack upon every evil man, whether politician or business man, every evil practice, whether in politics, in business, or in social life. I hail as a benefactor every writer or speaker, every man who, on the platform, or in book, magazine, or newspaper, with merciless severity makes such attack, provided always that he in his turn remembers that the attack is of use only if it is absolutely truthful. The liar is no whit better than the thief, and if his mendacity takes the form of slander, he may be worse than most thieves. It puts a premium upon knavery untruthfully to attack an honest man, or even with hysterical exaggeration to assail a bad man with untruth. An epidemic of indiscriminate assault upon character does no good, but very great harm. The soul of every scoundrel is gladdened whenever an honest man is assailed, or even when a scoundrel is untruthfully assailed. /4

Now, it is easy to twist out of shape what I have just said, easy to affect to misunderstand it, and, if it is slurred over in repetition, not difficult really to misunderstand it. Some persons are sincerely incapable of understanding that to denounce mud-slinging does not mean the indorsement of white-washing; and both the interested individuals who need whitewashing, and those others who practice mud-slinging, like to encourage such confusion of ideas. One of the chief counts against those who make indiscriminate assault upon men in business or men in public life is that they invite a reaction which is sure to tell powerfully in favor of the unscrupulous scoundrel who really ought to be attacked, who ought to be exposed, who ought, if possible, to be put in the penitentiary. If Aristides* is praised overmuch as just, people get tired of hearing it; and overcensure of the unjust finally and from similar reasons results in their favor. /5

*See the Second Part of John Bunyan's famous allegory, *The Pilgrim's Progress.* Roosevelt preserved much of Bunyan's language in his paraphrases of the original description. *(Editor's note)*

*Athenian statesman and general, also called Aristides the Just. *(Editor's note)*

Any excess is almost sure to invite a reaction; and, unfortunately, the reaction, instead of taking the form of punishment of those guilty of the excess, is very apt to take the form either of punishment of the unoffending or of giving immunity, and even strength, to offenders. The effort to make financial or political profit out of the destruction of character can only result in public calamity. Gross and reckless assaults on character, whether on the stump or in newspaper, magazine, or book, create a morbid and vicious public sentiment, and at the same time act as a profound deterrent to able men of normal sensitiveness and tend to prevent them from entering the public service at any price. As an instance in point, I may mention that one serious difficulty encountered in getting the right type of men to dig the Panama Canal* is the certainty that they will be exposed, both without, and, I am sorry to say, sometimes, within, Congress, to utterly reckless assaults on their character and capacity. /6

At the risk of repetition let me say again that my plea is, not for immunity to but for the most unsparing exposure of the politician who betrays his trust, of the big business man who makes or spends his fortune in illegitimate or corrupt ways. There should be a resolute effort to hunt every such man out of the position he has disgraced. Expose the crime, and hunt down the criminal; but remember that even in the case of crime, if it is attacked in sensational, lurid, and untruthful fashion, the attack may do more damage to the public mind than the crime itself. It is because I feel that there should be no rest in the endless war against the forces of evil that I ask that the war be conducted with sanity as well as with resolution. The men with the muck-rakes are often indispensable to the well-being of society; but only if they know when to stop raking the muck, and to look upward to the celestial crown above them, to the crown of worthy endeavor. There are beautiful things above and round about them; and if they gradually grow to feel that the whole world is nothing but muck, their power of usefulness is gone. If the whole picture is painted black, there remains no hue whereby to single out the rascals for distinction from their fellows. Such painting finally induces a kind of moral color-blindness; and people affected by it come to the conclusion that no man is really black, and no man really white, but that all are gray. In other words, they believe neither in the truth of the attack, nor in the honesty of the man who is attacked; they grow as suspicious of the accusation as of the offense; it becomes well-nigh hopeless to stir them either to wrath against wrongdoing or to enthusiasm for what is right; and such a mental attitude in the public gives hope to every knave, and is the despair of honest men. /7

To assail the great and admitted evils of our political and industrial life with such crude and sweeping generalizations as to include decent men in the general condemnation means the searing of the public conscience. There results a general attitude either of cynical belief in and indifference to public corruption or else of a distrustful inability to discriminate between the good and the bad. Either attitude is fraught with untold damage to the country as a whole. The fool who has not sense to discriminate between what is good and what is bad is well-nigh as dangerous as the man who does discriminate and yet chooses the bad. There is nothing more distressing to every good patriot, to every good American, than the hard, scoffing spirit which treats the allegation of dishonesty in a public man as a cause for laughter. Such laughter is worse than the crackling of thorns under a pot,* for it denotes not merely the vacant mind, but the heart in which high emotions have been choked before they could grow to fruition. /8

There is any amount of good in the world, and there never was a time when loftier and more disinterested work for the betterment of mankind was being done than now. The forces that tend for evil are great and terrible but the forces of truth and love and courage and honesty and generosity and sympathy are also stronger than ever before. It is a foolish and timid, no less than a wicked thing, to blink the fact that the forces of evil are strong, but it is even worse to fail to take into account the strength of the forces that tell for good. Hysterical sensationalism is the very poorest weapon wherewith to fight for lasting righteousness. The men who, with stern sobriety and truth, assail the many evils of our time, whether in the public press, or in magazines, or in books, are the leaders and allies of all engaged in the work for social and political betterment. But if they give good reason for distrust of what they say, if they chill the ardor of those who demand truth as a primary virtue, they thereby betray the good cause, and play into the hands of the

---

*In 1906 construction of the Panama Canal was an exciting and problematical enterprise. Disease control was a paramount problem, and almost seven years of work lay ahead. (Editor's note)

*"It is better to hear the rebuke of the wise than for a man to hear the song of fools. For as the crackling of thorns under a pot, so is the laughter of the fool: this is also vanity." (Ecclesiastes 7:5-6) The allusion hinges on the fact that thorns burn up too quickly to provide much useful heat. (Editor's note)

very men against whom they are nominally at war. /9

In his "Ecclesiastical Polity" that fine old Elizabethan divine, Bishop Hooker,* wrote:

"He that goeth about to persuade a multitude that they are not so well governed as they ought to be shall never want attentive and favorable hearers, because they know the manifold defects whereunto every kind of regimen is subject; but the secret lets and difficulties, which in public proceedings are innumerable and inevitable, they have not ordinarily the judgment to consider." /10

This truth should be kept constantly in mind by every free people desiring to preserve the sanity and poise indispensable to the permanent success of self-government. Yet, on the other hand, it is vital not to permit this spirit of sanity and self-command to degenerate into mere mental stagnation. Bad though a state of hysterical excitement is, and evil though the results are which come from the violent oscillations such excitement invariably produces, yet a sodden acquiescence in evil is even worse. At this moment we are passing through a period of great unrest—social, political, and industrial unrest. It is of the utmost importance for our future that this should prove to be not the unrest of mere rebelliousness against life, of mere dissatisfaction with the inevitable inequality of conditions, but the unrest of a resolute and eager ambition to secure the betterment of the individual and the Nation. So far as this movement of agitation throughout the country takes the form of a fierce discontent with evil, of a determination to punish the authors of evil, whether in industry or politics, the feeling is to be heartily welcomed as a sign of healthy life. /11

If, on the other hand, it turns into a mere crusade of appetite against appetite, a contest between the brutal greed of the "have-nots" and the brutal greed of the "haves," then it has no significance for good, but only for evil. If it seeks to establish a line of cleavage, not along the line which divides good men from bad, but along that other line, running at right angles thereto, which divides those who are well off from those who are less well off, then it will be fraught with immeasurable harm to the body politic. /12

We can no more and no less afford to condone evil in the man of capital than evil in the man of no capital. The wealthy man who exults because there is a failure of justice in the effort to bring some trust magnate to an account for his misdeeds is as bad as, and no worse than, the so-called labor leader who clamorously strives to excite a foul class feeling on behalf of some other labor leader who is implicated in murder. One attitude is as bad as the other and no worse; in each case the accused is entitled to exact justice; and in neither case is there need of action by others which can be construed into an expression of sympathy for crime.* There is nothing more antisocial in a democratic republic like ours than such vicious class-consciousness. The multi-millionaires who band together to prevent the enactment of proper laws for the supervision of the use of wealth, or to assail those who resolutely enforce such laws, or to exercise a hidden influence upon the political destinies of parties or individuals in their own personal interest, are a menace to the whole community; and a menace at least as great is offered by those laboring men who band together to defy the law, and by their openly used influence to coerce law-upholding public officials. The apologists for either class of offenders are themselves enemies of good citizenship; and incidentally they are also, to a peculiar degree, the enemies of every honest-dealing corporation and every law-abiding labor union. /13

It is a prime necessity that if the present unrest is to result in permanent good the emotion shall be translated into action, and that the action shall be marked by honesty, sanity, and self-restraint. There is mighty little good in a mere spasm of reform. The reform that counts is that which comes through steady, continuous growth; violent emotionalism leads to exhaustion. /14

It is important to this people to grapple with the problems connected with the amassing of enormous fortunes, and the use of those fortunes, both corporate and individual, in business. We should discriminate in the sharpest way between fortunes well won and fortunes ill won; between those gained as an incident to performing great services to the community as a whole, and those gained in evil fashion by keeping just within the limits of mere law-honesty. Of course no matter of charity in spending such fortunes in any way compensates for misconduct in making them. As a matter of personal conviction, and without pretending to discuss the details or formulate the system, I feel that we shall ultimately have to consider the adoption of some such scheme as that of a progressive tax on all fortunes, beyond a

---

*Richard Hooker (1554?-1600), an English theologian. The work to which Roosevelt refers is *The Laws of Ecclesiastical Polity*. (Editor's note)

*The final sentences of this paragraph appear to have been added when the text was prepared for publication. (Editor's note)

certain amount, either given in life or devised or bequeathed upon death to any individual—a tax so framed as to put it out of the power of the owner of one of these enormous fortunes to hand on more than a certain amount to any one individual; the tax, of course, to be imposed by the National and not the State Government. Such taxation should, of course, be aimed merely at the inheritance or transmission in their entirety of those fortunes swollen beyond all healthy limits.* /15

Again, the National Government must in some form exercise supervision over corporations engaged in interstate business—and all large corporations are engaged in interstate business—whether by license or otherwise, so as to permit us to deal with the far-reaching evils of over-capitalization. This year we are making a beginning in the direction of serious effort to settle some of these economic problems by the railway rate legislation. Such legislation, if so framed, as I am sure it will be, as to secure definite and tangible results, will amount to something of itself; and it will amount to a great deal more in so far as it is taken as a first step in the direction of a policy of superintendence and control over corporate wealth engaged in interstate commerce, this superintendence and control not to be exercised in a spirit of malevolence toward the men who have created the wealth, but with the firm purpose both to do justice to them and to see that they in their turn do justice to the public at large. /16

The first requisite in the public servants who are to deal in this shape with corporations, whether as legislators or as executives, is honesty. This honesty can be no respecter of persons. There can be no such thing as unilateral honesty. The danger is not really from corrupt corporations: it springs from the corruption itself, whether exercised for or against corporations. /17

The eighth commandment reads, "Thou shalt not steal." It does not read, "Thou shalt not steal from the rich man." It does not read, "Thou shalt not steal from the poor man." It reads simply and plainly, "Thou shalt not steal." No good whatever will come from that warped and mock morality which denounces the misdeeds of men of wealth and forgets the misdeeds practiced at their expense; which denounces bribery, but blinds itself to blackmail; which foams with rage if a corporation secures favors by improper methods, and merely leers with hideous mirth if the corporation is itself wronged. The only public serv-

ant who can be trusted honestly to protect the rights of the public against the misdeeds of a corporation is that public man who will just as surely protect the corporation itself from wrongful aggression. If a public man is willing to yield to popular clamor and do wrong to the men of wealth or to rich corporations, it may be set down as certain that if the opportunity comes he will secretly and furtively do wrong to the public in the interest of a corporation. /18

But, in addition to honesty, we need sanity. No honesty will make a public man useful if that man is timid or foolish, if he is a hot-headed zealot or an impracticable visionary. As we strive for reform we find that it is not at all merely the case of a long up-hill pull. On the contrary, there is almost as much of breeching work as of collar work; to depend only on traces means that there will soon be a runaway and an upset. The men of wealth who to-day are trying to prevent the regulation and control of their business in the interest of the public by the proper Government authorities will not succeed, in my judgment, in checking the progress of the movement. But if they did succeed they would find that they had sown the wind and would surely reap the whirlwind, for they would ultimately provoke the violent excesses which accompany a reform coming by convulsion instead of by steady and natural growth. /19

On the other hand, the wild preachers of unrest and discontent, the wild agitators against the entire existing order, the men who act crookedly, whether because of sinister design or from mere puzzle-headedness, the men who preach destruction without proposing any substitute for what they intend to destroy, or who propose a substitute which would be far worse than the existing evils—all these men are the most dangerous opponents of real reform. If they get their way, they will lead the people into a deeper pit than any into which they could fall under the present system. If they fail to get their way, they will still do incalculable harm by provoking the kind of reaction which, in its revolt against the senseless evil of their teaching, would enthrone more securely than ever the very evils which their misguided followers believe they are attacking. /20

More important than aught else is the development of the broadcast sympathy of man for man. The welfare of the wage-worker, the welfare of the tiller of the soil—upon this depends the welfare of the entire country; their good is not to be sought in pulling down others; but their good must be the prime object of all our statesmanship. /21

Materially we must strive to secure a broader economic opportunity for all men, so that each shall

---

*These remarks and Roosevelt's implied threat of interstate commerce regulations in the next paragraph were heatedly discussed after this address. (Editor's note)

have a better chance to show the stuff of which he is made. Spiritually and ethically we must strive to bring about clean living and right thinking. We appreciate that the things of the body are important; but we appreciate also that the things of the soul are immeasurably more important. The foundation stone of national life is, and ever must be, the high individual character of the average citizen. /22

The speech

1. What *pattern of organization* (see Glossary) did Roosevelt use in developing the body of his speech?

2. It has been said that Roosevelt relied surprisingly little on fact or specific information to support the main headings and subheadings of his speeches. Is that true of this speech? What kinds of supporting material are used?

3. One way to test the generalization that Roosevelt "incessantly extolled some gospel" would be to discover whether the supporting materials he used in this speech are like those you would expect to find in a sermon or inspirational speech. Are they? Illustrate.

4. It has been said of Roosevelt's speeches that: "They are essayish in that they are spun around the mood that was upon him whether of moral righteousness, patriotism, or preparedness." How accurately does this description suit "The Man with the Muck-Rake"?

5. Theodore Roosevelt was widely admired for his ability to use colorful and memorable metaphors or labels to express abstract ideas. What terms, other than "muck-raker," can you find in his address?

6. It has been said that Roosevelt's management of sentences, phrases, and words, rather than his management of reasoning and logical arrangement, gave strength to his speaking. Is this true of "The Man with the Muck-Rake"? Support your answer.

7. What portion of the speech do you consider to be the conclusion? Does it fulfill the functions of a good conclusion for this speech and speaker?

8. Theodore Roosevelt was reputed to have formulated his public statements with care. Identify several points in this speech where great pains seem to have been taken to avoid vagueness and possible misunderstanding.

9. What reasons, other than impulse or poor planning, might have led Roosevelt to include his controversial reference to income and inheritance taxes in a speech ostensibly about journalism?

For further study and discussion

1. Robert M. Hutchins, as Chairman of the Fund for the Republic, proposed in 1955 that an independent Commission on the Freedom of the Press should be established "to appraise and report annually upon the performance of the press" in the United States. Hutchins felt such a Commission could bring pressure on the press to devote more attention to "enlightening the public about current events." Would such an agency be useful today? How might it improve modern journalistic practices?

2. Explore *McClure's* magazine for January 1903 or some of the other muckraking magazines such as *Pearson's* or *Collier's Weekly* in the period just prior to Roosevelt's speech. Do you find his criticisms of these publications accurate and just?

3. Should government license and regulate newspapers and magazines (as Roosevelt tentatively suggested) in the manner by which radio and television are licensed and regulated? Why have we never regulated the press but always regulated broadcasting?

4. Do we need stronger libel laws or other legislation to protect individuals against unfounded criticisms published through our mass media of communication?

5. Explore Great Britain's legislation covering the reporting of criminal cases. Is their system or ours the wiser? Why?

6. What is a responsible journalist's duty? To report facts without interpretation? To interpret the news with a view to enlightening the public? To function as a political or social critic?

7. Is there any evidence that highly publicized legislative and journalistic investigations are discouraging qualified persons from serving in government today?

8. Do you think business receives fair treatment in the press today? Labor? Government officials?

9. Some have said that the federal regulation of railways, inaugurated under Theodore Roosevelt, has outlived its usefulness. What support or refutation can you find for this view?

10. What advances, if any, have we made since 1906 toward establishing truly equal justice before the law for rich and poor alike?

Suggestions for further reading

Edwin Emery, *The Press and America,* 2nd ed. (Englewood Cliffs, N.J., 1962)

Leonard W. Levy, *Legacy of Suppression* (Cambridge, Mass., 1960)

John Milton, *Areopagitica,* ed. by J. W. Hales (Oxford, 1917)

Frank L. Mott, *American Journalism,* 3rd rev. ed. (New York, 1962)

Arthur E. Rowse, *Slanted News* (Boston, 1957)

Frederick S. Siebert, Theodore Peterson, and Wilbur Schramm, *Four Theories of the Press* (Urbana, Ill., 1963)

Harvey Swados, ed., *Years of Conscience: The Muckrakers,* Meridian M129 (Cleveland, 1962)

Bernard A. Weisberger, *American Newspaperman* (Chicago, 1961)

Newspapers of the U.S.A. —an appraisal

W. SPRAGUE HOLDEN

The International Association of Torch Clubs was founded in 1924 to encourage members of the various learned professions to broaden their public and cultural awareness by sharing their knowledge with one another. Speeches by the members are a prominent feature of the meetings. Since the clubs are nonpartisan and do not associate themselves with causes, these speeches are usually on topics connected with the speaker's profession or avocation. Thus the speaking situation is one in which a specialist undertakes to inform nonspecialists concerning interesting or significant features of his subject.

The following speech, which was delivered to the members of the Detroit Torch Club on May 14, 1964, was such an address. The speaker, W. Sprague Holden, an experienced journalist, is Professor of Journalism and Chairman of the Department of Journalism at Wayne State University, Detroit. His speech should be read as an effort to enlighten and interest nonjournalists in American journalism. It is a popular address on a professional subject.

Holden was born in Grand Rapids, Michigan, in 1909. He received the A.B. degree from the University of Michigan (1930), where he also received the senior class rhetoric medal; and he was awarded the A.M. degree by Columbia University (1932). From 1926-1946, he held a variety of reportorial and editorial assignments with newspapers and news magazines, among them *Time,* the Akron (Ohio) *Beacon Journal,* and the Detroit *Free Press.* In 1956-1957, Holden was awarded a Fulbright grant to study Australian daily metropolitan newspapers. His *Australia Goes to Press,* published in 1961, is based on this research.

Professor Holden counts among his most important lessons in public speaking the following "revelations," which came to him on the occasion of his first public speech: "(1) The audience was neither Mass nor Monster. It was composed of individual humans. If I talked with them individually, I wouldn't be afraid; I would think nothing of it. (2) They weren't hostile. They weren't waiting to jeer at my first fluff. They *wanted* me to get what I had to say across to them. (3) If I talked

to the man way up there in the last row center of the balcony—if I could make him hear me—then everyone else would be able to hear me."*

The address that follows was published in edited and condensed form in *The Torch,* January 1965; the text appearing here reproduces the actual manuscript from which Professor Holden spoke.

Gentlemen of Torch:

My subject tonight is so big that I am going to start out by stating the limits I have set upon it. /1

First I shall give you a bit of history and a few statistics, to set the foundation. Then I shall discuss some of the principal functions of a free press in a democracy. After that, I shall talk about some of the huge problems that face the press. Then I shall deal with some of the principal criticisms of the press. Finally, I shall try to do a little crystal ball gazing and talk about the future. /2

I confine myself to these few points in order to resist the temptation of talking too long, or of talking too long about any one of my subtopics. /3

I shall speak tonight only of the *daily newspaper* of *general-interest.* It is the kind with which you are most familiar. But let me suggest that the word *newspaper* today covers far more in meaning than it used to cover, and that no viable newspaper that speaks to an audience, however small or however specialized in our democracy, is without importance. /4

We have weekly general-interest, daily special-interest (*Legal News, Women's Wear*), metropolitan-area, suburban and country weeklies of general-interest, labor, religious, ethnic-group, trade, professional and heaven knows how many other kinds of newspapers of special or particular interest. I am excluding them all, except for perhaps side references. /5

What *is* the general-interest daily newspaper press of the United States? /6

It is made up of 1,754 units,[1] dividing into 311 morning and 1,453 afternoon newspapers. Last year, despite the 114-day New York strike and the long Cleveland strike, plus a few others, these 1,754 published a daily total of almost 59 million separate

---

*From W. Sprague Holden, "The Man with the Jug-Handle Ears."
[1] Three hundred eleven plus 1,453 equals, of course, 1,764, not 1,754. The reason for the discrepancy is that ten U.S. dailies are published around the clock. They are rated as single papers, as to name and ownership, but as two papers in the morning and evening dailies totals.

newspapers—and that does not include Sunday papers, for these are six-day publication figures. Four dailies were begun in 1963. Fifty-nine million is one paper for every 3.2 population. /7

Daily newspapers vary greatly in size, in amounts of circulation and advertising, in format, concept, appearance and tone. The largest in circulation in the U.S. is the New York *Daily News* with more than two million copies per day. I can't tell you the name of the smallest, but there are some newspapers in Michigan of not much more than 3,000 circulation and they are doing pretty well. /8

What about Michigan? /9

In our state we have 53 daily newspapers. Only one of them is a morning newspaper—The Detroit *Free Press.* Michigan lost its only other morning paper when the Grand Rapids *Herald* was purchased by the Booth Newspapers a few years ago and then quietly terminated. By the rule-of-thumb definition of a metropolitan newspaper—daily circulation of 100,000 or more—we have in Michigan only four that qualify: Detroit *News* (703,000), Detroit *Free Press* (590,000), Grand Rapids *Press* (126,000) and the Flint *Journal* (98,000). The Detroit *Times* was also a metropolitan paper until its death in 1960. /10

We have one large chain operation in Michigan—the Booth Newspapers with nine units—Ann Arbor *News,* Bay City *Times,* Flint *Journal,* Grand Rapids *Press,* Jackson *Citizen Patriot,* Kalamazoo *Gazette,* Muskegon *Chronicle,* Saginaw *News* and Ypsilanti *Press.* Federated Newspapers has two papers in Michigan—Battle Creek *Enquirer and News,* and Lansing *State Journal* (it used to have three in Michigan, with the Grand Rapids *Herald*), and one or two outside the state. There are some associated ownerships. Detroit is the only Michigan city with more than one daily paper. Grand Rapids was the next to the last to have two. /11

Michigan's weekly newspapers swell the state total greatly. Michigan has upwards of 300 weeklies of general-interest. The figure is difficult to determine exactly, because some papers in metropolitan areas publish different editions for different circulation areas, changing only a few pages and using different names. Here in Detroit one company has nine different weekly papers of this nature. Another complication is the free-circulation paper. These don't get listed in the standard annuals of Michigan Press, American Newspaper Representatives and N. W. Ayers; yet they are often bigger than the paid-circulation weeklies. The Mellus newspapers downriver are an example. /12

The nation's dailies have shrunk from a high of 2,200 in 1910 to today's 1,754, but total circulation has steadily mounted with the population's increase. The shrinkage has increased the monopoly phase of the industry. As of 1962, only 155 newspapers were in competition; and with the recent demise of a big daily in Texas, only three cities in the U.S. had competing ownerships in the morning and evening fields. One more figure: There are 550 Sunday papers with total circulation of 47,000,000. Most are adjuncts to dailies, as you know. /13

So much for statistics. /14

We leave the firm ground of figures when we talk about the social role of newspapers, and go into the reasons that readers read them. There is no common denominator. The goal is something for everyone. For Reader A it is city-hall news; for Reader B, football and baseball. Reader C sticks to the finance-business phases. Reader D likes the Women's pages; reader E, the comics. /15

And so it goes from advertisements to astrology, from Walter Lippmann to Ann Landers, from Doc Greene to Doctor Molner. A newspaper is like a department store. No customer wants to buy everything in the store, but what each customer wants had better be there; to him that is the store's only importance. What the reader wants had better be there in the paper, too, whether it is the obit column or Hudson's sales or the used-car classifieds. To the reader who reads with his lips, Dick Tracy and Li'l Abner are just as important as are James Reston's or Bill Kelsey's comments to the serious-minded reader. That is to put readership on its broadest base. /16

That is also one reason that picking the "best ten" or "best 100" is such an exercise in futility. *Time* Magazine tried it last January[2] and spent much of the appended story saying how meaningless such lists are. The New York *Times* was on the list, but so was the New York *Daily News;* and most knowledgeable news folk would share agreement with the first choice and astonishment at the second. /17

The *Daily News* talks to the Sweeneys, as the bromide goes, and the *Times* talks to the Stuyvesants. The unhappy fact of the matter—for those who say that the New York *Times* is the standard and that all newspapers should be like it—is that out of 190,000,000 Americans there are only enough persons to support *one* New York *Times.* We had

[2]Alphabetically: *Sun,* Baltimore; *Cleveland Press; Los Angeles Times; Courier-Journal,* Louisville; *Milwaukee Journal; Minneapolis Morning Tribune; Daily News,* New York; *New York Times; St. Louis Post-Dispatch;* and *Washington Post.*

clear, proof-positive of this only a few weeks ago, when the *Times* folded its West Coast edition, a noble experiment that failed. And just for the record, the *Daily News'* two million-plus circulation compares with the *Times'* 681,000, a daily total that is much less than the Detroit *News'* circulation. /18

Newspapers have been important to the United States even before there was a United States. Benjamin Harris was not only a pioneer in 1690 with his single issue of *Publick Occurrences,* the first newspaper ever issued in the American colonies; he was symbolic. Harris' newspaper was promptly suppressed because he had no license to print it; it was not "Published by Authority." U.S. newspapers have been in there, slugging it out with government ever since but with more conspicuous success than Harris had. Only during the periods of the French war scare in 1798, with its accompanying Alien and Sedition Laws, and during the Civil War on a few occasions, has the U.S. government succeeded in shutting up the press or any part of it. /19

It is a question whether newspapers have played a bigger role by reporting events or by influencing them. In the days of the nation's infancy, when the pulpit and the pamphlet were the dominant opinion molders, the young newspapers of America helped to set in motion the Revolution and independence from Britain. When in 1783, the daily newspaper came into being in the U.S. (the same year that the Revolution ended), it quickly became the most important medium; first, for persuading Americans that constitutional government must replace Confederation; then, for the new Constitution's acceptance. The press crystallized the basic Jefferson-Hamilton debates, with a free-swinging no-holds-barred partisan press that guaranteed the amazing outcome—with both Federalists and anti-Federalists winning their dispute, and the young nation winning as a consequence. /20

The press led the historic states' rights-slavery-union-freedom debate from the Missouri Compromise of 1820 right up to Appomattox. Its performance wasn't always clean or pretty, and Lincoln had a hair shirt in even such a "friend" as Horace Greeley, but there isn't much question that the press helped to keep the Union together. /21

After 1865, with the dizzying swing from rural to urban, from an agrarian to an industrial order, with the change from 92 per cent rural society to 92 per cent urban society, the press played a leading role. It has sometimes been a wrongheaded role. It was sometimes a vengeful, irresponsible, irrational role;

but the influence, for good or evil, was always there —the printed word in a newspaper. /22

If I were asked to pick out one period in American history as more decisive in respect to the role of the press than any other, I think I would choose the years beginning with 1833. That was when Ben Day launched the New York *Sun* and began what was known as the *penny press.** Modern journalism began then. Earlier, the newspapers were small in circulation and were edited, more or less, for one of two groups—for the commercial-business community or for political factions. They also were priced beyond the average worker's ability to buy. /23

Day's *Sun* changed all that. His paper not only sold for a penny and thus was within reach of the man in the street; it talked his language. It told him about himself. The *Sun* was an instant success. Then came James Gordon Bennett with his *Herald*, Horace Greeley with his *Tribune,* and others, and the day of the mass-produced, mass-circulation newspaper, edited for a vast and growing general public, was launched. /24

Consider the moment. This was in the first year of Andrew Jackson's second term. His predecessor, John Quincy Adams, was the last of the genteel-gentleman-upper crust-Virginia-Massachusetts group of presidents. Jeffersonian democracy had yielded to the rough-frontier Jacksonian kind. It was only three years after Webster's reply to Hayne,** when the Union seemed on the brink of dissolution. West of the Mississippi, only Louisiana and Missouri had achieved statehood. Michigan's admission was still four years away. The population of the whole nation was less than 13,000,000. The growth of the country was to be explosive in the years up to the Civil War—the population would more than double, one criterion of many. /25

The 1830s were a period when democracy was being tested as never before on earth. The chief question was not whether the Union would hold together, but whether the man in the street, the voter, the "mechanic," as the laboring man was then called, could measure up to the demands of the most demanding, and the freest, kind of government ever invented. This was the era when a perceptive Alexis de Tocqueville was publishing his cautious praises and profound doubts about our American democracy.*** /26

---

*Benjamin Henry Day (1810-1889). The *Sun* sold for one cent per copy; competing papers sold for six cents per copy. (Editor's note)

**Daniel Webster replied in the U.S. Senate January 20, 27, 1830, to Robert Y. Hayne, who opposed growing federal powers. (Editor's note)

***Tocqueville (1805-1859) was the author of *Democracy in America,* first published in French and in English in 1835. (Editor's note)

The first thing the man in the street needed to know was the *facts*. He needed to know the issues and the men. He had to know how to vote and which way to argue with his fellows about the little issues that would decide the big ones. The country had long since outgrown the town-meeting phase. Hundreds of miles of wilderness, mountains, lakes and streams divided the Maine voter from the voter in Louisiana, the Missourian from the New Yorker. How could the American democrat know all that he *had* to know? /27

The penny press was one answer. And because invention responds to need, all manner of change began to occur in the newspaper craft, and all of the changes helped to improve the product. The railroads and the telegraph began to bring in the domestic news faster. Steamships cut the time of Atlantic passage from weeks to days. The rotary press was invented. The stereotype plate, the web-perfecting printing process—and all the other aspects of modern journalism—began to come after the 1830s. /28

The penny press had its bad features. Its high priest, James Gordon Bennett, put his impress on American journalism as few men have before or since. He broadened the field of journalism, but he also planted the seeds of yellow journalism. But there was a Greeley to balance a Bennett, and Uncle Horace's weekly *Tribune* achieved the unheard of circulation of 200,000 (the daily New York *Tribune* was in contrast, 25,000); and led Ralph Waldo Emerson to say that the farmers didn't know how to think about the issues of the day until they had read Mr. Greeley. /29

In our time, as we all know, the newspaper has become many things. It tells us what happened on the other side of the earth only a few hours ago. It brings us news of civil rights debates in Congress, apportionment squabbles in Lansing, riots in Birmingham, Alabama, Mr. Khrushchev's quasi-triumphant tour of Egypt, and what Mayor Cavanagh and the Common Council are going to do about the new state income tax law. /30

The social force of the press may be measured in one way by the effects of a newspaperless period. You will remember some of them from shutdowns here in Detroit, the one that lasted from December 1, 1955, to late January 1956, for example. You may have cussed out your paper every day for the month preceding, for all its sins and crimes of commission and omission. But when it suddenly wasn't there, there was a large void in life. /31

After the New York strike of 1963 was settled, the *New Yorker,* in that eccentric, oblique, sometimes brilliant manner of thinking that makes it an interesting magazine, thought about the effects of the strike for a while, then came up with this view:

[Paragraphs 32-33 were from *The New Yorker* Magazine for February 9, 1963, p. 23. The omitted passage (permission to reprint the paragraphs was refused) stressed the importance of newspapers in alleviating the city dweller's feeling of isolation and of insignificance in his "dirty, lonely, overcrowded, expensive, and hostile surroundings."]

In one sense that's a pretty terrifying picture—in its implications of the city as prison—but it is also a thoughtful one, and, I think, in its newspaper implications, a perceptive one. The *New Yorker* is describing one of the large end-products of the process that Ben Day began in 1833. The newspaper is a habit. America's per capita readership is among the highest on earth. The newspaper, as has been charged, may even be a narcotic, with the user, when deprived of it, in jeopardy of becoming a gibbering ruin. But it is part of our lives, and it is a large part. If, like the shadows on Plato's cave,* the newspaper tends to become more real than the events it reports, then that is again a measure of its hold upon us. /34

If I seem to be saying that our democracy would be impossible without the press, that is exactly my view. Thomas Jefferson wrote of Philip Freneau's *National Gazette* that it had saved us from galloping into a monarchy; and Freneau and his paper were regarded as loathsome and scabrous by the Federalists, including Hamilton and Washington. Joseph Pulitzer broke a Federal law once to keep England and the United States from going to war over a dispute about a Venezuela boundary.** The St. Louis *Post Dispatch* won a Pulitzer Prize for uncovering the Teapot Dome scandal; and a long roll call of other winners of that prize and such other prizes as the Elijah P. Lovejoy awards, attest to the great work in keeping government honest in our democracy that our newspapers have accomplished. And are accomplishing every day. /35

The newspapers today share with television and radio the great responsibility of keeping our public

*The allusion is to Plato's image of men who mistake shadows on the wall of a cave for reality. See *The Republic,* Book 7. (Editor's note)

**In 1895, Pulitzer violated legislation against private citizens' entering into communication with foreign powers on matters of public policy. He addressed appeals for forbearance in the Venezuela-British Guiana boundary dispute to members of the royal family and to the foreign office of Great Britain. U. S. Secretary of State, Richard Olney, publicly complained of Pulitzer's action, but no formal charges were made. (Editor's note) informed, of interpreting complex events and of influencing public opinion into good courses. The three media may snarl at each other occasionally, but each has found or is finding its role in our society. They complement one another. The quickness of the electronically-spoken word, the permanence of the printed word—the first with its dispatch, the second with its depth and ability to be returned to: these make a matchless team. It is a matter of record that, within four hours of the horrible tragedy in Dallas last November 22, every person in the Republic capable of understanding anything knew about President Kennedy's assassination. But hearing and seeing were not enough; as you well know, newspaper readership zoomed: the American people had to read the details that the loudspeaker and the glass screen could not present as well. /36

We have come a long way since Ben Day launched his *Sun* and Andy Jackson gave a new twist to democracy. Even then, Americans read more newspapers than did the peoples of any other nation in the world. The habit that began with the early eighteenth century is strong upon us still, stronger than ever. And it is one of the reasons that we have the strongest government in the world, and the highest standard of living. /37

I would like now to talk about some of the newspaper press's problems and some of the matters for which it draws criticism, sometimes exceedingly sharp. /38

When James Gordon Bennett started his New York *Herald*, he could do everything himself—and did, more or less, except print and deliver the edition. There wasn't much to write about. Local news was gathered on foot. Cities were small. National and foreign news were clipped and reprinted from exchanges. There was leisure time for the reader to read the few prose pieces that made up the paper. /39

Today the news editor is asked to do the impossible every time he takes off his coat and goes to work. It is a hoary truism that two and three times —or more—words are available to editors for printing than there is space to print them in. About 60 per cent of the column inches are dummied for advertising. Everything else—including comics, editorial page, pictures, departments and so on—must go into the remaining 40 per cent. In a 48-page paper, that means the news editor is lucky if he has 35 to 40 columns to work with in live news. Into these must go all the local, county, state, national and foreign news, all the pictures, with space allowed for headlines. /40

In point of fact, it all doesn't go. It simply won't fit. So news judgment gets a fierce workout—usually with department editors drawing blood over the contest for space—and there may be anywhere up to 100 per cent as much good unused stuff on the spikes as the amount that gets into the paper. News comes from 122 different nations today, and in the U.S. alone 190,000,000 persons are making it. /41

Related to the problem of such conspicuous waste is what might be called bits-and-pieces editing. The usual reasoning is that readers like stories short. So it's better to run ten snippets of news than one long detailed story. One consequence is that even the conscientious reader is left in mid-air on later chapters of stories. /42

A near-fatal accident is reported today; the victim dies and the follow story lasts one edition. Most readers don't get the chance to read about it. There is fierce fighting in Yemen or Cyprus or South Viet Nam today. The fate of civilization hangs on the result, if the headline is to be believed. Tomorrow, no fighting, no story, but somehow civilization has wiggled through. A prominent person comes to address the city's leading club on a major subject. If the story gets in at all, it may well be a pre-address interview. If it doesn't get in at all, "Ah, well, radio and TV carried it." /43

But what of the busy person who wanted to read what the distinguished visitor had to say and who missed the electronic reports? One of the deplorable effects upon news coverage, in my view, is this easy rationalization by editors that if the speech gets on the air it doesn't have to get onto paper. /44

Bits-and-pieces journalism may be a headache to the reader. It can be a nightmare to the conscientious news editor. Caught on the horns of the old dilemma of giving the public what it wants or what he thinks it ought to have, he may find himself leaning to the first because it sells papers, or slimming things so that only the unhappy bones of stories are offered to readers, with no flesh on them. /45

Newspaper thinking, like many another kind, sometimes is the prisoner of tradition and custom. "We've always done it that way, so we'll continue to do it that way." In the old days, for example, when fierce competition ruled newspapers, there was justification for the screaming headline and the jazzed-up story. You had to beat the opposition on street sales, and the big headline was the way to do it. /46

What is the justification for the eight-column line in a paper occupying a monopoly position, in morning or evening field, with most of its circulation home-delivered? It does of course give the reader a clear indication of what the editors think is the biggest news of the moment, and their ideas about what he, the reader, ought to be most interested in. But if newspaper research has turned up anything on the past two or three decades—and it has turned up plenty—it is that readers go their own sweet way, and have their own well seasoned, bullheaded ideas about what they are interested in—and they don't need 96-point Gothic headlines to tell them. /47

The population explosion has presented the metropolitan newspaper with one of its toughest problems. In the old days, again, the city limits, plus peripheral suburbs, were the daily's recognizable circulation area. Where do we stop today? What for example, is Detroit? Is Detroit today the 138 square miles of territory in the eastern end of Wayne County it used to be? I don't think so. /48

If I am wrong, then more than half of the membership of the Detroit Torch Club are not Detroiters, and I think we all consider ourselves to be. I did an informal nose-count from our yearbook and I found that of the 111 members listed this year, 73—more than one-half—live in some governmental unit that is not the City of Detroit. Many of us do not even live in Wayne County. Are we Detroiters or not? /49

In the seven southeastern counties of Michigan live about 4,500,000 persons of our state population of seven million-plus. Something more than half of the 4,500,000 live in the one or two largest cities of these seven counties. The rest of us are residents of what has been variously called suburbia, exurbia and disturbia. And it is this part of the population that is troubling the sleep of some publishers and bringing sweet dreams to others. Principally, it is a problem for the dailies. And this is the reason: /50

The big metropolitan dailies no longer can cover the Detroit area adequately. Our metropolitan sprawl is so big that nobody can say where Detroit, physically, spiritually, actually—or what you will—ends. There are more than half a hundred separate governmental subdivisions—cities, villages, towns—in the area bounded by 14 Mile on the north, the Monroe-Wayne County line on the south, Farmington Road on the west and Lake St. Clair and the Detroit River on the east and south. And this doesn't begin to take in all the Detroit metropolitan area. /51

My point is this: it is physically impossible for a Detroit daily to cover this vast sprawl, and these scores of communities, adequately. They try hard. They have zoned editions. They have suburban editors and reporters. They do their best. But the job is simply too big. /52

For those of us who want to keep up with the news of Detroit, and of our suburban areas, there is a special problem. At a certain point it becomes difficult, physically difficult, to deliver a paper produced in Detroit to the central city's suburban, far-out periphery. I live 22 miles from the point where the *News* and *Free Press* are produced. I subscribe to both of them. They are delivered to my home with admirable regularity, but it is not very often that I find in them much news about Farmington Township or Oakland County that affects me. For that, I have to subscribe to three weeklies—the Birmingham *Eccentric*, the Farmington *Enterprise* and the Southfield *News*. /53

I indulge in this rather personal aside only because what has happened to me is symptomatic of what has happened to persons in more than 200 of what the Census Bureau calls "SMSA"s—Standard Metropolitan Statistical Areas: population clusters in the U.S. with core cities of more than 50,000 and large adjacent suburbs. /54

What is happening to Michigan, in the population sprawl in Wayne, Oakland, Macomb, Monroe, Washtenaw, St. Clair and Livingston Counties, is happening in more that 200 other places in the country. /55

The other day a speaker at Wayne State University startled his audience by saying that megalopolis is yielding to a new monster—ecumenopolis. That means, I think, world city. We won't be simply a city stretching from Toledo to Bay City with Detroit as core. There won't be any breaks between cities at all. How can we tell, then, where the Detroit *News* and Detroit *Free Press* territories leave off and the Chicago *Daily News* and the New York *Times* territories begin? /56

Two of the beneficiaries in the change, at least for now, are the small-city daily and the progressive weekly. They are doing, if they are on their toes, what the metropolitan daily cannot do because it hasn't the space, the staff or the facilities to do. The Royal Oak *Daily Tribune* has more than doubled its circulation in the last couple of decades. The Pontiac *Press* has grown prodigiously. Such weeklies as the Birmingham *Eccentric*, The East Side Newspapers, the Dearborn *Press*, among others, have stepped in to provide the local news of their respective areas in a way that the mets simply cannot do. The population explosion is working its way on these smaller papers as well as upon the dailies. /57

And what is true around here is true of the areas around New York, Chicago, Philadelphia, Los Angeles, Cleveland and every other metropolis where suburbia is more than a word; where suburbia is people. /58

Many other problems face the daily newspapers. I shall mention only one more. Perhaps it is the most serious. It is the problem of keeping good papers alive, and it is directly related to the costs of producing a new newspaper every day. Labor, newsprint, ink, special services, everything connected with newspapers, cost more than they used to cost. Rising costs are the reason usually given for the deaths of papers. /59

Two papers in Los Angeles, the New York *Daily Mirror* (despite a circulation of more than 900,000), the Grand Rapids *Herald*, the Cleveland *News*, these and scores of other honorable and venerable newspapers have succumbed in recent years because they could not stay in the black. Survival is basic to the good work of any newspaper. It can't do *anything* if it dies, so staying in the black is the first problem. /60

How will all these problems be met? My crystal ball is clouded. But I am perfectly willing to make a few predictions, based on what is happening. If I'm wrong no one will remember, and if I'm right it won't matter for I am talking about decades, not years. /61

I think we will see a few more disappearances, or mergers. But I think we will not see any town of appreciable size, which is now serviced by one newspaper, suddenly deprived of that paper. No newspaper, to my knowledge, has directly succumbed to the competition of either radio or television. I think we will see, as the population sprawl stretches farther out, more weeklies becoming bi-weeklies, bi-weeklies becoming tri-weeklies and then four-, five-, and six-days-a-week newspapers. /62

We will see small dailies become bigger. Elsewhere in the U.S., some of these things have happened and some of them have happened right here. /63

The Copley newspapers in southern California, the Paddock chain in Chicago, and *Newsday* in Long Island have grown from little or nothing to impressive strength. I think their pattern will be repeated. /64

But I also expect that the drive toward automation will be speeded up in newspapers. Teletypesetting is now old stuff in newspapers. This is a process whereby letters and figures are punched out on a tape by an operator at a distant point, and received on tape simultaneously in many newspaper offices. The tape is then fed through a gadget on a conventional linotype machine and the type is set speedily and accurately. Both our big Detroit dailies set their stock market quotations this way now, untouched by human hands. A number of small papers now have press association news stories punched out on tape in their news rooms and then feed the tape through the linotype machines. Many critics take a jaundiced view of this, for the editor abdicates too much in the automated process. There is good reason to resist a trend which lets someone 500 or 1,000 miles away decide what a story is worth and how it should be set. /65

Cold-type, litho-offset printing is being used by more and more weeklies. This process by-passes the composing room completely. Pages of body type and head type and pictures are pasted up on cardboard sheets; these are photo-engraved and the plates put onto offset printing presses. This process was used with a fair degree of success in the Chicago daily papers' strike in the late 1940's, but it is slow and cumbersome and can be messy when not in expert hands. But many weeklies print by litho offset regularly now and do a fine job of it. The Greenville *Daily News* and the Wyandotte *News-Herald* are two that use and like the process. We had a Wayne State University Press Club Workshop on the subject last January and much interest was generated among visiting editors. /66

New and cheaper ways of engraving are being developed. There are increasingly exciting developments in all the graphic arts. And all these will have an effect upon newspapering. /67

But let us get back to the editorial phases. I think there are changes ahead in editing techniques. The newsmagazines have shown the way here in part. *Time, Newsweek, U.S. News* don't try to cover every dib and dab of news that breaks in the world. They are selective; and the way people respond to them is not lost on daily newspaper editors. Editing must get tighter. A sharper selectivity of subject and manner of treatment must prevail. Time, the measure of our hours and days, is the enemy; and time must be conquered. The readers must be given more of the things that matter, in ways that will cut the least severely into the hours of their days. /68

Newspapers are constantly measuring their readership, the appeal of their features and the attention span accorded their news stories. The pressure is increasing upon them to deal more effectively with the daily Niagara of words that pours into their editorial rooms. That may be the key to everything else. /69

If we are to continue as a vigorous, mature democracy we must have a citizenry that has a full supply of information and of interpretation about the big issues of the day. /70

Newspapers continue to be the principal source of that information and interpretation, although now they share the role with radio and television. /71

In order to continue in that role, there must be more concentration on information and interpretation, and less and less upon entertainment. Newspapers should stick to their role of vending the news and let television, radio, the movies and the theater do the entertaining. A balance of news and entertainment is a good thing; but get an imbalance on the side of entertainment and it is questionable whether you have a *news*paper. /72

That's my stint at the crystal ball. I have only one more prediction and it is a short one. /73

Newspapers are here to stay. They'll continue to improve. They will stay because there is no substitute for them and because, if they go, our democracy is finished. Their form may be as different 50 years from now as our present-day papers are different from those of the early penny press period. But they *will* be newspapers and they will be as good as the society they are informing and interpreting. /74

The speech

1. Comment on the use of statistics in paragraphs 7 through 14. Are they essential for an answer to Holden's question: "What *is* the general-interest daily newspaper press of the United States?" Would visual aids have helped listeners remember this information? Was establishing this information in detail Holden's objective? How would you have designed visual aids? Why?

2. By what specific means does Holden inject *activity* (see Glossary) into his account of how the modern daily newspaper emerged (paragraphs 19-30)?

3. List the major topics that form the main heads of this speech. Evaluate and improve, if possible, the *transitions* (see Glossary) by which listeners' thoughts are moved from one major topic to the next major topics.

4. What section do you consider to be the conclusion? Could it have been strengthened? By what specific means?

5. Identify the ways in which Holden has enlivened his explanation of the news editor's job (paragraphs 40-41) by injecting *conflict* (see Glossary) into the discussion.

6. Identify the *facts, allusions,* and *examples* (see Glossary) that would have special interest for Holden's audience. Did he make the speech "better" for his listeners by such inclusions? "Better" for you? Why or why not? How true is it that what a speaker must do to make his speech effective for a particular audience may weaken its value for general publication? If possible study the edited and condensed speech in *The Torch,* January 1965. Which version did you enjoy more? Why?

7. To what extent does this speech achieve the primary goals of *exposition* as described in the Glossary?

For further study and discussion

1. Is the steady decline in the number of daily newspapers, especially in cities, a cause for concern? Why or why not?

2. What evidence is there that advertisers exercise serious influence over editorial policies of newspapers? Over programs presented on radio and TV? Cite specific examples, if possible.

3. What truth is there in the allegation that we have a one-party press in the United States? Cite several reputable sources to support your answer.

4. For many years public opinion polls have shown that most Americans have more confidence in radio-TV news than in newspaper reporting. On the other hand, a 1965 *Newsweek* survey indicated that a fifth of all college students had "a great deal" of confidence in "the press" as an institution, but that only an eighth had "a great deal" of confidence in television as an institution. Are there justifications for either kind of preference?

5. The famous physicist and Nobel prize winner P. W. Bridgman wrote, "It seems to me that society tries to formally control, by means of laws, too many sorts of things. Popular sentiment has ways of getting results which are effective and more flexible. . . . " (*The Way Things Are,* Cambridge, 1959, p. 307). Do you agree? Do you think this applies to regulation of public information agencies like newspapers, radio, television, book publishing? Why or why not?

6. What is the history and present value of the Second Class mailing privilege? Do publishers use it responsibly? Does it contribute to improving public knowledge and taste as originally intended?

7. Why was the Sedition Act passed in 1798? What was the effect?

8. Explore the career of one of these famous journalists: James Gordon Bennett, Horace Greeley, William Randolph Hearst, Sr., Joseph Pulitzer, Edward Bok. What did he contribute to his profession? To political and social development in the United States?
9. Make a critical evaluation of the daily newspaper most widely read in the region where your college or home town is located.
10. Should newspaper or other reporters be allowed to conceal their sources of information from officers of government? From the courts?

Suggestions for further reading

George C. Bastian and others, *Editing the Day's News,* 4th ed. (New York, 1956)

Silas Bent, *Newspaper Crusaders: A Neglected Study* (New York, 1939)

J. Edward Gerald, *British Press under Government Economic Controls* (Minneapolis, 1956)

Theodore E. Kruglak, *The Foreign Correspondents* (New York, 1956)

Harry M. Scoble, *Press and Politics* (Boston, 1957)

Gilbert Seldes, *The Public Arts* (New York, 1956)

Leon Svirsky, ed., *Your Newspaper: Blueprint for a Better Press* (New York, 1947)

Images of the consumer's changing mind on and off Madison Avenue

MILTON ROKEACH

Like several other speeches in this book, the following address by Milton Rokeach is a "convention paper" and was presented to a professional association. In this case, however, the speaker's role and the nature of the occasion were in several respects distinctive. Professor Rokeach spoke as an invited expert-critic to a special session of the annual convention of the American Association of Advertising Agencies, Eastern Region, on November 6, 1963. Early in 1963, the Governors of the Association had directed that the November convention feature a program on "Our Changing Consumer Society," at which speakers

Reprinted by permission from *ETC: A Review of General Semantics,* Vol. XXI, No. 3; copyright, 1964, by the International Society for General Semantics. By permission also of Milton Rokeach.

from outside the field of advertising could be asked "to examine the faults, virtues, and future of advertising in terms of our changing economy and social values." Rokeach was one of four academic specialists invited to appear on this program. Following their formal presentations, the four speakers engaged in a brief, informal panel discussion with Dr. Howard Bursk, editor of *The Harvard Business Review,* as moderator.

Arthur C. Fatt, Chairman of the Board of Governors, American Association of Advertising Agencies, Eastern Region, presided at the program. When he introduced the speakers, Mr. Fatt said: "The aim of this session . . . is to take time out from our daily tasks and look at the consumer more objectively. And so we have turned to the campus. We want to expose ourselves to the stimulation of brilliant minds from outside the advertising orbit." The special roles the speakers had been asked to fill were noted in *Advertising Age.*[1] According to this journal, it was especially significant (see also Rokeach's paragraph 38) that all of the speakers had been urged to speak boldly and critically.

Milton Rokeach's training and experience made him an excellent choice for this program. He is Professor of Psychology at Michigan State University, where he has been a faculty member since 1947. Born in Poland in 1918, he is a naturalized citizen of the United States. He received the B.A. (1941) from Brooklyn College and the M.A. (1941) and Ph.D. (1947) from the University of California, Berkeley. In 1961-1962 he was a fellow at the Center for Advanced Study in the Behavioral Sciences at Stanford, California. Professor Rokeach's special field of interest is social psychology, and he has written extensively on subjects relating to the psychology of social attitudes. *The Open and Closed Mind* (Basic Books, 1960) is his most widely known work.

The text has been taken from *Papers from the 1963 Region Conventions,* American Association of Advertising Agencies, Eastern Region Annual Conference, November 6-8, 1963, New York City, pages 3-12.

The advertising man is not the only person who seeks to shape and change other people's beliefs, attitudes, and behavior. There are many kinds of people in our society, professional and non-professional, working for pay and for free, who for various combinations of altruistic and selfish reasons are vitally interested in the theory and in the practice of shaping and changing other people's values, beliefs,

[1]Volume 34 (November 11, 1963), p. 3.

attitudes, and behavior. Let me point by way of illustration to the psychotherapist, to the teacher, the missionary, the politician, and the lobbyist. All these have in common with the advertising man at least the desire to influence and to persuade others to believe and to act in certain ways they would not otherwise believe and act. /1

But this does not mean that the advertising man wants to change the same sorts of beliefs which, say, the therapist or the politician wants to change. Every human being has many different kinds of beliefs, and every advanced society seems to have encouraged the growth of different kinds of persuaders who specialize in trying to change some kinds of belief and not other kinds. /2

What, then, are the different kinds of beliefs which all men have and what kinds of beliefs does the advertising man wish most to influence? What are the properties of the different kinds of beliefs, and how easily is one kind changed compared with another kind? And what are the special problems which arise to plague the advertising man because of the fact that he specializes in trying to change certain kinds of beliefs and not other kinds, and what can he do about these problems? /3

To answer these questions, I would like to tell you about five kinds of beliefs which we have thus far isolated in our work at Michigan State University. This work is part of a larger, ongoing program of research extending over the past decade on the nature of man's systems of belief, how such systems of belief are formed, organized, and modified, and how such systems differ from one person to the next. /4

To begin with, all persons are assumed to have belief systems, and each belief system contains tens of thousands of beliefs. These beliefs cannot all be equally important to the person possessing them. It is necessary to assume that beliefs vary along a continuum of importance or centrality. Further, we must assume that the more important a belief the more it will resist change and the more trivial a belief the more easily it can be changed. And, finally, we must assume that the more important a belief which is changed the more widespread the repercussions in the rest of the person's belief system, because many of the beliefs "hooked up" with it will change too. /5

The five kinds of beliefs which I will describe may be represented by five concentric circles with the key beliefs at the center and the more inconsequential beliefs along the outside circle. To help keep track of them let me call the innermost beliefs

Type A, which is then followed by Type B, and so on, until we get to Type E along the outside circle.* /6

At the core are Type A beliefs, which I call primitive beliefs. These are beliefs we all share with one another about the nature of physical reality, social reality, and the self. For example, *I believe this is a table. I believe this is an audience listening to a speech. I believe my name is Milton Rokeach.* These are all supported by one hundred per cent social consensus. Type A beliefs are our taken-for-granted axioms which are not subject to controversy because we believe, and we believe everyone else believes. Such primitive beliefs are fundamental and we have evidence which shows that they are more resistant to change than any other type of belief. And we have obtained additional evidence suggesting that we become extremely upset when Type A beliefs are seriously brought into question. /7

And then there is a second kind of primitive belief—Type B—which is also extremely resistant to change. Such beliefs do not depend on social support or consensus but instead arise from deep personal experience. Type B beliefs are incontrovertible and we believe them regardless of whether anyone else believes them. Many of these unshakable beliefs are about ourselves and some of these self-conceptions are positive ones—Type B+—and some are negative ones—Type B−. The positive ones represent beliefs about what we are capable of, and the negative ones represent beliefs about what we are afraid of. /8

Let me illustrate some Type B+ beliefs which most of us here probably have. Regardless of what others may think of us, we continue to believe ourselves to be intelligent and rational men, able and competent, basically kind and charitable. Type B+ beliefs represent our positive self-images which guide our aspirations and ambitions to become even better, greater, wiser, and nobler than we already are. /9

But many of us also have Type B− beliefs—negative self-conceptions—which we cling to primitively regardless of whether others may agree with us. We are often beset by phobias, compulsions, obsessions, neurotic self-doubts, and anxieties about self-worth, self-identity, and self-competence. These are the kinds of primitive beliefs which we only wish we were rid of, and it is these Type B− beliefs which the specialized psychotherapist is often asked to

---

*At this point in his speech, Professor Rokeach supplied his listeners with copies of the table on page 117. (Editor's note)

Types of Beliefs

		Definition	Examples
Type A	Primitive beliefs	A belief which is uncontroversial because everyone in a position to know believes it too.	I believe this is a table. I believe this is an audience listening to a speech. I believe my name is Milton Rokeach.
Type B+			I believe I am intelligent. I believe I am rational. I believe I am a kind person.
	Primitive beliefs	A belief which is uncontroversial because I continue to believe it regardless of what others may think.	
Type B−			I believe I am abnormal. I believe others cannot be trusted. I believe I am no good.
Type C	Authority beliefs	Beliefs about which authorities can and cannot be trusted.	the Church, Kennedy, Einstein, scientists, parents, etc.
Type D	Peripheral beliefs	Beliefs which are derived from authority.	I believe divorce is immoral. I believe Jupiter has 12 moons.
Type E	Inconsequential beliefs	Beliefs which, if changed, leave other beliefs unaffected.	I believe a vacation at the beach is more enjoyable than one in the mountains. I believe Sophia Loren is prettier than Elizabeth Taylor.

change. Other specialized persuaders are generally not trained or interested in changing Type B− beliefs, but they may be interested in exploiting them without trying to change them. /10

A third kind of belief—Type C—we call authority beliefs, beliefs we all have about which authorities to trust and not to trust. Many facts of physical and social reality have alternative interpretations, are socially controversial, or are not capable of being personally verified or experienced. For these reasons all men need to identify with authorities who will help them to decide what to believe and what not to believe. Is communism good or bad? Is there a God or isn't there? How do we know the French Revolution actually took place? What about evolution? /11

No man is personally able to ascertain the truth of all such things for himself. So, he believes in this or that authority—parents, teachers, religious leaders, scientists—and he is often willing to take authority's word for many things. Thus, we all somehow develop beliefs about which authorities are positive and which are negative, differing from one person to the next, and we look to such authorities for information about what is (and is not) true and beautiful and good for us. /12

A fourth kind of belief—Type D—we call peripheral beliefs, beliefs which are *derived* from the authorities we identify with. For example, a devout Catholic has certain beliefs about birth control and divorce because he has taken them over from the authority he believes in. I believe Jupiter has twelve moons not because I have personally seen them but because I trust certain kinds of authorities who have seen them. I am quite prepared to revise my belief about Jupiter's moons providing the authorities I trust revise their beliefs. /13

Many people adhere to a particular religious or political belief system because they identify with a particular authority. Such peripheral beliefs can be changed providing the suggestion for change emanates from one's authority, or providing there is a change in one's authority. /14

Finally, there is a fifth class of beliefs—Type E—which I call inconsequential beliefs. If they are changed, the total system of beliefs is not altered in any significant way. I believe, for example, that you can get a better shave from one brand of razor blade than another; I believe that a vacation at the beach is more enjoyable than one in the mountains; I believe Sophia Loren is prettier than Elizabeth Taylor. But if you can persuade me to believe the opposite, the change is inconsequential because the rest of my belief system is hardly likely to be affected in any important way. /15

Let me now briefly summarize the five kinds of beliefs: every person's total system of beliefs is composed of beliefs that range in importance from the inconsequential, through the peripheral, to beliefs about authority and, finally, at the core, to primitive beliefs which are extremely resistant to change either because they do not at all depend on social support or because they enjoy universal social support. All these five kinds of beliefs, considered together, are organized into a remarkable piece of architecture which I call the belief system. It has a definable content and a definable structure. And it has a job to do; it serves adaptive functions for the person, in order to maximize his positive self-image and to minimize his negative self-image. Every person has a need to know himself and his world insofar as possible, and a need not to know himself and his world, insofar as necessary. A person's total belief system, with all its five kinds of beliefs, is designed to serve both functions at once. /16

You might wonder what objective evidence there may be that the five kinds of beliefs I have just described really exist. There is not enough time here to tell you about all our research addressed to this question, but I would like to report that the best evidence we have comes from a study as yet unpublished in which we tried to change the five kinds of beliefs I have described through hypnotic suggestion. This work was done in collaboration with my colleagues Dr. Joseph Reyher and Dr. Richard Wiseman at Michigan State University and the results we obtained are quite clear. Our data show that all five kinds of beliefs change under hypnosis. But, as we had expected, the amount of change in belief varies with the centrality of belief, the primitive beliefs—Types A and B—changing the least as a result of hypnotic suggestion, beliefs about authority—Type C—changing more, peripheral beliefs—Type D—changing yet more, and inconsequential beliefs—Type E—changing the most. /17

The results also show that changing one kind of belief leads to changes in the other kinds of beliefs, but changes in Types A and B beliefs exert the greatest consequences on other beliefs, changes in Type C beliefs exert lesser consequences, changes in Type D beliefs exert yet lesser consequences and, finally, Type E beliefs—inconsequential beliefs, the ones most easy to change—exert the least effect on other beliefs. /18

Now, given these five kinds of beliefs as a frame of reference, it is possible to obtain a somewhat clearer picture of what society's specialized persuaders are trying to do, and which kinds of beliefs they wish most to act upon, to influence, and to change. As far as I can tell, there are no specialized persuaders whose main business it is to change the first kind of belief I have described, the Type A beliefs which are universally supported by social consensus. But as already stated, it is the business of the professional psychotherapist to change the second kind of primitive belief. The psychotherapist's job is to help us get rid of our negative self-conceptions—Type B— beliefs—and to strengthen our positive self-conceptions—Type B+beliefs. /19

Then there are other specialized persuaders—the political and religious partisans and ideologists of various persuasions. What sorts of beliefs are they mostly concerned with? I would suggest that their main focus is on the Type C and Type D beliefs, those I have called authority beliefs and peripheral beliefs. /20

By now, you can perhaps anticipate what I am about to say next about the kinds of beliefs which that specialized persuader—the advertising man—tries to form and to change. Without in any way wishing to deny that the results of advertising may have important economic consequences, it could be stated from a psychological standpoint that the advertising man has concentrated mainly on changing Type E beliefs—inconsequential beliefs—to the extent that his purpose is to meet the competition, and he has concentrated mainly on Type D—peripheral beliefs—to the extent his purpose is to give information. Furthermore, the more competitive the advertising the more it addresses itself to changing psychologically inconsequential beliefs about the relative merits of one brand over another. /21

Let me now try to explore with you some implications which seem to follow from the preceding analysis. It is tempting to suggest that at least some of the unique characteristics, problems, and embarrassments besetting the advertising industry stem directly or indirectly from its heavy specialization in changing psychologically inconsequential beliefs, and stem from the additional fact that beliefs which are psychologically inconsequential to the average consumer are highly consequential to all those who economically need to advertise. /22

I have already mentioned our finding that inconsequential beliefs are generally easier to change than other kinds of beliefs. This does not mean, however, that the consumer will passively yield to others' efforts to change such beliefs. We generally resist changing *all* our beliefs because we gain comfort in clinging to the familiar and because all our beliefs, as I have tried to suggest, serve highly important functions for us. So the advertising man, while he has a psychological advantage over other persuaders specializing in changing more central beliefs, still has to find economical ways of changing the less consequential beliefs he specializes in. This he has often tried to do by developing methods for shaking the consumer loose from his belief regarding the inconsequential virtues of a particular brand over a competitor's in order to make him believe instead that the difference does make a difference. He tries to convince the consumer that there are important benefits to be gained by changing brands, that deeper beliefs and needs will be better satisfied. The advertising industry has frequently been successful in achieving this aim and, sometimes, miraculously so. /23

How? In line with my analysis, I would suggest that the advertiser's goal is achieved by associating the fifth kind of belief—Type E, the inconsequential beliefs—with other kinds of beliefs tapping psychologically more consequential beliefs and wants. But what are the other kinds of beliefs which are most frequently associated with Type E beliefs? Theoretically, it is possible to associate the inconsequential beliefs with Type D, or C, or B+, or B−, or A beliefs, but the advertising industry does not use all these combinations with equal frequency. The associations which seem to come up most often in competitive advertising are those between Types E and C—the authority beliefs—as in testimonials, and between Types E and B−, as in the old Lifebuoy ads on B.O.,* or in the more sophisticated Maidenform Bra ads which exploit primitive fears or primitive self-conceptions concerning insufficient femininity. /24

Why should these two combinations come up more often than the other possible combinations? I suspect that this is due to the fact that the advertising industry has been heavily influenced by two theories in psychology—behaviorism and psychoanalysis—both having in common an image of man who is fundamentally an irrational creature, helplessly pushed around on the one hand by irrational guilt, anxiety, self-doubt, and other neurotic self-conceptions—B− beliefs—and, on the other hand, helplessly pushed around by external stimuli, which, through reward and punishment, condition him to form arbitrary associations. /25

Advertising has borrowed from psychoanalysis its laws of association, and from behaviorism its principles of conditioning; psychoanalysis tells you what to associate with what, and behaviorism tells you how to stamp it in. I would suggest that it is because the advertising profession has taken over such an irrational image of man from behaviorism and psychoanalysis that the inconsequential beliefs have been so often associated with the authority beliefs—Type C—and with the primitive beliefs—Type B−. In doing so, the advertising industry has come in for a great deal of criticism—to my mind, justified—from various sources for a style of advertising which encourages conformity, which is exploitative, debasing, lacking in taste, and insulting to the dignity of man. /26

Given the facts of our industrial society and given what Harry C. Groome has, in a recent issue of the *Saturday Review*, called the *inevitability* of advertising, the advertising man's general strategy of associating the psychologically inconsequential with the consequential is probably the only one open to

---

*Through their advertising, Lifebuoy soap manufacturers made the initials B. O. (standing for "body odor") commonplace in the American language. (Editor's note)

him and seems psychologically sound in principle. But in line with my presentation of the five kinds of beliefs it is now possible to at least explore systematically the other possible combinations to see where they might lead us. What would an ad look like which tries to associate an inconsequential belief, Type E, with a primitive belief which we all share, Type A? /27

I recall having seen only one example of such an advertisement which has caught my eye like no advertisement has in many years. /28

It is an advertisement for *London Fog:* "How to keep water off a duck's back," appearing in *The New Yorker*, September 7, 1963, page 138, showing a duck wearing a raincoat. I might add that children seem to get an unusual delight in looking at this picture. Here we see an inconsequential belief about a particular brand of raincoat associated with a primitive physical belief about the fundamental nature of a certain animal called a duck. By the process of association our primitive belief about the stark-naked duck is momentarily violated; our sanity is threatened and it is virtually impossible to turn away from the ad until our primitive belief is somehow re-established or restored to its original state. In the process the viewer is entertained and *London Fog* gains attention. Whether *London Fog* also gains customers remains to be seen. /29

In this connection, too, let me also draw attention to the television program *Candid Camera* and to the fact that it often entertains mass audiences by having them watch what happens when there is a momentary disruption of a person's primitive belief about physical and social reality—Type A beliefs, those everyone believes. I am rather surprised that the advertising industry has not consciously applied the *Candid Camera* ideas for its own uses. The *London Fog* ad is the only one I remember seeing which seems to use a similar principle. /30

To end on a more serious note, let me next draw your attention to some psychological considerations which would favor an increasing emphasis in advertising on associations between the inconsequential beliefs, Type E, and the primitive beliefs, Type B+, which refer to the positive conceptions we strive to have of ourselves. /31

Since the end of World War II, an increasing number of distinguished psychologists have revolted against the image of Irrational Man which behaviorism and classical psychoanalysis have both helped build. Contemporary psychoanalysts talk more and more about the conflict-free sphere of ego functioning; the Gestalt psychologists have empha-

sized for a long time man's search for meaning, understanding, and organization. Carl Rogers has emphasized the drive for growth and maturity within all individuals; Abraham Maslow has familiarized us with man's drive for self-actualization; Gordon Allport and the existentialists talk about being and becoming; Robert White, Harlow, Berlyne, Festinger, and many others, have pointed to the fact that man has a need to know, to understand, and to be competent. I would say that the major way in which contemporary psychology differs from the psychology of twenty years ago is that Man is now seen to be not only a *rationalizing* creature but also a *rational* creature—curious, exploratory, and receptive to new ideas. This changing image of man I have represented by the B+ type of beliefs, which exist side-by-side with the B− type within the belief system. /32

I can see the barest beginnings of this changing image of man on the part of the advertising industry in certain advertisements, and it may surprise you to learn which advertisements I have in mind: the Pepto-Bismol and Anacin ads. There are probably millions of Americans walking around right now with a conception of a stomach that looks like a hollow dumbbell standing on end, and with a conception of a mind composed of split-level compartments.* In these ads we see an image of man on the part of the advertising man which concedes that consumers, at least the ones with bellyaches and headaches, have a need to understand why they have bellyaches or headaches. But at the same time the advertising man is also cynically saying that the consumer is too stupid or irrational to understand anything well. /33

If you or I were to learn that our children were being taught such conceptions of the stomach or head by their teachers, we would demand that such teachers be immediately fired for incompetence. Why, then, should the advertising man be allowed to exploit for money the consumer's legitimate need to understand his bellyaches and headaches? /34

Is there not a better example of the advertising industry's changing conception of man? Yes, I think there is. David Ogilvy** has expressed a more dignified and respectful view of the consumer at a conference we attended on creativity early in 1962; he has expressed this view in his recently published

---

*The verbal images accurately describe schematic drawings used in some television commercials to "demonstrate" the functions of the body and of the advertised medications. (Editor's note)
**Advertising executive; founder and former president of Ogilvy, Benson, and Mather advertising agency. (Editor's note)

book *Confessions of an Advertising Man* and in his advertisements on Puerto Rico, and on travel in the United States and abroad. This dignified image of man is not true of all his famous advertisements. For example, his Schweppes ads and his Rolls Royce ads associate an inconsequential belief with unconscious primitive beliefs concerning snobbish striving of the self—Type E with Type B—. But his travel ads try to associate psychologically inconsequential beliefs with unconscious primitive beliefs —Type B+—concerning a self which strives to become better-realized, better-rounded, and more open to experience. These ads hold out a dignified promise to let the consumer be and become. /35

But the irrational image of man still predominates in the advertising world. The more inconsequential the benefits of one brand over a competitor's the more desperately the industry has harangued and nagged and, consequently, irritated its mass audience. It's not easy work to convince others that psychologically inconsequential matters are consequential. /36

The fact that the advertising industry attracts such highly talented people, pays them fabulous salaries, and puts them under such terrific pressure —these can all be attributed to the kinds of beliefs it specializes in changing. It is, consequently, no wonder that the advertising profession is reputed to be among the most guilt-ridden, anxiety-ridden, ulcer-ridden, and death-ridden profession in America. /37

I think it significant that four speakers* from the academic world have been invited to come here to speak about the *consumer's* interests, and I think it also significant that on no less than three separate occasions was I reminded in the process of being invited to address you that the agency leaders who organized this meeting "are in no way seeking a whitewash of the advertising business." /38

These facts would seem to suggest the advertising industry's alarm over its predicament, an eagerness to face up to its social responsibility, a search for conviction, and a courage somewhat in excess of conviction. /39

In closing, therefore, let me emphasize again— constructively, I hope—that the advertising man's image of the consumer requires revision in order to bring it more in line not only with the broader and

newer image of man I have all too briefly outlined here but also with the advertising man's image of himself. To the extent that the advertising man can bring himself to do so, he will gain a new respect from the consumer and in the process gain a renewed respect for himself. /40

The speech

1. Study the two following characterizations. Discuss the adequacy and accuracy of each as a capsule report of the content of Rokeach's message.
   a. He "chided the 4A admen for some psychological short-sightedness." *Sponsor*, 17 (November 11, 1963), p. 22.
   b. He told the advertising specialists that "their theories had fallen badly behind the times. . . . Madison Avenue," Dr. Rokeach concluded, "would do well to update its approach to human psychology and appeal to the consumer on a rational basis." The New York *Times*, November 7, 1963, p. 60.

2. Suppose Rokeach had not received assurances that "agency leaders . . . 'are in no way seeking a white-wash of the advertising business'" (paragraph 38), would it have been advisable for him to alter this speech in any way in order to adapt it to his audience? If so, what changes would be needed? If not, point out why and how the speech, as actually given, would suit any general gathering of advertising agency representatives.

3. Rokeach distributed a table of "Types of Beliefs" (p. 117). How necessary was this visual material for effectively communicating Rokeach's message? In what other ways might the content of this table have been presented? Compare, for relative advantages and disadvantages as aids to communication, these alternatives and the method Rokeach actually used.

4. Examine paragraphs 27 through 30 carefully. What is Rokeach seeking to accomplish at this point in his speech? Do his examples of the London Fog advertisement and Candid Camera program contribute fully to his purpose? Why or why not?

5. Has Rokeach given his listeners adequate explanation or identification when he refers in paragraphs 33 and 35 to the Pepto-Bismol and Anacin advertisements, to David Ogilvy, and to the advertisements on Puerto Rico, travel in the United States, Schweppes, Rolls Royce? Would the use of these examples have to be changed if this speech were given in your class? If so, what changes would you make and why?

6. In the first twenty-seven paragraphs of this speech

*The other three speakers on this program were Dr. Norman Martin, Professor of Business Administration, New York University; Dr. Persia Campbell, Professor and Chairman of the Economics Department, Queens College; and Dr. George Katona, Professor of Economics and of Psychology, University of Michigan. (Editor's note) text, Rokeach cites no evidence that does not come from his own and his colleagues' research. Review the points he makes, the occasion, and his relation to his audience. Did he need evidence from other sources in this situation? Why or why not?

7. Comment on Rokeach's introduction and conclusion. What improvements, if any, do you think could be made in his introduction? In his conclusion?

For further study and discussion

1. Are advertisers still failing to associate their products and services with Types B+ and A beliefs—as Rokeach alleged in 1963 that they were? Justify your answer.

2. Explore the hypotheses of behaviorism and classical psychoanalysis to determine how, if at all, these psychological positions contribute to an "image of Irrational Man."

3. Study basic writings by one or more of the psychologists (Carl Rogers, Abraham Maslow, Gordon Allport, Robert White, etc.) mentioned in paragraph 32. To what extent do your findings confirm Rokeach's general statements about the tendencies of modern psychological theories?

4. What application of Rokeach's remarks about advertising could you make in explaining the process of persuasive speaking?

5. Carefully examine one or more persuasive speeches in this book. To what extent, if at all, does the persuasion conform to the standards Rokeach proposes for advertising?

6. What criteria, in your opinion, should a newspaper publisher use in determining what kinds of stories he will emphasize and what kinds of advertising, if any, he will reject? What criteria should a radio or television station owner use in determining what kinds of programs and commercials he will select or reject?

7. What is the "code of good practice" of the National Association of Broadcasters? What does it require of a station or network? Is the code enforced? If so, how?

Suggestions for further reading

Stephen Baker, *Visual Persuasion* (New York, 1961)

Milton H. Biow, *Butting In: An Adman Speaks Out* (Garden City, N.Y., 1964)

Leonard W. Doob, *Public Opinion and Propaganda* (New York, 1948)

Daniel Katz, Dorwin Cartwright, Samuel Eldersveld, Alfred McClung Lee, eds., *Public Opinion and Propaganda* (New York, 1954)

David Ogilvy, *Confessions of an Advertising Man* (New York, 1964)

Charles H. Sandage, ed., *The Promise of Advertising* (Homewood, Ill., 1961)

Poyntz Tyler, ed., *Advertising in America,* Reference Shelf Series, Vol. 31 (New York, 1959)

Moppet manipulation

NANCY JEANNE MYERS

"Moppet Manipulation" is Nancy Jeanne Myers' expression of her reaction to mass media conditions that held the anxious attention of many Americans as the 1950's ended. A number of studies offered unflattering analyses of the attitudes being inculcated by these media. Miss Myers indicates her indebtedness to two of the most famous of these works, David Riesman's *The Lonely Crowd* (1950) and Vance Packard's *The Hidden Persuaders* (1957), books which had done much to create interest in and concern about the nature of television programming.

When Miss Myers prepared the following speech during the spring of 1959, investigations by the District Attorney of New York were revealing that several of the most popular quiz programs on television were "fixed." The scandals proved widespread. Whoever chose to speak about what television was doing to the American character could, in this period, expect to be heard with lively interest and, probably, with active concern.

Miss Myers' address was prepared for delivery at the Women's State Original Oratory competition at Wittenberg College, Springfield, Ohio, in February 1959. Subsequently, it was presented to the national Pi Kappa Delta Convention, to the student body at Otterbein College, and to several service club audiences in Ohio. Because of its special timeliness it was at once a "contest speech" and one with immediate meaning for general audiences. In this it differed from "The Haven of the Defeated" (pp. 148-151) and "The Inner City—Our Shame" (pp. 216-218), though the latter speeches were no less significant in content than "Moppet Manipulation."

Much can be learned about audience adaptation—its possibilities and difficulties—by studying how each of these three student speakers adapted his or her appeal for action to the peculiar requirements of the subject, judged against the events of the day and the audience's preëxisting attitudes and concerns. Miss Myers could appeal to her audience for direct action because events had already aroused anxieties about her subject; moreover, most listeners in any audience she addressed were, or soon would be, involved in rearing and teaching children. Karos and Dinwoodie had not these advantages.

Although only a sophomore at Otterbein College when she composed and delivered "Moppet Manipulation,"

Reprinted by permission of Miss Myers from a copy of her speech provided by Professor James A. Grissinger, Chairman of the Speech Department of Otterbein College, Westerville, Ohio.

Miss Myers was already an experienced speaker. In 1957 she had been a member of a national championship high school debate team, and in her first year in college she was awarded first place in the Ohio State Women's Extemporaneous Speaking Contest. She was also active in college dramatic productions.

Picture for a moment the playroom of a child. Scattered among the various use-worn pieces of furniture are the toys which amuse the room's owner during his hours of play. Two decades ago these objects would have been production-imitating equipment such as toy trucks and steam shovels, miniature printing presses and sewing machines, and Lincoln logs. Stop and think for a minute. What objects dominate the scene of our children's play area today? We would notice a definite increase in the range of the child's toys. They now include a whole new field of objects modeled after the service trades: toy Bell telephones, Sohio service stations, Revlon make-up kits, Toni dolls, and Roy Rogers voice recorders. David Riesman, a prominent psychologist, in his book, *The Lonely Crowd,* says this is a visible indication of the changing American emphasis on consumption. Formerly the nation's youth were trained for production and creation; today the mass media are training young minds in a different line. Today our moppets are being trained for the future positions of skilled consumers. No doubt some of you remember the famous "cheese-glut" of the mid-fifties. Senator Alexander Wiley of Wisconsin made a statement during this time that has been used resourcefully by the modern advertising agencies. He said, "Our problem is not too much cheese produced, but rather too little cheese consumed." This has become the contemporary American ideology. /1

This ideology is not confined to adults as you might expect. Today it is the youth of America who are bearing the brunt of the advertiser's campaign—a campaign designed to so condition our reflexes that we subconsciously prescribe a certain brand or brands . . . "Be sociable, be smart, be up to date with Pepsi!" "Wheaties—breakfast of Champions!" "Wonder bread builds strong bodies twelve ways!" "Kleenex pops up like a jack-in-the-box!" The American Marketing Association has said that it need not worry now about obtaining funds to penetrate the youth market, that its problem is instead the determining of the way in which they can most effective-ly penetrate it with lasting impression. After all, as an ad appearing in a TV manufacturer's trade journal once exclaimed, "Where else on earth is brand consciousness so firmly fixed as in the minds of four-year-old tots?" The Association has also pointed out, with some exultation by the admen, that today most children can, and do, memorize long strings of beer and other commercials even before they learn to sing the "Star-Spangled Banner" or pray the Lord's Prayer. Are these the ideals we wish to fix in our moppets' minds? /2

A more blunt statement of the liberties taken by admen in this subconscious direction of children's minds appeared in an edition of *Printer's Ink* several years ago. The following appeal was made to merchandisers and advertisers by a firm specializing in supplying such educational materials as manuals, room decorations and wall charts. It ran: "Eager minds can be molded to want your products. In the grade schools of America there are twenty-three million boys and girls. These children eat food, wear out clothes, use soap. They are consumers today and will be the buyers of tomorrow. Here is a vast market for your goods. Sell these children on your brand name and they will insist that their parents buy no other. Many far-sighted advertisers are cashing in today—and building for tomorrow by molding eager minds. . . ." through material supplied to teachers. /3

Is this the future toward which we wish to look? Will we be complacent enough to allow our children's minds to be conditioned in such a way? What can we do to dispel the growing characterization of America's youth as "consumer-trainees"? /4

You may question whether or not this control of children's minds by industry actually is a problem facing America at the present time. In other words, "What's wrong with it? The worst that can happen is that we'll end up with pantries full of breakfast cereal we don't need. In the field of commerce children are considered fair game and legitimate prey." Yet in the field of religion or politics, manipulation of children's minds would result in a storm of parental protest and a rash of congressional investigations. Can we be sure that the manipulation of our children's minds will end with merely the field of commerce? Especially when the other institutions recognize the success of depth or motivational research in this area. Already we can find evidences of motivational techniques being used by church and service groups and state and federal governments. Do we not adjust the dials on our TV set when the picture becomes distorted? What can we do to combat this threat to America's future before it too spreads and distorts our focus? /5

There are, as you have noticed, two major areas through which this "depth research" is attempting to etch itself in the children's subconscious—education, or the classroom, and TV. From this "mind-engraving" the admen desire two things: first, that the conditioning will result in ten million who, as adults, will be trained to buy a certain brand of product just as Alaskan huskies are trained to advance when they hear the word, "Mush." The other thing the admen want is that parents' consumption will shift and increase because of their children's submission to the siren song of the solicitor. /6

Certainly our first and major consideration should be as parents, for as parents we are affected not only by irrational demands for certain products, but also by the knowledge that minds are being molded without the knowledge of their owners. The first thing we must do as parents is keep a firm hand on the dial of the TV set. Too many parents are too satisfied with the golden moments of relaxation stolen during the time the kiddies are absorbed in the messages of the "electronic wonder"—too satisfied to be concerned with what their children are watching. It has been said that while children cannot be turned off, the set can. By keeping one eye on the TV screen and one hand on the dial of the set, we can prevent much of what is objectionable in depth research from reaching our impressionable "trainees." Second, because we will not always be able to stop the advertisers at their outlet, we should insist that our children have rational bases for requests for certain brands and particular products. In this way we can thwart the efforts of the TV commercials aimed at "impulse buying" at supermarkets and well-stocked grocery shelves. And third, we must as parents accept the "ruling relationship" that is ours in the modern family. Social research reports have shown that "to children, adults are a ruling class against which they cannot successfully revolt." We would do well to be what our children think we are. Let's put our proverbial feet down when it will do the most good. When Junior reaches for that new cereal package because he has seen the man on TV demonstrate the plastic space gun inside, and the kitchen pantry is already overflowing with buys of just such motivation, let's say "No!" and stick to it. It is easy to say "Yes" to a child's demands. The strength is needed when a time to deny his wishes approaches. /7

In this way we neutralize one of the two opportunities used to etch admen's images into America's youth—TV. What about the other—the classroom? What can we do there? /8

Well, first, as teachers, which many of us are or intend to be, we can select carefully the educational materials we use in our classrooms, minimizing "brands for brands' sake." This could be a major way of reducing the unconscious impression brand names make on pupils from wall decorations and materials. Then, secondly, and most important, we can include logic as a part of our curriculum. Logic is not restricted to the college professor's use as a classroom subject. Dr. Frances Horwich, "principal" of TV's "Ding Dong School," in her intimate conversation with the eager tots viewing her program advised them to insist that their mothers select the "right" bottle of vitamins the next time they went to the store. Teachers can turn this kind of experience into a fascinating logic lesson. It could be done simply by discussing kinds of pills and arriving at a rational decision about which kind was best. Such questions as: Can we tell which is best by the color? By the size? By how many are in a bottle? could eliminate the conditioning of impulses to buy a pill just because "Miss Frances" said so! Indeed, as instructors we are responsible and can do something about the distorting effect of consumerism. /9

If, then, we as parents and teachers have partially succeeded in tuning out the interference of moppet manipulators, can we not use another channel also —that of the consumer? /10

We all know that merchandisers offer inducements to encourage children to lead their parents into a salesroom. Vance Packard reminds us in his book, *The Hidden Persuaders,* how General Electric offers a sixty piece circus, a magic-ray gun, and a space helmet to children who bring their parents into dealers' stores to witness demonstrations of new GE refrigerators. Sylvania offers a Space Ranger kit complete with disintegrator, flying saucer, and space telephone to children who manage to deliver parents to the salesroom. And Nash offers a toy service station. We can "turn off" this method by refusing to be "conned" into buying, or even examining, unnecessary products. Also we, as consumers, have perhaps the loudest voice of all when we make our disapproval of such techniques known to manufacturers, advertisers, and broadcast media who are interested always in maintaining a contented public. Listening councils, P.T.A., and community groups, plus individual efforts can have considerable effect on the way in which advertising dollars are spent. /11

Just as we can turn the TV screen on and off,

change its focus and its brightness, we as parents, teachers and consumers have controls that can turn on and off and change the focus or brightness of the distorting and potentially subversive efforts of the admen employing depth research. By using these controls, we can provide the child in that playroom with hours of contented play—play with telephones, not Bell telephones—make-up kits, not Revlon products—and dolls, not Toni dolls. We can watch his future being molded by rational thinking . . . not by those who would be "moppet manipulators." /12

The speech

1. Review *appeal*, *attitude*, *motivation*, and *suggestion* in the Glossary, and then describe as precisely as possible the persuasive potentials of Miss Myers' choice of a title for her speech.

2. Like Karos' "The Haven of the Defeated" (pp. 148-151) and Dinwoodie's "The Inner City—Our Shame" (pp. 216-218), this speech was delivered in a public speaking contest. Compare Miss Myers' attempts to adapt to the active interests of her student-faculty audience with similar attempts by Karos and Dinwoodie. Which speaker succeeds best in breaking through the contest situation to genuinely involve the listeners in the problem discussed? What are the reasons for your answer?

3. David Riesman, Senator Alexander Wiley, and Vance Packard are cited as authorities in this speech. Does the speaker adequately qualify each as an authority? Which of these authorities probably has the greatest prestige and therefore lends the most suggestive support to Miss Myers' arguments?

4. What emotions and drives does Miss Myers rely on to insure that her listeners will take unfavorable views of the advertising methods she describes?

5. From paragraph 7 to the end of this speech "we" are pictured as being engaged in a kind of competition with "admen." What attention factors and interest value does this add to the speech?

6. Miss Myers' speech conforms rather closely to the pattern of organization called the "motivated sequence." (See the Glossary). Identify the five steps of the sequence in this speech.

7. "Moppet Manipulation" is a persuasive speech. Does it aim at changing attitudes, opinions, or emotions, or all three? Identify several points at which the speaker is clearly trying to effect these kinds of changes.

8. An analogy provides the framework for the conclusion of this speech (paragraph 12). Is the analogy used as argument or figurative illustration? How, if at all, does this analogy contribute to variety in the speech?

For further study and discussion

1. Most adults identify commodities by specific trade names or their derivatives: coke, kleenex, etc. Is this undesirable? Why? Is it more undesirable that children should do so? Why? Why not?

2. What criteria do you suggest for distinguishing improper from proper advertising addressed to children or adolescents? Should advertising addressed to these groups be prohibited?

3. Senator Wiley's "explanation" of the cheese surplus has been applied to most farm surpluses. Do you think federal and state departments of agriculture should continue to spend tax money to promote wider use of eggs, milk, corn, cotton, and like products? Does Miss Myers' implied criticism of "consumerism" properly apply in such circumstances?

4. What is your opinion of "built-in obsolescence"—building products to wear out earlier than necessary or changing models to render older but usable products less appealing? Does our competitive economy require such practices in order to prosper?

5. Make a survey of advertising addressed to children. Is Miss Myers right in implying that most such advertising encourages children to prefer one product over another for illogical reasons? If so, is this more nearly true when children are addressed than when adults are addressed?

6. Many corporations and industrial organizations offer so-called educational services and teaching aids for use in the classroom. Study some of these services and materials. Are they objectionable? How does one decide when "moppet manipulation" is involved and when it is not?

7. Miss Myers assumes that the young actually believe and imitate what they see and hear via the media of mass communication. Is this really true? To what extent and under what circumstances? Is there scientific evidence on the point?

8. It has been alleged that there is as much cruelty, horror, and dishonesty in a typical fairy tale taken from *Grimm's Fairy Tales* as in the most violent children's fare on television. Is this true? If so, should it make any difference in our opinion of television programs for children?

9. Would action by parents' groups, PTA groups, and others seeking to force changes in television advertising be open to charges of "pressure-group" cen-

sorship such as Preminger levels at the Legion of Decency (see "Movies and Censorship," pp. 128-130, paragraphs 27, 29, and 63)?

10. Compare Miss Myers' criticism of advertisers with that of Rokeach (pp. 115-121). Could this speech be changed sufficiently to make the speech suitable for Rokeach's audience? If so, how? If not, why not?

Suggestions for further reading

Leon Arons and Mark A. May, eds., *Television and Human Behavior* (New York, 1963)

Walter B. Emery, *Broadcasting and Government: Responsibilities and Regulations* (East Lansing, Mich., 1961)

Burton Paulu, *British Broadcasting in Transition* (Minneapolis, 1961)

Wilbur L. Schramm, ed., *The Impact of Educational Television* (Urbana, Ill., 1960)

Wilbur L. Schramm and others, *Television in the Lives of Our Children* (Stanford, Calif., 1961)

Charles A. Siepman, *TV and Our School Crisis* (New York, 1958)

UNESCO, *Screen Education: A Critical Approach to Cinema and Television,* International Documents Service, Columbia University Press, New York

Movies and censorship

C.B.S. "SMALL WORLD" TELECAST

Small World was a unique discussion program produced by Edward R. Murrow and Fred W. Friendly and broadcast over the Columbia Broadcasting System Television Network. From various parts of the world the *Small World* broadcasts brought together, electronically, outstanding personalities for half-hour discussions of significant issues.

The four participants in the *Small World* telecast "Movies and Censorship," of April 10, 1960, were separated from each other by thousands of miles, as indicated in the transcript below; but the effect of the production was, for the viewer, very nearly that of seeing a face-to-face discussion. The program's director

and engineers followed the discussion closely, broadcasting the image of each speaker as he or she began a contribution or when the remarks of one participant seemed to be making a strong impression on another. The conversation was spontaneous and unrehearsed, though there had been preliminary planning. Those who saw and heard the program could hear all participants at all times.

Each of the three guests on the program had first-hand knowledge of the subject being considered. Monsignor John J. McClafferty was born in New York City in 1906. He attended Xavier High School, received his A.B. from Cathedral College in 1927, attended St. Joseph's Seminary, was awarded his A.M. by the Catholic University in 1932 and a diploma by the New York School of Social Work in 1936. He was ordained a priest of the Roman Catholic Church in 1930, appointed Monsignor in 1943, and Domestic Prelate in 1953. Father McClafferty has had a special interest in education and in social work throughout his career. From 1936 to 1947 he was Executive Secretary of the National Legion of Decency; during part of the same period he was a consultant for the National Church of the Air, Columbia Broadcasting System. He has also been an adviser to other religious and educational programs. At the time of the broadcast, he was at the Catholic University of America, Washington, D.C., where he had been Dean of the National Catholic School of Social Service from 1947 to 1955. Father McClafferty is now pastor of St. Peter's Church, Staten Island.

Deborah Kerr is a highly successful actress. She was born at Helensburgh, Scotland, in 1921 and attended the Helensburgh schools and Northumberland House School in Bristol, England. She began her film career by appearing in the British motion picture *Major Barbara* in 1940. After considerable success in the cinema and on the stage in England, she came to the United States in 1947. Among the later films in which she has appeared are: *From Here to Eternity, Tea and Sympathy, The King and I, Bonjour Tristesse,* and *The Journey.* As she indicates in the discussion, Miss Kerr has from time to time found reason to protest against certain forms of film censorship.

Otto Preminger is an outspoken, eminently successful producer-director of motion pictures and stage plays. He was born in Vienna, Austria, in 1906, and he holds the LL.D. from the University of Vienna. He began his career as producer-director at the Max Reinhardt Theatre der Josefstadt in Vienna but came to the United States in 1935. In New York he directed several major stage productions, among them *Margin for Error* and *Outward Bound.* In recent years Preminger has been primarily engaged in producing and directing motion pictures and has been very successful, both artistically and commercially.

Reprinted by permission of CBS News, Miss Deborah Kerr, Mr. Otto Preminger, and Monsignor John J. McClafferty.

Some of his pictures have been universally praised while others have been the sources of controversy and even litigation. Among the more famous of his many films are: *Fallen Angel, Forever Amber, Whirlpool, The Moon Is Blue, Carmen Jones, Saint Joan, Anatomy of a Murder,* and *Bonjour Tristesse.*

The text of "Movies and Censorship" that follows is from a typescript of the broadcast, supplied by the Columbia Broadcasting System. It is an accurate rendering-in-print of actual, spontaneous conversation. It can, therefore, be studied as an unedited representation of the language used by educated, articulate persons engaged in serious discussion. The organizational and stylistic qualities found here can be compared and contrasted with similar qualities found in transcripts of formal discussion, public speaking, or the various forms of written discourse. And, since the oral styles of the three major participants in this discussion are very different, these differences may themselves be the objects of profitable study.

ANNOUNCER: *Small World* is a four way transoceanic conversation filmed and edited by Murrow and Friendly. /1

DEBORAH KERR: This is Deborah Kerr, speaking from Klosters in Switzerland. /2

OTTO PREMINGER: This is Otto Preminger in Rome. /3

JOHN J. MC CLAFFERTY: This is Father McClafferty at the Catholic University of America, Washington, D.C. /4

EDWARD R. MURROW: This is *Small World,* and this is Ed Murrow in Hong Kong. /5

COMMERCIAL

MURROW: Good evening. Today on *Small World:* "Movies and Censorship"—or perhaps I should say "classification." From Washington, Monsignor John J. McClafferty, of the Catholic University of America, former head of the Legion of Decency. Monsignor, may I present that very fine actress, Miss Deborah Kerr. We all remember her in *Tea and Sympathy* and *From Here to Eternity*—two movies that are perhaps bench marks in the continuing controversy as to what the general audience should and should not see. Miss Kerr is in Klosters, Switzerland, tonight. Deborah, how's the snow? /6

KERR: Lovely, thank you. I understand from the skiers, it's great. /7

MC CLAFFERTY: How do you do, Miss Kerr. /8

KERR: How do you do, Monsignor. /9

MURROW: Our third guest ought really to be in Israel tonight, because he is filming *Exodus* there, but he's flown to Rome because the circuits from there are a little more reliable. Otto Preminger produced *Anatomy of a Murder* and *The Moon Is Blue.* Both of these pictures brought him into very considerable controversy with the Legion of Decency and other organizations. Mr. Preminger, I'm delighted that three people of such differing views have agreed to appear on *Small World* and disagree agreeably about the subject of censorship and movies. /10

PREMINGER: I am happy to be here and I can add to the conversation about the weather. The weather in Haifa, Tel Aviv, and in Rome, today, is delightful and very warm. /11

MURROW: Well, since we are going to talk about censorship or classification,* I suggest we begin by trying to define it. /12

PREMINGER: I think that censorship is an evil institution, where the State or other authorities try to impose their will on people who otherwise should enjoy the free expression of a medium of communication. I think that censorship is the first step in totalitarian government, regardless of whether the government is from the right or from the left, and therefore, I call it evil. When we speak about censorship today, we speak mainly about pre-censorship. It is a submission of some work or expression that we want to put into communication (like books, newspapers, or a speech on radio or a motion picture)—to submit it before we show it to the public, for permission to be shown. /13

MC CLAFFERTY: Yes. I gather, then, that Mr. Preminger, you make a distinction between censorship in respect to prior restraint and censorship in respect to post restraint. /14

PREMINGER: Naturally, I think that the laws of the United States give the police, in every State, the right, if somebody shows something obscene—whether it is in a magazine, in a book, or on the screen—to confiscate it, and to start criminal procedure. /15

KERR: It's not done enough then—is it? /16

PREMINGER: Huh? /17

KERR: That's not done enough. I'm always astounded at how many obscene magazines there are. /18

---

*As used here this term refers to the practice of classifying and publicly announcing the kind of audience for which a film is intended. See also paragraph 48. (*Editor's note*)

PREMINGER: Well, I am there with you as far as magazines are concerned, because I have suffered, personally, probably as much as you, Deborah, but I must say that the freedom of the press is probably worthwhile taking a little abuse, personally. /19

KERR: Yes, I agree with you there, but it's so difficult this whole business of censorship. Isn't it? I feel like the Libran* that I am, on the scales between you, Otto, and you, Monsignor, in that I always see both sides of the question, and . . . /20

PREMINGER: Well, I don't think it's really so difficult, because, at least in the United States, the Supreme Court has very often, in almost all cases, expressed, as far as the movies go, the opinion that pre-censorship is illegal, and whenever the Supreme Court was asked, it has declared censorship unconstitutional. /21

MC CLAFFERTY: I think I would differ with you with regard to that, because as far as I know, the Supreme Court has not definitively determined, up to the present time, with regard to the constitutionality, per se . . . /22

PREMINGER: That is true—because the Supreme Court . . . /23

MC CLAFFERTY: . . . of censorship. /24

PREMINGER: . . . tries to avoid making laws. But you must admit, Monsignor, that in no case has a Censorship Board won in front of the United States Supreme Court, at least not since 1923, since the Supreme Court has made it clear that motion pictures are a means of communication. /25

MC CLAFFERTY: In a ruling of the Supreme Court, fairly recently, in *Kingsley vs. Brown,* that Court held that prior restraint should be considered in the case of the particular analysis of each film, and in the case of *Roth* and in the case of *Alberts,* the Supreme Court has undertaken to define rather precisely what obscene is, in terms of a regulation or a control with regard to the exhibition of films. /26

PREMINGER: There is, of course, in the United States, another unofficial censorship. There are private groups which I may call pressure groups, which have never been very successful with books, magazines or newspapers, but have been very successful with the motion pictures during the last thirty years, telling them what they may

and may not show on the screen. I don't want to seem or sound like a crusader, and I would like to keep the perspective of good humor in this, but I made a small comedy called *The Moon Is Blue,* and both the Code Administration in Hollywood and the Legion of Decency declared that this cannot be shown on the screens of the United States. In the United States there was a great, great, tremendous publicity campaign against the picture, and I was told by many people the picture would never be shown. /27

MC CLAFFERTY: May I make . . . /28

PREMINGER: So I played the picture anyway, and the picture was a very big success all over the world, and particularly in the United States, in spite of being banned by both the Motion Picture Code Administration in Hollywood and the Legion of Decency, and I really don't think that anybody's character has been corrupted by seeing this rather harmless little comedy.* /29

MC CLAFFERTY: We have to enter at this point a discussion of fundamental moral values, and also make a consideration of the nature of the film as a medium of entertainment in terms of theme and thesis, but before entering into that . . . /30

PREMINGER: But films are not a medium of entertainment. They are mediums of communication. /31

MC CLAFFERTY: That it is. /32

PREMINGER: In fact, the theatre is the same medium or a very similar medium, and why did nobody object to people seeing the same comedy in the theatre, and why should it be sinful to see it in the movies? /33

KERR: Isn't it because there are so many more people involved? /34

MC CLAFFERTY: Yes, definitely. /35

PREMINGER: Why shouldn't the people—this is a, a very—I am surprised, Deborah, this is a rather, a rather snobbish and rather reactionary point of view. /36

KERR: No, No. /37

PREMINGER: Why shouldn't many people see the same thing as a few? /38

KERR: Well, I don't mean many people. I think there are more children involved. /39

MC CLAFFERTY: Yes, and adolescents. /40

KERR: And I am with you entirely, Otto. I have suf-

---

*From Libra, the seventh sign of the zodiac. Miss Kerr was born on September 30, a date that falls under the sign of Libra, a balance or pair of scales. (Editor's note)

*This film and Rossellini's *The Miracle* were among the most controversial pictures shown in the United States during the 1950's. Recent history of film censorship is virtually epitomized in the record of local, state, and federal decisions concerning *The Moon Is Blue, The Miracle,* and the French film *La Ronde.* (Editor's note) fered myself, from a very lovely play—it was *Tea and Sympathy*—being censored as far as the movie is concerned, and consequently being ruined as a movie, and yet its message that it carried was one of great, great compassion and tenderness, and really a message for the world, put through perhaps rather startling means. So, I am with you on that, but I have to say that I do see both sides of the question. I can see that in a mass medium, which television is, and movies are, I think you have got to have some form of control. Should I say control rather than censorship? /41

PREMINGER: But, darling, who should control it? /42

MC CLAFFERTY: Now, a State, and this is true, historically, has the right of self-protection and self-preservation. It must exercise certain kinds of responsible controls, whether it be in the field of public safety; whether it be in the field of public morals. But in the United States, with our cherished tradition, and thanks be to God for this tradition, the tradition of freedom, the central issue is the right balance between freedom and restraint. /43

PREMINGER: Well, there is no . . . /44

MC CLAFFERTY: Now, this freedom must be a responsibly exercised freedom with due cognizance taken of the social and moral welfare of the community; with due cognizance taken of the impressionable young people who view films, whose lifes' habits and attitudes are being formed and shaped. For their own welfare and for society's well-being, these considerations should counsel us to be socially and morally responsible in this exercise of one of the most precious freedoms that we have. /45

PREMINGER: Monsignor, your speech would have converted me if it had been necessary. I agree with you in everything you said, but it does not touch the real, practical problem that we are trying to discuss here. /46

KERR: No, I don't think so either. /47

PREMINGER: Censorship becomes in almost all cases —or I would say in all cases—a political question and a political football, and that is the danger. Now, I must say that I, personally, think that no grown-up man or woman should be told what they can see. There is another question that Deborah has brought up before about children. Now, strangely enough, as much as I am against any kind of censorship, particularly private censorship by pressure groups, I am very much for self-

classification of pictures, and wherever I can, I classify my own pictures and ask the exhibitors to, in their publicity, have a warning to parents . . . /48

KERR: Yes, well . . . /49

PREMINGER: . . . because I feel that parents should have a right to bring up their children in their own way, and if they don't want them to see pictures of some kind, they shouldn't see them. /50

KERR: But think about—think—there are too many parents that don't seem to have enough control over their children to stop them going to these pictures. /51

PREMINGER: But this cannot be helped by motion picture producers. /52

KERR: This is—this is the—this is the trouble, isn't it? /53

PREMINGER: I mean, there must be somebody else helping these parents. You cannot blame everything on—on motion pictures. If parents cannot control their children, then the motion picture censorship certainly won't help it, because there are many, many other areas where these children probably will be sinning and doing very bad things, regardless of motion pictures. /54

KERR: Yes, I agree. After all, we can—we can censor ourselves. We don't have to buy a newspaper if we find its policy offensive to us. /55

PREMINGER: That's right. /56

KERR: And we could just as well, you know, not go into the cinema if we don't like the subject. /57

MURROW: Excuse me. I am afraid I must censor all of us for one moment while we hear from Olin Mathieson. /58

COMMERCIAL

ANNOUNCER: *Small World* continues with Deborah Kerr, Otto Preminger, Monsignor John J. McClafferty, and Ed Murrow. /59

MC CLAFFERTY: I like very much, Miss Kerr, what you say about the individual having a responsibility to choose well and to not choose that which he may deem to be morally harmful to himself. I think that you can conceive of these ways of control in a series of expanding concentric circles. The first control, of course, is the control by the individual, according to the light of his conscience, and according to the information which he has at hand about the particular film in question. Then, of course, there is the area of parental control and the area of the counsel of voluntary associations. I don't term such counsel "censorship" or "pressure." /60

PREMINGER: No. I agree with you, as long as the Legion of Decency would tell only their members what to see and what not to see, I would never object to it. /61

MC CLAFFERTY: The Legion of De . . . /62

PREMINGER: But when the Legion of Decency threatens the theatres with boycott if they play certain pictures, then I think they go beyond what should be permissible. /63

MC CLAFFERTY: Yes. The Legion of Decency counsels its own members and, exercising its right of free association and free expression and free communication, makes known to its followers what its moral estimate of a given film is, but again, may I backtrack in the discussion, to something—or rather two things that you said, Mr. Preminger? First of all, you indicated that you felt you had a right to produce and exhibit whatever you wished. I do not think that that is an absolute right. I think that that is a right that must be exercised in a morally and socially responsible way in the light of the commonweal. /64

PREMINGER: That's right, but I must be the sole judge of what is morally responsible. /65

MC CLAFFERTY: Yes. And secondly, you said that each adult has the right to see what he wishes. Again, I do not think that that is an absolute right. I think that that is a right which must be exercised intelligently, prudently and wisely by the individual. /66

PREMINGER: But Monsignor, why should the censor's character not be corrupted when he sees these things, in order to tell people not to see them? And why should any other adult be corrupted when he sees them? /67

MC CLAFFERTY: Well, I . . . /68

PREMINGER: What makes the censor so special? /69

MC CLAFFERTY: I do not wish to be put into any position of advocating or sustaining, necessarily, official censorship. My own personal opinion is this (and I want to make it clear that I am not speaking for any group of any organization when I say it)—my own personal opinion would be against federal censorship of motion pictures. I would like to . . . /70

PREMINGER: I am all for that. /71

KERR: Otto, I am dying to ask you something. /72

PREMINGER: Yes? /73

KERR: About—you know, one has often thought, "Right, abolish censorship!" What happens if you abolish censorship? /74

PREMINGER: But we don't have censorship in the United States, Deborah. /75

KERR: No. What I was going to say, Otto, what I really wanted to ask you about was this, which has always bothered me. Were—it's all to do with censorship. If you have no censorship, or even if you have it in a very strict form, how can you— how can we . . . You are a sincere person. When you make your films, you do it with sincerity and you do it with taste, and I think taste is probably the keynote of this whole thing. I mean, anything, any message, can be given and point made if it's done with taste, but we are so wide open in our medium, and certainly in television, it seems to me, or perhaps less at the moment, I don't know, to the unscrupulous, half-talented person who sees in the making of a movie a great deal of money. /76

PREMINGER: Deborah, may I say that I personally believe in the good taste of the great masses? I have never heard of anybody becoming rich because he sold dirty books or dirty postcards, and I don't think anybody has ever become rich by making really dirty or obscene motion pictures. /77

KERR: Well, not rich—shall we say done rather well. /78

MURROW: Monsignor McClafferty, is it admissible that any group should attempt to control or influence what those who are not members to that group should see or hear? /79

MC CLAFFERTY: Well, it would be my thought that the voluntary group, exercising its right of free comment and moral evaluation, ought to communicate that moral evaluation to those who follow it, and communicate it likewise to the media of communication, so that that opinion may be communicated to the public at large. /80

PREMINGER: I must say that I would not object to it at all. /81

MC CLAFFERTY: I just wanted to make this point: I do not think that voluntary groups would wish to exercise coercive methods, but rather that they would wish to exercise persuasive methods. /82

PREMINGER: May I repeat my question which you did not answer, Monsignor, before? Then why does then the Legion of Decency, when it condemns a picture, also threaten the theatres that play it with boycott for their next pictures? Do you think this is right? /83

MC CLAFFERTY: First of all, I am not here as the spokesman of the Legion. /84

PREMINGER: No, but—but you are familiar with the practices of the Legion. /85

MC CLAFFERTY: I want to clarify the position in

which I express myself. I express myself as an individual. /86

PREMINGER: I realize this, but I still, for information, would like to ask you this question—what your personal opinion about it is. /87

MC CLAFFERTY: The Legion does not go, according to my recollection of its operation, to a motion picture company and make demands that this or that be done, or that this or that not be done. /88

PREMINGER: But it's my own picture, *The Moon Is Blue*. Here both—both Archbishops of New York and Philadelphia published letters in the newspapers, threatening theatres which played the picture to be boycotted by the members of the Legion of Decency—also for future exhibitions which by themselves were not condemned. /89

MC CLAFFERTY: The action of the Legion, under the leadership of such spiritual leaders that you mention, was in furtherance of the pastoral Ministry of the Church, namely, the spiritual well-being of those who are members of the Church, and those and others who follow the Legion classifications. I do not know of any central policy of the national office of the Legion which imposes any boycott or abstention for a period of time. There may be efforts on the local level for such supplementary action, but that is within the discretion and within the freedom of those subsidiary local efforts, because the national office of the . . . /90

PREMINGER: Do you, personally, approve of such actions? /91

MC CLAFFERTY: . . . Legion would give to those local efforts the freedom which all of us would like to see observed in all of the sectors of society, namely, a responsibly used freedom. /92

PREMINGER: Do you, personally, Monsignor, approve of such actions? /93

MC CLAFFERTY: Well, I don't explicitly understand what you mean by "such actions." You mean boycott? /94

PREMINGER: Yes. /95

MC CLAFFERTY: I, personally, would prefer that such voluntary associations utilize persuasive and interpretative methods rather than coercive methods, but it may be that the judgment of prudent men on the . . . /96

PREMINGER: I am very glad to hear that. /97

MC CLAFFERTY: . . . on the local level—that they have high responsibilities and the highest within a given territory, to see to it that their people are protected morally and spiritually, and that the people not be roadblocked in their progress towards spiritual perfection—roadblocked by any

such thing as a film that might be immoral or obscene. /98

PREMINGER: You agree, though, that this should only be done to members, by members, of a certain group, and should not extend to people who do not belong to the same creed, the same Legion, or the same group of people? /99

MC CLAFFERTY: Well, we must remember this—that just as the Code is based upon generally accepted moral standards, so too, the work of the Legion, generally, is based upon the fundamental Ten Commandments which should guide our relations to our neighbor in terms of rights and duties, and our relation to God in terms of our rights and duties. I believe, Mr. Preminger, that a great majority of the pictures which have been deemed worthy of receiving a so-called Oscar, have been rated in the "A" category by the Legion of Decency. I think this is a tribute not only to the good judgment of the Legion, but also to the good judgment of the audience, in having such a coincidence of opinion with respect to films that are judged to be worthwhile and outstanding. /100

PREMINGER: I want to state here, that neither Greta Garbo nor Ernest Lubitsch, nor Chaplin ever received an Oscar, and these certainly are three geniuses of the motion picture business. /101

KERR: Hear! Hear! /102

PREMINGER: Does anyone disagree? /103

KERR: No—not me! /104

PREMINGER: I think a producer has a right to make social comments, and it still can be very entertaining. As, for instance, recently, a picture *On the Beach* has proved—which made considerable social comments and still seems to be doing very, very well at the box office—and I do feel that pictures can be controversial and attack certain principles that might be very dear to certain segments of the population, without really insulting those segments of the population, if they are done in good taste and with the right feeling for drama. /105

MC CLAFFERTY: There is also the hazard, I believe, that when certain subject materials are shown on the screen, certain impressionable and perhaps unstable audience members may be tempted toward an experimental adoption of such a way of life . . . /106

KERR: Yes. /107

MC CLAFFERTY: . . . or toward an experimental use of such a way of life. /108

PREMINGER: But that is always true. We live in a very hazardous world. /109

KERR: That's why I would do away with horror films. I think they are much worse . . . /110

MC CLAFFERTY: Yes. /111

KERR: . . . all the dreadful tortures they practice and horrible things they do to people—ugh! /112

MC CLAFFERTY: When the Senate was investigating juvenile delinquency, a number of clinical experts testified, and in their opinion, there was a likely connection, a presumed connection between the amount and character of violence and horror on the screen, and the rising tide of juvenile delinquency, and I believe that this rising tide of juvenile delinquency is one of the reasons why there has been some resurgence of opinion and pressure within the population for some forms of control on the mass media of communication. /113

KERR: Yes. /114

MURROW: I'm sorry. Monsignor McClafferty, Miss Deborah Kerr, Mr. Otto Preminger, thank you all very much, indeed. Next week's guests in just a moment. /115

COMMERCIAL

ANNOUNCER: Next week on *Small World*, Professor Harold Urey of the University of California; Dr. Wernher von Braun of the National Aeronautics and Space Administration; and John Davy, Scientific Correspondent of the London Observer, discuss the problems of space and why should man want to get to the moon. /116

Tonight's conversation between Deborah Kerr, Otto Preminger and Monsignor John J. McClafferty was recorded and filmed simultaneously in Klosters, Switzerland; Rome; and Washington, D.C. Again, next week, Olin Mathieson brings you *Small World*. /117

The telecast

1. This discussion follows the *reflective* pattern of organization in some but not all respects (see Glossary). Which phases of reflection have the participants neglected? With what results for their listeners?

2. Evaluate the ways in which McClafferty and Preminger handle evidence in paragraphs 21 through 26. Which speaker has the better evidence? Which handles it more persuasively? Why?

3. In paragraph 27 Preminger seems to propose a change in what he calls "unofficial censorship." Does he thus assume the burden of proof on this point for the rest of the discussion? If so, does he effectively discharge that burden during the discussion?

4. Mr. Preminger and Miss Kerr contend that Monsignor McClafferty has missed "the practical problem we're trying to discuss here" (paragraphs 46-47). Can you identify that problem? What could have been done to make it easier for listeners to be sure of what these speakers meant?

5. Speeches, whether long or short, are most easily understood if they have central ideas, are related to their settings by introductions of some sort, and are concluded in a way that reminds the listener of the point that has been made. Using these criteria, evaluate the structure of the "speeches" that form paragraphs 13, 27-29, 41, 43-45, and 90-92.

6. This program evolved into a kind of debate between Monsignor McClafferty and Mr. Preminger, with comment and questions from Miss Kerr. In the remarks of the two "debaters" identify examples of each of the following methods of argument: dilemma, refutation, rebuttal.

7. Review the topic of *implication* in the Glossary. Is there any ground for thinking that in this discussion there is too much argument by implication and too little direct statement of propositions? If so, what are the principles and the evidence on which such a judgment is to be made?

8. The transcript of this discussion accurately represents an "animated conversation as carried on among educated persons" (see *conversational quality*, Glossary). Identify three or four passages having the directness, spontaneity, and informality a good public speaker might well copy. Identify three or four passages that illustrate uncertainty in language and organization that public speakers in more formal circumstances should avoid even while aiming at conversational quality.

9. What principles of formal speechmaking, if any, do *not* apply to informal, discussional speaking of the kind represented by this transcript?

10. Had you been the moderator of this program, would you have intervened in the discussion more often than Murrow did? If so, where and for what purpose?

For further study and discussion

1. Trace the history of F. Hugh Herbert's play *The Moon Is Blue* as a theatrical and then as a film production, or trace the court battles leading to the United States Supreme Court's decision on censorship of *The Miracle* by New York State. Can you draw any conclusions from these records as to whether censorship of motion pictures is desirable or legal?

2. Professor Fred B. Millett said in a speech entitled "The Vigilantes," "That the censorship of literature is usual-

ly self-defeating is so obvious as hardly to need explication. The very fact that a censor openly designates a work as dubious . . . is enough to draw the attention . . . of the public to a work that might otherwise have gone unnoticed." Do you agree or disagree? On what evidence? If Millett was right, is Preminger's practice of warning parents concerning some pictures equally self-defeating?

3. What is the Motion Picture Producers' Code? What is its history and how does the Code Administration work? Has it significantly affected the quality of motion pictures?

4. What is the Legion of Decency? What are its objectives and how does it work? What have been the results of its efforts?

5. Do you agree with Miss Kerr and Monsignor McClafferty that the standards of acceptability cannot be the same for the legitimate theater and for movies and television? Why?

6. What taboos other than those concerning sex are observed in television and motion picture production? Is there any clear evidence that the taboos of these industries directly affect the creation of original and significant works?

7. Explore the history of federal action through antitrust suits aimed at breaking the connection between the agencies producing films and those distributing them. What was the reason for these suits? What have been the results?

8. What significance have these films in the history of cinematic art: *The Great Train Robbery, Birth of a Nation, Intolerance, Nanook of the North, The Covered Wagon, The Jazz Singer?* What technical advances or creative ideas made each of these films a "landmark"?

9. How has the advent of television affected the organization and economy of the motion picture industry? How did the development of the motion picture industry affect the legitimate theater?

10. Assume that Preminger is right in saying that a good film is not an entertainment but a "communication." What was being communicated in the most impressive motion picture you have recently seen?

Suggestions for further reading

Robert B. Downs, ed., *The First Freedom: Liberty and Justice in the World of Books and Reading* (Chicago, 1960)

Morris L. Ernst and Alan U. Schwartz, **Censorship; The Search for the Obscene** (New York, 1964)

Harold C. Gardiner, *The Catholic Viewpoint on Censorship* (Garden City, N.Y., 1958)

Walter Kerr, *Criticism and Censorship* (Milwaukee, 1956)

Murray Schumach, *The Face on the Cutting Room Floor; The Story of Movie and Television Censorship* (New York, 1964)

Elmer E. Smead, *Freedom of Speech by Radio and Television* (Washington, D.C., 1959)

United States Congress, House Committee on Interstate and Foreign Commerce, **Political Broadcasts: Equal Time,** Hearings before the Committee, 86th Cong., 1st Sess. on HR5389 and other bills. . . . June 29, 30, and July 1, 1959 (Washington, D.C., U. S. Govt. Printing Office, 1959)

Alan F. Westin, *The "Miracle" Case: The Supreme Court and the Movies* (University, Ala., 1961)

The philosophy of social justice through social action

FRANKLIN D. ROOSEVELT

In June 1932 when the Democratic and Republican parties met one after the other in Chicago's Coliseum to nominate their candidates for president in the approaching election, the country was in the depths of the Great Depression. Falling steadily since the stock market crash of October 1929, railroad and industrial stocks stood at less than 20 percent of their former value. Factory payrolls had been cut in half. Government reports recorded 85,000 business failures, with total liabilities amounting to some 4.5 billion dollars. Five thousand banks were closed; private construction had practically ceased; annual corporate income was down from 11 billion dollars to 2; wages from 55 billion to 33; gross national income from 85 billion to an estimated 37. Worst of all, 11.5 million men and women were unemployed, and thousands more were losing their jobs daily. Bread lines, tar-paper shack villages, and street corner apple sellers became common sights in the cities; farmers poured milk on the ground and burned grain and produce in protest against sinking agricultural prices.

Believing that the roots of the depression lay in international economic and political causes over which the United States had no control and convinced that the economic policies of the current administration were sound, the Republicans reaffirmed their faith in the incumbent President, Herbert Hoover, by nominating him for a second term. The Democrats, after eliminating such other prominent contenders as Alfred E. Smith and Albert Ritchie, on the fourth ballot nominated Franklin D. Roosevelt (1882-1945), then governor of New York.

From the beginning, the campaign of 1932, centering on the issues of recovery, relief, and the repeal of the Eighteenth Amendment, was a dramatic one. Upon learning of his nomination, Roosevelt broke precedent by flying from Albany to Chicago to deliver a stirring speech to the convention delegates. During the campaign Roose-

velt traveled more than twenty-five thousand miles, visiting thirty-seven states and delivering twenty major addresses and sixty-seven briefer speeches, in addition to making almost a thousand rear-platform appearances as his campaign train moved about the country.

The speech that follows marked the close of Roosevelt's western tour of September 12 through October 3. On this tour he had made major addresses at Topeka, Sioux City, Seattle, Portland, and San Francisco, dealing with such subjects as agriculture, the tariff, public utilities, and his philosophy of government. Coming to Detroit on Sunday, October 2, for the final appearance of his trip, Roosevelt chose to deal with a subject he had not specifically treated in any of these other speeches—that of social justice through social action. It may well be that he deliberately selected Detroit as the place most suitable for an exposition of his ideas on this subject. Certainly this industrial city was one of the economic sore spots of the nation, with many thousands of its citizens unemployed and many more inadequately fed and housed.

Roosevelt's day in Detroit followed the typical campaign pattern. It began with a parade from the railroad station to the Statler Hotel, where he was guest of honor at a luncheon and informal reception. And following this speech, which was delivered at the Naval Armory, there was a second parade as the cavalcade of official cars moved back to Roosevelt's hotel. In the evening the newspaper correspondents who had accompanied Roosevelt on his trip gave him a farewell dinner.

The Detroit *News* reported that the streets were thronged with friendly and enthusiastic crowds that "waved and shouted words of welcome and cheer" as Roosevelt passed by on his way to the Naval Armory. The Armory itself was packed with an audience of more than six thousand persons, while outside there were four or five thousand more who had been unable to find seats. So dense was this crowd around the building that Rabbi Leo Framm, who had been scheduled to deliver the invocation, was unable to make his way through it, and Father Charles Coughlin of radio fame was pressed into service as a substitute. Mayor Frank Murphy introduced Roosevelt in glowing phrases, describing him as "a great spiritual figure in the political life of our country."

Considered historically, Roosevelt's speech on this occasion is notable as one of the first systematic statements of the social philosophy of the New Deal—the social philosophy that in the following decade was to revolutionize the American way of life and give rise to one of the bitterest and most prolonged disputes in our political history. The speech is interesting rhetorically as an example of Roosevelt's unusual resourcefulness as a campaign orator. Attempting to remove the discussion from the arena of partisan politics by identifying it with "fundamentals that antedate parties," he skillfully adapted his remarks to a Sunday afternoon audience and at the same time gained strong moral support for his views by showing they were no more advanced than the views held by the leaders of the major religious faiths. Moreover, he took advantage of his achievements as a New York legislator and as governor of that state to enhance his own prestige, and within the framework of an essentially philosophical and professedly nonpolitical address he still was able to direct telling jabs at his opponents.

The Detroit audience was warm and friendly, and the speech was enthusiastically received, being interrupted at many points by prolonged applause, laughter, and cheers. According to a reporter for the New York Times, the statement which drew the loudest ovation was Roosevelt's declaration that when all other methods had failed the federal government must see to the well-being of its citizens. This response to what was then a new and revolutionary doctrine becomes all the more significant when we realize that in 1932 Roosevelt himself was still relatively unknown outside of New York and that public reaction to his policies as governor had been mixed.

All accounts agree that although Roosevelt was at the close of an arduous three-week campaign trip, he looked tanned and fit, except for dark circles under his eyes, as he arose to speak. His voice was clear and fresh, and his articulation, as always, was sure and precise. Because of the crippled condition in which he had been left many years before by polio, he stood in one spot while speaking, his hands grasping the sides of the high reading desk on which his manuscript lay. Although he used few arm gestures, his typical head and shoulder movements and mobile facial expression helped to communicate his ideas forcibly.

The text of the speech as presented here was established by LeRoy Cowperthwaite and represents a synthesis of the official stenographic report with the "reading copy" used by Roosevelt in delivery.[1] A transcription of the speech preserved in the National Archives was apparently made either before or after its actual delivery since no applause or background noise is present.

[1] Lowery LeRoy Cowperthwaite, "A Criticism of the Speaking of Franklin D. Roosevelt in the Presidential Campaign of 1932" (Unpublished Ph.D. thesis, State University of Iowa, 1950), 2 vols., I, 8-9; II, Preface and 558-567.

My old friend Mayor Murphy, my old friend Governor Comstock, (*Applause*) and you—many of you—my old friends of Detroit and of Michigan: (*Applause*) /1

I have had a wonderful reception today, and I am awfully glad to be back in Detroit, and I am especially glad to be once more the guest of the Navy. (*Applause*) There is only one fly in the ointment, and I might just as well be perfectly frank with you—I would much rather be cruising the Great Lakes on the U.S.S. DuBuque. (*Laughter, applause*) /2

You know today is Sunday, and I am afraid that some of you people today in Detroit have been talking politics. (*Laughter*) Well I am not going to. My friends, I want to talk to you about Government. Well, that is a very different thing. (*Laughter, applause*) And I am not going to refer to parties at all. /3

But, I am going to refer to some of the fundamentals that antedate parties, and antedate republics and empires, fundamentals that are as old as mankind itself. They are fundamentals that have been expressed in philosophies, for I don't know how many thousands of years, in every part of the world. And today, in our boasted modern civilization, we are facing just exactly the same problem, just exactly the same conflict between two schools of philosophy that they faced in the earliest days of America, and indeed the earliest days of the world. One of them—one of these old philosophies—is the philosophy of those who would "let things alone," and the other is the philosophy that strives for something new—something that the human race has never attained yet, but something which I believe the human race can and will attain—social justice, through social action. (*Prolonged applause*) /4

Now the philosophy of "letting things alone" has resulted in the days of the cave man, and in the days of the automobile—has resulted in the jungle law of the survival of the so-called fittest. But this philosophy of social action results in the protection of humanity and the fitting of as many human beings as possible into the scheme of surviving. And in that first philosophy of "letting things alone" I am sorry to say that there are a lot of people in my community back home—which is a little village—and in the farming districts of the Nation and in the great cities of the country, such as yours—we can fit a great many splendid people into that category, splendid people who keep saying, not only to themselves and to their friends, but to the community as a whole, "Why shouldn't we 'let things alone'? In the first place they are not as bad as they are painted, and in the second place they will cure themselves. Time is a great healer." An easy philosophy! The kind of philosophy, my friends, that was expressed the other day by a Cabinet officer of the United States of America,* when he is reported to have said, "Our children are apt to profit rather than suffer from what is going on." (*Applause*) /5

While he was saying that, another branch of your Government and mine, the United States Public Health Service, which believes in my kind of philosophy, I think—telling the truth—said this: "Over six million of our public school children do not have enough to eat. Many of them are fainting at their desks. They are a prey to disease. Their future health is menaced." (*Applause*) /6

What school do you believe in? /7

And in the same way, there are two theories of prosperity and of well-being: The first theory is that if we make the rich richer, somehow they will let a part of their prosperity trickle through to the rest of us. (*Applause*) The second theory—and I suppose this goes back to the days of Noah—I won't say Adam and Eve, because they had a less complicated situation—(*Laughter and applause*) but, at least, back in the days of the flood—there was the second theory that if we make the average of mankind comfortable and secure, their prosperity will rise upward, just as yeast rises up, through the ranks. (*Applause*) /8

Now, my friends, the philosophy of social justice that I am going to talk about this Sabbath day, the philosophy of social justice through social action, calls definitely, plainly, for the reduction of poverty. And what do we mean when we talk about the reduction of poverty? We mean I think the reduction of the causes of poverty. When we have an epidemic of disease in this land in these modern days, what do we do? We turn to find out in the first instance the sources from which the disease has come; and when we have found those sources, those causes of the disease, we turn the energy of our attack upon them. /9

We have got beyond the point in modern civilization of merely trying to fight an epidemic of disease by taking care of the victims after they are stricken. We do that; but we do more. We seek to prevent it; and the attack on poverty is not very unlike the attack on disease. We are seeking the causes

---

*Secretary of the Interior Wilbur. (Editor's note)

and when we have found them, we must turn our attack upon them. What are the causes? What are the causes that destroy human beings, driving millions of them to destruction? Well, there are a good many of them and there are a good many of us who are alive today who have seen tremendous steps taken toward the eradication of those causes. /10

For instance, ill health: You and I know what has been accomplished by community effort, state effort, and the efforts and association of individual men and women toward the bettering of the health of humanity. /11

We have spent vast sums upon research. We have established a wholly new science, the science of public health; and we are carrying what we call today "instruction in health" into the most remote corners of our cities and our country districts. Well, the result is what? It is two-fold: First an economic saving. It has been money which has been returned to the community a thousand times over. You and I know that a sick person—a man, woman or child, who has to be taken care of—not only takes the individual who is sick out of active participation and useful citizenship, but takes somebody else, too. And so, from the purely dollars and cents point of view that we Americans are so fond of thinking about, public health has paid for itself. /12

And what have we done along other lines for the prevention of some causes of poverty? /13

I go back twenty-two years to a day when, in my State of New York, we tried to pass in the Legislature what we called a Workmen's Compensation Act, knowing, as we did, that there were thousands of men and women who every year were seriously injured in industrial accidents of one kind or another, who became a burden on their community, who were unable to work, unable to get adequate medical care—and a lot of us youngsters in the Legislature in those days were called radicals. We were called Socialists—they didn't know the word Bolshevik in those days, but if they had known that, we would have been called that, too. (*Applause*) And we put through a Workmen's Compensation Act, and the courts, as some courts do, thinking in terms of the Seventeenth Century, declared it to be unconstitutional. So we had to go about amending the Constitution, and the following year we got a Workmen's Compensation Act. /14

What has it done? We were not the first state to have it. One of the earliest States, by the way, was New Jersey, which, the year before the action in the

State of New York, passed a Workmen's Compensation Act at the bidding of that great humanitarian Governor, Woodrow Wilson. (*Prolonged applause*) But the result has been that almost every State of the Union has eliminated that cause of poverty among the masses of the people. /15

Take another form of poverty in the old days. Not so long ago, you and I know, there were families in attics—in every part of the Nation—in country districts and in city districts—hundreds and thousands of crippled children who could get no adequate care, crippled children who were lost to the community and who were a burden on the community. And so we have, in these past twenty or thirty years, gradually provided means for restoring crippled children to useful citizenship; and it has all been a factor in going after and solving one of the causes of poverty and disease. /16

And then in these later years, we have been wondering about old people; and we have come to the conclusion in this modern civilization that the theory and the idea of carting old people off to the county poorhouse is not perhaps the best thing after all. (*Applause*) /17

I will tell you what sold me on old age pension insurance—old age pensions. Not so long ago—about ten years—I received a great shock. I had been away from my home town of Hyde Park during the winter time and when I came back I found that a tragedy had occurred. One of my farm neighbors, who had been a splendid old fellow—Supervisor of his town, Highway Commissioner of his town—one of the best of our citizens. And before I had left, around Christmas time, I had seen the old man, who was eighty-nine, and I had seen his old brother, who was eighty-seven, and had seen his other brother, who was eighty-five, and I had seen his "kid" sister, who was eighty-three. /18

And they were living on a farm; I knew it was mortgaged. I knew it was mortgaged to the hilt; but I assumed that everything was all right, for they still had a couple of cows and a few chickens. But when I came back in the spring, I found that in the heavy winter that followed there had been a heavy fall of snow, and one of the old brothers had fallen down on his way out to the barn to milk the cow, and had perished in the snow drift, and the town authorities had come along and they had taken the two old men and they had put them into the county poorhouse, and they had taken the old lady and had sent her down, for want of a better place, to the insane asylum, although she was not insane, she was just old. /19

That sold me on the idea of trying to keep homes intact for old people. (*Applause*) /20

And then in another respect modern science has been good to us. It is not so very long ago that a young person, or an old person, who had anything the trouble with their mentality—they were put into what was called an asylum and not long before that they used to call it a "madhouse." Even when I was a boy, the States of the Nation used to provide asylums. And when anybody was not entirely complete mentally—when anyone was a mental defective as we call them today, in any shape, manner or form,—he used to be carted off to the asylum and they would always stay there until he came out to go to the graveyard. /21

Today that is not true. Medical science today is now doing two things: first, that the young people, the young people who are not mentally deficient but who require special mental training, and when schools allow them to remain in most cases in the bosom of their own families, we are applying special treatment and special education to them so that, instead of becoming a burden when they grow up, they are going to be useful citizens. (*Applause*) /22

And then, on the other side of it, there are the older people, the people who do have to go to hospitals for mental troubles—and the other day, just before I left Albany, I got a report from my State Department that showed that instead of the old-fashioned system by which the rule was observed of "once in, always in," this past year in the State of New York we had sent back to their families 23 per cent of all those in our hospitals for mental cases, sent them back cured to their families. (*Applause*) /23

Now, these are some of the causes, the causes that have destroyed in past ages countless thousands of our fellow human beings. They are the causes that we must attack if we are to make the future safer for humanity. We can go on taking care of the handicapped and the crippled and the sick and the feeble-minded and the unemployed; but common sense and humanity call on us to turn our back definitely on these destroyers. Poverty resulting from these destroyers is largely preventable, but, my friends, poverty, if it is to be prevented, requires a broad program of social justice. (*Applause*) /24

We cannot go back, we cannot go back to the old prisons, the old systems of mere punishment under which when a man came out of prison he was not fitted to live in our community alongside of us. We cannot go back to the old system of asylums. We cannot go back to the old lack of hospitals, the lack of public health. We cannot go back to the sweatshops of America. We cannot go back to children working in factories. (*Applause*) Those days are gone. (*Applause*) /25

And there are a lot of new steps to take. It is not a question of just not going back. It is a question also of not standing still. (*Applause*) /26

For instance, the problem in the long run, and I am not talking about the emergency of this year, but the problem of unemployment in the long run can be and shall be solved by the human race. (*Applause*) Some leaders have wisely declared for a system of unemployment insurance throughout this broad land of ours; and we are going to come to it. (*Applause*) /27

But I do not believe the Secretary of the Interior [Wilbur] would be for it. (*Laughter and applause*) He would say that great good is coming to this country because of the present situation. (*Laughter*) Yes, the followers of the philosophy of "let alone"—these people have been decrying all of these measures of social welfare. What do they call them? They call them "paternalistic." All right, if they are paternalistic, I am a father. (*Laughter and applause*) /28

They maintain that these laws interfere with individualism, forgetful of the fact that the causes of poverty in the main are beyond the control of any one individual, any czar, either a czar of politics or a czar of industry. (*Applause*) And the followers of the philosophy of "social action for the prevention of poverty" maintain that if we set up a system of justice we shall have small need for the exercise of mere philanthropy. Justice, after all, first is the goal we seek. We believe that when justice has been done individualism will have a greater security to devote the best that individualism itself can give. In other words, my friends, our long-range objective is not a dole, but a job. (*Applause*) /29

At the same time, we have in this Nation—and I know you have in Detroit, because Frank Murphy has talked to me of it many times in the past year or two—widespread suffering which all of us in the city and country alike have got to do everything we can to tide over. All agree that the first responsibility for the prevention of poverty and the alleviation of distress and the care of its victims rests upon the locality, the individuals, the organizations and the Government. First of all, perhaps, upon the private agencies of philanthropy, just as far as we can drag it out of them, secondly, the other social organizations, and last, but not least, the Church. And yet all agree that to leave to the locality the entire burden would result in placing the heaviest proportion of the burden in most cases upon those who are the least able to bear it. In other words, the communities that have the most difficult problem, like Detroit, would be the communities that would have to bear the heaviest burdens. /30

And so the State steps in to equalize the burden by providing for a large portion of the care of the victims of the poverty and by providing assistance and guidance for local communities. /31

Above and beyond that the national Government has a responsibility. (*Applause*) /32

I would like to enlarge on that a lot, but that would be politics, and I cannot. (*Applause*) My friends, the ideal of social justice of which I have spoken—an ideal that years ago might have been thought over-advanced—is now accepted by the moral leadership of all of the great religious groups of the country. Radical? Yes, and I will show you how radical it is. I am going to cite three examples of what the churches say, the radical churches of America—Protestant, Catholic and Jewish. (*Applause*) /33

And first I will read to you from the Sunday sermon, the Labor Sermon sent out this year by the Federal Council of Churches of Christ in America, representing a very large proportion of the Protestants in our country. /34

Hear how radical they are: They say: /35

"The thing that matters in any industrial system is what it does actually to human beings. . . . /36

"It is not denied that many persons of wealth are rendering great service to society. It is only suggested that the wealthy are overpaid in sharp contrast with the underpaid masses of the people. The concentration of wealth carries with it a dangerous concentration of power. It leads to conflict and violence. To suppress the symptoms of this inherent conflict while leaving the fundamental causes of it untouched is neither sound statesmanship nor Christian good-will. /37

"It is becoming more and more clear that the principles of our religion and the findings of social sciences point in the same direction. Economists now call attention to the fact that the present distribution of wealth and income, which is unbrotherly in the light of Christian ethics, is also unscientific in that it does not furnish purchasing power to the masses to balance consumption and production in our machine age." (*Applause*) /38

And now I am going to read you another great declaration and I wonder how many people will call it radical. It is just as radical as I am. (*Applause*)

It is a declaration from one of the greatest forces of conservatism in the world, the Catholic Church. And it is a quotation, my friends, from the scholarly encyclical letter issued last year by the Pope, one of the greatest documents of modern times, and the letter says this: /39

"It is patent in our days that not alone is wealth accumulated, but immense power and despotic economic domination are concentrated in the hands of a few, and that those few are frequently not the owners but only the trustees and directors of invested funds which they administer at their good pleasure. . . . /40

"This accumulation of power, the characteristic note of the modern economic order, is a natural result of limitless free competition, which permits the survival of those only who are the strongest, which often means those who fight most relentlessly, who pay least heed to the dictates of conscience. (*Applause*) /41

"This concentration of power has led to a three-fold struggle for domination: First, there is the struggle for dictatorship in the economic sphere itself; then the fierce battle to acquire control of the Government, so that its resources and authority may be abused in the economic struggle, and finally, the clash between the Governments themselves." /42

And finally, I would read to you from another great statement, a statement from Rabbi Edward L. Israel, Chairman of the Social Justice Commission of the Central Conference of American Rabbis. (*Applause*) Here is what he says: /43

"We talk of the stabilization of business. What we need is the stabilization of human justice and happiness and the permanent employment of economic policies which will enable us to preserve the essential human values of life amid all the changing aspects of the economic order. We must have a revamping of the entire method of approach to these problems of the economic order. We need a new type of social conscience that will give us the courage to act. . . . /44

"We so easily forget. Once the cry of so-called prosperity is heard in the land, we all become so stampeded by the spirit of the god Mammon, that we cannot serve the dictates of social conscience. . . . We are here to serve notice that the economic order is the invention of man; and that it cannot dominate certain eternal principles of justice and of God." (*Applause*) /45

And so, my friends, I feel a little as if I had been preaching a sermon. I feel a little as if I had been talking too much of some of the fundamentals, and yet those fundamentals enter into your life and my life every day. More, perhaps, than we can realize. If we realized that far more, it would result throughout this country in a greater activity, a greater interest on the part of the individual men and women who make up our Nation, in some of the problems which cannot be solved in the long run without the help of everybody. /46

We need leadership, of course. We need leadership of people who are honest in their thinking and honest in their doing. We need leadership if it is straight thinking—that is, unselfish; but in the last analysis we have got to have the help of the men and women all the way from the top to the bottom, especially of men and women who believe in the school of philosophy which is not content to leave things as they are. /47

And so, in these days of difficulty, we Americans everywhere must and shall choose the path of social justice—the only path that will lead us to a permanent bettering of our civilization, the path that our children must tread and their children must tread, the path of faith, the path of hope and the path of love towards our fellow man. (*Prolonged applause*) /48

The speech

1. What use does Roosevelt make of contrast in the opening passages of the speech? Is this an effective means of introducing and developing his theme? Why or why not?

2. How does Roosevelt's reference to his activities as a member of the New York legislature help to enhance his prestige with his listeners? How does this reference help to support the central idea of his speech?

3. Form a general estimate of Roosevelt's style. What are its dominant characteristics? What are its strengths? Its weaknesses? Is it suitable to the subject matter of the speech? To the audience and occasion? What part, if any, does it play in furthering his purpose? What, in particular, do you think of the phrase "social justice through social action"? Does it accurately epitomize the philosophy Roosevelt is attempting to present? What suggestive or persuasive power does it have?

4. What references does Roosevelt make to local conditions in Detroit? Would more such references have helped or hindered him in achieving his purpose?

5. What end is served by introducing the quotations from church leaders? Do you think it was a good idea to re-

peat these verbatim, or should Roosevelt have restated them in his own words? Was Roosevelt wise to save these quotations for near the close of his speech, or would it have been better to introduce them earlier?

6. How well does Roosevelt's address conform to our general notion of a campaign speech? What specific marks of a campaign speech are present? What things that you might expect to find in the average campaign speech are missing?

7. Comment on the structure or organization of the speech as a whole. Is it clear? Coherent? Do the important ideas and arguments receive proper emphasis? Are the rules of correct subordination observed? Would the speech outline easily?

8. Evaluate the anecdote Roosevelt uses to explain why he is "sold" on old age insurance. How clearly and strikingly is it presented? How well does it actually prove the need for a system of government-supported old age pensions?

9. How does Roosevelt turn to his advantage the charge that his proposals are "paternalistic"?

10. Trace the reasoning process by which Roosevelt arrives at the conclusion that the federal government "has a responsibility" in "the alleviation of poverty and distress." What are his premises? What inferences does he draw from them? Granted his premises, does he reason from them clearly and cogently?

For further study and discussion

1. What are some of the ways in which Roosevelt's philosophy of "social justice through social action" was implemented during his years in the White House and since? What were the principal criticisms of these implementing measures? To what extent do you think these criticisms were justified?

2. Compare the "two theories of prosperity and of well-being" Roosevelt mentions—the one which holds that "if we make the rich richer, somehow they will let a part of their prosperity trickle through to the rest of us," and the other which says that "if we make the average of mankind comfortable and secure, their prosperity will rise upward, just as yeast rises up, through the ranks." Point to some of the evidence that might be cited to support each view. Which, if either, would present-day economic theory accept as true? Must the alternative be as sharp as Roosevelt pictures it? Within limits, could both processes operate simultaneously?

3. Evaluate Roosevelt's argument that fighting poverty is like fighting disease and should be gone about in the same way. Can we isolate and control the causes of poverty? Is the prevention of poverty possible in the same sense and to the same extent that the prevention of disease is?

4. To what extent can any individual nation fight poverty and distress by a program of social action or by any other program? Aren't all of the nations of the world so bound together economically that the prosperity and well-being of each is directly dependent upon the prosperity and well-being of all?

5. Do you agree with Roosevelt "that the causes of poverty in the main are beyond the control of any one individual"?

6. Is it always true that the concentration of wealth carries with it the concentration of power? If so, is this necessarily bad? Are people who are successful economically also likely to be successful in running the affairs of a community or a nation?

7. Roosevelt strongly disagrees with the notion that sometimes people may actually benefit from adversity. What do you think?

8. Has the United States government gone as far as the governments of certain other democracies in trying to insure the social and economic well-being of its citizens? How are these attempts working out in other countries?

9. Should the government have the right to remove foodstuffs from the market if there is a possibility that they might be poisonous—as it did with cranberries just before Thanksgiving in 1959? Should it issue public warnings about the possible connection between cigarette smoking and lung cancer?

10. Admitting that a certain measure of governmental regulation is inevitable in the modern world, how can we yet preserve our individual rights and freedoms?

Suggestions for further reading

Sheldon Glueck, ed., **The Welfare State and the National Welfare,** A Symposium on Some of the Threatening Tendencies of Our Times (Cambridge, Mass., 1952). Contains statements by Bernard Baruch, John Foster Dulles, Dwight D. Eisenhower, Herbert Hoover, and others.

Robert Edwards Lane, **The Regulation of Businessmen; Social Conditions of Government Economic Control,** Yale Studies in Political Science, Vol. I (New Haven, 1954)

Herbert L. Marx, comp., **The Welfare State,** The Reference Shelf, Vol. XXII, No. 4 (New York, 1950)

Arthur M. Schlesinger, Jr., **The Age of Roosevelt** (Boston, 1957-). Vol. I, **The Crisis of the Old Order;** Vol. II, **The Coming of the New Deal;** Vol. III, **The Politics of Upheaval.**

Dixon Wecter, **The Age of the Great Depression, 1929-1941** (New York, 1948)

Recordings

Rendezvous with Destiny. NBC Documentary Recording (New York: Linguaphone Institute, 1946). Selections from more than twenty of Roosevelt's speeches, from the First Inaugural, March 4, 1933, to the Report to Congress on the Crimea Conference, March 1, 1945.

The Voice of F. D. R. (1932-1945), the Presidential Years (Decca Gold Label). Special narration by Quentin Reynolds.

Crime and criminals

CLARENCE DARROW

Clarence Darrow (1857-1938) is perhaps the most famous trial lawyer America has produced. He is best remembered today for his dramatic defenses of the Mc-Namara brothers (1911), of Loeb and Leopold (1924), and for his jousts with William Jennings Bryan in the Scopes "evolution" trial at Dayton, Tennessee (1925). During a legal career of more than half a century, however, he appeared in hundreds of cases, in nearly all of which he was fantastically successful, and in most of which his unusual speaking ability contributed in a major way.

In addition to his work as a lawyer, Darrow was an active platform speaker. He lectured extensively throughout the country and engaged in numerous public debates with some of the leading men of his day—among them T. V. Smith, Will Durant, John Haynes Holmes, Albert Edward Wiggam, and George B. Foster.

Not only as a speaker but as a prolific writer of books and articles, Darrow habitually expressed views which on the surface seemed to be at wide variance with majority opinion but in reality often represented the suppressed attitudes and desires of his listeners. This, perhaps more than any other single factor, accounts for the remarkably persuasive power of his discourses and explains the success of his highly unorthodox methods. He attacked big business, capital punishment, religious fundamentalism, prohibition, and the doctrine of free will, marking himself as a social maverick and winning such titles as "attorney for the damned," "the big minority man," and "the friendly enemy."

The speech presented here represents Darrow's unusual views concerning the causes and cures of crime, and reflects the thinking of his long-time friend and eventual law partner, John Peter Altgeld, as expressed in Altgeld's book Our Penal Machinery and Its Victims (1884).[1] It was delivered in as bizarre a situation as can be imagined. In 1902, when Darrow was forty-five years old and had already gained wide recognition as a criminal lawyer, the warden of the Cook County Jail in Chicago invited him to address the inmates. Eager to propagate his unusual views where they might have some effect, Darrow accepted the invitation and delivered the following lecture to the prisoners.

Aside from the ideas expressed, the speech is interesting as an example of skillful audience adaptation. The language is uniformly clear and simple; examples are numerous and appropriate; and the many thrusts of wit and humor are used to good effect. Moreover, the address is organized in such a way that its central purpose stands out clearly and is strongly reinforced by repetition and restatement.

How well the speech was received by the majority of the inmates, we can only conjecture. One prisoner when asked for his reaction is reported to have shaken his head and declared the ideas altogether "too radical." When reports of what Darrow had said were circulated among his friends, they were much distressed and argued that his theories, even though they might contain some measure of truth, should not have been presented to criminals in a jail.[2]

Darrow responded to this criticism by having the lecture printed at his own expense, affixing to it this introductory paragraph: "Realizing the force of the suggestion that the truth should not be spoken to all people, I have caused these remarks to be printed on rather good paper and in a somewhat expensive form. In this way the truth does not become cheap and vulgar, and is only placed before those whose intelligence and affluence will prevent their being influenced by it." As Arthur Weinberg reports, the pamphlet sold for five cents.

Although Darrow never repeated in quite so dramatic a form the ideas developed in this address, the same basic philosophy is to be found in a number of his later writings, notably Crime, Its Causes and Treatment (1922) and The Story of My Life (1932).

Darrow's delivery was as unorthodox as his ideas. Violating nearly all textbook precepts, he was careless in dress and grooming and for many of his lectures and debates made little or no preparation. He slouched and shuffled and lounged upon the speaker's stand, his head down and his left hand deep in coat or trouser pocket. His voice was low-pitched and unvaried, falling now and again into a monotonous drone. He drawled his words and generally spoke softly, although at times he could crack out a sentence like a whip. His vocal quality was husky and harsh. Yet, withal, Darrow held the attention and interest of his audiences as few speakers have done, and he drove home his ideas with an emotional force that was often overpowering. At the conclusion of his plea in the Loeb-Leopold case, for example, many of his spectators were in tears. As T. V. Smith, his opponent in many debates, summed it up, "He was at his prime a great speaker, not because he had much strategy about it, but be-

From Address to Prisoners in Cook County Jail, by Clarence Darrow, 3rd reprint, Charles H. Kerr and Company, Chicago, 1913.

[1]For the influence of Altgeld on this speech, see Irving Stone, Clarence Darrow for the Defense (New York, 1941), pp. 169-170, and Harry Barnard, Eagle Forgotten: The Life of John Peter Altgeld (Indianapolis, 1938), p. 88.

[2]Arthur Weinberg, ed. Attorney for the Damned (New York, 1957), p. 15.

cause he was a massive man with good glands, a fine heart, and mind enough to give priority to his heart and glands. His speech was impressive because he himself was impressive. We shall not soon see his full like again."[3]

If I looked at jails and crimes and prisoners in the way the ordinary person does, I should not speak on this subject to you. The reason I talk to you on the question of crime, its cause and cure, is because I really do not in the least believe in crime. There is no such thing as a crime as the word is generally understood. I do not believe there is any sort of distinction between the real moral condition of the people in and out of jail. One is just as good as the other. The people here can no more help being here than the people outside can avoid being outside. I do not believe that people are in jail because they deserve to be. They are in jail simply because they can not avoid it on account of circumstances which are entirely beyond their control and for which they are in no way responsible. /1

I suppose a great many people on the outside would say I was doing you harm if they should hear what I say to you this afternoon, but you can not be hurt a great deal anyway, so it will not matter. Good people outside would say that I was really teaching you things that were calculated to injure society, but it's worth while now and then to hear something different from what you ordinarily get from preachers and the like. These will tell you that you should be good and then you get rich and be happy. Of course we know that people do not get rich by being good, and that is the reason why so many of you people try to get rich some other way, only you do not understand how to do it quite as well as the fellow outside. /2

There are people who think that everything in this world is an accident. But really there is no such thing as an accident. A great many folks admit that many of the people in jail ought to be there, and many who are outside ought to be in. I think none of them ought to be here. There ought to be no jails, and if it were not for the fact that the people on the outside are so grasping and heartless in their dealings with the people on the inside, there would be no such institution as jails. /3

[3]T. V. Smith to John Buckley Roberts, Urbana, Illinois, March 12, 1941, in John Buckley Roberts, "The Speech Philosophy of Clarence Darrow" (Unpublished master's thesis, State University of Iowa, 1941), p. 168.

I do not want you to believe that I think all you people here are angels. I do not think that. You are people of all kinds, all of you doing the best you can, and that is evidently not very well—you are people of all kinds and conditions and under all circumstances. In one sense everybody is equally good and equally bad. We all do the best we can under the circumstances. But as to the exact things for which you are sent here, some of you are guilty and did the particular act because you needed the money. Some of you did it because you are in the habit of doing it, and some of you because you are born to it, and it comes to be as natural as it does, for instance, for me to be good. /4

Most of you probably have nothing against me, and most of you would treat me the same as any other person would; probably better than some of the people on the outside would treat me, because you think I believe in you and they know I do not believe in them. While you would not have the least thing against me in the world you might pick my pockets. I do not think all of you would, but I think some of you would. You would not have anything against me, but that's your profession, a few of you. Some of the rest of you, if my doors were unlocked, might come in if you saw anything you wanted—not out of any malice to me, but because that is your trade. There is no doubt there are quite a number of people in this jail who would pick my pockets. And still I know this, that when I get outside pretty nearly everybody picks my pocket. There may be some of you who would hold up a man on the street, if you did not happen to have something else to do, and needed the money; but when I want to light my house or my office the gas company holds me up. They charge me one dollar for something that is worth twenty-five cents, and still all these people are good people; they are pillars of society and support the churches, and they are respectable. /5

When I ride on the street cars, I am held up— I pay five cents for a ride that is worth two and a half cents, simply because a body of men have bribed the city council and the legislature, so that all the rest of us have to pay tribute to them. /6

If I do not want to fall into the clutches of the gas trust and choose to burn oil instead of gas, then good Mr. Rockefeller holds me up, and he uses a certain portion of his money to build universities and support churches which are engaged in telling us how to be good. /7

Some of you are here for obtaining property under false pretenses—yet I pick up a great Sunday paper and read the advertisements of a merchant prince—

"Shirt waists for 39 cents, marked down from 3.00." /8

When I read the advertisements in the paper I see they are all lies. When I want to get out and find a place to stand anywhere on the face of the earth, I find that it has all been taken up long ago before I came here, and before you came here, and somebody says, "Get off, swim into the lake, fly into the air; go anywhere, but get off." That is because these people have the police and they have the jails and the judges and the lawyers and the soldiers and all the rest of them to take care of the earth and drive everybody off that comes in their way. /9

A great many people will tell you that all this is true, but that it does not excuse you. These facts do not excuse some fellow who reaches into my pocket and takes out a five dollar bill; the fact that the gas company bribes the members of the legislature from year to year, and fixes the law, so that all you people are compelled to be "fleeced" whenever you deal with them; the fact that the street car companies and the gas companies have control of the streets and the fact that the landlords own all the earth, they say, has nothing to do with you. /10

Let us see whether there is any connection between the crimes of the respectable classes and your presence in the jail. Many of you people are in jail because you have really committed burglary. Many of you, because you have stolen something: in the meaning of the law, you have taken some other person's property. Some of you have entered a store and carried off a pair of shoes because you did not have the price. Possibly some of you have committed murder. I can not tell what all of you did. There are a great many people here who have done some of these things who really do not know themselves why they did them. I think I know why you did them—every one of you; you did these things because you were bound to do them. It looked to you at the time as if you had a chance to do them or not, as you saw fit, but still after all you had no choice. There may be people here who had some money in their pockets and who still went out and got some more money in a way society forbids. Now you may not yourselves see exactly why it was you did this thing, but if you look at the question deeply enough and carefully enough you would see that there were circumstances that drove you to do exactly the thing which you did. You could not help it any more than we outside can help taking the positions that we take. The reformers who tell you to be good and you will be happy, and the people on the outside who

have property to protect—they think that the only way to do it is by building jails and locking you up in cells on week-days and praying for you Sundays. /11

I think that all of this has nothing whatever to do with right conduct. I think it is very easily seen what has to do with right conduct. Some so-called criminals—and I will use this word because it is handy, it means nothing to me—I speak of the criminals who get caught as distinguished from the criminals who catch them—some of these so-called criminals are in jail for the first offenses, but nine-tenths of you are in jail because you did not have a good lawyer and of course you did not have a good lawyer because you did not have enough money to pay a good lawyer. There is no very great danger of a rich man going to jail. /12

Some of you may be here for the first time. If we would open the doors and let you out, and leave the laws as they are to-day, some of you would be back to-morrow. This is about as good a place as you can get anyway. There are many people here who are so in the habit of coming that they would not know where else to go. There are people who are born with the tendency to break into jail every chance they get, and they can not avoid it. You can not figure out your life and see why it was, but still there is a reason for it, and if we were all wise and knew all the facts we could figure it out. /13

In the first place, there are a good many more people who go to jail in the winter time than in summer. Why is this? Is it because people are more wicked in winter? No, it is because the coal trust begins to get in its grip in the winter. A few gentlemen take possession of the coal, and unless the people will pay $7 or $8 a ton for something that is worth $3, they will have to freeze. Then there is nothing to do but to break into jail, and so there are many more in jail in the winter than in summer. It costs more for gas in the winter because the nights are longer, and people go to jail to save gas bills. The jails are electric lighted. You may not know it, but these economic laws are working all the time, whether we know it or do not know it. /14

There are more people go to jail in hard times than in good times—few people comparatively go to jail except when they are hard up. They go to jail because they have no other place to go. They may not know why, but it is true all the same. People are not more wicked in hard times. That is not the reason. The fact is true all over the world that in hard times more people go to jail than in good times, and in winter more people go to jail than in summer. Of course it is pretty hard times for people who go to jail at any time. The people who go to jail are almost always poor people—people who have no other place to live first and last. When times are hard then you find large numbers of people who go to jail who would not otherwise be in jail. /15

Long ago, Mr. Buckle, who was a great philosopher and historian, collected facts and he showed that the number of people who are arrested increased just as the price of food increased. When they put up the price of gas ten cents a thousand I do not know who will go to jail, but I do know that a certain number of people will go. When the meat combine raises the price of beef I do not know who is going to jail, but I know that a large number of people are bound to go. Whenever the Standard Oil Company raises the price of oil, I know that a certain number of girls who are seamstresses, and who work after night long hours for somebody else, will be compelled to go out on the streets and ply another trade, and I know that Mr. Rockefeller and his associates are responsible and not the poor girls in the jails. /16

First and last, people are sent to jail because they are poor. Sometimes, as I say, you may not need money at the particular time, but you wish to have thrifty forehanded habits, and do not always wait until you are in absolute want. Some of you people are perhaps plying the trade, the profession, which is called burglary. No man in his right senses will go into a strange house in the dead of night and prowl around with a dark lantern through unfamiliar rooms and take chances of his life if he has plenty of the good things of the world in his own home. You would not take any such chances as that. If a man had clothes in his clothes-press and beefsteak in his pantry, and money in the bank, he would not navigate around nights in houses where he knows nothing about the premises whatever. It always requires experience and education for this profession, and people who fit themselves for it are no more to blame than I am for being a lawyer. A man would not hold up another man on the street if he had plenty of money in his own pocket. He might do it if he had one dollar or two dollars, but he wouldn't if he had as much money as Mr. Rockefeller has. Mr. Rockefeller has a great deal better hold-up game than that. /17

The more that is taken from the poor by the rich, who have the chance to take it, the more poor people there are who are compelled to resort to these means for a livelihood. They may not understand it, they may not think so at once, but after all they are driven into that line of employment. /18

There is a bill before the legislature of this State to punish kidnaping children, with death. We have wise members of the Legislature. They know the gas trust when they see it and they always see it,—they can furnish light enough to be seen, and this Legislature thinks it is going to stop kidnaping children by making a law punishing kidnapers of children with death. I don't believe in kidnaping children, but the Legislature is all wrong. Kidnaping children is not a crime, it is a profession. It has been developed with the times. It has been developed with our modern industrial conditions. There are many ways of making money—many new ways that our ancestors knew nothing about. Our ancestors knew nothing about a billion dollar trust; and here comes some poor fellow who has no other trade and he discovers the profession of kidnaping children. /19

This crime is born, not because people are bad; people don't kidnap other people's children because they want the children or because they are devilish, but because they see a chance to get some money out of it. You cannot cure this crime by passing a law punishing by death kidnapers of children. There is one way to cure it. There is one way to cure all the offenses, and that is to give the people a chance to live. There is no other way, and there never was any other way since the world began, and the world is so blind and stupid that it will not see. If every man and woman and child in the world had a chance to make a decent, fair, honest living, there would be no jails, and no lawyers and no courts. There might be some persons here or there with some peculiar formation of their brain, like Rockefeller, who would do these things simply to be doing them; but they would be very, very few, and those should be sent to a hospital and treated, and not sent to jail; and they would entirely disappear in the second generation, or at least in the third generation. /20

I am not talking pure theory. I will just give you two or three illustrations. /21

The English people once punished criminals by sending them away. They would load them on a ship and export them to Australia. England was owned by lords and nobles and rich people. They owned the whole earth over there, and the other people had to stay in the streets. They could not get a decent living. They used to take their criminals and send them to Australia—I mean the class of criminals who got caught. When these criminals got over there, and nobody else had come, they had the whole continent to run over, and so they could raise sheep and furnish their own meat, which is easier than stealing it; these criminals then became decent, respectable people because they had a chance to live. They did not commit any crimes. They were just like the English people who sent them there, only better. And in the second generation the descendants of those criminals were as good and respectable a class of people as there were on the face of the earth, and then they began building churches and jails themselves. /22

A portion of this country was settled in the same way, landing prisoners down on the southern coast; but when they got here and had a whole continent to run over and plenty of chances to make a living, they became respectable citizens, making their own living just like any other citizen in the world; but finally these descendants of the English aristocracy, who sent the people over to Australia, found out they were getting rich, and so they went over to get possession of the earth as they always do, and they organized land syndicates and got control of the land and ores, and then they had just as many criminals in Australia as they did in England. It was not because the world had grown bad; it was because the earth had been taken away from the people. /23

Some of you people have lived in the country. It's prettier than it is here. And if you have ever lived on a farm you understand that if you put a lot of cattle in a field, when the pasture is short they will jump over the fence; but put them in a good field where there is plenty of pasture, and they will be law-abiding cattle to the end of time. The human animal is just like the rest of the animals, only a little more so. The same thing that governs in the one governs in the other. /24

Everybody makes his living along the lines of least resistance. A wise man who comes into a country early sees a great undeveloped land. For instance, our rich men twenty-five years ago saw that Chicago was small and knew a lot of people would come here and settle, and they readily saw that if they had all the land around here it would be worth a good deal, so they grabbed the land. You cannot be a landlord because somebody has got it all. You must find some other calling. In England and Ireland and Scotland less than five per cent own all the land there is, and the people are bound to stay there on any kind of terms the landlords give. They must live the best they can, so they develop all these various professions—burglary, picking pockets and the like. /25

Again, people find all sorts of ways of getting rich. These are diseases like everything else. You look at people getting rich, organizing trusts, and making a million dollars, and somebody gets the disease and

he starts out. He catches it just as a man catches the mumps or the measles; he is not to blame, it is in the air. You will find men speculating beyond their means, because the mania of money-getting is taking possession of them. It is simply a disease; nothing more, nothing less. You can not avoid catching it; but the fellows who have control of the earth have the advantage of you. See what the law is; when these men get control of things, they make the laws. They do not make the laws to protect anybody; courts are not instruments of justice; when your case gets into court it will make little difference whether you are guilty or innocent; but it's better if you have a smart lawyer. And you can not have a smart lawyer unless you have money. First and last it's a question of money. Those men who own the earth make the laws to protect what they have. They fix up a sort of fence or pen around what they have, and they fix the law so the fellow on the outside can not get in. The laws are really organized for the protection of the men who rule the world. They were never organized or enforced to do justice. We have no system for doing justice, not the slightest in the world. /26

Let me illustrate: Take the poorest person in this room. If the community had provided a system of doing justice the poorest person in this room would have as good a lawyer as the richest, would he not? When you went into court you would have just as long a trial, and just as fair a trial as the richest person in Chicago. Your case would not be tried in fifteen or twenty minutes, whereas it would take fifteen days to get through with a rich man's case. /27

Then if you were rich and were beaten, your case would be taken to the Appellate Court. A poor man can not take his case to the Appellate Court; he has not the price; and then to the Supreme Court, and if he were beaten there he might perhaps go to the United States Supreme Court. And he might die of old age before he got into jail. If you are poor, it's a quick job. You are almost known to be guilty, else you would not be there. Why should any one be in the criminal court if he were not guilty? He would not be there if he could be anywhere else. The officials have no time to look after all these cases. The people who are on the outside, who are running banks and building churches and making jails, they have no time to examine 600 or 700 prisoners each year to see whether they are guilty or innocent. If the courts were organized to promote justice the people would elect somebody to defend all these criminals, somebody as smart as the prosecutor— and give him as many detectives and as many assistants to help, and pay as much money to defend you as to prosecute you. We have a very able man for State's Attorney, and he has many assistants, detectives and policemen without end, and judges to hear the cases—everything handy. /28

Most of all our criminal code consists in offenses against property. People are sent to jail because they have committed a crime against property. It is of very little consequence whether one hundred people more or less go to jail who ought not to go—you must protect property, because in this world property is of more importance than anything else. /29

How is it done? These people who have property fix it so they can protect what they have. When somebody commits a crime it does not follow that he had done something that is morally wrong. The man on the outside who has committed no crime may have done something. For instance: to take all the coal in the United States and raise the price two dollars or three dollars when there is no need of it, and thus kill thousands of babies and send thousands of people to the poorhouse and tens of thousands to jail, as is done every year in the United States,—this is a greater crime than all the people in our jails ever committed, but the law does not punish it. Why? Because the fellows who control the earth make the laws. If you and I had the making of the laws, the first thing we would do would be to punish the fellow who gets control of the earth. Nature put this coal in the ground for me as well as for them and nature made the prairies up here to raise wheat for me as well as for them, and then the great railroad companies came along and fenced it up. /30

Most of all the crimes for which we are punished are property crimes. There are a few personal crimes, like murder—but they are very few. The crimes committed are mostly those against property. If this punishment is right the criminals must have a lot of property. How much money is there in this crowd? And yet you are all here for crimes against property. The people up and down the Lake Shore have not committed crime, still they have so much property they don't know what to do with it. It is perfectly plain why those people have not committed crimes against property; they make the laws and therefore do not need to break them. And in order for you to get some property you are obliged to break the rules of the game. I don't know but what some of you may have had a very nice chance to get rich by carrying the hod for one dollar a day, twelve hours. Instead of taking that nice, easy profession, you are a burglar. If you had been given a chance to be a banker you would rather follow that. Some of you

may have had a chance to work as a switchman on a railroad where you know, according to statistics, that you can not live and keep all your limbs more than seven years, and you can get fifty dollars or seventy-five dollars a month for taking your lives in your hands, and instead of taking that lucrative position you choose to be a sneak thief, or something like that. Some of you made that sort of choice. I don't know which I would take if I was reduced to this choice. I have an easier choice. /31

I will guarantee to take from this jail, or any jail in the world, five hundred men who have been the worst criminals and law-breakers who ever got into jail, and I will go down to our lowest streets and take five hundred of the most abandoned prostitutes, and go out somewhere where there is plenty of land, and will give them a chance to make a living, and they will be as good people as the average in the community. /32

There is a remedy for the sort of condition we see here. The world never finds it out, or when it does find it out it does not enforce it. You may pass a law punishing every person with death for burglary, and it will make no difference. Men will commit it just the same. In England there was a time when one hundred different offenses were punishable with death, and it made no difference. The English people strangely found out that so fast as they repealed the severe penalties and so fast as they did away with punishing men by death, crime decreased instead of increased; that the smaller the penalty the fewer the crimes. /33

Hanging men in our county jails does not prevent murder. It makes murderers. /34

And this has been the history of the world. It's easy to see how to do away with what we call crime. It is not so easy to do it. I will tell you how to do it. It can be done by giving the people a chance to live—by destroying special privileges. So long as big criminals can get the coal fields, so long as the big criminals have control of the city council and get the public streets for street cars and gas rights, this is bound to send thousands of poor people to jail. So long as men are allowed to monopolize all the earth, and compel others to live on such terms as these men see fit to make, then you are bound to get into jail. /35

The only way in the world to abolish crime and criminals is to abolish the big ones and the little ones together. Make fair conditions of life. Give men a chance to live. Abolish the right of private ownership of land, abolish monopoly, make the world partners in production, partners in the good things of life. Nobody would steal if he could get something of his own some easier way. Nobody will commit burglary when he has a house full. No girl will go out on the streets when she has a comfortable place at home. The man who owns a sweatshop or a department store may not be to blame himself for the condition of his girls, but when he pays them five dollars, three dollars, and two dollars a week, I wonder where he thinks they will get the rest of their money to live. The only way to cure these conditions is by equality. There should be no jails. They do not accomplish what they pretend to accomplish. If you would wipe them out there would be no more criminals than now. They terrorize nobody. They are a blot upon any civilization, and a jail is an evidence of the lack of charity of the people on the outside who make the jails and fill them with the victims of their greed. /36

The speech

1. Describe as fully and as accurately as you can the nature of the speaking situation Darrow faced. Estimate the probable attitude of the audience toward him and his subject. Point out at least four specific ways in which—through his choice of ideas, organization, and language—Darrow attempted to adapt his speech to this attitude.

2. What is the central idea of Darrow's speech? Where is it first explicitly stated? How many times and in what ways is it reiterated? What advantage is gained by these repetitions? Might it have been better to state the central idea earlier in the speech? Give reasons for your answer.

3. Where in the speech do you find instances of humor? How do these aid Darrow in achieving his purpose?

4. Would you regard this speech as primarily persuasive or expository? As primarily a logical argument or an emotional harangue? As primarily a refutation of generally received beliefs or a constructive development of the speaker's own ideas and convictions?

5. Does the speech move toward a discernible climax? If so, at what point does the climax occur?

6. Do you think that Darrow's strong attacks on "preachers," the gas and oil trusts, Rockefeller, etc., are essential to the achieving of his purpose? Do they sometimes pass the bounds of good taste and responsible statement?

7. In what specific way does Darrow use language to try to create the impression that people outside of jail are just as bad as those who are in jail?

8. Find in the speech at least three statements which seem to you to stand as completely unsupported assertions.

Find two places at which, in your opinion, an example would have helped to clarify Darrow's meaning.

9. Where does the conclusion of the speech begin? What method does Darrow use in developing his conclusion?

10. If you had to cut this speech by six or seven paragraphs in order to fit it within a restricted time limit, which paragraphs would you eliminate? Why?

For further study and discussion

1. Does the ordinary person today look "at jails and crimes and prisoners" in the same way that Darrow says the ordinary person looked at them in 1902? If so, why have these views remained stable? If not, what has happened to change them?

2. If you were called upon to present additional arguments in favor of Darrow's position, what would they be? If you were called upon to refute his position, how would you proceed?

3. What are some of the leading theories today concerning the causes of crime and its cures? How do these compare with Darrow's views?

4. Do you think it wise or unwise to present to the inmates of a jail or prison the views Darrow expressed in this speech?

5. What do you think Darrow means by these statements? "In one sense everybody is equally good and equally bad. We all do the best we can under the circumstances."

6. If someone were to point out to Darrow that many present-day juvenile delinquents come from wealthy homes, what do you think his answer would be?

7. When Darrow implies that "pretty nearly everybody" outside of jail would pick his pockets if there were an opportunity, he is taking a decidedly pessimistic view of his fellow men. Is such a view justified? Why or why not?

8. Should the purpose of a prison sentence be to punish a man or to attempt to rehabilitate him?

9. How do the crime rates of the major countries correlate with the severity of their penal codes? In what states in our country is capital punishment outlawed? Do they have more or fewer murders than states with capital punishment?

10. In what ways may the practices and policies of our law enforcement agencies sometimes tend to foster rather than prevent crimes?

11. In what ways may conditions within the prisons themselves cause persons to return to a life of crime after they are released? How might prisons be reformed so as to eliminate these conditions?

12. Do statistics show that the crime rate is correlated with economic conditions? Does it, as Darrow's speech

would suggest, rise during periods of depression and fall during periods of prosperity?

13. Is there such a thing as "a criminal type"—a sort of person who will turn to a life of crime, irrespective of the social and economic conditions under which he lives?

Suggestions for further reading

Aristotle, "The Causes of Wrongdoing," *The Rhetoric*, Book 1, Chapters 10-14. The most readily accessible—and also perhaps the best—translations of *The Rhetoric* are those by Lane Cooper (New York, 1932) and Rhys Roberts (New York, 1954).

Harry Elmer Barnes and Negley K. Teeters, *New Horizons in Criminology*, 3rd ed. (Englewood Cliffs, N.J., 1959)

George Bernard Shaw, *Crime of Imprisonment* (New York, 1946)

Gresham M. Sykes, *Crime and Society* (New York, 1956)

Arthur Weinberg, ed., *Attorney for the Damned* (New York, 1957). A collection of Darrow's courtroom and platform speeches, including his debate with Judge Alfred Terry, "Is Capital Punishment Necessary?" his summation in the Loeb-Leopold trial, and his summation and examination of William Jennings Bryan in the Scopes case.

The haven of the defeated

PETER A. KAROS

In June 1890, in response to an invitation issued by the University of Michigan, delegates from the University of Wisconsin, Northwestern University, and Oberlin College assembled at Ann Arbor to organize the Northern Oratorical League, one of the oldest and most distinguished of the many associations designed to promote extracurricular speaking activities among college students. Since the first annual contest at the University of Michigan in 1891, the League has varied considerably in membership. Today the League consists of six schools: Iowa, Michigan, Minnesota, Northwestern, Western Reserve, and Wisconsin.

In 1901 the Honorable Frank O. Lowden, later United States congressman and governor of Illinois and in 1920 a leading contender for the Republican nomination for the Presidency, endowed the League with a sizable sum of money. The interest from this endowment has since been used to provide cash prizes for the first, second, and third

From *Winning Orations of the Northern Oratorical League, 1945-1950,* The Northwestern Press, Minneapolis. By permission of the Northern Oratorical League.

place winners in the annual speaking competition. These prizes are still known by their original name the "Lowden testimonials."

Being named to represent one's school in a Northern Oratorical League contest is among the highest honors that can come to a student speaker. The list of participants who later achieved distinction in public life or the professions is impressive. In 1913 Paul Blanshard, author and sociologist, represented the University of Michigan with a speech entitled "Christianity and the Social Order." In 1923 Senator Wayne Morse, then a student at the University of Wisconsin, spoke on "The Supreme Court and the People." In 1927 Harold Stassen, representing the University of Minnesota, discussed "National Will or International Good Will?"

The speech that follows won second place in the League's competition for 1950 and was delivered by Peter A. Karos, a student at the University of Minnesota. It is included here because of the unusual nature of its subject matter and because it provides a good example of a so-called "personal involvement" speech—a speech rooted in the first-hand experience of the speaker. In addition to its clear organization and rapidly moving style, this speech is notable for the vivid descriptive passages in which Karos depicts skid row and its inhabitants and for the skillful fashion in which he relates his subject to his listeners, arousing their sympathy as well as their interest in the problems of the men he describes. Structurally, the speech illustrates the disease-remedy or problem-solution pattern of organization.

While reading "The Haven of the Defeated," keep in mind the severely restricted time limits to which Karos was confined by the contest situation and the fact that the speech was written out and memorized. Even within these limitations, Karos' address provides a good example of how interesting and impressive a short student speech may be when the speaker selects a subject which he knows well and about which he has deep convictions.

How many of you have a nickel for a cup of coffee? When you stop to consider, five cents is really a very small amount. Yet I have known many men who had to beg for a cup of coffee, men who have degenerated to one of the lowest possible strata of life, a life spent on skid rows such as Washington Avenue in Minneapolis. To these rejected people skid row is both a physical and mental condition; physical, in that they are down and out. They have skidded to the depths of the pit. Mental, in that it's a continuous state of mind that forces them to consider themselves as shameful outcasts. /1

These havens of defeat constitute a major disgrace to our country, and a disgrace to every city which has them. The men inhabiting these jungles are living—if you call it that—in momentous fear, in terrible remorse, in a hell on earth. They're more than failures, for they have hit the rock bottom of despair after attempting to climb up again and again. /2

I sense this evening that your relationship towards them may be different from mine. Most of you have probably visited skid row areas. Outwardly you express sympathy for these men, but somehow I can't help believing that inwardly you are experiencing a deep sense of satisfaction at being superior to those human derelicts. My relationship was once like yours. Now it's different because as a restaurant owner on skid row I made many acquaintances with these so-called "bums." Although I've now sold the restaurant I still visit them from time to time. /3

If the majority of our respected citizens continue secretly to view them with scorn and contempt, then these sorrowful jungles will always remain in our cities. If I'm able to change your attitude to one of sympathy and understanding—then we have taken the first step towards eliminating these ghettos and raising these former exiles to a respectable level in life. /4

Let me take you behind the scenes on skid row. Many of you have expressed dissatisfaction with the boredom and daily routine of your lives. But as we move down skid row I wish you would constantly compare the occasional unhappiness of your lives to the constantly deplorable and frustrating conditions under which this forsaken population must exist. /5

First let's see where they live. A typical example is the Anchor Hotel on lower Nicollet Avenue in Minneapolis. This "hotel" has over 100 dingy, airless, and gloomy rooms on one floor, rooms which are separated only by thin plywood. The walls extend six or eight feet towards the ceiling of the large room. Each cubicle is covered across the top by chicken wire, and contains a bunk-like bed, a battered dresser, and perhaps a crate box for a chair. That's all. Fourteen windows provide ventilation for these one hundred rooms. The stench which exists, particularly in the summer time, is nauseating and repugnant. It doesn't sound very pleasant, does it? /6

Next, let's see what they do in their spare time. You and I have many social outlets. But what about these men—because of the conditions in which they find themselves they have long ago lost their families and friends. Having no responsibility except existing, and no friends or families to visit, they have

large amounts of free time. They can read or they can go to a cheap show, but the main attraction is the ample number of saloons accessible to them. There they can go and drink their dime beers, or perhaps one of their "pink ladies"—canned heat strained through a rag to eliminate impurities. /7

We have seen where they live and how they spend their days. I'd like to introduce you to some of the people who frequent these saloons. Actually in most cases their alcoholism is an effect rather than a cause —the causes including homosexuality, physical deformities, marital difficulties, and business disappointments; in short, all things of our complex society which produce frustration and result in social misfits. Remember, I'm not speaking of freaks of nature, because, you see, they're human beings the same as you and I. They, too, have been endowed with a heart, a body, and a soul. /8

Meet Sam Running. Sam is one of a large family which was unable to meet the financial strain brought about by the depression. As a result, his education was interrupted and he was forced to seek employment. Resentment and loneliness started his drinking. He worked in garages and became an accomplished body and fender man. Any employer would be glad to hire Sam—but Sam is a "deehorn." That is, he drinks anything with alcohol in it—anything from vanilla extract to bay rum. When sober, Sam is quiet, clean and respectable. However, when drunk a transformation occurs; a transformation which I cannot fully describe. He's then troublesome, dirty and repulsive. /9

Next, shake the hand of William Nelson. I met Bill when he washed dishes for me. Bill is a man who has had three years of college. He's intelligent, a good-looking man, and has a most pleasing personality. He was a conscientious worker. I could never quite figure out why Bill was on skid row. I soon got my answer. One day I was talking with a friend of Bill's. It seems that Bill had been a successful merchant in a small Minnesota town. However, because of general economic conditions his business failed. Shortly thereafter his wife became ill and required expensive medical treatment which Bill couldn't provide. Possibly because of the lack of medical treatment— she died. This dual misfortune caused Bill to withdraw to the irresponsible life of the bowery. I wonder how many of us here tonight could have met this test. /10

Now I would like you to meet Alfred "Buck" Jones. Buck is forty-three years old, married, has two children, and ran away from his faithless wife. I've known Buck, who is a machinist, for several years, and Buck is a person who attempts to give the impression he's enjoying the life of a derelict on Washington Avenue. But he's not. Oftentimes Buck would become serious and say, "Pete, whatever you do, don't ever start drinking. Look at me." After one of his periodic sprees Buck would come in and borrow fifty cents "to straighten out." I would place the half dollar on the counter, but his hands trembled so that he would be unable to pick it up. Then he would once more repeat his sincere advice. "Don't ever start drinking—look at me." /11

Yes—I could go on giving you many more examples of men like Sam, Bill, and Buck. I merely wanted to suggest that many men on skid row have the ability and capacity to become productive human beings. But without human help, their hopeless conviction that "once on skid row, always on skid row" will be more deeply rooted within them. I'm not attempting to make rash generalizations or excuses for them, and maintain that every man on the bowery can be rehabilitated to a useful citizen, because I don't believe that's true. But there are many men who, with the proper guidance and support, can be made good citizens. /12

Before we can attack this problem intelligently it's necessary to determine why these ports of loneliness harbor thousands of people. Skid row inhabitants seem to fall into two general categories: Those with dormant productivity and those unable to produce. /13

The first class includes ex-criminals, people with physical deformities, and fugitives from their former lives. Why is it that these particular types are universally found on skid rows? Because nearly all business men refuse to employ former convicts; because we shun people with physical deformities; because people, like those of us here tonight, shut these derelicts out of our lives, our minds, our consciences, and put them into association only with their own kind. /14

In the second class, those of sub-marginal incomes, we find people who are unable to produce. They are old-age pensioners and those on relief. The responsibility for their welfare lies with the federal and state governments. Relief or pension payments are simply below the minimum standards for decent living. Would you care to try living on a salary of forty dollars a month? /15

We must now ask—what can we do about the problem? Before anything constructive can be done we must conquer our ignorance concerning skid rows as we have regarding prisons and mental hospitals. Doing this will provide the foundation upon which the rest of the structure can be built. /16

Let's look and see what changes have occurred in prisons and mental hospitals. In the former, the men in prisons are no longer simply confined to cells. On the contrary, they have farms on which they work cooperatively, they have a form of government, they practice vocations in which they can become skilled. They're taking active parts in group activities. They're being prepared to assume a place in society. /17

In mental hospitals strait jackets and confinement are being eliminated. Patients are permitted hobbies, they're given responsibilities, discussion groups are encouraged. Institutions are attempting to change futile hopelessness to anticipation of the future. /18

As a people we have learned slowly and painfully, but we have learned, that men in prison cells cannot be returned to good citizenship by being shut off from human associations and productive work. We have learned that men in mental hospitals cannot be returned to good health in confinement and segregation. We must learn the similar truth that men on skid row can be returned to society only if that society opens the doors for them for useful work and healthy association with other men. /19

Civic projects must be undertaken in skid rows. Business men must hire people from the bowery to help them feel they can live as other people do. This can be done! Brown and Bigelow, a large corporation in Minneapolis, has successfully employed several hundred ex-criminals. /20

Well established churches must change their attitudes concerning skid rows and organizations like the Salvation Army. How would a dignified congregation react if a bowery bum came to church? How many churches have tried to aid the Salvation Army, a sincerely purposeful, religious organization that has successfully changed lives of skid row people? /21

Let's assume an enlightened public attitude and eager cooperation by various civic organizations. Specifically, what could be done? /22

First: Establish a farm in the state for the derelicts. As it is today, a person attempting to reform hasn't a place to go where he can stay away from the temptation of "slipping." /23

Second: The state or city can erect some new, sanitary, and livable rooming houses. By so doing, we will be helping to restore the dignity and respect which a human being is entitled to have. /24

Third: Establish a vocational guidance center, staffed with trained psychologists and sociologists, who can analyze the downfall of the people on the bowery and help them readjust to life. /25

If the feeling of the American public remains unchanged—and in our democracy this means our personal attitudes—skid rows will always be a discredit to our communities. /26

Let's give these fallen men an opportunity to live as human beings, an opportunity to serve useful ends in society, and possibly, an opportunity to help someone else. /27

The speech

1. Evaluate Karos' introduction. Is it well calculated to arouse interest in his subject? Does it have a sufficient amount of concrete material? Does it give a clear indication of what the speech is to be about? Does it move the listener easily and rapidly into a consideration of the subject, or does it bog him down in unnecessary or irrelevant details? Is it closely related to the body of the speech by means of a clear and smooth transition?

2. What specific steps does Karos take early in the speech to counteract any unfavorable attitudes his listeners may have toward his subject and to win a sympathetic hearing for his point of view? What means does he use at various points throughout the speech to relate his subject to his listeners and to arouse their sympathy?

3. In which paragraph is the central idea or specific purpose of the speech stated? Is it stated clearly, concisely, and accurately?

4. How successful would you say Karos is in describing skid row for us—in actually enabling us to see the street and its inhabitants? What specific methods and techniques does he employ in developing this description?

5. What do you think of Karos' plan of introducing Sam, Bill, and Buck to us as if we were actually meeting them face to face? Do you think this device is appropriate and effective, or is it excessively dramatic—too obviously a rhetorical trick or technique?

6. How would you evaluate the analogy which Karos draws between the reforms he would like to see for skid row and the reforms made in our prisons and mental hospitals? What specific point is he trying to prove? How successful is he in proving it?

7. Would you say that Karos adequately substantiates his contention that ex-convicts make good employees?

8. Consider the three-point program Karos sets forth for solving the problem of the skid row derelicts? Is it sufficiently clear and specific? Does he prove to your satisfaction that it would work—that if put into effect it would help solve the problem? Does he give adequate consideration to various objections that might be raised against it?

9. Is the style of the speech always as natural and conversational as one might wish? If you answer no, rewrite several passages to show how they might be improved in this respect.

10. Would you say that Karos has used a "summary" conclusion, an "appeal" conclusion, or that he has combined the two types? Defend your answer.

For further study and discussion

1. Mr. Karos seems to imply that, except for the crippled and mentally deficient, most of the men on skid row are there through no fault of their own, but because fate has dealt with them unkindly. Do you agree with this, or is it perhaps too sympathetic a view? What about the thousands of persons who have surmounted adversities and personal tragedies without losing their ambition and self-respect?

2. What do you think of the proposal that "new, sanitary, and livable rooming houses" be built for skid row inhabitants at municipal expense? Is the rehabilitation of these men a public responsibility or should it be carried on primarily by private social and religious agencies? What are the policies of some of our major cities in this respect?

3. Have the pressures and tensions of modern industrial society significantly increased the number of persons who are unable to compete successfully? Are there more "defeated" individuals today than there were fifty or a hundred years ago? Didn't ancient Rome, medieval Paris, and every other great city of every age always have a large number of "rabble" living on the edge of respectability?

4. What are the latest and most authoritative facts concerning chronic alcoholism? Would most authorities agree with Karos that it is "an effect rather than a cause" of man's downfall? Is alcoholism regarded as primarily a physical or a mental disease. What forms of treatment are thought best? How successful are they?

5. Do you think that men like Sam Running, William Nelson, and Alfred "Buck" Jones could be rehabilitated? Why? If you believe they could be, outline what you would consider to be an ideal rehabilitation program. Be as specific as you can, and stand ready to explain and defend your proposals.

6. Why do you suppose that although men of the type Karos describes are constantly in trouble with the law for drunkenness, vagrancy, and petty crimes, they do not often commit such major crimes as armed robbery or murder?

7. Are the "beatniks" only "skid rowers" in another form? What particular social and economic forces have contributed to the creation of the so-called "beat generation"?

8. Do social workers, ministers, and policemen who have worked with "skid rowers" believe most of them can be rehabilitated? What would they probably think of Karos' proposals?

9. Are there any facts available concerning the employability of ex-convicts? Do they make good employees? Are many companies hiring them successfully? What about the employability of the physically handicapped?

10. What, in general, are the churches doing to help skid row inhabitants? Should they be doing more? If so, how and what?

Suggestions for further reading

Alton L. Blakeslee, *Alcoholism, A Sickness That Can Be Beaten,* Public Affairs Pamphlet No. 118 (New York, 1952)

Earl Jerome Ellison, "The Shame of Skid Row," *Saturday Evening Post,* December 20, 1952, pp. 13-15, 48-51.

Hyman Feldman, "What Can We Do about Skid Row?" *Today's Health,* XXXV (December 1957), 18-21.

Sara Harris, *Skid Row, U.S.A.* (Garden City, N.Y., 1956)

J. M. Jellinek, ed., *Alcohol Addiction and Chronic Alcoholism,* Research Council on Problems of Alcohol (New Haven, 1942)

I have a dream

MARTIN LUTHER KING, JR.

By any measure, Wednesday, August 28, 1963, was a memorable day in the prolonged struggle for civil rights for the Negro, and by any measure, the climax of that day was the following speech by Dr. King.

More than 200,000 white and Negro citizens from all parts of the United States and from all walks of life had poured into the nation's capital by plane, train, bus, and automobile, and on foot. There, after gathering at the base of the Washington Monument, they marched en masse down Constitution and Independence Avenues to the Lincoln Memorial, where, in the presence of some seventy-five members of Congress and before the eyes of

Reprinted by permission of Dr. King.

the nation, they were addressed by such civil rights leaders as Roy Wilkins of the NAACP (National Association for the Advancement of Colored People), A. Philip Randolph of the Brotherhood of Sleeping Car Porters, John Lewis of SNCC (Student Nonviolent Coordinating Committee), and, last and most dramatically, by King.

The march and the demonstration of which it was a part were planned on a gigantic scale. Many diverse and often rival groups buried their differences to cooperate. One out of every ten marchers was white. Labor unions, at the urging of Walter Reuther and other leaders, advanced nearly half of the $110,000 budgeted for expenses. The National Council of Churches volunteered to prepare 80,000 box lunches (a cheese sandwich, an apple, and a slice of pound cake) to sell for fifty cents. Marchers who brought their own lunches were advised to make sandwiches of jelly and peanut butter because mayonnaise "deteriorates, and may cause serious diarrhea." They also were reminded to wear low-heeled shoes and to bring hats, raincoats, and sunglasses.

The Health Department of the District of Columbia provided 292 outdoor toilets and, with alcoholic refreshments banned, 21 portable water fountains capable of giving 35,000 people an hour "a good long drink." Forty doctors and 80 nurses manned 22 first-aid stations. Incoming groups were met by police escorts at the city limits, while 5,600 policemen reinforced by 350 club-carrying firemen patrolled the march area. At nearby bases, 4,000 soldiers and marines and 1,700 National Guardsmen stood by in case of trouble.

The purpose of the march was twofold. First, and in a general way, it was intended to symbolize the entire civil rights struggle—to suggest by the sheer presence of countless thousands, both white and black, that the struggle was one in which all Americans were deeply involved. Second, it was aimed at securing action on at least four specific matters: (1) passage "without compromise or filibuster" of the Kennedy civil rights bill, then pending in Congress; (2) integration of all public schools by the beginning of 1964; (3) a federal program to "train and place all unemployed workers—Negro and white—in meaningful and dignified jobs at decent wages"; and (4) a federal Fair Employment Practices Act that effectively barred all discrimination in employment. In line with these more specific purposes, the battle cry of the day was "Now." On placards and orally, the marchers demanded equality and action, not months or years in the future, but "Now."

Twenty minutes before the scheduled departure time of 11:30 A.M., groups of marchers began to stream down Constitution and Independence Avenues and along the sides of the Reflecting Pool toward the Lincoln

Memorial. "Some marchers," *Time* reported, "wept as they walked, [but] the faces of many more gleamed with happiness."[1] There were no bands, and though nearly everyone chanted or sang and a group of "denim-clad" youngsters from Plaquemine, Louisiana, danced all the way, on the whole the march was orderly and the marchers dignified and serious. Only four persons were arrested during the course of the day, and of the 1,720 treated in the first-aid stations nearly all were suffering from fatigue or from the heat.

As it gradually spread itself out around the Lincoln Memorial, the crowd was entertained by folk singers Joan Baez, Josh White, Odetta, Bob Dylan, and Peter, Paul, and Mary. Author James Baldwin and actors Marlon Brando, Paul Newman, Burt Lancaster, and Charlton Heston made brief appearances. The official program began at 1:59, though by this time Ralph Bunche, Dick Gregory, and several others already had spoken. By prearrangement each speaker was to limit his remarks to four minutes; nearly all, however, talked longer. The least restrained of the speeches was delivered by John Lewis of SNCC. Randolph's address was described by *Newsweek* as "visionary."[2] Wilkins spoke quietly but with deep conviction and great effect.

Following Wilkins' address, part of the huge crowd, which had been standing shoulder to shoulder for several hours, began to drift away. They were arrested, however, by singer Mahalia Jackson, who, with the gospel song "I've Been Buked and I've Been Scorned," alternately aroused laughter and tears. It was Miss Jackson's singing that set the emotional tone for King's speech. "Mahalia," said *Time*, "was hard to follow—and there probably was only one person in the civil rights world who could have done it quite so successfully."[3]

King's speech was short, as befitted the lateness of the hour and the weariness of the crowd. Moreover, it was heavily emotional, the emotion deriving in part from the ideas and in part from the resonant and highly figurative style in which they were expressed.

After a perfunctory and somewhat disappointing introduction, King plunged immediately and almost abruptly into the body of the address. This fell into three major divisions. In the first division (paragraphs 2-6) King spoke to the nation as a whole and to its leaders, recalling the "promissory note" of freedom for all as written into the Constitution and Declaration of Independence, and warning that it would be "fatal" to misjudge the urgency of the moment. Beginning with paragraph 7, he shifted his focus and appealed directly to his own "people," the Negroes, reviewing the indignities under which they suffered and reaffirming his faith in nonviolence as the strategy they must follow in redressing their wrongs. With paragraph 9, King introduced a gradual transition into the third and longest section of the address, in which, though he continued to speak to his "people," his concern shifted from their present plight to their future prospects. Reminding them of the depressing and restrictive conditions under which they lived, he promised them that "the situation can and will be changed." Interlacing his predictions with the recurrent phrase "I have a dream," he visualized for them a happier day when justice and brotherhood would reign. Then with the refrain "Let freedom ring," he built to a high emotional climax that culminated with the words of the old Negro spiritual, "Free at last! free at last! thank God almighty, we are free at last!"

Although the results of the march and of the demonstration as a whole are difficult to assess, there can be no question that King's speech was a resounding success. After the first few moments, *Time* reported, the audience was "enslaved" and "roared 'Yes, yes!' to almost everything he said."[4] The refrain "I have a dream," reported *Newsweek*, was greeted with cries of "Dream on! Dream on! . . . I see it! . . . Keep dreaming."[5]

In the following appraisal for the New York Times, James Reston summed up his impression of the speech:

"It was Dr. King, who, near the end of the day, touched the vast audience. Until then the pilgrimage was merely a great spectacle. . . . For many the day seemed an adventure, a long outing in the late summer sun. . . .

"But Dr. King brought them alive in the late afternoon with a peroration that was an anguished echo from all the old American reformers. Roger Williams calling for religious liberty, Sam Adams calling for political liberty, old man Thoreau denouncing coercion, William Lloyd Garrison demanding emancipation, and Eugene V. Debs crying for economic equality—Dr. King echoed them all.

" 'I have a dream,' he cried again and again. And each time the dream was a promise of our ancient articles of faith: phrases from the Constitution, lines from the great anthem of the nation, guarantees from the Bill of Rights, all ending with a vision that they might one day all come true.

"Dr. King touched all the themes of the day, only better than anybody else. He was full of the symbolism of Lincoln and Gandhi, and the cadences of the Bible. He was both militant and sad, and he sent the crowd

---

[1]*Time*, September 6, 1963, p. 14.
[2]*Newsweek*, September 9, 1963, p. 22.
[3]*Time*, p. 15.

[4]*Time*, p. 15.
[5]*Newsweek*, p. 22.

away feeling that the long journey had been worthwhile."[6]

As a speaker, King's principal asset is a rich baritone voice which, though naturally soft and musical, at times rises to impassioned climaxes. Normally he gesticulates only moderately and moves little. Although he prefers to speak extemporaneously and without notes, on important occasions he uses a manuscript. Parts of "I Have a Dream" are extemporaneous departures from his text.

King was born in Atlanta, Georgia, on January 15, 1929. He received his undergraduate education at Morehouse College, his theological training at Crozer Seminary, and his Ph.D. at Boston University. In addition to many honorary degrees, he has won numerous citations and awards, the most notable of which is the Nobel Peace Prize, in 1964. He is pastor of the Dexter Avenue Baptist Church in Montgomery, Alabama, and president of the Southern Christian Leadership Conference.

The text of King's speech as here reproduced is based upon a recording made at the scene. It has been edited to represent as closely as possible his actual phrasing.

I am happy to join with you today in what will go down in history as the greatest demonstration for freedom in the history of our nation. /1

Five score years ago, a great American, in whose symbolic shadow we stand today, signed the Emancipation Proclamation. This momentous decree came as a great beacon light of hope to millions of Negro slaves, who had been seared in the flames of withering injustice. It came as a joyous daybreak to end the long night of their captivity. /2

But one hundred years later, the Negro is still not free. One hundred years later, the life of the Negro is still sadly crippled by the manacles of segregation and the chains of discrimination. One hundred years later, the Negro lives on a lonely island of poverty in the midst of a vast ocean of material prosperity. One hundred years later (*Applause*), the Negro is still languished in the corners of American society and finds himself an exile in his own land. So we have come here today to dramatize a shameful condition. /3

In a sense we've come to our nation's Capitol to cash a check. When the architects of our republic wrote the magnificent words of the Constitution and the Declaration of Independence, they were signing a promissory note to which every American was to fall heir. This note was a promise that all men—yes, black men as well as white men—would be guaranteed the unalienable rights of life, liberty, and the pursuit of happiness. /4

It is obvious today that America has defaulted on this promissory note insofar as her citizens of color are concerned. Instead of honoring this sacred obligation, America has given the Negro people a bad check; a check which has come back marked "insufficient funds" (*Applause*). But we refuse to believe that the bank of justice is bankrupt. We refuse to believe that there are insufficient funds in the great vaults of opportunity of this nation. So we've come to cash this check—a check that will give us upon demand the riches of freedom and the security of justice (*Applause*). We have also come to this hallowed spot to remind America of the fierce urgency of *now*. This is no time to engage in the luxury of cooling off or to take the tranquilizing drug of gradualism. *Now is the time* to make real the promises of Democracy. *Now is the time* to rise from the dark and desolate valley of segregation to the sunlit path of racial justice. *Now is the* (*Applause*) *time* to lift our nation from the quicksands of racial injustice to the solid rock of brotherhood. *Now is the time* to make justice a reality for all of God's children. /5

It would be fatal for the nation to overlook the urgency of the moment. This sweltering summer of the Negro's legitimate discontent will not pass until there is an invigorating autumn of freedom and equality. Nineteen sixty-three is not an end, but a beginning. Those who hope that the Negro needed to blow off steam and will now be content will have a rude awakening if the nation returns to business as usual (*Applause*). There will be neither rest nor tranquility in America until the Negro is granted his citizenship rights. The whirlwinds of revolt will continue to shake the foundations of our nation until the bright day of justice emerges. /6

But that is something that I must say to my people who stand on the warm threshold which leads into the palace of justice. In the process of gaining our rightful place we must not be guilty of wrongful deeds. Let us not seek to satisfy our thirst for freedom by drinking from the cup of bitterness and hatred (*Applause*). /7

We must forever conduct our struggle on the high plane of dignity and discipline. We must not allow our creative protest to degenerate into physical violence. Again and again we must rise to the majestic heights of meeting physical force with soul

[6] New York *Times*, August 29, 1963, p. 1. (Late City edition)

force. The marvelous new militancy which has engulfed the Negro community must not lead us to a distrust of all white people, for many of our white brothers, as evidenced by their presence here today, have come to realize that their destiny is tied up with our destiny (*Applause*). And they have come to realize that their freedom is inextricably bound to our freedom. We cannot walk alone. /8

And as we walk, we must make the pledge that we shall always march ahead. We cannot turn back. There are those who ask the devotees of civil rights, "When will you be satisfied?" We can never be satisfied as long as the Negro is the victim of the unspeakable horrors of police brutality. We can never be satisfied as long as our bodies, heavy with the fatigue of travel, cannot gain lodging in the motels of the highways and the hotels of the cities (*Applause*). We cannot be satisfied as long as the Negro's basic mobility is from a smaller ghetto to a larger one. We can never be satisfied as long as our children are stripped of their selfhood and robbed of their dignity by signs stating "For Whites Only" (*Applause*). We cannot be satisfied as long as a Negro in Mississippi cannot vote and a Negro in New York believes he has nothing for which to vote (*Applause*). No, no, we are not satisfied, and we will not be satisfied until justice rolls down like waters and righteousness like a mighty stream (*Applause*). /9

I am not unmindful that some of you have come here out of great trials and tribulations. Some of you have come fresh from narrow jail cells. Some of you have come from areas where your quest for freedom left you battered by the storms of persecution and staggered by the winds of police brutality. You have been the veterans of creative suffering. Continue to work with the faith that unearned suffering is redemptive. /10

Go back to Mississippi, go back to Alabama, go back to South Carolina, go back to Georgia, go back to Louisiana, go back to the slums and ghettos of our northern cities, knowing that somehow this situation can and will be changed. Let us not wallow in the valley of despair. /11

I say to you today, my friends (*Applause*), so even though we face the difficulties of today and tomorrow, I still have a dream. It is a dream deeply rooted in the American dream. /12

I have a dream that one day this nation will rise up and live out the true meaning of its creed: "We hold these truths to be self-evident; that all men are created equal" (*Applause*). /13

I have a dream that one day on the red hills of Georgia the sons of former slaves and the sons of former slaveowners will be able to sit down together at the table of brotherhood; I have a dream— /14

That one day even the state of Mississippi, a state sweltering with the heat of injustice, sweltering with the heat of oppression, will be transformed into an oasis of freedom and justice; I have a dream— /15

That my four little children will one day live in a nation where they will not be judged by the color of their skin but by the content of their character; I have a dream today (*Applause*). /16

I have a dream that one day, down in Alabama, with its vicious racists, with its governor having his lips dripping with the words of interposition and nullification, one day right there in Alabama little black boys and black girls will be able to join hands with little white boys and white girls as sisters and brothers; I have a dream today (*Applause*)— /17

I have a dream that one day every valley shall be exalted, every hill and mountain shall be made low, the rough places will be made plane and crooked places will be made straight, and the glory of the Lord shall be revealed, and all flesh shall see it together. /18

This is our hope. This is the faith that I go back to the South with. With this faith we will be able to hew out of the mountain of despair a stone of hope. With this faith we will be able to transform the jangling discords of our nation into a beautiful symphony of brotherhood. With this faith we will be able to work together, to pray together, to struggle together, to go to jail together, to stand up for freedom together, knowing that we will be free one day (*Applause*). /19

This will be the day (*Applause*). . . . This will be the day when all of God's children will be able to sing with new meaning "My country 'tis of thee, sweet land of liberty, of thee I sing. Land where my fathers died, land of the pilgrim's pride, from every mountainside, let freedom ring," and if America is to be a great nation—this must become true. /20

So let freedom ring—from the prodigious hilltops of New Hampshire, let freedom ring; from the mighty mountains of New York, let freedom ring—from the heightening Alleghenies of Pennsylvania! /21

Let freedom ring from the snowcapped Rockies of Colorado! /22

Let freedom ring from the curvaceous slopes of California! /23

But not only that; let freedom ring from Stone Mountain of Georgia! /24

Let freedom ring from Lookout Mountain of Tennessee! /25

Let freedom ring from every hill and mole hill of Mississippi. From every mountainside, let freedom ring, and when this happens (*Applause*). /26

When we allow freedom ring, when we let it ring from every village and every hamlet, from every state and every city, we will be able to speed up that day when all of God's children, black men and white men, Jews and Gentiles, Protestants and Catholics, will be able to join hands and sing in the words of the old Negro spiritual, "Free at last! free at last! thank God almighty, we are free at last!" (*Thunderous applause.*) /27

The speech

1. Outline the speech and comment in detail on its organization. What are the major ideas? Are there too many? Too few? According to what principle are they arranged? In your opinion, is this the best possible arrangement? Why or why not?

2. King's speech has practically no concrete supporting material in the form of facts, statistics, quotations, and the like. Does the absence of such material detract from its effectiveness? Defend your answer.

3. To what particular sentences or phrases do you think James Reston may have been referring when he described King's speech as "full of the symbolism of Lincoln and Gandhi, and the cadences of the Bible"?

4. What is your evaluation of King's use of figurative language? Does it add to or detract from the effectiveness of the speech? Does King use figurative language too abundantly? Justify your answer.

5. Comment on the way in which King introduces the theme of the day, "Now," into his speech. Does he do it skillfully or unskillfully? Can you think of any ways in which his use of this theme might have been improved?

6. Evaluate the adequacy of King's introduction in terms of the purpose of his speech, his place on the program as a whole, etc. If King's had been the only speech delivered that day, do you think he would have used the same introduction? Explain your answer.

7. If you were a newspaper reporter describing King's speech, which of his ideas or themes would you single out for the "lead paragraph" of your story?

8. Write as complete and accurate a description as you can of the speaking situation King faced. See the accounts in such magazines as *Time*, September 6, 1963; *Newsweek*, September 9, 1963; *U.S. News and World Report*, September 9, 1963; *Life*, September 6, 1963; and in such newspapers as the New York *Times*, August 29, 1963.

For further study and discussion

1. Review thoroughly the guarantees of political equality for the Negro as written into the Constitution of the United States. Be sure to examine all pertinent clauses and amendments.

2. Investigate the history and the present state of racial integration in the South—in the schoolroom, on public transportation, in hotels and restaurants, in employment practices, in voting rights, in the election of colored men and women to public office, etc.

3. Review recent legislation—the Civil Rights Act of 1964, the Voting Rights Act of 1965, etc.—aimed at guaranteeing the Negro his civil liberties.

4. Evaluate public demonstrations, freedom marches, sit-ins, and the like as means of promoting racial equality. Are they effective? Are they ethically defensible? What limits and restrictions, if any, should be placed upon them?

5. What countries besides the United States still have serious problems of race relations to solve? What may we learn from their experience?

6. Where in the United States outside the South are we confronted with problems in race relations and the integration of minority groups? Are we solving these problems successfully?

7. What in your judgment is the best thing the white people of the South could do to promote harmony among the races? How could the white people of the North help most? What course of action should the Negroes follow?

8. Investigate the aims and methods of the various groups now engaged in the civil rights struggle—the NAACP, SNCC, CORE, etc.

Suggestions for further reading

W. Haywood Burns, *The Voices of Negro Protest in America* (New York, 1963)

James G. Cook, *The Segregationists* (New York, 1962)

Martin Luther King, Jr., *Strength to Love* (New York and Evanston, Ill., 1963)

_____, *Stride Toward Freedom* (New York, 1958)

_____, *Why We Can't Wait* (New York and Evanston, Ill., 1964)

Ashley Montagu, *Race, Science, and Humanity* (Princeton, N.J., 1963)

Lawrence Dunbar Reddick, *Crusader Without Violence: A Biography of Martin Luther King, Jr.* (New York, 1959)

Joseph Tussman, ed., *The Supreme Court on Racial Discrimination* (New York, 1963)

Rout the forces of hate

LeRoy COLLINS

On December 3, 1963, LeRoy Collins addressed the annual meeting of the Greater Columbia Chamber of Commerce at Columbia, South Carolina. Although Collins was at that time president of the National Association of Broadcasters, he did not appear in his role as czar of the broadcasting industry. Instead, drawing upon his background as a native Southerner and former governor of Florida, he spoke on the problems which confronted the South as it attempted to adjust to a new system of race relations and to the extension of civil rights to all.

As a Southerner speaking in the South to an audience which contained many old friends and associates, Collins had an initial advantage. He realized, however, that his speech probably would arouse antagonism in many of his listeners, for the burden of his remarks was critical of those educated and responsible Southerners who had "remained cravenly silent or lamely defensive" while less responsible elements of the population by word and action had created an unfavorable image of the South.

Following one of the common traditional methods for organizing a speech to a skeptical or hostile audience, Collins approached his leading ideas gradually, so that his first proposition—that the better elements in the South should step forward—was not mentioned until paragraph 16 and not brought to a climax until paragraph 22. Moreover, early in the speech he identified himself with his audience through the repeated use of the word "we," and he identified his audience with that group of Southerners who he thought should assume leadership. At the same time, he ingratiated himself with his listeners by mentioning the relative peacefulness with which integration was proceeding in the educational institutions of South Carolina; he focused upon the promise of the future as a means of burying a bitter past; he relieved the strong indictment of paragraphs 16-24 with an extended illustrative story; he declared that civil rights were a Northern as well as a Southern problem; and he skillfully emphasized the urgency and the challenge of the moment by repeated references to the tragedy of a few days before, the assassination of President Kennedy on November 22, 1963 (paragraphs 5, 7, 22, 66ff.). Finally, it was only near the close of his speech that he reminded his listeners of the harsh fact that the law of the land was

forcing changes upon the South whether it willed them or not, and he challenged his fellow Southerners to cease "sulking" and to "become a more vital part of the nation's efforts for the fulfillment of national goals" (paragraph 65).

Viewed as a whole, therefore, the speech is a good example of an address designed for a potentially unfriendly or critical audience. But it is more than a bag of tricks or techniques. Its high moral tone, its evident sincerity, and its clear idealism raise it above the ordinary and make it a dignified and challenging document in its own right.

Collins was born in Tallahassee, Florida, on March 10, 1909. Educated as a lawyer, he served in the Florida House of Representatives from 1934 to 1938 and in the Florida Senate from 1940 to 1944. Reëlected to the Senate in 1946, after two wartime years in the Navy, he combined political activities with the practice of law in Tallahassee until 1954, when he was elected governor of Florida to fill out the term of Governor Dan McCarty, who had died in office. In 1956 he was reëlected governor for a four-year term.

After serving as permanent chairman of the Democratic National Convention in 1960, Collins was appointed to a three-year term as president of the National Association of Broadcasters. In July 1964, President Johnson invited him to assume the directorship of the Community Relations Service, a federal agency designed to aid communities in solving problems resulting from compliance with the Civil Rights Act of that year. In June 1965 he was appointed Under Secretary of Commerce.

Although loyal to his Southern background and training, as this speech suggests, during recent years Collins has become increasingly identified as a spokesman for Southern "moderates."

The text of the speech as here printed is based upon a tape recording made at the time of delivery. A slightly edited version was printed in pamphlet form and reproduced in the *Congressional Record* for December 13, 1963.

It is a high privilege for me to be here in Columbia, and to participate in this Greater Columbia Chamber of Commerce Annual Meeting of 1963. /1

I like South Carolina, and I always have. Yours is a state rich in history and exciting in opportunity. /2

Your distinguished Governor, Donald Russell, who honors us all here tonight and has especially honored me by his introduction, is a public leader of conspicuous competence and of uncommon dedication, and he is known as that far beyond the boundaries of South Carolina. /3

I would like to add too, President Hudson, my warm congratulations to all of your Chamber of Commerce officers and committees. You have had a remarkably successful year; and, while the rank-and-file support of your membership doubtless has been excellent, I agree with you that special praise is due all of these men who have supplied this great leadership. /4

My message this evening is being carried by many broadcasters here and across this state, and I am grateful to them, and I also salute them, along with all other broadcasters, for their enormous efforts in reporting to the American people and to the world the story of our nation in the agony of its trial after the assassination of President Kennedy. As soon as the first dastardly shot was fired in Dallas, response of news broadcasters was immediate. It became complete, and reflected the highest skill and dedication. /5

This was the free broadcaster at his finest. No one from the government had to make the slightest move to get him going, or to keep him at his task, or to hold out any hope that his commercial losses would be offset in any way or shared by anyone else. It was his job. And in performing it, he asked not what the country could do for him, but what he could do for his country. /6

I do not believe anyone is more genuinely proud of his southern birth and "raising" than I am. I love this land. But some thoughts have been brooding in my mind lately, especially in the few mad days since the murder of our young President, and I think South Carolina and Columbia are good places for me to talk these out. /7

As Governor Russell has indicated, not all of you will agree with what I have to say. This does not trouble *me*, and it should not trouble *you*. /8

I have tried to be a Southerner who speaks plainly on sensitive issues, and you are sons and daughters of a state, which, from the time of Sumter and Pickens and Calhoun, has been characterized by forthright debate. /9

Doubtless as you have detected down the years, a number of people in other neighborhoods of America have not always agreed with the forthright talk emerging from South Carolina. But debate, if it is honest and thoughtful, refines the decisions in our republic and makes them more intelligent. /10

I have not come to address old grievances. It is the future of the South and of our nation that I wish to take up with you here tonight. And the one is inseparable from the other. /11

I would hope first that we might consider as our own the creed of our new President, Lyndon Johnson, who, once exasperated by his critics in the Senate when he was the leader of that forum, sought to explain himself in these terms: "I am a free man, an American, a United States Senator and a Democrat in that order." /12

Most of us, when we talk about the South, find the *easy* things to say. We like to recall the handicaps our region has suffered in the exploitation of its natural resources; the impoverishment which followed the Civil War, and the later unjust and repressive efforts made to thwart our growth and development. Then we like to speak of the happier days of our recent dynamic economic growth and prosperity—of the "new South," a land of vast new opportunities. And these things are all true. We can prove them by the bank deposits, by the new factories, by the lines on the charts, by the clothes we see children wearing to school. /13

We also like to speak of the "new, new South," which glitters with projections of future prosperity almost beyond comprehension. And I firmly believe that you and I will see this come to pass in our lifetimes. /14

But let us think together this evening about things more personal than material progress. /15

I do not like it when people speak of Southerners as if they are not human parts of the United States. But the prime reason they do this is that for too long we have permitted the South's own worst enemies to speak for it. /16

We have allowed the extremists to speak for the South—the very ones against whom we in the South have had to struggle in our towns and in our state capitals for much of the progress we have made. /17

They have done it in speeches on the floor of the Congress which have sounded like anti-American diatribes from some hostile foreign country. /18

They have done it in the national press and on the national radio and television to such an extent that citizens outside the South would be entitled to wonder if they might not need visas to pass through our region. /19

And all the while, too many of the rest of us have remained cravenly silent or lamely defensive while Dixie battle cries have been employed to incite sick souls to violence—egged on by the rabble-rousers' call to "stand up and fight!" /20

It is little wonder that other Americans fail to regard us on occasions as being in the mainstream of American life and citizenship. /21

And I ask you tonight, how long are the majority of Southerners going to allow themselves to be caricatured before the nation by these claghorns? How many Sunday School children have to be dynamited to death? How many Negro leaders have to be shot in the back? How many governors have to be shot in the chest? How many Presidents have to be assassinated? /22

All those evil happenings have been the products of environments where hatred has been preached and lawlessness extolled—environments which you and I know are foreign to the South—the South, for which we care deeply—and are repugnant to most Southerners. Violence and disorder will occur anywhere, regardless of the issue, when reason and discussion are allowed to give way to hate and personal acrimony. /23

It is time the decent people in the South, with all their might and strength, told the bloody-shirt-wavers to climb down off the buckboards of bigotry. It is time we started speaking and acting together more like loyal Americans and self-respecting Southerners. /24

You here in South Carolina have shown in many ways that you understand—that you are moving forward. /25

The cities of Oxford, Birmingham, Little Rock, New Orleans, Dallas—and Philadelphia and Chicago, for that matter—are not to be found in the State of South Carolina. /26

And that fact, as all of you well know, is no accident of geography. /27

It is because the leadership of this community and this state reached a rational decision that South Carolina was not going to allow bigotry and lawlessness to pervade your society and pollute your bloodstream. /28

There has been no need for federal marshals patrolling your university campuses, thanks to the good sense and respect for law among the people of this state. /29

You have demonstrated to the rest of the nation, which includes the rest of the South, and to yourselves, that a Deep-South community does not have to throw itself onto a funeral pyre of hate. /30

Yes, there are forces at work in the South—men and women who do not have their faces turned backward, stalwart men and women who have not received the headlines and public notices which have been accorded the more sensational examples of lack of progress, but who have been in the vanguard of progress nonetheless. /31

There is a story which came out of World War I. I do not vouch for its literal accuracy. In fact, there are many reasons for doubting its truth in detail. But to me, its message rings true. /32

Three American soldiers—one a Protestant, one a Catholic and one a Jew—became fast friends as they marched and fought together in France. They entered into a pact committing the survivors to do everything possible for the family of any one of them who might be killed in action. /33

In a battle soon afterward, on the outskirts of a small French village, the Protestant boy was killed. The only place of worship was a little Catholic church. The Catholic boy and the Jewish boy asked the priest of this little church for permission to have their friend buried in the church cemetery adjoining. But when the priest learned that the dead boy was not a Catholic, he regretfully declined, pointing out that under the regulations of the Church the cemetery had been established and blessed for the burial of Catholics only. /34

After considerable discussion of the point, the priest suggested as an alternative that the burial be made just outside the fence of the cemetery and he said, "Here we will be sure to see that the grave is cared for and not desecrated; we'll do this just as faithfully as we care for the graves on the inside." /35

The arrangement was worked out, and the two boys who survived went on through the war. When peace came, they returned to their homes in the United States. /36

They had the understanding, however, that three years from the date their friend was killed they would meet in this little French village and together visit the grave. /37

When this day came, they met as agreed and soon came to the little church. But when they arrived just outside the fence where they had buried their friend, they were shocked to see no sign of the grave. Angrily, they found the old priest and scolded him for his neglect. /38

Then the old father took the two young men out into the cemetery and he led them down the inside of the fence, and there was the grave just as the soldiers had left it. Then he said, "You know, some time after you boys left, I went back and studied our regulations further. I found it to be very clear that while I was not permitted to allow the burial inside the fence, there was nothing which prevented me from later moving the fence over." /39

Fellow Southerners, we can talk about our mores, about our local laws and customs, about the low standards of many Negroes, but the time has come when we must move some fences. /40

The soul of man is beyond the reach of a court order or a legislative act. But while courts and laws cannot change the innermost dictates of the human conscience, courts and laws most certainly can control the acts of men. /41

This task of assuring racial justice is no easy one for us in the South—nor is it for those in the North. But Americans everywhere must recognize that this is a national commitment and a national necessity. It is not going away. /42

The advancement of all rights of national citizenship, as we well know, will occur with the overt aid of the national government if local citizens and local and state governments do not move effectively to accomplish this on their own. /43

Yet, too many politicians down our way have been hoodwinking the people on the civil rights issue. They have been trying to pretend, for their own personal political advantage, that the changes which are coming over the hill really are not there. They talk defensively of "states' rights" when they and we well know that there can be no such thing as a state's right to default on a national duty. /44

Any rational man who looks at the horizon and sees the South of the future segregated is simply seeing a mirage. /45

"That all men are created equal" is not an empty cliché. It was not put in our Declaration of Independence by Jefferson merely to stir our revolutionary forces to greater sacrifice. /46

It is a mighty idea that is the keystone of our nation's whole meaning and perpetual commitment. It is the basic idea which supports the dignity of man as an individual. /47

It is an idea that can never be stopped—not by custom—not by prejudice—not by hate—not by murder—not by armies—not by any mortal force. /48

It may be thwarted—it may be delayed—its triumph may be at great cost and sacrifice—but it will keep coming on and on and on, for it has the invincibility of simple truth, justice and right. /49

Aside from human attitudes the most basic change which must occur to aid us in resolving our racial difficulties is the improvement of the standards of living of all underprivileged Americans. The taproot of future progress is greatly expanded and improved public education for all American youngsters. /50

While in the Florida Legislature many years ago, I undertook the leadership for the passage of legislation known as the Minimum Foundation Program. Under it, the state government guaranteed to every child in Florida, regardless of where he lived or how poor his county, a public education of no less quality than certain prescribed standards. This has worked quite well, and other states have developed similar plans. /51

There was talk at the time that a program like this would rob local communities of local interest and influence, but this did not turn out to be the case. /52

Now, I feel that we should mount in this country a massive National Minimum Foundation Plan under which the nation would assure to every child an education adequate to the full development of his talents. /53

This would call for the supplementing of local resources in proportion to need. It could enable us to close our educational gap and to bring to an end our vicious cycle of ignorance breeding more ignorance with resulting impoverishment of body, intellect and spirit. /54

This is not a national need; I say it is a national necessity. We must do this to enable the nation better to meet its adversaries in a hostile and competitive world. But, more importantly, we must do it to provide for American children a seed bed of simple justice which is now their rightful heritage, although for millions it has not been their inheritance. /55

Our country has a right to expect the best from all of us, regardless of where we live. /56

And just as it is wrong for anyone, including some Southerners, to sell the South short, by the same token we in the South have no right to go off in a corner and sulk. /57

Southerners, like Americans from every section of this land, have a solemn obligation to make whatever general and unique contributions they can to advance national good. /58

It is high time the South rid itself of any political inferiority complex. /59

Leadership in the South—business, professional, educational and political—instead of being rejected out of hand nationally must be regarded as a valuable resource in the role which America must play in meeting the challenge of history. /60

Some politicians in other regions of the nation are contending that the South now bears such a stigma before the nation that it is incapable of producing national leadership. And you know there are even some Southerners who parrot the same fallacy. /61

After all, I ask these, where was this republic founded? By whom were our nation's principles of freedom and individual dignity hammered out? /62

So much of this came from the minds of Washington and Jefferson and Henry. The young republic was nourished by the philosophies of Madison and Monroe and Jackson. Southerners all. /63

The South should be bright and optimistic, indeed, as we face the future. /64

To become a vital part, a more vital part, of the nation's efforts for the fulfillment of national goals will not demean our posture as states, but enhance it. It will not be a retreat, but an advance. It will not be a defeat, but a victory. /65

My fellow countrymen, a few long days ago our young President was struck down on the street of an American city. Good men have differences, and many Americans had differences with John Kennedy. But I do not know of any fellow countryman who, after rendezvousing with his soul, would not share the sweet dream of John Kennedy for a better America or his dedication to move his dreams toward reality. He was the unusual, heroic person in politics, who thought not in terms of years, but in terms of generations and of what America must be for our children and the children of our children. /66

Just a few days before his death, President Kennedy was talking to one of our leading Southern editors—a very close friend—Bill Baggs of the Miami *News*, about the year 2000 A.D., and of what we, in our generation, must plant and plow up to make this country right for its sons and daughters in 2000 A.D. /67

I say to you tonight that above all else it is the moral duty of our generation to plow under racial injustice everywhere in the United States and to plant new opportunities for the generations which will come along after us and reside in this green part of our old planet. /68

Now, this has not been anything like the speech that I first expected to make to you here tonight. /69

But the other day, as I followed the caisson drawn by the six white horses to Arlington's green hillside and listened to the bugler's mournful cry and saw the flame lighted on the grave as if to hold back at least a tiny part of the approaching darkness, my conscience grew heavy—grew heavy with the long promise of history: /70

"Beyond the sundown is tomorrow's wisdom;
Today is going to be a long, long ago." /71

Oh, God of all mankind, help us to find this wisdom. Help us to make today count for more than its sorrows. Thank you. /72

The speech

1. Evaluate Collins' opening remarks (paragraphs 1-4). Were they appropriate to the audience and to the occasion? Did they extend the usual courtesies? Could they have been improved? If so, how?

2. The references to broadcasters in paragraphs 5 and 6 undoubtedly were introduced because at the time of the speech Collins still was president of the National Association of Broadcasters. It could, however, be argued that these remarks were irrelevant to his subject and purpose, and that they should have been omitted. Do you think they should have been included? Discuss the question pro and con.

3. Study paragraphs 7 through 10, in which Collins first announces that not all of his audience will agree with what he is going to say. What general strategy or technique did he employ in making this announcement? Was it wisely chosen? Could you improve upon it?

4. Consider the various references which Collins makes to the assassination of President Kennedy (paragraphs 5, 7, 22, 66 ff.). In your opinion, what part do these references play in the overall strategy of his address? Do you think they probably helped Collins achieve his purpose?

5. Evaluate the unity and coherence of the speech. Does the story about the three soldiers distract attention from the central idea? In your opinion, do the paragraphs about a higher standard of living for all underprivileged Americans and about the Florida Minimum Foundation Program (paragraphs 50-56) directly further the speaker's purpose?

6. Comment on the conclusion of the speech (paragraphs 69-72). Do you think Collins should have admitted that the speech he actually gave was not "anything like" the speech he had intended to make? Do you think the citation of poetry and the appeal to the Deity for wisdom strike too emotional a tone for the rest of the speech and for the circumstances in which it was delivered?

7. Judging from the printed text of the speech alone, rate the speaker's sincerity and the earnestness with which he urged his ideas. Defend your answer by referring to specific sentences and passages.

8. Although the speech as a whole is expressed in literal language and in a conversational style, at

several points Collins uses figurative expressions. Locate these expressions, define them as to type, and evaluate their effectiveness. (See Glossary, *Figures of speech.*)

For further study and discussion

1. In your opinion, what effect will the increased industrialization and urbanization of the South have on relations between the races? Explain your answer.
2. To what extent do you agree with Collins that the good people of the South too often have allowed the "extremists" to speak and act for them, while they have remained silent or "lamely defensive"? How and under what circumstances should these persons make themselves heard?
3. Collins asserts that civil rights are a Northern as well as a Southern problem. Give evidence and examples to substantiate this assertion.
4. How would closing the "educational gap" and bringing to an end the "vicious cycle of ignorance breeding more ignorance" help guarantee civil rights to persons of all races?
5. What has the federal government done and what can it do to guarantee civil rights to citizens when these rights are denied by state or local governments?
6. To a certain extent the South always has been a discrete region, culturally and economically as well as geographically. Explain why this has been true. In what various ways have the culture and economy of the South changed in recent years?
7. Compare the attitudes of the people as they have affected the problems of racial integration and civil rights in the Deep South and in the Border States; in urban and in rural areas; in the so-called Black Belt and in areas where Negroes are a minority of the population. Which areas have the most serious problems? Explain your answer.
8. It is often said that legislation cannot solve the problem of race relations. Do you agree or disagree? Why?

Suggestions for further reading

Wilbur Joseph Cash, *The Mind of the South* (New York, 1941)

Thomas D. Clark, *The Emerging South* (New York, 1961)

Brooks Hays, *A Southern Moderate Speaks* (Chapel Hill, N.C., 1959)

William B. Hesseltine and David L. Smiley, *The South in American History,* 2nd ed: (Englewood Cliffs, N.J., 1960)

Valdimer Orlando Key, *Southern Politics in State and Nation* (New York, 1949)

Ralph McGill, *The South and the Southerner* (Boston, 1963)

Allan P. Sindler, ed., *Change in the Contemporary South* (Durham, N.C., 1963)

William D. Workman, *The Case for the South* (New York, 1960)

Apathy today and yesterday

In recent years sociologists, public officials, and religious leaders have expressed increasing concern over a vaguely defined syndrome of collective behavior which, for want of a better name, they call "apathy" or "social indifference."

Although the symptoms within this syndrome are numerous, most often they take one of two forms: (1) a refusal to intercede in situations in which an individual has been injured or is being subjected to indignity or bodily harm, and (2) an unwillingness to assume the full obligations of citizenship.

Various hypotheses have been advanced to account for this "apathy." Some experts believe that with the development of great urban communities and of modern systems of communication the problems of other persons impinge upon an individual so persistently that he must erect a psychological barrier against them. Other students of apathy as it manifests itself today point to man's increasing adherence to purely economic values or to a failure on the part of religious and educational institutions.

The problem of social indifference, however, is not new, nor is it confined to our larger cities. On the following pages are two speeches, one concerned with the apathy syndrome as it existed in a small American town over fifty years ago, and the other concerned with it as it exists today both in our society at large and on the campus of a state university.

The first of the two speeches was delivered in Coatesville, Pennsylvania, in 1911, by John Jay Chapman, an American critic and essayist, as part of a service which he conducted to mark the anniversary of a lynching that had occurred in Coatesville the year before.

Chapman, who had read vivid accounts of the lynching in the New York papers, was agitated not only by the brutality of the act itself, but also because no one intervened to prevent it, while, later, the citizens of the community, thinking such "publicity" bad for "business," refused to discuss the matter or to admit guilt. Chapman believed that by going to Coatesville and holding a memorial service he himself might, in some measure, do "penance" both for the town and for the country as a whole.

After unsuccessful efforts to hire a hall, Chapman succeeded in renting an empty store building. There, on the morning of Sunday, August 18, 1911, he presented his address. The audience consisted of three persons: an aged Negress who was visiting Coatesville from Boston, a man assumed by Chapman to be a local spy, and Miss Edith Martin, a friend who had accompanied Chapman from New York.[1]

Chapman's speech later was printed in *Harper's Weekly* for September 21, 1912, and in his book *Memories and Milestones* (New York, 1915). The text here reproduced is taken from the latter source.

The second speech, page 164, that by Phyllis Estep, was delivered to a class of undergraduates at Pennsylvania State University on March 17, 1965. Miss Estep was a junior, majoring in secondary education (English and French). She prepared these remarks in response to the following general assignment: "Deliver extemporaneously a ten- to twelve-minute talk in which you develop your personal views on any aspect of the following topics: politics, religion, sex, social relations, the arts, or your personal philosophy of life. Your objective may be to explain, to persuade, or to aim at inducing your audience to engage with you in further inquiry on a problem you present."

Miss Estep's audience consisted of eighteen students enrolled in Effective Speech, a course in oral communication required of all Pennsylvania State University students. Seven of these listeners were women and eleven were men, all in their freshman, sophomore, or junior years. Six were majoring in the liberal arts or sciences, four in education, three in business administration, three in engineering, and one each in agriculture and hotel administration. The classroom instructor and two teacher-interns also were in the audience.

The text of the speech was transcribed from a tape recording and has not been edited.

Coatesville

JOHN JAY CHAPMAN

We are met to commemorate the anniversary of one of the most dreadful crimes in history—not for the purpose of condemning it, but to repent of our share in it. We do not start any agitation with regard to that particular crime. I understand that an

From *Memories and Milestones*, New York, 1915.
[1]For fuller accounts of the circumstances under which the speech was delivered, see Jacques Barzun, ed., *The Selected Writings of John Jay Chapman* (New York, 1957), pp. v-x; Richard B. Hovey, *John Jay Chapman—An American Mind* (New York, 1959), pp. 209-212; M. A. DeWolfe Howe, *John Jay Chapman and His Letters* (Boston, 1937), pp. 215-219. An extended criticism of the speech may be found in Edwin Black, *Rhetorical Criticism* (New York, 1965), pp. 78-90.

attempt to prosecute the chief criminals has been made, and has entirely failed; because the whole community, and in a sense our whole people, are really involved in the guilt. The failure of the prosecution in this case, in all such cases, is only a proof of the magnitude of the guilt, and of the awful fact that everyone shares in it. /1

I will tell you why I am here; I will tell you what happened to me. When I read in the newspapers of August 14, a year ago, about the burning alive of a human being, and of how a few desperate, fiend-minded men had been permitted to torture a man chained to an iron bedstead, burning alive, thrust back by pitchforks when he struggled out of it, while around about stood hundreds of well-dressed American citizens, both from the vicinity and from afar, coming on foot and in wagons, assembling on telephone call, as if by magic, silent, whether from terror or indifference, fascinated and impotent, hundreds of persons watching this awful sight and making no attempt to stay the wickedness, and no one man among them all who was inspired to risk his life in an attempt to stop it, no one man to name the name of Christ, of humanity, of government! As I read the newspaper accounts of the scene enacted here in Coatesville a year ago, I seemed to get a glimpse into the unconscious soul of this country. I saw a seldom revealed picture of the American heart and of the American nature. I seemed to be looking into the heart of the criminal—a cold thing, an awful thing. /2

I said to myself, "I shall forget this, we shall all forget it; but it will be there. What I have seen is not an illusion. It is the truth. I have seen death in the heart of this people." For to look at the agony of a fellow-being and remain aloof means death in the heart of the onlooker. Religious fanaticism has sometimes lifted men to the frenzy of such cruelty, political passion has sometimes done it, personal hatred might do it, the excitement of the amphitheater in the degenerate days of Roman luxury could do it. But here an audience chosen by chance in America has stood spellbound through an improvised *auto-da-fé*, irregular, illegal, having no religious significance, not sanctioned by custom, having no immediate provocation, the audience standing by merely in cold dislike. /3

I saw during one moment something beyond all argument in the depth of its significance. You might call it the paralysis of the nerves about the heart in a people habitually and unconsciously given over to selfish aims, an ignorant people who knew not what spectacle they were providing, or what part they were playing in a judgment-play which history was exhibiting on that day. /4

No theories about the race problem, no statistics, legislation, or mere educational endeavor, can quite meet the lack which that day revealed in the American people. For what we saw was death. The people stood like blighted things, like ghosts about Acheron, waiting for someone or something to determine their destiny for them. /5

Whatever life itself is, that thing must be replenished in us. The opposite of hate is love, the opposite of cold is heat; what we need is the love of God and reverence for human nature. For one moment I knew that I had seen our true need; and I was afraid that I should forget it and that I should go about framing arguments and agitations and starting schemes of education, when the need was deeper than education. And I became filled with one idea, that I must not forget what I had seen, and that I must do something to remember it. And I am here to-day chiefly that I may remember that vision. It seems fitting to come to this town where the crime occurred and hold a prayer-meeting, so that our hearts may be turned to God through whom mercy may flow into us. /6

Let me say one thing more about the whole matter. The subject we are dealing with is not local. The act, to be sure, took place at Coatesville and everyone looked to Coatesville to follow it up. Some months ago I asked a friend who lives not far from here something about this case, and about the expected prosecutions, and he replied to me: "It wasn't in my county," and that made me wonder whose county it was in. And it seemed to be in my county. I live on the Hudson River; but I knew that this great wickedness that happened in Coatesville is not the wickedness of Coatesville nor of to-day. It is the wickedness of all America and of three hundred years—the wickedness of the slave trade. All of us are tinctured by it. No special place, no special persons, are to blame. A nation cannot practice a course of inhuman crime for three hundred years and then suddenly throw off the effects of it. Less than fifty years ago domestic slavery was abolished among us; and in one way and another the marks of that vice are in our faces. There is no country in Europe where the Coatesville tragedy or anything remotely like it could have been enacted, probably no country in the world. /7

On the day of the calamity, those people in the automobiles came by the hundred and watched the torture, and passers-by came in a great multitude and watched it—and did nothing. On the next morning the newspapers spread the news and spread the paralysis until the whole country seemed to be helplessly watching this awful murder, as awful as anything ever done on the earth; and the whole of our people seemed to be looking on helplessly, not able to respond, not knowing what to do next. That spectacle has been in my mind. /8

The trouble has come down to us out of the past. The only reason that slavery is wrong is that it is cruel and makes men cruel and leaves them cruel. Someone may say that you and I cannot repent because we did not do the act. But we are involved in it. We are still looking on. Do you not see that this whole event is merely the last parable, the most vivid, the most terrible illustration that ever was given by man or imagined by a Jewish prophet, of the relation between good and evil in this world, and of the relation of men to one another? /9

This whole matter has been an historic episode; but it is a part, not only of our national history, but of the personal history of each one of us. With the great disease (slavery) came the climax (the war), and after the climax gradually began the cure, and in the process of cure comes now the knowledge of what the evil was. I say that our need is new life, and that books and resolutions will not save us, but only such disposition in our hearts and souls as will enable the new life, love, force, hope, virtue, which surround us always, to enter into us. /10

This is the discovery that each man must make for himself—the discovery that what he really stands in need of he cannot get for himself, but must wait till God gives it to him. I have felt the impulse to come here to-day to testify to this truth. /11

The occasion is not small; the occasion looks back on three centuries and embraces a hemisphere. Yet the occasion is small compared with the truth it leads us to. For this truth touches all ages and affects every soul in the world. /12

Apathy

PHYLLIS M. ESTEP

On March 13th of last year, in Queens, New York, Catherine Genovese was murdered as she was

Reprinted by permission of Phyllis Estep.

returning home from work at 3:00 A.M. These facts in themselves do not seem too extraordinary, but this case is unusual. And it's unusual because no less than thirty-eight people witnessed that murder and did not attempt to go to her aid or even to call the police. When the police were finally called—after she was dead—they arrived in two minutes. It's almost certain that if someone had called them sooner, her life would have been saved. What is even more appalling are the answers these people gave when asked why they didn't do anything—such answers as: "I didn't want my husband to get involved." "I was tired; I went back to bed." And I think the worst one of all: "I don't know." /1

This was a case of apathy in the extreme. Is this the "apathy" we hear so much about? Is it affecting us? /2

Apathy is indifference—lack of emotion—toward other people and the things around us. I think of it as a disease which, if we allow it to infect us, will grow in us and can become a very serious thing. Certainly it exists in many different aspects of life, but I would like to point out three that I think are very important. /3

First, there's the apathy toward crime. The case of Catherine Genovese might be extreme, but in this same area of New York a group of people watched a teen-aged gang beat up a high school boy, and no one did anything about it. And the witnesses who saw Miss Genovese murdered last year were asked just last week—a full year afterward —what they would do in the same situation. They said that they didn't know! They still aren't sure they'd act any differently than they did before! /4

Deputy Police Commissioner Walter Arm, of New York, says that many people after witnessing a crime and being questioned by the police reply that they didn't see anything. Some may be a bit more honest and say, "I saw it, but I didn't do anything about it." /5

Secondly, I think we find apathy in our attitudes toward government, and this is particularly shown in voting. We're often preached at about the necessity of getting out to vote, or getting our parents to vote. In the last presidential election the statistics were rather impressive. Seventy-eight percent of the registered voters voted, and this represented 60 per cent of our total population of voting age. This broke the record of 1960. But when we think about it, what about that other 40 per cent of our population who were of voting age? Where were they on election day? And how many of them aren't even registered? /6

I think we're all aware of the typical excuses for not voting: "I didn't have time." "I was tired after a hard day's work." "I didn't feel like standing in line at the polls." "Besides, everyone knows so-and-so's going to win. My vote wouldn't count." I think, too, we are all well enough aware of the danger of such an apathetic attitude among a supposedly freedom-loving people. /7

Thirdly, we find apathy toward our fellow men. A prime example of this is in the civil rights situation today. Most of us would profess to believe in civil rights—the equality of men and such abstract ideas. But when it gets right down to it—to doing something concrete that involves us personally—how many of us are really willing to do anything? /8

We all know that places such as Harlem or Bedford-Stuyvesant or other ghettos exist in our major cities. Representatives in our legislatures may even pass vague legislation for these areas. But how much are we as individuals willing to do? Are we even concerned enough to donate a little money toward civil rights work in Mississippi? Or toward a war on poverty for needy areas? /9

So we know that apathy exists in our society in several different ways. But what about Penn State? Penn State is a friendly school. People here are concerned with one another. I think this is true, but I also think you can find apathy here, and I think you can find it in each of the major areas that I discussed for the nation as a whole: apathy toward crime, toward government, and toward our fellow men. /10

The chances are that we're not going to have anything as spectacular as a Catherine Genovese murder. But how often have you been sitting in your dorm studying at night and heard a scream outside? Usually, we assume that somebody is just "carrying-on." But how many ever are concerned enough to check it out to make sure it's not really someone who does need help? How often are we aware of a person who is cheating or stealing—however petty the act? Do we do anything about it, even to the extent of warning the offender or letting him know we know what's going on? /11

As far as government goes, University Student Government is becoming quite a force on our campus. But we're willing to sit back and complain that our government isn't providing for the student body, yet we aren't willing to participate in it ourselves. Or do we get out to vote for representatives we think will give us still better student government? /12

Then, we complain of exorbitant prices charged

by downtown book stores. But when a group on campus tried to start a campus book store, how much support did they get? /13

Well, how about apathy toward our fellow men? Here, again, we can think of the civil rights situation. How many here are concerned that one of our fellow students is in jail right now in Mississippi because he went there to be a civil rights worker? Would we be concerned enough to give—maybe a quarter—toward his bail money? I think we—most of us—tend to sit back and mock such groups as SENSE and CORE and SURE because these people are actively participating in what they believe in. It's a lot easier, of course, to be indifferent—and give lip service to supposed beliefs. /14

So apathy exists not only in society, but it exists here at Penn State. But why does it exist? What fears underlie it? I think there are four major fears that people have, which cause them to be apathetic. /15

First is the fear of rejection. This particularly applies to our campus. We're afraid that if we get too involved in politics or in a movement such as SENSE, people are going to think we're oddballs. We'll stand out from the crowd, and we don't like this. /16

Second, there's fear of reprisal. If we turn someone in for something, he may want to get back at us. We'll be in danger. It's a lot easier just not to notice. /17

Third, there's fear of getting mixed up with the police—with "the authorities." I think this is responsible for a lot of the general apathy toward crime. People fear having their names dragged into publicity relating to crimes. /18

Fourth, and I think most important, is the fear of "being involved." People just don't want to "be involved." Just listen some day. How often you can hear people say: "I just didn't want to get involved in it"—whatever the "it" may be just then. /19

The fact is apathy is a type of psychological protection. Today masses of people constantly impinge on us. This is particularly true in metropolitan areas, but here at Penn State it's true also. If we allowed ourselves to become concerned with the problems and troubles of each of these people we come in contact with, we couldn't stand it psychologically. So, we build a shell of indifference and apathy around us. /20

What can we do about it? I think it's purely an individual matter. Each of us must decide for himself how much other people mean to him. But, don't forget, as Miss Cooley pointed out the other day, *we* aren't much without other people! For me, "other people" are at least 90 per cent of life, for I think if

we want to *live* in this world, we *must* have compassion and concern for our fellow men. If we maintain only attitudes of indifference and apathy, we'll become like so many machines, each running on its own motor and doing its own job, completely independent of every other. /21

A. N. Rosenthal, the metropolitan editor of the New York *Times*, made a statement concerning the Genovese murder. He said there were two ways to look at the apathy displayed there. I think his two ways of looking at that situation can be applied to apathy in general and to our own apathy. He said:

"There are, it seems to me, only two logical ways to look at the story of Catherine Genovese. One is the way of the neighbors on Austin Street: 'Let's forget the whole thing.' The other is to recognize that the bell tolls even on each man's individual island, to recognize that every man must fear the witness in himself that whispers, 'Close the window.'" /22

The speeches

1. M. A. DeWolfe Howe calls the Coatesville address a thing of "austere and tragic beauty." Edmund Wilson describes it as "strange and moving." Jacques Barzun declares that it makes Coatesville "an historic name in . . . the country's . . . literary biography."[1] Point to qualities in the address which may have influenced these judgments.

2. How would you describe the principle or plan according to which Chapman's speech is organized? Do you think this plan is appropriate to the subject and to the occasion?

3. After consulting the Glossary entry Ends of Speaking, classify Chapman's speech as to type. Be ready to defend your classification.

4. Find one or more examples of striking *imagery* in Chapman's speech and explain the methods by which the imagery is achieved (see Glossary).

5. In commenting on Chapman's speech as a piece of rhetoric, Edwin Black says that it violates nearly all of the textbook rules.[2] Do you agree? Why?

6. As was pointed out in the introduction, Chapman's speech drew an audience of only three persons. Are we to conclude from this fact that it is an unimportant document unworthy of study?

7. Comment critically on Miss Estep's use of (a) direct discourse and (b) rhetorical questions. Do these com-

[1]Howe, *John Jay Chapman and His Letters*, p. 219; Wilson, *The Triple Thinkers*, p. 159; Barzun, ed., *The Selected Writings of John Jay Chapman*, p. v.
[2]Black, *Rhetorical Criticism*, pp. 82-83.

positional devices enhance or impair the effectiveness of her speech? Why?

8. In what way does Miss Estep endeavor to identify herself with her listeners? What efforts does she make to relate the subject to them directly?

9. What are the principal forms of support used in the Estep speech? Are they the best that could have been chosen? Are they used effectively?

10. Miss Estep breaks her discussion of the problem of apathy into two steps, dealing with apathy in our society as a whole and then with apathy at Pennsylvania State University. Considering the audience to which she was speaking, was this the best order in which to handle these subjects? Why or why not?

11. Evaluate Miss Estep's solution to the problem of apathy, as set forth in paragraph 21.

For further study and discussion

1. Two possible causes of social apathy or indifference were mentioned in the introduction (p. 162). Do you agree that these actually are causes of the phenomenon? Why or why not? What other causes would you suggest?

2. In her speech Miss Estep points to examples of apathetic behavior on the part of students at her university. Can the same charges be brought against students on your campus? Cite actual instances to support your answer.

3. Are college students as a whole more apathetic than their elders?

4. It has frequently been said that persons who are part of a mob will perform and permit acts which as individuals they never would perform or permit. Do you agree that this is true? If so, how do you account for such behavior? What are some of the views advanced by sociologists on this point?

5. Is it fair to say that the only reason people do not vote is that they are lazy or indifferent? Could our election laws and campaign practices be revised so as to encourage voting?

6. Should voting be made compulsory?

7. Why do doctors who happen to be passing the scene of an accident sometimes refuse to treat the accident victims?

8. If you were traveling on a dark and lonely road at night and someone signaled you to stop to help fix a flat tire, would you do so?

9. In earlier days people in rural communities always helped one another at barn raisings, harvesting, logging, etc. Do you think they did this out of altruism or necessity?

Suggestions for further reading

Eugene L. Burdick, *American Voting Behavior* (New York, 1959)

John W. Caughey, ed., *Their Majesties, the Mob* (Chicago, 1960)

Arthur L. Harding, ed., *Responsibility in Law and Morals* (Dallas, 1960)

A. M. Rosenthal, *Thirty-Eight Witnesses* (New York, 1964). The complete account of the Genovese murder mentioned in Miss Estep's speech.

See also Hadley Cantril, *The Psychology of Social Movements* (New York, 1963), Chapter IV, "The Lynching Mob." C. R. M. MacIver, *The Ramparts We Guard* (New York, 1950), p. 77. P. K. Merton, *Social Theory and Social Structure* (New York, 1957), p. 36. T. Parsons, *The Social System* (New York, 1951), p. 39.

6 / ETHICS AND MORALS

Comfort and fun: morality in a nice society

DANIEL LERNER

Daniel Lerner (1917-   ), a social scientist, has taught at various schools in the United States and France. During World War II he served in Europe with the U.S. Army in the Psychological Warfare Division and during that period received the Bronze Star and the Purple Heart.

A member of numerous learned societies, Lerner has received from France the *Palmes Academique* and has been designated *Officier d'Academie*. At present he is Ford Professor of Sociology and International Communications at the Massachusetts Institute of Technology. He is author of *Sykewar: Psychological Warfare Against Germany* (1949); *Propaganda in War and Crisis* (1951); *The Policy Sciences*, with H. D. Lasswell (1951); *The Nazi Elite* (1951); *France Defeats EDC*, with Raymond Aron (1957); *The Passing of Traditional Society in the Middle East* (1958); *The Human Meaning of the Social Sciences* (1959); *Evidence and Inference* (1960); *Quantity and Quality* (1961); and *Parts and Wholes* (1963).

This speech was originally delivered from notes and then written in its present form. Lerner wrote that his talk was given in January 1958 to the Faculty Seminar of The Institute for Social and Religious Studies, a group of people from universities, foundations, business, and public affairs who met for several years under the chairmanship of the late Lyman Bryson to discuss questions of ethical and responsible behavior in the contemporary world.

Normally, Lerner went on to say, he speaks only to groups with a high degree of interest and at least semiprofessional competence in current world affairs. Such speaking occasions have ranged over recent years from a small selected panel of high government officials at the International Affairs Seminar (sponsored by the American Friends Service Committee) to an audience of several hundred colonels at the Air War College and Army War College. According to Lerner, "For such groups, the rule to follow is very simple: since these are meat-and-potatoes people, I try to deliver a nutritious and satisfying main dish, and go light on the trimmings."

In the following speech Lerner said he tried to show "that as a society we are not doing nearly so bad as some of our critics would have us believe."[1]

The living generation of Americans has quietly acquired a new human right—the right to be constantly entertained—which is conferred upon us by the mass media and underwritten by the business structure of radio, movies, picture magazines, digests, book clubs and, surpassing all others, television. This is a quiet right because it has not yet figured in any ideological manifestoes. The Atlantic Charter, the Four Freedoms, and the Declaration of the United Nations are all equally silent upon the right to be continuously entertained. But this does not impede the rapid spread of this particular right, which is quietly working the largest sort of transformation possible in the affairs of any society—by altering the levels of desire, the categories of contentment, and the criteria of judgment among its citizens. /1

Some of the symptoms of this transformation have been widely noted and just as widely attacked. Few among our intellectual spokesmen have many kind words to say for the mass media. Their impact, while widely discussed, is rarely studied, usually deplored and not too well understood. Juvenile delinquency has been attributed to movies and comics. Television, in its brief career, has already been found guilty of the New Illiteracy. A terribly stern justice has given public floggings to the "other-directed organization man in the gray flannel suit." /2

[1]Letter to the editors, June 16, 1960.

But these summary judgments may be too hasty. They may relieve the anguish of those who respect the old austerities by overlooking the virtues that others find in the new conveniences. In reading the rash of morality plays about executives and suburbanites coinciding with the work of David Riesman, Erich Fromm, William Holly Whyte, I am reminded of the carol "God Rest You Merry, Gentlemen!" There it is suggested that "to save us all from Satan's power" we must heed the "tidings of comfort and joy." Those who struggle so mightily with the diabolical mass media sometimes fail to notice their tidings of comfort and fun. /3

There is no room for dogma in such matters, but there is much room for inquiry. Is the "other-directed" man really the "other-respecting" man? Is the "organization man" really the "organized man"? There has been a change in America's psychic weather, no doubt, but perhaps the change is not so joyless as some suppose. What we need, paraphrasing Spinoza, is neither to weep nor to laugh—but to understand. /4

In the transformation of American morality, now well advanced, the mass media are both index and agent. Every facet of each person's and each family's daily round is touched in some way, and it is the whole "style of life" that needs study. An apt phrase that has been proposed is "fun morality." Under the dispensation of fun morality, the old key proposition about "being good" is transformed into "having a good time." There is little doubt that Americans today are more deferential than their ancestors were, or any other living people are, toward the virtues and values of having a good time. /5

This small shift in vocabulary represents a large shift in American practices and perspectives. Perhaps basic is the drive to transform the notion that ours is an "economy of abundance" from a fine phrase to an everyday reality. There is nothing new to American ideology in the high valuation placed upon widespread sharing of wealth. Jefferson based the stability of democratic society upon possession, by a substantial majority, of a real stake in its economic life. Herbert Hoover, or his aides, popularized the phrase "two chickens in every pot." The new thing is that this desire for a wide sharing of wealth has, in the present American generation, come closer to realization than ever before in history. There is only slight exaggeration in the propaganda put out by the New York Stock Exchange that we are a "nation of investors" and "every man a shareholder." Celebrating this state of affairs is the new direction that the American social conscience appears to have taken. /6

In the early days of the New Deal, America's social conscience was heavily preoccupied with the survival of "one third of the nation." Since that time, with employment and income running at all-time highs, the social conscience has shifted to assuring every man's *comfort*. The objective is to create conditions under which nearly all can be "haves"—and in which "have-nots" do not become an "internalized proletariat," as Toynbee claims to be the historic rule. The public welfare now is looked after by public and private organizations, and this requires organization men. /7

The theory that every man has a right to comfortable conditions of life is the economic counterpart of the theory that every man has the right to be continuously entertained. Comfort and fun go together. This leads to a quite different perspective than that which has governed most societies in the past. We appear to be, as a nation, committed to the lifeways of *non*adversity. The Spencerian gloss on the Darwinian doctrine has lost its claim to credence. We no longer believe that life needs to be a struggle in which only the fittest survive. On the contrary, we seem to have become convinced that life can be relatively pleasant for all and that all may survive at a rather high level of contentment. /8

This, right or wrong, is a revolutionary new idea in the world. It directs effort toward creating those conditions of life which enable people to "take things easy." The old puritan ethic (or perhaps, more exactly, simply "Protestant"), with its emphasis on effort, ambition, achievement, struggle and success, has yielded to a whole new array of words expressing the new conception of right conduct and the good life. The shift is from "getting on" to "getting along." The emphasis is on "being nice." /9

Naturally, the puritan ethic dies hard. For the past three centuries it governed conceptions of right conduct in much of the Western world—and particularly in those countries which made the greatest technological and industrial progress. It had come to seem, indeed, the only possible view of morality. To those of us still committed to an ethic of effort and achievement, the new "fun morality" seems a form of moral degeneracy. We are concerned about "conformism." We attack the "adjusted man" as a mere unthinking Babbitt. We inflict heavy verbal scars upon the "organization man," who represents a model of success other than that on which most of us were raised. /10

But the attack on fun morality is perhaps itself less thoughtful and less virtuous than we imagine. Associated with fun morality are many practices which those who don't love Lucy and disdain Elvis would *not* like to see abandoned. Would those who scorn "consumer mentality" also prefer less real consumption? It is quite possible that we cannot have our kind of society without some version of fun morality. I do not say that this *is* so. I say only that there are plausible reasons for thinking it may be so. The hypothesis merits more consideration than it has been given. The burden of responsibility for acquiring knowledge, not manufacturing stereotypes, falls most heavily on precisely those of us who suspect the symptoms of a popular culture without wishing to undermine a consumer's economy and a representative democracy. /11

How did this new American mixture come about? The crucial word in the dramatic transformation of American lifeways is "mobility." This nation of immigrants was founded upon the mobility of the individual. Such mobility became possible in the New World only when the Old World had achieved conditions of life which unbound men from their native heath. Once ordinary men found themselves free to move from their ancestral soil, they began to move in huge numbers from farms to flats and from fields to factories. As the physical means for transporting people improved, they began to move overseas in growing numbers. America was the goal of many millions. This bore little resemblance to the migrant or crusading hordes of earlier centuries, driven by war and famine. This was movement by individuals, each having made a personal choice to seek elsewhere his own version of a better life. /12

Physical mobility of this type induced ideas of *social mobility* previously unknown in the Old World. Stirred by new desires, these new Americans voiced new demands. Each wanted his own stake in the new society and his own say in how it was to be organized. So there came to prevail in this country ideas of equal opportunity and democratic governance which would have been "unseemly" in the Old World. Perhaps no single institution so clearly expressed this new spirit as the victory of free public education for all who wanted it. This certified the idea that every man was entitled to a fair chance at winning for himself a good life by his own efforts and merits. Thus developed a new kind of participant society—a secular and rational society based on equal rights for each individual. Along with it, through the generations, developed a new style of personality. /13

A mobile society has to be rational, for the calculus of choice shapes individual behavior and conditions its rewards. People come to see social arrangements as manipulable rather than ordained, and to gauge their own prospects in terms of achievement rather than heritage. The test of merit is skill, not birth. Ways of thinking and acting are instruments of intention, not articles of faith; they succeed or fail by the test of what they accomplish, not what they worship. So whereas traditional men tended to reject innovation by saying "It has never been thus," modern Americans were more likely to ask only "Does it work?" and try the new way without further ado. /14

The psychic gap between these two postures is vast. It took long interweaving of ways of doing with ways of thinking before men could work out a style of living daily with change that *felt* consistent and seamless. Mobile society required a mobile personality, a self-system so adaptive to change that rearrangement is its permanent mode. It required the experience of psychic mobility through many generations to evolve participant institutions which, to ordinary men, felt "normal." /15

The mobile person shows a high capacity for identifying himself with new and strange aspects of the environment. He is capable of handling unfamiliar demands upon himself outside his habitual experience. The capacity for psychic mobility tends to enlarge a man's identity in two ways: *projection* facilitates identification by assigning to others certain preferred attributes of the self (others are "incorporated" because they are "like me"); *introjection* enlarges identity by attributing to the self certain desirable attributes of the object (others are incorporated because "I" am like them, or would like to be like them). We use the term "empathy" as shorthand for these techniques of enlarging a man's "self-system." In ordinary parlance, empathy is the capacity to see oneself in the other fellow's situation. This capacity leads us to put a high value on negotiation, mediation, compromise—on "getting along." /16

Empathy is the psychic instrument which enables newly mobile persons to act effectively in the world we live in. This is why the mobile personality is not to be regarded as mere psychic aberration or moral degeneration, but as a social phenomenon with a history. Our concern must be with the large historical movement (which started in the West and is now becoming apparent elsewhere)—a movement in which a strong capacity for empathy is the distinctive psychic component. And it is useful to study the way in which the person who possesses this quality to a high degree tends to become also the cash customer, the radio listener, the voter and the "nice person." /17

This emphasis upon empathy is dominant only in modern society—which is distinctively industrial, urban, literate and participant. (A society is participant if most people in it go through school, read newspapers, receive cash payments in jobs they are free to change, buy goods in a free market, vote in free elections, and express opinions on many matters which are not their business.) Any society develops a predominant personal style which people find most appropriate for daily life; the "style" of modern society is distinctive for its capacity to rearrange the "self-system" on short notice. /18

This is the style partially characterized by David Riesman as "other-directed." But the term "other-direction" has acquired, among our self-abnegating intelligentsia, a negative moral charge. The term "empathy" more nearly does justice to the elements of skill and the positive social functions of other-direction. Empathy enables people to respond efficiently to strange and varied stimuli; in so doing it enlarges the self-system of ordinary people. By enabling them to "see" the other fellow's situation more readily, empathy provides the psychological underpinning for the participant lifeways of modern society. The latent statistical assertion involved here is this: in modern society *more* individuals exhibit a *high* empathic capacity than in any previous society. In brief, there has been a *net increase in human imaginativeness,* as construed, in modern society (whether the society be favorably interpreted as "participant," or unfavorably as "conformist"). /19

To identify psychic mobility with the proposition that there has been an increase in empathy—that more people now command a greater skill at imagining themselves in strange situations than did people in any previous historical epoch—is to assign a large function to popular culture, notably elementary education and mass media. The technical history of the popular arts illuminates their function as an empathy multiplier. A generation before Columbus sailed to the New World, Gutenberg set up his printing press. Press, radio, film and television today climax the evolution thus set into motion. The mass media opened to mankind the infinite *vicarious* universe. Many more millions of persons in the world were to be affected directly, and perhaps more profoundly, by the communication media than by the transportation agencies. For the vicarious universe not only involves more people; it involves them in a different order of psychic experience. /20

Vicarious experience requires other skills and stimulates other psychic mechanisms from those used in travel. Travel involves direct personal exposure to a complex natural environment, whereas mediated experience explores mainly the simplified settings contrived by those who have prepared the "experience." Thus, while the traveler is apt to become bewildered

by the profusion of strange sights and sounds, the radio listener or movie viewer is likely to be enjoying a composed and orchestrated version of some new reality. He has the benefit of more facile perception of the new experience as a "whole," with the concomitant advantage (which is sometimes illusory) of facile comprehension. /21

On the other hand, the reader-listener-viewer loses the traveler's pragmatic advantage of being physically present in the strange environment, of having to make responsive action toward the stimuli it presents. The passive receiver of mediated communications finds his response to new stimuli necessarily confined to his own interior. Thus, while the stimuli he receives are usually less complex, the demands of exclusively interior response are often much more strenuous. The inhibition of overt response is a learned behavior and a difficult one. It was common, in the early days of movies, for persons strained beyond endurance to throw themselves or some objects at the screen to stop the villain from strangling the heroine. Even our sophisticated youngsters today will sometimes, at an agonizing moment in the television show, hide their faces. /22

The point is that mediated experience simplifies *perception* (what we "see") while greatly complicating *response* (what we "do"). In this way the media have helped to shape the modern, highly responsive self-system, ready to rearrange itself on short notice from a variety of cues. As history's great teacher of the skills of empathy, the mass media have multiplied psychic mobility among men in the West. (This is not to be construed as genial endorsement of current media operations, which too often tend to routinize, not stimulate, imagination.) /23

This capacity to empathize, to see ourselves in the other fellow's situation, is essential to our "nice person" morality. Its spread has made America a society in which most people can "take things easy"—can make it a rule of life to "get along with everybody." It underlies the national distrust of odd-balls, eight-balls and screwballs. It has made "puritanism" a pejorative word and "straitlaced" not less so. It leads to suspicion of a person who is "too ambitious," who "tries too hard" to overcome an obstacle instead of simply "sweating it out." The course of life in a nice society is "give and take"; the rule is "live and let live." /24

Popular attitudes of this sort can be painful for intellectuals and others who still live by (or at least believe they do) the old puritan ethic as compared with, in Holly Whyte's phrase, a "social ethic." But it may well be that the older ethic is obsolescent, not merely because the newer morality is more comfortable for most people but, possibly, because it is genuinely superior as a guide to life in an abundant society. Some clues to the newness of American lifeways are furnished by the attitudes toward America expressed in other countries. There is, for example, the attack launched from the highly "sophisticated" culture of contemporary France. /25

Because American intellectuals have borrowed ideas from France over the past three centuries, they have seen no reason to change their ways during the past three decades. Many postwar slogans deprecating American conformism and vulgarity have spread from France over much of the world, and even into our own country. These slogans have been more repeated than scrutinized. For some years there was much talk about American "bathtub culture"; but this left wide open the question of whether greater morality necessarily attaches to a population with a significantly higher proportion of microbes. There was also a period of talk about "Coca-Cola culture"; but this did not explore the question of whether a people is more virtuous because even more heavily alcoholic than we are. It is not without interest that Coca-Cola, in fact, spread rapidly through France, as all over the world, and remains, so far as I know, the only drink which can be bought by people almost anywhere for the equivalent of a nickel (except, of course, in the heavily protected French beverage market). /26

Much of this fancy talk about American vulgarization of taste and standardization of mind stems from a potent distrust, among French intellectuals, of our extraordinarily developed "popular culture." The fear of the mass media seems to me a *class* attitude of the least admirable variety. In its simplest form, this may be only the fear of technological unemployment: the mass media require skills quite different from those usually found among the traditional intelligentsia. On a somewhat more complex level, the French intelligentsia defends certain standards constructed largely by itself over past centuries and attacks everything which appears to threaten the institutional arrangements by which those standards are maintained. These standards express traditional and class aesthetic preferences, but often they parade as ethical judgments and are delivered in a high moral tone. A fine case study could be made of the "TV snob," usually a person with some pretentions to intellectuality, and nowhere more numerous than among the French intelligentsia. It is not irrelevant that artistic life in France has failed to flourish under the continued prevalence of this attitude. I refer here not only to the failure of the French intelligentsia to develop new creative lines in the modern arts of the mass media, but even the drying up of the old French creative spirit in the traditional arts. /27

This is not to be construed as a counterattack on French anti-Americanism. My own Francophilia lies too deep to be uprooted by the current show of petulance among a people who gave our modern world its great Cartesian myth of rationality. It is no easy thing to "speak for" a great power which has been diminished, a lovely culture which has been bypassed; and French intellectuals today have a tough assignment. But one who shares their heritage has a right to expect, a duty to demand, better of them than the defensive negativism they have been producing. In any case, the slogans created and diffused by an ambivalent intelligentsia ought to be scrutinized and evaluated before they are merely repeated by Americans. For there is a point underlying French petulance that goes deeper than French—or American—parochialism. It is a point on which may turn the future of Western civilization. /28

The great dialogue of the Western tradition has been "the dialogue of Self with Self"—in a word, conscience. If it is agreed that the dialogue has taken a new turn in modern times, has become a "dialogue of Self with Others," what does this mean for the future of Western civilization? Can *social* conscience—responsibility to others—adequately perform the functions historically assigned to individual conscience, which was responsible only to God or to the God-within-oneself? /29

The question is too important for a glib solution. It is all too easy to settle such problems by facile, derogatory references to hell fixation or stargazing. There are many people, less concerned with damnation or salvation than with the prospects for a decent future on this earth, who want reasonable answers, not easy quips. /30

The question has been posed, but even the few serious efforts to deal with it base their judgment on untested assumptions. It is not at all clear that Riesman's "other-directed" man is incapable of "autonomy" (as Riesman himself, if not his acolytes, has pointed out). It is even less clear why Whyte's "organization man" should not be taken as a highly moral man in a new sense—as an approximation of a model for the rational fusion of individual with social conscience. Of the treatises by Sloan Wilson, Vance Packard and A. C. Spectorsky, one must say that suburbia merits better than clever travesties lacking wit or insight. /31

Suburbia is, in parochial terms, the fulfillment of

the American Dream for the full range of "middle" classes of our society. Its concern with nice houses and cars, with the competition between school and TV for the education of its children, with community relations and civic activities—all these occur on a quasi-educated level of discourse that makes an easy mark for the American intelligentsia. But American suburbia, in global terms, may be the functional equivalent of what most peoples of the world seem, nowadays, to want. For suburbia may be the highest reach of civilized life that has yet been represented as within the grasp of common humanity. /32

A few years ago I visited a walled village of Iran, whose daily life-ways antedate the Christian era. There, among peasants in rags, a uniquely enterprising soul had just returned from the distant market town, where he had sold his crop for cash. Overstimulated by the sight of a city, he had spent his first cash on a battery radio, baubles for his wife, a ready-made suit for himself (the first in his village), and a calendar for their mud hut. The calendar now decorating their wall (it had been reproduced by a Teheran bank) portrayed the American Family—Dad, Mom, Junior and Sister—on the lawn in front of their ranch house with a station wagon parked in the driveway. O bright dream of suburbia! /33

Item: In suburbia *everybody has cash—or credit!* Decisions as to the desirable ratio to be maintained between cash and credit elicit real ingenuity in family conclaves. In traditional society there is no cash; in "modern" France there is no credit; in "modern" Russia there is no choice. Only in America is the great dialogue between present pleasure and future felicity thrown open for discussion and decision by the generality of individuals and families. "You pays your money and you takes your choice"—there resonates, in uncultivated but understandable tones, the American music of humanity. /34

Item: In suburbia *everybody has opinions!* As a student of the Middle East, I first learned what a giant step this was from the stoic, isolate silence of the constricted peasant in traditional society. Only in the lowest reaches of America's slums is there still any question as to whether people ought to have opinions. In the climactic scene of *Sweet Thursday*, John Steinbeck relates how the madam of a whorehouse prepares one of her hustlers, not really made for the business, to go out into the world of respectability. The first rule is to keep her mouth shut:

"Next thing is opinions. You and me is always busting out with opinions. Hell, Suzy, we ain't got no opinions! We just say stuff we heard or seen in the movies. We're scared we'll miss something, like running for a bus. That's the second rule: lay off opinions because you ain't really got any."

But in suburbia everybody has opinions, however acquired, and his right to them is beyond challenge. As a social psychologist somewhat wearied by the theories of my trade, I have sat through hours of P.T.A. meetings, bemused by the easy familiarity of my neighbors with the views of Doctors Spock, Gesell, Dewey and Freud. It is not necessary to be impressed by the technical skill displayed in handling these ideas in order to be overwhelmed by their extraordinary diffusion among a population which, not so many years ago, got their ideas on these matters mainly from Mother. /35

If all this sounds too much like a paean, I want to make it clear that the praise is for what freedom has accomplished in America until now. What may follow is another matter. Arnold Toynbee assures us that the passing of the Judaeo-Christian tradition spells the end of the West. That admirable Jesuit Father La Farge suggests that the new secularized dialogue of Self with Others can only sustain an afterglow" of the scintillant Western epoch. But how do they know? Toynbee, by a series of brilliantly executed tautologies which mainly recapitulate his own characterological preferences; Father La Farge, with his broader tolerance, by his wish that humanity shall not sin against itself. These are fine, decent, intelligent men. So are David Riesman and Holly Whyte. They care for men and worry for their humanity. But I am not sure that any of them has knowledge surpassing his own anxieties. /36

Nor have I. My exhortation is no counsel of unbounded optimism. But it does advise against selling short, in a time of crisis, the good portfolio of stocks that we hold. I think we can weather the storm of a clamorous world population wanting our dividends while they do not share our calculations, risks, investments. I think we can do so by sharing our dividends with others while they learn how to calculate risks, by sharing our know-how about getting on while getting along. I think that man's responsibility to others may produce a superior civilization even to that which evolved under the aegis of man's responsibility to himself—that reshaping the great dialogue as Self with Others can have a happy outcome for common humanity. I think that the mass media may be the principal instrument whereby men around the world can swiftly acquire the human skills needed to cope with their accelerating hopes and dreams. I think; but who, as yet, knows? /37

The speech

1. How do Lerner's opening remarks set the stage for his talk?
2. What was Lerner's audience like? What kind of background could he assume they had?
3. Prepare a précis of the speech that will bring out the main points and show their relation.
4. What pattern of organization is employed in this talk?
5. List at least five familiar phrases to which Lerner has given a new twist. What is the rhetorical effect of this device?
6. Comment on Lerner's use of irony. Who or what is treated ironically? Does this ironic treatment prepare you for the central idea stated in the conclusion? Does the title prepare you for the content and tone of the conclusion?
7. What is Lerner's scale of values? What, for example, does he prize most highly in American life? Least highly?
8. What precisely is the rhetorical effect of the speech on you? Does it confirm your present thought? Change it? Not affect it?

For further study and discussion

1. Do you agree that our society prizes comfort and fun above all? Expand your answer with illustrations.
2. Explain the seeming paradox in the phrase "fun morality." Demonstrate to what extent the phrase can be applied to American life.
3. What is the basis for contemporary criticism of business executives, ad men, and suburbanites by such writers as Riesman, Fromm, Packard, and Whyte? Is the criticism primarily on moral grounds?
4. To what extent do you believe the puritan ethic is dying out? Develop your answer with as many facts and examples as you can assemble.
5. How long do you think our physical mobility will continue to increase? Cite supporting evidence.
6. Do you believe social mobility is still on the increase? Explain your answer.
7. Do you agree that we have a "Coca-Cola culture"? Before answering this question, tell what the term means to you.
8. Do you agree that everyone in suburbia has opinions? If so, what are the implications as you see them?
9. Does the shift from man's responsibility to himself to man's responsibility to others imply for you a decline in moral standards? Explore the question in detail. (For the most direct statement in this book of man's responsibility to himself, read Emerson's "The American Scholar," pp. 39-47.)

10. What are the best things that can be said of contemporary American society? The worst things?

Suggestions for further reading

Ruth Anshen, ed., *Moral Principles of Action* (New York, 1952)
Erich Fromm, *Man for Himself* (New York, 1947)
————, *The Sane Society* (New York, 1955)
John H. Hallowell, *The Moral Foundation of Democracy* (Chicago, 1954)
H. L. A. Hart, *Law, Liberty and Morality* (Stanford, 1963)
Arnold H. M. Lunn, *Enigma; A Study of Moral Rearmament* (London, 1957)
Reinhold Niebuhr, *Moral Man and Immoral Society* (New York, 1932)
Harold Prichard, *Moral Obligation* (Oxford, 1949)
David Riesman, *Individualism Reconsidered, and Other Essays* (Chicago, 1954)
Arnold Toynbee, *A Study of History,* an abridgment of Vols. 1-10 by D. C. Somervell (New York, 1946-1957)
William H. Whyte, *The Organization Man* (New York, 1956)

The three parts of morality

C. S. LEWIS

Clive Staples Lewis was born in Belfast, Ireland, in 1898, and entered Oxford in 1918. After serving in the First World War, he became a lecturer at University College, Oxford, and in 1926 a fellow and tutor at Magdalen College. From 1954 until his death in 1963, he was Professor of Medieval and Renaissance English at Cambridge. A shy, sensitive, scholarly man, he devoted much of his life to writing, his works including novels and children's books as well as historical, critical, and religious works. He is probably best known for *The Screwtape Letters* (1942) and *Mere Christianity,* parts of which are included here. His autobiography, *Surprised by Joy,* appeared in 1955. Of *The Screwtape Letters,* C. E. M. Joad said: "Mr. Lewis possesses the rare gift of being able to make righteousness readable."

In 1942 Lewis gave several talks over the British Broadcasting Corporation system which were subsequently published in 1943 as *Christian Behavior* and later anthologized in *Mere Christianity*. In his talks Lewis concerned himself with morality in relations between man and man, in the things inside each man, and in relations between man and the power that made him. Two talks are reprinted here: "The Three Parts of Morality" and "Social Morality."

Lewis' talks were widely discussed at the time of their delivery. In the *New Republic* (April 24, 1944) British correspondent Alistair Cooke, commenting on the reception of Lewis' speeches, said: "From the way the talks were received in Britain and from the eagerness of American networks to have Mr. Lewis shed light on our own dark continent, it may be assumed that the personal values of several million Britons and Americans stand in imminent danger of the befuddlement at which Mr. Lewis is so transparently adroit." In contrast, F. J. Moore, writing in *Christian Century* (January 26, 1944), insisted that "Mr. Lewis' special characteristics in thought and style are exhibited at their best in the discussion of ethical questions." A careful study of the following speeches should help you decide whose judgment—Joad's and Moore's or Cooke's—seems most just.

There is a story about a schoolboy who was asked what he thought God was like. He replied that, as far as he could make out, God was "The sort of person who is always snooping round to see if anyone is enjoying himself and then trying to stop it." And I am afraid that is the sort of idea that the word Morality raises in a good many people's minds: something that interferes, something that stops you having a good time. In reality, moral rules are directions for running the human machine. Every moral rule is there to prevent a breakdown, or a strain, or a friction, in the running of that machine. That is why these rules at first seem to be constantly interfering with our natural inclinations. When you are being taught how to use any machine, the instructor keeps on saying, "No, don't do it like that," because, of course, there are all sorts of things that look all right and seem to you the natural way of treating the machine, but do not really work. /1

Some people prefer to talk about moral "ideals" rather than moral rules and about moral "idealism" rather than moral obedience. Now it is, of course, quite true that moral perfection is an "ideal" in the sense that we cannot achieve it. In that sense every kind of perfection is, for us humans, an ideal; we cannot succeed in being perfect car drivers or perfect tennis players or in drawing perfectly straight lines. But there is another sense in which it is very misleading to call moral perfection an ideal. When a man says that a certain woman, or house, or ship, or garden is "his ideal" he does not mean (unless he is rather a fool) that everyone else ought to have the same ideal. In such matters we are entitled to have different tastes and, therefore, different ideals. But it is dangerous to describe a man who tries very hard to keep the moral law as a "man of high ideals," because this might lead you to think that moral perfection was a private taste of his own and that the rest of us were not called on to share it. This would be a disastrous mistake. Perfect behaviour may be as unattainable as perfect gear-changing when we drive; but it is a necessary ideal prescribed for all men by the very nature of the human machine just as perfect gear-changing is an ideal prescribed for all drivers by the very nature of cars. And it would be even more dangerous to think of oneself as a person "of high ideals" because one is trying to tell no lies at all (instead of only a few lies) or never to commit adultery (instead of committing it only seldom) or not to be a bully (instead of being only a moderate bully). It might lead you to become a prig and to think you were rather a special person who deserved to be congratulated on his "idealism." In reality you might just as well expect to be congratulated because, whenever you do a sum, you try to get it quite right. To be sure, perfect arithmetic is "an ideal"; you will certainly make some mistakes in some calculations. But there is nothing very fine about trying to be quite accurate at each step in each sum. It would be idiotic not to try; for every mistake is going to cause you trouble later on. In the same way every moral failure is going to cause trouble, probably to others and certainly to yourself. By talking about rules and obedience instead of "ideals" and "idealism" we help to remind ourselves of these facts. /2

Now let us go a step further. There are two ways in which the human machine goes wrong. One is when human individuals drift apart from one another, or else collide with one another and do one another damage, by cheating or bullying. The other is when things go wrong inside the individual—when the different parts of him (his different faculties and desires and so on) either drift apart or interfere with one another. You can get the idea plain if you think of us as a fleet of ships sailing in formation. The voyage will be a success only, in the first place, if the ships do not collide and get in one another's way; and, secondly, if each ship is seaworthy and has her engines in good order. As a matter of fact, you cannot have either of these two things without the other. If the ships keep on having collisions they will not remain seaworthy very long. On the other hand, if their steering gears are out of order they will not be able to avoid collisions. Or, if you like, think of humanity as a band playing a tune. To get a good result, you need two things. Each player's individual instrument must be in tune and also each must come in at the right moment so as to combine with all the others. /3

But there is one thing we have not yet taken into account. We have not asked where the fleet is trying to get to, or what piece of music the band is trying to play. The instruments might be all in tune and might all come in at the right moment, but even so the performance would not be a success if they had been engaged to provide dance music and actually played nothing but Dead Marches. And however well the fleet sailed, its voyage would be a failure if it were meant to reach New York and actually arrived at Calcutta. /4

Morality, then, seems to be concerned with three things. Firstly, with fair play and harmony between individuals. Secondly, with what might be called tidying up or harmonising the things inside each individual. Thirdly, with the general purpose of human life as a whole: what man was made for: what course the whole fleet ought to be on: what tune the conductor of the band wants it to play. /5

You may have noticed that modern people are nearly always thinking about the first thing and forgetting the other two. When people say in the newspapers that we are striving for Christian moral standards, they usually mean that we are striving for kindness and fair play between nations, and classes, and individuals; that is, they are thinking only of the first thing. When a man says about something he wants to do, "It can't be wrong because it doesn't do anyone else any harm," he is thinking only of the first thing. He is thinking it does not matter what his ship is like inside provided that he does not run into the next ship. And it is quite natural, when we start thinking about morality, to begin with the first thing, with social relations. For one thing, the results of bad morality in that sphere are so obvious and press on us every day: war and poverty and graft and lies and shoddy work. And also, as long as you stick to the first thing, there is very little disagreement about morality. Almost all people at all times have agreed (in theory) that human beings ought to be honest and kind and helpful to one another. But though it is natural to begin with all that, if our thinking about morality stops there, we might just as well not have thought at all. Unless we go on to the second thing—the tidying up inside each human being—we are only deceiving ourselves. /6

What is the good of telling the ships how to steer so as to avoid collisions if, in fact, they are such crazy old tubs that they cannot be steered at all? What is the good of drawing up, on paper, rules for social behaviour, if we know that, in fact, our greed, cowardice, ill temper, and self-conceit are going to prevent us from keeping them? I do not mean for a moment that we ought not to think, and think hard, about improvements in our social and economic system. What I do mean is that all that thinking will be mere moonshine unless we realise that nothing but the courage and unselfishness of individuals is ever going to make any system work properly. It is easy enough to remove the particular kinds of graft or bullying that go on under the present system: but as long as men are twisters or bullies they will find some new way of carrying on the old game under the new system. You cannot make men good by law: and without good men you cannot have a good society. That is why we must go on to think of the second thing: of morality inside the individual. /7

But I do not think we can stop there either. We are now getting to the point at which different beliefs about the universe lead to different behaviour. And it would seem, at first sight, very sensible to stop before we got there, and just carry on with those parts of morality that all sensible people agree about. But can we? Remember that religion involves a series of statements about facts, which must be either true or false. If they are true, one set of conclusions will follow about the right sailing of the human fleet: if they are false, quite a different set. For example, let us go back to the man who says that a thing cannot be wrong unless it hurts some other human being. He quite understands that he must not damage the other ships in the convoy, but he honestly thinks that what he does to his own ship is simply his own business. But does it not make a great difference whether his ship is his own property or not? Does it not make a great difference whether I am, so to speak, the landlord of my own mind and body, or only a tenant, responsible to the real landlord? If somebody else made me, for his own purposes, then I shall have a lot of duties which I should not have if I simply belonged to myself. /8

Again, Christianity asserts that every individual human being is going to live for ever, and this must be either true or false. Now there are a good many things which would not be worth bothering about if I were going to live only seventy years, but which I had better bother about very seriously if I am going to live for ever. Perhaps my bad temper or my jealousy are gradually getting worse—so gradually that the increase in seventy years will not be very noticeable. But it might be absolute hell in a million years: in fact, if Christianity is true, Hell is the precisely correct technical term for what it would be. And immortality makes this other difference, which, by the by, has a connection with the difference between totalitarianism and democracy. If individuals live only seventy years, then a state, or a nation, or a civilisation, which may last for a thousand years, is more important than an individual. But if Christianity is true, then the individual is not only more important but incomparably more important, for he is everlasting and the life of a state or a civilisation, compared with his, is only a moment. /9

It seems, then, that if we are to think about morality, we must think of all three departments: relations between man and man: things inside each man: and relations between man and the power that made him. We can all co-operate in the first one. Disagreements begin with the second and become serious with the third. It is in dealing with the third that the main differences between Christian and non-Christian morality come out. For the rest of this book I am going to assume the Christian point of view, and look at the whole picture as it will be if Christianity is true. /10

The speech

1. What is the specific purpose here? How does this talk set the context for the subsequent talks?
2. What assumptions does the speaker make? For instance, does he assume we have freedom of will? That life is purposeful? That the soul is immortal?
3. Show in detail whether the argument is primarily deductive or inductive.
4. Evaluate the analogy of the ships, commenting especially on its aptness and its rhetorical effectiveness.
5. Comment on the style. Do you find it especially adapted to radio speaking? What special demands, if any, does radio presentation make on a speaker, and how are they different from the requirements of television presentation?

For further study and discussion

1. Define *morality*. How does it differ from *ethics*? From *religion*?
2. In your opinion is one a Christian by living according to the Golden Rule?
3. How do one's beliefs about the nature of the universe affect his moral standards? Develop your answer with examples.
4. Evaluate the college students you know, using Lewis' "three parts of morality" as your criteria.

Suggestions for further reading

Crane Brinton, *A History of Western Morals* (New York, 1959)
Matthew, "The Sermon on the Mount"
Plato, *Phaedo*
George N. Shuster, *Education and Moral Wisdom* (New York, 1960)

Social morality

C. S. LEWIS

The first thing to get clear about Christian morality between man and man is that in this department Christ did not come to preach any brand new morality. The Golden Rule of the New Testament (Do as you would be done by) is a summing up of what everyone, at bottom, had always known to be right. Really great moral teachers never do introduce new moralities: it is quacks and cranks who do that. As Dr. Johnson said, "People need to be reminded more often than they need to be instructed." The real job of every moral teacher is to keep on bringing us back, time after time, to the old simple principles which we are all so anxious not to see; like bringing a horse back and back to the fence it has refused to jump or bringing a child back and back to the bit in its lesson that it wants to shirk. /1

The second thing to get clear is that Christianity has not, and does not profess to have, a detailed political programme for applying "Do as you would be done by" to a particular society at a particular moment. It could not have. It is meant for all men at all times and the particular programme which suited one place or time would not suit another. And, anyhow, that is not how Christianity works. When it tells you to feed the hungry it does not give you lessons in cookery. When it tells you to read the Scriptures it does not give you lessons in Hebrew and Greek, or even in English grammar. It was never intended to replace or supersede the ordinary human arts and sciences: it is rather a director which will set them all to the right jobs, and a source of energy which will give them all new life, if only they will put themselves at its disposal. /2

People say, "The Church ought to give us a lead." That is true if they mean it in the right way, but false if they mean it in the wrong way. By the Church they ought to mean the whole body of practising Christians. And when they say that the Church should give us a lead, they ought to mean that some Christians—those who happen to have the right talents—should be economists and statesmen, and that all economists and statesmen should be Christians, and that their whole efforts in politics and economics should be directed to putting "Do as you would be done by" into action. If that happened, and if we others were really ready to take it, then we should find the Christian solution for our own social problems pretty quickly. But, of course, when they ask for a lead from the Church most people mean they want the clergy to put out a political programme. That is silly. The clergy are those particular people within the whole Church who have been specially trained and set aside to look after what concerns us as creatures who are going to live for ever: and we are asking them to do a quite different job for which they have not been trained. The job is really on us, on the laymen. The application of Christian principles, say, to trade unionism or education, must come from Christian trade unionists and Christian schoolmasters: just as Christian literature comes from Christian novelists and dramatists—not from the bench of bishops getting together and trying to write plays and novels in their spare time. /3

All the same, the New Testament, without going into details, gives us a pretty clear hint of what a fully Christian society would be like. Perhaps it gives us more than we can take. It tells us that there are to be no passengers or parasites: if man does not work, he ought not to eat. Every one is to work with his own hands, and what is more, every one's work is to produce something good: there will be no manufacture of silly luxuries and then of sillier advertisements to persuade us to buy them. And there is to be no "swank" or "side," no putting on airs. To that extent a Christian society would be what we now call Leftist. On the other hand, it is always insisting on obedience —obedience (and outward marks of respect) from all of us to properly appointed magistrates, from children to parents, and (I am afraid this is going to be very unpopular) from wives to husbands. Thirdly, it is to be a cheerful society: full of singing and rejoicing, and regarding worry or anxiety as wrong. Courtesy is one of the Christian virtues; and the New Testament hates what it calls "busybodies." /4

If there were such a society in existence and you or I visited it, I think we should come away with a curious impression. We should feel that its economic life was very socialistic and, in that sense, "advanced," but that its family life and its code of manners were rather old-fashioned—perhaps even ceremonious and aristocratic. Each of us would like some bits of it, but I am afraid very few of us would like the whole thing. That is just what one would expect if Christianity is the total plan for the human machine. We have all departed from that total plan in different ways, and each of us wants to make out that his own modification of the original plan is the plan itself. You will find this again and again about anything that is really Christian: every one is attracted by bits of it and wants to pick out those bits and leave the rest. That is why we do not get much further: and that is why people who are fighting for quite opposite things can both say they are fighting for Christianity. /5

Now another point. There is one bit of advice given to us by the ancient heathen Greeks, and by the Jews in the Old Testament, and by the great Christian teachers of the Middle Ages, which the modern economic system has completely disobeyed. All these people told us not to lend money at interest: and lending money at interest—what we call investment —is the basis of our whole system. Now it may not absolutely follow that we are wrong. Some people say that when Moses and Aristotle and the Christians agreed in forbidding interest (or "usury" as they called it), they could not foresee the joint stock company, and were only thinking of the private moneylender, and that, therefore, we need not bother about what they said. That is a question I cannot decide on. I am not an economist and I simply do not know whether the investment system is responsible for the state we are in or not. This is where we want the Christian economist. But I should not have been honest if I had not told you that three great civilisations had agreed (or so it seems at first sight) in condemning the very thing on which we have based our whole life. /6

One more point and I am done. In the passage where the New Testament says that every one must work, it gives as a reason "in order that he may have something to give to those in need." Charity—giving to the poor—is an essential part of Christian morality: in the frightening parable of the sheep and the goats it seems to be the point on which everything turns.

Some people nowadays say that charity ought to be unnecessary and that instead of giving to the poor we ought to be producing a society in which there were no poor to give to. They may be quite right in saying that we ought to produce that kind of society. But if anyone thinks that, as a consequence, you can stop giving in the meantime, then he has parted company with all Christian morality. I do not believe one can settle how much we ought to give. I am afraid the only safe rule is to give more than we can spare. In other words, if our expenditure on comforts, luxuries, amusements, etc., is up to the standard common among those with the same income as our own, we are probably giving away too little. If our charities do not at all pinch or hamper us, I should say they are too small. There ought to be things we should like to do and cannot do because our charitable expenditure excludes them. I am speaking now of "charities" in the common way. Particular cases of distress among your own relatives, friends, neighbours or employees, which God, as it were, forces upon your notice, may demand much more: even to the crippling and endangering of your own position. For many of us the great obstacle to charity lies not in our luxurious living or desire for more money, but in our fear—fear of insecurity. This must often be recognised as a temptation. Sometimes our pride also hinders our charity; we are tempted to spend more than we ought on the showy forms of generosity (tipping, hospitality) and less than we ought on those who really need our help. /7

And now, before I end, I am going to venture on a guess as to how this section has affected any who have read it. My guess is that there are some Leftist people among them who are very angry that it has not gone further in that direction, and some people of an opposite sort who are angry because they think it has gone much too far. If so, that brings us right up against the real snag in all this drawing up of blueprints for a Christian society. Most of us are not really approaching the subject in order to find out what Christianity says: we are approaching it in the hope of finding support from Christianity for the views of our own party. We are looking for an ally where we are offered either a Master or—a Judge. I am just the same. There are bits in this section that I wanted to leave out. And that is why nothing whatever is going to come of such talks unless we go a much longer way round. A Christian society is not going to arrive until most of us really want it: and we are not going to want it until we become fully Christian. I may repeat "Do as you would be done by" till I am black in the face, but I cannot really carry it out till I love my neighbour as myself: and I cannot learn to love my neighbour as myself till I learn to love God: and I cannot learn to love God except by learning to obey Him. And so, as I warned you, we are driven on to something more inward—driven on from social matters to religious matters. For the longest way round is the shortest way home. /8

The speech

1. What does Lewis mean by "social morality"? What is its basic principle?

2. If Christian morality is simply a reassertion of old simple principles, where and when *did* these principles originate? Does Lewis make this clear? If so, how? Is it important that he should clearly point out the origins of these principles to accomplish his purpose?

3. Does Lewis believe reform should begin with the individual or with a change in the social structure? Cite passages to substantiate your answer.

4. What is the pattern of organization in this talk? Can the talk be easily outlined? If so, show that it can.

5. Show whether Lewis allows for varying standards of morality or whether he assumes a kind of absolute morality. To motivate a radio audience toward belief, would one of these assumptions about morality be a more compelling basis for argument than the other? Why?

For further study and discussion

1. Describe in some detail what you think a Christian Utopia might be.

2. How closely do our accepted principles of good business correspond to Christian morality? Give examples to support your contentions.

3. Is Christianity primarily socialistic in its implications? If so, why are so many American Christians antagonistic to the ideas of socialism?

4. Why do children almost always consider their parents "old-fashioned" about morals?

Suggestions for further reading

Edward Bellamy, *Looking Backward* (Boston, 1888)
Edward D. Eddy, Jr., and others, *The College Influence on Student Character* (Washington, D.C., 1959)
William Dean Howells, *A Traveler from Altruria* (New York, 1894)
Walter Kaufmann, *The Faith of a Heretic* (New York, 1961)
Martin Luther King, Jr., *Strength to Love* (New York, 1963)
Frederic R. White, *Famous Utopias of the Renaissance* (New York, 1946)

"What is truth?"

PAUL TILLICH

Paul Tillich, one of the most distinguished contemporary Protestant theologians and religious philosophers, was born in August 1886 in the Prussian province of Brandenburg. His father was a minister of the Prussian Territorial Church (Lutheran). After graduating from the Friedrich Wilhelm Gymnasium in Berlin, Tillich studied at the universities of Berlin, Tübingen, and Halle. Following the First World War, in which he served as a chaplain, he held professorships in various German universities until 1933, when he was dismissed from the University of Frankfurt-am-Main by Adolf Hitler.

Through the influence of Reinhold Niebuhr, Tillich then became a professor of philosophical theology at Union Theological Seminary, a nondenominational theological graduate school in New York City. He was at Union until 1955 and at Harvard University from 1955 to 1962. In 1962 he moved to the University of Chicago Divinity School, where he stayed until his death in October 1965. For many years Tillich had been a powerful intellectual force in both Europe and America. His last works include *Dynamics of Faith* (1957) and *The Eternal Now* (1963).

Tillich's philosophy is based upon his concept of the opposition of the essential and the existential in life and man's estrangement from the essential. Before the Fall, man was "essential being"; but exercising his freedom, he became estranged from the Ultimate, and his life became chaotic and meaningless. Sin is not transgression, but separation. The problem is how "existential being"—man as he exists on the earth—can be united with "essential being"—man as he previously existed. The answer lies in Tillich's conception of the New Being, uniting in his person both the existential and the essential. Jesus, as the Christ in which essential "Godmanhood" appears, conquers the gulf between God and man. God becomes manifest as Love, overcoming estrangement, transforming and illuminating the human situation.

The following sermon is an important expression of these ideas. It was first given in 1949 to the students and faculty at Union Theological Seminary.

And the Word became flesh and dwelt among us, full of grace and truth; . . . For the law was given

through Moses; grace and truth came through Jesus Christ. John 1:14, 17. /1

Why do you not understand what I say? . . . you are of your father the devil. . . . He was a murderer from the beginning, and has nothing to do with truth, because there is no truth in him. When he lies, he speaks according to his own nature, for he is a liar and the father of lies. John 8:43, 44. /2

Pilate said to him, "So you are a king?" Jesus answered, "You say that I am a king. For this I was born, and for this I have come into the world, to bear witness to the truth. Every one who is of the truth hears my voice." Pilate said to him, "What is truth?" John 18:37, 38. /3

Jesus said to him, "I am the way, and the truth, and the life." John 14:6. /4

He who does what is true, comes to the light. John 3:21. /5

And I will pray the Father, and he will give you . . . the Spirit of truth, whom the world cannot receive, because it neither sees him nor knows him; you know him, for he dwells with you, and will be in you. John 14:16, 17. /6

When the Spirit of truth comes, he will guide you into all the truth. John 16:13. /7

Let us love one another; for love is of God, and he who loves is born of God and knows God. He who does not love does not know God; for God is love. I John 4:7, 8. /8

Jesus then said to the Jews who had believed in Him, "If you continue in my word, you are truly my disciples, and you will know the truth, and the truth will make you free." John 8:31, 32. /9

In the above passages there are words in which Jesus speaks about truth. Another of these words shall be the center of our meditation, the word in which He combines truth and freedom: "The truth will make you free." /10

The question of truth is universally human; but like everything human it was first manifest on a special place in a special group. It was the Greek mind in which the passionate search for truth was most conspicuous; and it was the Greek world in which, and to which, the Gospel of John was written. The words, here said by Jesus, are, according to ancient custom, put into His mouth by the evangelist who wanted to show the answer of Christianity to the central question of the Hellenic mind: the question of truth. The answer is given also to us, for we, too, ask the question of truth. And some of us ask it as passionately, and sometimes as desperately, as the Greeks did. /11

It is often at an early age that we are moved by the desire for truth. When I, myself, as a fifteen-year-old boy received the words of our text as the motto for my future life from the confirming minister, who happened to be my father, I felt that this was just what I was looking for; and I remember that I was not alone in my group with this longing for truth. But I also observed, in myself and in others, that the early passion for truth is due to be lost in the adolescent and adult years of our lives. How does this happen? /12

The truth the child first receives is imposed upon him by adults, predominantly by his parents. This cannot be otherwise; and he cannot help accepting it. The passion for truth is silenced by answers which have the weight of undisputed authority, be it that of the mother or the father, or an older friend, or a gang, or the representatives of a social pattern. But sooner or later the child revolts against the truth given to him. He denies the authorities either all together, or one in the name of the other. He uses the teachers against the parents, the gang against the teachers, a friend against the gang, society against the friend. /13

This revolt is as unavoidable as was his early dependence on authority. The authorities gave him something to live on, the revolt makes him responsible for the truth he accepts or rejects. /14

But whether in obedience or in revolt, the time comes when a new way to truth is opened to us, especially to those in academic surroundings: The way of scholarly work. Eagerly we take it. It seems so safe, so successful, so independent of both authority and willfulness. It liberates from prejudices and superstitions; it makes us humble and honest. Where else, besides in scholarly work, should we look for truth? There are many in our period, young and old, primitive and sophisticated, practical and scientific, who accept this answer without hesitation. For them scholarly truth is truth altogether. Poetry may give beauty, but it certainly does not give truth. Ethics may help us to a good life, but it cannot help us to truth. Religion may produce deep emotions, but it should not claim to have truth. Only science gives us truth. It gives us new insights into the way nature works, into the texture of human history, into the hidden things of the human mind. It gives a feeling of joy, inferior to no other joy. He who has experienced this transition from darkness, or dimness, to the sharp light of knowledge will always praise scientific truth

and understanding and say with some great medieval theologians, that the principles through which we know our world are the eternal divine light in our souls. And yet, when we ask those who have finished their studies in our colleges and universities whether they have found there a truth which is relevant to their lives they will answer with hesitation. Some will say that they have lost what they had of relevant truth; others will say that they don't care for such a truth because life goes on from day to day without it. Others will tell you of a person, a book, an event outside their studies which gave them the feeling of a truth that matters. But they all will agree that it is not the scholarly work which can give truth relevant for our life. /15

Where else, then, can we get it? "Nowhere," Pilate answers in his talk with Jesus. "What is truth?" he asks, expressing in these three words his own and his contemporaries' despair of truth, expressing also the despair of truth in millions of our contemporaries, in schools and studios, in business and professions. In all of us, open or hidden, admitted or repressed, the despair of truth is a permanent threat. We are children of our period as Pilate was. Both are periods of disintegration, of a world-wide loss of values and meanings. Nobody can separate himself completely from this reality, and nobody should even try. Let me do something unusual from a Christian standpoint, namely, to express praise of Pilate—not the unjust judge, but the cynic and sceptic; and of all those amongst us in whom Pilate's question is alive. For in the depth of every serious doubt and every despair of truth, the passion for truth is still at work. Don't give in too quickly to those who want to alleviate your anxiety about truth. Don't be seduced into a truth which is not really your truth, even if the seducer is your church, or your party, or your parental tradition. Go with Pilate, if you cannot go with Jesus; but go in seriousness with him! /16

Twofold are the temptations to evade the burden of asking for the truth that matters. The one is the way of those who claim to have the truth and the other is the way of those who do not care for the truth. The first ones are called "the Jews" in our gospel. They point to their tradition which goes back to Abraham. Abraham is their father; so they have all truth, and do not need to be worried by the question which they encounter in Jesus. Many among us, Christians and secularists, are "Jews" in the sense of the Fourth Gospel. They point to *their* tradition which goes back to the Church Fathers, or to the popes, or to the Reformers, or to the makers of the American Constitution. Their church or their nation is their mother, so they have all truth and do not need to worry about the question of truth. Would Jesus tell them, perhaps, what He told the Jews—that even if the church or the nation is their mother, they carry with them the heritage of the father of untruth; that the truth they have is not the truth which makes free? Certainly there is no freedom where there is self-complacency about the truth of one's own beliefs. There is no freedom where there is ignorant and fanatical rejection of foreign ideas and ways of life. There is no freedom but demonic bondage where one's own truth is called the ultimate truth. For this is an attempt to be like God, an attempt which is made in the name of God. /17

There is the second way of avoiding the question of truth—the way of not caring for it, of indifference. It is the way of the majority of the people today, as well as at the time of Jesus. Life, they say to themselves, is a mixture of truth, half-truth and falsehood. It is quite possible to live with this mixture, to muddle through most of the difficulties of life without asking the question of a truth that matters ultimately. There may be boundary situations, a tragic event, a deep spiritual fall, death. But as long as they are far removed, the question of truth can also stay far away. Hence, the common attitude—a little bit of Pilate's scepticism, especially in things which it is not dangerous today to doubt, as, for instance, God and the Christ; and a little bit of the Jew's dogmatism, especially in things which one is requested to accept today, as, for instance, an economic or political way of life. In other words, some scepticism and some dogmatism, and a shrewd method of balancing them liberate one from the burden of asking the question of ultimate truth. /18

But those of us who dare to face the question of truth may listen to what the Fourth Gospel says about it. The first thing which strikes us is that the truth of which Jesus speaks is not a doctrine but a reality, namely, He Himself: "I *am* the truth." This is a profound transformation of the ordinary meaning of truth. For us, statements are true or false; people may *have* truth or not; but how can they *be* truth, even *the* truth? The truth of which the Fourth Gospel speaks is a true reality—that reality which does not deceive us if we accept it and live with it. If Jesus says, "I am the truth," he indicates that in Him the true, the genuine, the ultimate reality is present; or, in other words, that God is present, unveiled, undistorted, in His infinite depth, in His unapproachable mystery. Jesus is not the truth because His teachings are true. But His teachings are true because they express the truth which He Himself is. He is more than

His words. And He is more than any word said about Him. The truth which makes us free is neither the teaching of Jesus nor the teaching about Jesus. Those who have called the teaching of Jesus "the truth" have subjected the people to a servitude under the law. And most people like to live under a law. They want to be told what to think and what not to think. And they accept Jesus as the infallible teacher and giver of a new law. But even the words of Jesus, if taken as a law, are not the truth which makes us free. And they should not be used as such by our scholars and preachers and religious teachers. They should not be used as a collection of infallible prescriptions for life and thought. They *point* to the truth, but they are not a law of truth. Nor are the doctrines about Him the truth that liberates. I say this to you as somebody who all his life has worked for a true expression of the truth which is the Christ. But the more one works, the more one realizes that our expressions, including everything we have learned from our teachers and from the teaching of the Church in all generations, is not the truth that makes us free. The Church very early forgot the word of our Gospel that He *is* the truth; and claimed that her doctrines about Him are the truth. But these doctrines, however necessary and good they were, proved to be not the truth that liberates. Soon they became tools of suppression, of servitude under authorities; they became means to prevent the honest search for truth—weapons to split the souls of people between loyalty to the Church and sincerity to truth. And in this way they gave deadly weapons to those who attacked the Church and its doctrines in the name of truth. Not everybody feels this conflict. There are masses of people who feel safe under doctrinal laws. They are safe, but it is the safety of him who has not yet found his spiritual freedom, who has not yet found his true self. It is the dignity and the danger of Protestantism that it exposes its adherents to the insecurity of asking the question of truth for themselves and that it throws them into the freedom and responsibility of personal decisions, of the right to choose between the ways of the sceptics, and those who are orthodox, of the indifferent masses, and Him who *is* the truth that liberates. For this is the greatness of Protestantism: that it points beyond the teachings of Jesus and beyond the doctrines of the Church to the being of Him whose being is the truth. /19

How do we reach this truth? "By doing it," is the answer of the Fourth Gospel. This does not mean being obedient to the commandments, accepting them and fulfilling them. Doing the truth means living out of the reality which is *He* who is the truth, making His being the being of ourselves and of our world. And again, we ask, "How can this happen?" "By remaining in Him" is the answer of the Fourth Gospel, *i.e.*, by participating in His being. "Abide in me and I in you," he says. The truth which liberates is the truth in which we participate, which is a part of us and we a part of it. True discipleship is participation. If the real, the ultimate, the divine reality which is His being becomes our being we are in the truth that matters. /20

And a third time we ask, "How can this happen?" There is an answer to this question in our Gospel which may deeply shock us: "Every one who is of the truth hears my voice." Being "of the truth" means, coming from the true, the ultimate reality, being determined in one's being by the divine ground of all being, by that reality which is present in the Christ. If we have part in it, we recognize it wherever it appears; we recognize it as it appears in its fullness in the Christ. But, some may ask in despair: "If we have *no* part in it, if we are *not* of the truth, are we then forever excluded from it? Must we accept a life without truth, a life in error and meaninglessness? Who tells me that *I* am of the truth, that *I* have a chance to reach it?" Nobody can tell you; but there is one criterion: If you *seriously* ask the question, "Am I of the truth?" you *are* of the truth. If you do not ask it seriously, you do not really want, and you do not deserve, and you cannot get, an answer! He who asks seriously the question of the truth that liberates, is already on his way to liberation. He may still be in the bondage of dogmatic self-assurance but he has begun to be free from it. He may still be in the bondage of cynical despair, but he has already started to emerge from it. He may still be in the bondage of unconcern about the truth that matters, but his unconcern is already shaken. These all are of the truth and on their road to the truth. /21

On this road you will meet the liberating truth in many forms except in one form: you never will meet it in the form of propositions which you can learn or write down and take home. But you may encounter it in one sentence of a book or of a conversation or of a lecture, or even of a sermon. This sentence is not the truth, but it may open you up for the truth and it may liberate you from the bondage to opinions and prejudices and conventions. Suddenly, true reality appears like the brightness of lightening in a formerly dark place. Or, slowly, true reality appears like a landscape when the fog becomes thinner and thinner and finally disappears. New darknesses, new fogs will fall upon you; but you have experienced, at least once, the truth and the freedom given by the truth.

Or you may be grasped by the truth in an encounter with a piece of nature—its beauty and its transitoriness; or in an encounter with a human being in friendship and estrangement, in love, in difference and hate; or in an encounter with yourself in a sudden insight into the hidden strivings of your soul, in disgust and even hatred of yourself, in reconciliation with and acceptance of yourself. In these encounters you may meet the true reality—the truth which liberates from illusions and false authorities, from enslaving anxieties, desires and hostilities, from a wrong self-rejection and a wrong self-affirmation. /22

And it may even happen that you are grasped by the picture and power of Him who is truth. There is no law that this must happen. Many at all times and in all places have encountered the true reality which is in Him without knowing His name—as He Himself said. They were of the truth and they recognized the truth, although they had never seen Him who is the truth. And those who have seen Him, the Christians in all generations, have no guarantee that they participate in the truth which He is. Maybe they were not of the truth. Those, however, who are of the truth and who have encountered Him who is the truth have one precious thing beyond the others: They have the point from which to judge all truth they encounter anywhere. They look at a life which never lost the communion with the divine ground of all life, and they look at a life which never lost the union of love with all beings. /23

And this leads to the last word which the man who has written the Gospel and the Letters of John has to say about truth: that the truth which liberates is the power of love, for God is love. The father of the lie binds us to himself by binding us to ourselves—or to that in us which is not our true self. Love liberates from the father of the lie because it liberates us from our false self to our true self—to that self which is grounded in true reality. Therefore, distrust every claim for truth where you do not see truth united with love; and be certain that you are of the truth and that the truth has taken hold of you only when love has taken hold of you and has started to make you free from yourselves.

The speech

1. What do the Biblical selections at the beginning of the sermon have in common? What use is made of them in the sermon?

2. What is the general purpose ordinarily of a sermon? Does this one share this general purpose? What is the specific purpose of this sermon?

3. What is scientific truth as Tillich uses the term? What methods has he used to clarify his meaning? What are its strengths and weaknesses? What proofs does he use to support his views on this point?

4. What is meant by "Go with Pilate, if you cannot go with Jesus; but go in seriousness with him!"?

5. What, according to Tillich, are the two ways of avoiding the question of truth? What does Tillich gain in the sermon by mentioning these before tackling the problem of facing up to truth?

6. What arguments would Tillich use, or does he use, in showing that those who believe in Jesus are not placing themselves in intellectual bondage?

7. Put into your own words the distinction Tillich makes between seeing truth in Jesus and seeing it in the doctrines about Jesus. Why does he insist upon the former? Show in detail how his whole argument hinges upon this distinction.

8. What is truth as Tillich uses the term? How may it be grasped? Is Tillich suggesting that the best way to apprehend truth is through a mystical experience?

9. Describe the organization of the sermon. Comment especially on the nature and value of the introduction and the conclusion.

10. Discuss the style, noting especially the word choice and sentence structure. Despite the fact that the subject is highly abstract, does the style help to hold your attention? If so, why? Would you say that the style of this sermon is livelier or duller than the style of most sermons you have heard? Defend your answer with specific references.

11. Is the argument primarily deductive? If so, what are the basic premises? If inductive, what is the evidence upon which the reasoning is based?

For further study and discussion

1. In what respects have you revolted from "truth" you once accepted on authority? What were the reasons for the revolt? Were the reasons always relevant ones? Comment.

2. What is your belief about the nature of Jesus? Can you determine the origins of this belief?

3. Do you think there are different kinds of truth (e.g., religious truth, scientific truth, historical truth) or that truth is a term which should be reserved for only what is absolute and eternal?

4. What is similar about our age and that of Jesus? Why should both ages breed skepticism?

5. Would you say that we live primarily by myth rather than truth (e.g., myths about ourselves, our friends, our country, etc.)? Develop your answer in detail.

6. What is the relation of education to truth—in theory and in practice?

7. How can you explain the belief that has been widely held through the ages that truth is beauty? That truth is goodness? That truth is love?

8. Is the object of all art and literature, as well as religion, truth? Describe whatever differences you see between the aims of art and religion.

9. Why do so many people not want to face up to the truth in the sense of the known facts? Explore this by discussing both the nature of man and the nature of truth. What truth have you been unwilling to confront frankly and openly?

10. In what sense can the truth "set you free"?

Suggestions for further reading

Barrows Dunham, *Man Against Myth* (Boston, 1947)
David Greenwood, *Truth and Meaning* (New York, 1957)
William James, *The Meaning of Truth* (New York, 1909)
David Starr Jordan, *The Stability of Truth* (New York, 1911)
Francois Mauriac, *What I Believe* (New York, 1963)
Reinhold Niebuhr, *Faith and History* (New York, 1949)
Bertrand Russell, *An Inquiry into Meaning and Truth* (New York, 1940)
Albert Schweitzer, *The Quest of the Historical Jesus* (London, 1954)
Paul Tillich, *The Shaking of the Foundations* (New York, 1948)

from "The Apology"

PLATO

"The Apology" is Plato's account of the reply of Socrates to the Athenian court that had sentenced him to death. The passage given here is the conclusion of the speech.

Born in Athens about 469 B.C., Socrates grew up to be one of the most likable of men, and one of the most pestiferous. Homely to the point almost of grotesqueness, he developed great sympathy for the frailties of others. In battle he demonstrated memorable courage. He affected the simplest of clothes and yet was no ascetic; he could be the best of company at the tables of the well-to-do. Apparently he had a keen sense of humor. Yet he felt it his main function to attack the ignorance and pretentiousness he found in his fellow Athenians. Constantly he tried to show them the

From "The Apology," *The Dialogues of Plato*, translated into English with analyses and introductions by B. Jowett, M.A. Fourth edition, Oxford, 1953, Volume I, pp. 363-366. Reprinted by permission of The Clarendon Press.

difference between knowledge and opinion, and the dependence of goodness upon wisdom. It was inevitable that such a persistent moral gadfly should make enemies.

Although the underlying reason for his trial was probably political (he was an unsparing critic of the democratic leaders of the time), he was actually charged with corrupting the young and practicing religious "novelties." Socrates scorned the charges and was convicted by a vote, apparently, of 280 to 220. Although the prosecutor asked for death, a much lighter sentence would probably have been meted out had not Socrates offended the court by insisting that he be treated as a public benefactor. He was sentenced to death by an even larger vote. During his last days in prison, he continued to instruct his followers in temperance and justice, and demonstrated his own respect for law by refusing to escape when the opportunity offered. When the sun set on the appointed day, he calmly drank the cup of hemlock and died. He was seventy years old.

In the portion of "The Apology" preceding the passage given here, Socrates tells that he has won the animus of the politicians and poets and rhetoricians by being wiser than they: he recognizes his own ignorance whereas they do not recognize theirs. Continuing, he attempts to refute the various charges leveled against him, reminds his listeners that his main purpose has always been to seek wisdom and virtue, and announces that, under the circumstances, the sentence he prefers is death. He then moves into the concluding statements.

SOCRATES Not much time will be gained, O Athenians, in return for the evil name which you will get from the detractors of the city, who will say that you killed Socrates, a wise man; for they will call me wise, even although I am not wise, when they want to reproach you. If you had waited a little while, your desire would have been fulfilled in the course of nature. For I am far advanced in years, as you may perceive, and not far from death. I am speaking now not to all of you, but only to those who have condemned me to death. And I have another thing to say to them: You think that I was convicted because I had no words of the sort which would have procured my acquittal—I mean, if I had thought fit to leave nothing undone or unsaid. Not so; the deficiency which led to my conviction was not of words—certainly not. But I had not the boldness nor impudence nor inclination to address you as you would have liked me to do, weeping and wailing and lamenting, and saying and doing many things, such indeed as

you have been accustomed to hear from others, but I maintain to be unworthy of myself. I thought at the time that I ought not to do anything common or mean when in danger: nor do I now repent of the style of my defence; I would rather die having spoken after my manner, than speak in your manner and live. For neither in war nor yet at law ought I or any man to use every way of escaping death. Often in battle there can be no doubt that if a man will throw away his arms, and fall on his knees before his pursuers, he may escape death; and in other dangers there are other ways of escaping death, if a man has the hardihood to say and do anything. The difficulty, my friends, is not to avoid death, but to avoid unrighteousness; for that runs faster than death. I am old and move slowly, and the slower runner has overtaken me; my accusers are keen and quick, and the faster runner, who is wickedness, has overtaken them. And now I depart hence condemned by you to suffer the penalty of death,—they too go their ways condemned by the truth to suffer the penalty of villainy and wrong; and I must abide by my award—let them abide by theirs. I suppose that these things may be regarded as fated,—and I think that they are well. /1

And now, O men who have condemned me, I would fain prophesy to you; for I am about to die, and in the hour of death men are gifted with prophetic power. And I prophesy to you who are my murderers, that immediately after my departure punishment far heavier than you have inflicted on me surely awaits you. Me you have killed because you wanted to escape the accuser, and not to give an account of your lives. But that will not be as you suppose: far otherwise. For I say that there will be more accusers of you than there are now; accusers whom hitherto I have restrained: and as they are younger they will be more severe with you, and you will be more offended at them. If you think that by killing men you will stop all censure of your evil lives, you are mistaken; that is not a way of escape which is either very possible, or honourable; the easiest and the noblest way is not to be disabling others, but to be improving yourselves. This is the prophecy which I utter before my departure to the judges who have condemned me. /2

Friends, who would have acquitted me, I would like also to talk with you about the thing which has come to pass, while the magistrates are busy, and before I go to the place at which I must die. Stay then a little, for we may as well talk with one another while there is time. You are my friends, and I should like to show you the meaning of this event which has happened to me. O my judges—for you I may truly call judges—I should like to tell you of a wonderful circumstance. Hitherto the divine faculty of which the internal oracle is the source has constantly been in the habit of opposing me even about trifles, if I was going to make a slip or error in any matter; and now as you see there has come upon me that which may be thought, and is generally believed to be, the last and worst evil. But the oracle made no sign of opposition, either when I was leaving my house in the morning, or when I was on my way to the court, or while I was speaking, at anything which I was going to say; and yet I have often been stopped in the middle of a speech, but now in nothing I either said or did touching the matter in hand has the oracle opposed me. What do I take to be the explanation of this silence? I will tell you. It is an intimation that what has happened to me is a good, and therefore those of us who think that death is an evil must be in error. I have this conclusive proof; the customary sign would surely have opposed me had I been going to evil and not to good. /3

Let us reflect in another way, and we shall see that there is great reason to hope that death is a good; for one of two things—either death is a state of nothingness and utter unconsciousness, or, as men say, there is a change and migration of the soul from this world to another. Now if you suppose that there is no consciousness, but a sleep like the sleep of him who is undisturbed even by dreams, death will be an unspeakable gain. For if a person were to select the night in which his sleep was undisturbed even by dreams, and were to compare with this the other days and nights of his life, and then were to tell us how many days and nights he had passed in the course of his life better and more pleasantly than this one, I think that any man, I will not say a private man, but even the great king will not find many such days or nights, when compared with the others. Now if death be of such a nature, I say that to die is gain; for eternity is then only a single night. But if death is the journey to another place, and there, as men say, all the dead abide, what good, O my friends and judges, can be greater than this? If indeed when the pilgrim arrives in the world below, he is delivered from our earthly professors of justice, and finds the true judges who are said to give judgement there, Minos and Rhadamanthus and Aeacus and Triptolemus, and other sons of God who were righteous in their own life, that pilgrimage will be worth making. What would not a man give if he might converse with Orpheus and Musaeus and Hesiod and Homer? Nay, if this be true, let me die again and again. I myself, too, shall find a wonderful interest in there meeting and conversing with Palamedes, and Ajax the son of Telamon, and any other ancient hero who has suffered death through an unjust judgement; and there will be no small pleasure, as I think, in comparing my own experience with theirs. Above all, I shall then be able to continue my search into true and false knowledge, as in this world, so also in the next; and I shall find out who is wise, and who pretends to be wise, and is not. What would not a man give, O judges, to be able to examine the leader of the great Trojan expedition; or Odysseus or Sisyphus, or numberless others, men and women too! What infinite delight would there be in conversing with them and asking them questions! In another world they do not put a man to death for asking questions: assuredly not. For besides being happier than we are, they will be immortal, if what is said is true. /4

Wherefore, O judges, be of good cheer about death, and know of a certainty that no evil can happen to a good man, either in life or after death, and that he and his are not neglected by the gods. Nor has my own approaching end happened by mere chance; I see clearly that the time had arrived when it was better for me to die and be released from trouble; therefore the oracle gave no sign, and therefore also I am not at all angry with my condemners, or with my accusers. But although they have done me no harm, they intended it; and for this I may properly blame them. /5

Still I have a favour to ask of them. When my sons are grown up, I would ask you, O my friends, to punish them; I would have you trouble them, as I have troubled you, if they seem to care about riches, or anything, more than about virtue; or if they pretend to be something when they are really nothing,—then reprove them, as I have reproved you, for not caring about that for which they ought to care, and thinking that they are something when they are really nothing. And if you do this, I shall have received justice at your hands, and so will my sons. /6

The hour of departure has arrived, and we go our ways—I to die, and you to live. Which is better God only knows. /7

The speech

1. List the arguments Socrates compresses into his summation in the first paragraph.
2. What kinds of *proof* does he use? (See the Glossary.)
3. Characterize Socrates. Does he seem Christlike? Psychopathic? What?

4. Since it is clear that Socrates does not expect a change in the sentence, what could be his point in delivering so moving a speech?

5. Characterize the tone you find here. Does it change as Socrates turns from one group to another? Do you find it suitable to the purpose you identified in answering the preceding question? (Since this is a translation, you are of course dependent upon the translator's ability in catching the tone of the original. Why should catching the tone be one of a translator's hardest problems?)

For further study and discussion

1. What for Socrates was the highest good? The greatest evil? Are these concepts different today?

2. How would you explain Socrates' inner "oracle"?

3. Do you find Socrates' explanations of death satisfying? Which do you think is the true explanation? How does your concept of death affect your philosophy of life?

4. What convictions through the course of history have been analogous to that of Socrates? Do you find any analogous situations today?

5. Comment on the modernity of this discourse. Is there a single issue that is not fundamental today?

For further reading

Learned Hand, *The Spirit of Liberty* (New York, 1960)

O. W. Holmes, *The Mind and Faith of Justice Holmes,* edited by Max Lerner (Boston, 1943)

Roscoe Pound, *Justice According to Law* (New Haven, 1961)

Micheline Sauvage, *Socrates and the Human Conscience* (New York, 1960)

Laurence Stapleton, *Justice and World Society* (Chapel Hill, 1944)

Arthur E. Sutherland, *The Law and One Among Many* (Madison, Wis., 1956)

Paul Tillich, *Love, Power and Justice* (New York, 1954)

What can we prove about God?

LEON R. ZELLNER

Leon R. Zellner, a junior in business administration, presented this talk on March 7, 1965, in a course in oral

communication required of all undergraduates at Pennsylvania State University. His assignment was as follows: "Deliver extemporaneously a ten- to twelve-minute talk in which you develop your personal views on any aspect of the following topics: politics, religion, sex, social relations, the arts, or your personal philosophy of life. Your objective may be to explain, to persuade, or to aim at inducing your audience to engage with you in further inquiry on a problem you present."

Zellner's audience consisted of eighteen students, the classroom instructor, and two teacher-interns. Seven of the undergraduate listeners were women and eleven were men; all were in their freshman, sophomore, or junior years. Six were majoring in the liberal arts or sciences, four in education, three in business administration, three in engineering, and one each in agriculture and hotel administration.

As Zellner mentions (paragraph 2), several other students had already spoken on some phase of religion.

The text that follows is transcribed from a tape recording of Zellner's talk.

Many people have made their expressed purpose in life that of either proving or disproving the existence of God by the use of scientific data. Let me point out immediately that what I'm going to do today is neither of these. What I'm going to try to show is that man's scientific arguments, by which I mean arguments drawn from any natural phenomenon, cannot possibly prove or disprove the existence of God. /1

Several other speakers in the past three days have made speeches of religious content, and for this reason I feel I should define exactly what I mean when I use the word *God* in this talk. In what I say I'll take God to mean not only the God of the Judeo-Christian faiths, but the supreme being lying at the zenith of any religion whatever. One other point of clarification I feel is necessary before I go farther. That is the meaning of the word *prove*. To prove something means to demonstrate that thing to be a fact. So, what I'm trying to show you is that it is impossible for man through scientific reasoning and logic to prove that the existence of God is a fact or not a fact. Today, I'll deal primarily with the first of these proofs—that is, the proofs that say God *must* exist. However, I'd like you to keep always in mind that the refutations of these proofs can also be used to refute arguments that try to prove the nonexistence of God. /2

I feel the best way to make my point for you is to take two of the proofs that are most generally used and show you exactly what's wrong with them. The first of these proofs is called argument from design. People who use this type of reasoning about God generally choose some complex kind of natural mechanism and prove—or at least they assume they prove—that the mechanism must have been planned. Thereby, they imply the existence of a Planner. One of these complex systems often used is the solar system which we know—the rotation of earth around the sun, the moon around the earth, and so forth. Another mechanism used is the eye, wherein you have the retina. Were it a little differently shaped, we wouldn't be able to see. Or, there are various other mechanisms of the eye which, if changed, would cause the loss of sight. One other mechanism used is the existence of the protein molecule, which is, indeed, the basis for all life. Had the atoms within this molecule been arranged in any degree differently, life as we know it could not possibly exist. /3

To refute any one of these arguments from design is actually the equivalent·of refuting them all, since they all follow the same basic lines of logic. Therefore, I'll deal primarily with the solar system because we know it better. The followers of this train of thought, of which Sir Isaac Newton was one, say that because the earth and the sun and all the other planets have specific masses and specific velocities, they follow a specific course. They also argue that these courses could not possibly have been selected through the forces of chance. They say these particular orbits were predesigned by some super-being which they call God. /4

Let me illustrate. Suppose, for example, that this line

represents the orbit of the earth around the sun. These people argue that for the earth to take this course by chance is infinitely improbable. Basically, they argue this because in the vastness of what we call space, there's so much room that this earth could have as easily spiraled into the sun, gone straight out into nowhere, or followed a parabolic or hyperbolic curve. But this orbit is the path it chose. Since that path is infinitely improbable, it must have been predesigned. That's the argument. /5

Now, suppose the earth, rather than following its orbital path, had instead followed this one:

What are the chances that the second path might have been taken? They are equally infinitely impossible. Therefore, the arguers are actually not proving anything, since they are saying, in fact, that all possible courses are infinitely impossible. They aren't proving anything by saying just one of them was chosen. The probabilities for any one path are equal. /6

This line of thought brings up an idea which may seem a bit curious. It is that no matter what happens in nature, it is infinitely improbable. This is to say if we try to figure out the probabilities for the fact that it's now snowing here at this moment, it can be proved that it's infinitely improbable that it would snow here today. It is necessary for a whole complex chain of events to occur before it can possibly snow in State College. If the earth weren't rotating at its particular speed, we wouldn't be here with the snow. If the earth were not revolving around the sun as it is, perhaps the climate would be warmer and it would be impossible for it to snow here. If the masses of air had any other set of molecules than they have at this instant, it would be impossible for it to snow. This kind of argument can be applied to anything in nature. Take the existence of a flower in a particular spot. There are an infinite number of places where that flower could grow. So, for a flower you don't plant but which just happens to grow, it is infinitely improbable that that flower could grow where it does. /7

There are two basic fallacies in all this arguing. The first is that you cannot explain, just by the complexity of a situation, that the complex had to be planned by some all-knowing mind. The second fallacy here is one that is more or less implied rather than expressed. Anyone who reads a great deal on this subject or explores a number of these "proofs" finds that the proponents of the "proofs" are always proving the existence of God by means of things which man considers noble, advantageous, beautiful, or virtuous. Men make this argument under the assumption that if a God does exist, by our definitions of God he must necessarily produce good and virtuous things. Their next step is to reverse this logic and say that since virtuous things do exist, they must have been produced by God. This is a fallacy as old as logic itself. Because we know that lightning can cause a house to burn, we're not justified, when we see a house burning, to conclude that the cause of that fire was lightning. You *can* argue from cause to effect, but you cannot argue *necessarily* in the reverse direction. /8

The second proof often used for the existence of God is that there are miracles. A miracle, as you know, is some breach of a natural law. In one of the articles I've been reading the author cites the fact that as soon as you mention miracles those you talk to tend to think, "What about people who have regained sight or have been able to walk after years without being able to use their legs?" These events prove nothing. They may, indeed, be miracles. They may be the intervention of some power, affecting what *we* call natural laws. However, they may as easily be the results of natural laws we don't yet know. The only time we can ever be sure some extraordinary event is a miracle is when we are one hundred percent sure that we know every natural law that exists. Since this is a condition we'll never attain, because we can never know there is a natural law we don't know, it is impossible to say that "miracles" are or aren't breaches of natural law. /9

So what have I shown you? Have I shown that God does not exist? Certainly not. I've shown only one thing—that to believe in a God requires, not some type of scientific proof, but rather a faith. Imagine a small child trying to "prove" Einstein's theory of relativity. He may, if he is highly intelligent, be able to understand something of this and take it on faith. He may think, "I know Einstein was supposed to be an important man, so I'll accept what he said as true." Now, I'm saying to you that man, trying to prove the existence of God, is like a small child trying to prove a theory far more complex and far greater than Einstein's theory of relativity. /10

If we could *prove* the existence of God, if we could take him down and put him in this chair and compile statistics that state his IQ is 130, his height such-and-such and his weight so much, and assert that he has specific personality traits—if we could do that, we'd have taken away the fact that he is a *god*. If I can take any one of you and prove *anything* about you—that you do exist, that I can see you are six feet two, or that your weight is 130—when I can start taking you apart, dissecting you and looking into your character, you cannot possibly be a god. /11

In the Book of Proverbs, in the Bible, chapter 3, verse 5, there is a line which says, "Trust in the Lord with all thine heart; and lean not unto thine own understanding." To me, what this means is this: "Trust" is the equivalent of faith—to believe. Believe in the Lord, have faith that he exists, but when you're trying to believe this, don't depend on your understanding. Don't try to *prove* it, because that's impossible. By the very definitions which we apply to a god, he's omnipotent, he's perfect goodness, perfect righteousness; a god is unattainable to man. This is the point that's really important: a god is something unattainable to man. This is what makes him a god. If we could pinpoint God and say what he is, he would be no god because he wouldn't be all-powerful. So I'd like to repeat again that any proof of God comes through faith and believing; it is not something for which we find proof or disproof through the usages of science, logic, or reason. /12

For discussion

1. What is the speaker's basic purpose? Is it narrowed sufficiently for a short classroom talk? Is it clear at every point in the speech?

2. In your own words summarize the speaker's argument that God's existence cannot be proved. In denying "proofs" of God's existence, the speaker could easily give the impression that he is denying God's existence. How does he try to avoid giving this impression? Does he succeed?

3. In the last half of the speech Zellner argues for the necessity of faith. Is this argument as strong as the one in which he denies the applicability of reason? Should it be? Explain your answer.

4. Do the statements in paragraph 11 accord with the definition of God in paragraph 2? Do they accord with the definition in paragraph 12? Are the definitions in paragraph 2 and paragraph 12 harmonious? Would the speech have been stronger had the definition in paragraph 12 appeared in paragraph 2? Defend your answers.

5. Indicate statements you think need strengthening. For example, is there any chance that listeners would not understand the last sentence in paragraph 2 without some elaboration? And how effective is a phrase like "in one of the articles I've been reading" (paragraph 9)?

6. The speaker uses "science," "logic," and "reason" at the very end of the speech as though they were coordinate elements. Does this rather sloppy use of words ruin the effectiveness of his conclusion? Explain your answer.

7. Do you find the style of the talk suitable to the subject? Consider diction, tone, syntax, rhythm, and sound.

8. What assumptions lie behind the speech? For example, is the speaker assuming that there is a God, and that we must have faith that there is?

9. Why is a speech on God difficult to deliver to a college audience? Or to any audience, for that matter, except one gathered together for religious purposes?

10. Speculate on the effect that this speech would have upon your own speech class. Would it be convincing to them? If not, how would you change it to make it convincing?

Pericles' funeral speech

This famous address to the people of Athens is a powerful expression of political ideals which were never fully attained in Athens or elsewhere but are striven for today as they were in ancient Greece. The text of what Pericles said in honor of those who had died in war has not come down to us, but the historian, Thucydides, reconstructed the speech as part of his *History of the Peloponnesian War*. Thucydides was a contemporary and a supporter of Pericles, and he probably heard the address when it was delivered. Most historians believe Thucydides was faithful to the spirit and argument of Pericles' "Funeral Speech"; at the very least, it is a speech that a great historian believed would have deeply touched and encouraged an Athenian audience in 431 B.C.

Pericles was born about 495 B.C. and died during the great plague of 429 B.C. He studied with distinguished Athenian teachers of music, science, and philosophy and psychology; they, it is said, freed Pericles "from the superstitions of the multitude whom it was his task to guide." His active political career in Athens began about 470 B.C. By knowledge, restraint, and eloquence he rose to leadership in Athenian politics. The expansion of Athenian naval and commercial influence abroad and the development of culture and tolerance at home were leading objectives of Pericles' policies, and he sought to attain these ends through the support and consent of the Athenian citizens. Although he was not always successful in maintaining popular support, he was indisputably the first citizen of Athens at the time when he delivered his famous "Funeral Speech."

The long series of struggles among the Greek states, which is known as the Peloponnesian War, began in March, 431 B.C. In the winter of that year the Athenians arranged the customary public funeral for all who had died in battle during the year. It was at this funeral that Pericles spoke, under circumstances that Thucydides describes in some detail:

From *The Peloponnesian War*, tr. by Rex Warner, Penguin Books Ltd., 1954. By permission of The Bodley Head Ltd.

"These funerals are held in the following way: two days before the ceremony the bones of the fallen are brought and put in a tent which has been erected, and people make whatever offerings they wish to their own dead. Then there is a funeral procession in which coffins of cypress wood are carried on wagons. There is one coffin for each tribe, which contains the bones of members of that tribe. One empty bier is decorated and carried in the procession: this is for the missing, whose bodies could not be recovered. Everyone who wishes to, both citizens and foreigners, can join in the procession, and the women who are related to the dead are there to make their laments at the tomb. The bones are laid in the public burial-place, which is in the most beautiful quarter outside the city walls. . . .

"When the bones have been laid in the earth, a man chosen by the city for his intellectual gifts and for his general reputation makes an appropriate speech in praise of the dead, and after the speech all depart. . . . Now, at the burial of those who were the first to fall in the war Pericles, the son of Xanthippus, was chosen to make the speech. When the moment arrived, he came forward from the tomb and, standing on a high platform so that he might be heard by as many people as possible in the crowd, he spoke as follows":

Many of those who have spoken here in the past have praised the institution of this speech at the close of our ceremony. It seemed to them a mark of honour to our soldiers who have fallen in war that a speech should be made over them. I do not agree. These men have shown themselves valiant in action, and it would be enough, I think, for their glories to be proclaimed in action, as you have just seen it done at this funeral organized by the state. Our belief in the courage and manliness of so many should not be hazarded on the goodness or badness of one man's speech. Then it is not easy to speak with a proper sense of balance, when a man's listeners find it difficult to believe in the truth of what one is saying. The man who knows the facts and loves the dead may well think that an oration tells less than what he knows and what he would like to hear: others who do not know so much may feel envy for the dead, and think the orator overpraises them, when he speaks of exploits that are beyond their own capacities. Praise of other people is tolerable only up to a certain point, the point where one still believes that one could do oneself some of the things one is hearing about. Once you get beyond this point, you will find people becoming jealous and incredulous. However, the fact is that this institution was set up and approved by our forefathers, and it is my duty to follow the tradition and do my best to meet the wishes and the expectations of every one of you. /1

I shall begin by speaking about our ancestors, since it is only right and proper on such an occasion to pay them the honour of recalling what they did. In this land of ours there have always been the same people living from generation to generation up till now, and they, by their courage and their virtues, have handed it on to us, a free country. They certainly deserve our praise. Even more so do our fathers deserve it. For to the inheritance they had received they added all the empire we have now, and it was not without blood and toil that they handed it down to us of the present generation. And then we ourselves, assembled here to-day, who are mostly in the prime of life, have, in most directions, added to the power of our empire and have organized our State in such a way that it is perfectly well able to look after itself both in peace and in war. /2

I have no wish to make a long speech on subjects familiar to you all: so I shall say nothing about the warlike deeds by which we acquired our power or the battles in which we or our fathers gallantly resisted our enemies, Greek or foreign. What I want to do is, in the first place, to discuss the spirit in which we faced our trials and also our constitution and the way of life which has made us great. After that I shall speak in praise of the dead, believing that this kind of speech is not inappropriate to the present occasion, and that this whole assembly, of citizens and foreigners, may listen to it with advantage. /3

Let me say that our system of government does not copy the institutions of our neighbours. It is more the case of our being a model to others, than of our imitating anyone else. Our constitution is called a democracy because power is in the hands not of a minority but of the whole people. When it is a question of settling private disputes, everyone is equal before the law; when it is a question of putting one person before another in positions of public responsibility, what counts is not membership of a particular class, but the actual ability which the man possesses. No one, so long as he has it in him to be of service to the state, is kept in political obscurity because of poverty. And, just as our political life is free and open, so is our day-to-day life in our relations with each other. We do not get into a state with our next-door neighbour if he enjoys himself in his own way, nor do we give him the kind of black looks which, though they do no real harm, still do hurt people's feelings. We are free and tolerant in our private lives; but in public affairs we keep to the law. This is because it commands our deep respect. /4

We give our obedience to those whom we put in positions of authority, and we obey the laws themselves, especially those which are for the protection of the oppressed, and those unwritten laws which it is an acknowledged shame to break. /5

And here is another point. When our work is over, we are in a position to enjoy all kinds of recreation for our spirits. There are various kinds of contests and sacrifices regularly throughout the year; in our own homes we find a beauty and a good taste which delight us every day and which drive away our cares. Then the greatness of our city brings it about that all the good things from all over the world flow in to us, so that to us it seems just as natural to enjoy foreign goods as our own local products. /6

Then there is a great difference between us and our opponents, in our attitude towards military security. Here are some examples: Our city is open to the world, and we have no periodical deportations in order to prevent people observing or finding out secrets which might be of military advantage to the enemy. This is because we rely, not on secret weapons, but on our own real courage and loyalty. There is a difference, too, in our educational systems. The Spartans, from their earliest boyhood, are submitted to the most laborious training in courage; we pass our lives without all these restrictions, and yet are just as ready to face the same dangers as they are. Here is a proof of this: When the Spartans invade our land, they do not come by themselves, but bring all their allies with them; whereas we, when we launch an attack abroad, do the job by ourselves, and, though fighting on foreign soil, do not often fail to defeat opponents who are fighting for their own hearths and homes. As a matter of fact none of our enemies has ever yet been confronted with our total strength, because we have to divide our attention between our navy and the many missions on which our troops are sent on land. Yet, if our enemies engage a detachment of our forces and defeat it, they give themselves credit for having thrown back our entire army; or, if they lose, they claim that they were beaten by us in full strength. There are certain advantages, I think, in our way of meeting danger voluntarily, with an easy mind, instead of with a laborious training, with natural rather than with state-induced courage. We do not have to spend our time practising to meet sufferings which are still in the future; and when they are actually upon us we show ourselves just as brave as these others who are always in strict training. This is one point in which, I think, our city deserves to be admired. There are also others: /7

Our love of what is beautiful does not lead to extravagance; our love of the things of the mind does not make us soft. We regard wealth as something to be properly used, rather than as something to boast about. As for poverty, no one need be ashamed to admit it: the real shame is in not taking practical measures to escape from it. Here each individual is interested not only in his own affairs but in the affairs of the state as well: even those who are mostly occupied with their own business are extremely well-informed on general politics—this is a peculiarity of ours: we do not say that a man who takes no interest in politics is a man who minds his own business; we say that he has no business here at all. We Athenians, in our own persons, take our decisions on policy or submit them to proper discussions: for we do not think that there is an incompatibility between words and deeds; the worst thing is to rush into action before the consequences have been properly debated. And this is another point where we differ from other people. We are capable at the same time of taking risks and of estimating them beforehand. Others are brave out of ignorance; and, when they stop to think, they begin to fear. But the man who can most truly be accounted brave is he who best knows the meaning of what is sweet in life and of what is terrible, and then goes out undeterred to meet what is to come. /8

Again, in questions of general good feeling there is a great contrast between us and most other people. We make friends by doing good to others, not by receiving good from them. This makes our friendship all the more reliable, since we want to keep alive the gratitude of those who are in our debt by showing continued goodwill to them: whereas the feelings of one who owes us something lack the same enthusiasm, since he knows that, when he repays our kindness, it will be more like paying back a debt than giving something spontaneously. We are unique in this. When we do kindnesses to others, we do not do them out of any calculations of profit or loss: we do

them without afterthought, relying on our free liberality. Taking everything together then, I declare that our city is an education to Greece, and I declare that in my opinion each single one of our citizens, in all the manifold aspects of life, is able to show himself the rightful lord and owner of his own person, and do this, moreover, with exceptional grace and exceptional versatility. And to show that this is no empty boasting for the present occasion, but real tangible fact, you have only to consider the power which our city possesses and which has been won by those very qualities which I have mentioned. Athens, alone of the states we know, comes to her testing time in a greatness that surpasses what was imagined of her. In her case, and in her case alone, no invading enemy is ashamed at being defeated, and no subject can complain of being governed by people unfit for their responsibilities. Mighty indeed are the marks and monuments of our empire which we have left. Future ages will wonder at us, as the present age wonders at us now. We do not need the praises of a Homer, or of anyone else whose words may delight us for the moment, but whose estimation of facts will fall short of what is really true. For our adventurous spirit has forced an entry into every sea and into every land; and everywhere we have left behind us everlasting memorials of good done to our friends or suffering inflicted on our enemies. /9

This, then, is the kind of city for which these men, who could not bear the thought of losing her, nobly fought and nobly died. It is only natural that every one of us who survive them should be willing to undergo hardships in her service. And it was for this reason that I have spoken at such length about our city, because I wanted to make it clear that for us there is more at stake than there is for others who lack our advantages; also I wanted my words of praise for the dead to be set in the bright light of evidence. And now the most important of these words has been spoken. I have sung the praises of our city; but it was the courage and gallantry of these men, and of people like them, which made her splendid. Nor would you find it true in the case of many of the Greeks, as it is true of them, that no words can do more than justice to their deeds. /10

To me it seems that the consummation which has overtaken these men shows us the meaning of manliness in its first revelation and in its final proof. Some of them, no doubt, had their faults; but what we ought to remember first is their gallant conduct against the enemy in defence of their native land. They have blotted out evil with good, and done more service to the commonwealth than they ever did harm in their private lives. No one of these men weakened because he wanted to go on enjoying his wealth: no one put off the awful day in the hope that he might live to escape his poverty and grow rich. More to be desired than such things, they chose to check the enemy's pride. This, to them, was a risk most glorious, and they accepted it, willing to strike down the enemy and relinquish everything else. As for success or failure, they left that in the doubtful hands of Hope, and when the reality of battle was before their faces, they put their trust in their own selves. In the fighting, they thought it more honourable to stand their ground and suffer death than to give in and save their lives. So they fled from the reproaches of men, abiding with life and limb the brunt of battle; and, in a small moment of time, the climax of their lives, a culmination of glory, not of fear, were swept away from us. /11

So and such they were, these men—worthy of their city. We who remain behind may hope to be spared their fate, but must resolve to keep the same daring spirit against the foe. It is not simply a question of estimating the advantages in theory. I could tell you a long story (and you know it as well as I do) about what is to be gained by beating the enemy back. What I would prefer is that you should fix your eyes every day on the greatness of Athens as she really is, and should fall in love with her. When you realize her greatness, then reflect that what made her great was men with a spirit of adventure, men who knew their duty, men who were ashamed to fall below a certain standard. If they ever failed in an enterprise, they made up their minds that at any rate the city should not find their courage lacking to her, and they gave to her the best contribution that they could. They gave her their lives, to her and to all of us, and for their own selves they won praises that never grow old, the most splendid of sepulchres—not the sepulchre in which their bodies are laid, but where their glory remains eternal in men's minds, always there on the right occasion to stir others to speech or to action. For famous men have the whole earth as their memorial: it is not only the inscriptions on their graves in their own country that mark them out; no, in foreign lands also, not in any visible form but in people's hearts, their memory abides and grows. It is for you to try to be like them. Make up your minds that happiness depends on being free, and freedom depends on being courageous. Let there be no relaxation in face of the perils of the war. The people who have most excuse for despising death are not the wretched

and unfortunate, who have no hope of doing well for themselves, but those who run the risk of a complete reversal in their lives, and who would feel the difference most intensely, if things went wrong for them. Any intelligent man would find a humiliation caused by his own slackness more painful to bear than death, when death comes to him unperceived, in battle, and in the confidence of his patriotism. /12

For these reasons I shall not commiserate with those parents of the dead, who are present here. Instead I shall try to comfort them. They are well aware that they have grown up in a world where there are many changes and chances. But this is good fortune —for men to end their lives with honour, as these have done, and for you honourably to lament them: their life was set to a measure where death and happiness went hand in hand. I know that it is difficult to convince you of this. When you see other people happy you will often be reminded of what used to make you happy too. One does not feel sad at not having some good thing which is outside one's experience: real grief is felt at the loss of something which one is used to. All the same, those of you who are of the right age must bear up and take comfort in the thought of having more children. In your own homes these new children will prevent you from brooding over those who are no more, and they will be a help to the city, too, both in filling the empty places, and in assuring her security. For it is impossible for a man to put forward fair and honest views about our affairs if he has not, like everyone else, children whose lives may be at stake. As for those of you who are now too old to have children, I would ask you to count as gain the greater part of your life, in which you have been happy, and remember that what remains is not long, and let your hearts be lifted up at the thought of the fair fame of the dead. One's sense of honour is the only thing that does not grow old, and the last pleasure, when one is worn out with age, is not, as the poet said, making money, but having the respect of one's fellow men. /13

As for those of you here who are sons or brothers of the dead, I can see a hard struggle in front of you. Everyone always speaks well of the dead, and, even if you rise to the greatest heights of heroism, it will be a hard thing for you to get the reputation of having come near, let alone equalled, their standard. When one is alive, one is always liable to the jealousy of one's competitors, but when one is out of the way, the honour one receives is sincere and unchallenged. /14

Perhaps I should say a word or two on the duties of women to those among you who are now widowed. I can say all I have to say in a short word of advice. Your great glory is not to be inferior to what God has made you, and the greatest glory of a woman is to be least talked about by men, whether they are praising you or criticizing you. I have now, as the law demanded, said what I had to say. For the time being our offerings to the dead have been made, and for the future their children will be supported at the public expense by the city, until they come of age. This is the crown and prize which she offers, both to the dead and to their children, for the ordeals which they have faced. Where the rewards of valour are the greatest, there you will find also the best and bravest spirits among the people. And now, when you have mourned for your dear ones, you must depart. /15

The speech

1. Epideictic or ceremonial speakers usually praise extensively those whom the ceremony honors, but Pericles spends little more than a paragraph for direct praise of the dead. What reasons might he have had for such a neglect of customary practice?

2. Among the standard topics of praise commonly used in ceremonial speeches are: uniqueness deserves praise, moderation deserves praise, bravery deserves praise, to do things for others rather than for one's self deserves praise. Does Pericles use these topics? Where? Does he use others like them?

3. Are there any sections of Pericles' address which, if adapted slightly, could be incorporated in a Memorial Day address in the United States? Which sections, if any?

4. Most funeral orators talk about the dead first and, after that, about the living. Pericles speaks of the living first and last and comments on the dead in a middle section of the speech. Suggest ways in which his specific purpose may have made this arrangement seem desirable.

5. Pericles cites relatively little concrete evidence to prove his statements. Can a speech be great without such evidence? Justify your answer.

6. Thucydides said of Pericles, "Because of his position, his intelligence, and his known integrity, [he] could respect the liberty of the people and at the same time hold them in check." Where, in this speech, do you find Pericles apparently trying to check popular feelings?

7. Do you think Pericles' final statement is an appropriate concluding remark for this occasion? Why or why not?

8. The famous scholar Richard C. Jebb described Pericles' speech as "tranquil, stately . . . but varied by occasional bursts having the character of lofty poetry." What sections of this speech illustrate each of these qualities?

9. The speeches Thucydides included in his history were intended to display the motives and beliefs of the important men of whom he wrote. What Periclean motives and beliefs has he illustrated by including this speech?

10. Among historic speeches Pericles' "Funeral Speech" has been especially admired by the English and the Americans. In the last three hundred years it has been repeatedly translated into English and has continued to be a favorite with successive generations. What are some of the qualities that may have given it this high popularity?

For further study and discussion

1. What are the most important traditions or practices we have inherited from the founders of this country (Puritans, framers of the Constitution, etc.)?

2. How far do we have equality before the law in the sense that Pericles claims it for Athens?

3. Do you think public office is open to all in the United States without regard for class or wealth?

4. How successful was the Athenian democracy as a form of government?

5. What degree of democracy do you think is practicable for a country as large as the United States?

6. Is it for the virtues Pericles enumerates that the modern world honors ancient Athens? If not, why did Athens influence the Western world so deeply?

7. Do you think the United States should become less concerned than it is about military security? Why or why not?

8. What social or spiritual uses have such public ceremonies as weddings, funerals, Independence Day observances, holy days, and the like?

9. Which comes closer to the Periclean ideal, Athens in Pericles' time or the United States at the present time? Why?

10. Woodrow Wilson said, "Loyalty means you ought to be ready to sacrifice every interest that you have and your life itself, if your country calls upon you to do so." Pericles would have agreed with Wilson. Do you? Why or why not?

Suggestions for further reading

W. R. Agard, *What Democracy Meant to the Greeks* (Madison, Wis., 1960)

Aristotle, *Politics* (New York, 1943)

Paul F. Lazarsfeld, *The People's Choice*, 2nd ed. (New York, 1948)

Bertrand Russell, *Human Society in Ethics and Politics* (New York, 1962)

Graham Wallas, *Human Nature in Politics* (Lincoln, Nebr., 1962)

T. H. White, *The Making of the President 1964* (New York, 1965)

The future of liberalism: a debate

The two discourses that follow were composed and printed as essays. They were addressed to readers of *The Reporter*, a magazine for relatively well educated people who tend to identify themselves as liberals in politics. Each author adapts to the predispositions of this audience. Each rightly assumes that he need not defend the merits of liberalism itself; each derives his supporting materials from the presumed common knowledge and assumptions of *The Reporter's* readers; each tries to adapt to and redirect his readers' somewhat nostalgic approval of the victorious liberalism of the New Deal in the 1930's. In these and other ways the essays of Arthur M. Schlesinger, Jr., and Max Ascoli resemble speeches and serve to illustrate how closely popular, adaptive, personal writing can approach the spoken word in substance and in manner.

These articles were first published in 1956, an election year. The national political conventions had not yet been held, but it was a foregone conclusion that President Eisenhower would be renominated by the Republicans. The chief contenders for the Democratic presidential nomination were Governor Adlai E. Stevenson of Illinois, the Democratic candidate in 1952, and Senator Estes Kefauver of Tennessee. The leadership in both parties, the political record of previous years, and the public opinion polls made it clear that the White House was almost certain to be occupied again by a confirmed "moderate." That Congress would operate under moderate leadership was equally plain. The astute political analyst, Samuel Lubell, had written in 1952 that a "conservative revolution" had taken place in the United States. To liberals this seemed all too true.

The political atmosphere of 1956, when these two essays were written, was in many respects like that of 1965. It caused liberals to reflect upon the role of liberalism in an affluent society. Schlesinger drew upon his historical studies and political experience to redefine the liberal creed, and his essay moved Ascoli, an equally ardent liberal, to reply. The exchange forms a debate-in-print on issues which remain moot a decade later.

Arthur M. Schlesinger, Jr., was born in Columbus, Ohio, in 1917. He is the son of the distinguished historian, Arthur M. Schlesinger, Sr., and has, himself, achieved distinction by his studies in American history. He received his A.B. from Harvard College in 1938 and was a member of the

Harvard Society of Fellows from 1939 to 1942. During World War II he served in several United States intelligence agencies, and in 1946 he joined the Harvard faculty, where he is now Professor of History. He has been a consultant to various departments of the federal government and was a member of Adlai E. Stevenson's campaign staff in the presidential election contests of 1952 and 1956 and a member of John F. Kennedy's staff in the presidential election contest of 1960. He was also a special assistant to President Kennedy from 1961 until the President's death.

Schlesinger has received numerous awards for historical research and writing, including the Pulitzer Prize for History in 1946. *The Age of Jackson* and *The Coming of the New Deal* are probably his best known historical works.

Max Ascoli was born in Ferrara, Italy in 1898. He attended the University of Ferrara where he received his LL.D. in 1920. In 1928 he was awarded his Ph.D. by the University of Rome. After serving as a professor of jurisprudence in Italian universities, he came to the United States in 1931 and was naturalized in 1939.

Since 1933 Ascoli has been a member of the Graduate Faculty of the New School for Social Research in New York City and in 1940 and 1941 served as Dean of that Faculty. He became editor and publisher of *The Reporter* in 1949 and has since continued in these positions. Ascoli is a recognized scholar in political theory as well as a teacher and journalist.

The challenge of abundance
ARTHUR M. SCHLESINGER, JR.

Rarely have the experts differed so sharply about the nature of the American political mood as they do today. I suppose that of living Americans the two men who have shown themselves the most penetrating diagnosticians of the nation's political state of mind have been Harry S. Truman and Samuel Lubell. President Truman's victory over fantastic odds in 1948 establishes him as the most astute professional in the politics of this generation. Mr. Lubell's *Future of American Politics*, published in 1952, remains the most illuminating analysis of the movements of political sentiment in this country written in recent years. Yet President Truman and Mr. Lubell are today in flat disagreement in their reading of the present temper of the country. /1

Arthur M. Schlesinger, Jr., "The Challenge of Abundance," *The Reporter*, Vol. 14, May 3, 1956, pp. 8-11. Copyright © 1956 by The Reporter Magazine Company. By permission of the author.

As Mr. Lubell sees it, "The people are in a conservative mood. They don't want 'more' so much as they would like to keep things as they are. Nobody wants war; nobody wants a depression. Few people even want reform. They are content to hold things as they are." Mr. Truman, on the other hand, evidently feels that the people are fed to the point of exasperation with government of the rich, by the rich, for the rich, and that they want more and better New Deals and Fair Deals* in the interests of the worker, the farmer, and the small businessman. /2

Now undoubtedly much of what both Mr. Lubell and Mr. Truman contend is true. There are millions of people in this country who are satisfied with things as they are and see no need for change. And there are millions who are dissatisfied with things as they are and feel that government can do much more to equalize opportunities and benefits. Both groups have existed for a long time—the Republican vote has not fallen under 15 million or the Democratic under 20 million in the last generation—and there is no reason to assume that either has substantially diminished. What is important rather are the 20 or 25 million voters in the middle. How do they feel? Are they perfectly happy with society as it is? Or do their eyes light up and their hearts beat faster when they hear the slogans and appeals of the New Deal and Fair Deal? /3

One is compelled to conclude that for this middle group neither the analysis of Mr. Lubell nor that of President Truman is wholly adequate. It is obvious that these people, most of whom live in tolerable economic circumstances and are not particularly mad at anybody, do not respond very strongly to the rhetoric of the liberalism of the 1930's. But it would seem equally obvious that they are by no means in a condition of unlimited spiritual equability. If there is anything plain about our middle-class society today, it is the evidence on every hand of widespread internal anxiety and discontent. Billy Graham and Senator McCarthy have both been beneficiaries of this tormenting uncertainty;** the so-called religious revival is a significant manifestation of inner unrest; and, indeed, the role of President Eisenhower as a national father image only emphasizes the extent to which many Americans have become today passionate seekers after some form of spiritual reassurance. /4

It thus seems hard to deny that widespread discontent of some kind exists. It seems equally hard to assert that the liberalism of the 1930's has the answer to this discontent. Plainly the problem for the liberalism of the 1950's is to identify the sources of discontent and to develop a program and a philosophy capable of meeting the challenge of a new era. /5

The old brand

The liberalism of this generation was born in the depression. It came of age at a time when social thought was urgently directed toward problems of unemployment, poverty, and want. Liberals were concerned with providing food for the hungry, shelter for the homeless, work for the jobless. The characteristic issues were those involved in refueling the economic machine, raising mass living standards, setting minimum wages, pegging farm prices, refinancing mortgages, vindicating collective bargaining, establishing systems of old-age insurance and social security. The liberals of the 1930's aspired to create a new society characterized by full employment, rising national income, and expanding economic opportunity. /6

Let me call this for a moment "quantitative liberalism." I mean by this that it was a liberalism that thought primarily—and necessarily—in quantitative terms. It had to deal with immediate problems of subsistence and survival. And it had another characteristic too. In dealing with these problems, it had to face the fierce resistance of the business community of the nation—an experience that stamped this liberalism with the conviction that the "special interests" were determined to block or sabotage every advance toward a more decent social order. /7

This liberalism was, in the main, a brilliant success. It overhauled the American economy, equipped it with a set of built-in safety devices and stabilizers, rolled back poverty, instituted a fair measure of social and economic security, and tamed and educated the business community. It laid the foundations for a new age in America. /8

But that new age is now largely upon us. And, ironically, it is the very success of the older liberalism that is the essential cause of its present irrelevance. For the experience of the 1930's gave it the assumption that poverty and reaction were the essential sources of social discontent—an assumption that is in part responsible for the bafflement of many liberals today, when both poverty and reaction have receded from the forefront of our national life. Suppose that the New Dealers of 1936 could have envisaged America twenty years later—a nation with nearly sixty-three million men and women at work, a gross nation-

---

* The Truman Administration called its reform program the Fair Deal. (*Editor's note*)

** The reference is to Reverend William (Billy) Franklin Graham's evangelistic campaigns in the United States and abroad and to Senator Joseph R. McCarthy's charges that large numbers of Communists had infiltrated governmental services. (*Editor's note*) al product of 387 billion a year, business progressive and enlightened, trade unions solid and respectable, minimum wages, maximum hours, and farm-price supports written into the law of the land. Transported into so rich and overflowing a society, they might well have supposed that the "more abundant life" had been at last achieved. If people had jobs, and unions, and enough to eat, and prospects for security in case of unemployment or old age—and if all this was accepted by the business community—what more could anyone ask? The dream of plenty seemed to promise a solution for all the problems of life. /9

Today we dwell in the economy of abundance—and our spiritual malaise seems greater than ever before. As a nation, the richer we grow, the more tense, insecure, and unhappy we seem to become. Yet too much of our liberal thought is still mired in the issues, the attitudes, and the rallying cries of the 1930's. It is as if Franklin Roosevelt and his associates, instead of inventing a New Deal of their own, had insisted on repeating the incantations of Woodrow Wilson's New Freedom and Theodore Roosevelt's New Nationalism.* Liberals today must be as alert in identifying the problems of the 1950's as the New Dealers, who were courageous and uninhibited thinkers, were alert in identifying the problems of the 1930's. /10

New strategies for new wars

What is required today is a new liberalism, addressed to the miseries of an age of abundance. I would not mean to suggest by this for a moment that the job of "quantitative liberalism" is finished. There are unhappily still broad areas of poverty in our land. No American can be complacent when approximately four million American families are trying to make ends meet on incomes of less than $2,000 a year. The depressed areas in states like Massachusetts and West Virginia** now threaten to become stagnant industrial slums. There is no excuse for the continued instability in farm income; and, even worse, there remain ugly splotches of grinding rural poverty where farm families live outside the price-support system. Yet, while there is still much to be done in completing the battle against poverty, the central problems of our time are no longer problems of want and priva-

tion; and the central sources of discontent are no longer, as they were in the 1930's, economic in character. /11

Liberalism in an age of abundance must begin shifting its emphasis. Instead of the quantitative liberalism of the 1930's, rightly dedicated to the struggle to secure the economic basis of life, we need now a "qualitative liberalism" dedicated to bettering the quality of people's lives and opportunities. Instead of talking as if the necessities of living—a job, a square meal, a suit of clothes, and a roof—were still at stake, we should be able to count that fight won and move on to the more subtle and complicated problem of fighting for individual dignity, identity, and fulfillment in a mass society. The new liberalism implies no repudiation of the old; rather it respects, accepts, and absorbs the triumphs of the New and Fair Deals, regards them as the basis for a new age of social progress, and seeks to move beyond them toward new goals of national development. Nor, should I add, does the distinction between "quantitative" and "qualitative" mean that one form of liberalism requires taxation and spending while the other is cheap and painless. Obviously progress in the "qualitative" area will require government initiative almost as much as the other. Yet a significant difference remains between the two in mood and approach. /12

The issues of 1956 are no longer the issues of 1933—the issues that made the difference between starvation and survival. Depression is dead as an issue, and will remain so until another depression revives it. The question whether trade unions should exist, whether business should be regulated, whether social security should be established—these are no longer issues. Even bigness in business and reaction in the business community, if issues now, take a new form and require a new attack. All these were part of the crisis of the 1930's. Thanks to the liberalism of the 1930's we have surmounted that crisis. /13

The issues of 1956 are those which make the difference between defeat and opportunity, between frustration and fulfillment, in the everyday lives of average persons. They have to do with education, with medical care, with more equal opportunities for minority groups, with the better planning of our cities and our suburbs, with slum clearance and decent housing, with the improvement of life for the sick and the aged, with the freedoms of speech, expression, and conscience, with the bettering of our mass media and the elevation of our popular culture—in short, with the *quality* of civilization to which our nation aspires in an age of ever-increasing abundance and leisure. /14

---

*"The New Freedom" was a slogan Wilson used in the campaign of 1912. In 1913 he published a book by this title, and the phrase became the "tag" for the reforms of his first administration. Theodore Roosevelt's tag for his administrations was the "Square Deal," but others sometimes referred to his program as the "New Nationalism." (Editor's note)

**Some industries had moved from Massachusetts to Southern states. West Virginia epitomized the plight of Appalachia, toward whose problems President Johnson addressed his "War on Poverty" in 1964-1965. (Editor's note)

But issues are not enough. There is need too for a new spirit. The liberal program of the 1930's had necessarily to be presented in an atmosphere charged with class tension. The business community of the day was united and ruthless in its opposition to programs of liberal reform—an opposition whose imbecility is demonstrated by the fact that even the business community now back in power has not seriously tried to repeal a single basic New Deal measure. Nor did business behavior in the 1930's constitute a novelty in American history. The dislike of the "economic royalists" in Franklin Roosevelt's day corresponded to Theodore Roosevelt's detestation of the "malefactors of great wealth," to the Populist hatred of the trusts and the millionaires, and to Andrew Jackson's denunciations of "the rich and powerful." Nothing was more traditionally American about the New Deal than its conviction that the business community could not be trusted with undue power. /15

Reformed 'malefactors'

But the business community assumes a more amiable appearance in this age of prosperity. Businessmen plainly have a broader recognition of their social responsibilities than they had twenty-five years ago; and some liberals even think they see in the business world the beginnings of a permanent business conscience. Of course, much the same things were being said about business—and business was saying exactly the same things about itself—at the height of the prosperity of the 1920's. We will know the extent of the change of heart only if economic adversity strikes again. Then we will see whether the business "conscience" will not be, as it was in 1929, the first thing jettisoned by businessmen struggling to keep their heads above water. /16

Still, for the moment, the old anti-business exhortations do not apply in the same way as they did in the 1930's. Where the older liberalism inveighed against business domination per se, the new liberalism must make a subtler point—that is, that government by a single interest is bad, whatever the nature of the interest. And, where the older liberalism rebelled against business rule in the name of the manifestly abused sections of society, the new liberalism can hardly hope to persuade people who do not feel themselves mistreated that they are, in fact, the slaves of an economic tyranny. What the new liberalism must do is again something that is more subtle and perhaps more edifying: It must make the point that our country can grow only if we develop a positive philosophy of the public interest to be asserted against the parochial interests of any special group. /17

It is the rehabilitation of a sense of the public interest that will provide the moral impetus for the new liberalism's legislative program. Here is a nation richer than ever before, and getting even richer every moment, and yet devoting a *decreasing* share of its wealth to the public welfare. Our gross national product rises: our shops overflow with gadgets and gimmicks; consumer goods of ever-increasing ingenuity and luxuriance pour out of our ears. But our schools become more crowded and dilapidated, our teachers more weary and underpaid, our playgrounds more crowded, our cities dirtier, our roads more teeming and filthy, our national parks more unkempt, our law enforcement more overworked and inadequate. And we wonder why, for example, we have a growing problem of juvenile delinquency! /18

While we let the production of consumer goods for the sake of profit achieve a sort of moral priority in our culture, our Federal government is permitted to spend an average of $5 million a year since the war for slum clearance. While private wealth heaps up in our shops and homes, we refuse to undertake adequate programs to improve our schools, our hospitals, our cities, our natural resources, our public domain. While our business leaders, whose first duty is to make money for themselves, demand popular reverence as moral symbols and exemplars, those who serve us all—our public administrators, teachers, foresters, welfare officers, policemen, firemen (all, indeed, except our security officers)—are treated with condescension, when not with contempt. /19

The problem of rehabilitating the public sector of our national life is not financial. If our economic growth continues, and if we maintain taxes at current levels, we will have sizable funds available for public purposes. Each new $10 billion of national income should produce about $3 billion of new revenue. The issue is whether these gains of economic progress should be invested in the welfare of a few or in the general welfare. The Eisenhower Administration last year chose the welfare of the few, which is why the rich received tax reductions when the nation should have received schools, hospitals, and roads.* /20

So long as we refuse to assert the general welfare against the false notion that the unlimited pursuit of profit will guarantee the general welfare, we can expect that, while we privately grow richer, our nation will grow in proportion poorer. While we overstuff

---

* In 1955 the Eisenhower Administration refused to approve a general tax reduction for individuals or corporations but did recommend lower corporate taxes on income from foreign sources. It is possible, however, that the reference is to the Internal Revenue Act of 1954, a controversial feature of which was the exemption of the first fifty dollars of dividend income from taxation. (*Editor's note*)

ourselves as individuals, we will let the national plant run down. And it is the national plant—health, education, welfare, resources—on which our future so largely depends. /21

How to revive the conception of the general welfare, a conception sufficiently dear to the Founding Fathers that they inscribed it indelibly in the preamble to the Constitution? One thing is clear: that single-interest government is not likely to be the instrument of that revival. Single-interest government inevitably fosters that insidious optical illusion which leads sincere men to mistake their own for the public interest and to contend that what is good for General Motors is necessarily good for the country.* A passion for the *general* welfare is far more likely to emerge from a government that represents the diverse interests of the American community—whose decisions are made not only by representatives of business but by representatives of farmers, workers, professional men, and even, if I may use the word, of intellectuals. /22

The new challenge

Many liberals will agree that there are plenty of things to be done, but will add that we must have a depression before the people will ever again give government a license for reform. But this suggestion is surely one more example of the extent to which liberal thought has become frozen in the mold of the 1930's. Richard Hofstadter has recently developed a distinction between "interest politics"—the clash of material aims and needs among competing blocs— and "status politics"—the clashes arising from status aspirations and discontents. As periods of depression breed interest politics, so periods of prosperity breed status politics; but the dynamics of status politics can lead to reform as well as reaction. Indeed, until the New Deal, nearly every great burst of progressive enthusiasm in American history came in a time of relative prosperity—the age of Jefferson, of Jackson, of the Progressives at the turn of the century. It is the sheerest defeatism to suppose that depression must be the prerequisite to reform. /23

What liberalism requires is a program sharply focused to meet the qualitative discontents of the present age. It requires a spirit that aims not to indict any group in the community as a special obstacle to change but rather to rally men of good will in all groups behind programs designed to improve life in America for all Americans—a spirit that seeks, in other words, not to divide the country and aggravate its tensions, but to unite it around a revitalized sense of the public interest. /24

Above all it needs to commit itself to bringing about a new birth of freedom. In the first instance, this means equal rights for minorities. The great creative proposal of the Truman Administration in the domestic field was the civil-rights program of 1948 (though in time, perhaps, the Brannan farm plan and the Ewing health-insurance plan will receive new recognition).* President Truman perceived that if the coalition forged by depression was breaking up, a new coalition might be brought into being by abundance—a coalition founded not on a common fear of poverty but on a common desire for opportunity Assurance of equality of opportunity not only for Negroes but for all nationality groups must be an essential ingredient of the new liberalism. /25

And equally important is the issue of civil liberties. Now that the nonsense of the age of McCarthy has begun to clear away, there is a superb opportunity for men of conviction to consolidate the national sense of shame and to restore the Bill of Rights to its central position in our theory of society. The spectacle of the most powerful nation on earth frightening itself to death over Communists in its midst is as disgraceful as the spectacle of the richest country on earth pretending it cannot afford adequate systems of education, medical care, and housing. The United States in the last three years has succeeded in presenting both spectacles to a dismayed world. /26

I have said nothing about foreign affairs. In the immediate future, of course, the issues of peace and war far overshadow problems of justice and polity at home. But it can be said that a truly creative and progressive American foreign policy can only come from a truly creative and progressive America. In a free state, foreign policy can rarely be more effective than the character of the nation that stands behind it. No magic of psychological warfare is likely to persuade the rest of the world that we are different from what we are. /27

We will thus probably require a reawakening of the liberal conscience and the liberal will at home before we can offer positive and compelling alternatives to the world. We cannot convincingly champion freedom before the world so long as we kick freedom

---

* The allusion is to a statement made by Charles Erwin Wilson, Secretary of Defense, 1953-1957, and former President of General Motors. He had observed that he believed what was good for the country was good for General Motors and vice versa. This corruption of his statement quickly became a catch phrase among his critics. (*Editor's note*)

* Charles F. Brannan, Secretary of Agriculture, 1948-1953, recommended a controversial two-price farm commodity support program; Oscar R. Ewing, Federal Security Agency Administrator, 1947-1952, was an ardent advocate of federal health insurance legislation. (*Editor's note*)

around at home. We cannot convincingly champion equality abroad so long as we practice segregation at home. We cannot convincingly champion opportunity abroad when too many of our own people linger at home in cultural mediocrity and economic want. As we renew a fighting faith against the inequities of our own society, we will generate an enthusiasm that will reverberate across the world—as the New Deal made Franklin Roosevelt a world figure long before Hitler began his war. Nothing would go farther to restore world confidence in American leadership than a display of progressive conviction in our own society. /28

In its fundamentals, the liberal tradition in this nation is as old as the Republic itself. This tradition has been responsible for nearly all the acts of government that have contributed to the growth of freedom and opportunity in America. And its continuing vitality in the days since Jefferson and Jackson has been due to its perennial capacity to define new problems and acknowledge new challenges. /29

The liberalism of this generation has been for some years in the travail of redefinition. It is pointless, as some writers have rather self-righteously done, to dismiss contemporary liberalism as sterile and bankrupt because it hasn't come up with all the new answers overnight. Obviously the process of rethinking takes time, and it cannot be completed until the burden of responsibility gives thought the final instinct for reality. Liberalism seemed sterile and bankrupt in the 1920's, and even in the early years of the depression; but in the end it flowered in the New Deal. /30

Of course it is currently fashionable, among both liberals and conservatives, to patronize the New Deal. Still, if the liberals of our time can do half as well in meeting the problems of this age, they should be more than satisfied. But liberals will never meet the challenge of the 1950's until they realize that it is something essentially different from the challenge of the 1930's. /31

The scarcity of ideas

MAX ASCOLI

Life would be much easier for American liberals these days if Arthur Schlesinger's diagnosis of what's

Max Ascoli, "The Scarcity of Ideas," The Reporter, Vol. 14, May 3, 1956, pp. 12-16. Copyright © 1956 by The Reporter Magazine Company. By permission of the author.

wrong with American liberalism were as sound as it is plausible. /1

There is a comfortable, cozy quality in his conception of liberalism. His assumptions, as I understand them, have been with us for so long that they have acquired an aura of near-truth. They can be listed: /2

1. The major obstacle to general welfare and democratic progress is the Business System, which fosters the selfish interests of the few unless, bridled by government, it is made to work in the interests of the many. /3

2. The people best suited to be in charge of bridling, general welfare, improvement, and betterment at large are the liberals. /4

3. The Federal government works in the interests of society as a whole—if enough liberals hold positions of power in it. /5

4. The progressive and bettering job can best be done by government taxing and government spending. /6

There are other assumptions that for a long time have been the stock in trade of American liberalism —first of all the one that in the indivisible interest of nation, government, and individual, progress is ultimately inevitable. But lately the optimistic progressivism of many a liberal has been darkened by some reading of Reinhold Niebuhr. Moreover, the New Deal has made such pragmatists of all liberals that they shun adherence to any general theory—including pragmatism. They tend to shy away from problems that do not lend themselves to quick solutions. This is one reason why they prefer to stick to strictly domestic causes and remedies of our nation's ailments, as Schlesinger shows. /7

There are some other people—liberals and not-so-liberals—who are inclined to think that the widespread restlessness and spiritual malaise of our days is influenced and may even be caused by the precarious state of world affairs. But, if I understand Schlesinger correctly, the issue of war and peace which so overshadows all others "in the immediate future" should not—even in the present—distract us from curing our political and spiritual malaise through increased government spending. It would seem that McCarthy's rise to fame and Billy Graham's immense popularity were determined by inadequate housing projects and other inconveniences that qualitative liberalism can eliminate. /8

Leviathan on parole

Since the Republicans came to power, assumption No. 1 has been temporarily qualified, for this businessmen's Administration,* aside from taking some liberties with natural resources and tinkering with agricultural price supports, has failed to wreck the reforms of the New Deal. Schlesinger has put the Business System on probation: It all depends on how it behaves if and when a depression comes. At present, however, businessmen are in control of the government, in violation of assumptions Nos. 2, 3, and 4. A few liberals say that the greedy old Leviathan is acquiring something like a human soul. But Schlesinger keeps his fingers crossed. /9

The curious thing about this jaundiced view, widespread among American liberals, is that it considers the Business System both irredeemable and indestructible. The way of all business is to be profit-hungry in the interest of the selfish few. As in the Calvinistic concept of human destiny, there is no escape from this original sin. The only thing we can do is to be aware of it and, at times, manage to check it by keeping liberals in positions of governmental power. Our liberals recoil from any dream of ultimate redemption in a socialist heaven or purgatory. /10

This is why they deeply resent—and right they are—being accused of crypto- or creeping socialism. They have no socialist blueprint on hand, no timetable for the verification of a predetermined pattern of history. In fact, it is doubtful that they have much of a concept of history at all. Some may have flirted vaguely with socialist theories in their youth, just as some at present—particularly those who have had an opportunity to become familiar with Big Business—give serious evidence of crypto- or creeping capitalism. /11

By and large, however, all through depression and prosperity, New and Fair Deal, there has been little change in the liberal attitude toward the Business System. It is still considered, actually and potentially, the major obstacle to general welfare. It is to be the object of constant watching and constant nagging. But since it is to stay with us forever, it is to be looked at with gentle, sad, routinized hatred. /12

Private governments

If Schlesinger's article is to some degree representative—as I think it is—the liberal world is an enviably simple one. There is the Business System, there is the individual, and there is the government, which, whenever managed or influenced by liberals, can somehow redress the inequities of the Business System toward the individual. The other large-scale organizations catering to the masses' needs are in general objects either of sympathy or of scant attention. The private, nongovernmental entities that purport to represent the interests of the individual are seldom accused, as business is, of being self-perpetuating and selfish. This is the case with political machines—with the possible exception of Republican ones—as it is with interstate authorities. Other instances are Federally established authorities for power development and flood control of the TVA type. But the most cherished instance is labor. To the American liberal, labor is a prize exhibit of what is public-spirited, innately democratic, and good. /13

In this liberal mythology, labor had a prominent role even before the New Deal actually succeeded in fostering the enrollment of millions of workers into the trade unions. This was one of the major advances of Schlesinger's "quantitative liberalism," and led to the improvement of the workers' lot. But at present, at the time when "qualitative liberalism" should get started, Big Labor controls such a huge hunk of the workers' rights, welfare, and destiny that it may be properly called private government—obviously as fallible and as exposed to the temptations of power as that other private government which goes by the name of Big Business. /14

Yet there is not much evidence that American liberalism is ready or even disposed to tackle the intricacies of private government. There are vast areas of national life where new forms of power have entrenched themselves, unrestrained or inadequately restrained either by the Federal government or by the states. This applies eminently to Big Business, of course, but also to Big Labor, to the Federal and interstate authorities, and to many other public and private agencies, all of which exert sovereign influences on the citizen's life. /15

A man's job, the security of his job, the welfare funds that are to take care of his old age and sickness, his hope of getting adequate lodging, the condition of his neighborhood—all these crucial matters are dependent on decisions made by holders of power who can be forced only with difficulty to give an accounting of their stewardships. Actually, the multiplicity of the centers of power, public and private, territorial or functional, formal or informal, vertical or horizontal, has become so complex and unruly that it is hard to define the few zones where representative democracy still works according to the established principles of limited and responsible authority. Moreover, we have entirely new forms of power that operate with frightening effectiveness not at representing but at molding the people's opinions and habits. /16

---

* The number of businessmen whom President Eisenhower appointed to the cabinet and other posts in 1953 was a subject of complaint among political liberals. (*Editor's note*)

Feudalism is the proper name for the system, or lack of system, that rules us. Only a very few liberals —Adolf Berle* outstanding among them—are aware of such a state of affairs. Schlesinger too feels something is wrong, but his answer is that more Federal spending is needed, more taxes—and a greater expansion of the Federal bureaucracy. /17

Most of our liberals do not seem to worry about the dangers of an ever-expanding bureaucracy—particularly if it is the one of Big Government. Yet occasionally, some unusually farsighted liberal, like Franklin Roosevelt, has acknowledged how risky it is to expand the system of Federal controls, since the controlling or regulatory agencies may fall into the hands of people who can hardly be called liberals. Indeed, this has been the experience over and over again, following the ebb of a progressive or reforming wave. Our Business System would never have become so resilient and articulate had it not been for the regulatory agencies, which were first established to harness it. Invariably, with the coming to power of a conservative Administration, Big Business has drawn strength from its control of the harnessing equipment. /18

But there is no sign that an allergy toward Big Government has developed among our liberals, if for no other reason than that they were waiting for the next political upheaval that may give them a chance to gain control of Big Government and make it bigger. Usually such a chance comes after a depression. But now Schlesinger tells us that there is no reason why the liberals' reforming skill should be practiced on the government only in the wake of a depression. True, he admits, the liberals haven't done much thinking lately, but, he adds, under the burden of responsibility they will surely think. /19

What price abundance?

The need for sustained, hard thought about how our freedoms can be preserved and invigorated could not be more pressing—a need that is in direct relation to the well-being that an unprecedentedly large number of citizens enjoy and to the multitudinous complexity of the institutions that service them. Each one of these service institutions exacts a price that can hardly be measured in terms of the dollars and cents it charges; each demands allegiance on the part of the citizens. /20

What is, for instance, the real price we pay for the entertainment or the diversions provided at nominal cost or at no cost by the media of mass communica-

tion? Are our lives enriched or desiccated by them? What do we actually pay for the gadgets we think we buy at bargain prices—all these things which according to Schlesinger "pour out of our ears"—even when the payment is cash on the barrelhead? What is the cost of goods we acquire with token payments for token ownership? /21

It is the function of government—or at least it should be—to see to it that prices be fair and the ultimate cost to the community not exorbitant. This, however, because of the extraordinary degree to which our economy is based on confidence, and because of the never-ending commitments and relationships the citizens get into or are taken in—this is becoming a function with which government can scarcely keep up. /22

Yet lest we become driven by forces over which we have no measure of control, some order must be made out of this chaos. The powers that rule us and weigh on us—this increasingly cumbersome and increasingly secret government in which all the bureaucracies of government, of business, of labor, of religion, of education, of philanthropy, of entertainment, et cetera, combine to increase their hold on us —must be made limited, representative, and responsible lest our freedom turn out to be a rather ghostly thing. Our individual freedom is frittered away or mortgaged out at such a remorseless pace that at times the symbolic celebration of it in an election booth seems as incongruous as the re-enactment of a medieval pageant. /23

Liberals, incidentally, are supposed to have something to do with freedom. They are not necessarily the seasonal journeymen of Big Government, and liberalism is not supposed to mean the dispensation of government liberalities. Liberals are supposed to be at work whenever and wherever our freedoms are stunted. /24

There can be no more dangerous illusion for liberals than the continued adherence to the notion that the major protagonists of the human comedy are the individual and the government—the official political government which seems to have no other way of establishing its authority over its too many competitors than by getting bigger. Gone are the days when government was the only Leviathan standing in front of the individual, and gone also are the days when it made any remote sense to think that if good men were in control of this one big Leviathan, then there would be no further obstacle to ever-increasing prosperity and freedom. /25

The agenda for American liberalism is as vast as it is compelling. American liberalism must acquire a

---

*See his **The 20th Century Capitalist Revolution**. (Editor's note)

far greater sophistication toward power and learn how not to hate and not to love it. The liberals' antibusiness demonology is about as outdated as their —alas—frequently platonic love of government. /26

On the agenda of American liberalism a major item should be the delimitation of the various powers and governments now on the loose. We cannot rely optimistically on the hope that they will automatically balance and contain each other. Neither can we assume that the checking, containing job can be the monopoly of the Federal government. Among other reasons, some of these powers—eminently those which provide us with food for our tables and gas for our cars—are international or supranational in scope. /27

If liberty is to survive, the new feudalism which rules us must be replaced by a federal system, in which the economic and occupational powers—like those of business and labor—may become interlocked with the old ones of a political and geographic nature. Practices of diplomacy and administration must be developed that will allow each one of these governments, old and new, to work with responsible independence in its own and the commonwealth's interests. /28

In the sphere of old-fashioned or political government itself there are vast zones that ought to be resettled. Our huge metropolitan areas, for instance, are at the same time ungoverned and subjected to overlapping, wasteful governments. Our regions are not any longer just geographical names but have acquired a powerful economic reality; yet there is no evidence that anything is in the making that can be called regional government, with its own specific, limited authority. Our state governments collect every year more than fifteen billion dollars; yet they manage to operate so quietly that, to all intents and purposes, they have become an instance of semi-secret government. /29

The crowded center

Any list of "oughts" and "musts," of reforms and revaluations that are needed, indeed imperative, is bound to be dismissed as entirely theoretical and impractical—egghead stuff. Everybody wants to be a realist these days, including the eggheads, who don't want to have their utterances answered by silence or by yawns. /30

The few items on the liberal agenda that I have hinted at have all to do with governments, public and private. But it will be said there is no use defining the relationship all these governments have among themselves and the impact they exert togeth-

er on the citizens, since by and large the whole thing works spectacularly well. Our only trouble is abundance. /31

Why should anybody complain that this wondrous system of government we have is not only unwritten and informal but also unknown to those who operate it? What of it? Aren't we prosperous? Isn't the large majority of our people now increasingly conservative and firmly unwilling to have the existing order of things tinkered with by reforms? "Qualitative liberalism" will give not merely to a majority but to the whole citizenry the chance to be conservative. After that, I imagine, we shall sit down contentedly and contemplate the steady growth of our fat. /32

Yet there are still some liberals like myself who think that the fair or fairer distribution of well-being among the citizens should be one but by no means the major concern of liberals. For I believe it is the function of liberals—indeed, it is what entitles them to that name—to keep constant watch over all the agencies that are supposed to serve the individual and, if need be, to overhaul them, seeing to it that the individual is equally provided with the opportunity to play a role in the societies he belongs to and with the right to be left alone by them. /33

But, again, it is said we never had it so good, no other nation on earth ever had it so good. American liberals, so it seems, find no reason to object that our country is ruled by an oligarchy of feudal barons —the barons of government, of politics, of industry, of labor, of philanthropy, and so on. After all, the roster of the leading barons can be read on the letterhead of any nation-wide organization established to further any not-too-controversial, do-goodish cause. Moreover, quite a few of these barons had a liberal future in their pasts. /34

The barons, and the whole nation behind them, are magnificently united in the middle of the road, so huddled around the vital or dead center that, as we can see these days, it takes a considerable effort of partisan public relations to find enough differences between liberal conservatives and conservative liberals to provide the nation with a little electoral excitement and fun. /35

Schlesinger, a practical man, fully acknowledges the conservative, nonradical mood of the country. He agrees with the stated and restated Lubell diagnosis, but he believes that if the Truman technique of 1948 is used again, American conservatism can be brought—for keeps—under liberal management. He brings the spiritual element into the picture for reasons still unclear to me—unless he too is swayed by that revival of all words having to do with the spirit or with religion which is so masterfully managed by our President and Secretary of State.* /36

Schlesinger's article could serve as a succinct program for any Presidential candidate, were it not that his two key words, "qualitative" and "quantitative," are somewhat over the people's heads. Or maybe these two words can be used with equal effectiveness the other way around, since, if I understand Schlesinger correctly, he wants more quantity of the New-Fair Deal quality distributed to more people. /37

Back to Fortress America

Be that as it may, what really stirred me to pick a quarrel with Schlesinger was the offhand way in which he brushed off the impact of international affairs on the fortunes, well-being, and freedom of our country. Maybe what's new and surprising is not the new phase of liberalism he advocates but the rebirth of a virtuous "I-am-unholier-than-thou" isolationism. The idea that before getting messed up in other people's business, we ought to put our own house in order and realize in all its fullness the American dream is an old boiler plate of liberal rhetoric. It has come back into circulation lately, but at no time, because of the conditions prevailing at home and abroad, has it been so dangerous and foolish. /38

In Schlesinger's argument, as I see it, "the issues of peace and war" loom large on the horizon "in the immediate future," but this infatuation should be brought to an early end. According to him, we need qualitative liberalism at home "before" propounding democracy or liberalism abroad. That "before" must mean that Khrushchev and Bulganin** should be invited to take a rest and see to it that Communism is well implanted in their country before propagating it abroad. In fact, for those inclined to think this way, the time should be ripe: If the issue is just one of war and peace, the chances of war seem to have dwindled, while peace is still far off. Why shouldn't we take advantage of such a hiatus to leave wretchedly ungrateful allies to their destiny, and price ourselves out of the world market? /39

Schlesinger is not only skeptical about the role of international affairs in our nation's life now; he makes his skepticism retroactive. A historian of Roosevelt and of the New Deal, he seems to forget that in 1939 there were still ten million unemployed in our labor market. It is quite true, as he puts it, that in 1936 no New Dealer could possibly have envisaged the rich and overflowing society of today. For how could anyone at that time have imagined that our full employment and abundance would be obtained as a by-product of the effort to counteract two extraneous agents—first Adolf Hitler, then Joseph Stalin? /40

The infatuation with peace and war still seems to play some role in keeping our economy in high gear. In this year 1956, of each dollar spent by the government sixty-one cents go to check Communism. Since the end of the war, more than $363 billion has gone for our own and our Allies' protection. Of this tidy sum, I suppose more than a trickle has helped to keep business humming at home. /41

It is rather peculiar to see how Schlesinger is now falling into line with those who ignore the part military expenditure has been playing in energizing the nation's economy. Perhaps isolationism, like middle-of-the-roadism, has spread throughout our prosperous, predominantly middle-class nation. Perhaps isolationism had been only temporarily knocked out by the impact of this national emergency of unlimited duration, just as happens with some of the most evil viruses under the onslaught of antibiotics. /42.

Our system of alliances is in danger of falling apart. But here comes the new twist: Why not accept this trend as irreversible and make the best of it? Even for our defense, it is said, the need for foreign bases has become more than questionable, for we now have intercontinental bombers and soon we shall have intercontinental missiles. David Lawrence in his *U. S. News & World Report* never neglects a chance to show how hopeless is our situation abroad and how mischievous are the Allied leaders. The justifications for the drive back to Fortress America* are many, according to the nature of the various groups, but the drive is unquestionably on. Herbert Hoover can now afford to keep quiet, as he has found a large number of new disciples. /43

It may be somewhat disheartening to find that liberals too are moving gingerly toward Fortress America, but by no means surprising. Intervention in both World Wars—and particularly in the First—was bitterly opposed by large groups of our liberals, and their forebodings have been at least partly

---

* Secretary of State John Foster Dulles, who died May 24, 1959, and President Eisenhower were charged by some with undue moralizing about matters of state. (*Editor's note*)

** Nikolai A. Bulganin was Premier of the U.S.S.R. at this time, and Nikita S. Khrushchev was First Secretary of the Communist Party. In 1956 it was claimed by the Russians that the two men shared equally in the leadership of the country. (*Editor's note*)

*After World War II former President Hoover had recommended concentration on the defense of the Western Hemisphere to create a "Fortress America." Mr. Hoover died in 1964. (*Editor's note*) vindicated by what happened to them in the aftermath of both wars. /44

After the last war, American liberals did not have very much to contribute to the establishment of a new peace in the world that had become largely dependent on American initiative and means. Not much—aside from a few patented American prescriptions like TVA, trade unions unsoiled by class consciousness, and trust busting. There was also a large export of a curious watered-down Marxism, fervently advocated by internationalists of all political denominations—the firm belief that for any people, under any circumstances, the improvement of living conditions and the march toward democracy are one and the same thing. /45

Now some extraordinarily hard thinking is needed if the new Communist rampage is to be stopped and the network of alliances is to be rewoven around new supranational institutions. It is not surprising, therefore, that there are American liberals who do not relish this prospect and think that there is no use in taking up new troubles when a little bit of hell raising, a new moderate spurt of business baiting, can bring them back into power. Once they were in power, of course, the nation would become further isolated from the rest of the world—isolated not only by its wealth and by its widespread conservatism but also by its liberalism, both quantitative and qualitative. /46

All this would be attractive enough, at least to some, and the prospect of an ever-increasing, evenly distributed prosperity very alluring, were it not for two or three bothersome obstacles. The threat of Soviet Russia is not the greatest of these obstacles.* The power, the freedom, even the prosperity of our country are in danger because our system of government—that queer coexistence of governments and baronies—makes for the constantly diminishing freedom of the individual, who is the only bearer of freedom. Everyone who calls himself a liberal should know this. Our nation, far from being the only one afflicted by this unruly, unfree state of affairs, shares it with all the other democracies. /47

The conclusion, at least for liberals, should be that they must enter upon their task of reversing the trend and making freedom operational both at home and abroad—for there is no line of demarcation between home and abroad. /48

Maybe I'm all wrong. Maybe I'm just hearing things, and Schlesinger, who is a realist, has the answer. All that the future of American liberalism

needs, for itself and for the world, is that America remain prosperous and free. Schlesinger is paraphrasing Secretary Wilson and, as becomes a scholar, is bringing the Wilsonian principle into a near-universal or at least world-wide context: If liberals regain control of the government, then what's good for America is good for the world. /49

The essays

1. What are the typical differences between an essay and a speech? To what extent do these essays illustrate such differences?

2. Is Ascoli's essay more like a speech than Schlesinger's? If so, in what ways and for what reasons?

3. Identify three kinds of definition in Schlesinger's essay.

4. Which definitions in his essay seem designed to persuade by the "short circuit" of *suggestion* (see Glossary) and at the same time to clarify objective meanings? Of the kinds of definition, which are most likely to give this double effect and which are least likely to do so?

5. Is Schlesinger trying to win belief through evoking strong attitudes and feelings, or is he simply trying to inform? Support your answer with specific references.

6. Must Schlesinger and Ascoli adapt what they say to an occasion in the manner of a speaker? What generalizations can you make concerning the similarities and differences between speaking and writing in this respect?

7. Paragraph 23 of Schlesinger's essay and paragraphs 1-13 of Ascoli's exemplify the argumentative method called rebuttal. To what extent do they fulfill the requirements for this kind of argument?

8. Is "liberalism," as Schlesinger and Ascoli use the term, a *stereotype* (see Glossary)? Does each writer use it the same way? If not, what meaning does each give it?

9. What is the effect of Ascoli's use of such symbolic terms as "feudalism," "barons," "baronies," "demonology," and others associated with medieval life and with mythology?

10. Evaluate Ascoli's analysis of Schlesinger's arguments (see paragraphs 1-17). Do you think Ascoli has isolated a truly important feature of Schlesinger's case? Are Ascoli's rebuttal and refutation sharply enough focused on the arguments and assumptions isolated by analysis?

11. In part at least both of these essays aim at changing the attitudes of political liberals toward business and government. What are those attitudes? What change

---

*China's conflicts with Russia and her independent militancy in Asia were not clearly foreseen in 1956. (Editor's note)

is each writer trying to effect in them? By means of what alternative beliefs, motives, and attitudes?

12. What common ground does Schlesinger try to establish with his readers (see especially paragraphs 11 and 30)? Does Ascoli try to establish the same common ground? If not, how does that fact affect his potential persuasiveness with the readers of *The Reporter*?

13. What part does ethos play in rendering an essay credible? If each of these authors had delivered his composition in person to a convention of political liberals, what difference would there be in the role of ethos as a source of proof?

14. Remembering that both essays were addressed to political liberals, which author's position seems likely to have the greater initial credibility with the audience? Why?

15. How much truth do you think there is in this statement: "With a sprinkling of references to a place and time, either of these essays might easily be mistaken for a transcript of a speech"?

For further study and discussion

1. Who are the "independent voters" in national elections? What makes them independent of partisanship? Do they really decide the outcome of our national elections?

2. Do you think there is a "widespread internal anxiety" in the United States today? If so, what do you think is the cause? Are there any political actions that could remove the cause or causes?

3. Do you agree with Schlesinger that "depression is dead as an issue" in politics? Do you agree that we have surmounted most of the purely economic problems of our society? If so, how did this come about? If not, what important problems still remain to be solved?

4. Explore the history of one of the public welfare enterprises and professions Schlesinger mentions in paragraphs 18 and 19. Does it seem "depressed" in the midst of prosperity? If so, what has made it so? Is political action required? If so, what kind of political action?

5. Schlesinger and Ascoli disagree on whether we must attain perfection at home in civil liberty, education, economic equality, etc., before trying to promote these benefits intensively abroad. What is your opinion? Why?

6. Do you agree with Ascoli that we have "entirely new forms of power that operate with frightening effectiveness . . . at molding the people's opinions and habits"? If so, what is "frightening" about them? If you disagree, what is it that prevents unions, commu-

nications networks, corporations, and governmental agencies from exerting dangerous power?

7. What basis, if any, is there for Schlesinger's concession that business is developing a "social conscience" and for Ascoli's claim that the liberals' "antibusiness demonology" is out of date?

8. How do philanthropic foundations affect the conduct and conditions of higher education? Which of their effects are good for the students' interests and which interfere with these interests?

9. In what ways, if any, can governmental agencies and bureaus interfere with fundamental individual freedoms?

10. What basic differences divided the Republican and Democratic parties in the United States in 1960? In 1964? What differences divide them now? Is there justification for the charge that American voters have no real choice between political policies in national elections?

11. Schlesinger and Ascoli seem in mild disagreement about the New Deal's success in solving the economic problems of the 1930's. What historical support is there for the position of either writer?

12. Does President Johnson's "Great Society" program represent a "new liberalism"? If so, does it reflect Schlesinger's or Ascoli's definition of liberalism, or neither?

13. Both men seem to agree that economic well-being, alone, cannot produce political and social well-being. Is their position sound? If so, is our foreign aid policy sound? Should efforts to increase our standard of living have first priority in governmental policy?

14. What is the difference between a political "conservative" and a political "liberal"? What were the differences at the time of the French Revolution—in France? In England? In the United States?

15. What influence, if any, has Marxism had on modern liberalism? On modern conservatism?

Suggestions for further reading

Daniel Boorstin, *The Genius of American Politics* (Chicago, 1953)

James Burnham, *Suicide of the West: An Essay on the Meaning and Destiny of Liberalism* (New York, 1964)

Henry Steele Commager, *The American Mind* (New Haven, 1950)

Richard Hofstadter, *The Age of Reform* (New York, 1955)

Sidney Hook, *Political Power and Personal Freedom* (New York, 1959)

Valdimir O. Key, Jr., *Politics, Parties, and Pressure Groups*, 5th ed. (New York, 1964)

Russell Kirk, *The Conservative Mind*, rev. ed. (Chicago, 1954)

Samuel Lubell, *The Future of American Politics*, 2nd rev. ed. (Garden City, N.Y., 1956)

Eugene J. McCarthy, *The Liberal Answer to the Conservative Challenge* (New York, 1964)

Dexter Perkins, *The American Way* (Ithaca, N.Y., 1959)

Changing concepts of public service

WILLIAM O. FARBER

The following address was delivered by William O. Farber to the faculty, students, and friends of the State University of South Dakota on February 19, 1959, as the Seventh Annual College of Arts and Sciences Lecture on Liberal Education. It is a lecture for an educated audience that lacked specialized knowledge concerning public administration. The speaker's view of his subject is for this reason panoramic rather than particular. The possibilities and public consequences of administrative practice, not the technics of administration, are Farber's concern in this speech.

There are few assignments more difficult for a specialist than preparing a popular lecture on the general character of his specialty. This is what was asked of Farber. As you read the address consider some of the rhetorical problems speakers in Farber's situation always have to solve. If he treats his subject comprehensively, he will have many main headings and subheadings. How shall he keep the essential unity of these points before his listeners' minds? What supporting materials will be simple enough to be understood by laymen, yet true to technical fact? Shall he content himself with explaining the general nature of this, his favorite subject? Or shall he also try to make the subject impressive and urgently important?

Farber is head of the Department of Government and director of the Governmental Research Bureau at the State University of South Dakota, Vermillion, South Dakota. He was born at Geneseo, Illinois in 1910, received his B.A. and M.A. from Northwestern University, and in 1935 was awarded his Ph.D. by the University of Wisconsin. Although he has been a college teacher since 1935, he has also served in a variety of governmental capacities: as State Price Officer, Office of Price Administration; director, State Legislative Research Council; Public Administration Advisor, Seoul National University, Korea; minority counsel, U.S. Senate subcommittee on National Policy Machinery (1960-1961). He has been visiting professor at Northwestern University and the University of Wisconsin and has published works dealing with city manager and state governments and with Indian affairs.

From a reprint of Mr. Farber's address published by the College of Arts and Sciences, State University of South Dakota, October 1959. By permission of the author.

On the eastern side of the South Dakota Badlands there is a geologic feature labeled appropriately "The Door." From this entrance, carved long ago by nature's persistent forces, the traveler follows a trail winding past high pagoda-like columns into a maze of oddly shaped rock piles. And if one has the good fortune to take the excursion in early morning or late evening, when the shadows are the longest, the effect is startling and enchanting, substantiating again and again, Frank Lloyd Wright's observation that the Dakota Badlands "have more spiritual quality to impart to the mind of America than anything else in it made by man's God." /1

From "The Door," to guide and safeguard the traveler, yellow stakes have been driven at regular intervals so that the traveler may retrace his journey without fear of being lost. And, if one views the stakes from "The Door" at the start of his journey, they fade into a hazy obscurity and one wonders where the way really goes and what eventually it is like. /2

Just so, tonight, I propose to discuss with you the direction which our public service is taking and appears to be going, and I hope, with some careful focusing and delineation, to point out, as with the aid of a telephoto lens, the difficulties that lie ahead and what needs to be done if our public servants, our formal leaders upon whom our future depends, are to meet the ills and challenges of present as well as yet unopened Pandoran boxes. In short, I propose to present a descriptive analysis of the public service as it is now evolving, and to stress the obligation of the academic world in that development and in the training of responsible leaders. /3

The public service as I consider it here consists of all those persons engaged in the work of our national, state, and local governments and who are employed in government's many and varied activities and functions. Thus defined, public service includes federal, state, and local officials of all ranks and occupations,—governors and judges, mayors and policemen, cabinet members and postmen, school teachers and meteorologists, generals and presidents, county highway commissioners and social workers, city council members and legislators—all who, on the public pay roll, have a special obligation to serve their country. In short I'm talking about those people whom some describe as "those who couldn't find any other job, so they're working for the government." /4

Now public employment is obviously essential to us, because of the services rendered—traffic control, police protection, the construction of highways, the maintenance of public parks, and the like. Significant as these functions are, I would like to suggest that a more vital consequence of public service lies in the extent to which it will enable us to survive in the battles we now face. The competitive struggle with Russia and modified Soviet economic and social systems is only part of this picture. The inability to organize the world to provide employment, to educate it properly, to feed it, to clothe it, to house it, to ease tensions creates far more urgent problems. The importance of the public service lies, as I see it, in this urgency of present world problems and the ability or inability of the United States government through its public service to deal with them successfully. /5

On such an evening as this, one doesn't like to be pessimistic. But I am reminded of the middle-aged lady who, after hearing a discussion of the educational problem, exclaimed, "Oh dear, the critical crisis in education is so full of critical crises." /6

Unfortunately, the dear lady had pointed out the world situation exactly. The critical crisis is full of critical crises. In many areas, the world is sick. A battle is going on that is full of many battles. /7

Let us take stock of the present by considering briefly certain events that have occurred in the past thirty years. I'm referring to obvious things. There is an old Korean saying, "His view of the world is the view of a frog at the bottom of the well." Not only do we often have too limited a view restricted by the sides of the well, but only too often we want to close our eyes to the obvious. /8

The urgency of the present can be shown by reference to three significant recent events: the depression of the thirties, World War II, and the massacres of the Jews in Germany from 1935 to 1941. These tragic events are close enough at hand so that for many of us, only some brief reflection is needed to recall them as sad, to-be-forgotten memories. /9

I do not like to remember 1933, with its hunger and breadlines, its WPA and NYA,* when all the banks were closed and many a person existed only on what he had in his pocket. Somehow, in looking back, it seems impossible that the depression could have happened to a country as wealthy as the United States. With great resources, tremendous productive capacity, and people desiring and needing work, we were as a nation ill-clothed, ill-fed,

and ill-housed. Nor do I like to recall the time, when responding to a greeting from Uncle Sam, I found myself picking up cigarette butts in a hot barracks area in Texas, and, along with millions then and thousands since, almost completely bereft of civil rights, at the mercy of the caprice of a Pfc. /10

But most of all, I do not like to review the tragedy of Germany under Hitler, where over six million members of a minority race were put to death by various methods—tragic not alone because of *when* it took place, but because of *where* it took place—in a country known for its religion, its education, its culture. In 1955, I was privileged to be in a small group that asked Toynbee* in London how he accounted for this strange antithesis of civilized conduct. Toynbee responded, "We should never forget: Civilization is at best only a thin veneer, and underneath the man is the brute. It takes very little to remove the veneer." /11

There is no need to elaborate further. The inadequacy of human endeavor when called upon to meet the monumental problems of today is only too clearly evident. And as one surveys the exploding population bomb, the arms race, and the pathetic inability to cope with Berlin, Quemoy, and Panmunjon,** one can find much to worry about. /12

An Italian journalist took me to visit the Roman Forum. It was about eleven o'clock at night, and as one might anticipate, a moon had risen. It was one of those times when one could set his fancies free and one could almost see bold Caesar on the steps of stone across from the temple of the Vestal Virgins and imagine Roman citizens thronging through the narrow ways between the maze of buildings. Here was tangible evidence of what had been the capital of the world, but now was capital no longer. Nations rise and fall; they differ only as to rate. /13

Clearly there is no reason to believe that the United States can occupy its position of pre-eminence forever. There are signs the eclipse has already begun. A word like "co-existence" is a symbol of the distasteful reality. /14

President Eisenhower has observed, "For the first time in history, we have the power to end history." We are challenged not only by the other nations; we are challenged by the weapons we have developed. Certainly, there is little cause at the moment

---

* Works Progress Administration and National Youth Administration. (*Editor's note*)

* Arnold Joseph Toynbee, historian. (*Editor's note*)
**Quemoy: Chinese Nationalist island close to Chinese mainland. Panmunjon: symbol of divided Korea; a UN-North Korean armistice was signed here July 27, 1953. (*Editor's note*)

to be comfortable. The times will come again that will try men's souls. It is in the light of this urgency of the present and the future, when our society, our civilization is in the balance, that this examination of public service is made. /15

This is not the place to review in detail the development of the American public service. Much of this history has not been a proud one. The prestige of government service has been low. Mothers could say, "I didn't raise my boy to be on the public pay roll." The concept of His Majesty's Service has not become The President's Service—and if it had, I doubt if there would be any great struggle for more people to enter it. /16

Today we find some two million persons in national employ and many more, if we include our educational system, in state employ. The numerical rise of civil service employees as well as those in military service has been one of the significant developments of twentieth-century America. For the most part, despite the partial truths of *The Ugly American,* we can be proud of our individual public servants today. I confess, I had not quite realized how proud we should be until I examined the role of Institutes of Public Administration in the Far East. With some exceptions, government in the Far East is carried on as much under as over the table. At least our problem seems to center around electric refrigerators, rugs, and mink coats. /17

But if the individual servant seems properly the object of some admiration, the appropriate yardstick, I feel, is not what he does, but what needs to be done. In short, in the light of the urgent present, the public servant needs to be something more than he has been, if the challenges of the present are to be met. And somehow, the individual competence generally prevalent must be so organized as to minimize the collective incompetence too frequently prevailing. /18

Looking at our public service, certain characteristics seem clear—its increase in size, the growth of field as well as central government service, its developing career aspects, its emphasis on the merit principle and political neutrality as goals. But there are new aspects and needs of the American public service which are apt to be overlooked and which are emerging. And it is these I now wish to call to our attention. /19

First of all, public service has tended to become international. This has occurred in three different ways: first, an actual international public service has come into existence and flourished with the establishment of the League of Nations. This service is far more extensive than most people realize. /20

Secondly, those parts of our own national civil service dealing in international problems have become immeasurably more sizeable and important. In addition to the regular work of the State Department and other departments of the government, commerce and agriculture, for examples, which have important international functions, such specialized agencies as USIS and ICA* are tremendously influential. Indeed the whole technical assistance program is becoming increasingly regarded as one of the great hopes of the world. /21

Toynbee has said that the historian of the future looking back on this period might characterize this century not as a period when the methods of transportation made great advances, not as a time when the ravages of disease were greatly reduced, not as an era when the atom was split, but as the age when man first dared to think that the benefits of civilization might be distributed to all mankind. In line with this thinking, the American Point Four program was initiated, in the words of the President, as "a bold new program for making the benefits of our scientific advances and industrial progress available for the improvement and growth of under-developed areas." /22

Finally, and most important, public service has become international *locally*—in every Main Street in America. The influx of foreign travelers to the United States and their contact with officialdom is important, but an even greater significance is our own treatment of minority groups. I shall never forget the Bank of Korea clerk who was my guide to Kyongju, the Athens of Korea. We had had a wonderful excursion with temple exploration and verbal give and take. He had observed that this was his first opportunity to become really acquainted with an American and he liked the equality of it. "But," he said over the cups, "what about Little Rock?"** /23

Even in remote Kyongju, wherever you may go, the question remains, "But what about Little Rock?" /24

Or, to give another example, a young Korean major in the ROK army invited me to attend the great Yung Nak Presbyterian church in Seoul. It proved to be a thrilling experience. Over 1,500 Koreans were in the audience, and the old hymns were sung with an enthusiasm rare with us these days. After the service, in a Chinese tearoom, as we exchanged

*U.S. Information Service; International Cooperation Administration.
**In 1957, President Eisenhower sent federal troops to Little Rock to enforce a court order for school integration. (Editor's note)

confidences, expressing some sort of Christian brotherhood, Major Lee quite unexpectedly said, "I've heard the Presbyterians in the north part of the United States quarrel with those in the south. Is it true they are divided? If so, why?" /25

"If so, why?" Yes. "Why?" Our domestic difficulties have a way of boomeranging all the way back to us after spreading doubts around the entire world. /26

The point remains, our attitude, as expressed in law toward our foreign students, toward each other, toward foreign policy, all affect international goals and aspirations. Our public servants administering that law thus become international even though their duties seem ostensibly domestic. /27

I'm well aware that some students of administration would say that the first duty of a public official is to carry out orders, and that he cannot be solicitous of remote effects, when trivial, on international relations. Thus, a leading student of public administration has observed: "If an administrator, each time he is faced with a decision, must perforce evaluate that decision in terms of the whole range of human values, rationality in administration is impossible."[1] What I am thinking about is not so much the actual decision as the manner of making it. Thus, Koreans have asked, "Why don't University department heads in the United States answer letters of inquiry?" Such minute matters have a way of causing impact far beyond their original significance. My first observation then is that from top to bottom the public service has come to have international aspects, and public servants must be trained accordingly. /28

The second observation is that the modern public servant needs to be a humanitarian; he must be tolerant and possess a sympathetic understanding of the culture of other lands. He must have what Harlow Shapley* has called "reverence for humility." The conclusion is commonplace that the transition from nineteenth-century government to twentieth-century government was a shift from the police and defense functions to welfare activities. Thus, government, perhaps of necessity as the power of the voter has grown, has become concerned with people and what becomes of them. /29

Our approach to this in the world setting is cogently stated in President Truman's 1949 inaugural address: "More than half the people of the world are living in conditions approaching misery. Their food is inadequate. They are victims of disease. Their economic life is primitive and stagnant.

Their poverty is a handicap and a threat both to them and to more prosperous areas. For the first time in history, humanity possesses the knowledge and the skill to relieve the suffering of these people. . . ." /30

This humanitarian approach does not mean ignoring the law in bestowing governmental largess; it does not mean the winking at legal violations, but it does mean the exercise of administrative discretion where discretion exists to the benefit of mankind, and in a manner designed to promote human dignity. Institutions may be governed in theory and law by regulations designed to insure fairness, hearing, and equal and sympathetic treatment. In practice, as institutions must operate through men, the results may be quite different. /31

I think here of one of the most thought-provoking comments I have ever heard. In the course of investigating the off-reservation Indian problem, the three of us who constituted the research team interviewed an Indian woman, well known for her welfare work. We asked her why the Indian spent so much time in bars, drinking. She hesitated, and then said: "There is more Christianity in the bar than in the church. If the Indian attends church, no one will sit near him, no one will speak to him, no one will shake his hand; in a bar this is not true. Bars are friendly." /32

Thus, just as the rules of the church prescribe friendliness, unless the heart be in it, there is no friendliness; so, too, government can require equality of treatment, but unless the public servant feels that equality none will exist. The power to tear down is a terrible power. And no one has as much opportunity as the teacher to use it. As the scope of government has grown, as discretionary authority has become enlarged, so too the potential humanitarian character of both government and the public servant has increased immeasurably. /33

Let there be no mistaken notion about the extent of discretion in administration these days. Naive is the student who accepts the professor's answer, "I am sorry I cannot give you an 'A' "; or the professor who accepts the department head's statement, "You have not taught long enough to be recommended for promotion"; or the department head who accepts the dean's statement, "Sorry, there is no money left in the budget"; or the dean who accepts the president's statement, "No more out-of-state travel will be permitted this year"; or the president who accepts the governor's statement, "No new building will be recommended by me." To be compelled to accept a negative is simply an indication, for the most part,

---

[1] Herbert A. Simons, *Administrative Behavior* (Macmillan, 1957), p. 13.

* American astronomer. (*Editor's note*)

that one's political resources are insufficient for the occasion. /34

The third characteristic of public service is its multilateral nature. There was a time when we in political science exhibited a certain possessiveness when it came to civil service positions. Government and political science were synonymous, and government employment was political science employment. /35

Professionalization and the rise of technological education laid this pretense to rest. While certain organizational, financial, and personnel problems of civil service were still the primary concern of students of government, the greater problems became those of professional objectives and training. It was, for example, how the health, the highway, and the educational programs attained their goals that counted. /36

But now we have reached a still further stage in this development, when governmental positions in addition to being *multifarious* are *multilateral*. To be the specialist is not enough. The specialist must know something of language and culture, history and government, science and literature, and above all, he must possess the spirit of humanity, a kindly tolerance and humility, a realization that this is a human being's world. /37

All through the public service today one does find to an increasing degree the dedicated doctor, nurse, nutritionist, educator, social worker, economist, meteorologist, engineer, astronomer, aware of this larger role as leader he is called upon to play. I think, for example, of the large number of public servants taking foreign language courses. /38

Therefore, keeping pace with specialization has been the need for the specialist to be mindful of his international and humanitarian obligations, the multilateral or generalist aspects of his work. /39

One final characteristic of the new public service must be considered. The developments previously noted have occurred at a time when the demands that the public service "produce" are greater than ever before. The pragmatic test—"What does it do?" is supplying the answer for much of the world as to which camp a people wishes to be a part of. Can the United States outproduce Russia? Are the people of the United States happier? More moral? More content? "By their fruits ye shall know them" becomes a yardstick that Americans may properly apprehend and a new satellite around the sun becomes a symbol that has significance far beyond its scientific import. /40

From the viewpoint of the public servant, the challenge arises in how to do what policy declares should be done in spite of restrictive rules. Time and again the public servant—whether postal clerk, mayor, county commissioner, state geologist, attorney general, or president—is faced with the frustration of dubious legal sanction. /41

The easy way out is to treat doubtful legal potence as the excuse not to act. This is exactly what the good administrator should not do. "There are no hopeless situations; there are only people hopeless about them." In the public service, no less than in other activities, creativity has an important role to play. /42

Hence, as the final characteristic of the new public service, I would suggest creativity, meaning inventiveness or resourcefulness. The importance of this trait has received increasing attention. Dr. F. S. C. Northrop of Yale University has noted that Socrates regarded the philosopher as a thorn in the flesh, and he observed that nobody is a creative thinker unless continuously he has a thorn in the flesh, that is, unless he is disturbed by something. /43

It has been my experience that public servants have many thorns in the flesh and many, especially those engaged in field work, do something about them, both inside and outside the rules and the regulations. This resultant action is the essence of creativity. In an account of Dr. Arthur H. Compton's[*] analysis of conditions under which scientists are creative, it is pointed out that he found that each scientist has become conscious of his own "thorn in the flesh." Further, with reference to our own Ernest Lawrence,[**] Compton observed that Lawrence had more initiative than almost anyone else that he knew, a tremendous energy and a determination to get things done as he wanted them. Compton concluded with this comment: "Here then are the things that I see as I review this group of typical cases. First of all, to my mind, the thing which is the essence of creativity is the *decision* to do something about it when you are irritated. I would agree that irritation is the first step, but the decision to do something about it is the essence of creativity."[2] /44

Now in my own governmental experiences in the Office of Price Administration, both in the field and in Washington, D.C., on the regional loyalty board, with the state legislature, and my contracts with foreign aid agencies, have impressed me not only with the opportunity and the need of public servants to

---

* American physicist and Nobel Prize winner. (Editor's note)
** American physicist and Nobel Prize winner. Reference to "our own" is an allusion to the fact that Dr. Lawrence, a native of South Dakota, was a student at its State University. (Editor's note)
2 Cited in Fred Olson, "Introduction and Summary," *The Nature of Creative Thinking* (Industrial Research Institute, 2nd ed., n.d.), p. 6.

exercise inventiveness, but with the extent to which they actually use it. /45

Illustrations leap up, but the words cannot be put down, for to do so would be to betray illegal albeit humanitarian acts. The tragedy is, especially for our foreign service, that greater discretion has not been officially bestowed upon our public servants. It takes but little imagination to see that what has been called inventiveness is only an aspect, a neglected aspect, of what we more familiarly think of as leadership. /46

So much for the character of our present and incipient modern public servant who thus emerges as now needing to have international, humanitarian, generalist, and inventive or leadership traits. This is what we are getting in the way of a public servant, though in an inadequate way; this is what we need, to a much greater degree. /47

This leads me to the final group of observations. /48

I have tried to stress the urgency of contemporary social problems and the present character of the public service. I should like now to show the relationship of the new public service and the University community. /49

Emerson in his famous Phi Beta Kappa address, "The American Scholar," * said: "Books are the best of things, well used; abused, among the worst. What is the right use? What is the one end which all means go to effect? They are for nothing but to inspire. I had better never see a book than to be warped by its attraction clean out of my own orbit, and made a satellite instead of a system. The one thing in a world, of value, is the active soul." /50

The urgency of world problems and the type of public servant required to meet these problems make the development of "active souls" imperative. The need is great for men and women whose vision ignores the confines of intellectual disciplines, the harness of the classroom assignment, and the goose-step of fifty-minute periods. We should recruit men of the type of Ulysses, described in the Odyssey: "Many cities did he visit, and many were the nations with whose manners and customs he was acquainted." But the beneficial consequences of mere travel, unaccompanied by knowledge and appreciation of history, language, and culture, and the habit of thinking realistically mean little. Max Weber** in his essay on "Politics as a Vocation," in noting that the age of an individual is not significant, stated: "What is decisive is the trained relentlessness in viewing the realities of life and the ability to face such reality and to measure

up to them inwardly." Thus we must cease praising those who build houses by the side of the road to be a friend of man, and encourage the man who is out in the road fighting society's battle. /51

The function of higher education in times such as these is somehow to provide the meeting ground of theory and realities, to train the public servant broadly and generally, but preserve the relentless instinct to grapple with specific situations. The ivory tower comes into its own as a tower in times such as these. /52

"Comfort without vision is no match for the four horsemen riding in from beyond the hills. . . . Immunity without responsibility, vision without action, means eventual suicide. Human necessity, if no nobler motive, cries out for restoration of the tower, not as a monument to academic irrelevance, but as an indispensable vantage point of vision without which we perish as men. Though no bread may be baked in the tower, no baker is free to bake bread with integrity and peace without the trustworthiness of the tower's primary work and wisdom."[3] /53

I would hope that educators, regarding the ivory tower as part of the battlefield in considering their responsibility to provide public servants, would not lose sight of the need to produce well rounded public servants with an international, humanitarian, multilateral, and inventive orientation. This does not mean extroverts only are needed. Indeed, as Woodrow Wilson noted in his *Leaders of Men*, "a book is often quite as quickening a trumpet as any made of brass and sounded on the field." But it does mean that more and more in urgent times such as these, the stars and mud must be combined. Woodrow Wilson in the work just cited illustrated this point well: /54

"The captain of a Mississippi steamboat had made fast to the shore because of a thick fog lying on the river. The fog lay low and dense upon the surface of the water, but overhead all was clear. A cloudless sky showed a thousand points of starry light. An impatient passenger inquired the cause of the delay. 'We cannot see to steer,' said the captain. 'But all's clear overhead,' suggested the passenger. 'You can see the North Star.' 'Yes,' reflected the officer, 'But we are not going that way.' Politics must follow the actual windings of the channel of the river if it steer by the stars."[4] /55

---

[3] Glenn A. Olds, "View from the 'Ivory Tower,'" *The Saturday Review*, June 21, 1958, p. 26.

[4] Woodrow Wilson, *Leaders of Men*, ed. by T. H. Motter (Princeton University Press, 1952), pp. 47-48.

*See pp. 39-47. (Editor's note)
**Famous German sociologist. Died 1920. (Editor's note)

I have attempted tonight to present the changing nature of public service in the light of the urgency of present world problems and the place of the universities in these developments. The absorption of these concepts into our way of thinking of the public service as thus described would, I think, do much to improve the position of the United States internationally. /56

I remind you that we have been thinking of the public service broadly as including president, governors, mayors, congressmen, legislators, councilmen, and all federal, state, and local employees, including civil servants, university professors, and school teachers among others. Unless we look on the public servant as partaking and needing to partake to a greater or lesser degree of the developing traits described tonight, we will give the public servant, as a leader, less than his due, at a time when we can ill afford to detract from the dignity and dedication which should belong to him. /57

It takes but little imagination to appreciate that my "changing concepts" are really new *demands* on the public servant in his role as leader—that he be international, humanitarian, generalist, and inventive. And it takes but little more imagination to realize that these are demands which are actually confronting all of us whether public servant or not, if we are to carry the burden of our mission on earth. /58

The peoples of the world are observing critically how, locally, we meet such problems as education, housing, reorganization of government, civil liberties and segregation. If we are concerned about the international situation and sometimes feel that Washington is incompetent, we should not forget that our own failures in meeting local issues have an impact far beyond our national boundaries. /59

Measured against our great natural resources, how adequately do we provide higher education for poor but superior students? How successful have our slum clearance projects been? How satisfactory have been our attempts to safeguard personal liberty and promote human dignity? /60

All American citizens, as well as local and national officials, thus have an important international role to play. The choice between the American and Russian systems will be made by many undecided peoples on the basis of which system, in their opinion, is better able to demonstrate its ability to attain desired human and economic goals. /61

The continuous succession of international crises during the past thirty years emphasizes the urgent need to examine the demands made on our public servants and determine how these demands can best be met. Unless public servants are broadly trained and are recruited for their tolerance, resourcefulness, and understanding of international problems, we can lose to Russia in a race more important than launching satellites into space. /62

As we return to "The Door"—the start of our venture tonight—this final thought: If we continue to think of our own careers, as well as those of public servants, as wholly local, specialized, narrow, and mechanistic, the result will be, I think, disastrous. We need to recognize what the human venture is becoming and needs to become and to train accordingly. We need to appreciate the discretion that is ours, that we all partake of the mission of leadership. As public power, as government continues to grow, as the earth continues to shrink and we must live closer together, these changing concepts, needing and demanding acceptance and appreciation, afford a way to a better and happier world. /63

The speech

1. What is the function of paragraphs 4-15 in the overall plan of this speech? Could the speech have achieved its purpose with these sections omitted?

2. Identify the internal summaries in the speech. Do you think the listeners needed the help of these recapitulations in order to keep the main headings of the speech in mind? Why or why not?

3. Comment on the use of authorities in this speech. Which citations of authority are made more credible by the speaker's remarks about them and which have such prestige that the speaker gains credibility simply by citing them?

4. Does Farber do anything within the speech to make his listeners view him more favorably? Are there any features of the speech that could detract from the listeners' favorable impressions of the speaker?

5. Farber amplifies the humanitarian qualities of the civil servant by definition, authority, assertion, and analogy (see paragraphs 29-33). Identify each form of support in this section and comment on how well it contributes to a clear understanding of the humanitarianism required of the civil servant of modern society.

6. Review the following topics in the Glossary: *conciseness, periodic sentences, rhythm,* and *style.* What general observations can you make about the oral style of this speech?

7. Farber uses a number of anecdotes as supporting material. How do they make his main headings more believable or understandable? Should any have been longer?

For further study and discussion

1. Farber suggests that the British attitude toward public service is different from the American attitude. What is the difference?

2. Study a curriculum for training administrators or public service personnel: the case study system at the Harvard Business School, British Foreign Service selection and training programs, the Brookings Institution seminars in government, or others. Does the program seem likely to produce public servants with the qualifications Farber thinks are needed?

3. What are some recent events that support Farber's proposition that even the local decisions made by American public officials are of national and international importance?

4. Note the series of questions asked in paragraph 60 of this speech. From these questions, compose several topics for speeches and discussions.

5. In view of the multilateral nature of modern public service, should all persons appointed to civil service posts requiring college training also be required to have spent a specified period studying the liberal arts?

6. What was the "American Point Four Program"? How did it come to be established? Does it still exist? If so, what is its present character and how successful is it?

7. How do conditions of employment (wages, advancement, tenure, opportunity to make one's own decisions, etc.) in civil service compare with conditions for similar work in private enterprise? Which kind of career seems more inviting to you?

8. How might our methods of nominating candidates for public office be improved? Review some of the plans proposed for changing the electoral college system. What merits, if any, do these have?

9. Study the history of the "Authority" as an administrative agency in public service: the Port of New York Authority, Tennessee Valley Authority, various highway and turnpike authorites, etc. How do these agencies function? What is their relation to municipal, state, or national governments?

10. What caused the separation of several Protestant denominations into Northern and Southern branches or associations? Is there any tendency for these church groups to reunite today? Do you think it is important that they should? Has religious leadership become "public service" in Farber's sense too?

Suggestions for further reading

Frederick Lewis Allen, *The Big Change; America Transforms Itself, 1900-1950* (New York, 1952)

Foreign Policy Association, *Careers in World Affairs: At Home and Abroad* (Garden City, N.Y., 1961)

Franklin P. Kilpatrick and others, *The Image of the Federal Service* (Washington, D.C., 1964)

Robert E. Lane, *Political Life: Why People Get Involved in Politics* (Glencoe, Ill., 1959)

Harold D. Lasswell, *Who Gets What, When, and Why* (Chicago, 1958)

Robert E. Merriam and Rachel M. Goetz, *Going into Politics* (New York, 1957)

The inner city—our shame

S. DAVID DINWOODIE

The following speech was delivered by S. David Dinwoodie at the final hearing for the Woodford Prize in Public Speaking at Cornell University in 1958. The Woodford Prize was established at Cornell in 1870 by Stewart Lyndon Woodford and is awarded annually by a faculty committee to the Cornell University senior who presents the best public address in an open competition.

Dinwoodie's speech was delivered in a setting that was relatively informal. He addressed about fifty students and faculty members assembled in one of the lounges of the student union building. Some listeners were seated in lounge chairs along three sides of the room and others sat before the speaker's stand in chairs more formally arranged. Although a prize was at stake, the "contest" features of the occasion were deëmphasized as much as possible. Both speakers and listeners were encouraged to assume that the meeting had been called in order that a group of seniors might address some final remarks to their fellow students and teachers before departing from the university community.

Like Karos' address, "The Haven of the Defeated" (pp. 148-151), Dinwoodie's speech grew out of a deeply moving personal experience. The discourses are alike, also, in that each depicts grave social ills from which urban society suffers, and each does so with art and sincerity.

Although Dinwoodie obviously believes that changes are needed desperately, he does not try to produce a solution for metropolitan overcrowding. Consider, then, whether "The Inner City—Our Shame" is really a message worth hearing for its own sake, or will it, as well as other speeches that offer only a "need step," however moving, inevitably disappoint the audience? Consider, too, whether Din-

Reprinted by permission of S. David Dinwoodie.

woodie's address and Stevenson's "The City—A Cause for Statesmanship" (pp. 219-224) would, if somehow blended, have formed a more complete and compelling case for urban renewal than either speech heard separately.

Dinwoodie holds a B.S. in Industrial and Labor Relations (1958) and an M.A. in English (1960), both from Cornell University.

Last summer I worked with a group of eight-year-old boys in East Harlem, New York, and tonight I want to share with you some of my impressions of that tragic place. /1

Let me begin by telling you of the incident that introduced me to this pathetic area. Of all the new and intriguing experiences that I had last summer none was more profoundly moving than this one. /2

It took place at Bob Vane's apartment. He was one of the boys in my group and I was getting acquainted with his family. The dimly lit apartment was thick with the sickening smells that come from too many people living in too small an area. The three small rooms housed two mothers, their eight copper-colored children—and a dog. As I learned later, no husband lived there permanently, but Bob did have a succession of "uncles" moving in and out with fair regularity. /3

I had been exchanging pleasantries with the mothers and playing and joking with the kids for about only ten minutes, when little Mary, a three-year-old with the kind of arresting beauty that makes you wish you were a poet, boosted herself up onto the sofa where I was sitting, crawled into my lap, planted her feet flat on my legs and stood up bringing her face on a level with mine. She raised her arms and entwined her hands about the back of my neck, gazing into my eyes through long dark lashes with a look that I can describe only as rapt adoration. She stood like that for at least a minute and then, drawing her face close to mine, she kissed me on the cheek. /4

I was overwhelmed—of course—but as I realized only at the end of the summer, after living for two months with many kids who have no permanent fathers, the same thing would happen to any male who gave East Harlem kids his attention and affection. To Mary and the many like her, East Harlem bequeaths a heritage of lovelessness. Such lovelessness is tragic because it warps lives, and as intelligent, sensitive people we can no more ignore the social tragedy of East Harlem than we can ignore the social problems of polio and economic recession. /5

Lovelessness, and a host of other evils, have led social scientists to call East Harlem the Inner City. For it must be distinguished from the rest of New York City and from the rest of our society. The Inner City is alienated and separated; it is walled off from the rest of society by barriers of language, race, religion, and culture. Like an eddy in a great river, East Harlem is swirled around and by-passed by the mainstream of society. It doesn't share the economic and cultural progress of society. It has conditions that work to degrade and defeat its people to an extent that is hard to imagine. /6

My work in the Inner City was an upsetting experience. Before last summer, when I heard or read about the Inner City, I was inclined to ignore the reports—after all, the poor are with us always. But after working in East Harlem's squalor, after living in the midst of its lovelessness, and its racial antagonisms; its dope addiction, and its juvenile delinquency, I can't be passive any longer. The Inner City is maintained at the expense of too many personalities. The Inner City destroys that which makes man great, his creative aspirations! /7

If these were the 1930's when students were hypersensitive to social problems and anxious to correct them, I would make a ringing appeal tonight for recruits to man a great crusade of social reform. If you were a philanthropic organization or a church group, I would ask you to contribute huge donations to the many social agencies working in East Harlem. But this is, after all, 1958, a time of relative peace, prosperity, and progress, when social reform doesn't seem to be a paramount concern of most students. And I'm talking to people whose main concerns are probably to develop personal life philosophies and critical faculties. /8

So, I'm not recruiting a group of reform-minded students to march on New York's City Hall. I am trying to make you aware of the social disgrace of the Inner City, feeling that you—as intelligent, sensitive people—will be moved to some kind of reform action. I don't expect immediate action although that would be desirable. I don't expect noisy radical action although that might help. I do hope for the kind of quiet but dynamic activity that springs from mature adults and citizens who feel responsible for shaping the destiny of their society and who, consequently, devote their energy and talents to that cause. I hope that in the near future—as voters, as teachers, as legislators, lawyers, and doctors—you will work to eliminate the Inner Cities like East Harlem, which can be found in every urban area. Let me tell you about other conditions that make the Inner City intolerable in our society. /9

East Harlem is crowded. On the block where I lived, four thousand people are housed in twenty-seven stinking, rotting tenements. If this people-per-block ratio of East Harlem were applied to the entire country, the nation's population could be put in half of New York City. As a result, East Harlemites are continually jammed, shoved, pushed, and packed together. Naturally, this increases the normal frustrations and tensions of living. Human beings need periods of privacy. We need to be alone once in a while to gain perspective on life. But the people of East Harlem have no place to be alone. And unable to relieve their tensions in solitude, they seek relief in escape—in escapes like liquor, sex, pentacostal religion, and dope. /10

Another result of crowded living conditions is that kids are thrown out onto the streets at a young age. Finding themselves in the asphalt jungle—without the parental protection that most of us of the middle class have known—they soon learn the law of this jungle. They learn to scrap and claw for survival—survival of the fittest—that's their philosophy of life. And if my boys lied, fought, and cheated during my time with them, it was only because they had had to do so all their lives. /11

The crowded living conditions lead to another regrettable characteristic, the school system. East Harlem schools are overcrowded and understaffed. There are forty pupils in classes that, because of the tremendous emotional problems of the kids, should have only five. As a result the schools are mere discipline factories. The harried teachers spend their time trying to maintain order and don't have time or energy to really teach. This situation accounts for the teenagers I met who couldn't read or write. It also helps produce the teenage dope addicts I knew—they were for the most part bright kids, who, attending schools that couldn't challenge their intellects, turned to narcotics to escape the boredom. /12

But the most tragic of all, East Harlem's people are apathetic—they are aimless—they seem unable or afraid to hold a vision of what they might become. I was always amazed by the large number of men who did nothing all day but hang around the stoops. But the lack of inspiration isn't hard to understand, really. Puerto Ricans and Negroes came north even as the Jews had hopefully set out for the promised land. There was opportunity, wealth, and freedom to the north. But what did the Puerto Ricans and Negroes find? When they did get work (which wasn't always), it was as elevator operators, busboys, dishwashers, and sewing machine operators in fly-by-night sweat shops. The small wages they did earn

were set upon by racketeering unionists and exploiting landlords. They were forced into ghettos by housing discrimination. But the biggest disappointment was the knowledge—not so much an explicit fact that one could touch, but more a feeling of constant, overwhelming pressure—the knowledge that the rest of society regarded them as second-class citizens. No wonder there is apathy and lack of vision. No wonder huge numbers of men avoid family responsibilities. No wonder they lounge on doorsteps all day and escape into dreamworlds of alcohol, sex, and dope at night. What is a man to do when so many social forces seem bent on destroying his self-respect? /13

The women are lucky. They gain some measure of creative self-realization by having children. And they indulge in this fulfillment with great abandon, knowing that welfare checks will take care of them if transient lovers won't. But what really hurts—what really hurts is to talk to 15 and 16 year old boys, to listen to them spin dreams of long Cadillacs and jobs where they can put their feet up on the desk; and then to see the glow of aspiration slowly fade from their eyes giving way to angry despair as they look at the men lounging about them and realize that this is the true vision of their future. /14

What then are my impressions of East Harlem? I saw the Inner City—an area walled off from the rest of society—an area of lovelessness, racial antagonism, and crowdedness, an area of abominable housing, inadequate educational facilities, escapism, and juvenile delinquency. I saw the Inner City—generating destructive feelings of hatred, fear, prejudice, and apathy. I saw the Inner City—destroying many, many lives. /15

And I saw my impressions brought together most strikingly in the tragic person of Tony. Tony is a 14 year old Negro boy—big for his age and not very bright. He can't read or write. Because of his backwardness, he is not accepted by his own age group and so he seeks companionship with younger boys. Unfortunately, his confused life has led him to make homosexual advances to the younger boys and they of course reject him, too. /16

One cold, drizzly night, I was walking to my apartment when I heard sobs coming from a nearby alley, and I found Tony there huddled against a wall among some garbage cans. I asked him what was wrong and in his convulsive, sobbing answer, I heard the distilled cry of an entire community that is rejected by the rest of society. "I don't know what to do," he cried. "Nobody wants me. Everybody—everything is against me." /17

It is sad when one person is shattered by life. It's

tragic when thousands feel crushed and without hope; the Inner City does this—it crushes and shatters thousands. Its existence is our shame. Its continuance is our shame compounded, and our reaction to this great social problem will be the test of our maturity. An anguished cry breaks into Cornell's comfortable, creative mood tonight. It's the Inner City echoing Tony's pathetic cry—"We don't know what to do. Nobody wants us. Everybody—everything is against us." /18

The speech

1. What is the introduction to this speech? Is the length of the introduction appropriate for the speaker's purpose, occasion, and audience?

2. Does Dinwoodie's explanation of what he expects of his audience occur in about the right place, too early, or too late? Why?

3. The speaker was deeply concerned about his subject, yet his listeners could not alone do much about the problem. In view of this was his plea for present awareness and future action well chosen? Was the plea too remote from the listeners' interests or was it simply realistic? Should he have given this speech to a college audience at all?

4. What could the substance of this speech have achieved if addressed to the ACTION conference that Adlai E. Stevenson spoke to in Newark (see pp. 219-224)? What parts of the speech would Dinwoodie have had to change in adapting to that audience?

5. Much of the persuasion in this speech is achieved through suggestion rather than through argument. To make his suggestion that overcrowding causes escapism logically acceptable, what attitudes and evidence do you have to supply from your own mind as you read paragraph 10? What form or forms of suggestion are used in this paragraph?

6. Review the topic of *proof* in the Glossary. What kinds of proofs does Dinwoodie use to establish that overcrowding leads to juvenile delinquency (see especially paragraph 12)?

7. What is your reaction to the use of the word "kids" in this speech? Is it overused? Should it be used at all? Do the circumstances of the speech make any difference?

8. Do the rather unpleasant qualities in the personality of Tony make you more or less sympathetic toward him? Would it have been more effective for the speaker to have found a different illustration with which to end the speech? Or do Tony's limitations make him an ideal voice for the "Inner City"?

9. Is Dinwoodie's a deliberative, forensic, or epideictic speech? Which of these kinds of speeches is Mr. Stevenson's Newark speech (pp. 219-224)? Will either speech secure specific actions by the audience? If not, were the speeches worth making to these audiences?

10. The force of this speech depends heavily on the speaker's credibility. How many specific points can you find at which what the speaker chooses to say or not to say adds to or detracts from your confidence in him?

For further study and discussion

1. Do you think overcrowding is really the basic cause of the social evils Dinwoodie describes? What about cultural influences?

2. The late Cardinal Meyer of Chicago said, "It is the [housing] restrictions against the most capable and self-reliant portions of the Negro population which call loudest for remedy." Will Negroes, Puerto Ricans, and Mexicans be able to move from tenements to better dwellings, as their Irish, Italian, or German predecessors have?

3. Has the creation of good, low-income housing had any effects upon family solidarity, quality of education, and individual ambition in cities where such housing programs have been tried?

4. What opportunities do Negroes, Puerto Ricans, Mexicans, and Orientals have to join craft and professional labor unions?

5. What is the governmental relationship between the United States and the Commonwealth of Puerto Rico? What bearing does this relationship have on situations such as Mr. Dinwoodie described?

6. Explore the political career of Vito Marcantonio, Adam Clayton Powell, or William Dawson. To what extent did the "alienation" of the "inner cities" form these political leaders and shape their careers?

7. Representative Powell has said, "The next fight [for civil rights] is in housing and that will come in the next five years. . . . There are a few things I'd like to do . . . for one thing unite the Negroes and the Puerto Ricans." Do you think united political action by such ethnic groups might contribute to the solution of modern urban problems?

8. Make yourself familiar with the activities of the Division of Juvenile Delinquency Services, United States Department of Health, Education, and Welfare. How has it contributed to solving youth problems since its establishment in 1955?

9. Are the urban problems discussed by Stevenson and Dinwoodie peculiarly American? Do they exist in cities of other lands? Are they inevitable features of metropolitan society?

10. In connection with President Lyndon B. Johnson's "War on Poverty," federally operated Job Corps camps were established to train unemployable youths. Some public officials have recommended a permanent National Youth Conservation Corps to provide work on public lands for city youths. Do you think these programs are needed? Desirable? Would it be better to modify child labor laws in states where they prevent teen-aged youths from taking full-time employment? Would it be better to raise the age limits for compulsory school attendance?

The city—
a cause for statesmanship
ADLAI E. STEVENSON

It has been rightly said that "not since William Jennings Bryan won the leadership of the Democratic Party in 1896 with his famous 'Cross of Gold' speech has public address contributed so much to establishing and maintaining a major presidential candidate's national prominence as in the case of Adlai E. Stevenson."[1] There can be little doubt that Stevenson's rise from the middle ranks of party life to national prominence came about largely because of his unique speaking abilities.

Adlai Stevenson was born in Los Angeles, California, in 1900, received his B.A. degree from Princeton University in 1922, worked briefly as a journalist, and then entered the study of law, receiving a J.D. from Northwestern University in 1926. From 1927 to 1933 he practiced law in Chicago, and from 1933 to the end of World War II he held a variety of governmental positions and practiced law in Washington, D.C. In 1946 and 1947 Stevenson was a delegate to the General Assembly of the United Nations. In 1948 he was elected governor of Illinois. In 1952 and again in 1956, the Democratic party nominated him for the presidency of the United States. From 1960 until his death July 14, 1965, he was head of the United States delegation to the United Nations.

From *Putting First Things First* by Adlai E. Stevenson. Copyright © 1960 by Adlai E. Stevenson. Reprinted by permission of Random House, Inc.
[1]Russel Windes, Jr., and James A. Robinson, "Public Address in the Career of Adlai E. Stevenson," *Quarterly Journal of Speech,* XLII (1956), p. 225.

Stevenson's great facility with language—his mastery of witty wordplay, the epigram, and satiric statement—probably derived from his lifelong interest in literature and writing. Whenever possible he wrote his own speeches, carefully revised them, and delivered them from manuscript. He professed not to have given much thought to the theory of public address, and he insisted that the art of speaking had been difficult for him to learn. He, himself, believed his early experience as a college and professional journalist had significantly affected his practice in speech composition. Of his rhetorical intent, he said, "My basic purpose in speaking is to inform."[2]

Political commentators sometimes alleged that Stevenson spoke over the heads of his audiences. Objective analysis shows that his vocabulary was not significantly more difficult than the vocabulary of other political speakers; nor were the topics he treated unfamiliar in political discourse. There is, indeed, no clear evidence that popular audiences found Stevenson difficult to understand, though his allusions may now and again seem perplexing at a first glance. It is more probable that Stevenson's unwillingness to make major adaptations in campaign speaking, his commitment to the texts of carefully molded compositions, and his editorial tone created in some listeners the impression that he was aloof, speaking *to* them rather than *with* them. On occasion these qualities almost disappeared from his speeches in the United Nations Security Council. Without doubt, Stevenson was a master of words; in this respect he probably excelled all American political speakers since Franklin D. Roosevelt.

The speech reprinted here was delivered on May 5, 1959, to an audience of about five hundred business leaders, members of a national group known as ACTION (American Council to Improve Our Neighborhoods), meeting in Newark, New Jersey. The aim of ACTION is to energize public agencies and private enterprises on behalf of urban reconstruction programs. Stevenson was the featured speaker at the Newark conference. In his address he met with consummate skill the audience's desire that its own policies and objectives be rendered urgent and impressive through fresh, exhilarating restatement.

You have assigned me an impressive title—"The American City—A Cause for Statesmanship." I despair, frankly, that any words of mine can satisfy the promise of this title, or that my grasp can equal its reach. /1

As for The American City: I am not expert in its

[2]Ibid., p. 232.

problems. I confess to not even living in it, but rather as far from it as the logistics of commuting permit.* I know this makes me, in the literature of the subject, a "fugitive from civic responsibility," a form of parasitical growth taking income and culture from the city, and in return only adding to the morning and evening traffic jams. /2

As for Statesmanship: again I pretend no expertise. If certain political adventures of mine—in my youth —may have seemed to involve pretenses of statesmanship, I recognize that issue as having been publicly settled—not once, but twice. /3

Yet surely the first charge upon statesmanship as it applies today to the American city is clear enough. It is the charge upon statesmen responsible for all of the cities of the world. It is that these cities be permitted to survive—that they not become, in a chain of blinding flashes, only smoking, gaping holes in the ground. The point does not bear laboring. But neither may it be forgotten—lest it become the ultimate irony that man's foregathering in the city was to simplify his self-destruction. /4

But survival isn't the only problem we have in common with the rest of the world. Urban renewal and a shortage of housing are universal problems. I was told everywhere from Central Asia to Leningrad that housing is the number-one problem of the Soviet Union. And I have seen the great boom towns in the exploding population areas from Damascus to Manila, and the new central cities that have arisen from the ashes of London, Warsaw, Berlin.** Everywhere on earth the city planners and officials are struggling with the same problems of the decay and death of old centers and the birth and growth of new ones. /5

In distant places, I have, like you, often thought about our fantastic standard of living, and that in spite of blessings that exceed the grasp, even the imagination, of most of the world's people, we in America have still fallen far short of even arresting the spread of blight and decay in our cities. Like you, I have often wondered how we can hope to solve the problems of maintaining our alliances, of meeting the Communist economic and scientific offensive, of extending a helping hand to the peoples now searching for national identity and independence, of standing firm against aggression anywhere, if we can't mobilize our domestic resources to meet the needs of day-to-day work and living. /6

We are not concerned just with the new low-income and minority ghettos in some cities, nor just with real-estate values in the downtown central business districts, nor the bedeviled commuter, nor the costly, growing traffic congestion, nor the general offensiveness of the urban sprawl. The deficiencies in our schools and communal services, like parks, playgrounds, hospitals, and the ugly outcroppings of juvenile violence, are all pleading for attention and are all part of the broader task of revitalization and reinvigoration of the city as a way of life. /7

It is not even a renaissance we seek; rather it is the construction of an entirely new mode of living—poles apart from the Victorian city of old. What we are concerned with is the exciting, exhilarating adventure of constructing economic, financial, social and political tools to build—not a city—but a metropolis. /8

But to return to "statesmanship" in this context—I would define it simply as the marking and the doing of the central thing that needs to be done—finding the right key—and turning it. /9

If there is a key to the answers to the problems which today beset our cities, I am sure I haven't got it. I don't think there is one key. But I think of Pope's line about a key to a drawer wherein lie other keys.* /10

Because, I suppose, many of the best years of my life have been devoted to the problems of government, the drawer I look to is the one marked "government"—government with a small g (which suddenly reminds me of Oscar Wilde's remark that nothing produces such pleasing effects as a good platitude). /11

Government with a small g does not mean, for me, the agencies of public government as distinguished from those of what we call business or private enterprise. I wish everyone could realize, as you do, how closely the functions of a corporation are related to "governmental" functions when—for example—a great insurance company takes over the clearing of a slum and its replacement with the facilities for decent, twentieth-century living. /12

The problems of the American city will be met when, and not until, we recognize that they are already and inexorably committed to the *joint* trusteeship of private enterprise and public responsibility; that they demand a shoulder-to-shoulder, two-fisted attack; that their solution depends entirely upon an alliance of private and public agencies—with each

---

*Mr. Stevenson's home was in Libertyville, Illinois, somewhat more than thirty miles from the heart of Chicago. (Editor's note)

**Stevenson had returned from a trip abroad in August 1958. On that particular journey, he had visited Russia and central Europe. (Editor's note)

* Pope's standard works contain no such references to ''keys,'' ''drawers,'' ''lock,'' or ''unlock.'' See Edwin Abbott, *Concordance to the Works of Alexander Pope.* Stevenson may have in mind a line from Pope's ''Translations from Greek and Latin,'' his ''Adaptations of Chaucer,'' or his ''Imitations of English Poets.'' *(Editor's note)*

respecting its own limitations and the capacities of the other, and with each acting in support of the other. /13

It is equally essential to recognize that the public agencies involved operate at three levels—federal, state and local—and that there is a similar problem of distributing responsibilities among these three, with each being equipped to do its appointed part. /14

America has the resources, the wealth, the raw materials, the intelligence, the technical know-how, the pressing need and the driving desire to solve all the problems which have so far prevented the remaking of the cities. Statesmanship's question here is not *what* to do but *who* is to do it—and how to make an alliance among the agencies involved, as you have evidently done with such spectacular success here in Newark. /15

There is no point in emphasizing at an ACTION conference the stake private enterprise—including every businessman in every city in America—has in the preservation and the strengthening of the urban structure. You, more than any other group, have pointed out that what is good for the American city is good for every businessman who operates there. /16

Part of these returns are direct—in profit on the building projects themselves. But more and more the business community is coming to realize that urban renewal also means more customers coming in the doors, that an equity investment in a slum clearance development project represents philanthropy—at a profit. We are beginning to recognize that not only charity, but investment as well, can best begin at home, *in* homes. /17

I suspect that in the long run the clearing of slums will come less as the result of public concern about the people there being poor people than as a product of the business community's concern about their being poor customers. This isn't cynical. It simply recognizes the fact that it is hard to sustain public concern—except when a school burns down or a rat bites a child—in a problem which neighbors can solve by moving away from it. But businesses can't easily do that. /18

So business, especially big business, has a great opportunity here to make a contribution—and to make a profit. /19

But there are some parts of this job that just cannot be done at a profit, and therefore will not be done privately. The necessary distribution of responsibilities for city saving will not come about as long as influential groups insist that any governmental financial aid, except to guarantee mortgages, is socialist sin—which you are either against in all if its manifes-

tations or for, all the way. For that matter we will never get our sights straight as long as influential people persist in the myth that all public spending is bad, all private spending good. I believe it was Justice Holmes who said: "I buy civilization with my taxes." /20

I came across, the other day, a speech I made at a Housing Day Conference in Chicago ten years ago. This line jumped out at me: "The public housing debate is over." That was shortly after, of course, the enactment under the sponsorship of Senators Taft, Wagner and Ellender, of the Housing Act of 1949—providing for the building of 135,000 public housing units a year for six years, or 810,000 in all. /21

But now, ten years later, only half of those 810,000 units have been built, and some of those who denounced Senator Taft as an "old Republican"[*] have brought in a housing bill providing for no public housing at all. /22

Nobody "likes" public housing. It is a mark of failure, and the nation will welcome and accept the views of those critics of public housing who will develop alternatives which are constructive and realistic. But mere insistence that private enterprise can do the job without public housing is no answer—unless this insistence is backed up with action. We are entitled to say here, with a new meaning, "either put up—or shut up." /23

There is reason for larger satisfaction about the increasing supply of middle-income housing. I saw a few days ago in New Haven the heartening spectacle of a beautiful new city rising from the ashes of ugliness and neglect. We have in Chicago now, as you have in a number of your cities, substantial developments which confirm the willingness and ability of private capital and enterprise to carry the job of reconstruction forward if public funds are available for the preliminary clearing of the old slum areas. /24

I am most encouraged, incidentally, by the reports of success in leasing these new accommodations on "open-occupancy" basis, for any realistic appraisal of the housing problem must take account of the serious danger that subsidized housing will become racially segregated housing and will thereby aggravate a problem as serious as the housing problem itself. /25

Last week a friend of mine who has done a great deal to rebuild Chicago showed me how the private equity investment of $4,725,000 per year for ten years will produce the capital required to completely

---

* Senator Robert A. Taft and General Dwight D. Eisenhower were competitors for the Republican nomination for President in 1952. Eisenhower's supporters insisted their candidate represented "modern Republicanism" and Senator Taft, the "old Republicans." (Editor's note)

rebuild an entire square mile of slums with fine, modern living accommodations which can be rented to low-middle-income families at a fair profit. I was sobered when he added that this proposition assumes a public subsidy to acquire this land and to write it down to use value, and that these costs will run to $8,000,000 per year. Yet this is the kind of cooperative venture, the kind of public-private alliance, which alone can do this job. It appeared, for a while, that there was solid recognition of the degree of aid that would have to come from federal sources to support local urban renewal, in both its private and its public aspects. Of late, there has been considerable doubt cast on both the extent of such aid and its character or continuance. The plain fact is that those who oppose federal aid for urban renewal are actually against urban renewal. For they know full well that many of the possibilities of local revenue have been pre-empted by federal and state taxing bodies, that the largest urban centers are operating under archaic revenue authority with little hope of relief from state legislatures dominated by non-urban lawmakers.* The vast sums urban renewal requires are just not available exclusively from private funds or from the local resources of the overwhelming majority of urban centers. /26

From administrative experience we have learned some lessons the hard way. It is clear now that the administrators of the federal program destroy the effectiveness of local authorities and discourage willing private investors when they keep changing the rules of the game, throwing out projects which were carefully devised to conform to the old rules but which don't meet the new ones. Too many of us here are familiar with the crippling effect in our own cities of arbitrary notices from Washington that all projects are to be scaled down by an arbitrary percentage. Too often the scaled-down project just doesn't make sense. Half a building is not better than none, and it is often the falsest economy to pick at a slum instead of rending a bulldozer all the way through it. /27

It is noteworthy, too, that these pending bills reflect the significance of the conservation principle that a dollar put into preventing urban decay is ten dollars saved in subsequent rebuilding. /28

Such legislation deserves support solely in terms of the human values that are involved. The juvenile delinquency a slum breeds infects a whole city. The tax bill for it—for police regulation, for fire protection, for relief payments—goes to every taxpayer. /29

You and I vote at each election with complacent

confidence that democratic capitalism means security and the supplying of life's purposes. But our votes count no more than the votes from slum victims which are not based on that faith. /30

I reread not long ago the story of the twenty-one American soldiers who chose not to return from the Korean Communist prison camp but to stay with those who had captured their minds as well as their bodies. Fifteen of those "21 Who Stayed" came from slums—some in the cities, some in the country. I could only think of Bret Harte's poetic dictum that nobody shoulders a rifle in defense of a boarding house. /31

But, we are being told, we can't afford these things. /32

I would, if it were necessary, say to this that there are emergencies in which you call the doctor without asking the cost, and that cancer in our cities is such a case. When somebody starts talking about the evil of passing a burden of public debt on to the next generation it makes me want to ask if it is better to pass on a burden of slums, of ignorance, of national weakness—and ultimately greater debt. We have a way of saying about reforms and changes that they were "inevitable." But with urban renewal as with everything else—"the mode by which the inevitable comes to pass is effort." /33

But to support a program of full-scale renewal and rebuilding of the cities is not to be soft-hearted (which seems to me no sin); it is also to be hardheaded. I am not a budget buster. But I do believe in America's greatness, and that this greatness can be traced to bold leaders and bold enterprises and the basic notion that money invested properly and adequately will multiply wealth. And every dollar of public funds that goes into slum clearance and urban renewal will be returned to the public coffers in increased revenues. /34

In the face of these great needs which are also great opportunities, I hope we are ready to stop the demagogic political debate which assumes that government and private enterprise are inherently antagonistic. I hope we are now ready to accept, instead, the demanding necessity for a confident alliance of public and private enterprise in meeting the problems of the city. /35

Money is not enough. Indeed the wrong amount of money at the wrong time and in the wrong place may hinder rather than help our efforts to construct the city of the future. We Americans have a penchant for believing that sufficient inputs of energy and dollars can solve any problem. We rush in where angels fear to tread and frequently we profit, but sometimes

---

* To secure reforms in the revenue authority of cities was one of the official objectives of ACTION. (Editor's note)

we learn why the angels, in their greater wisdom, have not joined us and preferred to stay aloft. Urban reconstruction is a case in point. /36

Despite the laudable efforts we have been making to deal with various aspects of the problem in the generation since the New Deal began, does the sum of these parts add up to a meaningful whole? Instead of developing a comprehensive program, are we in danger of creating a patchwork, a conglomeration of temporary and short-sighted solutions to pieces of a problem which cannot be handled piecemeal?* Even in that haven of generalities—a preamble to a federal law—we look in vain for a comprehensive statement of what we are after. /37

What do we want our downtown centers to become? What, in the long run, are the proper uses of the land in the "gray belt"? What kind of transportation system will best meet our needs? How do we want to use the remaining open spaces around our cities—for parks, for wild-life reservations, for industries or for the next wave of developments? /38

We shall have to look to groups like this for responsible, sustained help in finding the answers. But it will have to be left to the citizens of each urban community, acting through their own governments, to settle their own issues. And here we run into another familiar problem of government—the problem of too much government. At the local level the jumble of bureaus, municipalities, counties, commissions, authorities, corporations and officialdom generally has neither a sense of union nor a sense of direction. In most instances even the skeleton of a limp confederation is lacking. /39

At the very root of this problem is also the fact that although we have become a dominantly urban and suburban society, our political thinking and structure is still predominantly country minded. Coming from the country, I have no quarrel with rural people. But the fact is that one hundred million Americans live today in 168 metropolitan areas. This is over 60 percent of our total population. Yet in most legislatures the vote of a small town or rural citizen is worth substantially more than his city cousin's. /40

I know from my years as governor of a divided state how difficult this problem is. There are two sides to it. And yet there is bound to be a change. Local governments must be given the fiscal authority which the discharge of their responsibilities demands. There must be enlargement, in one way or another, of the revenue sources available to them. Gotham won't secede from New York, nor Chicago

* Major, rather than piecemeal, urban renewal was an official ACTION objective. (Editor's note)

from Illinois, but this is a serious problem and it is going to take ingenuity—and a willingness to seek out entirely new ways—to meet it. /41

These urban problems have today become metropolitan problems, problems that cross all lines between city and suburbs and between incorporated and unincorporated areas, problems that have no city limits. /42

The plain fact is that the resources on which our urban life depend—land, water and breathable air—are getting scarcer. The decisions about their use, like the decisions about transportation, are hard decisions. Any assumption that the city planners or high level commissions will devise the answers seems to me to go only halfway. For the answers, however wise, won't mean anything unless they are adopted —through the political decision-making process—by those affected by these decisions. /43

I know the difficulties which will be in the way of developing new machinery of decision. The sovereignties and vested interests of established local units and officialdom will be as hard to break down as they are at the national and international levels. The various suburbs which surround our major cities are already developing special ethnic and economic personalities, and this will make it harder and harder for the citizens of one area to be persuaded to submit their interests to a common vote which includes the citizens of another. /44

But I know, too, of the bold, effective way this problem has been met by Toronto. We are all watching eagerly the imaginative inquiry being conducted at Detroit. Other cities have taken the first essential steps toward metropolitan planning and are now looking to the possibilities of limited metropolitan government. /45

If building new instruments seems hopeless, then I must say that I think the other choice is to accept for our cities the fate of eternal worrying at the edges of our urban concerns, of everlasting plucking at ever broadening scabs of blight and decay; while more authority will remain at the higher state and federal levels. /46

A Balkanized metropolis can probably cope, in desperation, with the problems of urban survival. It can make our day-to-day difficulties tolerable. But I doubt if it can ever conceive the great plans, set the great policies, make the great decisions, which are essential if the cities are to be built and rebuilt according to the blueprints of our hopes. /47

I have tried to suggest that the problems of the American city demand the exercise of what is perhaps the most difficult art of democratic government:

the effective mobilization of all of the forces which make up the free body politic and the free body economic—not just to make the right decisions, but also to carry them out. /48

There are people in the world today who say that tough public problems are best solved behind closed doors, by dictators or central committees. But in our land we dare not even reach for a goal of human improvement in disregard of human values, human judgments. The central tenet of statesmanship in a democracy is that unless the people understand it and participate in it, no long-term program can endure. /49

The municipality of tomorrow must be renewed in the image of people's hopes and ambitions for a better life. The values to be recreated must have a sound political and economic pedestal, but they must flow from human needs. /50

Thus will we build and rebuild our cities, and in so doing renew and rekindle our faith in ourselves and in the limitless creativeness of free men. /51

The speech

1. Stevenson has sometimes been criticized for treating serious issues with too much humor. Identify the points at which he makes use of humor in this speech. Do you think these usages reflect undue casualness concerning the subject he is discussing?

2. What is the central idea of this speech? Is it an expository or persuasive thesis?

3. What are the main divisions of the body of the speech? What is the pattern of organization?

4. A distinctive feature of Stevenson's style is his use of connotations of a special kind, neither wholly familiar nor truly individual. Review the discussion of *connotation* in the Glossary, and then identify at least four such special connotations used in this speech. Could the occurrence of such usages make some listeners feel Stevenson talked "over their heads"?

5. Stevenson is expert at making epigrams. After reviewing the definition of an *epigram* in the Glossary, identify at least three epigrams in the speech. Do these epigrams reinforce the speaker's points?

6. Do you find any examples of satire in this speech? If so, what reactions were they likely to elicit from the ACTION audience?

7. It has been said that Stevenson's analyses and criticisms are clearer and more precise than his plans and programs. Is this true in this speech? Would plans and programs need to be spelled out in more detail for a popular audience in a political campaign than for the ACTION conference? Why?

8. Are there any passages in the speech that seem more like something you might read in a newspaper than hear from a public platform? If so, what characteristics distinguish those passages from others which you judge to have a clearly *oral* style?

9. Identify some of the points at which Stevenson deliberately tried to strengthen his own ethos before the ACTION audience. Do his references to his "escape" from city dwelling reduce his ethos with this audience?

10. Which of the ends of speaking did Stevenson probably achieve with his audience? To inform? To inspire? To persuade? To inquire?

For further study and discussion

1. What processes of population movement and sociological change produce what Stevenson calls "low-income and minority ghettos"? Are these processes different in northern and southern cities in the United States?

2. Inform yourself concerning a comprehensive urban renewal program in one of our cities—Hartford, Connecticut; Pittsburgh; Baltimore; or some other. How was the program started? How were costs shared? Were living conditions for low-income groups improved?

3. Do you agree with Stevenson and ACTION that only coordinated financing by federal, state, and local governments and by business can solve the planning and reconstruction problems of our major cities? Explain.

4. What is the difference, if any, between the positions of the Republican and Democratic parties on granting and administering federal assistance for slum clearance? If there is a difference, which position do you endorse?

5. What remedies have been proposed for "the jumble of bureaus, municipalities, counties, commissions, authorities, corporations, and officialdom" that constitutes the present government of metropolitan areas? Is the concept of city government, distinct from the government of its suburbs, sound?

6. Is there clear evidence that slums breed juvenile delinquency, or are causes other than housing conditions more important? What do authorities list as the major and the minor causes of juvenile delinquency?

7. What effects have power struggles between rural and urban groups had on the legislation of your state in the last ten years? Have these effects been generally good or bad? In what ways?

8. Is it true that the federal government has pre-empted so many sources of tax money that states and municipalities can no longer finance their proper responsibilities? If so, what should be done about it?

9. What kinds of taxes ought to be levied by federal and state governments in order to finance urban renewal programs?

10. Which do you think is the most critical domestic problem in America today: urban renewal, improvement of education, financing medical care, security for the aged, or highway construction? Support your choice.

Suggestions for further reading

Nels Anderson, *The Urban Community: A World Perspective* (New York, 1959)

David E. Christensen, *Urban Development* (New York, 1964)

Leonard A. Duhl, ed., *The Urban Condition: People and Policy in the Metropolis* (New York, 1963)

"Metropolis in Ferment," *Annals of the American Academy of Political and Social Sciences,* Vol. 314 (November 1957)

Wilfred Owen, *Cities in the Motor Age* (New York, 1959)

Oscar H. Steiner, *Our Housing Jungle and Your Pocketbook* (New York, 1960)

Frank Lloyd Wright, *The Living City* (New York, 1958)

Inaugural address

JOHN F. KENNEDY

Except in rare circumstances an inaugural address is a ceremonial rather than a persuasive speech. Audiences do not attend the installations of new officers to hear legislative plans debated, laws interpreted, or moral systems compared. They come to observe and to celebrate the assumption of duties they believe are important. Because this is so, inaugural speakers necessarily speak in general rather than specific terms, suggesting rather than contending for the courses of action they hope to further through the authority of their offices.

On January 20, 1961, John F. Kennedy admirably filled these rhetorical obligations in assuming the office of President of the United States. He addressed himself to all the citizens of the country and, indirectly, to all peoples of the civilized world, knowing that his real audience was vastly larger than the several thousands gathered in Washington to hear him. Although he drew upon ideas with which he and his political party had associated themselves during the election contest of 1960, he observed the ceremonial occasion by avoiding any show of partisanship. In campaigning for the presidency he had adopted the theme "New Frontier" and had found much fault with American foreign policy under the preceding Republican administration. Now, in his inaugural speech, he held to the same theme but magnified its least controversial aspects by sketching undoubted opportunities for new ventures in politics and economics and by devoting a greater proportion of time than any other peacetime president to unquestionable challenges in foreign relations.

Kennedy's address received generous praise. Adjectives commonly applied to it were "vigorous," "eloquent," "inspiring." Some commentators said it compared favorably with the great addresses delivered by Lincoln and Franklin D. Roosevelt. Others characterized it as "mood music" but conceded it was an impressive expression of the new president's aspirations and confidence.

As is customary at presidential inaugurals, Kennedy spoke in the open air. The day was unusually cold but clear. A snowstorm had impeded travel in and about Washington during the forty-eight hours preceding the inaugural ceremony, but a satisfactorily impressive audience gathered before the Capitol to hear the address. Millions heard and saw the new president on radio and television.

President Kennedy spoke slowly, in striking contrast to his rapid-fire delivery in impromptu discourse. Sometimes prolonging vowel sounds, sometimes repeating the same pattern of pitch inflections on successive phrases, he emphasized the cadence of his prose. Each major stress in phrasing was further reinforced by a sharp, downward thrust of his right forearm and hand. At points of greatest vocal force he rapped the reading desk sharply with knuckles or fist.

The style of the speech was in keeping with the delivery: again and again balanced and antithetical constructions rendered the language at once economical and rhythmical; direct questions and imperative sentences gave the address a sermonic or hortatory quality; the recurring religious and historical allusions reinforced the solemnity with which the speaker delivered his remarks.

John F. Kennedy was born in Brookline, Massachusetts, in 1917. He graduated with honors from Harvard University in 1940 and entered the Navy. He was severely wounded while commanding a PT boat during World War II. In 1946, he was elected to Congress from Massachusetts and served there until elected to the U.S. Senate in 1952. During his second term in the Senate he was nominated as the Democratic party's candidate for the presidency and in 1960 defeated Richard M. Nixon (pp. 241-247) in one of the closest presidential elections in American history. He was assassinated in Dallas, Texas, on November 22, 1963.

During a period of illness in 1954, Mr. Kennedy began preparation of his now famous book *Profiles in Courage.* It was published in 1956 and became a best seller. It and Mr. Kennedy's inaugural address are two of his most distinguished works.

My Fellow Citizens: We observe today not a victory of party but a celebration of freedom—symbolizing an end as well as a beginning—signifying renewal as well as change. For I have sworn before you and almighty God the same solemn oath our forebears prescribed nearly a century and three-quarters ago. /1

The world is very different now. For man holds in his mortal hands the power to abolish all forms of human poverty and all forms of human life. And yet the same revolutionary beliefs for which our forebears fought are still at issue around the globe—the belief that the rights of man come not from the generosity of the state but from the hand of God. /2

We dare not forget today that we are the heirs of that first revolution. Let the word go forth from this time and place, to friend and foe alike, that the torch has been passed to a new generation of Americans—born in this century, tempered by war, disciplined by a hard and bitter peace, proud of our ancient heritage—and unwilling to witness or permit the slow undoing of those human rights to which this nation has always been committed, and to which we are committed today at home and around the world. /3

Let every nation know, whether it wishes us well or ill, that we shall pay any price, bear any burden, meet any hardship, support any friend, oppose any foe in order to assure the survival and success of liberty. /4

This much we pledge—and more. /5

To those old allies whose cultural and spiritual origins we share, we pledge the loyalty of faithful friends. United, there is little we cannot do in a host of cooperative ventures. Divided, there is little we can do—for we dare not meet a powerful challenge at odds and split asunder. /6

To those new states whom we welcome to the ranks of the free, we pledge our word that one form of colonial control shall not have passed away merely to be replaced by a far more iron tyranny. We shall not always expect to find them supporting our view. But we shall always hope to find them strongly supporting their own freedom—and to remember that, in the past, those who foolishly sought power by riding the back of the tiger ended up inside. /7

To those peoples in the huts and villages of half the globe struggling to break the bonds of mass misery, we pledge our best efforts to help them help themselves, for whatever period is required—not because the communists may be doing it, not because we seek their votes, but because it is right. If a free society cannot help the many who are poor, it cannot save the few who are rich. /8

To our sister republics south of our border, we offer a special pledge—to convert our good words into good deeds—in a new alliance for progress—to assist free men and free governments in casting off the chains of poverty. But this peaceful revolution of hope cannot become the prey of hostile powers. Let all our neighbors know that we shall join with them to oppose aggression or subversion anywhere in the Americas. And let every other power know that this Hemisphere intends to remain the master of its own house. /9

To that world assembly of sovereign states, the United Nations, our last best hope in an age where the instruments of war have far outpaced the instruments of peace, we renew our pledge of support—to prevent it from becoming merely a forum for invective—to strengthen its shield of the new and the weak—and to enlarge the area in which its writ may run. /10

Finally, to those nations who would make themselves our adversary, we offer not a pledge but a request: that both sides begin anew the quest for peace, before the dark powers of destruction unleashed by science engulf all humanity in planned or accidental self-destruction. /11

We dare not tempt them with weakness. For only when our arms are sufficient beyond doubt can we be certain beyond doubt that they will never be employed. /12

But neither can two great and powerful groups of nations take comfort from our present course—both sides overburdened by the cost of modern weapons, both rightly alarmed by the steady spread of the deadly atom, yet both racing to alter that uncertain balance of terror that stays the hand of mankind's final war. /13

So let us begin anew—remembering on both sides that civility is not a sign of weakness, and sincerity is always subject to proof. Let us never negotiate out of fear. But let us never fear to negotiate. /14

Let both sides explore what problems unite us instead of belaboring those problems which divide us. /15

Let both sides, for the first time, formulate serious and precise proposals for the inspection and control of arms—and bring the absolute power to destroy other nations under the absolute control of all nations. /16

Let both sides join to invoke the wonders of science instead of its terrors. Together let us explore the stars, conquer the deserts, eradicate disease, tap the ocean depths, and encourage the arts and commerce. /17

Let both sides unite to heed in all corners of the earth the command of Isaiah—to "undo the heavy burdens . . . [and] let the oppressed go free." /18

And if a beach-head of cooperation may push back the jungles of suspicion, let both sides join in creating a new endeavor, not a new balance of power, but a new world of law, where the strong are just and the weak secure and the peace preserved. /19

All this will not be finished in the first one hundred days. Nor will it be finished in the first one thousand days, nor in the life of this Administration, nor even perhaps in our lifetime on this planet. But let us begin. /20

In your hands, my fellow citizens, more than mine, will rest the final success or failure of our course. Since this country was founded, each generation of Americans has been summoned to give testimony to its national loyalty. The graves of young Americans who answered the call to service surround the globe. /21

Now the trumpet summons us again—not as a call to bear arms, tho arms we need—not as a call to battle, tho embattled we are—but a call to bear the burden of a long twilight struggle, year in and year out "rejoicing in hope, patient in tribulation"—a struggle against the common enemies of man: tyranny, poverty, disease, and war itself. /22

Can we forge against these enemies a grand and global alliance, North and South, East and West, that can assure a more fruitful life for all mankind? Will you join in that historic effort? /23

In the long history of the world, only a few generations have been granted the role of defending freedom in its hour of maximum danger. I do not shrink from this responsibility—I welcome it. I do not believe that any of us would exchange places with any other people or any other generation. The energy, the faith, and the devotion which we bring to this endeavor will light our country and all who serve it—and the glow from that fire can truly light the world. /24

And so, my fellow Americans: ask not what your country can do for you—ask what you can do for your country. /25

My fellow citizens of the world: ask not what America will do for you, but what together we can do for the freedom of man. /26

Finally, whether you are citizens of America or citizens of the world, ask of us here the same high standards of strength and sacrifice which we ask of you. With a good conscience our only sure reward, with history the final judge of our deeds, let us go forth to lead the land we love, asking His blessing and His help, but knowing that here on earth God's work must truly be our own. /27

The speech

1. A number of critics have remarked that the dominant characteristic of this speech was balance—balance not only in style and organization but also in the policies expressed. What passages seem to confirm this appraisal? Are there any that tend to refute it?

2. Study closely the sequence of ideas in paragraphs 6-11, where President Kennedy speaks first to our allies, second to the newly formed nations of Africa and Asia, third to Latin America, fourth to the United Nations, and finally to those countries "who would make themselves our adversary." What rhetorical and psychological advantages does this sequence have? What disadvantages?

3. To what motive or motives does Kennedy appeal? At what points in the speech are the appeals made? Which of the appeals is strongest? What do you think of his choice of motives?

4. Comment on the introduction of the speech—its length, tone, transition into the body. What effort is made to heal some of the wounds that might have been left by the campaign?

5. The speech is dotted with *epigrams* and *figures of speech* (see Glossary). Find as many as you can. Do they help the speaker communicate his ideas or do they hinder him? Comment on Kennedy's word choice and sentence structure.

6. Before his election some of Kennedy's critics charged he was too young and inexperienced to be President. Can you find in the speech a passage which seems to refute this charge?

7. Except for the paragraph where Kennedy asks "both sides . . . [to] formulate serious and precise proposals for the inspection and control of arms," he speaks in general rather than specific terms. Do you regard the absence of concrete supporting materials as a defect in the speech? Present arguments both pro and con.

8. Study particularly paragraph 23 where Kennedy attempts to drive home his point by using a rhetorical question. Did this device add strength to his argument? If so, why; if not, why not?

9. Some persons believe that at places Kennedy was too idealistic (see, for example, paragraphs 11, 17-19, etc.) and that as a result listeners reacted unfavorably. Do you agree or disagree? Why? Can you find a passage in the speech where this idealism is tempered?

10. Compare this speech with Theodore Roosevelt's "The Man with the Muck Rake" (pp. 102-106). Does Kennedy

"extol . . . gospel, in a manner distinctly homiletical," as Roosevelt is said to have done? If so, what features of the speech give it this quality? Which are like, and which different from, the features of Roosevelt's address?

For further study and discussion

1. What practical difficulties stand in the way of an international system of arms inspection and control? How might some of these difficulties be effectively removed?

2. In what ways is atomic energy now used for peaceful purposes? How may the nations of the world cooperate to promote developments in this field?

3. What problems have arisen as new independent nations have been formed in Africa and Asia? What policy should the United States follow toward these new nations?

4. Review the present state of our relations with the countries of Latin America. In what respects has our present policy toward them worked well? In what respects has it failed? What recommendations would you make for the future?

5. What problems sometimes strain our relations with our traditional allies—England, France, Canada, etc.? In your opinion, how may these problems be minimized or solved?

6. Do too many people today ask what the government can do for them rather than what they can do for the government?

7. Discuss Kennedy's statement that "the same revolutionary beliefs for which our forebears fought are still at issue around the globe. . . ."

8. What are the advantages and disadvantages of "summit" meetings? Is "personal diplomacy" to be preferred to negotiations carried on through traditional channels?

9. Do you agree with Kennedy that present problems and responsibilities should be welcomed, or would you prefer to "exchange places" with some other people or some other generation?

10. Name some specific ways in which we might go about exploring with other nations "what problems unite us instead of belaboring those problems which divide us"?

Suggestions for further reading

James MacGregor Burns, *John Kennedy: A Political Profile* (New York, 1960)

The Joint Appearances of Senator John F. Kennedy and Vice President Richard M. Nixon and Other 1960 Campaign Presentations, Final Report of the Committee on Commerce, U.S. Senate, 87th Cong., 1st Sess., Report 994, Part 3 (Washington, D.C., 1961)

John F. Kennedy, *Profiles in Courage* (New York, 1956)

Victor Lasky, *J.F.K., the Man and the Myth* (New York, 1962)

Norman Mailer, *Presidential Papers* (New York, 1963)

Allan F. Westin and others, *Centers of Power* (New York, 1964)

Ethics in international relations today

DEAN ACHESON

Dean Acheson, former Secretary of State and foreign policy advisor to Presidents Kennedy and Johnson, has long been known for his trenchant and often iconoclastic views. In the following speech, delivered at Amherst College on the evening of December 9, 1964, he presents a fresh and provocative analysis of the role of ethics in international relations.[1]

While not denying the importance of strict ethical standards in the conduct of diplomats, Acheson maintains that "moralistic maxims" are not the criteria by which foreign policy should be formulated or judged. Instead, he advocates what he terms "the strategic approach"—an approach which evaluates policies pragmatically by asking whether they foster an environment "in which free societies may exist and flourish."

After a bold opening in which persons "who seek to deduce foreign policy from ethical or moral principles" are said to be as "misled" as are those "who would conduct our foreign relations without regard to them," the speech follows an indirect or inductive pattern of development. Paragraphs 2 through 7 point out the importance of openness and honesty in international negotiations; paragraphs 7 through 12 draw a distinction between the ethics of private and of public life; and paragraphs 13 through 22 criticize three of the "delusive . . . maxims" which pass for "ethical standards for governmental policies in foreign affairs." Finally, with paragraph 23, near the close of the address, the conception of "the strategic approach" is advanced and explained. Following this explanation, a brief conclusion, developed chiefly by reiteration, rounds out the address.

While the speech received wide attention in the press, comment upon it generally was critical. Typical of the more outspoken reactions was that offered editorially by the New York *Times*, which said that instead of being a measure of "weakness," moral restraints actually are "a measure of realism . . . in a world dominated by nuclear weapons."[2]

Acheson, who was graduated from Yale University and the Harvard Law School, held various government posts before becoming Secretary of State in the Truman cabinet. He now practices law in Washington, D.C.

The text of the address as here printed was supplied by Acheson and approved by him.

The discussion of ethics or morality in our relations with other states is a prolific cause of confusion. The righteous who seek to deduce foreign policy from ethical or moral principles are as misleading and misled as the modern Machiavellis who would conduct our foreign relations without regard to them. /1

Most of what we, and a good part of the noncommunist world, regard as ethical principles relates to conduct, the behavior of individuals toward one another. There is pretty general agreement that it is better to act straightforwardly, candidly, honorably, and courageously than duplicitously, conspiratorially, or treacherously. This is true of conduct toward friends and toward those who are ill-disposed to us. It is well that our government should give to foreigners as well as to our own people as clear an idea as possible of its intentions. To do so should inspire confidence and increase stability. One need not counsel perfection—for instance, to tell the whole truth; but it ought not to be too much to advise telling nothing but the truth—advice which might usefully have been given to President Eisenhower before he began issuing statements about the U-2 aircraft shot down some years ago over the Soviet Union. /2

The French school of diplomacy, founded by Cardinal Richelieu, the dominant school for nearly three centuries, and probably still the best ever devised, was based, as François de Callières stated, upon the principle that "open dealing is the basis of

Reprinted by permission of Dean Acheson.
[1]The speech was one of the featured events of a two-day symposium on "The Future of the Western Alliance."

[2]"Morality Is Realism," New York *Times*, December 12, 1964, p. 30 (Late city edition).

confidence" (a very different idea from President Wilson's ill-considered maxim, "open covenants openly arrived at"). He adds, "The negotiator therefore must be a man of probity and one who loves truth; otherwise he will fail to inspire confidence." And again, "Deceit is the measure of the smallness of mind of him who uses it . . . a lie always leaves behind it a drop of poison. . . . Menaces always do harm to negotiation. . . ." /3

It does not detract from the purity of his morals that he supports them with worldly wisdom:

"The diplomatist must be . . . a good listener, courteous, and agreeable. He should not seek to gain a reputation as a wit, nor should he be so disputatious as to divulge secret information in order to clinch an argument. Above all the good negotiator must possess enough self control to resist the longing to speak before he has thought out what he wants to say. . . . He should pay attention to women but never lose his heart . . . , possess the patience of a watch-maker . . . should not be given to drink . . . and be able to tell where, in any foreign country, the real sovereignty lies. . . . Finally . . . a good cook is often an excellent conciliator." /4

For any of you who are contemplating a career in the Foreign Service, François de Callières is as sound an adviser today as he was in 1716. /5

Without laboring the point further, I take it as clear that, where an important purpose of diplomacy is to further enduring good relations between states, the methods—the modes of conduct—by which relations between states are carried on must be designed to inspire trust and confidence. To achieve this result the conduct of diplomacy should conform to the same moral and ethical principles which inspire trust and confidence when followed by and between individuals. /6

The purpose of our own diplomacy, as of the French school, requires the inspiring of trust and confidence, for our governmental goal for many years has been to preserve and foster an environment in which free societies may exist and flourish. When we have said this, we had better stop and think before concluding that the policies which will advance us toward this goal can usefully be discussed or evaluated in terms of moral or ethical principles. /7

In the first place, a little reflection will convince us that the same conduct is not moral under all circumstances. Its moral propriety seems to depend, certainly in many cases, upon the relationship of those concerned with the conduct. For instance, parents have the moral right, indeed duty, to instill moral and religious ideas in their children and correct moral error. Ministers, priests, rabbis, and mullahs have much the same duties to their flocks, including that of correcting heresy, when they can make up their minds what it is. /8

But these same acts on the part of public officials —certainly in the United States—would be both wrong and a denial of the fundamental rights of the citizen. Indeed, even prayer prescribed and led by teachers in our public schools is condemned by our courts with the approval of some of our churches. The attempt of both governmental and religious bodies to censor literature, painting, sculpture, the theater, and the movies, under the aegis of those alliterative adjectives, lewd and lascivious, seems to me intolerable. Parents, if they are any good, can shield their children from whatever they choose. The rest of us had better take our chances with mortal sin, rather than to have policemen, trained to handle traffic and arrest criminals, become judges of what art we may see or read. And it is just as bad when the local watch and ward society or church body tries to do the same thing. /9

So, acts, moral in one human relationship, may become quite the reverse in another. Generally speaking, morality often imposes upon those who exercise the powers of government standards of conduct quite different from what might seem right to them as private citizens. For instance, the moral, and indeed the legal, duty of a judge in bringing to bear upon a party before him the coercive power of the state is not to do "what he thinks is right," or by his decision to mould the kind of society which seems to him to accord with divine will or high human aspiration. He has not been given this great power so that he might administer personal justice, even though his conscience be as clear as that of Harun al-Rashid or Henry the Second when they decided disputes by virtuous inspiration. Our courts are supposed to be courts of law; and whatever justice may be (I know of no satisfactory definition of it), it is to be achieved, as the phrase goes, "under law." It is our hope that the consciences of our judges will be guided, not by what they think is right, but by what they believe the law requires them to decide, whether they like it or not. /10

So, too, what may be quite proper and moral for a private citizen—for instance, the pursuit of personal advantage, or the advantage of a group—often, and rightly, is condemned if done when he assumes legislative or executive office. This distinction is not always perceived and has gotten many people into trouble. Even a candidate for office cannot expect the same latitude given private individuals in exposing his ignorance and stupidity. November 3rd last made that rather clear. /11

Moreover, the vocabulary of morals and ethics is inadequate to discuss or test foreign policies of states. We are told that what is ethical is characterized by what is excellent in conduct and that excellence may be judged by what is right and proper, as against what is wrong, by existing standards. But when we look for standards we find that none exist. What passes for ethical standards for governmental policies in foreign affairs is a collection of moralisms, maxims, and slogans, which neither help nor guide, but only confuse, decision on such complicated matters as the multilateral nuclear force, a common grain price in Europe, policy in Southeast Asia, or exceptions and disparities under the Kennedy Round of tariff negotiations. /12

One of the most often invoked and delusive of these maxims is the so-called principle of self-determination. In the continuing dispute over Cyprus it has been invoked by nearly all parties to the struggle to support whatever they were temporarily seeking to achieve—by all Cypriots to justify revolt against British rule, by Archbishop Makarios to support an independent government for the whole island, by Greek Cypriots as foundation for enosis (union) with Greece, and by Turkish Cypriots for partition of the island and double enosis, union of one part with Greece and the other with Turkey. /13

Despite its approval by Woodrow Wilson, this maxim has a doubtful moral history. He used it against our enemies in the First World War to dismember the Austro-Hungarian and Ottoman Empires with results which hardly inspire enthusiasm today. After the Second World War the doctrine was invoked against our friends in the dissolution of their colonial connections. In all probability these connections would inevitably have been dissolved. But the results were immeasurably improved when considerations other than moralistic maxims were brought to bear on the process. /14

On the one occasion when the right of self-determination—then called secession—was invoked against our own government by the Confederate States of America, it was rejected with a good deal of bloodshed and moral fervor. Probably you agree that it was rightly rejected. You would doubtless also agree that the dialogue now in progress between the British and French speaking sections of Canada upon the problems of a common national life together would not be helped by conducting it in terms of the principle of self-determination. /15

Furthermore, this moralistic doctrine is not merely no help to wise policy decisions, it can be a positive menace to them. "Hitler's appeal to national self-determination in the Sudeten crisis in 1938," writes Henry Kissinger, "was an invocation of 'justice,' and thereby contributed to the indecisiveness of the resistance; it induced the Western powers to attempt to construct a 'truly' legitimate order by satisfying Germany's 'just' claims. Only after Hitler annexed Bohemia and Moravia was it clear that he was aiming for dominion, not legitimacy; only then did the contest become one of pure power." /16

Another set of moralisms and maxims crops up to bedevil discussion and decision about what is broadly called "foreign aid." A good deal of trouble comes from the anthropomorphic urge to regard nations as individuals and apply to our own national conduct vague maxims for individual conduct—for instance, the Golden Rule—even though in practice individuals rarely adopt it. The fact is that nations are not individuals; the cause and effect of their actions are wholly different; and what a government can and should do with the resources which it takes from its citizens must be governed by wholly different considerations from those which properly determine an individual's use of his own. /17

This does not mean that considerations of compassion have no place in governmental decisions. It does mean that the criteria are generally quite different and far more complicated. Some of these criteria will determine what funds can be made available; others will determine their allocation among uses always exceeding amounts available. /18

The overriding guide must be achievement of a major goal of policy—in this case, creating an environment in which free societies may flourish and undeveloped nations who want to work on their own development may find the means to do so. This is an exceedingly difficult matter for both aiding and aided governments. The criteria should be hard-headed in the extreme. Decisions are not helped by considering them in terms of sharing, brotherly love, the Golden Rule, or inducting our citizens into the Kingdom of Heaven. /19

But, you will say to me, at least one moral standard of right and wrong has been pretty well agreed to be applicable to foreign policy. Surely, the opinion of the world has condemned the use and threat of force by one state against another, as the United Nations Charter bears witness. Does this not give us firm ground on which to stand? Well, does it? Ever since the Charter was signed, those whose interests are opposed to ours have used force, or the threat of it, whenever it seemed to them advisable and safe—in Greece, Czechoslovakia, Palestine, Berlin, Korea, Indochina, and Hungary. Each side used it in regard to Suez. /20

Is it moral to deny ourselves the use of force in all circumstances, when our adversaries employ it, under handy excuses, whenever it seems useful to tip the scales of power against every value we think of as moral and as making life worth living? It seems to me not only a bad bargain, but a stupid one. I would almost say an immoral one. For the very conception of morality seems to me to involve a duty to preserve values outside the contour of our own skins, and at the expense of foregoing much that is desired and pleasant, including—it may be—our own fortunes and lives. /21

But, however that may be, those involved in the Cuban crisis of October, 1962, will remember the irrelevance of the supposed moral considerations brought out in the discussions. Judgment centered about the appraisal of dangers and risks, the weighing of the need for decisive and effective action against considerations of prudence; the need to do enough, against the consequences of doing too much. Moral talk did not bear on the problem. Nor did it bear upon the decision of those called upon to advise the President in 1949 whether and with what degree of urgency to press the attempt to produce a thermonuclear weapon. A respected colleague advised me that it would be better that our whole nation and people should perish rather than be party to a course so evil as producing that weapon. I told him that on the Day of Judgment his view might be confirmed and that he was free to go forth and preach the necessity for salvation. It was not, however, a view which I could entertain as a public servant. /22

What, then, is the sound approach to questions of foreign policy? I suggest that it is what we might call the strategic approach—to consider various courses of action from the point of view of their bearing upon major objectives. On August 22, 1862, President Lincoln wrote to Horace Greeley in response to the latter's question as to how the President viewed the question of slavery in relation to the war then in progress, "my paramount object in this struggle is to save the Union, and is not either to save or destroy slavery. If I could save the Union without freeing any slave, I would do it; and if I could save it by freeing all the slaves, I would do it; and if I could do it by freeing some and leaving others alone, I would also do that. What I do about slavery and the colored race, I do because I believe it helps to save this Union; and what I forbear, I forbear because I do not believe it would help to save the Union. I shall do less whenever I shall believe what I am doing hurts the cause, and I shall do more whenever I shall believe doing more will help the cause." /23

This is what I mean by the strategic approach. If you object that is no different from saying that the end justifies the means, I must answer that in foreign affairs only the end can justify the means; that this is not to say that the end justifies any means, or that some ends can justify anything. The shifting "combinazioni," sought by the weak Italian city states of the Renaissance to plunder one another, not only failed to justify the means they used, but gave their diplomacy and its expounder, Niccolo Machiavelli, the bad name they have today. /24

The end sought by our foreign policy, the purpose for which we carry on relations with foreign states, is, as I have said, to preserve and foster an environment in which free societies may exist and flourish. Our policies and actions must be tested by whether they contribute to or detract from achievement of this end. They need no other justification or moral or ethical embellishment. To oppose powerful and brutal states which threaten the independence of others is not less admirable because it helps secure our own as well; nor is it less good to help others improve their lot because it is necessary to keep the free world free and to strengthen it. /25

In conducting our foreign affairs we can use any amount of intelligence, perseverance, nerve, and luck. But if we have an excess of moral or ethical enthusiasm or idealism, let us not try to find an outlet for it in the formulation of foreign policies. Rather in how we carry them out. In this country we have an unfortunate tendency to do fine and noble things in a thoroughly churlish way. Let us remember that often what we do may be less important than how we do it. "What one lives for may be uncertain," writes Lord Robert Cecil; "How one lives is not." We can be faulted far less in what we do, than in how we do it. /26

The speech

1. Find within the speech the one sentence which in your judgment best states the speaker's specific purpose. Defend your choice.

2. List and evaluate the principal methods and devices of persuasion which Acheson employs.

3. How would you classify the *introduction* (see Glossary)? Is it appropriate to the speaker, the subject, the audience, and the occasion?

4. Do you think that Acheson's audience probably was friendly, neutral, or hostile to his ideas? Why? What, in your judgment, would have been the probable attitude of an audience of clergymen? Of businessmen? Of military leaders?

5. In paragraphs 13-20 Acheson criticizes the principle of self-determination, attacks the "anthropomorphic urge to regard nations as individuals," and says it is wrong to deny ourselves the use or threat of force in all situations. If you were developing these three ideas, would you take them up in the order Acheson followed? Why or why not?

6. In your opinion, does the quotation from Lincoln (paragraph 23) furnish a germane and effective illustration of the so-called "strategic approach" to foreign policy? Why or why not?

7. Select the one aspect of the speech—its style, its arrangement, the arguments presented, etc.—which you think most detracts from its total persuasive impact. Try to rework the speech so as to improve it in this respect.

8. Is the conclusion of the speech effective or ineffective? Why?

For further study and discussion

1. If, as Acheson maintains, there is a special ethic that governs relations among nations, does it follow that there also is a special ethic of business transactions, of labor-management relations, of advertising, and the like? Are there no ethical standards which are applicable in all situations?

2. Acheson attacks the principle of self-determination because Hitler used it to deceive and the United States used it unsuccessfully (paragraphs 14-16). Do you agree that these experiences invalidate the principle? Why or why not?

3. Comment on Acheson's statement that although a nation should tell nothing but the truth, it need not tell "all" the truth.

4. Attack or defend this statement: "What passes for ethical standards for governmental policies in foreign affairs is a collection of moralisms, maxims, and slogans, which neither help nor guide, but only confuse. . . ."

5. Acheson mentions the Cuban missile crisis of 1962 as an instance in which "moral considerations" did not enter into a policy decision. Can you, on the other hand, name some instances in which the foreign policy of the United States or of some other nation appears to have been so guided?

6. Granting Acheson's view that "the same conduct is not moral under all circumstances," are there still certain acts on the part of nations or of individuals which you would consider as immoral under all circumstances, and therefore never acceptable?

7. In what ways have improved means of communication and the development of modern weapons systems complicated the problem of working out an acceptable ethic of international relations?

8. As long as the nations of the world represent diverse cultural and religious traditions and stand at widely varying stages of social development, can we ever hope to develop an ethic of international relations that will be universally recognized and accepted?

9. In your opinion are espionage and under-cover intelligence activities legitimate means of gathering information concerning the intentions and policies of other nations?

10. In commenting on Acheson's speech editorially, the New York *Times* (December 12, 1964, p. 30) declared: "Belligerence can be self-defeating if the rest of the world decides that the United States is reckless or ruthless in the use of its wealth and strength." Do you agree? Why or why not?

Suggestions for further reading

Dean Acheson, *Power and Diplomacy* (Cambridge, Mass., 1958)
———, *Real and Imagined Handicaps of Our Democracy in the Conduct of Its Foreign Relations* (Independence, Mo., 1962)
McGeorge Bundy, ed., *The Pattern of Responsibility* (Boston, 1962)
Richard A. Falk, *Law, Morality, and War in the Contemporary World* (New York, 1963)
Joseph Frankel, *The Making of Foreign Policy: An Analysis of Decision-Making* (New York, 1963)
Morton A. Kaplan, *System and Process in International Politics* (New York, 1957)

The minds of the non-Western world

VERA MICHELES DEAN

In the following lecture, delivered at San Francisco State College on June 26, 1962, Vera Micheles Dean attempts

Reprinted by permission of Vera Micheles Dean and the Board of Trustees of the Edith P. Merritt Memorial Lecture Fund.

to explain the attitudes and aspirations of non-Western peoples and to account for the forces that have shaped them.

Rhetorically, Mrs. Dean's remarks are both interesting and instructive. In a long introduction, divided into three parts, she first refers with grace and sincerity to the occasion for her address (paragraphs 1-4); second, she presents her unusual definition of *non-Western* (paragraphs 5-7); and, third, she provides a smooth transition into the body of the lecture (paragraphs 8-9).

The body itself is clearly organized. First, Mrs. Dean explains why we lack understanding of the non-Western world (paragraphs 10-12), why we must understand it (paragraph 13), and why we must understand not just a part of it, but all of it (paragraphs 14-15). Then she examines the basic attitudes shared by all non-Western peoples and sets forth four of the reasons for these attitudes—resentment of colonialism, authoritarian governments, backward economic and social conditions, and concern with domestic problems. Each reason is introduced with a clear subject sentence and then is developed by explanation or analogy.

Although the lecture lacks a separate solution step, Mrs. Dean, at various junctures, points out what we in the United States could and should do to promote better relations with non-Western countries, and she particularly stresses the contribution which might be made by the college students who composed a large part of her audience (paragraphs 30-31). In her final paragraphs, she suggests the sort of international community in which all nations, both Western and non-Western, some day may participate, and thus concludes the lecture on a strongly optimistic note.

Special mention should be made of Mrs. Dean's simple and exceptionally clear style; her use of rhetorical questions as transitional devices (paragraphs 9, 10, 13, 34, etc.); and the way in which she occasionally employs direct discourse to emphasize or enliven a point (paragraphs 6, 14, 18, etc.).

Mrs. Dean was born in St. Petersburg, Russia, on March 29, 1903. She came to the United States in 1919, and was educated at Radcliffe College and Yale University. Besides a Ph.D. from Yale, she holds nine honorary degrees.

Since 1962, Mrs. Dean has been Professor of International Development in the Graduate School of Public Administration, New York University; she was director of the Non-Western Civilizations Program, The University of Rochester, from 1954 through 1962, and was research director and editor of the Foreign Policy Association, from 1928 to 1961. She is the author of several books on world affairs, among them *The Nature of the Non-Western World*.

When asked to outline her views on public speaking, Mrs. Dean replied as follows.

"I regard every speech as a performance which must be prepared in such a way that it has a beginning, a middle, and a dramatic end, and is delivered in a tone of voice that holds the attention of the audience throughout. Early in my career I thought it necessary to write out texts of speeches—and then deliver them from the script. But my husband, a lawyer, firmly told me that I would never succeed by using this method, and urged me to speak extemporaneously, from a bare outline of what I intended to say.

"I was frightened to death when, in my 20's, I first tried out this method in a formal address before the imposing, all-masculine Economic Club of New York—but then found that I relished having direct communication with the audience, and have used this method ever since, to the despair of those who want a written text in advance. As a result, I feel that I am talking *with* those who listen to me, not *at* them. I also love to answer questions—in fact, this is for me the best part of a meeting—and at the advice of Frances J. Pratt, a wise friend who has skillfully guided my lecture career, have learned to make answers, which I once thought should be long and exhaustive, brief and pointed.

"But I would be less than honest if I said that, after years of experience, I am unafraid whenever I rise to speak. Quite the contrary. I am always nervous—and would be frightened if I were not. For a speaker who wants to communicate with an audience *must* be keyed up, like an actor, to give the best performance possible. And to dramatize the performance, I usually end every lecture with an appropriate quotation from some poem—often suggested to me by one or other of my many friends around the globe who know the delight I take in reciting poetry."

The following text is based upon a stenographic transcript made at the time of delivery. It has been approved by Mrs. Dean.

I am delighted to revisit San Francisco State College, where I spoke on a previous occasion several years ago. But today I feel particularly privileged to have been invited by the college to inaugurate this series of memorial lectures established in honor of Edith Merritt. /1

I regret that I did not have an opportunity to know Mrs. Merritt, but I have read about her life and about the outstanding work she had done in this college and in this community in the field of inter-cultural studies, which are of such vast importance to all of us today at all stages of education. /2

It is always extremely difficult for all of us to think of someone whom one loves and honors as passing from the scene of active life. Obviously, we all have to be prepared for this kind of situation ourselves. But it has always seemed to me that in looking beyond this life, whatever may be our personal religious beliefs, we can and should take comfort in the form of immortality which is given to those people who, when living, made such an imprint upon their friends and colleagues and students that their spirit, in effect, remains alive in the work of an institution and of a community. Clearly, this is the spirit which all who have been concerned with this memorial lectureship have felt in relation to Mrs. Merritt. And I hope that you will persevere in your endeavor of bringing to students here and to the community the kind of knowledge about what, for lack of a better word, we call the non-Western world, which Mrs. Merritt was communicating so brilliantly in the field of elementary education. /3

I think there is no time like the youngest time to make our children think about other people who are living under conditions entirely different from ours in vast areas of the world outside the United States. Their customs may be completely different from ours, but they are nevertheless rooted in the traditions and ideas of these peoples, just as our customs and our way of life are rooted in our traditions. This seems natural, and yet, we seem to find it very difficult, even today, to understand the peoples who live in the areas I call non-Western. /4

Now I should say right away that my definition of the word non-Western is somewhat unorthodox, as those of you who may have read my little book *The Nature of the Non-Western World* are aware. Under that term I group not only Asia and Africa and the Middle East—this is quite an orthodox way of doing it—but I also include in the non-Western world Russia, which cannot possibly be understood intelligently if we think of Russia as a Western country in 1917. Today Russia is being westernized, but this is quite a different matter. In 1917 it was not a Western country. /5

Even more controversially, I included Latin America in the non-Western world. Now this causes many arguments among some of my colleagues, who ask me a simple question. They say, "You do know, don't you, where Latin America is?" I say, "Yes, I do know it is in the Western Hemisphere. I have looked at the maps. I am aware of it." Then they ask, "How can you place Latin America in the non-Western world?" I answer: "For a very simple reason, and that is that social and economic conditions among our Good Neighbors to the south are very similar to those of Asia, the Middle East, and Africa today." And as a result, these conditions create political circumstances in Latin America which are very similar to those of Asia and the Middle East and Africa. To give only one example, let us look at the role of the military leader in Latin America. In a society where no middle class has yet developed, the military leader is the one who is educated, the one who really has control of what technology exists in his country, and so there are many similarities between, let us say, Colonel Peron in Argentina or Sergeant, later Colonel, Batista of Cuba, and Colonel Nasser in Egypt or Kasim in Iraq or Marshall Ayub Khan in Pakistan. So when I give examples of what I mean by the non-Western world, please bear in mind that from my point of view this term embraces a vast spectrum of the world. /6

When I speak of the non-Western world, my definition embraces those areas which have been little, or not at all, affected by the forces that have shaped Western civilization. We do know that Western civilization was shaped by the experience of Greece and Rome, and by the experience of Christianity—but let us remember that it was Roman Catholic Christianity, and not the Byzantine Christianity of Eastern Europe, of Russia. It was shaped by the Renaissance and the Reformation, by the impact of the three great political revolutions of the West—the English, French, and American Revolutions—and by the Industrial Revolution, which is only now beginning to penetrate into the non-Western world. If we bear this in mind, then we can approach the non-Western world with a historical perspective. /7

What is astonishing is that in spite of all our facilities for education at all levels in this country, in spite of our radio and television and newspapers, we are still just as much in the dark about understanding non-Western people as Europe was in the days of Marco Polo. I remember seeing an exhibition in Venice a few years ago which celebrated the 600th anniversary of Marco Polo's expedition to Asia. It was interesting to look at the maps of Marco Polo's time and to see that the only areas which were indicated on the maps were along the coasts, or here and there a little distance up a river, but for the rest of it, the interiors of Asia and Africa, the Middle East and Latin America were still completely empty spaces. They were empty spaces because no one had yet had an opportunity to explore these areas and to set down place names in these new non-Western areas which were only being discovered at this time. /8

Today there is no trouble in setting down place names in the interiors of non-Western continents. Geographers have been there; anthropologists have been there; we know the names and the places. But in spite of this knowledge, do we understand the peoples who live in the non-Western areas? This is the basic question we have to ask ourselves. I am sure all of you who are concerned with education realize that there is a vast difference between knowledge and understanding. You can know facts, but you may not understand anything about what these facts really add up to in human terms. /9

Why is it that we do not yet begin to understand the non-Western peoples? My own belief is that this is due to a reluctance on our part to accept the fact that the center of the universe has changed in the past decade. What do I mean by this? Well, until World War II we, like the peoples of Western Europe, had become accustomed to think that the West was the center of the universe, and we thought of the non-Western peoples as off center, so to speak, on the fringes of the great Western civilization developed in the Mediterranean and on the Atlantic and inherited by us in this country from the peoples of Western Europe. We continued to believe this in spite of the fact that we must surely be aware of the tremendous contributions that non-Western peoples have made to the heritage of civilized mankind. It is no diminution of the magnificent achievements of the West to recognize that the non-Western peoples have contributed some of the great religions of the universe—Hinduism, Islam, Buddhism, Shintoism, Confucianism—and, indeed, have contributed the faiths most of us practice in this country, Christianity and Judaism, which come, after all, from a non-Western area. These peoples, too, have contributed magnificently to the arts, to literature, to the philosophies of mankind, and in their day, many of them had systems of administration—in China, in India, in the Ottoman Empire—which compare very well with the systems of administration of the Western world. /10

And yet, we still cannot visualize clearly a world where these great peoples will be our equals in the world community. I believe that our reluctance to do so is due to some of the same emotions which were aroused in Western Europe at the end of the Renaissance and in the early part of the 17th Century when suddenly people felt the impact of the discoveries of Copernicus and Galileo, who had proved to their satisfaction that the earth was not the center of the universe. This was a terrifying experience for many Westerners. One can see this by reading some of the poets of England in the early 17th Century, for example, John Donne, who yielded to pessimism at this discovery, and wrote:

"And new philosophy calls all in doubt
'Tis all in pieces, all coherence gone."

But fortunately there were other poets in that period who saw the tremendous challenge and excitement of the new dimension in the universe opened up by the discoveries of Copernicus and Galileo. The poet Thomas Traherne wrote in quite a different mood when he said:

"The infinite I'll sing
Of time and space
My heart from joy doth spring
And all my spirits move
With pleasant trembeling." /11

Now it is going to be for us to decide whether we shall be gloomy and depressed at the thought that other peoples are emerging upon the world scene, challenging us in many ways, much of it for our own good, or whether we shall welcome the coming of these peoples back into the mainstream of world development. And let's face it, whether we are depressed or whether we are gay about it, these peoples are here and they will be here until the end of time. This is why it is essential that we who are concerned with education should make sure that every one of our citizens is aware of this tremendous change which has taken place in the universe. This is not a matter merely of an academic exercise. If that was all there was to it I would not try to sound as persuasive as I want to sound. I think it is a matter of life and death for all of us to understand the rest of the world. /12

Why is it a matter of life and death? Because today the peoples of the non-Western world are entering the world community in the United Nations, where each new nation can speak to us on a basis of equality no matter how small or weak it may be in terms of physical power. And let us face the fact that the majority of human beings in this world are, and will continue to be, non-white peoples. The white peoples are, and will remain, a minority. It is therefore essential that our children should be prepared to understand the majority among whom they will live, so that they, in turn, may hope to receive from them an understanding of ourselves, such as we have all too often in the past failed to give to non-Western peoples. /13

In trying to understand the minds of the non-Western peoples, it is not enough, as I see it, to study just one country or one area of the non-Western world. Some of my colleagues become alarmed when I make this point. They ask, "How shall we ever have the resources to study the whole non-Western world in this school or that college? Can't we just concentrate on one country and study, let us say Japan and, then, after we've studied Japan that will help us to understand China and Nigeria and Brazil." But I say, "No. You will understand Japan, perhaps, but you will certainly not understand China or India or Brazil or Nigeria." /14

Let me raise this question right now, because it occurs so often. How would you feel if you were an expert on Western Europe and you said, "Now I shall teach my students about Germany, and having understood Germany, children, you will all understand about Britain, and France and the Netherlands and Belgium and the Scandinavian countries, and also Italy." Of course they won't understand all these countries, because Germany is not France, and if you then try to tell me that by understanding even all of Western Europe, you would understand Britain, then I would have to smile sadly because Britain just isn't Europe, is it? It is Britain. So you would have to understand Britain just by itself. In the same way, it is insulting to the vast variety of experiences of the non-Western world to say, "Ah, I have understood the Japanese, and now the Nigerians are just as plain to me as could be." We'll just have to make an extra effort and understand as many of the non-Western peoples as possible, to become aware of their vast variety and diversity. /15

But let me reassure you. Because we would have to spend a few days here if I were to go through the entire world, I am going to emphasize today those factors which non-Western peoples do have in common, factors which may help us to approach non-Western peoples wherever we come in contact with them, and above all to understand their minds. /16

The first of these factors is resentment of colonialism. The interesting thing is that we in this country are astonished to find colonial peoples resent colonialism. No sooner, let us say, has Ghana achieved independence, than we say within 24 hours, "Why do you still dislike the British? Come on, love them. It's all over; you are independent." The people who say that—and many such write newspaper editorials or speak on TV—apparently did not have a course in American History, although American history is taught for four to six years. When I came to this country as a young immigrant and went to the fine institution of Radcliffe-Harvard—and that was not 100 years ago—even my professors used to twist the British lion's tail all the time, and tell about all the misdeeds of Britain including, of course, the fact the British had been here, the Redcoats had been here, and in Massachusetts. As far as I can see, even now many Americans have not yet gotten over the memory of British colonialism nearly 200 years after the American Revolution. We are beginning to be a little more gentle with the British now that we ourselves have become involved in the affairs of colonies, past or present. But we still do not understand why the non-Western peoples cannot forget colonialism overnight. /17

Actually, the miraculous thing is that non-Western peoples show so little resentment about colonialism. Once they become independent they are perfectly willing to work with Britain, or France, or even with Belgium in the Congo after barely two years, in spite of the utmost difficulties experienced there. One of the assumptions made about India after independence was that India would dislike the British for a long time, and we thought they would love us because we had not been there and would turn to us as their dearest friend, because we had said so often they should have independence. And then, what a surprise! The Indians loved the British. The moment the British left their dominion of India, the warmest friendship emerged between the two peoples. I remember one American diplomat who said, "I can't understand it. There's a love affair between the British and the Indians." By the way, there is one thing which we might just as well get used to, and that is that there cannot be such a thing as love among nations. This we must understand because so often we ask ourselves, "Why don't the Indians love us?" or "Why don't the Chinese love us?" So let us not seek for love in world affairs. /18

What the newly emerged non-Western countries do feel is that colonialism must end wherever it still exists and, therefore, they continue to press for an end to colonialism where it remains. This was particularly true during the bloody affair of Algeria, and is still true in the Rhodesias and in Portuguese Angola. There the non-Western peoples still feel their first task is to make sure that all other non-Westerners who remain under Western colonial rule are freed. /19

It is only after all remnants of Western colonialism have been liquidated that it will be possible to refocus the attention of the non-Western peoples on whatever Russia or China are doing with their forms of imperialism. And we must bear in mind that, in the past, colonialism came not in the guise of Russia or of China, but in the guise of white men who were Westerners. And, therefore, it will take some time for non-Westerners to get over the idea that colonialism is a purely white and Western phenomenon. The Indians have already understood that the Chinese are also imperialistic by looking at their own problems along the China border. Other non-Western peoples have not yet become aware of this point. /20

But we must not be impatient on this score. It is important, of course, that we ourselves should understand that wherever we are engaged today, as in Southeast Asia, we should deal with the peoples of the areas where we are operating on terms of equality. We must not look down upon them and we must avoid at all costs any intimation of racial discrimination, because to the non-Western peoples colonialism was irretrievably linked with racial discrimination against non-whites. This feeling still remains there, and it inspires what we call anti-Westernism, a feeling of opposition against Western peoples and against Western ways. This has nothing to do in the first instance with communism. Anti-Westernism existed in Russia long before Lenin came on the scene, and its most powerful exponent in Russia in the 19th century was the writer Dostoevsky, who felt that any contact Russia had with the West would destroy its way of life and its religious beliefs, which were so different from those of the West. So bear in mind that it is not necessarily the Russians who taught anti-Westernism to other peoples. They themselves had experienced it with respect to the West. We must also understand that nationalism took the form of anti-Westernism in many areas, and it is only when the non-Western peoples achieve independence that they can shake off their feeling of resentment against the West. /21

Another aspect which it is important for us to understand is the role of democracy or lack of it among non-Western peoples. As we look around the non-Western world, we are immediately struck by the fact that there are very few countries where one can speak of democracy in the Western sense. I would say that there are only four non-Western countries which can be described today as democracies: Japan, India, Israel and the Philippines. In the case of Japan, democracy of the Western type might not have come when it did if it had not been intro-duced at the end of a grueling war by General MacArthur, who to many people seemed an unlikely bearer of democracy, and yet who did exactly that, and did it well in Japan. /22

Whether or not Japan's democratic institutions are firmly rooted today in its own soil, it is still difficult to know. In India, both under Hindu and under Muslim rulers, there was the fortunate coincidence of a tradition of democratic attitudes on the part of the rulers towards the ruled, and of concern with the welfare of human beings. This experience happened to fit in a remarkable way with the concept of British liberalism brought to India in the 19th century. So in India you have an Anglo-Indian synthesis which brings together the best concepts of political development of both the West and of Asia, and in India democracy seems deeply rooted for the future. /23

But most of the other areas of the non-Western world have authoritarian governments. This alarms many of our editorial writers. They say, "It is dreadful that these people don't have democracy. They have authoritarian governments. Why didn't they learn democracy from the Western powers which ruled them?" To this question there is a very easy answer. The Western democratic countries did not rule democratically in the colonies. This was stated very simply by John Stuart Mill in his famous essay on liberty where, after describing all the joys and privileges of liberty he then added that, of course, the liberties he described are not for backward peoples who are still in their nonage (that is, in their childhood), nor are they for children and, he added, backward peoples, like children, must be taken care of for their own sake by the colonial powers. This gives us an idea of why democracy did not appear in the same guise in the colonial world as it did in the countries of Western Europe which enjoyed democracy. /24

But quite aside from the West's attitude about liberty, we need to bear in mind that democracy takes a long time to develop. It took a long time in the most advanced Western European nations. Take Britain, for example. If you accept Magna Carta in 1216 as your starting point, then I would say that it has taken Britain 700 years to move from Magna Carta to Harold Macmillan, to become a welfare state as well as a political democracy. Therefore, we cannot expect that the non-Western peoples will develop democratic institutions overnight. Many of them are today politically at the stage where England was in the days of Henry VIII, and I don't think he would be regarded as the prototype of modern democracy. If you ever wonder about this question, all you have to do is to stand in the courtyard of the Tower of London and look under your feet and see the plaques commemorating the names of all the people who were beheaded in the days of Henry VIII. It is already a great improvement today that the leaders of non-Western countries, for the most part, go no further than to imprison their opponents from time to time. /25

These countries are emerging from what would be comparable to the Middle Ages of Europe, and under such conditions strong authoritarian governments are far more effective than would be shaky and uncertain attempts at democracy for which peoples have not yet been prepared by their traditions, their education and their experience. The important thing to watch for is whether authoritarian governments can manage to escape becoming totalitarian, that is escape from becoming either Fascist or Communist, and refrain from trying to dominate the thinking and the whole way of life of their peoples. But why, you may ask, do governments have to wield strong power at this stage? /26

This brings us to a third aspect, and that is that the non-Western countries must at this stage alter their whole economic and social system if they are to emerge into the 20th century. They cannot carry their ancient institutions into the modern world. They are confronted with the fantastically difficult task of effecting a whole series of telescoped revolutions which the Western world was fortunate enough to space over several centuries. /27

Today these revolutions must happen all at once in the non-Western countries. These countries must modernize their agriculture, they must diversify their economy, they must introduce at least a modicum of industry, they must provide for the education of their people, they must assure them enough food, enough clothing, enough housing, so that they can really feel that their expectations of a better life will be eventually fulfilled. This means that the non-Western peoples are terribly pressed for time. Time is the thing they need most of all—time to provide for all the needs of their peoples. /28

Under these circumstances, the greatest contribution we can make is to help buy this time for them. This the Western world can do. We have the technology, the educational experience to offer the non-Western peoples. Very often we think of foreign aid primarily in terms of money. True, no one despises money. But money is not everything. Not only do the copybooks say it, but international experience points it out. It is not enough to give money to

people who are still illiterate, who are not yet trained for technical development. What they need is help in becoming educated and in becoming accustomed to using technological skills. /29

The non-Western peoples are more hungry for education than they are even for food. And it is here that those of you who are engaged in education will have in the future an unparalleled opportunity to serve the needs of these new countries—if you can spare a year or two of your active life by going to teach in the non-Western countries under circumstances which will be extremely difficult and sometimes very painful, but where one can really feel that assistance is being given in realistic and constructive terms. This is true, of course, also of those of us who have mechanical skills of any kind. /30

This would be a tremendous contribution on your part, but I hasten to add that not all underdeveloped areas are in the non-Western world. If you do not want to go to the non-Western world, do try to help the underdeveloped areas in the United States, the areas of our South and the slums of our cities. Too often we have been animated by a picturesque missionary zeal, thinking we could do better in China or Nigeria than we can do in Alabama or in the slums—not, of course, of San Francisco, which has none I assume, but of New York or Detroit. We can also serve there. /31

Under all these pressures for change, for complete transformation of economic and social conditions, the non-Western countries are ready to accept aid from any source where they can get it. They are seeking aid not only from the United States and Western European countries, but also from Russia and even from Communist China. And let us be frank about this. The experience of Russia and Communist China, which are themselves only now emerging from backward conditions, is far more valuable for non-Western peoples than our experience, because we are too advanced in many ways to understand some of the difficult problems of yet underdeveloped economies. /32

Many of us complain because the non-Western peoples go to Moscow or Peiping. But we have to recognize that they are in the happy position of trading in a bazaar. If they can't get aid in Washington, they say, "Well, that's too bad, we'll go to Moscow." And then we say, "Well, perhaps we'd better give them something so they don't go to Moscow." By then they are already in contact with Moscow, and Moscow says, "We haven't got a ruble left"; so they say, "All right, we are going back to Washington." Then Mr. Khrushchev presumably digs up a ruble or so, and this bargaining keeps on, but who can blame the new countries? They are so poor, they are so much in need, they welcome aid from all sides and from whatever source is available. /33

Does that mean that they are all going to go Communist in the future? This is, of course, the question we often ask ourselves. The fourth and final aspect that I want to mention is that, in my view, the non-Western countries are concerned today neither about being for the West nor being for the Soviet bloc. What they are concerned about are their own problems, and because of these problems they seek non-alignment. Non-alignment is often described as neutralism, but I think it is a misleading term. India, which first started the whole concept of non-alignment, does not like the word neutralism, because it is not neutralist as between democracy and communism, as it clearly indicated the moment it achieved independence when it voluntarily joined the British Commonwealth. Non-alignment means that the non-Western peoples feel they have so much to do at home, they are so much concerned with the tasks of economic and social and political development, that they cannot divert their limited resources of money, of human skills, and of educated leadership to struggling in the cold war. To them the mere possibility of war spells the end of their hoped-for independent existence which had been their lodestar during their struggle against colonialism, the end of everything they have sought to achieve in our generation. /34

What they want to do is to stay out of the conflicts between the Western and the Soviet blocs. But this does not mean that they are non-committed in international affairs. On the contrary, they are committed. They are committed not to one bloc or another. They are committed to the United Nations, which for them is the forum where they can meet the great powers on terms of equality, and which they regard as the shield and spear that will defend them against future encroachments. It is important to realize that many of the non-Western peoples, out of their meager resources, have aided the United Nations in its peace-keeping operations, in the Gaza Strip between Egypt and Israel where peace has been miraculously kept by the United Nations since 1956, and in the Congo operation. For example, India has contributed both to the Gaza operation since 1956, and to the operation in the Congo, where it maintains 7000 men, the bulk of the U. N. forces, spared with considerable difficulty from an army of 400,000 men at a time when Com-

munist China is menacing India's northern border. /35

In this respect I believe the non-Western peoples are actually a portent of the future—of a future society where all of us, while retaining our separate national values which are essential for the well-being and the stimulation of every people, will nevertheless all be committed to an international community of which we shall all be members as partners in the same enterprise. Meanwhile, all the vast changes which are shaking the world today often frighten and dismay some of us, and many begin to think that the outlook is grim, since the Western world may be in a state of eclipse. /36

For my part, I do not believe it is in a state of eclipse. And far from thinking the world is grim, I suggest that we raise our sights to those of Colonel Glenn and Yuri Gagarin who, when they orbited the earth, both reported exactly the same experience, saying that from the height at which they were "the world looks beautiful." The world does look beautiful, once we sense the beauty and the excitement of the vastly varied international where West and non-West can come together for mutual benefit. I hope that, looking at this world community, all of you will feel with the English poet that your spirits move with "happy trembeling." /37

The speech

1. How would you define the term *lecture*? How would you distinguish between a *lecture* and a *speech to inform*? Would you agree that *lecture* is an appropriate designation of Mrs. Dean's address?

2. If this lecture were to be delivered to a group of high-school students, what stylistic and organizational changes, if any, would you recommend? Why?

3. Are the forms of supporting material Mrs. Dean used the best she could have chosen to achieve her purpose? Are they sufficiently numerous and varied? Do they make the ideas they support clear and convincing? (See *Supporting material*, Glossary.)

4. Comment on the length of the lecture in relation to the speaker's purpose. Is it longer than it needs to be? Not long enough? If you were developing this topic for a similar audience, what, if anything, would you cut or add?

5. Do you consider Mrs. Dean's remarks purely informative or do you think they have elements of persuasion? If so, what and where? In what sense may information sometimes be persuasive?

6. Do you agree that the introduction extends through paragraph 9? If not, where do you think it ends? At

what point, in your judgment, does the conclusion begin?

7. Some authorities claim that there is a distinction between good oral style and good written style. Oral style, they say, should be less formal and more loose in construction than written style; it should be more conversational, freer to admit slang words, etc. Other authorities claim that the qualities which make for excellence in good oral style are the same as those which make for excellence in good written style.

   Test the validity of these competing positions by examining Mrs. Dean's lecture. If you were to rewrite it for publication in a book or magazine, what changes would you make? Why?

8. How well does the lecture adhere to the basic rhetorical rules of *unity, coherence,* and *emphasis* (See Glossary)? Defend your answer.

For further study and discussion

1. Comment on Mrs. Dean's use of the term *non-Western.* Do you think she is justified in including Russia and Latin America in the "non-Western world"? If not, in what category do they belong?

2. In your opinion, is the United States making any improvement in its understanding of the attitudes and aspirations of non-Western peoples? Do we understand them better today than we did in 1962, when Mrs. Dean delivered her lecture?

3. Has foreign aid won or lost us friends among the "non-Western" nations?

4. Evaluate American policy during the Suez crisis (1957); toward the Congo (1964); in Vietnam (1965); in Korea (since 1950).

5. Should the United States trade with Red China? Should we agree to admit Red China into the United Nations?

6. Is Russia's policy toward the emerging nations of Asia and Africa more successful than ours? If so, why? If not, why not?

7. Was "colonialism" the unmitigated evil that some non-Western peoples believe it to have been? What, if anything, can be said on its behalf?

8. How successful have various non-Western nations been over the past few years in solving their political, economic, and social problems?

9. Is the *Ugly American,* by William J. Lederer and Eugene Burdick, based on fact or fiction?

10. In 1960, Charles Malik, former President of the United Nations General Assembly, outlined the policy which he thought the United States should follow toward the new nations of Africa and Asia. Compare his recommendations with those of Mrs. Dean. See Charles H. Malik, "Developing Leadership in New Countries," *Representative American Speeches, 1963-1964,* ed. Lester Thonssen, (New York, 1964), pp. 115-131.

Suggestions for further reading

Vera Micheles Dean, *The American Student and the non-Western World* (Cambridge, Mass., 1956)
————, *Builders of Emerging Nations* (New York, 1961)
————, *The Nature of the Non-Western World* (New York, 1957)
————, and Harry D. Harootunian, eds., *West and Non-West: New Perspectives* (New York, 1963)
Charles H. Malik, *Man in the Struggle for Peace* (New York, 1963)
————, *The Problem of Coexistence* (Evanston, Ill., 1955)
Max F. Millikan and Donald L. M. Blackmer, eds., *The Emerging Nations: Their Growth and United States Policy* (Boston, 1961)

Address to the Russian people

RICHARD M. NIXON

Richard M. Nixon's "Address to the Russian People" was broadcast from a Moscow studio, August 1, 1959, the day before he left the Union of Soviet Socialist Republics. Officially Nixon, who was then Vice President of the United States, had come to the U.S.S.R. to open the American National Exhibition in Moscow; he had also conferred at length with Premier Nikita S. Khrushchev and in the course of his ten-day visit had been to several major cities. His speech on this occasion was delivered in English from a manuscript on which he had worked during much of the day preceding his television appearance. He departed from his text only once—to excuse himself for having preëmpted the time usually occupied by a popular comedy program. The New York *Herald Tribune* Bureau reported that the speech, including pauses for translation into Russian, took approximately forty-three minutes.

Nixon's speech was telecast over a network of stations covering the Russian capital and seven other cities within a radius of about two hundred miles; it was also filmed and recorded for rebroadcast on television and radio in other parts of Russia, in the United States, and in other countries. The full text of the address was printed in *Izvestia* and in newspapers outside the U.S.S.R. Nixon's immediate audience was, thus, Russian, but his ultimate audience was international. His problems of audience ad-

Reprinted by permission of Richard M. Nixon.

aptation were exceedingly complex for, as James Reston wrote in the New York *Times*, "It was necessary for him to balance his speech and meet sensitive political situations in both this country [U.S.S.R.] and the United States." Reston added, "The general feeling here among Westerners is that he managed to do so with considerable skill."

Nixon has been an exceptionally controversial figure throughout his political career, and the qualities of his speaking have often been at the center of disagreements concerning his personal and political merits. Within hours after his address, Russian radio commentators were charging that he had distorted the truth about American actions by omitting any mention of American air bases encircling the U.S.S.R. and that his analysis of Soviet policies was equally unfair. It was also said that his version of an offer to secure an American National Exhibition ticket for a Muscovite omitted mention that he had offered the Moscow worker money. In Moscow, as at home, Nixon's selection and arrangement of evidence quickly became the objects of both praise and criticism.

It is Nixon's habit to speak from notes, or to prepare his manuscripts from notes, in which topics, rather than logical subdivisions of the subject, form the main headings. His Moscow address reflects this practice in its topical organization. His skillful adaptation to the knowledge and interests of his possibly hostile Russian audience and the directness, concreteness, and simplicity with which he argues his propositions are also characteristic features of Nixon's popular speaking.

Nixon was born in Yorba Linda, California, in 1913, and was educated at Whittier College, California, and at Duke University Law School. Between 1937 and 1942 he practiced law in Whittier and in Washington, D.C. He served in the United States Navy from 1942-1946 and, after his discharge from the Navy, was elected to the House of Representatives from California. In 1950 he was elected to the Senate, and in 1952 and 1956 he was elected Vice President of the United States on the Republican ticket headed by Dwight D. Eisenhower. In 1960 he was narrowly defeated for the presidency by John F. Kennedy.

I first want to express my appreciation to the government of the USSR for giving me an opportunity to speak to the people of this country by radio and television just as Mr. Kozlov and Mr. Mikoyan spoke to the American people on their visits to my country. /1

I realize that nine days is much too brief a time for a visitor to spend in this great country. But in that period I have had the opportunity of having ex-

tended and frank discussions with Mr. Khrushchev and other leaders of your government. I have visited Leningrad, Siberia and the Urals and I have had the privilege of meeting thousands of people in all walks of life. /2

What I would like to do tonight is to answer for the millions of people who are listening to this program some of the questions which were asked me over and over again on this trip so that you may get a true picture of the policies of the American government and people. /3

I should like to begin by answering a question which I often heard: What are my impressions of this country and its people? /4

While my visit was brief I did have a chance in addition to visiting this great capital city of Moscow to see the beauty and culture of Leningrad whose brave people won the admiration of the world for their heroic defense of their city during the war; to savor the inspiring pioneer spirit of Novosibirsk; to witness firsthand the thriving productivity of the factory complex of the Urals. I was greatly impressed by the efficient modern equipment of your factories; your magnificent ballets in Leningrad and Novosibirsk; by the competitive drive for progress which is evident on every side. /5

But most of all I was impressed by your people; after all, the greatest asset of a country is not its forests, its factories or its farms but its people. /6

These are some of the characteristics of the Soviet people which I particularly noted on this trip. /7

First, their capacity for hard work, their vitality; their intense desire to improve their lot, to get ahead, is evident everywhere. /8

There was another feature about the Soviet people which I noted that may surprise you and that is in how many respects you are like us Americans. We are similar in our love of humor—we laugh at the same jokes. The people of your frontier East have much the same spirit of what was our frontier West. We have a common love of sports; the name of Vasily Kuznetsov, your great decathlon champion, is known in the United States as well as in the Soviet Union. We are both a hospitable, friendly people. When we meet each other we tend to like each other personally, as so many of our soldiers who met during the last great war can attest. /9

Above all, the American people and the Soviet people are as one in their desire for peace. And our desire for peace is not because either of us is weak. On the contrary, each of us is strong and respects the strength the other possesses. /10

This means that if we are to have peace it must be

a just peace based on mutual respect rather than the peace of surrender or dictation by either side. Putting it bluntly, both of our peoples want peace but both of us also possess great strength and much as we want peace neither of us can or will tolerate being pushed around. /11

That is why I was so surprised at a question that was asked me by a worker on the new scientific center outside of Novosibirsk. My heart went out to him as he told me that he had been wounded in World War II and that his father and mother had been killed by bombs. But then he said, "I don't believe you when you say America is for peace." /12

Nothing he could have said could have astonished or saddened me more. /13

And so to the millions of Soviet people who suffered or lost their loved ones in war, and to all of those in this great country who want peace, I say tonight, if you doubt that the American government and the American people are as dedicated to peace as you are, look at our record, examine our policies and you can reach only one conclusion—only aggressor nations have anything to fear from the United States of America. /14

We have fought in two World Wars and have demanded and received not an acre of territory or a cent in reparations. We enjoy the highest standard of living of any people in the world's history, and there is nothing whatever that we want from any other people in the world except to live in peace and friendship with them. No leader in the world today could be more dedicated to peace than our President. As his brother, who has honored us by making this visit with us, can tell you, President Eisenhower's whole life is proof of the stark but simple truth—that no one hates war more than one who has seen a lot of it. /15

We know as do you that in this age of nuclear weapons it is impossible for either of our nations to launch an attack which would not bring terrible destruction to itself. /16

In this age any leader who is so insane even to think of starting a war should well heed your proverb —"Do not dig a pit for another; you may fall into it yourself." /17

Why then is there any doubt that the American government and people are just as dedicated to peace as the people of the USSR? I think part of the answer is to be found in another question which was often asked of me on this trip and which Mr. Khrushchev, himself, raised in this manner in his speech on July 28 at Dnepropetrovsk. "If you believe in the peaceful intentions of our country, why do you con-

tinue the arms race, why do you construct new military bases around our borders?" /18

In answering this question, let me first point out that these bases are not maintained for purposes of attacking you but for purposes of defending ourselves and our allies. /19

Why did we think it was necessary to set up bases? Let us look at the record. We disarmed rapidly after World War II. Then came a series of events which threatened our friends abroad as well as ourselves. The Berlin blockade and the war in Korea are typical of the actions which led the United States and our allies to rearm so that we could defend ourselves against aggression. /20

We must also remember that these events occurred before the 20th Party Congress changed the line to the one Mr. Khrushchev enunciated again in his speech at Dnepropetrovsk—that Communism will now try to achieve its international objectives by peaceful means rather than by force. I could cite statement after statement made by previous leaders of the USSR which advocated and threatened the use of force against non-Communist countries in order to achieve Communist objectives. /21

A striking illustration of why we maintain bases and strong military forces is the fact that one-fourth of the entire production of the USSR goes into armaments. This in effect, means that every worker in the Soviet Union works one day out of four for armaments. And we in our country are also bearing a heavy burden of armaments. Think what it could mean to both of our countries if we could lift this burden from the backs of our people. /22

Some may ask, why don't we get rid of the bases since the Soviet government declares today that it has only peaceful intentions? The answer is that whenever the fear and suspicion that caused us and our allies to take measures for collective self-defense are removed, the reason for our maintaining bases will be removed. In other words, the only possible solution of this problem lies in mutual rather than unilateral action leading toward disarmament. /23

Another question which was often asked was—why won't the United States agree to stop the tests of atomic weapons? The answer in a nutshell is that the question is not whether we both should enter into an agreement to stop tests but whether that agreement is one which will make sure that the tests actually are stopped. /24

That is why we say that if both sides honestly want to stop tests, we must first agree to set up inspection procedures in both of our countries which will make certain that the agreement is not violated. We believe this position is the only one that gives assurance of accomplishing the objective of stopping tests rather than just signing an agreement to do so. /25

We are encouraged by the fact that at least in this area we are presently engaged in serious negotiations which have made some progress. I know that I express the sentiments of the people of both of our countries when I say that I am hopeful that these negotiations will finally end in agreement. /26

Another question that has often been asked me went something like this: "The United States says it is for peace, but what the world wants are deeds not words, and the United States is short on deeds and long on words." /27

Nothing could be further from the truth. It is possible that many of you listening to me are not aware of the positive programs the United States has proposed which were designed to contribute to peace. Let me tell you about just a few of them and what happened to them: /28

We had a monopoly on the atomic bomb when on June 14, 1946, we submitted the Baruch plan for international control of atomic energy. What happened? It was rejected by the USSR. /29

Under Article 43 of the United Nations Charter, provision was made for the establishment of the United Nations Armed Forces to keep the peace. On June 4, 1947, we made the first of many requests that agreement be reached. What happened? All have been rejected by the USSR. /30

At the Summit Conference in Geneva on July 21, 1955, President Eisenhower made his offer of open skies aerial inspection. What happened? It was rejected by the USSR. /31

On May 1, 1958, the United States offered an Arctic aerial inspection plan to protect both nations from surprise attack. What happened? It was rejected by the USSR. /32

I realize that your government has indicated reasons for its rejection of each of these proposals. I do not list these proposals for the purpose of warming over past history but simply to demonstrate the initiative that our government has taken to reduce tensions and to find peaceful solutions for differences between us. /33

I realize that my answers to these questions indicate that there are some very basic differences between us. But let me emphasize at the same time that the very fact that we have not made as much progress as we would like in the past in settling our differences is the strongest reason for us to redouble our efforts to create better understanding between our two countries; to remove fear, suspicion and miscon-

ception where they exist, and thereby, to pave the way for discussions and eventual settlement by agreement of some of the basic conflicts between us. /34

We should both frankly recognize that we have some very real differences; that they are not easily settled: But two men who are friends can settle an argument between them without using their fists and two nations who want to be friends can do so without war. /35

I should like to suggest tonight some practical steps which will contribute to the cause of peace to which we are both dedicated. /36

First there are some positive things we can do which will create better understanding between us. /37

We can start by removing the language barrier. Here is one place where you are ahead of us. I was amazed at the number of people I met on this trip who were studying English. What we need are millions of American students who understand Russian and millions of Soviet students who understand English. /38

Both the exchange of persons and the cultural exchange programs should not only be continued but sharply expanded. The more Americans who visit and get to know first-hand the people of the Soviet Union and the more Soviet citizens who do the same in the United States, the better understanding we shall have. /39

I believe also that visits by officials like the ones Mr. Mikoyan and Mr. Kozlov made to the United States and which I have just concluded can provide the means of frank and full discussion of some of our problems and the development of solutions for them. Consequently, we should explore ways of increasing contacts of this type. /40

Most important of all, we need a much freer exchange of information between our two countries so that misconceptions we may have about you and that you have about us may be removed. I was rather surprised that Mr. Khrushchev should raise a question about the failure of the Western press to report adequately one of his recent statements. I would estimate that at least 100 of Mr. Khrushchev's words are printed in our American press for every one word of President Eisenhower's speeches that are printed in the Soviet press. /41

Perhaps this is an area where the cause of better understanding would be served if we had a more equal exchange. Let us agree that all of Mr. Khrushchev's speeches on foreign policy be printed in the United States and that all of President Eisenhower's speeches on foreign policy be printed in the Soviet Union. /42

Why not go further and set up regular radio and television broadcasts by Mr. Khrushchev to the American people in return for President Eisenhower having the same privilege to talk to the Soviet people? /43

Let us put a stop to the jamming of broadcasts so that the Soviet people may hear broadcasts from our country just as the American people can hear forty hours of broadcasts a day from the Soviet Union. And let us have a freer flow of newspapers and magazines so that the Soviet people can buy American newspapers and magazines here just as we Americans purchased over one and one-half million Soviet publications in last year alone. /44

I recognize that freedom of information can be abused and that neither of us is free from blame in this respect. The press, radio, television and other means of communication such as film studios, have a heavy responsibility for maintaining the spirit of truth and for preventing misinformation. In the final analysis the misrepresentation of facts or distortion of the truth defeats itself. Let me give you an example from an experience that occurred to me on this trip. /45

There was a report in *Pravda* to the effect that on the morning after I arrived in Moscow I tried to give money to a poor Soviet citizen, with the hope that American press photographers might take pictures of the incident and send them around the world. There was not a shred of truth to this story. /46

Here is what actually happened. On an early morning visit to the Danilovsky Market, I had talked to scores of people and received a most friendly welcome. As I was about to leave, several of the people asked me for tickets to the American Exhibition. I told them I did not have any with me, but that I would be glad to buy some tickets for those present who wanted to attend the Exhibition. One of the group explained that it was not a question of their not having money for the tickets, but simply a question of their not being able to obtain them. I told him I would be glad to check into the matter and see if I could get tickets for him. /47

These are the simple facts as far as this incident was concerned, and I can only add that all irresponsible reporters should never forget that in the end the truth always catches up with a lie. /48

Through this greater exchange of information between our two peoples we not only learn from each other and improve our way of life but we reduce the suspicion, the mistrust, and fear and misunderstanding and assure the understanding and friendship which will lead to the peace we all want. That is why, to me, the concept of co-existence is completely inadequate and negative. Co-existence implies that the world must be divided into two hostile camps with a wall of hate and fear between. /49

What we need today is not two worlds but one world where different peoples choose the economic and political systems which they want, but where there is free communication among all the peoples living on this earth. /50

Let us expand the concept of open skies. What the world also needs are open cities, open minds and open hearts. /51

Let us have peaceful competition not only in producing the best factories but in producing better lives for our people. /52

Let us cooperate in our exploration of outer space. As a worker told me in Novosibirsk, let us go to the moon together. /53

Let our aim be not victory over other peoples but the victory of all mankind over hunger, want, misery and disease, wherever it exists in the world. /54

I realize that this era of peaceful competition and even cooperation seems like an impossible dream when we consider the present differences we have between us. But the leaders of our countries can help make this dream come true. So far as the leader of our country is concerned, I can assure you that President Eisenhower has no objective to which he is more dedicated. /55

As far as Mr. Khrushchev is concerned, as I am sure you know, we disagree sharply on political and economic philosophy and on many world problems. But these characteristics are evident to anyone who meets him—He is a self-made man who worked his way up from the bottom; he is an articulate spokesman for the economic system in which he believes; he has immense drive; in sum, he is one of those individuals who, whether you agree with him or disagree with him, is a born leader of men. Because he has these unique qualities and because the decisions he makes will affect not only the 200 million people of the USSR but the 3 billion people on this earth, he carries a tremendous responsibility on his shoulders. /56

I would not be so presumptuous as to try to give him advice on how he should fulfill that responsibility. But could I relate something that I noted on the trip I have just completed? In every factory and on hundreds of billboards I saw this slogan, "Let us work for the victory of Communism." /57

If Mr. Khrushchev means by this slogan working

for a better life for the people within the Soviet Union that is one thing. If, on the other hand, he means the victory of Communism over the United States and other countries, this is a horse of a different color. For we have our own ideas as to what system is best for us. /58

If he devotes his immense energies and talents to building a better life for the people of his own country, Mr. Khrushchev can go down in history as one of the greatest leaders the Soviet people have ever produced. But if he diverts the resources and talents of his people to the objective of promoting the communization of countries outside the Soviet Union, he will only assure that both he and his people will continue to live in an era of fear, suspicion and tension. /59

The Geneva conference is a case in point. It would not be proper for me to comment on the specific proposals that are pending before that conference at this time. But agreements between great powers cannot be reached unless they take into account the views and interests of all parties concerned. I was encouraged to note in my conversations with Mr. Khrushchev that he recognizes this fact and agrees that a successful outcome of this conference could be a great step forward in settling some of the problems I have discussed tonight. /60

I have one final thought to add. Mr. Khrushchev predicted that our grandchildren would live under Communism. He reiterated this to me in our talks last Sunday. /61

Let me say that we do not object to his saying this will happen. We only object if he tries to bring it about. /62

And this is my answer to him. I do not say that your grandchildren will live under capitalism. We prefer our system. But the very essence of our belief is that we do not and will not try to impose our system on anybody else. We believe that you and all other peoples on this earth should have the right to choose the kind of economic or political system which best fits your particular problems without any foreign intervention. /63

As I leave your country, I shall never forget an incident that occurred as I was driving through your beautiful Ural mountains. A group of children on the side of the road threw wild flowers into my car and cried in English the words "friendship," "friendship." Mr. Zhukov told me that the first word children who study English are taught is the word "friendship." There could be no more eloquent expression of the attitude of the Soviet people, an attitude which we share in common with you. /64

Finally, may I express on behalf of my wife and I, and all the members of our party, our deep appreciation for the warm friendship and boundless hospitality we have found everywhere we have gone in the Soviet Union. I pledge to you that in the years to come I shall devote my best efforts to the cause of peace with justice for all the peoples of the world. /65

The speech

1. Nixon says he intends to "answer for the millions of people who are listening . . . some of the questions which were asked me . . . ." Do you think this was his real purpose in speaking? If not, what was his specific purpose?

2. Good introductions should establish common ground between speaker and listeners. By what means does Nixon attempt to do this in his introduction? Where else does he establish such common ground?

3. What are the major divisions of this speech? Are these topics so closely related to one another that to mention the first makes it necessary or natural to discuss the next? Defend your answer.

4. Do you think Nixon used evidence in such a way as to overstate his country's peaceful behavior?

5. What do you think Nixon hoped to accomplish by the passage in which he seems to analyze Khrushchev's probable place in history?

6. What do you think Nixon was trying to suggest to his listeners when he discussed the slogan, "Let us work for the victory of Communism"?

7. A good conclusion ought to restate and vivify the speaker's central idea and re-emphasize his intentions toward his audience. By what means does Nixon try to gain emphasis in his conclusion?

8. One journalist said of this speech, "It may not have convinced them, but at least it gave them pause." In what ways and by what means might the speech raise self-doubts among convinced and loyal Russians?

9. Walter Lippmann called this speech "self-respecting and well directed to the Russians who heard it." What does Nixon do, or avoid doing, that adds to his own dignity as a high public official?

10. Nixon's development of the topic, the United States seeks peace, is predominantly refutational. What justification is there in this section for Lippmann's assertion that the speech was "well directed to the Russians who heard it"?

For further study and discussion

1. Why do you think the United States should or should not stop developing and testing nuclear weapons?

2. If there were an international disarmament agreement, would you be willing to allow Russian and other foreign representatives to travel freely in the United States as inspectors and enforcers of the agreement? Why or why not?

3. What good or harm could arise from regular, uncensored broadcasts by Russians over American networks and by Americans over Russian networks?

4. Why do you agree or disagree with Nixon's statement that millions of young Americans should learn Russian? Should every college student be required to master at least one foreign language? Why or why not?

5. What evidence is there that our newspapers, radio, and television give us a fair understanding of Russia and the Russian people?

6. Do you agree with Nixon that "free communication among all people" is more important than the political or economic systems they choose? Why or why not?

7. What limitations, if any, would you put on the policy that the United States should avoid all interference with other countries no matter what kind of economic or political systems they choose?

8. What reasons are there for believing or disbelieving that the development of missiles will make foreign air bases and troop concentrations unnecessary to American foreign and defense policies?

9. Do you think capitalism will eventually be replaced by socialism in the United States? Justify your opinion.

10. Do you think personal visits by and discussions among high public officials are more likely to advance world peace than traditional diplomacy or negotiations through the United Nations? Why or why not?

Suggestions for further reading

Herbert Agar, The Price of Power (Chicago, 1957)

"Asia and Future World Leadership," Annals of the American Academy of Political and Social Sciences, volume 318 (July 1958)

Hanson W. Baldwin, Power and Politics (Claremont, Cal., 1950)

George E. G. Catlin, What Does the West Want? (London, 1957)

Foster Rhea Dulles, America's Rise to World Power, 1898-1954 (New York, 1955)

Brooks Emeny, Mainsprings of World Politics (New York, 1956)

James M. Gavin, War and Peace in the Space Age (New York, 1958)

Louis J. Halle, Choice for Survival (New York, 1958)

Kenneth Ingram, History of the Cold War (London and New York, 1955)

William W. Kaufman, ed., Military Policy and National Security (Princeton, 1956)

Grayson Kirk and others, The Changing Environment of International Relations (Washington, D.C., 1956)

Edgar Ansel Mowrer, A Good Time to be Alive (New York, 1959)

Reinhold Niebuhr, The World Crisis and American Responsibility (New York, 1958)

"Resolving the Russian-American Deadlock," Annals of the American Academy of Political and Social Sciences, volume 324 (July 1959)

Science and Foreign Policy, pamphlet, Headline series (New York, 1958)

Arnold Wolfers, Alliance Policy in the Cold War (Baltimore, 1959)

Press conference

CHARLES DE GAULLE

A De Gaulle press conference has been described variously as a "rite," a "monologue," a "ritual ballet," and a "series of answers to which reporters are to think up questions."[1] Certainly, both in rigidity of procedure and in austerity of tone, these sessions differ from the Presidential press interviews with which American television viewers are familiar.

Despite their formal and rehearsed quality, however, De Gaulle's press conferences are eagerly anticipated by newsmen and diplomats as sources of important pronouncements concerning French views and policies in world affairs.

The conference reproduced below was held on July 23, 1964. It not only is a good example of the De Gaulle technic but also explains with unusual detail and clarity De Gaulle's (and presumably the French) position on three major questions then before the world: European unity and the role of the United States in Europe, French atomic developments, and the settlement of the war in Vietnam. In addition, a portion of the interview here omitted reviewed the state of the French economy and outlined plans for curbing inflation.

Following established custom, the conference was held in the Salle des Fêtes of the Elysée Palace. Approximately 800 reporters, cameramen, and officials, including members of the French cabinet, were crowded into the stuffy, ornate room. Promptly at 3 P.M., De Gaulle appeared and took his position behind a large desk. A bright raspberry red curtain hung at his back

From Speeches and Press Conferences, Tenth Press Conference, July 23, 1964, No. 208. Reprinted by permission of the French Embassy Press and Information Division.

[1]Time, January 18, 1963, p. 6, and July 31, 1964, p. 20; Newsweek, August 3, 1964, p. 36.

and a large cut-glass chandelier was directly overhead. The general wore a double-breasted dark gray suit and a striped tie. At the opening of the interview a number of previously prepared questions were read and then there was a pause while these questions were grouped by topics.

Drew Middleton of the New York *Times* describes De Gaulle's delivery during the conference as follows:

"By turns pleading, professional and pungent, the general gave a vintage performance. His heavy voice sank almost to a whisper as he explained why France needed atomic bombs. Then it boomed full and strong as he announced that she had them, with more terrible weapons to come. . . .

"The general often gestured to emphasize his points. He discarded the thick glasses that aid his failing sight until he left, then he slipped them on to see the short flight of steps leading off the platform."[2]

The most controversial parts of the one-hour and sixteen-minute interview were (1) the proposal that the United States, Russia, China, and France withdraw from Vietnam and submit the settlement of the Vietnamese problem to a second Geneva Conference (paragraphs 34-42), (2) the criticism of West Germany's continued desire for close ties with America (paragraphs 19-20), and (3) the pointed reminder to the United States that conditions in Europe had changed from the days when that continent was almost entirely dependent on Marshall Plan aid (paragraphs 9-11).

All three of these pronouncements aroused unfavorable reactions in world capitals. The German government issued a statement denying that its policy was in any way "subordinated" to the wishes of the United States, London was "cool" to the suggestion for neutralizing Southeast Asia, and in a press interview of his own the following day President Johnson rejected the proposal on Vietnam by declaring, "We do not believe in a conference called to ratify terror."

De Gaulle became prominent internationally at the time of the fall of France during World War II, when he was recognized by the British government as the leader of the Free French. In that capacity he headed French military resistance during the remainder of the war, and became president of the provisional French government organized after the liberation of Paris in August 1944.

After resigning from this post on January 20, 1946, De Gaulle formed the RPF (Rally of the French People), a right-wing movement designed to further his political views. He headed this organization until May 6, 1953,

when he withdrew from politics. On June 1, 1958, he was recalled as premier after a series of revolts by French nationals in Algeria threatened to spread to France itself. He became president of the Fifth French Republic on January 8, 1959, the position which he held at the time of this press conference.

Ladies and gentlemen, I am pleased to see you once again, and once again, if you please, we are going to conform to what has become a little like a ritual for the exchange of questions and answers between us. This means that I am here to enlighten you on what you would like to ask me and consequently I ask you to be so good as to formulate your questions now. As usual we will group them, and then I will endeavor to answer them. /1

* * *

There is the problem of our economic perspectives, on the one hand in themselves, and on the other hand with regard to the stabilization plan. /2*

There is everything concerning Europe in general, and in particular the French-German agreement. /3

There is the fact, capital at this time, of Southeast Asia and France's policy in relation to that of the United States in this area. /4

There is the point we have reached in our atomic development with regard to the (atomic) force. /5

Europe and the French-German agreement

QUESTION: Mr. President, what meaning do you attach to the pursuit of the political unification of Europe after your recent talks with Chancellor Erhard in Bonn? /6

QUESTION: Mr. President, what results has the French-German treaty produced in political, economic and military matters? Do you deem these results satisfactory, disappointing or simply insufficient? /7

In discussing Europe and in trying to distinguish what it should be, it is always necessary to ascertain what the world is. /8

At the end of the last World War, the distribution of forces in the world was as simple, as brutal as possible. It appeared suddenly at Yalta. Only Amer-

---

[2]New York *Times*, July 24, 1964, p. 2. (Late city edition)

*General De Gaulle's discussion of these purely domestic problems is omitted from the following text. (Editor's note) ica and Russia had remained powers, and all the more considerable powers in that all the rest found themselves dislocated, the vanquished engulfed in their unconditional defeat and the European victors destroyed to their foundations. /9

For the countries of the free world, threatened by the Soviets' ambition, American leadership could then seem inevitable. The New World was, of all of them, the great victor of the war. Under the command of the United States, owner of atomic bombs, the Atlantic Alliance ensured their security. Thanks to the Marshall Plan their economies were being revived. Wherever the colonial powers were effecting, under more or less violent conditions, the transfer of their sovereignty to self-governing regimes, there pressure was felt, openly or not, from Washington. At the same time, America was seen to assume the conduct of political and strategic affairs in all the regions where the free world found itself in contact with the direct or indirect action of the Soviets. It did this either unilaterally or through the channels of regional international bodies which in practice were at its disposal: in Europe, NATO; in Western Asia, CENTO; in Southeast Asia, SEATO; in America, the OAS; or, thanks to its supremacy in the North Pacific, or, finally, through military or diplomatic intervention, in Korea, in the Congo, or during the Suez crisis through the offices of the United Nations Organization which it dominated by its preponderance. /10

It is clear that things have changed. The Western States of our old continent have rebuilt their economies. They are rebuilding their military forces. One of them—France—is becoming a nuclear power. Above all they have become aware of their natural ties. In short, Western Europe appears likely to constitute a major entity full of merit and resources, capable of living its own life, indeed not in opposition to the New World, but right alongside it. /11

On the other hand, the monolithic nature of the totalitarian world is in the process of dislocation. China, separated from Moscow, enters on the world scene by its mass, its needs and its resources, avid for progress and consideration. The Soviet Empire, the last and the largest colonial power of this time, is seeing first the Chinese contest the domination it exercises over vast regions of Asia, and second is seeing the European satellites which it had subjugated by force moving further and further away. At the same time the Communist regime, despite the enormous effort it has been making in Russia for half a century and despite the results it has achieved in certain massive undertakings, is meeting with failure with respect to the standard of living, the satisfaction and the dignity of men in comparison with the system that applies in Western Europe which combines "dirigisme"* with freedom. Lastly, great aspirations and great difficulties are deeply agitating the developing countries. /12

The result of all these new factors, complicated and interrelated, is that the division of the world into two camps led by Washington and Moscow respectively corresponds less and less to the real situation. With respect to the gradually splitting totalitarian world, or the problems posed by China, or the conduct to be adopted toward many countries of Asia, Africa and Latin America, or the remodeling of the United Nations Organization that necessarily ensues, or the adjustment of world exchanges of all kinds, etc., it appears that Europe, provided that it wishes it, is henceforth called upon to play a role which is its own. /13

Undoubtedly, it should maintain an alliance with America in which, in the North Atlantic, both are interested so long as the Soviet threat remains. But the reasons which, for Europe, made this alliance a form of subordination are fading away day by day. Europe must assume its share of the responsibilities. Everything indicates, moreover, that this event would be in accordance with the interest of the United States, whatever may be its merit, its power and its good intentions. For the multiplicity and complexity of the tasks henceforth go beyond, and perhaps dangerously, its means and its capacity. That is why the United States declares that it wishes to see the old continent unite and organize itself while many among the Gallic, Germanic and Latin people cry out "Let us build Europe!" /14

But which Europe? That is the question. Indeed, the established conveniences, the accepted renunciations, the deep-rooted reservations do not fade away easily. According to we French, it is a question of Europe's being made in order for it to be European. A European Europe means that it exists by itself for itself, in other words in the midst of the world it has its own policy. But that is precisely what is rejected consciously or unconsciously by some who claim, however, to want it to be established. In reality, the fact that Europe, not having a policy, would be subject to the policy that came to it from the other side of the Atlantic appears to them, even today, normal and satisfactory. /15

---

*A neologism derived from the French verb *diriger* (to direct, control, conduct, steer, manage), and in this case used to refer to the direction of affairs by a strong central authority. (Editor's note)

We have seen many people—quite often, what is more, worthy and sincere—advocate for Europe not an independent policy, which in reality they do not visualize, but an organization unsuited to have one, linked in this field, as in that of defense and the economy, to an Atlantic system, in other words American, and consequently subordinate to what the United States calls its leadership. This organization, entitled federal, would have had as its bases on the one hand a council of experts withdrawn from the affiliation to the States, and which would have been dubbed "executive"; and on the other hand a Parliament without national qualifications and which would have been called "legislative." Doubtless each of these two elements would have supplied that for which it would have been fitted, that is to say, studies for the council and debates for the Parliament. But, without a doubt, neither of the two would have made what indeed no one wanted them to make, that is a policy, for if the policy must take the debates and studies into account, it is another thing entirely than studies and debates. /16

A policy is an action, that is to say a body of decisions taken, of things done, of risks assumed, all this with the support of a people. The governments of nations alone can be capable of and responsible for making policy. It is of course not forbidden to imagine that a day will come when all the peoples of our continent will become one and that then there could be a Government of Europe, but it would be ridiculous to act as if that day had come. /17

That is why France—refusing to let Europe get bogged down, becoming bogged down herself in a guileful undertaking that would have stripped States, misled peoples and prevented the independence of our continent—took the initiative of proposing to her five partners of the Rome Treaty a beginning for the organization of their cooperation. Thus we would begin to live in common, pending the time when habit and evolution would gradually draw the ties closer together. We know that the German Government adhered in principle to this project. We know that a meeting of the six States in Paris, then another one in Bonn, seemed at first on the road to success, but that Rome refused to call the decisive meeting, its objections, joined with those of The Hague and Brussels, being powerful enough to halt everything. Finally, we know that the opponents invoked two arguments, moreover contradictory. The first argument: the French plan, which maintains the sovereignty of the States, does not conform to our conception of a Europe having

as its Executive a commission of experts, and as its Legislative a Parliament cut off from national realities. The second argument: although Britain does not agree to lose its sovereignty, we will not enter into any European political organization to which it would not belong. /18

The French plan for European organization not being adopted by Italy and by the Benelux countries; moreover, integration not being able to lead to anything other than an American protectorate; finally, Great Britain having shown throughout the interminable Brussels negotiations that it was not in a position to accept the common economic rules and, by the Nassau agreement, that its defense force, particularly in the nuclear domain, would not be European for lack of being autonomous in relation to the United States—it seemed to the Government of the Federal Republic of Germany and to the Government of the French Republic that their bilateral cooperation could have some value. It was then that, on the proposal of the German Government, the French-German Treaty of January 22, 1963 was concluded, which I had the honor of signing right here with Chancellor Adenauer. /19

However, it must be noted that, if the French-German Treaty made possible limited results in some areas, also if it led the two Governments and their services to establish contacts, which, for our part, and altogether, we judge can be useful and which are, in any case, very pleasant, up to now a common line of conduct has not emerged. Assuredly there is not, and there could not be any opposition, strictly speaking, between Bonn and Paris. But, whether it is a matter of the effective solidarity of France and Germany concerning their defense, or even of the stand to take and the action to pursue toward the East, above all the Moscow satellites, or correlatively of the question of boundaries and nationalities in Central and Eastern Europe, or of the recognition of China and of the diplomatic and economic mission which can be opened to Europe in relation to that great people, or of peace in Asia and particularly Indochina and Indonesia, or of the aid to give to the developing countries in Africa, Asia and Latin America, or of the organization of the agricultural common market and consequently the future of the Community of the Six—one could not say that Germany and France have yet agreed to make together a policy and one could not dispute that this results from the fact that Bonn has not believed, up to now, that this policy should be European and independent. If this state of affairs were to last, there would be the risk, in the long run, of doubts among the French people, of misgivings among the German people and, among their four partners of the Rome Treaty, an increased tendency to leave things as they are, while waiting, perhaps, to be split up. /20

But, throughout the world, the force of things is doing its work. In wanting and in proposing the organization of a Europe having its own policy, France is sure of serving the balance, the peace and progress of the world. Moreover, she is now strong enough and sure enough of herself to be able to be patient, except for major external changes which would jeopardize everything and therefore lead her to change her direction. Besides, at the last meeting just held between the Governments in Bonn and Paris, Chancellor Erhard gave an indication of a forthcoming German initiative. In waiting for the sky to clear, France is pursuing, by her own means, that which a European and independent policy can and should be. It is a fact that people everywhere are pleased with it and that for herself it is not an unsatisfactory situation. /21

French atomic policy

QUESTION: Can you tell us, General, the present state of French policy in atomic matters, given the present circumstances, and particularly the project for a multilateral nuclear force which does not seem to be making visible progress? /22

Nineteen years ago, suddenly, an atomic bomb caused 100,000 deaths in Hiroshima. Then, in Nagasaki, another caused as many. Suddenly Japan—a great people, courageous in the highest sense of the word, still possessing powerful military means, whose territorial nature and national character lent themselves perfectly well to the defensive to the bitter end—was seen to capitulate unconditionally, to the extent of allowing itself to be entirely occupied, governed, even transformed by its enemy. /23

Thus there opened in the history of our world an entirely new phase, regarding the security of peoples, consequently regarding their policy and their respective relations. To possess the atomic weapon is for a country to be in a position to reduce relentlessly a nation which does not possess it. But it is also to deter any nation which possesses it from carrying out atomic aggression against it. For that would be tantamount to inflicting death only to receive it immediately. /24

Since America and Russia have both equipped themselves with such an atomic arsenal, there exists between them a kind of automatic deterrent balance. But this balance really covers only them and not the other countries of the world, even when they are linked to one or the other of the two colossal powers. For the cause and the integrity of each of the others might not seem to their great ally to be worth the trouble of being crushed itself in crushing its rival. And, nevertheless, those threatened by the ambition of one of the two giants are led to accommodate themselves, in relation to the other, with strategic and therefore political dependence in which they think they see the only chance for their security. /25

Certain were able to believe that the prospect of conflict was so terrible that the United States and Russia would in concert renounce that sort of arsenal. The fruitless and interminable Geneva conference arose from this illusion. But in the present state of the world, the hypothesis is unbelievable. /26

The fact that America and Soviet Russia possess their nuclear arsenal provides them with such security and moreover gives them, inside their respective camps, such a reason for exercising hegemony that they will not get rid of theirs, no more than any other State in their place would get rid of its arsenal, whatever its ideology, its nature and its propaganda. The result is that the countries which do not have an atomic arsenal believe that they have to accept a strategic and consequently a political dependency in relation to that one of the two giants which is not threatening them. /27

In these conditions France, while deploring the fact that the two giants in question do not disarm—except, of course, in the form of a momentary agreement which aimed only at a certain slowing down in the rate of production, but which continues to allow them to maintain and increase their gigantic power of destruction—France, I say, as soon as she was able to be herself, judged it necessary to begin the desired effort in order to become an atomic power in her turn. In this respect, it is true, she is suffering from the consequences of a long delay caused first by the war under the occupation, then by the reconstruction of everything that was demolished on her soil, and lastly by the procrastinations for her political, economic and financial recovery. Also in comparison with the United States and Russia, which have widely put to use in their time the assistance of European scientists and technicians, and with Great Britain, which profited from the American experience, France disposes of only French capacities. Lastly, it is clear that the total of our scientific, technical and industrial means is far from reaching that of the two giants. /28

However, we are on the road and we are advancing according to our plan. At the same time the vast research, invention and production activity that atomic development itself involves introduces a most effective stimulus into our scientific, technical and economic life. And here, at this very moment, we are reaching results. Our first atomic air unit becomes operational this year. In 1966 we will have enough Mirage IV's and refueling planes to be able to carry at one time, over a distance of thousands of miles, bombs with a total power exceeding that of 150 Hiroshima bombs. Furthermore, we are working on moving on from series A fission bombs to series H fusion bombs, the latter launched from either atomic submarines, surface vessels or land. This very day the Premier is on his way to inspect the distant and isolated sites where, under the best testing and security conditions, the necessary tests will take place in due time. We are in a position to think that six years from now our deterrent means will reach a total instantaneous power of 2,000 Hiroshima bombs. This is what certain, obviously unthinking, opponents call France's "little bomb." /29

The field of deterrence is thus henceforth open to us. For to attack France would be equivalent, for whomever it might be, to undergoing frightful destruction itself. Doubtless the megatons that we could launch would not equal in number those that Americans and Russians are able to unleash. But, once reaching a certain nuclear capability, and with regard to one's own direct defense, the proportion of respective means has no absolute value. Indeed, since a man and a people can die only once, the deterrent exists provided that one has the means to wound the possible aggressor mortally, that one is very determined to do it and that the aggressor is convinced of it. That is why France's modern arsenal not only constitutes for her the incomparable guarantee of her security, but also introduces into a dangerous world a new and powerful element of wisdom and circumspection. /30

However, our advent to the rank of an atomic power is not failing to arouse diverse opposition here. To condemn this new force, the classic marriage of eternal demagogy and eternal routine is taking place; a marriage which once caused the failure of our Army's transformation in the face of Bismarck's ambitions and which was thus greatly responsible for our defeat in 1870; a marriage which, before 1914, deprived us of heavy artillery, for the lack of which, during the World War, our human losses far exceeded those of the enemy until we were finally able, after three years of exhausting combat, to equip ourselves with the necessary cannon; a marriage which, on the eve of World War II, led the public powers and military command to refuse to build the mechanized armored force, while Germany gave itself Panzer divisions, the effects of which are known; a marriage which today loudly stigmatizes the so-called excessive cost of atomic weapons, while not only does this cost not annually exceed one hundredth of our national income, or one quarter of our military expenditures, or half what the State pays to its pensioners and retired people, or the total of the social benefits paid to farmers, but permits us to reduce by half our Army personnel and the length of military service. /31

However, this time the opposition does not come only from an oversimple refusal of reform. It is in reality inspired by adherents to two political prejudices, doubtless opposed, but both aimed at France's effacement under the hegemony of one or another foreign State. There are those, on the one hand, who would like to establish a totalitarian dictatorship in our country and who therefore desire to see us deprived of the means with which to defend ourselves against the East. There are, on the other hand, the partisans of the American protectorate who are alarmed at the prospect of a France mistress of herself with regard to her allies. But I believe, less than ever, that these objections coming from two very different horizons, but both originating with the intention that our country be subordinated, are persuading the French nation. We will thus continue our atomic effort over the short, medium and long term, convinced to be thereby helping the nation's scientific, technical and industrial development, to be reviving the body and soul of our army as modern times command, and to be giving France the means for her security and her independence, consequently those for her action in behalf of equilibrium and peace in the world. /32

Southeast Asia

QUESTION: General, taking into account the United States policy toward South Vietnam, do you hold to the suggestions which you have formulated since last year for Southeast Asia? /33

The Geneva Agreements concluded in 1954 put an end to the fighting in Indochina. At the time, everyone seemed to desire it sincerely. These agreements included provisions which varied according to the countries in question, but which had in common the absolute exclusion of all outside intervention. Cambodia pledged not to enter into any alliance and not to allow any base on its territory. Laos was to prohibit the presence of any foreign troops, with the exception of a French military mission and an airfield used by France in Seno. The two Vietnams could not ally themselves with anyone, or introduce on their soil any force from the outside, or receive armaments which would increase their potential. Moreover, general elections were scheduled to take place in Vietnam in 1956, so as to lead to the institution of a democratic Government and to reunification. /34

The 1954 agreements were not applied for long. That is the least that can be said about them. Cambodia alone—thanks to its national unity and to the very skillful and determined way in which it is led by its Head of State—has known how and been able to remain intact, neutral and relatively peaceful until now. But in Vietnam everything conspired to bring that country back to the troubled situation from which it had just emerged, while Laos in its turn was caught up in domestic conflicts, aided from the outside. /35

Concerning Vietnam, it must be said that the existence of a communist State installed in Tonkin, from where our troops withdrew in accordance with the agreements, and the shock caused in the south by the withdrawal of our administration and forces, exposed the country to new perils. It was a matter of knowing whether it could find, in itself, a national cohesion and a solid government. It was then that the Americans arrived, bringing their aid, their policy and their authority. /36

The United States, in fact, considered itself as being invested throughout the world with the burden of defense against communism. Since South Vietnam was running the risk of it, as the regime established in the north was aimed at imposing itself there, Washington wanted to put this State in a position to protect itself. It can be added, without any intention of being derogatory, that their conviction of fulfilling a sort of vocation, the aversion which they had to any colonial work which had not been theirs, and finally the natural desire in such a powerful people to ensure themselves of new positions, determined the Americans to take our place in Indochina. /37

We know that, back in 1954, they sponsored the Diem government, that Diem immediately and unfortunately assumed an unpleasant attitude toward us, that once Emperor Bao-Dai had left the country he replaced him, that he did not carry out

the scheduled elections and lastly that in all fields, particularly those of defense, economy and administration, he placed himself in the orbit of Washington. But, as this policy was more and more unpopular, the day came when Diem tried to disentangle himself from it, while the Americans began to have doubts about him. Then a military putsch removed the President and gave him a successor. After that, a new putsch invested another one, the latter closely linked with the war action which the United States is supporting, staffing, financing and arming. /38

War action, indeed, for although the subversive elements of the Vietcong had disappeared from South Vietnam after the 1954 agreements, they reappeared there under pretext that and as the agreements were not being applied. Guerrilla fighting and some action carried out by constituted units are spreading more and more over the territory. At the same time, the populations, whatever their opinion of communism, are less and less inclined to support a cause and an authority which in their view are intermingled with those of a foreign State. Thus it seems that, locally, a military solution cannot be expected. /39

Some people imagine, it is true, that the Americans could seek it elsewhere by carrying the war to the north as far as it would be necessary. But, although they certainly dispose of all the desired means, it is difficult to assume that they wish to take the tremendous risk of a generalized conflict. /40

Lacking a decision by war, it is peace which thus must be made. Now, this implies returning to what was agreed upon ten years ago and, this time, complying with it, in other words, this implies that in North and South Vietnam, in Cambodia and in Laos, no foreign power any longer intervene in any way in the affairs of these unfortunate countries. A meeting of the same order and including, in principle, the same participants as the former Geneva conference would certainly be qualified to make a decision and to organize an impartial control. That is what France is proposing to all the States concerned, certain that, unless plunging Asia first and without doubt, at a later date, the entire world into very serious trials, this will have to be done, and the sooner, the better. /41

This meeting, to which each must come without conditions or recriminations, would successively deal with the international aspects of the Laotian, Cambodian and Vietnamese situation and of which the essential is, in advance, their neutrality. No other road can be visualized which can lead to peace in Southeast Asia, provided that once the theoretical agreement is concluded, if it is to be, two practical conditions be realized. The first is that the powers which directly or indirectly bear a responsibility in what was or is the fate of Indochina and which are France, China, the Soviet Union and America, be effectively resolved to be involved there no longer. The second is that massive economic and technical aid be furnished to all of Indochina by the States which have the means for it, in order that development replace cruel division. France, for her part, is ready to observe these two conditions. /42

. . . . *

Ladies and Gentlemen, I thank you for your very kind attention, all the more as I fear that you have been made rather uncomfortable by heat in this large room. I thank you very sincerely for your attention. /43

The conference

1. Compare De Gaulle's method of conducting a press conference with the methods followed by President Kennedy and by President Johnson. Which of the three methods do you think best? What are the advantages and disadvantages of each? (Complete descriptions and lengthy excerpts from the press conferences of Presidents Kennedy and Johnson will be found in the New York *Times*.)

2. Evaluate the press conference as a method for informing the people of one's own nation as well as those of other nations of a government's decisions and policies. What advantages does it have over a prepared address? Over a written press release? What dangers does it entail?

3. Comment on the order in which De Gaulle took up the three questions of "Europe and the French-German Agreement," "French Atomic Policy," and "Southeast Asia." Do you think he chose this order deliberately or accidentally? Defend or attack this order (a) from a logical or substantive point of view, and (b) from a psychological or rhetorical point of view.

4. Allowing for difficulties in translation, how well do you think De Gaulle explains his views? Are you able to follow his explanations easily? In your opinion, does he leave any major questions unanswered?

5. In paragraph 37, De Gaulle says that the United States is adverse to any colonialism that is not its own. Is this an unnecessarily harsh and tactless statement? Might it have aroused needless antagonism between the two nations? Or is it a rhetorically strong and effective way of putting his point across?

6. This press conference is classified in the table of contents of this book as a "speech to inform." What grounds are there for classifying it as a "speech to persuade"? How would you classify it?

For further study and discussion

1. Review the aims and provisions of the Marshall Plan, and assess its achievements in reviving the economies of the European countries after World War II.

2. Is the desire of De Gaulle and like-minded persons for a "European Europe" free of American influence or domination to be attributed to mistakes in American foreign policy or is it a natural result of economic and political developments in the countries of Western Europe?

3. What is NATO? Which nations belong to it? What does NATO do? How successful has it been? What has been French policy with regard to NATO?

4. What were De Gaulle's reasons for vetoing Britain's entry into the Common Market?

5. Most observers agree that De Gaulle's aim is to reëstablish France as one of the great nations of the world. What obstacles stand in the way of achieving this aim? What forces and conditions operate in its favor? To what extent is the desired result being achieved?

6. Why does De Gaulle say he is opposed to a federated Europe? What does he propose instead?

7. Evaluate De Gaulle's proposal for settling the war in Vietnam (a) in terms of the situation as it existed at the time of the press conference, and (b) in the light of subsequent developments.

8. Trace De Gaulle's argument as to why it is necessary for France "to become an atomic power in her turn." Do you agree with his analysis? If so, why? If not, upon what grounds would you refute it?

Suggestions for further reading

Uwe W. Kitzinger, *The Politics and Economies of European Integration: Britain, Europe, and the United States* (New York, 1963)

Roy Macridis and Bernard E. Brown, *The De Gaulle Republic: A Quest for Unity* (Homewood, Ill., 1960)

Fritz Nova, *Contemporary European Governments* (Baltimore, 1963)

Ronald Steel, *The End of Alliance: America and the Future of Europe* (New York, 1964)

Alexander Werth, *The De Gaulle Revolution* (London, 1960)

Philip M. Williams and Martin Harrison, *De Gaulle's Republic* (London, 1960)

*Omitted here is a comment regarding De Gaulle's proposed fall visit to Latin America. (Editor's note)

Pan-Africanism, the Communists, and the West

COLIN LEGUM

The Royal African Society, a nonpolitical organization, was founded in 1901 to perpetuate the memory of Mary Kingsley, a pioneer African explorer and writer. Its announced aims are "to foster and encourage interest in Africa, particularly in those territories which form part of the Commonwealth; to form a link between those who are or have been concerned with Africa; and to assist the study of African affairs in the United Kingdom."

In carrying out these aims, the Society publishes a quarterly journal entitled *African Affairs*, arranges an annual conference on Africa, and sponsors a series of monthly lectures open to the public.

On March 5, 1964, the Society's lecturer was Colin Legum, African expert on the staff of the London *Observer*. Speaking on the subject "Pan-Africanism, the Communists, and the West," Legum presented a broad analysis of what he termed "the realities" of the African situation as it then existed and discussed the threat of Communist infiltration into that continent.

Although the lecture is loosely organized and at two points (paragraphs 16 and 22) lacks suitable transitions, it is comprehensive in view and incisively delineates the seven "realities" of present-day Africa. The style displays both the strengths and the weaknesses of extemporaneous speaking, its pleasing informality sometimes being marred by an awkward sentence or a grammatical error. The question-answer session, held at the close of the lecture, is typical of such "forum" periods, for while some of the questions seem to be genuine requests for additional information, others appear to be designed to embarrass the speaker or to call forth statements to support the questioner's views.

Legum was born in a village in the Orange Free State, South Africa, in 1919. Before moving permanently to England in 1949, he worked on various South African newspapers and was active in politics. In addition to being a writer for *The Observer*, Legum is a popular broadcaster and lecturer and the author of five books: *Must We Lose Africa?* (1954), *Congo Disaster* (1961), *Africa: A Handbook to the Continent* (1962), *Pan-Africanism* (1962), and *South Africa: Crisis for the West*, with Margaret Legum (1964).

The text of Legum's lecture is from *African Affairs*, LXIII (July 1964), 186-196.

Used by permission.

As one looks back at this slight distance of time to the reactions in this country to the mutinies in East Africa and the revolution in Zanzibar, one is struck by two astonishing facts: the first is that these events seem to have taken so many people by surprise, and one cannot help wondering what had happened to all the warnings that had gone up in recent years about the way things were being allowed to drift in East Africa. And the second is the way in which so many opinion-makers in the press, in Parliament—and of course on television and radio —seemed to have floundered in their attempts to analyse these events. Unfortunately, the majority of the opinion-makers in this country have only two frameworks within which they seem to be able to operate. The one is the framework of colonialism and of the old British Africa; the other is the framework of the cold war. Judging events within the first framework necessarily leads to judgments on Africa as if the events there were simply an extension of British problems in a black setting. Events are still being judged first as to what is thought to be in the best interests of the British, and not of the Africans. African leaders are categorised as "moderates" if they are pro-West and as "extremists" if they are not. /1

Thinking within such a framework produces two reactions. The moment something goes wrong, a shout goes up—what should Britain do about it? Not, what can Britain do about it? Not whether it is any of Britain's business any longer to want to do anything about it, or even whether she can do anything about it? Among those who ask this kind of question, thought is seldom given to what the African leaders themselves want to do about it, or whether they want us to do anything at all and, if so, what it is that they would wish us to do. The talk at this level is no different from what in fact it was in colonial times. Thinking within the colonial framework robs a person of one of the essential prerequisites for judging modern African affairs: the need to remember, above all, that African leaders no longer need or want us to look after them, or to tell them what to do. In this they might be wise or be foolish; but this is a fact of modern Africa. /2

A second reaction is the shout that goes up: "All this goes to show that we handed over power too soon; these people weren't ready for independence." Despite the generally funereally sober tones which such "I-told-you-so-ers" assume on these occasions, one cannot avoid the note of glee in their voices. One is left wondering when those who cling to the view that "we have handed over power too soon" are going to accept what they must know to be true —that Britain handed over power not because the Africans were ripe, or not ripe, for independence; but because it suited Britain's best interests to do so. A point had been reached where not to hand over power in Africa would have landed Britain in the same pickle as France had landed herself. The ghastly war in Indo-China was followed by the seven-year war in Algeria. France, which clung to power too long, drained the country materially and physically, destroyed democratic government in the Republic, committed the French Army to one disastrous campaign after the other for almost 14 years, and in the end they had to abandon the field just the same: to chaos in Indo-China and in a betrayal of the *colons* in Algeria. This is precisely the kind of situation in which we would have found ourselves in Africa if we had decided on a different course of action. /3

The second framework within which people operate in this country is that of the cold war. Every event is interpreted in terms of whether it is pro-West or pro-East. Politicians are judged entirely as to whether they are Communists or anti-Communists; every rebel movement is unfriendly if it is seen to go against what we regard as our moderate friends; and leaders of such movements are always either the agents of Moscow or of Peking. The idea that they might be the agents of nobody but themselves and of their own nationalism seldom seems to cross the minds of these analysts. /4

Now, I am not saying that the Communists are not busy in Africa and are not a threat to Africa. The Communists are busy, and they will become increasingly so. What I am saying are two things. First, that all the troubles in Africa at present are not due to the Communists, and that it is foolish and dangerous to think they are. It is this kind of thinking, which seeks to find the fault in everything that goes wrong as due to Communists, that leads Britain into serious errors in its relations with African leaders. /5

And second, that Africa's troubles are due to real problems in the continent which face the new governments. It is important, if we want to judge African affairs rightly, to see them not in the framework of the old colonial Africa, not in the framework of the Cold War, but in the framework of the realities of Africa. I mention seven realities as the most important factors affecting developments in Africa. I have no time to go into any of these fully, and I will mention them only briefly. /6

The first—and in the long term the most serious problem—is the balkanisation of Africa. The process of decolonisation has left behind a balkanised Africa in the sense of having produced there a large number of small and comparatively weak states, almost all of whom suffer more or less serious internal tensions as well as from external tensions due to disputes over questions of policy, frontiers, ethnic divisions, and so on. Africa, with a total population of perhaps 225-250 millions—only one-half of India's—already has 35 independent states, and by the time the process of decolonisation is over there might well be 50. Thus something like one-third of the world's states will be in Africa; on an average each of these states will have a population of perhaps 4½ million people—the size of a reasonable city in the industrialised world. But this average figure becomes even more disadvantageous if one takes into account that almost half the continent's total population live in five countries. The great majority of newly independent African states are, therefore, bound to be economically and militarily weak, unless they can create larger economic and political units. /7

The second problem is the general problem of underdevelopment and everything that arises from it. It gives rise to what we now describe as the "crisis of expectations" which comes to every newly independent country shortly after the transfer of power. Africa might be rich potentially—just how rich it would be hard to say; but at the moment it is extremely poor, and so far as its governments are concerned this raises great problems because of the aspirations of their own people and what they expected independence to bring to them. But it brings other problems as well, e.g., for the greater part, their major export crops are heavily subject to the vicissitudes of the rise and fall of commodity prices on the international market. If we remember that many of the new African states are politically but not yet economically independent, the conclusion is irresistible: that the new African governments are unable to exercise effective control over their own economies, and, as a Sierra Leone economist has put it: "To believe that Africa will accept the political independence without economic independence is moonshine." /8

The third reality is the revolutionary situation in Africa. It is not true, as people often believe, that Africa is in a state of peaceful evolution from colonialism to independence. The dynamics of African nationalism and Pan-Africanism, and the high aspirations Africans have set for themselves—especially the youth—make for a revolutionary situation. Changes in Africa are likely to be rapid and drastic. Its societies and its politics are in a state of flux, and will remain so until Africa establishes a new equilibrium, internally and with the outside world. It is impossible to predict how slow or how long the African revolution will run before it achieves its new equilibrium. In this situation it is necessary to remember that the present African governments or their leaders cannot be taken for granted; the possibilities of change are high. And here too one must avoid the danger of identifying a country with its present leadership. Ghana is not Nkrumah and Tanganyika is not Nyerere. /9

The fourth reality is the problem of white supremacy. Africa is deeply concerned, obsessed if you like, about the danger of neo-colonialism and about the need to destroy all vestiges of minority rule everywhere in the continent. The fear of a "second scramble" for Africa is widespread, and feelings about neo-colonialism rise whenever foreign powers combine to assist one side against the other in an African struggle such as we saw in Katanga. We stand on the threshold of what could become the worst disaster since Hitlerism and Stalinism: the possibility of a race war in South Africa. To ignore this possibility is to fly in the face of reality in Africa. If it should come to a race war the results will be cataclysmic—not only for Africa. /10

The fifth reality—and here I should mention that the notes I am speaking from now were originally read in a lecture in Germany nine months ago—is the military weakness of African states. Militarily, Africa is weak and vulnerable both to internal and to external attacks. Apart from South Africa, the U.A.R., Algeria, the Sudan, Ethiopia and Morocco, none of the African states has an armed force of any consequence; nor is it able to defend itself effectively against anything like an armed attack made against it from inside or from outside. /11

The sixth reality is the flood of international rivalry which plays on Africa's shores. Internationally, Africa is heavily courted by both the West and the East. And a new dimension in the courtship has been introduced by the split between Moscow and Peking. Considerations of cold war politics are bound never to be too far below the surface in decisions that are taken by any of the major powers in their relations with Africa. And so far as the Africans are concerned, although non-alignment is the aspiration of most of the African leaders, its practice is rather inconsistent. /12

The seventh reality is the irresistible rise of the single party state; because of its universality not only in Africa but in most of the newly independent countries—it seems that we must accept that their emergence meets a special need in the transition period after the ending of their dependency status. But whether the one party state can fulfill the wants as well as meet the needs of Africa is quite a different question. /13

These then are the realities which will determine the future shape of Africa. The objective conditions suggest that the continent needs a high degree of unity; that this is the only way in which the aspirations of African nationalism can be fulfilled; in other words, that Pan-Africanism is not just an ideal, but that it is the right answer to Africa's needs. To come to this conclusion, however, is not the same thing as concluding that this is in fact what will happen. One must take into account the negative factors operating against the consummation of unity. /14

Here one notices the fact that while the balkanisation of Africa is largely the result of historical processes and to a considerable extent of colonial policies as well, it is also a reflection of parochial nationalist aspirations. And one can say of Africa as Peter Calvocoressi has said of the Middle East: "There is a fission-fusion process at work. When fission is in the ascendant we get a host of small units whose quarrels may be dangerous; when fusion gains the day, the units are fewer, but they are also so large that they must be difficult to discipline." In Africa today we have both fission and fusion at work; and even as it is being balkanised the movement towards unification proceeds. Whether these states will prove amenable to the necessary disciplines still remains to be seen. /15

I now turn to the other aspect of my lecture which is the relationship between Pan-Africanism and Communism. The first thing that is to be said about Pan-Africanism is that this is much older than Communism in its modern form; that it has aspirations, desires and ends of its own. And the second point is that its confrontation with Communism is by no means new; it has been going on for forty years. What is new is the confrontation between Communism and Pan-Africanism inside Africa itself: this is the present phase which started only about five years ago. /16

Pan-Africanism is not, and never has been, a unified or a structured political movement. It is a movement of ideas and emotions: its recent political history has been a search for a viable political organisation. Its history can be broadly divided into four parts—and I am not going to spend a lot of time on this, but it does throw an important light on what we talked about. Those of you who have any real interest in Pan-Africanism might be interested in a book by that title, cost 22/6 and the fact that I am the author of it is not my only reason for mentioning it! The first is the period of its nascence from roughly the seventeenth century to the beginning of the twentieth century. The second period is the primary political stage—beginning with the first Pan-African conference in London in 1900—which was highlighted by the conflicting attitudes of the two giants of Pan-Africanist thinking—Marcus Garvey and W. E. B. DuBois.* And those of you who are *Sunday Telegraph* readers who read the story about Nkrumah** last week should not fail to notice that DuBois, who is presented as the great influence on Nkrumah's life, was not the leader of the "Back to Africa" movement, but in fact spent the whole of his life fighting Marcus Garvey who was. Thirdly, the period which might be called the period of synthesis, beginning with George Padmore's*** break with the Comintern in the middle 1930's, and with the start of his activities in London. This period reached its apogee in 1945 at the Manchester Pan-African Conference. Here one finds the first attempt at resolving basic conflicts within Pan-Africanist thinking, giving a greater coherent relationship between emotions and ideas, and establishing a sophisticated political framework for Pan-Africanism and especially its attachment to the idea of non-alignment. /17

And finally there is the fourth period which is also the first African continental period. It begins with the rooting of Pan-African ideas in Africa itself when the first Conference of Independent African States was convened by Dr. Nkrumah in Accra in 1958, and reached its high point in the first African Summit Conference of African Heads of State in Addis Ababa in May 1963. /18

So far as the Communists are concerned, they took an active interest in the second period of Pan-Africanism, trying hard to win over either Garvey or DuBois, who had managed to get considerable mass following among the American Negroes; since the Communists could not get a hold on the Negroes in America or on the Africans in South Africa, they concentrated all their efforts to win over Pan-

African leaders in these two countries, and they failed in both cases. /19

But the problems in Africa which faced the Communists in 1958—the moment when Pan-Africanism was set up in a proper form in the continent—are not difficult to understand. For almost forty years they had tried to ally these Negro movements, as I have just said, to the Communist International and failed. The analysis of the colonial liberation movement had led them widely astray. Having been guided by the Stalinist theory that the colonial revolution proceeds from the premise that the solution of the colonial problem and the liberation of the oppressed peoples from colonial slavery is impossible without a proletarian revolution and the overthrow of imperialism—they were almost wholly unprepared for the sudden disengagement by the Western colonial powers in Africa. Although they had always recognised the importance of the bourgeois nationalists as allied in the liberation struggle, the Communist theories did not allow for these forces to be capable of developing sufficient militancy to wrest independence without the cadres of what they called "the proletariat vanguard" to inspire them. The Communist International had forecast bitter struggles as the imperialists fought rearguard actions, as in Indo-China, during which time the revolutionary cadres would emerge to take over the leadership. But this did not happen in Africa. /20

It was only in 1955 that the Communists began to have serious doubts about the correctness of the diagnosis of colonial revolution. The Bandung conference, the successful challenge of the Naguib-Nasser officers' movement, and the relatively quick breakthrough by the CPP* in the Gold Coast caused them to revise their theories. But by then it was already too late. They were confronted by a totally new and unforeseen situation—a whole string of "bourgeois nationalist" governments, nearly all of which had outlawed the Communists in their own countries as one of their earliest acts. These new governments were, in fact, much tougher and more competent than the colonial powers had been in this particular field. And one can understand the mournful reactions of a Communist theorist who surveyed the African scene and commented of it: "Anti-Communism, Communist-phobia, the suppression of Marxism-Leninism as a system of thought, the attempt to crush the Communist organisation—all this is not only a limitation of de-

---

*Marcus Garvey (1887-1940) gained fame during the 1920's as leader of the Universal Negro Improvement Association. W. E. B. DuBois, American Negro educator and writer, founded the *Crisis*, journal of the NAACP. (Editor's note)
**Dr. Kwame Nkrumah is president of Ghana. (Editor's note)
***George Padmore is a Liberian diplomat. (Editor's note)

*The Convention People's Party, led by Nkrumah. (Editor's note) mocracy in Africa. It is no less a limitation on national development, a weakening of the national cause, of the truest interests of the mass of the people, and as assistance to the imperialists. It is regrettable that some African leaders have picked up this tattered mantle of the dictators and imperialists." So we see in Moscow, as in London, the Communists are not terribly happy with what has happened. /21

There are just a few points with which I wish to deal very briefly. One is the attitude or the mood of African nationalism which I believe is seriously misunderstood both in the Communist world and in the West. Modern African nationalism developed largely as a reaction to European nationalism, rooted in its ideas of European supremacy and of a world revolving around Western Europe. Its reaction therefore is not only against alien rule (anti-colonialism) but equally against race supremacy. For the African nationalist the ending of colonialism is the beginning not the end of a struggle—a point not sufficiently understood. How often does one hear the complaint: Now that colonialism is finished, what more do the Africans want? They want to abolish the status of inferiority—social, cultural, economic and political—cast upon Africa as a continent, and upon Africans as a people. African nationalism is a forceful assertion of the dignity of the individual African; it is a force struggling to establish real equality between Africa and the rest of the world, especially with its former alien rulers with whom it remains deeply entangled—and not altogether unwillingly so. /22

These aspirations give it two distinctive qualities. Externally, it operates as a force working for the total abolition of the old relationship as between superior and inferior—Europe and Africa—and as between European and African. Internally, it is a regenerating force seeking to destroy Africa's colonial mentality, and to uplift the African—economically, culturally and socially. It seeks to bring about a cultural Renaissance in Africa as well as an economic revolution. And an important aspect of African nationalism is its ambivalence towards Europe: the very nationalist leaders working actively to extrude Europe are at the same time willing to continue working with the former colonial powers and their allies. African nationalism does not reject Europe altogether; it seeks to create a new relationship based on true independence. There is a surprising lack of hatred and bitterness such as we have found as the result of the nationalism in Europe. /23

What I have really been trying to say throughout this talk comes down to this: that the majority of African leaders wish to be neither part of the west nor the east, that they will react against both, the strength of the reaction being determined by the pressures they feel placed upon them by one side or the other. Secondly, that African leaders see their interests not as an extension of the interests of Europe but as something totally separate. Thirdly, that whatever doubts Europeans might have about African capacity to defend their own interests against all comers, including the Communists, they themselves have no such doubt—and nothing causes greater resentment than the unfortunately frequent expressions of doubt about the African's capacity and ability to see who his real friends and enemies are. This is seen—and correctly seen—as a hangover from the old days when we regarded ourselves as superior in our wisdom over the Africans—and how many of us here in this hall today still do not hold this view to be true in our own hearts? Fourthly, that Africa is in for much worse troubles than anything we have yet seen. These are partly due to their inherited difficulties of balkanisation, economic and military weakness, to internal dissensions and to the forces of the cold war. These pressures make for revolutionary situations rather than for stability. /24

Finally, that the West should confine itself strictly to defending its own proper interests in Africa. These are confined only to three; economic interests; to the well-being of those white communities which still rest their dependence on the West rather than on the new African states; and to a proper concern that Africa should not turn in revulsion to the Communists. Such a revulsion might come—but if it does it will be principally against Western arrogance and lack of understanding of the true feelings and of the real economic and technical needs of Africa. /25

But these proper interests can only be defended in terms that are acceptable to the African leaders themselves. In other words, our actions must be guided by the reality that Africa is no longer a European colonial continent. We have given up being a colonial power—but we have not yet given up thinking in colonial terms. /26

Discussion

QUESTIONER: Does the speaker think we were right in recognising the new Zanzibar government and if so, does he think we should have done it more quickly? /27

SPEAKER: I most certainly think that we were right

and I most certainly think that we should have done it more quickly because I feel sure that, had anybody examined the situation within the new government, they would have known that the forces sympathetic to the Commonwealth—the forces that this country should have recognised in its own interests—were in the ascendant in the new government despite impressions to the contrary. It should also have recognised that their ascendancy could only be maintained by the immediate recognition as was given by the neighbouring African states. Unfortunately it was withheld—perhaps for too long—by this country. /28

QUESTIONER: Does Mr. Legum agree that even if the process of the nation-state had not been introduced into Africa by the colonisation, would it have been necessary to introduce it in order to facilitate decolonisation? /29

SPEAKER: If it hadn't existed I would certainly have agreed, but I think that scholars should re-examine two things about Africa. The one is the real nature of African nationalism which I think is completely misunderstood by European historians treating African nationalism in the same way as they treat European nationalism; it does not add up. The second is the idea that the nation-state was wholly exported from Western Europe to Africa. If this were so, one asks where did Moshoeshoe get his idea of the nation-state in developing Basutoland? Then, too, the formation of what we call empires, for want of a better term —Ghana, Songhai, Mali, etc.—which pre-date colonial Africa, had the effect of bringing together large numbers of people under strong central control: they introduced a central court, a universal religion (Islam), a common language and other unifying features. Thus there grew up under different circumstances and in ways that are not wholly akin to Western Europe, the fabric of the nation-state. Certainly, I believe that you cannot run a modern state without the concept of the nation-state. /30

QUESTIONER: Mr. Legum was careful not to differentiate between communism from Moscow and communism from Peking. Is it his contention that Russian and Chinese communism are working together in Africa? /31

SPEAKER: At one level they do work together; this is the level of propaganda to discredit all Western ideas, of all democratic ideas, and in building up their own ideas that authoritarian socialism is the only valid system to suit the needs of underdeveloped countries. In so far as these ideas are spread by both Moscow and Peking, they work together. But at the same time there are obviously clear differences between Peking and Moscow. These have been going on for at least three years, with Peking trying to get its separatist viewpoint established in the minds of the Africans in support of its own conflicts with Moscow in the international communist world. So, at one level they work together; at another level they oppose each other. Whether this "helps" or does not "help," I am not sure; perhaps it makes for a more revolutionary situation since both sides have to outbid each other. As against this, Africans are reacting against the attempts to involve them in disputes which they feel have nothing to do with them. /32

QUESTIONER: To what does the speaker attribute the general hostility of the West towards Pan-Africanism? The Western press, I beg your pardon. /33

SPEAKER: I think one should confine the answer by saying "a large part of the Western press." One must not get the idea that the entire Western press is hostile. A great deal of hostility, I imagine, is based on the fact that many simply do not know what Pan-Africanism is. It is generally identified in the minds of certain groups in this country—not only press groups—as representing the mobilisation of black power in order to oppress white people in Africa and to destroy European interests in general. I think it is this kind of confusion that leads to the antagonism towards Pan-Africanism. /34

QUESTIONER: Mr. Legum says that Ghana is *not* President Nkrumah, it was also said that Germany was *not* Hitler. We know that President Nkrumah is dismissing independent judges. What can the people of Ghana do about it, if they do not like it? And what does Mr. Legum mean by neo-colonialism which is a communist expression like fascist? /35

SPEAKER: The first thing is that I said "Nkrumah is not Ghana, Nyerere is not Tanganyika" and so on and so forth. This was a general assertion about the state of flux in Africa. I believe that there is almost no leader in Africa today who cannot be put on the expendable list. Since you raise the question of Ghana in particular and not of Tanganyika or any other country—in the case of Ghana there is no doubt that we are witnessing the rapid growth of authoritarianism. One finds the same process in perhaps a dozen other African states, mainly the Francophone states; but these are less remarked upon. There is considerable resistance to this process of authoritarianism, but for various reasons it has not yet become effective. I think one should never forget the important fact, that when discontent reaches a certain point, opposition to it will effectively assert itself. I recall a conversation I had with Dr. Nkrumah several years ago when he said that no African leader can forget that in the long run he would be swept aside by the change of opinion when the people reach a point of disaffection, where the bad outweighs the good. The process that made for destoolment of even powerful chiefs is still a factor to be contended with. Only it takes longer to achieve a broad unanimity of view because the unit of the "stool-lands" is so much larger. /36

I recall Dr. Nkrumah saying that if public opinion ever reached the point where it was no longer willing to put up with the existing authority, no bullets or police could stop them. He recognised that there was no alternative to "rule by consent." The real question is at what point consent is withdrawn? Former members of the colonial administration well know the kind of difficulty they had especially in West Africa where knowing a Chief was corrupt, or authoritarian, the people nevertheless refused all pleas to get rid of the Chief. In the end the official had no alternative but to come to terms with the Chief because the people would not undertake the process of destoolment. Then suddenly out of the blue and for no obviously good reason, the official found the tribal community had turned, and were insisting on destooling the Chief. This is the process by which change will come about in Africa. At a certain moment the people will have had enough, and when they reach this point the groundswell of discontent will remove the leadership. In this country we know the same process as "an election landslide." But at this stage in Africa, it will not be done through elections; it will come because people have become ungovernable. There have been examples of this already in the Congo (Brazzaville), in Dahomey and Gabon. There have also been popular movements in Ghana—but these were always localized. /37

On the question of neo-colonialism; it was invented by the early Pan-Africanists and picked up by the communists who have tried to make it a communist weapon. But it was not a communist invention. Neo-colonialism, in its classical form, means that there are people who while apparently willing to give up the old system of colonialism, seek to create new dependency relationships, usually of an economic kind—what is called "colonialism by the back-door." The truth is that neo-colonialism does operate to a considerable extent in Africa. Certain financial and other forces do pull the strings or at least try to do so. Neo-colonialism is not just a fantasy of the Africans or an invention of Communism. Neo-colonialism is a reality. Undoubtedly it becomes greatly exaggerated, as so many realities do get exaggerated. The best way of combatting neo-colonialism is to stop practising it; and that goes for the Communists no less than for the West. /38

QUESTIONER: Is there a tendency for economic planning at the centre to equate itself with Socialism? /39

SPEAKER: It is certainly true that there is a tendency to link economic centralisation or planning with the ideas of authoritarian socialism. But centralised economic planning is a perfectly valid and traditional Western idea: You do not have to go to the East for it. The trouble is that the Russians have persuaded some Africans, and certainly some African socialist leaders, to believe that central economic planning is taught and practised only by Marxists. /40

So far as economic totalitarianism is concerned, or any kind of totalitarianism for that matter, I do not think Africans have to go to Russia or anywhere else to learn about it. Africa is quite capable of providing its own totalitarianism. It has done so in the past and will no doubt, unhappily, do so in the future. But because Africans are no different from other people they will produce good and evil leaders as in any other continent. Why should this be a matter for surprise? One mentions it because there is the old idea still at large that Africans cannot think for themselves and that they must necessarily get their ideas either from the West or from the East. Modern African leaders are remarkably eclectic. They are choosing new ideas from all over the world and adapting them to their own ideas. But this pragmatic process is invariably adapted to African conditions. /41

QUESTIONER: We Africans are poor; we need all the help we can get. But if we go to the East we are attacked by the West, and *vice versa*. What should we do? /42

SPEAKER: Of course, the questioner (who is the High Commissioner for Uganda) does not expect an answer from me—he is doing a bit of teasing. He is in fact doing a satire on the days when he used to go to the District Commissioner in Uganda and say to him "Now you say this thing and the Chief says another thing. Either I am going to antagonise our Chief or our District Commissioner. Please tell me how I can avoid doing so." You do not want an answer because you know how to do this without anybody's advice. You are rightly drawing attention to a problem facing African leaders. In fact you have been successful in playing off the East against the West. Now this can be a dangerous game, but it can also be a profitable game—up to a point. You of course play it according to your rules, and I do not think for a moment that anything I tell you is going to change the way you make those rules. /43

QUESTIONER: What can be done to dispel the suspicion among Pan-African leaders that they have to fight a neo-colonialist plot? And how is Africa to be persuaded that Britain is not practising neo-colonialism? /44

SPEAKER: Well, Chief Arthur Prest is a veteran nationalist politician and government leader. When he puts a question like this one, he knows the answer better than I do! I think the main difficulty Africans have in trying to understand British policy is because it is still so largely equivocal; sometimes Africans seem to feel that British policy understands and is in tune with the ideas of modern Africa; at other times they read statements about South Africa, recently over East Africa, over Central African or Portuguese policy in Africa which raise serious doubts. Also they cannot follow the inconsistency in the role played by financial interests, say in Katanga. These might make perfectly good sense to British people reading their papers in this country; but they are awfully hard to understand if you are an African looking at the continent from a non-British angle. It is this apparent duality of policy which gives rise to the kind of difficulty that Chief Arthur Prest has talked about, and which makes it so difficult to persuade people that this country is not practising neo-colonialism—if indeed it is not. To some extent it does go in for neo-colonialism and to some extent it does not. What I am pleading for here this afternoon is that colonialism should be honestly ended; that it should be seen to be ended, and that we should act in every way as though it has indeed been ended. /45

QUESTIONER: Mr. Legum has given us a very interesting and thoughtful analysis of African aspirations and feelings, and of the present position in Africa. It seems to me that he has been thinking, perhaps naturally, of the relatively small group of more sophisticated Africans. Perhaps he would say something more specifically about what recent changes have meant to the ordinary men and women—in other words, to 90% of the people of these new African States. Are they actually better off, freer, and happier, and with the early prospect of higher standards of living? In short, are they consciously better off? /46

SPEAKER: I am very grateful to Lord Milverton for serving me up such a soft question this afternoon as well as such an important one. It is perfectly true that because so many people spend so much of their time worrying about Communism that they overlook the fact that Africans still draw so largely from Western schools of thought. That they adapt these ideas to their own needs and interests goes without saying. There is not the slightest doubt in my mind that more ideas are picked up about liberty and democracy than about the counter-ideas of authoritarianism and the dictatorship of the proletariat and the class struggle, etc. The question is what happens to ideas about liberty and democracy in a transitional society. After independence the leaders operate under great pressures which make it far from easy to live by the precepts of liberty and democracy. Nor should we forget that democracy is a by-product of plenty, and that it flourishes best in societies which are rich and homogeneous. The enemy of liberty is instability, sectionalism, poverty, an absence of national unity and discipline; yet these are the conditions which the great majority of African States have inherited. Small wonder that so many Africans, although they believe in liberty and democracy, find that these conditions make it hard to stand by their principles. But one would be wrong to conclude, therefore, that Africans do not believe in the basic tenets of liberty as much as we do. A country like Ghana has produced as many ardent champions of liberty as any other country I know of. Some of these people work within the governments, others have withdrawn. Some are in exile at the moment, having refused to go on holding their high posts because they were not prepared to compromise themselves personally. It is ridiculous to suppose that Africans neither prize liberty nor will they make the necessary sacrifices for freedom. Africans feel, as Lord Milverton knows from his own long experience in Africa, as deeply about the values of a free society as we do. These are not things that they have "learnt" from us.

The difficulty which faces African democrats is how to maintain the basic practises of democracy in the awkward situations which accompany independence. /47

I was asking earlier whether the one-party state can satisfy not only the wants but also the needs of Africa. I believe that in the end Africa will go through the same historical process as every other continent. It will go through periods of authoritarianism and it will swing away from authoritarianism. Its one-party states are going to be challenged in the course of time, and new political and constitutional processes will take over. Once we get used to the idea that Africans are no different from other people, we will stop trying and find in them unique qualities—whether uniquely good or uniquely evil. But this is still the hangover of the past—so many people cannot yet think of Africans as being no different from anybody else: in the end their political developments will be the same as everybody else's. /48

The speech

1. How well does Legum carry out his purpose of examining African affairs "not in the framework of the old colonial Africa, not in the framework of the Cold War, but in the framework of the realities of Africa"?

2. Would you say that Legum had or had not thought long and carefully about the ideas and judgments he presents? Point to specific passages that support your answer.

3. In your opinion, did Legum organize his major ideas effectively? If not, what changes would you suggest?

4. Because the lecture was delivered extemporaneously, it contains some awkward sentences and an occasional grammatical error. Would it have been better if Legum had read his lecture and thus avoided these defects? Explain your answer.

5. Do you think Legum scolds his audience too much in his opening remarks? Does he criticize too bluntly the current British attitude toward Africa? Do you think this criticism might have built unnecessary barriers between him and his audience?

6. In paragraph 5, Legum says that the Communists are not to blame for everything that "goes wrong" in Africa. Then in paragraph 12, he speaks of the "courtship" of Africa by Moscow and Peking, and of how "Cold War politics" influence African politics. Are these two statements inconsistent? Explain your answer.

7. How well does the summary-type conclusion (para-

graphs 24-26) cover the points made during the course of the lecture?

8. Evaluate the usefulness of forum periods in general and of this forum period in particular? What are their advantages and disadvantages? What are the various plans by which forum periods may be conducted? In your opinion, which plan is best? Why?

9. Do you think that Legum answers each question satisfactorily? If not, how might he have improved some of his answers?

For further study and discussion

1. What evidence, if any, is there of Communist activity in Africa at the present time? How successful have the Communists been in winning over the new nations of Africa?

2. Comment on American policy toward the new African nations. Do you approve or disapprove of it? Why?

3. Comment specifically on American policy at the time of the Belgian-United States rescue mission in the Congo during the fall of 1964. Should we have sent rescue teams into that area? Should we do the same thing again under like circumstances?

4. Compare the race problem in South Africa with the race problem in the United States.

5. Develop more fully the history of Pan-Africanism, as outlined in paragraphs 17-19. Refer specifically to the Manchester Pan-African Conference of 1945, the Conferences of the Independent African States at Accra in 1958 and at Addis Ababa in 1963. What roles did Marcus Garvey and W. E. B. DuBois play in the movement?

6. Report on the economic and trade problems faced by some of the new African nations. On their problems in the areas of agriculture, education, and health.

7. In paragraph 13, Legum asserts that "the single party state" meets "a special need" in a country that is just emerging from "dependency status." Do you agree? Why or why not?

8. What does Legum mean by "neo-colonialism"? Is it as serious a threat as he implies?

9. Do you think Legum would be in substantial agreement with Mrs. Dean's analysis of the non-Western world (see pages 234-240)? Explain your answer.

Suggestions for further reading

Paul Bohannan, *Africa and Africans* (Garden City, N.Y., 1964)
Zbigniew Brzezinski, *Africa and the Communist World* (Stanford, Calif., 1963)
Smith Hempstone, *Africa, Angry Young Giant* (New York, 1961)
Vernon McKay, *Africa in World Politics* (New York, 1963)
Arnold Rivkin, *Africa and the West: Elements of Free-world Policy* (New York, 1962)

The method of scientific investigation

THOMAS HENRY HUXLEY

(analysis by Walter Blair[1])

Trained as a physician, Thomas Henry Huxley (1825-1895) began his distinctive career as an assistant on an exploring and surveying cruise of the *Rattlesnake,* a vessel in the British navy. The cruise furnished him with exciting new information about marine biology which he wrote up in papers to the Linnaean and Royal societies. Almost immediately the papers made him famous. In 1854 he became Lecturer on Natural History at the Royal School of Mines, and in 1863 he became Fullerian Professor at the Royal Institution and also Hunterian Professor at the Royal College of Surgeons. Thereafter, he held many governmental and university posts; none of them, however, were so demanding that they cut seriously into his research, writing, and lecturing. In 1885 he was elected President of the Royal Society.

Huxley had the happy faculty of being able to speak informatively on his field to laymen as well as to other scientists. His lectures to workingmen in 1860 on the "Relation of Man to the Lower Animals" were models of scientific exposition. And subsequent lectures in which he explained and defended Darwinism to the general public were equally lucid. To this day he remains one of the greatest popularizers of science in the best sense of that term. The speech analyzed here was first delivered in 1866 to an audience of unread workingmen in England. Both as a speech and later as an essay, it has remained one of the finest statements of the method of scientific investigation.

The method of scientific investigation is nothing but the expression of the necessary mode of working of the human mind. It is simply the mode at which all phenomena are reasoned about, rendered precise

---

and exact. There is no more difference, but there is just the same kind of difference, between the mental operations of a man of science and those of an ordinary person, as there is between the operations and methods of a baker or of a butcher weighing out his goods in common scales, and the operation of a chemist in performing a difficult and complex analysis by means of his balance and finely graduated weights. It is not that the action of the scales in the one case, and the balance in the other, differ in the principles of their construction or manner of working; but the beam of one is set on an infinitely finer axis than the other, and of course turns by the addition of a much smaller weight. /1

ANALYSIS: After hearing only the first several sentences, the listener knows what the purpose of the whole lecture is—to explain to a lay audience "the method of scientific investigation." He also learns what the central idea is: that scientific study is a refined brand of common sense, a way of learning truth that every workman in the audience knows. The first paragraph offers proof that this is the central idea by reiterating it. Sentence 1 states it. Sentence 2 repeats it, but avoids monotony by using different words and by emphasizing a concept represented merely by the adjective "necessary" in sentence 1. (It does this by placing the words which paraphrase this one word in the most emphatic part of the sentence—at the end.) Sentences 3 and 4 take up a matter hitherto barely implied—the degree of difference between scientific and ordinary thinking, clarifying the matter by contrasting two common men, the butcher and the baker, with a particular kind of scientist, a chemist. Although the contrast is emphasized, the idea is restated for a second time, since the speaker points out that both workmen and scientists use scales. The listener, as the result of the reiterations, upon concluding the paragraph, has acquired one idea, with a few modifications—that scientists proceed as ordinary men do.

You will understand this better, perhaps, if I give you some familiar example. You have all heard it repeated, I dare say, that men of science work by means of induction and deduction, and that by the help of these operations, they, in a sort of sense, wring from Nature certain other things, which are called natural laws, and causes, and that out of these, by some cunning skill of their own, they build up hypotheses and theories. And it is imagined by many, that the operations of the common mind can be by no means compared with these processes, and that they have to be acquired by a sort of special apprenticeship to the craft. To hear all these large words, you would think that the mind of a man of science must be constituted differently from that of his fellow men; but if you will not be frightened by terms, you will discover that you are quite wrong, and that all these terrible apparatus are being used by yourselves every day and every hour of your lives. /2

There is a well-known incident in one of Molière's plays, where the author makes the hero express unbounded delight on being told that he has been talking prose during the whole of his life. In the same way, I trust that you will take comfort, and be delighted with yourselves, on the discovery that you have been acting on the principles of inductive and deductive philosophy during the same period. Probably there is not one here who has not in the course of the day had occasion to set in motion a complex train of reasoning, of the very same kind, though differing of course in degree, as that which a scientific man goes through in tracing the causes of natural phenomena. /3

The second and third paragraphs again restate the idea of the first paragraph and of the speech as a whole. They use new methods, however, and progress toward the next division. The second paragraph is built very differently from the first. Instead of starting with a topic sentence, Huxley holds the whole meaning in suspension. "I [will] give you some familiar example," he says, then, "You have all heard. . . . And it is imagined by many. . . . To hear all these large words, you would think . . . but. . . ." The word "but" is a pivot: only after this is it indicated that what has been heard, imagined, and thought is not so. In other words, this paragraph restates the thesis by setting forth an opposite one and then by denying the antithesis. And the third paragraph restates in still another way—by employing a literary allusion analogically: Prose, he suggests, is to Molière's character as inductive and deductive philosophy is to "you"—a lifelong instrument. Both paragraphs, in addition, forecast later divisions of the speech and thus prepare the listener for them. Paragraph 2 does this unobtrusively when it mentions "induction and deduction . . . hypotheses and theories," since these pairs of items, respectively, will be considered in the next divisions of the speech. Paragraph 3 also forecasts later divisions, once by mentioning "the principles of inductive and deductive philosophy" in the next to last sentence, and once

by mentioning "a complex train of reasoning" in the last sentence. The listener has now begun to comprehend the specific nature of the similarity between the scientist and the ordinary man which has been emphasized in these opening paragraphs.

A very trivial circumstance will serve to exemplify this. Suppose you go into a fruiterer's shop, wanting an apple—you take one up, and, on biting, you find it is sour; you look at it, and see that it is hard, and green. You take up another one and that too is hard, green, and sour. The shopman offers you a third; but, before biting it, you examine it, and find that it is hard and green, and you immediately say that you will not have it, as it must be sour, like those that you have already tried. /4

Nothing can be more simple than that, you think; but if you will take the trouble to analyse and trace out into its logical elements what has been done by the mind, you will be greatly surprised. In the first place, you have performed the operation of induction. You found, that, in two experiences, hardness and greenness in apples went together with sourness. It was so in the first case, and it was confirmed by the second. True, it is a very small basis, but still it is enough to make an induction from; you generalize the facts, and you expect to find sourness in apples where you get hardness and greenness. You found upon that a general law, that all hard and green apples are sour; and that, so far as it goes, is a perfect induction. Well, having got your natural law in this way, when you are offered another apple which you find is hard and green, you say, "All hard and green apples are sour; this apple is hard and green, therefore this apple is sour." That train of reasoning is what logicians call a syllogism, and has all its various parts and terms—its major premise, its minor premise, and its conclusion. And, by the help of further reasoning, which, if drawn out, would have to be exhibited in two or three other syllogisms, you arrive at your final determination. "I will not have that apple." So that, you see, you have, in the first place, established a law by induction, and upon that you have founded a deduction, and reasoned out the special conclusion of the particular case. Well now, suppose, having got your law, that at some time afterwards, you are discussing the qualities of apples with a friend: you will say to him, "It is a very curious thing —but I find that all hard and green apples are sour!" Your friend says to you, "But how do you know that?" You at once reply, "Oh, because I have tried them over and over again, and have always found them to be so." Well, if we were talking science instead of common sense, we should call that an experimental verification. And, if still opposed, you go further, and say, "I have heard from the people in Somersetshire and Devonshire, where a large number of apples are grown, that they have observed the same thing. It is also found to be the case in Normandy, and in North America. In short, I find it to be the universal experience of mankind wherever attention has been directed to the subject." Whereupon your friend, unless he is a very unreasonable man, agrees with you, and is convinced that you are quite right in the conclusion you have drawn. He believes, although perhaps he does not know he believes it, that the more extensive verifications are—that the more frequently experiments have been made, and results of the same kind arrived at—that the more varied the conditions under which the same results are attained, the more certain is the ultimate conclusion, and he disputes the question no further. He sees that the experiment has been tried under all sorts of conditions, as to time, place, and people, with the same result; and he says with you, therefore, that the law you have laid down must be a good one, and he must believe it. /5

In science we do the same thing;—the philosopher exercises precisely the same faculties, though in a much more delicate manner. In scientific inquiry it becomes a matter of duty to expose a supposed law to every possible kind of verification, and to take care, moreover, that this is done intentionally, and not left to a mere accident, as in the case of the apples. And in science, as in common life, our confidence in a law is in exact proportion to the absence of variation in the result of our experimental verifications. For instance, if you let go your grasp of an article you may have in your hand, it will immediately fall to the ground. That is a very common verification of one of the best established laws of nature—that of gravitation. The method by which men of science establish the existence of that law is exactly the same as that by which we have established the trivial proposition about the sourness of hard and green apples. But we believe it in such an extensive, thorough, and unhesitating manner because the universal experience of mankind verifies it, and we can verify it ourselves at any time; and that is the strongest possible foundation on which any natural law can rest. /6

Indicating, as it does, that a "trivial circumstance" will now "exemplify" the truth so frequently stated in earlier paragraphs, the opening sentence of paragraph 4 marks off a new division. Paragraph 4 recounts the "circumstance" in the form of a little story with "you" as the leading character; paragraph 5 shows the basic similarity between the mental activity in which "you" engage and that of the scientist; and paragraph 6, which concludes the division, reports that while there is such a similarity, the scientist's activity is more "delicate." In other words, the content of the three closely related paragraphs is a systematic development of the idea expressed in both the last sentence of paragraph 3 and the first sentence in paragraph 6. Note, however, that though Huxley expresses the same idea in both these sentences, he foreshadows the immediate emphasis by manipulating the position of the "though" elements. And a number of additional transitional devices also help to mark off as well as to relate the subdivisions. The word "suppose," for instance, is used twice—each time to introduce a story. In addition, words and phrases such as "in the first place," "having got your natural law in this way," "that train of reasoning," and others, as well as summarizing sentences, are skillfully used to aid the whole movement of the section—a movement from childishly simple illustration to a complex generalization for which the illustration has prepared.

Huxley, by following this procedure, interestingly enlightens the listener. The listener, from the simple story in paragraph 4, learns how the common man effortlessly uses induction and deduction in buying apples, but his understanding has not yet been complicated by his trying to attach labels. In paragraph 5, he learns about the applicability of the terms to the procedures of both the common man and the scientist. Further, by following the generalization in the paragraph, he gets a clear idea of what the terms mean. Then (a) by following another story which exemplifies "experimental verification" and (b) by generalizing with Huxley about this process, the listener acquires an understanding of this new term. By noting comparisons and contrasts as well as specific examples in paragraph 6, the listener becomes acquainted with the essential differences as well as the essential likenesses between common and scientific methods of verification and also learns how the great law of gravitation may be seen to rest upon "the strongest possible foundation." Thus, as a result of the whole orderly and carefully divided presentation in this division, the listener achieves a clear grasp of the meaning.

So much, then, by way of proof that the method of establishing laws in science is exactly the same as that pursued in common life. Let us now turn to another matter (though really it is but another phase of the same question), and that is, the method by which, from the relations of certain phenomena, we prove that some stand in the position of causes toward the others. /7

Paragraph 7, a transitional paragraph, has as its whole purpose marking off the end of a division and announcing a new division. "So much," it says, for this aspect of the subject; "Let us now turn to another matter"—the matter of the proof of cause-effect relationships. Carefully, though, the speaker informs the listener that this other matter "really . . . is but another phase of the same question," thus showing that the divisions are interrelated. The listener therefore knows that he is to shift his attention to a new topic, but that he is to be alert to interrelationships.

I want to put the case clearly before you, and I will therefore show you what I mean by another familiar example. I will suppose that one of you, on coming down in the morning to the parlor of your house, finds that a teapot and some spoons which had been left in the room on the previous evening are gone— the window is open, and you observe the mark of a dirty hand on the windowframe, and perhaps, in addition to that, you notice the impress of a hobnailed shoe on the gravel outside. All these phenomena have struck your attention instantly, and before two seconds have passed, you say, "Oh, somebody has broken open the window, entered the room, and run off with the spoons and the teapot!" That speech is out of your mouth in a moment. And you will probably add, "I know there has; I am quite sure of it!" You mean to say exactly what you know; but in reality you are giving expression to what is, in all essential particulars, an hypothesis. You do not *know* it at all; it is nothing but an hypothesis rapidly framed in your own mind. And it is an hypothesis founded on a long train of inductions and deductions. /8

Section three, which concludes the speech, follows almost exactly the same pattern as does section two—simple story of a commonplace happening (most of paragraph 8); consideration of the reasoning process involved in the illustration (rest of paragraph 8, paragraph 9); simple story of another happening which is the consequence of the one recounted at the start of the division (paragraphs 10 and 11); consideration of the reasoning processes involved in this second happening (paragraphs 12 and 13). It may be worth while to look at paragraph 8 to see how Huxley uses it to prepare the listener for the rest of the speech. The first sentence informs the listener what Huxley is going to do and why he is going to do it. Furthermore, it recalls a pattern which has been used twice before and thereby suggests that it may be followed again. "I will show you what I mean by another familiar example," he says. And in introducing his story, Huxley uses a word heretofore used to introduce stories: "I will suppose. . . ." Again the story is told without incidental comment; but at the end

of the paragraph, the mental processes which "you" had in the course of the happenings just set down are labeled: the listener therefore learns that the story showed the working out of a hypothesis. The last sentences repeat this new word twice, thus emphasizing the speaker's new concern. They do more: (a) They show why part 3 of the speech should have been placed last. The hypothesis which the listener has expressed about the burglar, says Huxley, is "founded on a long train of inductions and deductions." Now obviously, if the listener had had to take time out while, at this point, Huxley helped him understand "induction" and "deduction," he would have found the understanding of the speech pretty complicated. As it is, he needs to master only one new term at a time. (b) They show where the speaker will next turn—to another analysis of mental processes, this time the processes which lead to the forming of a hypothesis.

What are those inductions and deductions, and how have you got at this hypothesis? You have observed in the first place, that the window is open; but by a train of reasoning involving many inductions and deductions, you have probably arrived long before at the general law—and a very good one it is— that windows do not open of themselves; and you therefore conclude that something has opened the window. A second general law that you have arrived at in the same way is that teapots and spoons do not go out of a window spontaneously, and you are satisfied that, as they are now not where you left them, they have been removed. In the third place, you look at the marks on the window sill and the shoe marks outside, and you say that in all previous experience the former kind of mark has never been produced by anything else but the hand of a human being; and the same experience shows that no other animal but man at present wears shoes with hobnails in them such as would produce the marks in the gravel. I do not know, even if we could discover any of those "missing links" that are talked about, that they would help us to any other conclusion! At any rate the law which states our present experience is strong enough for my present purpose. You next reach the conclusion that, as these kinds of marks have not been left by any other animals than men, or are liable to be formed in any other way than by a man's hand and shoe, the marks in question have been formed by a man in that way. You have, further, a general law, founded on observation, and experience, and that, too, is, I am sorry to say, a very universal and unimpeachable one —that some men are thieves; and you assume at once from all these premises—and that is what constitutes your hypothesis—that the man who made the marks outside and on the window sill, opened the window, got into the room, and stole your teapot and spoons. You have now arrived at a *vera causa;*—you have assumed a cause which, it is plain, is competent to produce all the phenomena you have observed. You can explain all these phenomena only by the hypothesis of a thief. But that is a hypothetical conclusion, of the justice of which you have no absolute proof at all; it is only rendered highly probable by a series of inductive and deductive reasonings. /9

The opening sentence of paragraph 9 makes clear, more specifically than the sentence just before has, that the speaker will next analyze the inductions and deductions "you" used in getting the hypothesis mentioned in paragraph 8. A series of markings-off ("in the first place"; "a second general law"; "in the third place"; "you next reach"; "you have, further"; and "you have now arrived") set up guideposts which enable the listener to see how reasonings lead to "a general law," how other reasonings result in "another general law," and so on, until the hypothesis is formulated. The listener may wonder why Huxley used the phrase *vera causa* in addressing an audience who would be unlikely to understand it; but the listener will notice that frequent synonyms for "hypothesis" show that the reasoning has led to such a formulation.

I suppose your first action, assuming that you are a man of ordinary common sense, and that you have established this hypothesis to your own satisfaction, will very likely be to go off for the police, and set them on the track of the burglar, with the view to the recovery of your property. But just as you are starting with this object, some person comes in, and on learning what you are about, says "My good friend, you are going on a great deal too fast. How do you know that the man who really made the marks took the spoons? It might have been a monkey that took them, and the man may have merely looked in afterwards." You would probably reply, "Well, that is all very well, but you see it is contrary to all experience of the way teapots and spoons are abstracted; so that, at any rate, your hypothesis is less probable than mine." While you are talking the thing over in this way, another friend arrives, one of that good kind of people that I was talking of a little while ago. And he might say, "Oh, my dear sir, you are certainly going on a great deal too fast. You are most presumptuous. You admit that all these occurrences took place when you were fast asleep, at a time when you could not possibly have known anything about what was taking place. How do you know that the laws of Nature are not suspended during the night? It may be that there

has been some kind of supernatural interference in this case." In point of fact, he declares that your hypothesis is one of which you cannot at all demonstrate the truth, and that you are by no means sure that the laws of Nature are the same when you are asleep as when you are awake. /10

Well, now, you cannot at the moment answer that kind of reasoning. You feel that your worthy friend has you somewhat at a disadvantage. You will feel perfectly convinced in your own mind, however, that you are quite right, and you say to him, "My good friend, I can only be guided by the natural probabilities of the case, and if you will be kind enough to stand aside, and permit me to pass, I will go and fetch the police." Well, we will suppose that your journey is successful, and that by good luck you meet with a policeman; that eventually the burglar is found with your property on his person, and the marks correspond to his hand and to his boots. Probably any jury would consider those facts a very good experimental verification of your hypothesis, touching the cause of the abnormal phenomena observed in your parlor, and would act accordingly. /11

The word "suppose" at the start of paragraph 10, as it has before, reintroduces the story element. This piece of narrative, as it is unfolded in this paragraph, has dramatic interest, since it tells about some contentious friends who try to convince "you" that "your" hypothesis is invalid. Here Huxley was mixing in some persuasion—the arguments used by the two callers were quite similar to arguments which some people in Huxley's day were using to discredit hypotheses. When, therefore, in paragraph 11 Huxley indicates that such arguments are not guided by "natural probabilities," he is in reality attacking contemporary opponents of science. And when the listener hears the triumphant vindication of the hypothesis at the end of the paragraph, he learns that these arguments do not vitally affect "your" shrewd guess. Meanwhile the listener has mastered more facts about the nature of a hypothesis, the nature of arguments against it which may be ineffective, and the way it may be verified.

Now, in this supposititious case, I have taken phenomena of a very common kind, in order that you might see what are the different steps in an ordinary process of reasoning, if you will only take the trouble to analyse it carefully. All the operations I have described, you will see, are involved in the mind of any man of sense in leading him to a conclusion as to the course he should take in order to make good a robbery and punish the offender. I say that you are led, in that case, to your conclusion by exactly the same train of reasoning as that which a man of science pursues when he is endeavoring to discover the origin and laws of the most occult phenomena. The process is, and always must be, the same; and precisely the same mode of reasoning was employed by Newton and Laplace in their endeavors to discover and define the causes of the movements of the heavenly bodies, as you, with your own common sense, would employ to detect a burglar. The only difference is, that the nature of the inquiry being more abstruse, every step has to be most carefully watched, so that there may not be a single crack or flaw in your hypothesis. A flaw or crack in many of the hypotheses of daily life may be of little or no moment as affecting the general correctness of the conclusions at which we may arrive; but, in a scientific inquiry, a fallacy, great or small, is always of importance, and is sure to be in the long run constantly productive of mischievous if not fatal results. /12

Do not allow yourselves to be misled by the common notion that an hypothesis is untrustworthy simply because it is an hypothesis. It is often urged, in respect to some scientific conclusion, that, after all, it is only an hypothesis. But what more have we to guide us in nine-tenths of the most important affairs of daily life than hypotheses, and often very ill-based ones? So that in science, where the evidence of an hypothesis is subjected to the most rigid examination, we may rightly pursue the same course. You may have hypotheses, and hypotheses. A man may say, if he likes, that the moon is made of green cheese: that is an hypothesis. But another man, who has devoted a great deal of time and attention to the subject, and availed himself of the most powerful telescope and the results of the observations of others, declares that in his opinion it is probably composed of materials very similar to those of which our own earth is made up: and that is also only an hypothesis. But I need not tell you that there is an enormous difference in the value of the two hypotheses. That one which is based on sound scientific knowledge is sure to have a corresponding value; and that which is mere hasty random guess is likely to have but little value. Every great step in our progress in discovering causes has been made in exactly the same way as that which I have detailed to you. A person observing the occurrence of certain facts and phenomena asks, naturally enough, what process, what kind of operation known to occur in Nature applied to the particular case, will unravel and explain the mystery? Hence you have the scientific hypothesis; and its value will be proportionate to the care and completeness with which its basis has been tested and verified. It is in these matters as in the commonest affairs of practical life: the guess of the fool will be folly, while the guess of the wise man will contain wisdom. In all cases, you see that the value of the result depends on the patience and faithfulness with which the investigator applies to his hypothesis every possible kind of verification. /13

The opening sentences of paragraph 12 inform the listener what Huxley has done so far in this section and why—in terms of clarification—he has done it. The rest of the paragraph clarifies anew—by considering hypotheses rather than inductions and deductions—the main point of the speech, that science uses a refined version of the sort of thinking typical of the man of common sense. First the similarity is stressed, and then (beginning with the words, "The only difference is . . .") Huxley turns to the refinements upon everyday methods which scientists use. Paragraph 13 continues to make the distinction between ordinary hypotheses and scientific ones, chiefly by the use of example and argument. The use of argument in behalf of hypotheses here means, of course, that Huxley is again being an advocate, though now in a somewhat less subtle way than before. And the final paragraph summarizes once more, in a new way, the unifying idea of the speech. Thus, by Huxley's skillful setting forth of facts and ideas in familiar-to-unfamiliar organization, time arrangement, cause-effect arrangement, definition, analogy, comparison, and some persuasion at appropriate points in his speech, his audience has learned about the methods of science.

On the federal Constitution

JONATHAN SMITH

(analysis by Carroll C. Arnold)

On September 17, 1787, the Constitutional Convention of the United States of America heard a reading of the final draft of its proposed Constitution, which the delegates subsequently signed. The Convention then submitted the Constitution to the states, to be debated and approved or disapproved by specially elected state conventions. The approval of nine states was necessary to make the new form of government binding.

Pennsylvania, New Jersey, Connecticut, Georgia, and Delaware ratified the Constitution before the middle of January, the pro-Constitution forces having little difficulty in those conventions. The Massachusetts convention, which convened on January 9, 1788, was different. Historians agree that most of the Massachusetts delegates were opposed to the Constitution or had grave doubts about it when they first came together. Even John Hancock and Samuel Adams were undecided, but the strongest opposition came from farmers and artisans, particularly those from the western part of the state.

On January 24, 1788 (some sources say January 25), a relatively unknown man rose in the Massachusetts convention and made a short speech that still stands as one of the most refreshing and artful to be found in the records of American deliberative argument. What follows is a rhetorical analysis (see "Four Ways of Looking at a Speech," pp. 17-24) of this address. The object of this analysis is to discover what effects this speech probably produced and why.

To discover what probably occurred on January 24, 1788, when a man named Jonathan Smith spoke to some three hundred fifty delegates, we should know something about the man who spoke, the special expectations and purposes that dominated the occasion, the ideas and attitudes the audience had before the speech began, and what the speaker did when he spoke. That we cannot know these things in full detail means that we shall never be able to re-create the event of the speech entirely. How much of the event we can recover with limited information, the analysis that follows will illustrate.

Unfortunately we know little about Jonathan Smith. Were it not for his speech, he would be all but lost to history. He was from Lanesboro, Massachusetts, a tiny village in Berkshire County in the northwest corner of the state. He had fought in the Revolutionary War, entering service as an ensign and leaving as either a captain or a colonel (the records are conflicting on this point). He had held the office of justice of the peace, been a delegate to the convention that framed the Constitution of Massachusetts, and was now the elected delegate from his town to the convention on the federal Constitution. Lanesboro was one of only seven of the twenty-two Berkshire County towns to send pro-Constitution delegates to the convention in Boston. Smith was a farmer, but he may have had other occupations as well. This is all we know of him.

From even so little knowledge some conclusions about Jonathan Smith as a convention speaker are possible:

1. He would get special attention because he came from a part of the state where the Constitution was unpopular, yet he favored it.

2. He could easily establish common ground with some opponents of the Constitution because he was a western farmer.

3. He could probably gain some advantage in advising farmers from the fact that he had had special experience in the military and in government. (Note that in lines 41-44 he uses some of these advantages deliberately.)

So, from what little we know of Jonathan Smith, we can presume that when he rose and began to speak, farmers and perhaps some others found this "plain man" from the "opposition country" worthy of a careful hearing.

But Smith had to fit into a special kind of occasion. He was at a deliberative meeting. The convention was assembled to debate and to vote on a plan that would regulate the future conditions of life in Massachusetts. When its task was finished, the convention would adjourn forever. It had been created for this single purpose. Each Massachusetts town had its delegate or delegates, and all were free to speak their minds on the great subject. Samuel Adams and Fisher Ames might be bigger and more powerful men than a Berkshire County farmer, but on this speaking occasion the farmers and artisans were assured as respectful a hearing as the "learned and moneyed men." We can conclude, then, that a man like Jonathan Smith could speak confidently, with a real hope of influencing the course of events. Such was the occasion; his kind of speaker was not out of place as long as he directed attention to the important action the convention had to take.

What of his audience? No Gallup polls tested the opinions and attitudes of the delegates to the Massachusetts convention, but we can still tell something about their views and anxieties. A good source of information is the speeches they made before Smith spoke. Other sources are their newspapers and the personal records historians have now explored. Such evidence shows that Smith spoke to an audience in which the doubters would finally determine which side would win on the Constitutional question.

Opponents of the Constitution had tried to intensify the following doubts about the Constitution: (a) Congress might become a tyrannical clique; (b) to allow a federal government to set the time for elections and to tax the people might destroy the people's control over the government and over their own property; (c) the powers of Congress to regulate trade, create an army, collect duties, etc., might destroy the rights of states and create a federal tyranny. And the kinds of questions asked by doubters show they were worried about these possibilities and about such other things as whether it was safe to let Senators have terms as long as six years, whether the new government would hide its operations in secrecy, and whether a formal bill of rights was needed to protect the individual citizens against the national government. This kind of evidence, though scanty, tends to show us two most important facts about the audience:

1. The doubters were the people for all persuaders to concentrate on.

2. Since the doubters were fearful of too much government, persuaders would have to show them that there was more to fear from rejecting the Constitution than from ratifying it, that their fears about too much government were groundless.

One other fact about the audience must also be understood. Getting the farmers to support a new, more powerful government was certain to be a more than normally difficult and delicate task. The farmers, or some of them at least, had a record of opposition to strong government, even by the state. Some delegates had been involved in the famous Shays' Rebellion, a violent movement among farmers and artisans in Massachusetts to close the courts by force in order to prevent imprisonment of debtors and foreclosures on mortgaged property. The first threats occurred on September 12 and 13, 1786, at Taunton (Bristol County) and at Concord, both in the eastern part of the state. As Smith indicates in his speech, the violence swiftly spread westward. Berkshire County, in which Smith lived, was caught in the grip of severe anti-government, anti-court, anti-wealth raids in which several persons were killed. In February 1787 a company of rebels fought government troops on one of the Berkshire roads. It was there that the rebels put prisoners between themselves and the militiamen while they reloaded their firearms. With such events in the recent past, farmers and the subject of farmers would have to be handled with great delicacy by any speaker.

With this background concerning Smith, the convention as a speaking occasion, and the audience, we are ready to look at Smith's little composition. Ideally we should examine (a) his arguments and suggestions, (b) their organization, (c) the language he used, and (d) his delivery. About his delivery nothing seems to have come down to us, not even the testimony of any who listened. We cannot, therefore, make a full analysis of the speaking event, but we can at least secure a partial answer to what happened that day if we examine the following things about the text of the speech:

1. We must examine the arguments and suggestions in the speech to:

   a. Identify the kinds of proof used. We can do this by:

      1) Looking for and testing the probabilities of rhetorical syllogisms (deductions and causal relations) that support ideas.

      2) Looking for and testing the probabilities of arguments from example and analogy (inductions) that support ideas.

      3) Looking for statements and assertions that, though not parts of the reasoning, still have influence because of what they suggest to the listeners.

   b. Discover in the reasonings and "proofs" by suggestion:

      1) Whether the audience would think these reasonings and assertions credible, coming from Smith (ethos plus credibility of logic and feeling).

      2) Whether the reasonings and assertions are likely to move the listeners closer to approving the Constitution. The occasion and Smith's general purpose being deliberative, any proofs that move in another direction *may* be irrelevant and confusing, though not necessarily so.

2. We must examine the arrangement of ideas to see:

   a. Whether the main ideas are set forth in a way that listeners could follow easily.

   b. Whether by such means as building climaxes, arranging proofs cumulatively, etc., Smith has gained or lost any potential emphasis for his most important ideas and suggestions.

3. We must examine Smith's style, particularly how his language serves:

   a. To render all ideas clear.

   b. To give an appropriate and consistent reflection of Jonathan Smith, farmer, addressing a democratically elected and conducted meeting in Boston.

      1) Here, we cannot judge with certainty, for his delivery could have much effect on the appropriateness of his utterance.

      2) We must not apply standards of style, grammar, etc., that would not have been applied in 1788.

   c. To render the ideas interesting. (For standards see Glossary: *Activity, Concreteness, Conversational Quality, Figures of Speech, Imagery, Liveliness, Originality, Variety*.)

   d. To supply suggestive proof through connotations of words chosen.

The marginal notes accompanying the text of Jonathan Smith's speech below illustrate the kinds of judgments about the effects of a speech that can be reached by an inquiry of the sort just outlined.

Mr. President. I am a plain man, and get my living by the plough. I am not used to speak in public, but I beg your leave to say a few words to my brother ploughjoggers in this house. I have lived in a part of

5 the country where I have known the worth of good government by the want of it. There was a black cloud that rose in the east last winter and spread out over the west.

[Here Widgery, one of the opponents of the Constitution, interrupted: "Mr. President, I wish to know what the gentleman means by the east." Widgery was from New Gloucester and, like some others, was exceedingly sensitive to any blame thrown on his section (now Maine).]

I mean, sir, the county of Bristol; the cloud rose

10 there, and burst upon us, and produced a dreadful effect. It brought on a state of anarchy, and that led to tyranny. I say it brought anarchy. People that used to live peaceably and were before good neighbors, got distracted, and took up arms against government.

[Here Kingsley interrupted, asking what "the history of last winter" had to do with the Constitution. Several other members, including Samuel Adams, called out that Smith was in order and should "go on in his own way."]

15 I am going, Mr. President, to show you, my brother farmers, what were the effects of anarchy, that you

ANALYSIS: Emphasizes identification with farmers; doesn't even pretend to address his "betters."

Term of familiarity addressed to fellow farmers.

Ethos: claims qualification to judge what makes for practical happiness.

The metaphor at once suggests Shays' Rebellion but treats the issue euphemistically.

Is Widgery afraid the euphemism might pass without irking listeners who might vote against the Constitution?

Straight answer helps ethos.

Picks up metaphor just where he had left it, thus helping clarity, imagery, activity in his discourse.
Language suggests conflict and danger. So soon after the Revolution, "tyranny" had special, damning connotations. Cause-effect argument forecast.

Explains "anarchy" in concrete terms, adding clarity. If hearers know this is what happened, no proof is needed; so far none is offered.

Smith used no clear introduction and stated no central idea. Kingsley may be confused, or he may be trying to "gag" Smith.

Central idea now clearly stated. A more artful speaker might have stated it earlier to prevent confusion.

may see the reasons why I wish for good government.
People, I say, took up arms; and then, if you went to
speak to them, you had the musket of death presented

20 to your breast. They would rob you of your property;
threaten to burn your houses; oblige you to be on
your guard night and day; alarms spread from town
to town; families were broken up. The tender mother
would cry, "O, my son is among them! What shall I

25 do for my child!" Some were taken captive, children
taken out of their schools, and carried away. Then
we would hear of an action, and the poor prisoners
were set in the front, to be killed by their own
friends. How dreadful, how distressing was this!

30 Our distress was so great that we would have been
glad to snatch at anything that looked like a government. Had any person, that was able to protect us,
come and set up his standard, we should have
flocked to it, even if it had been a monarch; and

35 that monarch might have proved a tyrant; so that
you see that anarchy leads to tyranny, and better
have one tyrant than so many at once.

Now, Mr. President, when I saw this Constitution,
I found that it was a cure for these disorders. It was

40 just such a thing as we wanted. I got a copy of it, and
read it over and over. I had been a member of the
Convention to form our own state Constitution, and
had learnt something about the checks and balances

Builds suggestion of active danger, narrating events very concisely. Note the metaphor.

Events narrated gain force from cumulative arrangement.

This attempt to evoke emotion may have seemed less "stagy" in 1788. Such use of direct discourse was common.

Narrative builds to climax: suggestion is that there is little worse than child-stealing . . .

. . . there is one worse thing, after all. But on reaching the climax, Smith does not accuse or blame. To do so would offend some he hopes to persuade.

Emphasizes the *effect*, not blame: lack of good government leads to violence and violence leads to unwise choices (cause-to-effect, cause-to-effect). Hearers will accept if they believe the story as Smith tells it.

"Monarch" had threatening connotations in 1788.

"Tyrant" was even more threatening. Smith repeats those threatening words, then concisely restates the pair of cause-effect arguments he has been proving. Everything since line 5 is neatly unified as an argument, but the vigor of it was achieved through suggestion.

Now it emerges that lines 4-37 were a "need argument." The Constitution is the "remedy."

Ethos: he looked for himself. Note how he stresses his independence in later lines.
Ethos: his special qualifications to judge, modestly expressed.

Many former Revolutionists had strong favorable attitudes toward "checks and balances" as curbs on government.

of power, and I found them all here. I did not go to
any lawyer, to ask his opinion; we have no lawyer in
our town, and we do well enough without. I formed
my own opinion, and was pleased with this Constitution. My honorable old daddy there [points to Amos
Singletary who had spoken in opposition to the Constitution just before Smith rose] won't think that I
expect to be a Congressman, and swallow up the liberties of the people. I never had any post, nor do I
want one. But I don't think the worse of the Constitution because lawyers, and men of learning, and
moneyed men, are fond of it. I don't suspect that they
want to get into Congress and abuse their power.
I am not of such a jealous make. They that are honest
men themselves are not apt to suspect other people.
I don't know why our constituents have not as good
a right to be jealous of us as we seem to be of the
Congress; and I think those gentlemen, who are so
very suspicious that as soon as a man gets into power
he turns rogue, had better look at home.

We are, by this Constitution, allowed to send ten
members to Congress. Have we not more than that
number fit to go? I dare say, if we pick out ten, we
shall have another ten left, and I hope ten times ten;
and will not these be a check upon those that go?
Will they go to Congress, and abuse their power, and
do mischief, when they know they must return and

The opposition had sniped at lawyers in the pro-Constitution forces. Smith dissociates his judgment from lawyers,
adding to ethos.

Refutation of opposing arguments begins here but opens
with colloquial deference to his older opponent.

Independence and identification with ordinary people suggested.

Opponents had also tried to arouse suspicion of wealthy
and college-educated supporters of the Constitution.

Smith uses the ethos he has built up; now he turns it against
suspiciousness of opponents.

Rhetorical syllogism (enthymeme) that also suggests an accusation against opponents.

Analogy "turns the tables" on opponents: argument plus
suggestion.

Suggests the fault is in the ethos of opponents, not in
Constitution.

Refutation (lines 48-63) ends.

Constructive argument resumes: the "remedy" is safe.

Rhetorical questions plus an assertion evoke attitudes of
pride in selves and predispose listeners favorably toward
checks on government.

A rhetorical syllogism is being suggested but not fully
stated: whoever is checked will behave; we have a check,
so members will behave.

look the other ten in the face, and be called to ac-

count for their conduct? Some gentlemen think that

our liberty and property are not safe in the hands of

moneyed men, and men of learning. I am not of that

75 mind.

Brother farmers, let us suppose a case, now: Sup-

pose you had a farm of 50 acres, and your title was

disputed, and there was a farm of 5000 acres joined

to you, that belonged to a man of learning, and his

80 title was involved in the same difficulty; would you

not be glad to have him for your friend, rather than

stand alone in the dispute? Well, the case is the same.

These lawyers, these moneyed men, these men of

learning, are all embarked in the same cause with us,

85 and we must all swim or sink together. And shall we

throw the Constitution overboard because it does not

please us alike? Suppose two or three of you had

been at pains to break up a piece of rough land, and

sow it with wheat; would you let it lie waste because

90 you could not agree what sort of a fence to make?

Would it not be better to put up a fence that did not

please every one's fancy, rather than not fence it at

all, or keep disputing about it until the wild beasts

came in and devoured it?

95 Some gentlemen say, "Don't be in a hurry; take

time to consider"; and "Don't take a leap in the dark."

I say, "Take things in time; gather fruit when it is

Sums up "safety" argument.

Again addresses his particular audience—farmers.

Analogy: an argument to prove that the *supporters of the Constitution are reliable.* Analogy is as close to farmers' experience as possible.

Mild variation on an old metaphor saves Smith from falling into clichés while clinching "reliability" argument.

Another analogy: to prove Constitution is *desirable.* Smith is moving gently toward an action step, using an experience especially familiar to the western farmers on the frontier. How is suggestion working here?

Action step is reached as conclusion begins. Which proverbs would evoke the more favorable attitudes in farmers?

ripe." There is a time to sow and a time to reap; we

sowed our seed when we sent men to the Federal

100 Convention; now is the harvest. Now is the time to

reap the fruit of our labor. And if we won't do it now,

I am afraid we never shall have another opportunity.

Rhetorical syllogism formed from proverb (lines 97-98), an analogy (lines 98-100), and conclusion (line 100).

Conclusion of the rhetorical syllogism restated, then reinforced by suggestion that need is urgent.

From such a reading of this speech, what new knowledge is unearthed about the event that occurred as Jonathan Smith spoke in Boston in 1788? At least these things can be said:

1. Smith was the right man to make this speech; he could and did, in all reasonable ways, identify himself with that part of his audience he could most probably persuade.

2. Each of Smith's arguments was relevant to the convention's purpose: deciding for or against the Constitution. He never drifted into condemnation or praise for its own sake. His argumentation was efficient.

3. Whether deductions or inductions, his arguments were the kind farmers would most easily understand and readily believe. They did not prove his case scientifically, but they were the kind to establish enough probability to give some doubting listeners reason to endorse the Constitution.

4. His assertions, arguments, and individual words were freighted with suggestion capable of magnifying the dangers of weak government, criticizing opponents of the Constitution as too suspicious and not rational enough to be the best advisers, and calling forth favorable attitudes toward such features of the Constitution as its "checks and balances," its system of responsible representation, its general reasonableness.

5. All the materials of the speech were assembled in a clear, psychologically inviting pattern, except that Smith was somewhat slow to clarify his central idea. In other respects the introduction met most requirements of a satisfactory opening. The body of the speech offered an easy-to-follow and clearly emphasized "disease-remedy" arrangement of ideas, with proper attention to the safety and desirability of the plan the listeners feared unsafe. The conclusion summed up Smith's position in colorful but familiar ways and also constituted an "action step."

6. Of Smith's style we would have to say that though it was colloquial and somewhat rustic, it was never unclear. To those he addressed it seems likely to have appeared entirely appropriate to a "plain man" and hence to make Smith, himself, more credible.

Our conclusion must be that on January 24, 1788, Jonathan Smith was convincing to at least some of the doubting farmers, perhaps even to others. He could scarcely have done more as a speechmaker. Although we do not know whom he convinced, if anyone, we now know that if speechmaking could sway votes in the convention, Smith's speech must have swayed some and so contributed to the final, narrow majority of nineteen by which the Massachusetts convention ratified the Constitution on February 5, 1788.

Address to Congress

DOUGLAS MAC ARTHUR
(analysis by Douglas Ehninger)

At 1:00 A. M. on the morning of April 11, 1951, in the midst of the Korean War, the following statement was released by President Harry S. Truman:

"With deep regret I have concluded that General of the Army Douglas MacArthur is unable to give his whole-hearted support to the policies of the United States Government and the United Nations in matters pertaining to his official duties. In view of the specific responsibilities imposed upon me by the Constitution [and] the added responsibility which has been entrusted to me by the United Nations,[1] I have decided that I must make a change of command in the Far East. . . . Full and vigorous debate on matters of national policy is a vital element in the constitutional system of our free democracy. It is fundamental, however, that military commanders must be governed by the policies and directives issued them in the manner provided by our laws and Constitution. . . . General MacArthur's place in history as one of our greatest commanders is fully established. The nation owes him a debt of gratitude. . . . I repeat my regret at the necessity for the action I feel compelled to take in this case."

Twice during the preceding months General MacArthur had been indirectly reprimanded by the White House for expressing views critical of the announced United States and United Nations policy of fighting only a "limited war" in Korea. The immediate cause of his dismissal, however, was in all probability a letter addressed to House Minority Leader Joseph W. Martin. In this letter the General advocated using Chinese Nationalist troops to establish a second front against Red China, pointedly derided the statements of prominent United Nations diplomats, and said in effect that an all-out war in Asia was not only the surest defense against the spread of communism in Europe but also the policy best calculated to save all free nations.

World reaction to MacArthur's dismissal was immediate and sharp. The British House of Commons greeted the announcement with applause. Paris, Rome, The Hague, Stockholm, and New Delhi approved. Most United Nations delegates were obviously pleased. In the United States the press generally supported the President's action on the ground that civilian control of the nation's foreign policy must be insured. Hearst and Scripps-Howard papers, however, were vociferously opposed. Using the strongest language of all, Colonel Robert R. McCormick's Chicago *Tribune* editorialized, "President Truman must be impeached and convicted. . . . He is unfit, morally and mentally, for his high office."

In Congress, where reaction tended to run along partisan lines, there were also demands for the impeachment of the President and of Secretary of State Acheson and Secretary of Defense Marshall as well. From coast to coast the great mass of the American people made their views known by flooding Washington with more than 125,000 telegrams on the two days following the dismissal. As Richard H. Rovere and Arthur M. Schlesinger, Jr., say in their book *The General and the President*, "It is doubtful if there has ever been in this country so violent and spontaneous a discharge of political passion. . . ."[2]

Unmoved by the turmoil, on the evening of April 11, just two and a half hours after issuing his statement, President Truman hastened to address the nation by radio and television. It would be "tragically wrong," he declared, "for us to take the initiative in extending the war."

The General's supporters in Congress also moved swiftly. Following a morning-long policy meeting in which Representative Martin and Senator Robert A. Taft of Ohio played prominent parts, a resolution was introduced that MacArthur be invited to address a joint session of the two houses. After a short delay the resolution was passed, and the invitation issued and accepted.

On April 16, accompanied by his wife and thirteen-year-old son, General MacArthur left Tokyo to return to the United States and to retirement from a military career that had extended over fifty-two years. The trip home has been described as "a series of triumphant send-offs and welcomes."[3] In Tokyo a crowd of 230,000 persons waved farewell as his private plane, the *Bataan*, left the runway; 180,000 greeted the General in Honolulu; and more than 500,000 lined the streets of San Francisco as he passed. In New York, police estimated that MacArthur was seen by 7,500,000 people—nearly twice as many as had greeted President Eisenhower on his return from Europe after World War II. Following the welcoming parade, street cleaners swept up 16,600,000 pounds of paper and ticker tape that had been showered upon him. The previous record was a mere 3,600,000 pounds. On April 26 nearly 4,000,000 Chicagoans greeted MacArthur as a hero.

It was while these homecoming festivities were at their height and while the passions stirred by his dismissal still

---

[1] On July 7, 1950 the United Nations Security Council authorized the United States government to set up a unified military command in Korea. General MacArthur was appointed to this post on July 8.

[2] Richard H. Rovere and Arthur M. Schlesinger, Jr., *The General and the President* (New York, 1951), p. 5.
[3] *Facts on File*, April 20-26, 1951.

boiled that on April 19, 1951, General MacArthur, accompanied by his aid and adviser Major General Courtney Whitney, flew down to Washington from New York to deliver the following address to Congress. Detailed descriptions of the speech and speech occasion were published in the newspapers and news magazines.[4]

At precisely 12:00 noon the House solemnly assembled. At 12:13, as the members "rose and cheered," Mrs. MacArthur entered the gallery. At 12:18 the General's son, accompanied by a group of officers who had served under the General in the Pacific, walked down the aisle and took a seat immediately in front of the rostrum. The members of the Senate appeared in a body at 12:20. Finally, at 12:31 as the blinding beams of a dozen floodlights were suddenly turned on, the seventy-one year old general, relaxed but erect, his "gladitorial features stony," strode into the Chamber escorted by a courtesy committee of Representatives and Senators and by House Doorkeeper William F. Miller. More than six feet tall, he was dressed in dark military slacks and a battle jacket bare of decorations. Only the insignia of his rank as a five-star general was visible on his shoulders. Following a two-minute ovation Speaker Sam Rayburn introduced him with these words: "Members of the Congress, I deem it a high privilege, and I take great pleasure in presenting to you General of the Army Douglas MacArthur."

General MacArthur delivered his address from a prepared manuscript, standing in the place customarily occupied by chiefs of state when they appear before Congress. As all reports agree, from his first words he was in complete control of the speaking situation. Poised and alert, he read slowly and in a low voice—a voice that sometimes rasped and once or twice fell almost to a whisper. Except when turning the pages of his manuscript, the General's hands were anchored firmly to the sides of the lectern. Once he reached for a glass of water, and the tremor with which he had been afflicted since the middle of World War II was discernible.

Even MacArthur's severest critics admitted that his delivery was impressive—his inflections meaningful and precise, his sense of timing superb, and his eye contact with his listeners excellent. The address lasted forty minutes and was interrupted some thirty times by applause. When he had finished speaking the General handed his manuscript to a clerk and walked rapidly out of the Chamber through a "moist" and cheering audience.

Representative Dewey Short, educated at Harvard, Oxford, and Heidelberg, enthusiastically declared, "We saw a great hunk of God in the flesh, and we heard the voice of God." Ex-President Herbert Hoover, hardly less restrained in his comment, saw in MacArthur "a reincarnation

of St. Paul into a great General of the Army who came out of the East."

Following the speech MacArthur rode down Pennsylvania Avenue to the Washington Monument under an air cover of jet fighters and bombers flying in formation. In ceremonies held on the Mall he was presented with a silver tea service and the official key to the city while a seventeen-gun salute boomed out. When he left Washington at 8:20 that evening to return to New York, a cheering crowd gathered at the airport.

In addition to the immediate audience packed into the House chamber, it has been estimated that some forty-nine million Americans heard MacArthur's speech over radio and television. This was by all odds the largest audience ever assembled by the mass media up until that time. Ball parks were empty. The Boston marathon which usually attracts a quarter of a million spectators had less than half that number, and most of these were equipped with radios. Work in stores, offices, and factories stopped as men and women everywhere listened. The final paragraph of the address, with its memorable phrase that old soldiers never die but merely fade away immediately became a part of the nation's folklore.

Douglas MacArthur was born January 26, 1880, at Little Rock (Arkansas) Barracks. His father, Lieutenant General Arthur MacArthur, was a Civil War hero and Congressional Medal of Honor winner who later became military governor of the Philippines. Educated at West Texas Military Academy and at West Point, where he earned the highest four-year average ever acquired (98.14), MacArthur first saw active service in the Far East and in the Mexican border action of 1916. When World War I broke out, he organized and led the famous Rainbow Division, composed of National Guard units from throughout the country, becoming at thirty-seven the youngest divisional commander in the American army. Between wars MacArthur served as the youngest commandant in the history of the United States Military Academy and from 1930 to 1935 was Army Chief of Staff. In 1932, under orders from President Hoover, he led troops against the hundreds of World War I veterans who had descended upon Washington to demand a bonus for their military service.

Retiring from the United States Army in 1937 at the age of fifty-seven, MacArthur went to the Philippines to direct the development of the military forces of this newly independent nation. He was recalled to active duty with the American army in July of 1941 and almost immediately was promoted to four-star rank. After escaping from Corregidor in 1942, he led the "island hopping" campaign by which Allied troops gradually regained the areas lost to the Japanese early in the war. In 1945 he presided over the formal Japanese surrender on the battleship *Missouri*. Between the close of World War II and the outbreak of the

---

[4] See especially the New York *Times* for April 20, 1951, and *Time*, April 30, 1951.

Korean struggle, MacArthur directed the American occupation of Japan. In Korea he was the first commander ever to head a United Nations force composed of troops from a number of nations. His characteristic trademarks, much loved by cartoonists and caricaturists, were a gold-braided military cap and a corncob pipe. These, too, have become a part of America's folklore.

Mr. President, Mr. Speaker, and distinguished members of the Congress: I stand on this rostrum with a sense of deep humility and pride—humility in the wake of those great architects of our history who have stood here before me, pride in the reflection that this home of legislative debate represents human liberty in the purest form yet devised. /1

Here are centered the hopes and aspirations and faiths of the entire human race. /2

I do not stand here as advocate of any partisan cause, for the issues are fundamental and reach quite beyond the realm of partisan considerations. They must be resolved on the highest plane of national interest if our course is to prove sound and our future protected. /3

I trust, therefore, that you will do me the justice of receiving that which I have to say as solely expressing the considered viewpoint of a fellow American. /4

I address you with neither rancor nor bitterness in the fading twilight of life, with but one purpose in mind: To serve my country. /5

ANALYSIS: Paragraphs 1-5 constitute the *introduction* of the speech.

In paragraphs 1 and 2, MacArthur establishes contact with his listeners by referring to the historic place in which his address is being delivered.

In paragraphs 3-5 MacArthur declares himself non-partisan and asks for a fair hearing, thus developing a strong personal or "ethical" appeal.

The issues are global, and so interlocked that to consider the problems of one sector oblivious to those of another is but to court disaster for the whole. While Asia is commonly referred to as the gateway to Europe, it is no less true that Europe is the gateway to Asia, and the broad influence of the one can not fail to have its impact upon the other. There are those who claim our strength is inadequate to protect on both fronts, that we cannot divide our effort. I can think of no greater expression of defeatism. /6

If a potential enemy can divide his strength on two fronts, it is for us to counter his efforts. The Communist threat is a global one. Its successful advance in one sector threatens the destruction of every other sector. You can not appease or otherwise surrender to communism in Asia without simultaneously undermining our efforts to halt its advance in Europe. /7

The *body* of the speech is composed of paragraphs 6-53. The overall plan of the body of the address is gradually to narrow the listeners' focus of attention, moving from (1) a brief consideration of the general world situation, to (2) a survey of recent social and political changes in Asia, to (3) a statement concerning the "strategic potential" of the Pacific area, and finally to (4) a discussion of the Korean War itself.

In developing his ideas on these subjects MacArthur employs exposition or explanation as his principal form of supporting material and relies almost exclusively upon his own ethical proof to establish the validity of his conclusions.

In paragraphs 6-7, MacArthur gives his analysis of the general world threat posed by communism. This analysis serves as a premise upon which his more specific views concerning the situation in Asia, in the Pacific, and in Korea are based.

Beyond pointing out these general truisms, I shall confine my discussion to the general areas of Asia. /8

Paragraph 8 is a transition, focusing the attention of his listeners upon Asia.

Before one may objectively assess the situation now existing there he must comprehend something of Asia's past and the revolutionary changes which have marked her course up to the present. Long exploited by the so-called colonial powers, with little opportunity to achieve any degree of social justice, individual dignity, or a higher standard of life such as guided our own noble administration in the Philippines, the people of Asia found their opportunity in the war just past to throw off the shackles of colonialism and now see the dawn of new opportunity, and heretofore unfelt dignity, and self-respect of political freedom. /9

Mustering half of the earth's population, and 60 per cent of its natural resources, these peoples are rapidly consolidating a new force, both moral and material, with which to raise the living standard and erect adaptation of the design of modern progress to their own distinct cultural environments. /10

Whether one adheres to the concept of colonialization or not, this is the direction of Asian progress and it may not be stopped. It is a corollary to the shift of the world economic frontiers as the whole epicenter of world affairs rotates back toward the area whence it started. /11

In this situation, it becomes vital that our own country orient its policies in consonance with this basic evolutionary condition rather than pursue a course blind to reality that the colonial era is now past and the Asian peoples covet the right to shape their own free destiny. What they seek now is friendly guidance, understanding and support, not imperious direction, the dignity of equality and not the shame of subjugation. /12

Their pre-war standard of life, pitifully low, is infinitely lower now in the devastation left in war's wake. World ideologies play little part in Asian thinking and are little understood. /13

What the people strive for is the opportunity for a little bit more food in their stomachs, a little better clothing on their backs and a little firmer roof over their heads, and the realization of the normal nationalist urge for political freedom. /14

These political-social conditions have but an indirect bearing upon our own national security, but do form a backdrop to contemporary planning which must be thoughtfully considered if we are to avoid the pitfalls of unrealism. /15

Employing abstract rather than concrete language (except in paragraph 14), MacArthur, in paragraphs 9-15, describes social, economic, and political conditions in Asia.

Of more direct and immediate bearing upon our national security are the changes wrought in the strategic potential of the Pacific Ocean in the course of the past wars. /16

Paragraph 16 furnishes a transition, again narrowing the listeners' focus by centering attention on changes wrought in the "strategic potential of the Pacific Ocean in the course of the past wars."

Prior thereto the western strategic frontier of the United States lay on the littoral line of the Americas, with an exposed island salient extending out through Hawaii, Midway and Guam to the Philippines. That salient proved not an outpost of strength but an avenue of weakness along which the enemy could and did attack. The Pacific was a potential area of advance for any predatory force intent upon striking at the bordering land areas. /17

All this was changed by our Pacific victory. Our strategic frontier then shifted to embrace the entire Pacific Ocean, which became a vast moat to protect us as long as we held it. Indeed, it acts as a protective shield for all of the Americas and all free lands of the Pacific Ocean area. We control it to the shores of Asia by a chain of islands extending in an arc from the Aleutians to the Marianas, held by us and our free allies. /18

From this island chain we can dominate with sea and air power every Asiatic port from Vladivostok to Singapore—with sea and air power, every port, as I said, from Vladivostok to Singapore—and prevent any hostile movement into the Pacific. /19

Any predatory attack from Asia must be an amphibious effort. No amphibious force can be successful without control of the sea lanes and the air over those lanes in its avenue of advance. With naval and air supremacy and modest ground elements to defend bases, any major attack from continental Asia toward us or our friends in the Pacific would be doomed to failure. /20

Under such conditions, the Pacific no longer represents menacing avenues of approach for a prospective invader. It assumes, instead, the friendly aspect of a peaceful lake. /21

Proceeding by the method of contrast, MacArthur, in paragraphs 17-21, explains this "strategic potential of the Pacific Ocean."

Our line of defense is a natural one and can be maintained with a minimum of military effort and expense. It envisions no attack against anyone, nor does it provide the bastions essential for offensive operations, but, properly maintained, would be an invincible defense against aggression. /22

The holding of this littoral defense line in the western Pacific is entirely dependent upon holding all segments thereof, for any major breach of that line by an unfriendly power would render vulnerable to determined attack every other major segment. This is a military estimate as to which I have yet to find a military leader who will take exception. /23

For that reason, I have strongly recommended in the past, as a matter of military urgency, that under no circumstances must Formosa fall under Communist control. Such an eventuality would at once threaten the freedom of the Philippines and the loss of Japan and might well force our western frontier back to the coast of California, Oregon, and Washington. /24

General Douglas MacArthur addresses the Joint Session of Congress on April 19, 1951.
Seated on the rostrum behind him are Alben Barkley, the Vice President, and Sam Rayburn, the Speaker of the House. (Acme Photo)

In paragraphs 22-24, the defense obligations which this "potential" imposes upon the United States are reviewed.

To understand the changes which now appear upon the Chinese mainland, one must understand the changes in Chinese character and culture over the past 50 years. China up to 50 years ago was completely nonhomogeneous, being compartmented into groups divided against each other. The war-making tendency was almost nonexistent as they still followed the tenets of the Confucian ideal of pacifist culture. /25

At the turn of the century under the regime of Chang Tso-lin efforts toward greater homogeneity produced the start of a nationalist urge. This was further and more successfully developed under the leadership of Chiang Kai-shek, but has been brought to its greatest fruition under the present regime to the point that it has now taken on the character of a united nationalism of increasingly dominant aggressive tendencies. /26

Through the past 50 years the Chinese people have thus become militarized in their concepts and in their ideals. They now constitute excellent soldiers, with competent staffs and commanders. This has produced a new and dominant power in Asia,

which, for its own purposes, is allied with Soviet Russia but which in its own concepts and methods has become aggressively imperialistic with a lust for expansion and increased power normal to this type of imperialism. /27

There is little of the ideological concept either one way or another in the Chinese make-up. The standard of living is so low and the capital accumulation has been so thoroughly dissipated by war that the masses are desperate and eager to follow any leadership which seems to promise the alleviation of woeful stringencies. /28

Abruptly and without a unifying transition, MacArthur, in paragraphs 25-28, turns to an explanation of "the changes [which have occurred] in Chinese character and culture over the past 50 years."

I have from the beginning believed that the Chinese Communists' support of the North Koreans was the dominant one. Their interests are at present parallel with those of the Soviet, but I believe that the aggressiveness recently displayed not only in Korea but also in Indo-China and Tibet and pointing potentially toward the south reflects predominantly the same lust for the expansion of power which has animated every would-be conqueror since the beginning of time. /29

Paragraph 29 gives MacArthur's conclusions about the actions and intentions of Red China.

The Japanese people since the war have undergone the greatest reformation recorded in modern history. With a commendable will, eagerness to learn and marked capacity to understand, they have from the ashes left in war's wake erected in Japan an edifice dedicated to the supremacy of individual liberty and personal dignity, and in the ensuing process there has been created a truly representative government committed to the advance of political morality, freedom of economic enterprise, and social justice. /30

Politically, economically, and socially Japan is now abreast of many free nations of the earth and will not again fail the universal trust. That it may be counted upon to wield a profoundly beneficial influence over the course of events in Asia is attested by the magnificent manner in which the Japanese people have met the recent challenge of war, unrest, and confusion surrounding them from the outside and checked communism within their own frontiers without the slightest slackening in their forward progress. /31

I sent all four of our occupation divisions to the Korean battlefront without the slightest qualms as to the effect of the resulting power vacuum upon Japan. The results fully justified my faith. /32

I know of no nation more serene, more orderly and industrious, nor in which richer hopes can be entertained for future constructive service in the advance of the human race. /33

Paragraphs 30-33 give MacArthur's estimate of the situation in Japan, again entered upon without benefit of an explicit transition and, as in the case of all preceding expositions and inferences, advanced with no supporting material except the speaker's own authority.

Of our former ward—of our former ward the Philippines—we can look forward in confidence that the existing unrest will be corrected and a strong and healthy nation will grow in the longer aftermath of war's terrible destructiveness. We must be patient and understanding and never fail them, as in our hour of need they did not fail us. /34

A Christian nation, the Philippines stand as a mighty bulwark of Christianity in the Far East, and its capacity for high moral leadership in Asia is unlimited. /35

On Formosa the government of the Republic of China has had the opportunity to refute by action much of the malicious gossip which so undermined the strength of its leadership on the Chinese mainland. The Formosan people are receiving a just and enlightened administration with majority representation on the organs of government, and politically, economically, and socially they appear to be advancing along sound and constructive lines. /36

In paragraphs 34-36, the situation in the Philippines and Formosa is sketched in brief and general terms.

With this brief insight into the surrounding areas, I now turn to the Korean conflict. /37

Paragraph 37 provides a transition, the final narrowing of focus to "the Korean conflict" itself.

While I was not consulted prior to the President's decision to intervene in support of the Republic of Korea, that decision, from a military standpoint, proved a sound one. As I say, it proved a sound one, as we hurled back the invader and decimated his forces. Our victory was complete, and our objective within reach, when Red China intervened with numerically superior ground forces. /38

This created a new war and an entirely new situation, a situation not contemplated when our forces were committed against the North Korean invaders; a situation which called for new decisions in the diplomatic sphere to permit the realistic adjustment of military strategy. Such decisions have not been forthcoming. /39

Paragraphs 38-39 review our initial successes in Korea and the new and unfavorable situation produced by Red China's intervention.

While no man in his right mind would advocate sending our ground forces into continental China, and such was never given a thought, the new situation did urgently demand a drastic revision of strategic planning if our political aim was to defeat this new enemy as we had defeated the old one. /40

Apart from the military need, as I saw it, to neutralize the sanctuary protection given the enemy north of the Yalu, I felt that military necessity in the conduct of the war made necessary (1) The intensification of our economic blockade against China; (2) The imposition of a naval blockade against the China coast; (3) Removal of restrictions on air reconnaissance of China's coastal area and of Manchuria; (4) Removal of restrictions on the forces of the Republic of China on Formosa, with logistical support to contribute to their effective operations against the Chinese mainland. /41

In paragraphs 40-41 the steps which MacArthur regarded as necessary to meet this altered situation are summarized.

For entertaining these views, all professionally designed to support our forces committed to Korea and bring hostilities to an end with the least possible delay and at a saving of countless American and Allied lives, I have been severely criticized in lay circles, principally abroad, despite my understanding that from a military standpoint the above views have been fully shared in the past by practically every military leader concerned with the Korean campaign, including our own Joint Chiefs of Staff. /42

I called for reinforcements, but was informed that reinforcements were not available. I made clear that if not permitted to destroy the enemy built-up bases north of the Yalu, if not permitted to utilize the friendly Chinese force of some 600,000 men on Formosa, if not permitted to blockade the China coast to prevent the Chinese Reds from getting succor from without, and if there was to be no hope of major reinforcements, the position of the command from the military standpoint forbade victory. /43

Paragraphs 42-43 tell how MacArthur's views were received, and give his reply to his critics.

We could hold in Korea by constant maneuver and in an approximate area where our supply line advantages were in balance with the supply line disadvantages of the enemy, but we could hope at best for only an indecisive campaign with its terrible and constant attrition upon our forces if the enemy utilized its full military potential. /44

I have constantly called for the new political decisions essential to a solution. /45

Paragraphs 44-45 give MacArthur's general criticism of the policy he was obliged to follow.

Efforts have been made to distort my position. It has been said in effect that I was a warmonger. Nothing could be further from the truth. I know war as few other men now living know it, and nothing to me is more revolting. I have long advocated its complete abolition, as its very destructiveness on both friend and foe has rendered it useless as a means of settling international disputes. /46

Indeed, on the second day of September, 1945, just following the surrender of the Japanese nation on the battleship *Missouri*, I formally cautioned as follows:

"Men since the beginning of time have sought peace. Various methods through the ages have been attempted to devise an international process to prevent or settle disputes between nations. From the very start workable methods were found in so far as individual citizens were concerned, but the mechanics of an instrumentality of larger international scope have never been successful. Military alliances, balances of power, leagues of nations, all in turn failed, leaving the only path to be by way of the crucible of war. The utter destructiveness of war now blocks out this alternative. We have had our last chance. If we will not devise some greater and more equitable system, our Armageddon will be at our door. The problem basically is theological and involves a spiritual recrudescence and improvement of human character that will synchronize with our almost matchless advances in science, art, literature and all the material and cultural developments of the past 2,000 years. It must be of the spirit if we are to save the flesh." /47

But once war is forced upon us, there is no other alternative than to apply every available means to bring it to a swift end. War's very object is victory, not prolonged indecision. /48

In war there is no substitute for victory. /49

In paragraphs 46-49, MacArthur disavows the charge that he is a "warmonger" but reiterates his philosophy that in war "there is no substitute for victory."

There are some who for varying reasons would appease Red China. They are blind to history's clear lesson, for history teaches with unmistakable emphasis that appeasement but begets new and bloodier wars. It points to no single instance where this end has justified that means, where appeasement has led to more than a sham peace. Like blackmail, it lays the basis for new and successively greater demands until, as in blackmail, violence becomes the only other alternative. Why, my soldiers asked of me, surrender military advantages to an enemy in the field? I could not answer. /50

Some may say, to avoid spread of the conflict into an all-out war with China. Others, to avoid Soviet intervention. Neither explanation seems valid, for China is already engaging with the maximum power it can commit, and the Soviet will not necessarily mesh its actions with our moves. Like a cobra, any new enemy will more likely strike whenever it feels that the relativity of military and other potentialities is in its favor on a world-wide basis. /51

In paragraphs 50-51 the view that we should "appease" Red China is refuted, two figurative analogies being used as supporting material.

The tragedy of Korea is further heightened by the fact that its military action was confined to its territorial limits. It condemns that nation, which it is our purpose to save, to suffer the devastating impact of full naval and air bombardment while the enemy's sanctuaries are fully protected from such attack and devastation. /52

Of the nations of the world, Korea alone, up to now, is the sole one which has risked its all against communism. The magnificence of the courage and fortitude of the Korean people defies description. They have chosen to risk death rather than slavery. Their last words to me were: "Don't scuttle the Pacific." /53

MacArthur, in paragraphs 52-53, praises the part Korea has played in the conflict and reports the Korean people's plea to the democracies.

I have just left your fighting sons in Korea. They have met all tests there, and I can report to you without reservation that they are splendid in every way. /54

It was my constant effort to preserve them and end this savage conflict honorably and with the least loss of time and a minimum sacrifice of life. Its growing bloodshed has caused me the deepest anguish and anxiety. Those gallant men will remain often in my thoughts and in my prayers always. /55

Paragraphs 54-56 are the conclusion:
In paragraphs 54-55, MacArthur, displaying increasingly the emotional tone evident in paragraphs 52-53, praises the "splendid" behavior of our "gallant" men in Korea, and expresses his solicitude for their welfare.

I am closing my 52 years of military service. When I joined the army, even before the turn of the century, it was the fulfillment of all of my boyish hopes and dreams. The world has turned over many times since I took the oath on the Plain at West Point, and the hopes and dreams have long since vanished, but I still remember the refrain of one of the most popular barracks ballads of that day which proclaimed most proudly that old soldiers never die; they just fade away. And, like the old soldier of that ballad, I now

close my military career and just fade away, an old soldier who tried to do his duty as God gave him the light to see that duty. Good-by. /56

Paragraph 56 gives MacArthur's moving personal farewell to military life and to national service.

Suggestions for further reading

John Gunther, *The Riddle of MacArthur; Japan, Korea, and the Far East* (New York, 1951)

Richard H. Rovere and Arthur M. Schlesinger, Jr., *The General and the President* (New York, 1951)

John W. Spanier, *The Truman-MacArthur Controversy and the Korean War* (Cambridge, Mass., 1959)

Charles Andrew Willoughby, *MacArthur, 1941-1951* (New York, 1954)

Recordings

MacArthur, Douglas. *Speech to Congress* (Washington, April 19, 1951) (C). Capitol, H274. Also (C). Columbia, ML4410. Also (C). Victor, LPM5. Also (C). Mercury, MGMCM.

————. "Speech Aboard USS Missouri" (September 1, 1945) (E: 2 min. 46 secs). *Those Historic Years.* Panacoustic, A100.

————. "Formal Japanese Surrender" (Tokyo Bay, September 2, 1945) (C). *Those Historic Years.* U. S. Recording, H9485.

————. Fragments in *I Can Hear It Now,* Vol. 1. Columbia, MM800. Also in *Mr. President.* Victor, LM1753.

General MacArthur's speech:
a symposium of critical comment
FREDERICK W. HABERMAN

The forty-nine million Americans who composed the radio, television, and face-to-face audience that heard General Douglas MacArthur's address to the Joint Session of Congress on April 19, 1951, became speech critics overnight. Their criticism had quantity and it had intensity. It ranged from Representative Dewey Short's statement in the *Congressional Record* (April 19, p. 4238): "We saw a great hunk of God in the flesh, and we heard the voice of God" to the opinion that the speech was Satanic in its power to

Frederick W. Haberman, "General MacArthur's Speech: A Symposium of Critical Comment," *Quarterly Journal of Speech,* Vol. XXXVII, October 1951, pp. 321-331. By permission of the Speech Association of America and Professor Haberman.

evoke chaos. Like these two examples, much of the criticism was a blend of happy emotionalism and the urge to formulate dicta; but much of it was aesthetic and philosophical. To gather a set of comments on this extraordinary speech and to obtain some samples of contemporary criticism, I invited critics from three groups to contribute to this symposium. The Congressional critics include Joseph W. Martin, Jr., Minority Leader of the House of Representatives; Senator Robert S. Kerr, of Oklahoma; Senator Karl E. Mundt, of South Dakota (formerly Professor of Speech); Senator Hubert H. Humphrey, of Minnesota; Senator Alexander Wiley, of Wisconsin; and Representative Robert J. Corbett, of Pennsylvania (formerly a coach of forensics). The Journalist critics include Richard H. Rovere, contributor to *The New Yorker;* Quincy Howe, School of Journalism and Communications, University of Illinois; and William T. Evjue, editor and publisher of *The Capital Times,* Madison, Wisconsin. Included in the third group— the Academic critics—are W. Norwood Brigance, Wabash College; Herbert A. Wichelns, Cornell University; Wilbur Samuel Howell, Princeton University; Henry L. Ewbank, University of Wisconsin; and A. Craig Baird, State University of Iowa. In my letter of invitation to these critics, I made one suggestion— that the commentary be brief.

I. Congressional critics

JOSEPH W. MARTIN, JR.

In politics, the effectiveness of a speech is measured by its ability to strengthen friendships and win converts. Usually the most effective political speeches contain comprehensive thought, breadth of viewpoint, humor, warmth of words, and emotional impact. All too frequently, political addresses "sound" better than they "read."

The address of General MacArthur to the Joint Meeting of Congress was a masterpiece of content and delivery, possibly the great address of our times, certainly surpassing, in my opinion, the first Roosevelt Inaugural speech in 1933 and the Winston Churchill address to the Joint Session of Congress in 1942. When a speech moves Members of Congress to tears, its impact cannot be denied. In my 27 years in Congress, there has been nothing to equal it.

The MacArthur address not only "sounded" in a masterful fashion, it "reads" even better. Each sentence is freighted with thought; each word is at work. Its logic, its simple directness, its clear-cut statement of the issues, and its orderly exposition make the structure of the speech a model for all to follow.

It was a monumental effort.

ROBERT S. KERR

I listened earnestly and carefully to General MacArthur's speech. I looked for unity. I didn't find it. I watched for an acknowledgment of the necessity to maintain the integrity of civilian control of the military power. It was not there. I searched for language that would give hope of a limited conflict and a purpose to prevent the spread into world-wide conflagration. He did not provide it.

I listened for words which would promote cooperation between this nation and our allies for collective security. Those words were not spoken. I expected him who had been in command of the United Nations forces to acknowledge and report on his stewardship and tell how to strengthen the common front. He did not even mention the United Nations or a single ally.

I hoped he would show the way to promote peace and prevent more or larger war. He was not looking in that direction.

Instead, if I understood him, he sounded a call for an expanded war, a second front for sure, and a third front, if it came. The General spoke sadly, but I was much sadder because I was convinced that his plan would not lead us upward to the goal of peace, but would hurl us downward to the awful road of total war.

KARL E. MUNDT

The speech Douglas MacArthur delivered to the joint meeting of the Houses of Congress upon his return from Korea seems destined to become one of the classics of the English language.

Sitting as I did about twenty feet directly in front of General MacArthur as he stood at the front of the chamber of the House of Representatives I had an opportunity to view at close range the presentation of an oratorical masterpiece which was excelled in its composition only by the skillful prowess with which it was delivered to those who heard it in person and to the many millions who gave it their rapt attention via radio and television. Without any apparent oratorical effort, MacArthur from the very beginning and by the very force of his sincerity and his magnetic personality held the intense attention of the audience he was to go on to inspire and captivate. He was the complete master of the occasion all the way.

What were the superb qualities of the great speaker that MacArthur so vividly exemplified? High on the list of factors contributing to MacArthur's mastery of the situation was the sincerity and the obvious earnestness he radiated. His choice of vivid words, his balanced phraseology, his great reserve power, his facial expressions, and the eye contact he managed to maintain with the audience without doing violence to his manuscript all contributed to the excellence of his delivery and the convincing impact of his message. Even those who were later to disagree with him and to criticize his recommendations were caught in the magnetism of the occasion; there were very few who had temerity enough to offer quick rejoinder to the arguments presented.

My experience as a college speech teacher impelled me to rate Churchill, Roosevelt, and Madame Chiang-Kai-Shek—in that order—as the most impressive speakers I had heard before joint meetings of the Congress in my fourteen years there prior to the MacArthur speech. Without question, and by general agreement of most of us who had heard all four of them in person, Douglas MacArthur stood out spectacularly above them all.

Perhaps it was the near perfect control of his inflections, perhaps his impressive posture and actions, perhaps the emphasis with which he stressed his points without ever appearing to approximate his full powers of expression—whatever it was, no other speaker in our generation has moved strong men of politics to open tears and caused even those who disagreed with his position to praise his oratorical ability with unhesitating superlatives. In brief, the MacArthur address to Congress demonstrated once again the prowess of the spoken word; it gave new proof that men can still be moved and policies determined by those who excel in the arts of speech.

HUBERT H. HUMPHREY

General MacArthur's speech was a masterful presentation by a persuasive man rising at a dramatic occasion to give reason and justification for his life's work and life's reputation. There is no doubt that it affected every member of the Congress who heard him. His manner, poise, language, and the strength of his voice helped create an impression favorable to him and consistent with the myth associated with him and carefully developed over the past few years.

The issues represented by General MacArthur's speech, however, are far more important than the personality questions involved and more significant than the techniques of speech he has so artistically developed. It is to those issues I enter my dissent.

In my judgment, the basic issue involved in the controversy is one of civilian versus military control over our foreign policy. In a democracy, the elected representatives of the people are responsible for determining foreign policy, and this responsibility is not vested in the military leaders. This is one of the essential elements of our historical tradition. It is part of our Constitution. In dismissing General MacArthur, President Truman, as Commander in Chief under our Constitution, had no choice. The General—a brilliant and able military leader—disagreed with our government's foreign policy and with the recommendations of General Marshall and the Joint Chiefs of Staff. No government can exist so divided in policy since no government can be guided by two inconsistent foreign programs. General MacArthur, as an individual, has a perfect right to disagree with our government's foreign policy but he has no right and no prerogative as a military commander to formulate his own policy in opposition to policy established by our government.

I welcomed General MacArthur's arrival in the United States and his address to the Congress. It brought with it a complete re-examination of our foreign policy, particularly as it affected the Far East. There is no doubt in my mind that at the conclusion of the debate, with the fading away of emotions and the supremacy of reason, the American people will come to see that President Truman was correct in removing General MacArthur. It is my hope that, even as they come to disagree with the General's policies and regret his human failings, they will not allow it to interfere with their judgment of him as a great military leader.

ALEXANDER WILEY

The basic standard by which to evaluate a speech is whether or not it actually succeeds in its objective. Does it sell the speaker's ideas, the speaker's personality? Does it win the audience?

Based on that standard, General MacArthur's address to the Congress and to the American people was a masterpiece of effectiveness. It has been stated that at many times during his speech there was hardly a dry eye in the entire audience—so emotional was its impact.

It should be remembered that although the General had the sympathetic admiration of practically all Americans in view of his fifty-two years of honored military service, he faced a seen and unseen audience which was sharply divided (then as now) as to the major policy points he was recommending. Many members of Congress particularly on the Democratic side of the aisle knew that their every favorable manifestation—applause, cheers, etc.,—might be interpreted as an implied slap at their Chief Executive, the head of the Democratic Party. Nevertheless, they gave themselves almost unrestrainedly in rousing general support of the General even though they did not completely reflect Republican enthusiasm for MacArthur's specific suggestions.

Rarely has a divided audience been so attentive to a speech. Judged from every technical standpoint, the General's comments came across with brilliant diction, masterly timing, keen logical sequence, splendid choice of words. Because he was the thorough master of his subject and of the specific phrasing of his speech, he could look up at the television cameras and at the audience in such a way as to maintain perfect rapport.

MacArthur's speech helped, moreover, to disprove many false ideas about him. To those individuals who had swallowed the false line about MacArthur's arrogance, he came to be respected as a man of great humility. To those individuals who were convinced that he was anxious to precipitate a partisan controversy, he emerged as a true statesman who avoided all references to personalities and who gallantly accepted the cruel dismissal action. To other individuals who had assaulted his basic motives, MacArthur's objective approach knocked the ground from under them. Douglas MacArthur in summary, made an historic address which will be reviewed by future generations as one of the great expositions in the history of oratory.

It should be remembered that not just any individual could have made a speech of such stature. It was a great speech, delivered by a great American, at a great time in the history of our country and of the world. Assuming that combination of circumstances, the speech was a masterpiece. Had it been offered by any individual other than MacArthur, and at any other time, under any other circumstances, it would not have "come off." As it is, it has become a classic in American history.

ROBERT J. CORBETT

The address of General of the Army Douglas MacArthur to the Joint Meeting of Congress was one of the outstanding speeches of modern history. This is true, not because of extraordinary eloquence, excellent delivery, masterful phrasing, or thought-compelling philosophy. The speech was great because it met the situation exactly as it was designed to do.

The situation was as tense and drama-packed as any that ever happened. Tens of millions had waited since the hour of his dismissal for this moment. Few had ever seen or listened to this almost mythical person. Here at last he stood in the Halls of Congress after years of absence from the country, and after a long trip, punctuated with tremendous receptions and covered in minutest detail in the press and on the radio. He could fall or triumph. His case could be lost completely. His whole career could end in a sorry flop. Seldom has so much depended on a single speech.

The speech was great because it met that tremendous situation with unbelievable perfection. The speech did what it was supposed to do. It explained the General's point of view clearly and persuasively. It said what is was necessary to say and little more. It matched and multiplied the tense emotional feeling that gripped the nation. The speech was the test of the whole man and his whole career. He and it measured up.

I do not believe that MacArthur's speech should be dissected and analyzed. It can't be studied as a thing apart from the whole circumstance with any hope of understanding or appreciation. It was a great speech because it did a great job.

II. Journalist critics
RICHARD H. ROVERE

As a literary critic and political observer, I view the speech solely from the literary and political points of view. I am not qualified to criticize oratory or elocution.

As a piece of composition, the speech seemed to me a good deal but not a great deal better than the general run of public prose in the United States today. MacArthur has eloquence of a kind, but it strikes me as a rather coarse eloquence. He never shades his meanings, never introduces a note of humor, never gives the feeling that he is one man, only one, addressing himself to other men. His language is never flat and bloodless; neither is it flabby and loose-jointed, as so much writing of this sort is. But to me there is rather a fetid air about it. It does not leave me with the impression that a cool and candid mind has been at work on difficult matters of universal concern. Instead, it leaves me with the impression that a closed and in a sense a rather frantic mind has been at work to the end of making an appeal to history—not neglecting to use any of the rule-book hints on how to do it. I think not of history but of second-rate historian as I read the speech.

Form and content are, if not inseparable, very closely related. Politically, MacArthur's speech seemed extremely weak to me. This is not, I think, because I am opposed to his politics; I believe he could have made out a much stronger case for himself. But he never came to grips with the issues. For example, he wanted to have it that he was being persecuted for "entertaining" his particular views. This, of course, is rubbish. He got into trouble not for the political and military views he entertained (no doubt he was right in saying they were entertained by many of his colleagues) but for seeking to usurp the diplomatic function. He never sought to answer the objections to his position that rest on political and economic facts recognized by both sides: that if we followed him, we would be abandoned by several allies; that if Russia invaded Europe, which he has admitted might be an early consequence of his policy, the industrial balance would favor the Communist world; that, like it or not, American power does have its limitations. MacArthur's policy may be sounder than Truman's. But this contention cannot be sustained without facing these stubborn facts about the world today. MacArthur, in his speech, never faced them.

QUINCY HOWE

In a period that produced Winston Churchill and Franklin D. Roosevelt, General MacArthur stands out as perhaps the greatest actor of them all. Churchill and Roosevelt knew how to express many different moods. MacArthur has less versatility, but greater power within his own field. It is perhaps no accident that his first wife chose as her second husband the professional actor, Lionel Atwill, for MacArthur might also have made a great career for himself on the stage. But he had wider interests and abilities and chose soldiering instead. Finally, at the tragic climax of a dramatic career, he found himself called upon to play before both Houses of Congress the part of the old soldier who did his duty as God gave him to see that duty. By a coincidence, rare in the history of drama, the man who acted the part of the old soldier happened himself to be an old soldier whose experiences precisely resembled the experiences of the old soldier whose part he was enacting. The result was a fusion of man and actor, of reality and illusion, unique in the history of politics and drama. The qualities that make a man a great actor require a student of the drama to define. But the student of history with any experience or interest outside his special field can hardly fail to recognize that MacArthur certainly belongs in the company of Edwin Booth and William Jennings Bryan. His position as a statesman seems to this observer measurably lower than that of Harry S. Truman.

WILLIAM T. EVJUE

An injustice is being done to Abraham Lincoln by those who are claiming that General MacArthur's speech to the Congress is "another Gettysburg address." There is a great difference in the two speeches, as there is a great difference in the two men. One was a humble, sincere, and warmly human man of the people. The other is a mighty warrior, a showman conscious of the part he is playing and the destiny which he seeks to fashion for himself. The climax of Lincoln's greatest speech was a deathless expression of the ideal of democracy. The center of Douglas MacArthur's speech was Douglas MacArthur. The climax was a plea for sympathy for an "old soldier" "fading away."

There is a vast difference between the beautiful simplicity of Lincoln's address and the straining for colorful expression found in MacArthur. Some of it is downright hammy and some would not pass muster in a college freshman theme. For example, MacArthur's statement that the last words of the Korean people to him were: "Don't scuttle the Pacific," belongs in the department of statements that were never made. This is corn. In developing his hunch that the Russians would not enter a war on the side of the Chinese, MacArthur said: "Like the cobra, any new enemy will more likely strike whenever it feels that the relativity in military or other potential is in its favor on a worldwide basis." The simile reveals a striving for effect that makes the thought ridiculous. It conjures up the ludicrous picture of a cobra looking over reports from its intelligence service before it strikes to make sure that the "relativity in military or other potential is in its favor on a worldwide basis."

Outstanding in MacArthur's address was the obvious and amazing lack of knowledge of China. The general in the past has been given to speaking of the "Oriental mind"—an expression, incidentally, of which the Orientals deeply disapprove. It is a concept without foundation, just as much as the "Occidental mind," or the "American mind," or the "Wisconsin mind," or the "Madison mind" is baseless in social psychology.

In his speech the general said that the Asian people seek "friendly guidance . . . not imperious direction." But in a letter to the V.F.W. on August 28, 1950, he wrote that it is "in the pattern of the Oriental psychology to respect and follow aggressive, resolute and dynamic leadership." The general said that sixty per cent of the world's resources lie in Asia. Does he include the inaccessible coal and the nonexistent steel? He said that the "war-making tendency [up to 50 years ago] was almost non-existent, as they still followed the tenets of the Confucian ideal of pacifist culture." Any student of Chinese history knows that this "pacifist culture" was chiefly marked by centuries of bloody strife between competing warlords. Actually Confucianism is no more pacifist than Christianity. Would a Chinese speaker be right if he told his people that the Christian nations did not make war because Christ taught the ways of peace?

Students of Chinese history are shocked that the general in his discussion of the unification of China failed to mention the name of Sun Yat-sen. MacArthur gave credit to Chang-Tso-lin, thus choosing a Manchurian warlord in preference to Dr. Sun, who was a great scholar and statesman and whose dream was the establishment of a progressive democracy for his people.

In short, it is inconceivable that his address, with its obvious shortcomings in knowledge of essential historical background, its attention to easy and empty sociological concepts, its emotional preoccupation with vainglory and its regrettable theatrics, could even be compared to any of Lincoln's great masterpieces.

III. Academic critics

W. NORWOOD BRIGANCE

Three times within the past 15 years high army commanders have found themselves in disagreement with their chief executives. The first, Francisco Franco, led the army against the government, overthrew it by civil war, and set up himself as dictator. The second, Erwin Rommel, was handed a pistol by the executive's agent and told to shoot himself, else he with his family would be executed. The third, Douglas MacArthur, returned from the field of action and presented his case to Congress and to the American people without reprisal or threat of reprisal from the Chief Executive. This is the larger setting for MacArthur's speech. It was not merely a momentous speech. It was not merely the first momentous speech to be delivered to a combined television and radio audience in America. It was also a demonstration of public address as a force in a free society.

MacArthur's audience might be classified into four groups. First, was the noncritical mass of people to whom he was an abused war hero. Second, were the Republicans—until now hopelessly divided on foreign policy, with Hoover's American Gibraltar wing at one end and the Dulles' world leadership wing at the other—who suddenly and unexpectedly found an issue and a man behind whom they could unite. Third, were the Democrats, stunned by the public fury over MacArthur's dismissal, definitely on the defensive, yet hoping that MacArthur would discredit himself before Congress and the nation. Finally, were a few thinking critical people who respected MacArthur as a great military leader, but who were half convinced that many years in the Far East had conditioned him to think of issues primarily in terms of Asia only.

Within the first 10 minutes, the Democrats knew that they were in a fight for their survival as a majority party. In a voice that sometimes rasped, seldom rose from a low flat pitch, yet swelled with resonant confidence, he came almost at once to the ultimate issue in the minds of critical listeners. "The issues are global . . . there are those who claim our own strength is inadequate to protect on both fronts, that we cannot divide our effort. I can think of no greater expression of defeatism."

Interrupted by applause some thirty times, he marched with a soldier's precision from point to point . . . the Asiatic background, the Korean invasion, his call for reinforcements and for political decisions, a resulting military campaign that "forbade victory."

The climax of "old soldiers never die" was perhaps overdone for critics who heard the speech by radio. Some sneered at it as "corn." To those who saw it on television, however, it was emotionally effective, if not indeed spine-tingling and "beyond the limits of ordinary present-day oratory."

The President was probably right in his decision to dismiss MacArthur. MacArthur was probably wrong in his claim that his position was supported by the Joint Chiefs of Staff. In the immediate aftermath of the speech neither of these important issues counted for much. By this speech MacArthur had seized the initiative even as he had done by the audacious landing at Inchon.

HERBERT A. WICHELNS

Demosthenes had the problem, too: how much to spell out, how formal and explicit to make his proposals. At times Demosthenes judged it best not to "make a motion," but merely to offer comment and advice at large. MacArthur made a similar choice. In the main he chose not to debate, in the sense of formulating proposals and defending them in full. Instead he indicated the heads for debate, leaving no doubt as to the direction of his policy. Definite proposals were few, and sharply limited to Formosa and Korea. Supporting reasons were very sparingly given, and sometimes confined to bare assertions (as on the extent of China's present military commitment and Russia's probable course). But the call for a harder and more aggressive policy is plain from the beginning ("no greater expression of defeatism").

The chief support for that policy is neither logical argument nor emotional appeal, but the self-portrait of the speaker as conveyed by the speech.

It is an arresting portrait. Certain colors are of course mandatory. The speaker respects Congress and the power of this nation for good in the world. He is free from partisanship or personal rancor. He sympathizes with the South Koreans and with his embattled troops. He prefers victory to appeasement. He seeks only his country's good. He hates war, has long hated it. If these strokes are conventional, they take little time, except for the last, on which the speaker feels he must defend himself.

More subtle characterizing strokes are found in the "brief insight into the surrounding area" which form a good half of the speech. Here the General swiftly surveys the nature of the revolution in Asia, the island-frontier concept and Formosa's place in the island-chain, the imperialistic character of the Chinese communities, the regeneration of Japan under his auspices, the outlook for the Philippines, and the present government of Formosa. All this before reaching Korea. Most of these passages have no argumentative force. But all together they set up for us the image of a leader of global vision, comprehending in his gaze nations, races, and continents. The tone is firmest on Japan ("I know of no nation more serene, orderly and industrious"), least sure on the Philippines, but always positive.

Rarely indeed have the American people heard a speech so strong in the tone of personal authority. "While I was not consulted . . . that decision . . . proved a sound one." "Their last words to me"—it is the Korean people with whom the General has been talking. "My soldiers." The conduct of "your fighting sons" receives a sentence. A paragraph follows on the General's labors and anxieties on their behalf. The pace at which the thought moves, too, is proconsular; this is no fireside chat. Illustration and amplification are sparingly used; the consciously simple vocabulary of the home-grown politician is rejected. The housewife who "understood every word" was mistaken; she missed on *epicenter* and *recrudescence* and some others. But having by the fanfare been jarred into full attention, she understood quite well both the main proposition of the speech—a harder policy—and the main support offered—the picture of a masterful man of unique experience and global outlook, wearing authority as to the manner born.

WILBUR SAMUEL HOWELL

No prominent speech of the post-war era has contained so strong an appeal to emotion as MacArthur's

did. Here was the old soldier in the fading twilight of life still seeking at the end of a career of fifty-two years in the Army to serve his country, even though she had deprived him of command, even though he was the reluctant advocate of an expanded war. Here was the veteran warrior recalling his boyish hopes and dreams on the plain at West Point a half-century earlier, and concluding his speech in part from the words of a popular barracks ballad of his youth and in part from the celebrated accents of Lincoln in the peroration of the Second Inaugural Address.

But these dominant and recurrent appeals would have been more persuasive if they had not clashed with that which he more briefly developed when he spoke of America's fighting sons in Korea. "I can report to you without reservation," he said, "that they are splendid in every way." He then mentioned his own anguish and anxiety at the growing bloodshed of the savage conflict in Korea. Such words would have the effect of arousing similar anguish and anxiety in his audience, and these powerful sympathies would cancel out those which he was bent upon creating towards himself as part of his program of advocacy of what might produce still greater bloodshed.

Ethical ambiguities in his speech tend also to weaken the effect he wanted to have. The only one of these that I shall deal with is so plainly at work that one wonders why he or his political advisers did not correct its injurious influence in advance. Those who listened to him on April 19 may have shared in part at least my feeling of elation when he urged America not to pursue "a course blind to reality that the colonial era is now past and the Asian peoples covet the right to shape their own free destiny." Here is an ethical standard to which the wise and just can repair. But hardly had these words reached our ears when he declared that from our island chain between the Aleutians and the Marianas "we can dominate with sea and air power every Asiatic port from Vladivostok to Singapore." We do not have to be Asiatics ourselves to feel at this point that in MacArthur's denunciation of colonialism the voice is Jacob's voice, but in his assertion of our power to threaten Asia the hands are the hands of Esau.

As for logic, MacArthur's speech tends to expand into propositions that are easy to grasp and hard to defend. One of these is that all-out war with Communist China should be risked at once, not avoided as long as we can. MacArthur discounts this risk in eleven words—"China is already engaging with the maximum power it can commit." Does not the General miscalculate his rhetorical strategy when he allots so few troops to such a crucial position? An even more crucial position which his strategy requires him to occupy is that America should deliberately risk war with Soviet Russia at this time. But again he does not man the position in strength. He sees that his four recommendations might cause Russia to intervene on the side of China; and then he deals with that grim eventuality so as to discount its possibility, not to calculate its final result. He merely says, "the Soviet will not necessarily mesh its actions with our moves." Even if this is right so far as it goes, it gives our moves a significance that we as a nation have to estimate in terms more exact than those used by the General. Thus it may happen that, with the applause now over and done with, the General's thesis will seem less and less attractive as time goes on.

HENRY L. EWBANK

It is difficult to imagine a more dramatic speech situation. A great military hero and speaker of unusual power, just relieved from his command for reasons not generally understood, broadcasts over all major networks his criticisms of the Department of State and the President. It couldn't happen in Russia. We are glad it can happen here.

This speech is part of a "great debate" on our foreign policy and who should determine it. In the main, MacArthur stuck to the issues, labelled his opinions as such, avoided *ad hominem* attacks, and presented his case with poise and dignity.

By way of objective analysis I applied Rudolf Flesch's criteria of readability. He has devised two scales: one measuring "ease of reading," the other "human interest." The reading ease score is based on sentence length and the number of syllables per hundred words. Possible scores range from zero (practically unreadable) to 100 (easy for any literate person). MacArthur's average sentence length is 24.5 words. The shortest has six; the longest, eighty. The number of syllables per hundred words ranges from 130 to 190; the average is 161. His score is 46 (difficult) compared with 70 (fairly easy) for the Gettysburg Address. The human interest score is based on the percentages of "personal words" and "personal sentences." Possible scores range from zero (very dull) to 100 (of dramatic interest). MacArthur's score is 20, on the borderline between "mildly interesting" and "interesting." Listeners who rated the speech higher in clarity and interestingness were probably reacting to the speaker's prestige, the content of his speech, and the excellence of his delivery.

The style is uneven. There are direct, skillfully constructed sentences: "It assumes instead the friendly aspect of a peaceful lake"; "We have had our last chance"; "They are blind to history's clear lesson . . ."; "In war there can be no substitute for victory"; "These gallant men will remain often in my thoughts and in my prayers always."

But there are a few words strangers to the average listener, an occasional awkward phrase and some sentences whose precise meaning is not readily apparent: ". . . the whole epicenter of world affairs rotates back toward the area whence it started"; "These political-social conditions . . . form a backdrop to contemporary planning which must be thoughtfully considered if we are to avoid the pitfalls of unrealism"; "China . . . was completely non-homogeneous, being compartmented into groups . . ."; ". . . efforts toward greater homogeneity produced the start of a nationalist urge"; ". . . I formally cautioned as follows"; "The problem . . . involves a spiritual recrudescence. . . ."

One must, it seems, say something about the concluding paragraph. It does not fit our stereotyped picture of Douglas MacArthur, nor has he just faded away. But let him who has not waxed sentimental as he bade his fraternity brothers farewell, or reached the end of his professional career, cast the first stone.

In many ways this was, and is, a great speech. But it will not find an enduring place in our literature as a model of speech composition.

A. CRAIG BAIRD

General Douglas MacArthur will be ranked as one of America's outstanding military orators. Partly because of disciplinary and strategic restraints, few modern soldiers have achieved reputations as outstanding speakers. Exceptions occur when military command and political leadership have merged, or when American public opinion of the present decade has invited nation-wide, untrammeled reports from such five-star heroes as George Marshall, Dwight Eisenhower, and Douglas MacArthur.

General of the Army MacArthur, before the Joint Session of Congress, on April 19, 1951, was deeply eloquent in his Apologia. His defense was in the tradition of Robert Emmet, before the Dublin court that had condemned him.

The general adequately fulfilled the speaking demands of the situation, with its expectancy of powerful eloquence that should exist "in the man, in the subject, and in the occasion." He is an orator by temperament, by habit, and by long exercise. Before Congress he realized Webster's criterion of the orator as one who possesses boldness, manliness, and energy.

The mode of his discourse, in spite of its logical texture, was primarily personal and ethical—a vindication of his intellectual integrity, wisdom, and good will. The historical-philosophical overview, the delineation of the new strategic frontier in the Pacific, the speech structure and movement, the language at times somewhat Churchillian—all these exalted the mature judgment and common sense of the speaker. The general's understanding of the vast Eastern populations, his sympathy for them, his implications of his own destiny strongly enforced his assumptions about his own character.

MacArthur in this dramatic setting was heroic in his bearing, movements, and gestures. His voice was by turns self-confident, convincing, stern, scornful, righteous.

What were his limitations? His sonorous delivery, occasional volatile phrasing, and calculated peroration were defects due to Asian rather than to Attic style. Pericles would presumably have composed and delivered this oration with more artistic subtlety, sense of order, freedom from extravagance, with more intellectual severity and emotional balance.

If MacArthur had not been a soldier for the past fifty-two years, he could have become a statesman of stature. For he has much of the parliamentary grand manner and an eloquence that the age has not outgrown.

When you speak in public, you usually want others to be entertained, to understand, to believe, or to act. To achieve your purpose as fully as possible, you must work for originality—in ideas, their management, their expression, and their presentation. A good original speech is the result of good methods consciously applied, and good methods come from the study of principles, guided application of them, sound criticism of their use, and discriminating observation of how others use them. The moments of actual speaking are few but exacting; the hours of preparation are many and equally exacting.

To be an effective public speaker, you must know how to choose a suitable subject for your speech, determine its overall purpose, and gather materials for it quickly and systematically. You must be able to organize your speech in a clear, coherent pattern; express your ideas in accurate, appropriate, lively language; and deliver your speech in a natural, interesting manner. In this Handbook we will examine some of the basic methods you can use to achieve each of these essential functions.

Choosing a subject

How do you select a subject for a speech? Purposeful observation and thoughtful analysis, combined with a liberal dash of imagination, will help you find suitable subjects and aid you in exploring their possibilities. For example, study the pencil in your hand. It invites you to learn and share new knowledge about graphite, wood, rubber, communication, the art of writing. Even in so simple a subject there will be "news" of interest to most speakers and listeners.

After you unearth a potential subject, you should test it by asking two questions: Does it interest me? Can I make it meaningful to other people? If either answer is negative, you should discard the subject. If your answers are affirmative, test the subject further by examining it in the light of the principles suggested in the Glossary under *Subject* and *Originality*. Always seek your subject early, and seek it carefully and methodically. And do not abandon a promising subject at the first sign of difficulty. Remember that it takes time to command a subject thoroughly and to comprehend all of its facets and trace all of its implications.

Audience analysis and purpose

Next come the twin problems of analyzing the audience and determining the precise nature of the response you want from your listeners. This response becomes the specific purpose of your speech.

Here again, you need to ask the right questions: What do I most want to accomplish in speaking on this subject? What does the audience most need to understand or believe concerning it? The answers to these questions will help point the way toward efficient research, fresh ideas that are significant and useful, and a speech pattern that will be closely adapted to the needs and interests of your listeners.

In determining what you as a speaker most want to accomplish in talking on a given subject, proceed as follows:

1. Decide tentatively which of the *ends of speaking* (see Glossary) is most suitable to your subject, audience, and occasion.

2. Decide whether the audience will be willing and able to respond as you would like. To reach this decision, ask yourself the following questions:

A. What attitudes will my listeners probably have toward me, my subject, and the occasion? (Men in the prime of life seldom relish instruction from youth; minorities are not amused by accounts of their difficulties or peculiarities; wedding parties are not occasions for political advocacy.)

B. Has the audience too little, enough, or too much knowledge to respond as I would like? (Children can be informed about rocks but are little amused by geologists' "inside jokes.") Has the audience the authority or power to act as I wish? (Students can be convinced about foreign policy, but there is little they can do to carry out their convictions.)

C. Will my listeners have a sense of common interest or feel themselves strangers to one another's concerns? (Labor union members might agree unanimously on a proposal affecting their working hours but be widely divided on a political or a religious issue.)

D. Will age, sex, socioeconomic status, or similar factors influence my listeners' readiness to respond to my preferred purpose? (The old are often more cynical than the young; women may be less interested in high finance than men; the poor usually respond to "pocketbook motives" more readily than the well-to-do.)

Above all, remember that as a public speaker you are never entirely the master of your own purpose. Only after studying the probable audience can you decide whether the purpose you prefer is wise and realistic. You may wish to *amuse* by poking fun at modern architecture, but what if your hearers have seen few modern buildings? Or what if some architects will be in the audience? Given these conditions, your "realistic" purpose cannot be to amuse. Some of your listeners know too little about the subject, and others know too much. What can you do? You can modify or adjust your purpose to meet the situation. You might *explain* a layman's reaction to modern architecture. And doubtless you could add some amusing touches that would enliven your expository discourse. In a speech with this modified purpose, there would be "news" for all. A moderate shift of your central idea directs your speech toward the true ground on which you, your subject, and your audience can meet, realistically and to mutual advantage.

Gathering materials

Once you have chosen your subject, analyzed your audience, and located a practical purpose, you must turn researcher. Where are the facts, figures, and arguments you will need to influence your listeners—to win from them the response of understanding, belief, or action which you seek? Sound methods of research will save hours of time and will help uncover the best materials available. There are four great repositories of potentially useful information:

1. The storehouse of your own memory; you must think about your subject and remember what you have already learned about it.

2. The world outside yourself; you must take a look about you.

3. The minds of friends, acquaintances, and available experts; you must talk with them.

4. The vast resources of printed materials; you must read.

Speakers who have the most trouble finding materials for their speeches are usually those who do not explore these repositories systematically. They wish they knew all, but they do not take inventory of the bits of relevant knowledge they already possess. They look without seeing and touch without feeling;

they pass by pertinent information insensitively. They talk at random; they do not interview. They read without remembering the purpose of their speeches and the characteristics of their prospective listeners.

What specific method should you use in your search for speech materials? You cannot do better than direct your energies as Emerson urged "The American Scholar" to manage his. Read paragraphs 11 through 17, pages 40-41, of this address. Make "the scholar of the first age" your model in research.

In addition, you will find that you can save much time and confusion by taking careful notes. The extra minutes you spend in recording ideas and their sources, *completely and accurately*, on separate slips of paper or note cards, will be minutes quickly won back when you begin to compose your speech. Here is an example of well-recorded information:

> Persuasion   Common Ground
>
> J. A. Winans, ~~Speech~~-Making (1938), p. 370.
>
> "... to persuade a man is largely a matter of identifying the opinion or course you wish him to adopt with one or more of his established beliefs or customary courses of conduct." (Italics W's.)

You can take such a note quickly, from a book or during a conversation. If you write your information on a note card, you can file it easily, carry it to the speaker's stand, put it out of the way if unneeded, or save it for later use and refer to it with confidence months or years later. Sheets of miscellaneous and fragmentary notations offer none of these conveniences.

Reading is very important. Since public speeches are often about public affairs, you as a student of public speaking should keep informed about current questions. You will find that reading good sources of information regularly is enjoyable as well as educational. In each geographical region there is a "best" newspaper; it is the paper with the widest and least biased coverage of both world and local news. The one "newspaper of record" in the United States is the New York *Times,* which not only has a comprehensive index but publishes the texts of major, newsworthy documents and speeches. For stimulating and authoritative information also study such magazines as the following: for general information *The*

Atlantic, Harper's Magazine, Yale Review; for conservative opinion on public questions the *U.S. News & World Report* and the *National Review;* for liberal opinion *The Nation, New Republic, The Reporter;* for the viewpoint of business *Business Week* and *Fortune.* Some journals specialize in publishing analyses of public issues: *Vital Speeches of the Day* offers the texts of significant current speeches; the *Congressional Digest* presents analyses of current problems, often in debate form; more authoritative articles on such problems can be found in *The Annals of the American Academy of Political and Social Science* and *Foreign Affairs.*

Planning the speech

If you gather your material carefully, think about it, and apply imagination to it, you will usually be able to produce a clear speech plan that will reflect sound and original views—views you can express in your own best language and can relate to your listeners' lives and experiences. If need be, you will also be able to expand or defend these views, because you will understand how and why you came to hold them. On the other hand, when your knowledge is sketchy, reflection meager, and imagination lacking, your speech plans will probably be cloudy and your ideas shallow. In short, you cannot prepare and organize a speech quickly. Success or failure hangs in the balance as you engage in each of the tasks extending from the first search for raw materials to the final shaping of the finished discourse.

Outlining the body of the speech. These are the basic steps in planning the body of a speech:

1. Give final form to the specific purpose of the speech by stating it in a precise, carefully limited sentence. (See Glossary: *Central Idea, Specific Purpose.*) Sometimes your research will prove that the purpose you selected initially was too inclusive, too narrow, or otherwise unsatisfactory. Not infrequently your opinions will change as your study of the subject continues. You *must,* therefore, re-examine your original intention before turning to the other stages of speech planning.

2. Study the relation of the materials collected to the proposed purpose of the speech in order to determine the leading ideas or main divisions.

  A. As guides to this process read these sections of the Glossary, preferably in the following order: *Analysis, Main Headings, Subheadings, Subordination, Patterns of Organization, Motivated Sequence.*

  B. Discover the arrangement of ideas which best supports or explains the purpose of the speech as finally determined in Step 1. The so-called "standard" patterns of organization are simply the arrangements speakers are most in the habit of using. You must judge by your own intelligence and experience which pattern best serves your needs. How you may arrive at this choice methodically is suggested in the Glossary under *Reflective Thinking.*

3. As a result of Step 2 you should have a rough outline of the body of your speech, one in which the organization of the main headings will probably conform to one of the patterns of organization discussed in the Glossary.

4. With the proposed main headings and, perhaps, some of their subheadings coordinated and subordinated in outline form, fill in any subheadings still needed and insert relevant *supporting material* (see Glossary) from the fund of facts and ideas gathered in research. Ask yourself:

  A. Will the main headings, if the audience believes them all, win assent for the central idea?

  B. What needs to be proved or clarified to win assent for each main heading? The answers will suggest the subheadings and supporting materials that are still needed.

  C. Do unused or previously discarded research materials offer better answers to the questions asked in Step 4B? If so, perhaps a weaker heading or less pertinent piece of supporting material should be discarded and a new one put in its place.

  D. Do the subheadings and supporting materials as now revised prove or clarify the main headings and make them striking enough to command the attention of your audience? Does the speech as a whole strongly support the specific purpose? If not, what additional materials might help? At this point some supplementary facts and figures may have to be gathered or some new and stronger arguments formulated; the first phase of research seldom produces every item actually needed for adequate proof and sufficient motivation.

Checking the main sections. With this done, examine each main section of the speech as finally developed. Test it for:

1. Redundancy. Eliminate excess materials, saving only *enough of the best* to win the specific response proposed. No audience wants to hear in a single sitting all that a competent speaker knows.

2. Lack of variety in supporting material. In some instances examples may be needed to replace statistics, or statistics needed to replace authority. Each main heading should be strongly and variously supported.

3. Motivational and suggestive force. The main headings and their subdivisions must make the hearers *want* to understand, believe, or act. (See Glossary: *Adaptation, Motivation, Emotion, Suggestion, Drive, Attitude, Stereotype, Appeal.*)

It is in making these decisions and choices that superior speakers prove themselves and poor speakers proceed by guess rather than informed judgment. To derive and arrange the materials of a speech requires intelligence, command of method, and sensitivity to the nature of audiences. It is an art that you can learn only through long and dedicated practice.

Introductions and conclusions. As a final step in planning your speech, you must compose an introduction and conclusion, being guided both by the nature of your subject and by the needs of the audience. For the essential requirements of a good *introduction* and *conclusion,* see the Glossary.

Style

When you give a speech extemporaneously, you must develop the wording by experimentation in a series of oral or sub-vocal rehearsals (see the following section, "Extemporaneous delivery"). If you deliver the speech from manuscript, or from memory, you may perfect the stylistic elements as writing and rewriting progress. A fourth and probably ideal procedure is to write the speech in full, from the outline, carefully evaluate and perfect the language used, then destroy the manuscript and rehearse the ideas extemporaneously. With this process you are likely to use the carefully worked out expression of the manuscript naturally in the actual speech without destroying the still greater advantages of flexibility in both style and delivery. For the extemporaneous speaker this process of writing enlarges language resources while repeated rehearsals intensify the sense of plan and direction.

As you write a speech or experiment in rehearsals for extemporaneous speaking, you should work for language that is at once accurate, clear, appropriate, and lively. Your experience with words, your common sense, your good taste, must guide the search. No one can give exact instructions suited to all cases, but you can learn, in advance of making any particular language decision, what kinds of useful language are available and what standards influence the best speakers when they make similar choices. Some of these considerations are discussed in the Glossary under such topics as: *Abstraction, Activity, Clarity, Conciseness, Concreteness, Connotation, Conversational Quality, Emphasis, Figures of Speech, Force,* *Imagery, Impressiveness, Liveliness, Originality, Style, Suggestion, Variety.*

Good oral style requires plentiful and carefully formulated transitions and internal summaries. It is more difficult to achieve clarity in oral discourse than in written because listeners must grasp the full import of a word or sentence instantaneously. They cannot reflect and re-examine as readers constantly do. You must, then, take special pains to keep the relationships among ideas clear by using frequent transitions and summaries. These tell the listeners where the speaker has been, where he is now, and where he is going. They are not integral parts of the organization of a speech; they are verbal bridges between parts, placed there to aid the listener who otherwise might not be able to make the crossing. Since the transition usually restates part of what the speaker has already said, it functions both as a connective and an internal summary. You should plan such aids to listeners in detail—including them in your outline for the speech and consciously inserting them orally as you rehearse. For examples of such transitional and summary statements, see the Glossary under *Transition.*

Extemporaneous delivery

The extemporaneous speaker is more versatile, more adaptable, and, usually, more convincing than the speaker who has memorized his speech or who reads from manuscript.

Rehearsing the speech. Planning and outlining are the backbone of the extemporaneous method. For good delivery you must have total command of your basic speech plan and must be fortified by a series of thoughtful rehearsals. Thus equipped, you can come to the platform confident of your preparation. Having been through the speech many times and having met its difficulties in different ways each time, you know you have a full, diverse fund of thoughts and a ready supply of words with which to meet any problems that may arise during the presentation. To arrive at this enviable frame of mind, prepare as follows:

1. When the speech plan is complete, read it over several times, from beginning to end, always concentrating on how each idea is related to the idea which precedes it and the one which follows it.

2. Next place the speech plan before you and try to talk through the speech, *aloud if possible.* No matter how much trouble you have at any point, do not pause to correct it but proceed from beginning to end without stopping. To do otherwise will establish a psychological block at the point of difficulty.

3. Having made your way through the speech plan, however haltingly, study it again, working out smoother connections between the ideas and planning clearer, more fitting, more lively ways of expressing each point.

4. Now repeat Step 2 exactly as before, moving from the beginning of the speech to the end without stopping. Then review once more the plan and the manner of handling it, just as you did in Step 3. As you rehearse and adjust the speech, constantly keep in mind the audience you will be addressing and the response you seek.

5. When, after alternating Steps 2 and 3, you feel that the speech plan is firmly fixed in your mind, make a set of brief "speaker's notes," based on the detailed speech outline. These notes should consist of cue words and phrases that will help you recall the order of the main headings and the several subheadings that fall under each. They must be brief enough to be read at a glance. To go with these notes, assemble those quotations, statistics, and other detailed materials which you wish to use in the speech but which it would be difficult or impossible to commit wholly to memory.

6. Finally, rehearse the speech again, this time using only your notes and special reference cards. Make the necessary final adjustments in timing, language, emphasis, and delivery. When you are satisfied with these adjustments, you are ready to face your audience. The leading ideas of the speech and their supporting materials will now be old friends. Moreover, you now know the "marching orders" embodied in the detailed speech plan; you know them so well that as the speech is being delivered to the audience you can make minor changes without destroying its essential character.

Delivering the speech. Before taking the platform, you probably will be nervous. You should be. You will have "butterflies." You should have. Like an athlete, you are keyed to your task—a task important enough to be nervous about. Your salvation, like the athlete's, is that you know what the plays are; most of them are in your well-practiced plan. Your nervous tension is a fact, but no more a fact than your thorough familiarity with the ideas you wish to communicate. And if you have rehearsed the speech as you should have, you already have met and conquered most of the difficulties that can confront you on the platform. This, too, is a fact as significant as your nervousness.

But it is uncomfortable to be nervous while waiting to speak. What can be done to bring a little comfort without destroying the keyed-up feeling so essential to effective extemporaneous speaking? Here are some suggestions:

1. Breathe deeply. More oxygen helps. Also, using the large muscles of the chest and abdomen discharges some of the pent-up energy that contributes to discomfort.

2. Drop the arms; let the hands dangle loosely beside the body; let the head droop too if no one is looking. Concentrating on relaxing takes the mind off the task that is causing nervousness.

3. Remember some of the successes of rehearsals; try to recapture the ideas, feelings, and language of those moments. This encourages you and also provides review.

4. When introduced, walk—don't shamble or rush —to the speaker's stand. Take time—time to recapture one of the several good beginnings made in rehearsal. Keep your mind on the response you wish to win from the audience, and why. *You* are not very important now; your business with the audience is.

5. When you are ready, and not until then, "lean into your audience" and begin working on *them*. A speech is not a "performance"; it is a transaction carried on with other minds. The sooner this business relationship becomes your entire preoccupation, the sooner the tensions of speaking will be channeled out of discomfort-producing paths and into paths that make the body obedient to the mind.

Such is the experience of most effective extemporaneous speakers. Experience does not dull the excitement. Experience does not even make the process of preparation less time consuming. The experienced extemporaneous speaker differs from his less experienced brother chiefly because he knows that careful advance planning can solve most problems. He knows that properly used, his tensions can help, not thwart, him. Convinced of these things, his mind is free to re-create the thoughts of his preparation, and his spirit is free to *mean* them.

Other modes of delivery

Few speakers memorize their speeches today. The hurry of modern living does not allow them time. Happily, nothing of great value is lost in consequence. The only good memorized speeches are those in which every idea is an old and familiar friend. Only when words need not be consciously remembered can ideas be delivered with meaning; so it is not until a speech is completely, flawlessly memorized that one arrives at the equivalent of Step 6 in the extemporaneous speaker's program of rehearsal. From this point on, the speaker with a memorized speech prepares himself and focuses his nervous energies in much the same manner as the extemporaneous speaker. For the extra effort of memorization he earns a more perfect control over style, but he also sacrifices much freedom in adapting ideas and appeals to audience responses.

The speaker who reads from a manuscript may believe that he has chosen the easiest mode of speech preparation and delivery. He hasn't if he means to be effective. He has chosen the quickest path to detailed control over style but the most difficult path to vibrant, communicative delivery. Moreover, if he means to speak with genuine effect, he must struggle with his habits to avoid writing an essay rather than a speech; he must rework his written draft as carefully as the extemporaneous speaker reworks his modes of expression. Unless he is already a well-trained, gifted reader, he must spend much time in rehearsal. President Franklin D. Roosevelt's "War Message" of December 8, 1941, was exceedingly brief (about 45 lines), yet he put it through three written drafts within twenty-four hours, before he was willing to read it to Congress and the nation. Those who propose to speak from manuscript should be guided by the fact that Roosevelt, the finest manuscript speaker in modern American history, normally insisted that each speech be rewritten five to eight times and carefully rehearsed aloud before it was finally delivered.

Effective oral reading is a special art that cannot be examined here, but it is an art that must be mastered if speeches are to be meaningfully delivered from manuscript. That this necessity is seldom met by public figures, painful memories and painful anticipations attest.

Impromptu speaking—that is, speaking without formal preparation—is sometimes necessary. Few, if any, effective speeches have ever been so delivered, however—except on subjects about which the speaker had already thought long and clearly. The test of adequacy in impromptu speaking is simple: Is the speaker so well grounded in the subject and the art of speech composition that not even the unexpected call for a speech upsets his command of substance and method? Impromptu speaking may afford excellent drill in the methods of effective speaking; but except when done by the best informed and ablest speakers, it is usually an imposition upon the listeners.

Physical aspects of delivery

The physical aspects of delivery concern the proper use of voice and body.

The voice. All listeners, but only some speakers, seem to know that the speaker must speak loudly enough to be heard or his breath is wasted. If you have normal vocal equipment, you are capable of speaking so that you can be heard by a hundred listeners in a moderately quiet hall. You can, if you are willing to work at it, establish habits of using the breathing apparatus, the vocal folds, and the resonators efficiently—even pleasingly. This may require drill, but the drills are best conducted as specially prepared exercises, not in the public speaking situation itself.

It is also plain that your pronunciation and articulation of words must be reasonably conventional or understanding will be impaired. Again, if you have unconventional habits or are handicapped by physical or other difficulties so that your speaking manner distracts from the communication of your meaning, you must retrain yourself. This kind of retraining is best undertaken under the supervision of a speech rehabilitation specialist and, except under special circumstances, conducted apart from attempts to learn the art of influencing audiences through public speaking.

The speed or rate at which you speak is a function of the duration of sounds and of the duration of the pauses between those sounds. Up to a point, intelligibility depends more on clear articulation than on the control of rate. Speakers who articulate clearly often can be understood when speaking well over 200 words a minute; some can speak no more than 160 words a minute before listeners begin to complain of their speed. On the other hand, fluent speakers seldom are thought to speak too slowly until they fall well below 100 words a minute. As a public speaker, you must learn by observation, study, and drill what kinds of emphasis and mood can be suggested by changing the duration of words and pauses, thus changing the overall rate of utterance. Here, as everywhere in public speaking, manageable variety is the goal.

Body action. The problem of when and how to use gestures has plagued aspiring speakers for centuries. Charts have been drawn, rules have been proclaimed, taboos have grown up. Elaborate "sciences" or "arts" of gesture have won fanatic followers. But direct, meaningful oral communication has seldom resulted from these efforts. Neither has it come from the opposite extreme—from the purists of the nature-will-take-care-of-you-if-you-only-let-it-alone persuasion. A few propositions about communication through physical movement may, however, be given.

1. People who don't *want* to communicate with others seldom communicate effectively—physically or in any other way. You must have the will to communicate—or a "lively sense of communication," as it has been called—before you can use gestures meaningfully.

2. People strongly bent on communicating with others sometimes use one means in preference to another, and do so effectively. Some speakers prefer to rely much on vocal resources and little on physical movement; some rely on head-and-shoulder emphasis but little on movements of the arms. Always, however, your bodily actions must be motivated by the ideas you seek to communicate. Gestures, bodily movements, muscle tension, and facial expression come from the inside out; they are not superimposed upon the speech by a predetermined formula.

3. Although different styles of physical emphasis and different patterns of gestures may be equally communicative, three qualities are necessary if you expect to reinforce your ideas effectively through bodily action:

A. Your communicative activity must be coordinated. Bodily movements must serve the same meanings as the accompanying verbal language, or they will distract from, rather than add to, what is said.

B. Your bodily activity must be well timed. Our natures seem to dictate that a gesture which is really meant just precedes or exactly coincides with the utterance it reinforces. The wonderfully comic effects of ill-timed movement are sufficient evidence that meaningful gestures have a subtle time relationship to the ideas or feelings that generate them.

C. Your posture and position on the platform must allow expressive movements to develop easily, whenever meaning demands them. This is why you should carry your weight on the balls of the feet, keep your hands free, and stand somewhat away from a lectern.

Self-evaluation. In all aspects of delivery, self-observation and self-criticism are continuously necessary—for the experienced speaker as well as for the inexperienced. Unless you constantly evaluate yourself, you may develop distracting mannerisms in your vocal or bodily behavior. You must learn what your personal resources are, blend them into what is for you the most communicative speaking style, and then guard that style against faulty habits and annoying behaviors. Often this requires self-conscious drill, preferably apart from actual speechmaking. When you are delivering a speech, most of your energies must be concentrated on the meaning of the ideas you are communicating and on the people to whom you are communicating them. Your body will then contribute added meaning insofar as it is trained to serve your mind. Its further retraining may well deserve attention after the speech is over, but you can hardly deliver an effective speech and at the same time pass judgment on the behavior of an arm or leg.

A final word

Studying a textbook, reading a student's handbook, and analyzing the texts of speeches will not, even together, make you an effective public speaker. But these undertakings will furnish you with a body of sound ideas about how men influence others through speech. From such ideas you may learn much that will be of use as you confront audiences in the classroom and in later life. Do not look, however, for sure-fire tricks and devices. There are none. *There is no way to make a good speech without having something to say that is so much worth saying that you want others to know it too.* Given this kind of worthiness in intention, methodical, thoughtful preparation and a well-disciplined body will mediate between your meaning and the listener's experience so that your message is clearly and impressively communicated. The study of speaking and speeches can contribute much to your understanding, method, and principles of discipline; only you can supply the practice that is necessary to turn such knowledge into productive, influential behavior. "The only way that promises success in the long run is to become intelligent about speech-making."[1]

---

[1] J. A. Winans, *Speech-Making* (New York, 1938), p. 8.

For the student's convenience, glossary terms are italicized wherever they are referred to in the following discussions.

a

Abstraction Dealing with nonsensory concepts, such as truth, honesty, democracy. See "What Is Truth?" pp. 180-183; "The Challenge of Abundance," pp. 200-201, par. 28 (except the reference to Roosevelt). See also *Concreteness*.

Action Step See *Conclusion, Motivated Sequence*.

Activity Action or *movement* in communication conveyed through the choice and forms of language as well as through *gestures* and other physical behavior. Movement or progression can be suggested by the arrangement of ideas and images, as in climactic order; through special arrangements of thought units, as a *periodic sentence;* and through choosing images that suggest things in motion. Listeners pay the most attention to those communications that set pictures moving within their minds. See "The Inner City—Our Shame," p. 216, par. 6, "Like an eddy . . . mainstream of society." See also *Climax, Liveliness*.

Adaptation Generally, the adjustment of all elements of discourse to the capacities and expectations of the listeners. Effective speaking requires that ideas, arrangement, style, and delivery be adapted to the audience, occasion, purpose, and speaker—with a view to securing responses favorable to the end the speaker has chosen. See an address popularizing a subject for a local audience, "Newspapers of the U.S.A.—An Appraisal," pp. 107-114; address to jail inmates, "Crime and Criminals," pp. 142-147; address to an alien audience, "Address to the Russian People," pp. 242-246; see also "The Haven of the Defeated," p. 149, pars. 3, 5, and 8, "Remember, I'm not . . . the same as you and me"; "Rout the Forces of Hate," pp. 157-158, pars. 1-10; "Apathy," pp. 165-166, pars. 10-19; "The Minds of the Non-Western World," p. 239, pars. 30-31; "Culture and Communication," p. 22, par. 13 ff.

Allegory A somewhat extended communication, usually *narrative*, in which events, characters, or objects have figurative or metaphorical as well as literal meanings. A *parable* is likely to be a metaphorical narrative used as *supporting material*, an allegory is a still more extensive metaphorical unit that often constitutes the entire *amplification* of a major point. Allegories rarely appear in modern public addresses, though they are sometimes found in sermons and speeches to entertain. John Bunyan's *Pilgrim's Progress* and Jonathan Swift's *A Tale of a Tub* are among the most familiar allegories in literature. See also *Figures of Speech*.

Alliteration Repetition of initial sounds in words or of sounds in stressed syllables within words. "Mock morality" and "denounces bribery but blinds itself to blackmail" in "The Man with the Muck-Rake," p. 105, par. 18, illustrate achievement of subtle emphasis by means of alliteration. Compare "The Writer's Duty," p. 53, par. 4, "ding-dong of doom"; "Rout the Forces of Hate," p. 159, par. 24, "buckboards of bigotry." Alliteration that calls attention to itself distracts from meaning.

Allusion A brief reference to some fact or event or character to clarify or vivify a thought. Note the many allusions to specific suburbs, counties, and newspaper writers used in "Newspapers of the U.S.A.—An Appraisal," pp. 107-114, to define geographical areas or to identify types of writing. Here, as with all allusions, the hearer must be able to supply details of the thing alluded to from his own knowledge if he is to understand the reference. See "The Man with the Muck-Rake," p. 102, pars. 2-3, and p. 103, par. 8, "Such laughter . . . to fruition"; "Rout the Forces of Hate," p. 159, par. 26; "The Novel and the Fairy Tale," pp. 57-58, pars. 19, 21, 23-24.

Ambiguity Obscurity or vagueness created by use of equivocal, inexact, or little understood words or propositions. Speaking becomes ambiguous when listeners cannot supply ready "translations" for specialized vocabulary. In "Speech as a Liberal Study," p. 3, par. 7, "Thought is usually conveyed through rhetorical-behavioral reflections of each character's moral and intellectual choices" would be ambiguous to anyone unfamiliar with concepts found in Aristotle's *Rhetoric and Poetics*. Where key terms are subject to various interpretations, ambiguity results; consider "dramatic transformation of American lifeways," in "Comfort and Fun: Morality in a Nice Society," p. 170, par. 12.

Amplification Literally, enlargement or extension. In rhetoric, amplification is usually thought of as the discussion which provides the details, illustrations, and other clarifying material concerning an idea. There is no necessary distinction between that which "proves" a point and that which amplifies it, but the term "amplification" is usually applied to developmental material without regard to its strength as "proof." See "The Inner City—Our Shame," p. 217, pars. 10-14, for an illustration of amplification that "proves" largely by suggestion; "Changing Concepts of Public Service," p. 211, pars. 29-33, for an illustration of a variety of amplifying methods within one segment of a speech; "The Method of Scientific Investigation," pp. 265-266, pars. 4-6, for an especially apt instance of clarification through amplification. See also *Allegory, Allusion, Analogy, Anecdote, Concreteness, Definition, Epigram, Evidence, Example, Figures of Speech, Imagery, Parable, Proof, Proverb, Repetition*.

Analogy A moderately extended comparison, either literal or figurative, used either to clarify or to "prove." An extensive figurative analogy is usually called a *parable* or an *allegory*. Analogy connotes a comparison more complex or extensive than a simile or metaphor. See "Crime and Criminals," p. 145, par. 24; "The Three Parts of Morality," pp. 175-176, pars. 3-4; "The Challenge of Abundance," p. 200, par. 23; "Culture and Communication," p. 21, par. 7; "What Can We Prove about God?" p. 189, par. 10; "Newspapers of the U.S.A.—An Appraisal," p. 108, par. 16. See also *Amplification, Figures of Speech*.

Analogy as Argument The use of circumstances existing in one place or sphere of experience as the basis for an inference about the circumstances existing elsewhere. Such argument usually runs: what is true of A must also be true of B since A and B are known to be similar. The validity of such an argument depends (1) on the truth of what we say about A; (2) on the similarity of A and B in all significant respects; (3) on whether the causative forces that work in A are also at work in B. Because of the difficulty of establishing these matters beyond reasonable doubt, argument from analogy is often called the weakest of the forms of argument, yet it is one of the commonest. Many analogies that fail the tests of logical validity contain enough probability to help sustain arguments that are also supported by other methods. See "The Haven of the Defeated," p. 150, pars. 17-19; "The Apology," p. 185, par. 1, "For neither in war . . . to say and do anything"; "The Minds of the Non-Western World," p. 237, par. 15. See also *Argument, Persuasion, Proof.*

Analysis A term used in several senses and contexts. Practically, the term refers to the division of anything into its constituent parts. In rhetoric, analysis is the process by which the discussable aspects of a subject—the *central idea,* the *main headings,* and even the *subheadings*—are discovered and revealed. Analysis of a subject involves discovering what, of all that it is possible to say about the subject, should be said to a specific audience on a particular occasion. The experience of centuries proves that many subjects can be analyzed by dividing them according to one of several standard patterns. See *Patterns of Organization, Partitioning.*

Anecdote Usually, a brief *narrative* supporting or amplifying a thought or *proposition.* Anecdotes used in introducing or concluding a speech or essay should be subordinate to the *central idea* of the discourse. An anecdote may serve either or both of two rhetorical functions: to make the idea more vivid and interesting or to support the idea as a *proof* by providing an illustration. See "Moppet Manipulation," p. 124, par. 9; "The Philosophy of Social Justice Through Social Action," p. 137, pars. 18-20; "The Three Parts of Morality," p. 175, par. 1; "Address to the Russian People," p. 246, par. 64.

Animation In oral or written composition, the quality of *liveliness* or *activity.* Expressive utterance, facial vivacity, and physical movement are the chief elements of animated delivery. Note the animation in style attained by the use of *direct discourse* in "The Minds of the Non-Western World," pp. 235, 239, pars. 6, 33, etc.

Antithesis A form of expression in which opposing terms or ideas are set against one another. Antithesis is especially valuable in argumentative discourse since it points up the sharp contrast between two viewpoints. In his *Rhetoric* Aristotle makes the point that lively expression in persuasive speech must be especially marked by "antithesis, metaphor, and actuality [*concreteness*]." See "The Apology," p. 185, par. 1, "I would rather die . . . and live"; "Inaugural Address," p. 227, pars. 19, 22, 25, 26. See also *Contrast.*

Appeal A term commonly and somewhat loosely used to mean evoking a reasoning or feeling state by means of something said or done. The phrases "emotional appeal" and "logical appeal" are frequently used to describe the process by which a speaker seems to invite a given kind of response from his audience.

By means of ideas, language, and delivery speakers can cause listeners to have mental experiences within themselves; and to these experiences, in turn, the listeners may react—sometimes with much and sometimes with little intellectual calculation. That these reactions are exclusively emotional or rational seems improbable. The same phrase or action may arouse very different experiences in different listeners. There is even evidence to show that trained listeners cannot agree with themselves or with others when they try to identify portions of a communication as "logical" or "emotional."

It is true one can find segments of printed speeches in which the purpose seems to have been to make the listeners feel more than think, or vice versa. This tells us the speaker's probable purpose, but not how the listeners reacted—how they translated the "appeal." In general, both speakers and critics must remember that normal respondents react to what they see and hear with mixed, often individualistic, feelings and thoughts; and it is the *effect* to which speaker and critic must pay most attention. To describe a child on an operating table may evoke highly professional calculations in a listening surgeon and deep emotion in the surgeon's wife, though they sit side by side in the same audience. Is the appeal of the description, then, "logical" or "emotional"?

For an authoritative discussion of processes commonly called "appeal," read "Images of the Consumer's Changing Mind on and off Madison Avenue," pp. 115-121. To understand the sweeping inclusiveness of "appeal" as a descriptive term, note that in "The Inner City—Our Shame," pp. 217-218, pars. 10-18, description and narrative at once appeal for sympathy and form evidence that action is needed; in "Address to the Russian People," p. 243, pars. 20-21, the series of factual statements constitute *evidence* but also could stir up feelings of guilt; in "The City—A Cause for Statesmanship," p. 221, pars. 21-22, there is appeal against an allegedly inconsistent opposition's *ethos* and, indirectly, to the listeners' belief in their own better logic. See also *Attitude, Emotion, Empathy, Loaded Language, Logic, Persuasion, Proof, Set.*

Appropriateness The quality of being suitable. In rhetoric this term usually refers to *style:* "Effective oral style must be clear, appropriate, and lively." Whatever language is at once suitable to the speaker, his subject matter, the *occasion* on which he speaks, and the particular audience he addresses will be called appropriate. Usually appropriateness, as distinguished from *clarity,* refers to such subjective qualities as propriety, good taste, level of difficulty, etc. See also *Liveliness.*

Argument It is doubtful that any distinction between argument and persuasion is psychologically defensible in rhetoric. Nonetheless, in composing a persuasive communication, one must often concentrate on the discovery and arrangement of *propositions* and the *evidence* for their support. In this phase of creativity the composer is usually said to be developing "arguments." Also, listeners and readers tend to classify as "arguments" those parts of a communication in which extensive reasoning and evidence are introduced. In "Address to the Russian People," p. 244, pars. 27-32, an allegation is refuted chiefly by adducing the evidence of examples; but by repeating "It was rejected by the USSR" at the end of each item of proof, a strong suggestion of blame is injected into the argument. See also *Analogy as Argument, Causal Relationship, Deduction, Inference, Persuasion, Sign, Syllogism.*

Arrangement See *Patterns of Organization.*

Articulation The production and blending of speech sounds. Good articulation results when the sounds of the language are uttered conventionally and clearly, but not in such a manner as to call attention to themselves. Faults of articulation fall into four classes: sound omission, sound distortion, sound substitution, and sound addition.

Assertion Any statement or declaration for which no support except the authority of the communicator is offered. In rhetoric, unlike scientific discourse, many assertions are entirely acceptable to audiences because experience or common knowledge supplies *proof* to support the assertion. Theodore Roosevelt's "There is nothing more distressing to every good patriot . . . ," p. 103, par. 8, only asserts an alleged fact. In ''The Challenge of Abundance,'' p. 197, par. 8 consists largely of assertions. Note how each listener's political bias will govern the acceptability of these statements. See also *Proposition.*

Attention The act of noticing or becoming aware of something. It is especially important for speakers to remember that (1) a listener's attention must be aroused before ideas can have any influence upon him; (2) human attention is selective, not diffuse—a listener perceives only what seems important or interesting to him at the moment; (3) unless ideas, language, and delivery constantly renew the listener's interest in what is being said, his attention will be lost very quickly. The attention of listeners is even less stable than the attention of readers; therefore, the speaker, even more than the writer, must know and constantly use all the resources of arrangement, style, and delivery to direct his listener's attention to whatever is most important in the speech. See also *Adaptation, Emphasis, Factors of Attention, Interest, Motivation, Persuasion, Variety.*

Attitude A predisposition to respond favorably or unfavorably to a stimulus. Attitudes are learned. Once we have learned them, we are ready to act approvingly or disapprovingly whenever the stimulus that created them recurs. Having formed a distaste for cabbage, we no longer experiment with it; no menu that contains cabbage seems wholly good to us. What is commonly called an *appeal* in speaking is usually an attempt by the speaker to evoke some set of strong attitudes that his listeners share. By this means the speaker hopes to arouse his listeners' feelings, including perhaps a desire to reason. There are several facts about attitudes that are especially important to speakers: (1) each listener possesses attitudes that are inconsistent with one another, but, at any given moment, the attitudes actively influencing a listener will tend to be consistent; (2) people who share similar attitudes tend to congregate together, and often what is called the speech ''occasion'' can be defined best by describing the particular attitudes that made the people gather to hear the speaker; (3) we often have attitudes—even strong ones—that we would rather not put into words, so what people say they favor or disapprove does not always reflect their true attitudes; (4) to create new attitudes or to change old ones is always a slow process, almost never accomplished by a single speech. Note Jonathan Smith's adaptation to both favorable and unfavorable attitudes in ''On the Federal Constitution,'' pp. 273-274, ll. 41-46, ''I had been a member. . . . well enough without.'' See also *Opinion, Persuasion, Suggestion.*

Audience Broadly, those reached by any communication. Audiences for speeches are listeners and, usually, viewers; their ways of apprehending a communication are neither as efficient nor as sustained as those of readers. Speakers who secure and maintain *attention* and *belief* adjust their communicative behavior to counteract the special problems and weaknesses of listening audiences. Among such special adaptations the following are especially important: (1) distinguishing in relatively obvious fashion between important and less important ideas; (2) expressing ideas in especially striking or otherwise memorable ways in order to assure swift, clear understanding; (3) offering *proof* that is evident rather than subtle; (4) exhibiting behavior that suggests trustworthiness, good will, and intelligence; (5) providing ample opportunities for review, relaxation, and refreshment of *interest.* See also *Adaptation, Attention, Attitude, Credibility, Motivation, Occasion.*

Audience Contact See *Directness.*

Audio-visual Aids Any resources other than the speaker's own person used to clarify or reinforce ideas by sight or sound. In ''The World of Jazz,'' pp. 67-76, an orchestra and its music were used as audio-visual aids to reinforce the speaker's discourse.

Authority The source from which *opinion* or expert testimony is derived. Although we tend to think of authorities as individual people, agencies such as the Bureau of the Census or the New York *Times* serve as authorities in many speeches. The *credibility* of an authority usually depends on the general *prestige,* the known or demonstrated competence, and the consistency of the source. Thus, whether a speaker introduces direct quotations from his authority or cites the authority indirectly, he ought to state the qualifications of his source unless the authority is already well known to his listeners. The *supporting material* drawn from a well-qualified and eminent authority not only serves as a form of *evidence* but also constitutes a form of *suggestion* because men tend to believe readily and often uncritically those whom they respect. Lincoln paraphrased Jesus when he said, ''A house divided against itself cannot stand.'' The quotation probably had more suggestive than logical force for his listeners; the same opinion is doubly convincing today, for we give it the authority of both Jesus and Lincoln. Who, now, analyzes the evidence behind the quotation? Note the use of eminent authorities to provide evidence and to lend impressiveness to various topics in ''Changing Concepts of Public Service,'' p. 211, par. 30; p. 212, par. 44; and p. 213, pars. 54-55; ''The Philosophy of Social Justice Through Social Action,'' pp. 138-139, pars. 33-45; ''Ethics in International Relations Today,'' pp. 229-232, pars. 3-4, 16, 23, 26; ''The Minds of the Non-Western World,'' p. 236, par. 11; ''Pan-Africanism, the Communists and the West,'' p. 256-257, pars. 8, 15; ''Culture and Communication,'' pp. 21, 23, pars. 12, 23. For examples of testing and qualifying authorities, see ''Comfort and Fun: Morality in a Nice Society,'' p. 173, par. 36; ''What Is Truth?'' pp. 180-181, pars. 10-11; ''The Challenge of Abundance,'' pp. 196-197, pars. 1-3.

b

Barbarism A nonstandard word such as ''disremember'' or ''irregardless'' that has been irregularly formed. Because barbarisms often becloud meaning, distract attention, and impair the speaker's *ethos,* they should be avoided. See *Impropriety, Vulgarism.*

Belief Any idea accepted with confidence and trust. In rhetoric, it is common to distinguish between speaking intended to create belief and speaking which aims at responses that go beyond belief to seek reinforcement, stimulation, or action. For an analysis of various types of beliefs, see ''Images of the Consumer's Changing Mind on and off Madison Avenue,'' pp. 116-118, pars. 3-16. See also *Ends of Speaking, Opinion, Proof, Refutation.*

Body That portion of a speech or essay containing the support or explication of the *central idea* or thesis. In an informative communication the body explains or develops the central idea. A persuasive speech or essay will always contain some proposition, stated or implied, and a proof of the proposition. This proof forms the body of the composition. To the proposition and proof, an introduction and a conclusion may be appended as the audience requires. ''The Challenge of Abundance,'' p. 196, has no introduction; par. 1 begins the body with proof that there is a problem. See *Discussion.*

Both-Sides Persuasion Persuasion in which viewpoints at variance with the speaker's main thesis are deliberately mentioned and then refuted or neutralized. Experimental evidence indicates that this recognition of ''other views'' is more persuasive than one-sided persuasion unless the listeners already agree with the persuader's thesis, are poorly educated, and are not likely to be exposed to counterargument at a later time.

Burden of Proof The responsibility for providing full, affirmative support in argument. In almost all situations those who propose something are expected by their hearers or readers to furnish convincing proofs in favor of their proposal. This is the general burden of proof that goes with initiating ideas, but sometimes there are also special rules or customs that prescribe more exactly where and how the burden of proof shall fall. In United States courts whoever prosecutes is required to prove guilt, while the defendant need only maintain the innocence the law already presumes in his favor. In certain parliamentary situations and in school debate it is the custom to require that those who advocate a change from existing practices shall assume the burden of proving the change better than any alternative. Except where there are special rules of this sort, persuaders must study their audiences to discover just what burdens of proof must be assumed. Since commencement speakers usually praise education—as is almost expected of them—they need not prove to their audiences that education is necessary and desirable unless they recommend further education. See *Presumption*.

Burlesque See *Satire*.

C

Causal Relationship The relationship between things or ideas that answers the question "Why?" Persons of Western culture tend to assume that whatever exists must have had a cause and that if any force is exerted some effect must follow. It is therefore necessary in any discourse to be explicit about why alleged effects came into being and what consequences follow from any "cause" that is discussed. The basic conditions to be proved about an alleged causal relationship in *persuasion* are these: (1) that the relationship between the supposed cause and its supposed effect is a steady and invariable one, and (2) that the supposed cause is sufficiently strong to produce the alleged effect. In *exposition* the communicator's chief task is sometimes to show simply and clearly how causes and their effects are interrelated, as when the thrust of a jet engine is to be explained. Even in a *narrative* it is essential to clarify why the events of the narrative flow as they do. Causality, then, is either a relationship that has to be clarified or proved or a relationship that suggests a way of dividing and organizing a discourse. See "The Inner City—Our Shame," p. 217, pars. 10-12, where the speaker amplifies the effects of an alleged cause (overcrowding); "Science and Society," pp. 78-80, pars. 1-12. See also *Patterns of Organization*.

Cause to Effect, Argument from That form of argument in which the communicator first shows that a given force (cause) is at work and then undertakes to prove that some consequence was or will be produced by the cause. See "The Philosophy of Social Justice Through Social Action," pp. 136-137, pars. 12-15; "The Challenge of Abundance," pp. 197-198, par. 9. See also *Causal Relationship, Effect to Cause, Patterns of Organization*.

Central idea A *proposition* or statement that expresses the essential meaning of an entire communication. To reveal its truth is the function of all *amplification* and *proof* in the discourse. In *persuasion* the central idea is the proposition to be proved; in *exposition* it is the statement to be clarified; in *description* it is a statement characterizing the spatial relations which the discourse will detail. Because of the limitations of auditory *attention*, the central idea of a speech must be especially explicit and frequently deserves repetition. In persuasive

discourse, especially when the audience is hesitant or hostile, the central idea may be withheld until the proofs have rendered it acceptable, but it should still dominate the persuader's planning and presentation. Other terms synonymous with central idea are subject sentence, thesis, and theme statement. In "Changing Concepts of Public Service," pp. 208-214, the central idea is stated in different ways in pars. 3, 5, 15, 18, 51, 56; in "Culture and Communication," it is stated in par. 12, pp. 21-22. There is no explicit statement of the central idea in "Address to the Russian People," pp. 242-246, a speech to a presumably hesitant or hostile audience. See *Specific Purpose*.

Character of the Speaker See *Ethos*.

Chronological Pattern See *Patterns of Organization*.

Clarity The quality of being fully understandable. In rhetoric this term is most often used in reference to style. Clarity in style is attained through precise and familiar language, conventional usage and word order in grammatical construction, and simplicity and directness in all the functions of composition and presentation. Because of the instability of listeners' *attention* speakers must seek to make all they say so clear that it will be instantaneously intelligible. For examples of especially luminous styles, see "The World of Jazz," pp. 67-76, and "The Minds of the Non-Western World," pp. 234-240. See also *Appropriateness, Liveliness*.

Classification, Definition by See *Definition*.

Cliché Any term or phrase that is trite or hackneyed. "Those immutable laws which down the corridors of Time have guided the destiny of man" is pure cliché. *Figures of speech* and *epigrams* are especially likely to become clichés after being so widely used that familiarity destroys the imagery or originality that first made them strikingly communicative. See "Science and Society," p. 82, par. 32, first sentence.

Climax A culmination or high point. In rhetoric the term usually refers to the point in a discourse at which the greatest force or impact is achieved. Although we usually think of a climax as coming late in an experience, there is reason to believe that this is not always desirable in a speech. Experimental studies and speeches themselves show that the point of greatest impact comes sometimes with the first main point of a speech. It is, in any case, impossible to say that the climax of a speech must necessarily appear near the conclusion. In "The Man with the Muck-Rake" the climax of the speech seems to come in pars. 12-13, p. 104; for a climax at the end of the speech, see "The Inner City—Our Shame," pp. 217-218, pars. 16-18, or "I Have a Dream," pp. 155-156, pars. 21-27. See also *Attention, Interest, Patterns of Organization*.

Coherence Literally, sticking together. In discourse, the quality of relevance—all parts being relevant to the *central idea* and to each other. Note how carefully the sentences and the main divisions are locked together in "Science, Technology, and World Development," pp. 83-87.

Common Ground Any belief or feeling about which speaker and listener have shared *interests* or *attitudes*. Whenever speakers can show that their knowledge, views, or values are the same as those of the people they address, they may expect *arguments* and *amplifications* based on these topics to be favorably received. See "Address to the Russian People," p. 242, pars. 9-10; "The City—A Cause for Statesmanship," p. 223, par. 41, "I know . . . this problem is"; "Rout the Forces of Hate," p. 158, pars. 13-20. See also *Adaptation, Appeal, Attention, Ethos, Identification, Persuasion, Suggestion, Syllogism*.

Communication An inclusive term which, broadly applied, may be used to describe virtually any kind of human or nonhuman interaction. Thus it may even be said that the appearance or manner of another individual "communicates" the sort of behavior that will be appropriate toward him, or that the parts of a machine "communicate" with one another. In recent years the word has acquired special signification in such fields as psycholinguistics, rhetoric, computer technology, etc. Communication theorists often visualize communication as the sequence of events in which a "source" of information "encodes" a "message," sends it through a "channel" to a "receiver" who "decodes" it, "interprets" it, and "responds" to his understanding of it. Viewed according to such a model of communication, speaking-listening relationships may be described thus: a speaker selects ideas, encodes them in verbal and gestural signals, transmits these through the channels of air and light waves to a listener who decodes the signals, interprets them, and responds to them—perhaps by feeding back his own coded message to the original speaker. There are a variety of "communication models"; their general purpose is to identify and order the events of communication so that these may be analyzed scientifically. See also *Rhetoric*.

Comparison See *Analogy, Figures of Speech*.

Concept A general notion or idea formed by associating details that seem to belong together and deriving from these associations an abstract generalization concerning the collective nature of the details. The term "man" represents a concept, for it designates no particular man nor class of men, but represents the sum of our abstract generalizations about any and all men. In "The American Scholar," pp. 39-40, pars. 5-7, Emerson tries to build an intelligible concept of "Man Thinking" by using as his starting point the more familiar and more general concept "Man." A *stereotype* is a concept that has become commonplace.

Concession The voluntary yielding of a disputable point for the sake of gaining a strategic advantage in an argument or in order to win a hearing from listeners who are hostile to the speaker or his proposal. In making concessions, the speaker must take care not to concede any of the major points upon which his case rests nor to concede so many minor points that its strength is impaired. See "The Challenge of Abundance," p. 199, pars. 16-17; "Rout the Forces of Hate," p. 158, pars. 13-14. See also *Common Ground, Yes Response*.

Conciliation In rhetoric, any of the several processes by which potential or actual hostility to ideas, language, or persons may be allayed. See *Appeal, Common Ground, Credibility, Motivation, Persuasion, Suggestion*. See especially "Rout the Forces of Hate," pp. 157-158, pars. 1-14.

Conciseness Compactness of expression. A speech is concise when, because of the precision of the wording, the meaning may be grasped as easily and quickly as possible. The concise speech is not necessarily a brief speech. The speaker wishing to speak briefly cuts down on his ideas and supporting material; the speaker wishing to speak concisely keeps all the ideas and supporting material he thinks necessary for his purpose but communicates them in wording that is as exact and pithy as he can make it. The following sentence fails to be concise because of its many useless words. "In the case of Abraham Lincoln we find that he had a marked tendency to enjoy stories that can best be described as having a humorous character." All it says is that Lincoln enjoyed humorous stories. Words that in one fashion or another mean the opposite of conciseness are wordiness, verbosity, redundancy, and tautology. Note the ultraconciseness in Urey's list of intellectual developments, "Science and Society," pp. 80-81, pars. 16-25; contrast the condensed but highly suggestive expression in "The

Writer's Duty," pp. 52-53. See also "On the Federal Constitution," pp. 272-276.

Conclusion The last of the three major divisions of a speech, and as such to be distinguished from the *introduction* and the *body*. The conclusion usually takes the form of a summary or reiteration of the principal ideas presented in the body, or of an appeal for belief or action based upon those ideas. It should (1) grow out of the body easily and naturally, (2) be relatively brief, (3) touch once again upon the principal interests and concerns of the listeners, and (4) bring the speech to a satisfying termination esthetically as well as logically. For a "summary" type of conclusion, see "Crime and Criminals," pp. 146-147, par. 36. For an example of an "appeal" conclusion, see "The Haven of the Defeated," p. 151, pars. 26-27. An emotionally moving conclusion growing out of a personal experience on the part of the speaker may be found in "Rout the Forces of Hate," p. 161, pars. 69-72. "Apathy" appropriately concludes with a quotation, p. 166, par. 22; "Culture and Communication," with an illustration, p. 25, pars. 40-42; "Newspapers of the U.S.A.—An Appraisal," with a prediction, p. 114, par. 74.

Concreteness Possessing the power to evoke sense impressions. Considered in absolute terms, concrete expressions evoke sense impressions (sight, hearing, touch, taste, smell) whereas abstract expressions do not. Considered in relative terms, concrete expressions are more specific than abstract terms and hence tend to evoke sense impressions to a higher degree. Notice how this works in the following series in which the words range from the general and abstract to the more specific and concrete thing: *vehicle—automobile—Buick—Buick hardtop—a white and gold Buick hardtop*. Abstractions are necessary for ideas and concepts, but concrete words suggest the world of actual experience. Both are necessary in the typical speech. The weakness in many speeches is that the speaker slights the concrete. For examples of concreteness, see "Address to the Russian People," p. 242, par. 9. Note also the concreteness in Zimmermann's speech, "Mingled Blood," pp. 98-100.

Conflict Actual or potential clash, opposition, antagonism. Conflicts of most sorts are interesting to humans; consequently, representations or even hints of conflict become a *factor of attention* and add to the probability that listeners will attend to the ideas. The language form called *antithesis* is interesting in part because it always expresses some degree of conflict. References to dangers, threats, and differences derive force from explicit or implicit conflict. "On the Federal Constitution," pp. 272-276, contains a number of such descriptions, narratives, and examples; see especially lines 10-14, 18-29, 76-94. Even the mention of "belligerent," "wary," and "suspicious" faculty members in "What Every Freshman Should Know," p. 36, par. 7, may make these people—and the speaker's real point—more interesting because opposition among students, faculty, and administration is suggested. The refutations of proofs of God's existence in "What Can We Prove About God?" pp. 188-189, pars. 3-9, present conflicts in ideas and therefore enhance the interest of the address.

Connectives See *Transition*.

Connotation A complex of associations brought to mind by a word. A connotation is distinct, therefore, from a denotation, which is the dictionary definition of a word, stripped of its emotional overtones. *The American College Dictionary* gives the same denotations for "sweat" and "perspire": to excrete watery fluid through the pores. But the connotations of the words are quite different. "Sweat" brings to mind such things as laborers, athletes, horses, and locker rooms. "Perspire," on the other hand, suggests more genteel persons, or at least more genteel activities: a hot night at a dance, a girl with a moist forehead, a man's dress shirt getting wet under the arm.

Connotations can be roughly divided into two classes: group connotations and individual connotations. The first are the connotations common to a large number of people because of shared experience. For example, "red" suggests danger or communism to many people; "green" suggests "go" or envy; "Cadillac" suggests wealth and refined living. Because of your unique experience, however, "red" may suggest to you alone a red sports car you smashed up the night after buying it. Obviously, speakers cannot capitalize on the individual connotations their listeners have for words, because they do not know what they are. But they can and do capitalize on group connotations. That is, if they want a favorable reaction to a man, they call him a "statesman" instead of a "politician," "firm" instead of "stubborn," "a public servant" instead of "a bureaucrat," "a man who is loyal to his friends" instead of "a tool of the interests that elected him." See "The City—A Cause for Statesmanship," p. 220, par. 7, ". . . the new low-income and minority ghettos"; par. 8, "metropolis"; p. 222, par. 27, "Half a building . . . through it"; "Press Conference," p. 249, par. 12, "monolithic"; "Pan-Africanism, the Communists and the West," p. 256, par. 7, "balkanisation . . . balkanised." Note also the extensive use of connotative words throughout "I Have a Dream," pp. 154-156.

Content A term normally used to designate the ideas of any discourse, as distinguished from their arrangement, style, or manner of presentation. The substance or proof in a communication.

Context, Definition by See *Definition*.

Contiguity Literally, the nearness of one thing to another. In rhetoric, the term normally refers to the tightness of relationships which ideas have to one another. Since listeners cannot hold specific statements in mind for very long, it becomes necessary for speakers to emphasize the closeness or contiguity of important relationships. Clear *patterns of organization, transitions,* and *summaries* are useful in stressing the contiguity of related ideas; see, for example, "The World of Jazz," p. 73, par. 32.

Contrast The placing of two incompatible ideas side by side in order to make them stand out in vivid opposition. See "The Philosophy of Social Justice Through Social Action," pp. 135-136, pars. 4-8; "Crime and Criminals, pp. 145-146, pars. 27-28; "The Novel and the Fairy Tale," pp. 54-55, pars. 4-5. See also *Antithesis*.

Conversational Quality Having the tone and spirit of an animated conversation as carried on among educated persons. It is generally regarded as being the opposite of an "oratorical" pattern of style or delivery.

Suggesting that a speech should have a conversational quality does not mean that it is to be worded and delivered in exactly the same manner as when one converses. Although good conversation usually has the desirable properties of directness, spontaneity, and informality, more often than not even the best conversation is marred by slovenly articulation, inadequate projection, imprecise word choice, awkward sentence structure, and the presence of colloquialisms and slang. Conversational quality, as the recommended spirit of good public speaking, does not include these undesirable qualities of conversation but emphasizes its desirable qualities to meet the demands of the more formal public situation.

Many of the elements that make for conversational quality are especially well exemplified in "The World of Jazz," pp. 67-76; "The Philosophy of Social Justice Through Social Action," pp. 135-139; and "Crime and Criminals," pp. 142-147.

Counter Words In *Writer's Guide and Index to English*, Porter G. Perrin defines counter words as ones "which also have more restricted precise senses but are used frequently as general terms of approval

or disapproval. . . . Their popularity is a matter of fashion and is related to slang, except that they are ordinary English words and lack the element of surprise that good slang has. . . . *fabulous, definitely, mixed-up* have had such currency. In ordinary speech *colossal, cute, fine, fix, grand, lousy, lovely, nice, gorgeous, poor* are samples, and in more educated circles words like *adjusted, creative, dynamic, structure, vital, challenge, charismatic,* and often epithets like *red, radical, conservative, reactionary* are used as vague expressions of like or dislike without regard to more exact meaning."[1]

Creativity See *Originality*.

Credibility Inherent probability or likelihood. The power of an assertion to win acceptance in its own right and prior to the introduction of any evidence or argument designed to support it.

An assertion may possess credibility because (1) it appears, to the best of the listeners' knowledge, reasonable or true to fact; (2) it is made by a person or a group of persons whose judgment and integrity the listeners respect; (3) the listeners wish to believe it since it contributes to their happiness or security, or flatters their ego, or accords with their predispositions and prejudices.

A speaker should carefully gauge the probable degree of credibility an assertion will have for his listeners, and stand ready to introduce proof in support of any statement that does not seem likely to win ready acceptance in and of itself. See also *Probability*.

Cumulation A massing of specific details in an effort to clarify a complex matter, or a heaping up of many independent proofs to accumulate an overwhelming preponderance of evidence in favor of a disputable *proposition*.

Cumulation as a technique for winning assent by "piling on" a preponderance of independent proofs aims at a variety or multiplicity of support, and is to be distinguished from so-called "straight-line" reasoning, in which a speaker advances a single, carefully drawn argument to show that a certain conclusion must inevitably follow from admitted facts. A typical use of cumulation in argument is found in "Address to the Russian People," p. 244, pars. 28-32. Compare "The Minds of the Non-Western World," p. 239, par. 28. See also *Cause to Effect, Deduction, Induction*.

Deduction The process of reasoning from two established or admitted propositions to a conclusion. For example, one may deduce that since virtually all humans have some form of spoken language, the people of a little-known Eskimo tribe probably have such a language. If this kind of reasoning is to seem reliable to those who hear it, at least two conditions must be met: (1) the audience must agree that virtually all humans do have some spoken language, and (2) they must accept the tribe in question as one that consists of humans. The full statement of a deduction is called a *syllogism*. Deductions may use premises of various types. In popular speech or writing the materials of deductive reasoning are usually only probably true, and they are generally so familiar to the audience that a part of the syllogistic form may be omitted without causing confusion. The illustration of a deduction given in the second sentence of this definition is of the abbreviated type. See *Syllogism* for alternative forms of deduction. See "The Price of Excellence," p. 33, par. 30; "In Defense of Abstract Art," p. 64, par. 12; "Science and Spiritual Values," p. 93, par. 28, "As a conceptual . . . facts of human history"; "Address to the Russian People," p. 245, pars. 49-53. See also *Inclusion-Exclusion, Induction, Logic*.

---

[1] *Writer's Guide and Index to English*, Fourth Edition (Chicago, 1965) p. 565.

Definition A clarification of the meaning of an unusual word or phrase, or an explanation of the sense in which a term will be employed. Because communication cannot take place unless language is meaningful, the framing of clear and precise definitions may be an essential part of a speaker's task.

Common methods of definition employed by speakers include:

Definition by classification. Explaining the term to be defined by assigning it to a similar group of items or by dividing it into its natural subgroups. ("Mankind may be defined as consisting of all males and females of the human species.") See "Changing Concepts of Public Service," p. 208, par. 4.

Definition by context. Using the term in such a way that the sentence or passage makes its meaning clear. ("He who is *impetuous* will live to rue his hasty actions.")

Definition by etymology. Explaining the derivation of a term. ("*Propeller* comes from the Latin *pro* meaning 'forward, and *pellere*, which means 'to drive.' Therefore a *propeller* is something that drives a movable object forward.")

Definition by genus and differentum. Putting the term to be defined into a genus or class and then differentiating it from other things in that class. ("Democracy is that form of government [genus] in which sovereignty resides not in a single man or class but in the people as a whole [differentum].")

Definition by negation. Making clear what a term does not mean. ("Socialists, who believe in public ownership of the major means of production, are not to be confused with Communists, who believe in the common ownership of all goods.") See "Science and Spiritual Values," p. 90, par. 7, "The problem . . . by human action"; "The Scarcity of Ideas," p. 203, par. 24; "The Minds of the Non-Western World," p. 240, par. 34.

Definition by synonym. Supplying a word closely related in meaning to the term being defined. ("A campanile, or bell tower.")

Stipulative definition. A definition more or less arbitrarily adopted by a speaker in order to develop a particular line of explanation or argument. ("For purposes of this discussion, let us define 'inflation' as that state of affairs in which too many dollars are chasing too few goods.") See the definition of "speech" in "Speech as a Liberal Study," p. 3, par. 3; "The Challenge of Abundance," p. 197, par. 7. See also "The Minds of the Non-Western World," p. 235, pars. 5-7; "What Can We Prove About God?" p. 187, par. 2.

Deliberative Speaking Speaking concerned with the formulation of public policy—the selection or rejection of courses of common action to be followed by a community, state, or nation. Characteristically persuasive in nature, oriented toward the future rather than the past, and centering in considerations of cost, feasibility, moral obligation, and the like.

Deliberative speaking is to be distinguished from *forensic speaking*, which deals with the justice or injustice of past actions; from informative speaking, which conveys knowledge or gives instructions; and from *epideictic speaking*, which is essentially "occasional" or ceremonial in nature. See "On the Federal Constitution," pp. 270-276, for critical comment on the deliberative nature of this speech.

Demonstration Full or apodictic proof, as contrasted to the contingent or probable proofs normally found in discussions of human affairs. The proof of a theorem in geometry would be called a demonstration by almost everyone. The kind of proof of which Huxley speaks in "The Method of Scientific Investigation," pp. 264-269, could more reasonably be called demonstration than could the proofs Jonathan Smith adduces in "On the Federal Constitution," pp. 272-276. Smith's "proofs of probability" cannot approach Huxley's proofs in reliability because the conditions and forces Smith must reason about are less predictable.

Denotation The dictionary or scientific definition of a word. See *Connotation.*

Description A word picture of a person, scene, event, object, situation, or feeling; a systematic enumeration of the essential qualities of a thing in an effort to make listeners understand how it looks, feels, tastes, smells, or sounds.

In order to convey a picture accurately through language, a speaker must (1) mention crucial rather than trivial details; (2) select words that represent these details precisely, and that can be understood easily by the audience; (3) order the selected details into a systematic pattern (space order, time order, etc.); and (4) observe the traditional requirements of coherence and emphasis. See "Mingled Blood," p. 99, pars. 10-11; "The Haven of the Defeated," p. 149, par. 6; pp. 149-150, pars. 9-11. See also *Coherence, Emphasis, Imagery, Narrative.*

Dialectic Originally, a formal method of philosophical investigation and/or debate of which Plato's dialogues are the best extant examples. In modern usage somewhat broader meanings are sometimes assigned to the term. These meanings include: reasoned conversation, argumentation, the reasoning processes that precede communication, logic.

Diction Style as achieved through word choice or simply words themselves. A second meaning, common when speech is being discussed, is: the distinctness with which sounds are enunciated. See *Articulation.*

Didactic Literally, instructive. Stating a conclusion and then supporting it by evidence or reasoning is called "didactic organization" by some writers on rhetoric. Others call any pattern of organization didactic if informative or motivational materials precede statement of conclusions.

Dilemma An argument that poses two equally undesirable alternatives, one of which must, as a practical matter, be selected. ("If you always speak the truth, men will despise you; if you do not, the Gods will despise you.")

The dilemma is frequently used by speakers as a "special method of *refutation*" to show that a policy advocated by an opponent can have only two results, either of which would be undesirable. ("If, as Mr. Jones proposes, we reduce our present air strength, either we shall have to double or triple appropriations for our already expensive rocket development program, or we shall be entirely without means of retaliation in case we are attacked.")

If a dilemma is to have validity as an argument the alternatives to which it points must (1) follow as necessary effects of the policy proposed, (2) be all-inclusive, and (3) be mutually exclusive. Occasionally, speakers employ trilemmas. These are like dilemmas in all respects except that they proffer three choices instead of two. See "Pan-Africanism, the Communists and the West," pp. 255-256, pars. 2-6. See also *Causal Reasoning.*

Direct Discourse Discourse in which the speech or writing of another person is quoted exactly. It is to be distinguished, therefore, from indirect discourse and paraphrase. Indirect discourse is discourse in which the phrasing of another is imbedded in the speaker's sentence with such adjustments as are necessary to maintain coherence. Paraphrase is a free rendering of the discourse of another.

Direct discourse (in quotation marks). Alexander Pope wrote: "To err is human; to forgive divine." See "Social Morality," p. 177, par. 1; "Apathy," pp. 165-166, pars. 1, 5, 7, 19; "The Minds of the Non-Western World," pp. 235, 237, 239-240, pars. 6, 14-15, 33.

Indirect discourse. Alexander Pope once wrote that to err is human, to forgive divine. See "Moppet Manipulation," p. 124, par. 9, "Dr. Frances . . . to the store."

Paraphrase. To make mistakes is a consequence of our humanity, but to forgive mistakes is a sign of our divinity. See "The Man with the Muck-Rake," p. 102, par. 2.

Directness Sometimes referred to as "audience contact." That quality in speech which causes a hearer to believe that the speaker is aware of his presence and is earnestly attempting to communicate with him. Directness has both "physical" and "mental" components. The speaker who habitually gazes at the floor or ceiling is physically indirect; the speaker who adopts an exhibitory oratorical manner or who appears to be immersed in his own thoughts erects mental barriers between himself and his auditors.

Discussion This term has both general and technical meanings. In general use it may refer to any systematic or even casual conversation. Sometimes everything said on a matter, whatever the medium of expression, is called discussion. Writers on oral communication usually use the term in one of two more restricted senses: (1) to designate the *body* of a speech—that which is neither *introduction* nor *conclusion*; (2) to designate some form of relatively systematic oral communication dealing more or less reflectively with a specific subject and participated in by two or more people. An example of discussion in this second sense is "Movies and Censorship," pp. 127-129.

Division See *Analysis, Partitioning, Patterns of Organization.*

Drive Persistent goal-directed behavior, arising from an internal stimulus and terminating when the desired goal is achieved. Often referred to as a "basic wish" or "motive."

Most psychologists classify drives as "primary" or "secondary." Primary drives (hunger, thirst, etc.) arise out of recognized physiological needs; secondary drives (desire for ego satisfaction, security, property, etc.) are socially or environmentally produced. Authors of textbooks on public speaking list "drives" in many different ways, some recognizing only four or five, and others cataloging as many as thirty. Among the drives most commonly named, however, are health and personal well-being, self-advancement, security of property and possessions sex, and ease and personal enjoyment. These also are probably the drives most frequently invoked in speeches to persuade, stimulate, or actuate.

When a public speaker tries to make use of a drive or motive he says in effect, "Do as I recommend, and you will be secure or rich or happy or healthy or will attain a higher status." "Images of the Consumer's Changing Mind on and off Madison Avenue," pp. 115-121, sheds much light on this subject. See also *Appeal, Motivation.*

e

Effect to Cause, Argument from That form of argument in which the speaker first points to some result or consequence and then undertakes to show the cause that produced it. The speech "Apathy," pp. 164-166, illustrates how the entire argument of a speech may be organized in this manner. For individual effect-to-cause arguments see "Crime and Criminals," pp. 143-144, pars. 14-15; "The Haven of the Defeated," p. 150, par. 14. See also *Causal Relationship, Cause to Effect, Patterns of Organization.*

Elimination See *Patterns of Organization.*

Emotion Very loosely, any "feeling." More precisely, an emotion is any response of such strength that it is accompanied by physiological changes such as changes in pulse rate, breathing rate, perspiration, etc. Emotions, understood in this sense, not only change our biological processes (making possible "lie-detecting" instruments), but they also incline us toward more complex behaviors such as sobbing, wringing the hands, running, thinking, speaking. Ideas and even single words can be emotion-producing stimuli; the emotions they produce within us may cause us to seek relief through fearful, angry, affectionate, thoughtful, or other kinds of behavior that relieve the psychological tensions produced by what we hear. When this happens, it is sometimes said that what we heard "appealed" to fear, or to hate, or to love, or to reason. The speaker's business, then, is to try to control the emotional responses of his listeners, for, as Aristotle insisted, an important part of persuasion "is effected through the audience, when they are brought by the speech into a state of emotion; . . . we give very different decisions under the sway of pain or joy, and liking or hatred." See also *Appeal, Attitude, Common Ground, Connotation, Drive, Humor, Identification, Motivation, Persuasion, Proof.*

Empathy This psychological term refers to the processes by which we enter mentally into the feeling or spirit exhibited by someone or something other than ourselves. Leaning forward when we watch a runner approach the finish line may be a symptom of our empathy with the runner; sharing a speaker's indignation, or feeling bored because he appears bored, are empathic responses common among listeners. One may empathize with a character in a well told narrative or with persons or things vividly described, as well as with persons and things directly observed. Note the role of empathy in "Mingled Blood," pp. 98-100, or "The Inner City—Our Shame," pp. 216-218.

Emphasis Forcefulness; the means by which anything is made to stand out or to seize the *attention.* Modern research suggests that among the most effective ways to achieve emphasis in speaking are: (1) to give an idea the first position in the *body* of the speech; (2) to repeat an idea three or four times, preferably at intervals, during the speech; (3) to call special attention to an idea, as by saying, "This is the point I especially want you to remember"; (4) to give a larger portion of one's time to one idea than to others. Since any change tends to seize the attention, ideas may also be emphasized if they are delivered with gestures, pauses, or other behaviors even slightly out of the ordinary. Any method of emphasis, of course, can become boring or absurd if used too often; hence, there must be *variety* even in methods of emphasis. "Address to the Russian People," p. 244, pars. 29-33, ". . . rejected by the USSR," illustrates emphasis by repetition. Note also the emphasis gained by the repetition of words and phrases in "I Have a Dream," pp. 154-156. See also *Climax, Force, Impressiveness, Patterns of Organization, Repetition, Rhythm, Vividness.*

Ends of Speaking The aims or general purposes for which men speak, called by some writers "the rhetorical purposes." Most writers classify the ends of speaking according to the kinds of audience response a speaker wishes to elicit; thus, one finds the ends of speaking divided in such ways as these: to please, to inform, and to move; to inform, to convince, to persuade, and to entertain; to inform, to stimulate, to actuate, and to entertain; or to report, to inquire, to persuade, and to evoke. Any of these classifications can be useful if it reminds the speaker that he must make some single aim, and only one, dominate each speech.

Enthymeme See *Syllogism*

Epanorthosis The sudden retraction or cancelling of what one already has said. The effect may be humorous or sarcastic: "He was clearheaded about life. Wealth was his goal." Most often, in speaking, the retraction is simply introduced to correct a previous inaccuracy: see "Movies and Censorship," p. 129, par. 48.

Epideictic Speaking Literally, to show forth; display. The name traditionally given to speaking done on commemorative or patriotic occasions (at dedications and commencement exercises; on Memorial Day, the Fourth of July, etc.), and including speeches of tribute or eulogy. As generally used today, the term "epideictic" also refers to the more specialized "forms" of public address—speeches of presentation, acceptance, welcome, and the like. See also *Deliberative Speaking, Forensic Speaking, Occasional Speaking.*

Epigram A terse, witty statement. An epigram can be especially useful in pinning down a point because its ingenuity attracts attention and its brevity makes it easily remembered. The following are two examples from Mark Twain:

"The man who is a pessimist before forty-eight knows too much; if he is an optimist after it, he knows too little."

"Let us so live that when we come to die even the undertaker will be sorry."

See "The Philosophy of Social Justice Through Social Action," p. 138, par. 28, ". . . if they are paternalistic, I am a father." Epigrams in Emerson's "The American Scholar," pp. 39-47, can be numbered by the score. See also *Slogan.*

Ethos The *proof* or persuasiveness that comes from the source of a communication. This influence may spring from the reputation of a speaker or the group he is known to represent; it will always grow or shrivel, depending on his behavior, as he appears before his audience. Aristotle said of these influences, "We might almost affirm that ethos is the most potent of all the means of persuasion." Modern research demonstrates that he was right, at least concerning immediate responses to a communication. Just how "ethical proofs" affect our delayed responses to things said is not yet understood in psychology or rhetoric. The fact of greatest importance to the speaker is that all his behaviors—selection of ideas, their arrangement, their expression in language, and their delivery—inevitably add to or detract from the ethical reinforcement he, himself, gives to his message. See also *Attitude, Authority, Credibility, Identification, Motivation, Persuasion, Suggestion.*

Etymology See *Definition.*

Euphemism A mild or prestigious term substituted for one considered unpleasantly direct. We live in a world of euphemisms: "pass away" for "die," "powder room" for "women's toilet," "lower level" for "basement," "mortician" for "undertaker," and so on. Euphemisms tend to draw a veil over reality. They should be strenuously avoided unless the more direct word is likely to give pain to a listener or unless an effect such as *irony* or *understatement* is deliberately sought. See "The Inner City—Our Shame," p. 216, par. 3, "uncles."

Euphony Agreeableness to the ear, especially of speech sounds uttered in combination. One may suppose Adlai Stevenson strove for some degree of euphony in choosing the words "Thus *will* we *build* and rebuild . . ." and "*renew* and *rekindle* our faith in ourselves. . . ." "The City—A Cause for Statesmanship," p. 224, par. 51.

Evidence Those matters of *fact* and *opinion* that underlie and support argument; the data upon which a speaker bases his *proof* of a contention.

As employed in speeches, evidence usually takes one of three forms: *statistics,* quotations from *authorities,* or *examples.* To be of value in proof, evidence must be (1) recent, (2) sufficient in quantity, (3) germane to the point to be established, and (4) derived from a reliable source. Moreover, a speaker has the moral obligation to report fully and fairly the evidence upon which his argument rests. "The City—A Cause for Statesmanship," pp. 221-222, par. 26, "Last week . . . can do this job," illustrates use of statistical evidence

within an example that rests on the authority of "a friend." See also *Argument, Supporting Material.*

Example An instance or sample specimen selected from a larger group of items of the same general class. A leaf may be held up as an example of foliage, or the work of a mechanical engineer may be given as an example of what engineers do. Examples of this sort clarify general ideas and are especially useful in *exposition.* Some writers use the term "illustration" for such examples to distinguish them from examples used as *proof.* A single example usually forms a weak proof; audiences are more impressed by several examples than by only one, no matter how representative the single example is shown to be. Only the naïve believe that the first swallow to arrive proves that summer has also come. The rhetorical effectiveness of examples lies primarily in their concreteness. "Apathy," pp. 164-166, and "What Can We Prove About God?" pp. 187-189, are speeches especially replete with examples. See also "Crime and Criminals," pp. 142-143, pars. 5-8; pp. 144-145, pars. 21-24; and "The Scarcity of Ideas," p. 202, pars. 15-16; "The Minds of the Non-Western World," pp. 235-236, 238-239, pars. 6, 8, 25; "Culture and Communication," pp. 22-23, pars. 20-24.

Explanation See *Exposition.*

Exploration In rhetoric, discourse having inquiry rather than exposition, persuasion, or entertainment as its primary purpose. Exploratory speaking is also sometimes called "speaking to induce inquiry." For the characteristic methods of this kind of speaking, see *Reflective Thinking.*

Exposition The term applied to a class of rhetorical processes and also to the compositions produced by these processes. Expository processes show the nature or character of something by revealing how its parts are related to each other, how the parts form the whole, how a thing is produced or evolves through a series of interrelated stages, etc. A composition, written or oral, in which the chief object is to inform others by means of these processes is also called an exposition. *Clarity* is the foremost requirement in successful exposition; the special forms of support most commonly used to attain clarity in exposition are comparison, *definition, example, statistics,* and visual aids (such as graphs, charts, pictures, and the like). "The World of Jazz," p. 67-76, is an outstanding expository speech using virtually all the resources available to the informative speaker. See also "The Novel and the Fairy Tale," pp. 54-67. In "Ethics in International Relations Today," pp. 229-232, quotations, examples, and *analogies* are used as means of exposition. See also "The Minds of the Non-Western World," pp. 237-238, pars. 20-23. The entire text of "Press Conference," pp. 248-254, may be regarded as an extended exposition, as may the text of "Pan-Africanism, the Communists and the West," pp. 255-263. See *Amplification, Analogy, Causal Relationship, Central Idea, Contiguity, Patterns of Organization.*

Extemporaneous Speaking That mode of speech composition and delivery in which the speech is planned in detail but not committed to memory or delivered from a manuscript. Extemporaneous speakers normally memorize *patterns of organization* and sometimes crucial *transitions* and *summaries.* Their primary concern in composition and rehearsal is to fix the sequence of ideas firmly in mind. They rehearse their speeches if possible, not to learn them word by word but to gain full command over the speech as outlined and to experiment with alternative ways of expressing ideas in language. The advantage of extemporaneous speaking over manuscript or memorized speaking is that the extemporaneous speaker retains a flexibility which will allow him to adapt to the demands of audience and occasion during the presentation of his speech. Contrast with *Impromptu Speaking.*

Fable A short tale designed to teach a moral. Frequently it uses animals or inanimate objects as characters. Some of the best known are such fables of Aesop as "The Tortoise and the Hare" and "The Fox and the Grapes." Fables are useful in a speech to draw attention to moral considerations. Their rather childlike simplicity makes them easy to follow and to remember. Compare with *Parable*.

Fact An item of knowledge; something known with reasonable certainty. A fact is capable of objective confirmation and so is to be distinguished from *opinion*. See *Evidence*. Compare with *Presumption*, *Opinion*.

Factors of Attention Special characteristics or qualities of discourse that tend to enhance its interest value and hence to capture the spontaneous attention of listeners. Generally, attention factors include such qualities as *activity*, conflict, novelty, primacy, proximity, and recency. Thus a speaker who gives activity and movement to his ideas, or who brings ideas into *conflict*, or who deals with novel matters or treats old matters in a new way, or who selects a subject close to the interests of his audience or recent in time, will, as a general rule, hold attention better than one whose ideas are static, or hackneyed, or not immediately related to the concerns of his listeners. See "Address to the Russian People," pp. 244-245, pars. 41-44, in which the speaker uses the listeners' high interest in things American as an attention factor.

Fallacies Errors in reasoning; violations, usually unintentional, of the rules of valid inference. Not to be confused with *stratagems*, tricks of argument consciously employed to hide the absence or insufficiency of proof. See *Inference*.

Feedback A term borrowed from electronic engineering and ordinarily used in speech to refer to any signals of audience response which the speaker can detect. See also *Communication*, *Empathy*, *Identification*, *Yes Response*.

Figures of Speech Expressions which make their point not literally and directly but in terms of something else. Consider these two sentences: *She's a very attractive girl* and *She's a doll*. They both mean the same thing, but in the first the words all carry their literal, dictionary meaning. In the second "doll" does not have its literal meaning of a toy puppet but a figurative meaning which colorfully suggests the girl's attractiveness. As this example suggests, figures of speech are useful because they can be vivid and memorable and because they often catch the quality of the object or action much more dramatically and economically than a literal statement can. They have to be used with some caution, however, because (a) if too many of them are used, they call attention to themselves and make a speech seem artificially ornamented, and (b) if they are not reasonably original, they give the speech a dull, hackneyed flavor. (See *Cliché*). The most common figures of speech are these:

Simile. A stated comparison between things which, except for a particular quality, are essentially dissimilar. Usually a simile is introduced by *like* or *as*. *He kept after me just as if he were a badger. He kept after me like a badger.* See "What Is Truth?" p. 183, par. 22, "Suddenly, true reality . . . finally disappears"; "I Have a Dream," p. 155, par. 9; "Coatesville," p. 164, par. 5.

Metaphor. An implied comparison between two essentially dissimilar things. In a metaphor, *like* and *as* are omitted. *The man is a badger if ever I saw one. He badgered me incessantly.* A mixed metaphor is a silly combination of two or more metaphors. *Let's set our helm and stay on this course until we reach the mountain peak of success.* See "What Is Truth?" p. 183, par. 22, "New darknesses . . . by the truth"; "I Have a Dream," p. 154, pars. 2-7, passim; "Newspapers of the U.S.A.—An Appraisal," pp. 113-114, pars. 69, 73; "Rout the Forces of Hate," pp. 160, 161, pars. 55, 68.

Personification. The attribution of human characteristics to animals or inanimate objects. *When a badger is sitting still, thinking about its sins, that's the time to be wary of it.* See "What Is Truth?" p. 183, par. 22, "Or you may be . . . acceptance of yourself"; "The City—A Cause for Statesmanship," p. 223, par. 46, "of everlasting . . . decay," and par. 47, "a Balkanized metropolis." See also *Allegory*, *Irony*, *Overstatement*, *Understatement*.

Force Energy or vigor of expression and, as such, a quality of style, as well as of delivery. In delivery a forceful manner results from appropriate arm and head gestures, alert muscle tension, animated facial expression, a faster than average speaking rate, and a volume adjusted to the meaning and mood of the material being presented. Forcefulness in style depends primarily upon the compelling quality of the speaker's ideas, but it may be enhanced if he employs many concrete words, uses short declarative sentences, casts selected passages into the active voice, omits unnecessary connectives, and uses with restraint and judgment a few epithets, *metaphors*, hyperboles, and *rhetorical questions*.

Contrary to the opinion sometimes held, force in delivery is not attained simply by shouting, nor does force in style result from exaggeration or bombast or from the uncontrolled use of exclamations and other strong figures. Rather, forcefulness springs from compelling ideas presented in an earnest and animated manner. Pars. 22-25 of John F. Kennedy's "Inaugural Address," p. 227, achieve force through expressing sweeping ideas in imagistic language framed in *parallel constructions* often producing *antitheses*. "Address to the Russian People," p. 245, pars. 51-54, illustrates how short, balanced statements in series produce forcefulness.

Forensic Speaking A term having two common but different meanings. In the loosest sense, forensic speaking or forensics may mean almost any kind of debate under formal rules. Thus used the term may refer to courtroom speaking, to highly organized parliamentary debate, to school debate, or even to oratory under contest rules.

The older and more exact use of the term refers only to the kind of speaking in which the speaker tries to prove that an accepted rule or code has or has not been broken sometime in the past. Accusing and defending, pleading the justice or injustice of past acts, are the commonest functions of such speaking; courtrooms, hearing rooms, and the like are the places where forensic speaking is most frequently heard. This meaning of the term goes back at least to the time of Aristotle and is the meaning still used in the study of rhetoric. Forensic speaking, in this sense, differs from *deliberative* and *epideictic speaking* in both subject and aim, for the forensic speech treats chiefly past events and "laws," with the object of securing a judgment of "right" or "wrong."

Forms of Discourse See *Deliberative Speaking*, *Discussion*, *Epideictic Speaking*, *Exploration*, *Exposition*, *Forensic Speaking*.

Generalization A statement about a group or class rather than about a particular member of the group or class. ("People seem to care less about the arms race than they used to." "European schools have high academic standards.") See "Science and Society," pp. 78-79, par. 2. See *Induction*.

Genus and Differentum, Definition by See *Definition*.

Gestures Easily discernible movements of the arms, head, shoulders, and torso. Although gestures play an important role in clarifying and reinforcing ideas presented orally, they should not be imposed upon a speech artificially. Instead, they should be natural and should spring from an inner impulse to communicate effectively. See also *Activity*.

Good Will, Speech of A speech designed to deepen the listeners' appreciation of some profession, organization, or institution, thus unobtrusively securing their support for it.

h

Humor Most broadly conceived, anything that is amusing. Chiefly, humor arises from a sudden perception of the incongruous, provided the perception does not bring a sense of pain. Any joke, therefore, is simply a sudden break in the listener's pattern of expectancy. He expects one thing and gets something quite incongruous to his expectation. Note how this works in an old wheeze used by Freud: Two men met near a European municipal bathing establishment. "Have you taken a bath?" asked one. "Why?" replied the other. "Is one missing?"

The basic uses of humor in speech are these: to entertain, to help explain a point, to affect the listener's thinking or conduct. Inexperienced speakers often find their humor gets no response from the audience. Most frequently the reason is that it has too little bearing on the subject and hence seems forced or that it has been introduced too formally. The casual touch is best in handling humor. See "The Philosophy of Social Justice Through Social Action," p. 135, pars. 2-3. See also *Irony, Overstatement, Satire, Understatement*.

Hypothetical Illustration or Example An imaginary or fictitious illustration or example, as distinguished from a factual or actual illustration or example. See "The Method of Scientific Investigation," pp. 267-268, pars. 8-11, for an extended hypothetical illustration. See *Example*.

i

Identification Literally, the act of showing that one thing is the same as another; hence, in rhetoric the term usually applies to any process by which listeners or readers are brought to see that their interests, goals, or judgments are shared by a speaker or writer. Some writers use the term "identification" as a synonym for *common ground*. "I Have a Dream," pp. 154-156, permits an interesting study of ways a speaker may shift his identification relative to immediate and remote listeners. Compare the ways in which the speaker identifies with the Negro people in pars. 2-6, p. 154; pars. 7-8, pp. 154-155; pars. 9-27, pp. 155-156.

Illustration See *Example, Hypothetical Illustration or Example*.

Imagery The sensory details of a speech. Imagery includes all specific sensations suggested by a speech, i.e., those of sight, sound, touch, taste, and feeling. These sensations can be suggested either literally or figuratively. Images are useful rhetorically because they inevitably carry emotional overtones and hence help to affect the listener's feelings and attitudes. A speaker arguing for slum clearance, for example, might profitably attempt to evoke in the minds of his audience images of the sights, sounds, and odors characteristic of the local slum. These might well have more rhetorical effect than any amount of well-knit argument. See "The Haven of the Defeated," p. 149, par. 6; "The Inner City—Our Shame," p. 216, par. 3; "Coatesville," p. 163, par. 2.

Implication A form of argument (or series of arguments) in which the writer or speaker offers *proofs* without emphasizing the propositions they support. A speaker argues by implication if, without urging that we do the same, he tells us of a community that reduced its juvenile delinquency problem when a group of college students volunteered to assist in its youth centers. Entire speeches and essays are sometimes organized in this way; for example, a speaker wishing to stir enthusiasm for better schools may do so by presenting an *exposition* of conditions in the existing schools. In "Address to the Russian People," p. 246, par. 59 is an indirect or implicative argument about what is the wisest Soviet policy; "The Inner City—Our Shame," pp. 216-218, is also developed chiefly by implication. See also *Amplification, Appeal, Argument, Patterns of Organization, Persuasion, Suggestion*.

Impressiveness That quality of a speech, or of some passage within a speech, which causes it to have a deep and lasting influence upon the listener. Impressiveness does not derive from pompousness or oratorical display, but from significant ideas expressed in a manner appropriate to the topic, the audience, and the occasion. Style or delivery that is exhibitory or highly dramatic may render ideas momentarily striking, but it seldom makes them permanently impressive.

Impromptu Speaking Speaking with little or no preparation. Typically, the impromptu speaker prepares his thoughts and selects his language just before and during his speech. Contrast with *Extemporaneous Speaking*.

Impropriety An incorrect use of a word; a violation of standard practice, such as "We *suspicioned* that his motives were not of the best." See *Barbarism, Vulgarism*.

Inclusion-Exclusion In logical analysis two or more statements may be connected logically if the meaning of one entails the meaning of the other in such a way as to suggest a third meaning. The shared meaning need not encompass all the meaning of either statement; its extensiveness is what distinguishes what is shared (included) from what is not shared (excluded) in the relationship of the statements. The first two sentences of par. 6, "Address to the Congress," p. 279, show General MacArthur defining his subject by this process: identifying the inclusive-exclusive relationships of Asiatic defense and world defense. See *Deduction, Syllogism*.

Induction The process of reasoning from specific cases. The reasoning may be from one instance to another, as in *analogy*, or from a number of instances to a general conclusion. The reliability of all such reasoning depends on the representativeness of the cases used and the accuracy of one's information about them. Reliability in inductions is difficult to obtain because completely analogous instances are rare and because generalizations always must be inferred from a selected sample of known instances. The following example illustrates three degrees of reliability in generalizations based on the same data. A study of eight clothing and shoe factories shows all individual workers aged fifty-five to sixty are more productive than the average of the best and fastest group of young workers. From this we may induce that workers aged fifty-five to sixty are more productive than any similar group of young workers in these eight factories. This induction is highly reliable if the facts were correctly gathered. If we reason that in all clothing and shoe factories workers aged fifty-five to sixty are likely to be more productive than young workers, our induction will be fairly reliable if our eight factories are representative of the clothing and shoe production industries. To reason that elderly men make better workers than young men in all factories would be entirely unjustified, for there is no reason to think that our sample is representative of all workers and all factories. In offering inductions as *proofs* speakers must take special pains to satisfy their audiences that (1) the reasoning rests on truly representative cases, (2) the facts about the cases were accurately gathered, and (3) the conclusions offered claim no more than the sample will justify. See "Address to the Russian People," p. 244, pars. 28-33; "The City—A Cause for Statesmanship," p. 221, par. 24. See also *Deduction*, *Logic*.

Inference The process of reasoning by which a conclusion is drawn from facts or evidence. See *Analogy as Argument*, *Causal Relationship*, *Deduction*, *Demonstration*, *Inclusion-Exclusion*, *Induction*, *Reflective Thinking*, *Sign*, *Argument from Syllogism*.

Information, Informative See *Evidence*, *Exposition*, *Fact*.

Inquiry See *Discussion*, *Ends of Speaking*, *Exploration*, *Patterns of Organization*.

Interest The focusing of one's attention. Whatever seems even momentarily important or pleasing arouses us—it attracts our attention because it interests us. No feature of speaking is ever without some positive or negative influence upon the listeners' interest in the whole message; hence every speaker should incorporate into his presentation all relevant qualities that arouse and sustain interest. Among the most important of these qualities are those that can be introduced through astute and sensitive composition; a number of such resources are identified above as factors of attention. See also *Activity*, *Common Ground*, *Imagery*, *Motivation*, *Variety*.

Intonation The movement of the voice up and down the scale while speaking. Although it is possible for a speaker to have an exaggerated or artificial melodic pattern, the more common fault is vocal monotony resulting from a narrow pitch range. The melody of speech should not be planned, but like *gestures* and *movement*, should be a natural response springing from an earnest desire to communicate.

Introduction The first of the three major divisions of a speech, the other two being the *body* and the *conclusion*. The purpose of the introduction is to catch the *attention* of the listeners, arouse their interest in the subject under discussion, and prepare them to understand and appreciate the ideas that will be set forth in the body of the address.

An introduction which performs these functions well usually consists of highly concrete material, is striking without being cheap or sensational, and is closely related to the body of the speech in thought and mood. Common methods of developing the introduction include telling a story (serious or humorous), making a startling statement, asking a question or a series of questions, reading a quotation, or making a reference to the subject, audience, place, or occasion. Common faults of introductions are excessive length, abstractness in language or ideas, effusiveness, feigned sincerity, and the absence of an adequate *transition* into the body of the speech. The introduction to "Apathy," pp. 164-165, pars. 1-3, illustrates a typical pattern for introducing a subject: a startling incident, deftly made more striking by "editorial comment," catches attention; the incident is related to the general subject and (rather weakly) to the audience; the subject is then defined, and the speaker's central idea and immediate purpose are stated.

A low-keyed but interesting introduction is exemplified by the first paragraphs of "The Novel and the Fairy Tale," p. 54. The introduction to "Rout the Forces of Hate," pp. 157-158, combines references to the audience and occasion with the indirect or conciliatory development appropriate for a speech to a hostile audience. For an introduction in the form of a personal greeting, see "The Minds of the Non-Western World," pp. 234-235, pars. 1-3; compare "Excellence in Teaching," p. 48, par. 1. "Pan-Africanism, the Communists and the West" opens with a direct reference to the subject, p. 255, par. 1; "Culture and Communication" with a story or anecdote, pp. 20-21, pars. 1-5.

Irony A figure of speech in which for the purpose of derision, however slight, the literal meaning is something other than the intended meaning. Often an ironic statement is the opposite of what is intended. "Let's spend more and more money on athletics so that American education can get better and better." It may, however, simply involve some obvious disparity or *understatement*. Any kind of material can be treated ironically: the light and playful, the deadly serious. The special value of irony is that its indirect approach calls attention to the material and, when ingeniously handled, provides intellectual pleasure at the same time that it persuades rhetorically. Socratic irony is irony in which the speaker pretends to be more naïve or ignorant than he really is. See "The Scarcity of Ideas," pp. 201-202, par. 9. See also *Sarcasm*.

Jargon The stylistic fault of using language peculiar to a particular class, sect, trade, or profession when more generally understood terms would convey meaning more directly or more clearly. "Malfunctions and breakdowns can be avoided if the equipment is ruggedized before it is used" can be translated out of jargon into more meaningful English by saying "Ruggedly built equipment breaks down less often than poorly built equipment" or "Only well-built equipment will withstand the shocks of hard use." See also *Provincialisms*.

Language In one sense, any code used in signaling; in another sense, the body of commonly accepted meanings (denotative and connotative) which signals symbolize. In the sense most immediately important to speakers, language is the total fund of verbal and gestural symbols by means of which speakers and listeners share experience. Speakers use and listeners respond to two "language systems" at the same time: (1) meanings represented or suggested by speech sounds and (2) meanings represented or suggested by visible behavior—action. One of a speaker's special problems is so to control himself that the meanings he symbolizes in one of his two languages do not distract from or contradict the meanings he is symbolizing in the other language.

Liveliness Vivacity or sprightliness of expression; a language pattern marked by animated thought, vivid words, crisp form, and rapid movement. The opposite of a ponderous, unimaginative style.

Liveliness of expression depends ultimately upon a stock of fresh and lively ideas, but it may be enhanced by appropriate stylistic devices, such as *metaphor*, *antithesis*, and hyperbole, provided these are used in moderation and always to help communicate ideas rather than to embellish them. See also *Force*, *Impressiveness*, *Interest*.

Loaded Language Language capable of evoking strong attitudes and emotions. All verbal language is in some degree "loaded" because virtually all words have connotative as well as denotative meanings.

The term "loaded language" is usually applied in circumstances where the user of language seems to have made unusual efforts to evoke powerful attitudes and feelings by means of the words and phrases he chooses. There is, for example, markedly more "loading" of language in "Mingled Blood," pp. 98-100, or "I Have a Dream," pp. 154-156, than in "Changing Concepts of Public Service," pp. 208-214, or "The City—A Cause for Statesmanship," pp. 219-224.

Logic Logic can be practically defined as the science of reasoning reliably. When a connection is alleged to exist between two or more things or events, it becomes important to ask, "How reliable are the thought processes by which this connection was 'discovered'?" This is the basic question that logical rules and procedures explore; for example, one logical procedure for testing whether we may safely reason about A from what we already know about B is to explore the essential likenesses and dissimilarities of A and B. (See *Analogy*.) Some of these methods of testing the ways we think are fairly simple and familiar; others, like those of statistical analysis, are highly complex. Audiences apply at least the simpler logical tests to what they hear, especially in moments of doubt or disagreement with the speaker. With a speaker's help most audiences are also able to follow and to apply moderately complicated logical procedures, a fact of great value to speakers who must offer unfamiliar reasonings or who must criticize the logic of an opponent in *refutation*. When a speaker encourages his listeners to use logical procedures in validating conclusions, he is said to be using a "logical appeal." See *Inference*.

M

Main Headings Usually, the statements that express the chief divisions of the body of the speech or essay. The term derives from the prominence these statements have in an outline, where they are assigned special symbols and indentations. Arrangements of main headings that are especially common are called standard *patterns of organization*. If a speech is organized in topical order, each major statement to be developed constitutes a special "topic" and, hence, is a main heading. If the disease-remedy pattern is used, the statements specifying the need, recommending a solution, and, perhaps, asserting the desirability of a solution will form the main headings. For *clarity* and *coherence* the main headings, taken together, must form a complete and sufficient justification of the *central idea*; the *proofs* and *amplifications* associated with each main heading should justify or clarify the main heading itself. In "Changing Concepts of Public Service," pp. 208-214, main headings are clearly announced in pars. 20, 29, 35, 40, 49. Compare "Apathy," pp. 165-166, pars. 4, 6, 8, 16-19.

Melody See *Intonation*.

Metaphor See *Figures of Speech*.

Mock-Epic See *Satire*.

Motivated Sequence A comprehensive *pattern of organization* based upon "the normal process of human thinking," and for this reason assumed to be particularly effective in motivating listeners to respond to the speaker's purpose.

As developed by its principal exponent, Professor Alan H. Monroe (*Principles and Types of Speech*, 5th ed. [Chicago: Scott, Foresman and Co., 1962]), the motivated sequence provides a basic pattern by which all types of speeches may be organized, "needing only to be modified by omitting or lengthening certain parts according to the particular situation." In speeches to actuate, all five steps of the sequence are present. These bear the functional names of Attention, Need, Satisfaction, Visualization, and Action. The first step catches the

"attention" of the listeners; the second points to the existence of a problem or "need"; the third advances a proposal that will "satisfy" this need; the fourth "visualizes" the benefits to be derived from adopting the proposal; and the fifth, drawing upon the groundwork thus laid, makes a direct *appeal* for "action." In speeches to inform, only three steps—Attention, Need, and Satisfaction—are present. The function of the first is again to catch "attention"; the second shows the listeners why they "need" to know the information that is to be presented; and the third "satisfies" this "need" by presenting the information. Speeches to entertain may be either an extended development of the Attention Step or a mock-serious treatment of the speech to inform, convince, or actuate.

Motivation Generally, an inducement or incentive. In rhetoric the terms "motive" and "motivation" usually refer to very broad and overlapping descriptions of the goals for which human beings strive. Thus, it is said that among the strongest and most universal motivations of man are his desires for self-protection, love, admiration, comfort, etc. Such general listings of human motives are always loose and imprecise, but they serve to remind speakers of the predictable tendencies of most listeners. The wise speaker knows his hearers must be motivated by their own desires or *drives*; he should discover what their desires are likely to be, how strong they are, and whether any of them can be gratified by the actions he expects to urge. Franklin Roosevelt, in asking public support for foreign aid, once argued that only a churlish man would refuse the loan of his garden hose when his neighbor's house was on fire; his hint that to refuse the aid would bring ill repute added one more inducement to the case he had already made on England's behalf. A less astute speaker might have rested his case on England's need alone, neglecting to touch the always present desire to be well thought of. See *Appeal*, *Drive*.

Movement Getting from place to place on the platform. The amount and kind of movement a speaker employs are important aspects of delivery. Just as he should not stand rooted to one spot during a five- or ten-minute speech, so he should not constantly pace about. Movement, like *gestures*, should not be planned, but should spring from an inner impulse to communicate more effectively. Often a speaker will feel impelled to move as he makes a transition from one major point to another or as he emphasizes a particularly important idea. See *Gestures*.

N

Narrative The recounting of a connected succession of events, usually with a description of the persons involved and of the environment in which the events occurred. Occasionally an entire speech—particularly a speech to entertain or inform—may be developed as a narrative. Persuasive speeches often contain one or more narrative passages in which happenings that explain or support the speaker's contentions are related.

Narratives usually possess the attention factors of *activity* and *conflict* and may also have elements of suspense, *humor*, or surprise. Hence, they are high in interest value and may under appropriate circumstances be used to enliven almost any sort of speech. Listeners, however, are sometimes slow to grasp the point of a narrative or to see how it relates to the ideas and arguments being developed. Whenever a speaker suspects that the significance or relevance of a story may not be evident, he should pause to make these matters entirely clear. For an example of the most usual use of narrative in speaking, see "The Inner City—Our Shame," p. 217, par. 17; for an example of historical narrative, see "Newspapers of the U.S.A.—An

Appraisal,'' pp. 109-110, pars. 19-30; for use of narrative method with what might be called non-narrative materials, see ''What Is Truth?'' p. 183, par. 22. Compare ''Rout the Forces of Hate,'' p. 159, pars. 32-39.

Needs See *Drive, Motivation.*

Negation, Definition by See *Definition.*

O

Occasion The circumstances in which a speech occurs, including whatever reasons brought the audience together. This term is often used to refer to the entire environment in which a speech is set. Each set of conditions for speaking offers distinctive opportunities and imposes distinctive limitations; each setting affects the expectations and predispositions of the audience and prescribes forms and precedents that speakers may not safely violate. If, for example, the occasion is a legislative debate, the speaker must accomplish his purpose within the rules enforced by the legislative body; on the other hand, legislative speakers may choose their proofs more freely than courtroom pleaders, whose procedures and rules of evidence are more detailed and restrictive. Each ceremonial occasion also prescribes in some degree what may be said and how: the commencement speaker is not free to oppose education or to adopt the tone he might use in addressing a club smoker. Even physical circumstances are influential: the bishop is more impressive and the political fanatic more ridiculous when speaking from beneath an ancient Gothic arch; the highly personal anecdote needs an intimate and conversational setting, while the sonorous phrase sounds best from a somewhat distant platform. All these considerations and more are encompassed in the injunction that every effective speech must be adapted in all its details to its subject matter, audience, and occasion. Contrast the differing requirements of the speaking occasions for ''The Place and the Price of Excellence,'' pp. 28-34; ''I Have a Dream,'' pp. 154-156; ''Crime and Criminals,'' pp. 142-147; ''Address to the Russian People,'' pp. 242-246; and ''Rout the Forces of Hate,'' pp. 157-161. See also *Adaptation, Set.*

Occasional Speaking The various kinds of speaking appropriate to special occasions—the Fourth of July, the retirement of a valued employee, etc. Also the speaking demanded by the rituals of organized groups. Speeches of welcome (for an example see ''Excellence in Teaching,'' pp. 48-51), responses, presentation speeches, farewells, eulogies, speeches of good will, after-dinner speeches, and the like are frequently classed together as ''occasional speeches.'' ''The Writer's Duty,'' pp. 52-53, is an occasional speech. See *Epideictic Speaking.*

Onomatopoeia Use of words, for rhetorical effect, whose sounds suggest the literal meanings of the terms; e.g., *whisper, boom, rustle, cuckoo.* See also ''pounding, squeezing,'' and ''bombs'' in ''Mingled Blood,'' p. 99, par. 11.

Opinion A judgment grounded in inconclusive evidence and, therefore, dependent, to a greater or lesser extent, upon a subjective evaluation of the meaning and worth of that evidence.

Opinions may be classified as sound or unsound, according to the amount and quality of the evidence on which they are based and the accuracy and objectivity with which that evidence is interpreted. Even the soundest of opinions, however, are disputable in a sense that ''facts'' are not.

The public speaker who expresses an opinion has the moral obliga-

tion of reporting the evidence upon which it rests and of evaluating that evidence as precisely and fairly as possible. For examples of opinions based on the speaker's own experience, see ''The City—A Cause for Statesmanship,'' p. 223, pars. 41-42. Note also the extent to which ''Ethics in International Relations Today,'' pp. 229-232, reflects the speaker's personal opinions. For a second sense in which the term ''opinion'' is commonly used by writers of textbooks on public speaking, see *Attitude.*

Organization See *Patterns of Organization.*

Originality Freshness in ideas, interpretations, judgments, or proposals, and in the language in which these are communicated to listeners. The speaker who is original in his thinking does not rehearse facts and conclusions reported by others but, as a result of long study and reflection, advances worth-while creative insights of his own. Original expression conveys ideas in a fresh and sprightly manner and is free of overworked phrases, bromides, and *clichés.* Originality is an important quality in a speech not only because fresh ideas freshly expressed are more likely to prove interesting to listeners, but also because the speaker who thinks creatively makes a greater contribution to the intelligent solution of the problems with which he deals. Theodore Roosevelt's use of the image from *Pilgrim's Progress* met the standards of rhetorical originality and contributed to the lasting influence of the speech ''The Man with the Muck-Rake,'' pp. 102-106.

Overstatement Exaggeration or hyperbole. Overstatement has the same value as caricature: it calls attention to an important aspect of the subject through gross exaggeration. To be successful, overstatement must be gross enough so that it is absurd, and original enough so that it attracts by its ingenuity. Mark Twain described a jack rabbit he shot at in this form: ''He dropped his ears, set up his tail, and left for San Francisco at a speed which can only be described as a flash and a vanish! Long after he was out of sight we could hear him whiz.'' Ascoli is probably indulging in overstatement when he describes the liberal's ''jaundiced view'' of the business system and equates it with religious dogma, in ''The Scarcity of Ideas,'' p. 202, par. 10.

P

Parable A short tale designed to convey a moral truth. Easily the most famous examples are the parables of Jesus, such as that of the prodigal son, the tares and the wheat, or the mustard seed. Although parables oversimplify reality, they are useful in putting across a single, unadorned idea. See also *Fable.*

Parallel Construction Construction in which ideas of equal worth are given the same syntactical form. That is, two or more ideas are said to be in parallel construction if they appear, for example, as independent clauses, as dependent clauses, as participial phrases, or as a series of nouns, verbs, etc. The connectives most used in parallel construction are *and, but, for, either . . . or,* and *neither . . . nor.* Parallel construction is especially useful in pairing items, in listing a series, or in establishing an *antithesis.* It tends to make prose rhythms more regular than they usually are, and for this reason it is often employed at the end of a speech to provide emotional intensity. For good examples of the extended use of parallel construction, turn to the Lord's Prayer in the King James Version of the Bible or to The Gettysburg Address.'' See ''The Haven of the Defeated,'' p. 150, par. 14; ''Inaugural Address,'' p. 227, pars. 25-26; ''I Have a Dream,'' pp. 154-156, passim. See also *Sentence Movement.*

Parody See *Satire*.

Partitioning *Analysis* of a subject and selection of the issues or *main headings* to be developed in the *body* of the speech. Sometimes the term is used to include determination of what points shall be made in the *introduction* and *conclusion*. For many centuries, rhetorical theorists argued that virtually all speeches ought to contain sections in which the speakers formally outlined and defended their chosen ways of partitioning their subjects. This, it was thought, should be done before beginning the body of a speech. Contemporary theory tends to advise such discussion only when listeners need special help in understanding or finding justification for the way in which the speaker has chosen to treat his subject. See ''Newspapers of the U.S.A.—An Appraisal,'' p. 107, par. 2. See also *Patterns of Organization*.

Patterns of Organization The structural plan or framework of a speech. In selecting the pattern of organization to be followed in any given speech, the speaker should carefully consider not only the ideas to be communicated but also his purpose (to entertain, inform, persuade, etc.) and the attitude of the audience (friendly, neutral, hostile). Standard patterns, which may be adapted or modified to meet specific speaking situations, include these:

Cause to effect order. Pointing first to a generative or causal force and then to the result it may be expected to produce. (''Wages in the steel industry continue to rise. Therefore, we may expect the price of steel products to increase.'')

Chronological order. Describing events in the order in which they occurred, or giving instructions by telling what to do first, what second, etc. (''On the evening of the murder Jones left home at seven o'clock and went to the filling station. From there. . . .'') ''Newspapers of the U.S.A.—An Appraisal,'' pp. 107-114, is developed in a roughly chronological order.

Deductive order. Urging the acceptance of a controversial claim on the ground that its truth, justice, or practicability follows of necessity from an accepted principle. (''If, as we believe, all Americans are entitled to religious freedom, then members of all religious sects, however unpopular, should be allowed to worship as they please.'')

Disease-remedy or *problem-solution order.* Pointing first to the existence of a problem or evil, and then offering a program to correct it. (''Our city is overrun with slums. We should have an urban renewal program.'') The corrective program that is set forth must meet two principal criteria: (1) it must be practicable—that is, capable of being put into effect and of actually eliminating the evil in question; (2) it must be desirable—that is, it must not introduce new and worse evils of its own. The farmer who burns down his barn to rid it of rats adopts a practicable solution but not a desirable one. See ''The Haven of the Defeated,'' pp. 148-151; ''On the Federal Constitution,'' pp. 272-276.

Effect to cause order. Accounting for an existing situation by explaining the cause that produced it. (''Today our military establishment is inadequate and outmoded. Why? Because in recent years we have not made adequate appropriations for defense.'') See ''Apathy,'' pp. 164-166.

Elimination order. Sometimes called the ''method of residues.'' Considering all possible interpretations of a subject or all possible solutions to a problem, and then showing that all except one are incorrect, impracticable, or undesirable. (''We could solve the problem of overcrowded schools by increasing the size of classes, running double shifts, making wider use of televised instruction, or by hiring more teachers and constructing more school buildings. Of these possible remedies, however, all except the last would seriously impair the quality of education our children receive.'') See ''What Can We Prove About God?'' pp. 187-189.

Inductive order. Using a number of individual cases or instances as the basis for a generalization concerning additional members of the same class. (''A concentration of funds and research efforts was effective in curbing polio. The same thing happened with tuberculosis, typhoid, and the diseases of infancy. Therefore, in all probability, cancer can be conquered through similar efforts.'')

Reflective order. Organizing a speech according to the five steps in ''reflective thinking'' as outlined by the philosopher John Dewey: (1) recognition of problem; (2) description and delimitation of problem; (3) suggestion of possible solutions; (4) comparative evaluation and testing of solutions; (5) selection of preferred solution. (''1. The sharp drop in farm income poses a problem. 2. This is primarily a problem of overproduction. 3. To solve this problem, we could ship more food abroad, consume more at home, move families off the farm, or continue our policy of price supports. 4. But shipping more food abroad would glut the world market. We cannot consume more at home. Moving families off the farm would seriously disrupt their lives. 5. On the whole, therefore, the best solution is to continue our program of price supports.'') See ''Science, Technology, and World Development,'' pp. 83-87.

Space order. Describing how something looks by proceeding systematically from left to right, top to bottom, front to back, etc., mentioning each part or aspect in order. (''At the front of the great hall stands the golden throne. To its left is an impressive Flemish tapestry. Immediately in front of the tapestry is a carved table, and to its right a stool.'')

Topical order. Arranging ideas in an order dictated by the subject being discussed. (''Intelligent reading requires understanding the general purpose and structure of a book, as well as mastering the detailed information it presents. Let us consider, first, how to discover a book's purpose and structure; then how to master its details.'') See ''Changing Concepts of Public Service,'' pp. 208-214; ''Address to the Russian People,'' pp. 242-246.

Chronological, space, and topical orders lend themselves most naturally to informative speeches; cause to effect, deductive, disease-remedy, effect to cause, elimination, inductive, and reflective orders are best adapted to persuasive speeches. See also *Motivated Sequence*.

Periodic sentence A sentence in which the meaning is not completed until the end. Because they are more formal, periodic sentences are less common in our conversation than loose sentences, which continue after the main clause is completed. But they can be helpful in a speech requiring suspense and great emphasis on the word or words which come last.

Periodic sentence: ''Whatever you may say of me or whatever you do to me, I will not retract.''

Loose sentence: ''I will not retract, no matter what you say about me or what you do to me.''
See also *Sentence Movement*.

Personification See *Figures of Speech*.

Persuasion In general, any form of discourse that influences others in a predetermined way through some combination of information, reasoning, and emotion. To persuade through speech requires that one make his listeners give *attention* to those ideas, images, words, manners, etc., which will lead them to feel that accepting the recommendations of the speaker will be more satisfying than rejecting them. Some writers on *rhetoric* and *logic* seek to distinguish persuasion from *argument* and *propaganda*, but few are clearly agreed on how these processes differ from one another, if they do. It is generally agreed, however, that discourse ought to be called persuasive if it aims at modifying *attitudes*, *opinions*, and perhaps *conduct*. Most authorities also agree that to ''be persuaded'' of anything, one must have adopted some new way (to him) of responding to a situation or idea. For changes of this kind to occur there must be, somewhere, an incentive or *motivation* strong enough to make the change seem gratifying. These incentives or motivations may be brought to a listener's attention through the reasonings, the *suggestions,* and the *ethos* and *prestige* of the speaker. Thus, whatever meaning is assigned to the term "persuasion," it is clear that when speakers undertake to change any aspect of human behavior, they must find and offer their listeners the kinds of incentives that will make the new behavior seem more satisfying than the old. See also *Appeal, Both-Sides Persuasion, Common Ground, Logic, Proof, Set.*

Pitch See *Intonation.*

Posture A speaker's stance or bearing. Good posture for speaking does not result from placing the feet or arms in any particular position, but from standing in such a way that attention is not split away from the ideas being presented. By and large, listeners find most natural, and therefore least distracting, a posture that is dignified and alert, yet relaxed enough to avoid the appearance of military stiffness.

Precedent A type of authority drawn from previous actions or decisions, as of a court of law. See *Supporting Material.*

Premise Any statement from which a conclusion is drawn by reasoning. See *Deduction, Inference, Syllogism.*

Prestige The power of arousing admiration or esteem that influences acceptance of spoken or written materials. The sources of such prestige include but often go beyond the *ethos* of a speaker. The reputations of those who help a speaker communicate his message and the impressiveness or unimpressiveness of the *occasion* are additional sources of prestige affecting the response to a speaker's message. If, for example, a speaker addresses his audience by radio or television, his prestige may be increased or diminished by the trust people have in these media of communication; also, the prestige of the program on which he appears and the reputation of the broadcasting station or network may add to or detract from his stature. Similarly, speakers gain or lose prestige according to the reputations of those who sponsor their appearances on public platforms. If others are known to have assisted a speaker in preparing his address, their reputations may also affect the esteem in which speaker and speech are held. In the persuasive process called *suggestion,* prestige is the most important single factor determining favorable or unfavorable audience response. The prestige of the Presidency gave weight to ideas expressed in "The Man with the Muck-Rake," pp. 102-106; the prestige of religious office and leadership in the civil rights movement reinforced criticisms and claims in "I Have a Dream," pp. 154-156; and, probably, the prestige of the Russian broadcasting services affected the credibility of "Address to the Russian People," pp. 242-246, in the eyes of the Russian audience.

Presumption An ambiguous term, both in the law and in nonlegal argument. In its first and primary sense, presumption defines the rights and obligations of the parties to a controversy. In law, for example, a person accused of a crime is "presumed" to be innocent, and therefore is not called upon to defend himself until the plaintiff has made out a prima facie case establishing his guilt. Similarly, in nonlegal argument an existing institution, value, or practice is by convention assigned the presumption and hence may rest secure until sufficient doubt concerning its usefulness, practicability, or desirability has been established. In a second and derived sense, a presumption is an inference that may or must be drawn from certain sorts of evidence. Thus a person absent and unheard of for seven years is "pre-

sumed" by the law to be dead, a child born in wedlock is "presumed" to be legitimate, etc. In nonlegal argument this second use of the term makes it practically synonymous with "assumption." In "The Scarcity of Ideas," p. 201, pars. 1-8, Max Ascoli discusses whether the "assumptions" of Arthur Schlesinger, Jr., any longer have "presumption" in their favor. See *Burden of Proof.*

Probability A degree of likelihood greater than possibility, but less than certainty; that which is more likely than not to be true, but concerning which we have no absolute assurance.

Since the choices and actions of men cannot be predicted accurately, speakers dealing with problems lying in the realm of human affairs or involving future events cannot be expected to prove their *propositions* conclusively (for example, to show that uniform marriage and divorce laws will *certainly* reduce the divorce rate; or that the introduction of an honor system on a college campus will *certainly* reduce cheating). Even in criminal law, where a man's life may be at stake, only proof "beyond reasonable doubt" is required. A speaker does, however, have the obligation of introducing a preponderance of *proof* to support any proposition that is not self-evident—the burden of showing that it is more likely than not to be true. His proof should always approach certainty to the fullest extent his subject matter permits. See also *Credibility.*

Proof Broadly, anything about a speech that induces *belief* or action. This general meaning is common in *rhetoric,* although in *logic* and science proof usually refers only to the result of *evidence.* Aristotle's view that rhetorical proof takes four forms is still widely accepted: there is proof (1) arising from the logic of reasoning and evidence; (2) arising from the feelings aroused in the audience *(emotion);* (3) arising from the reputation of the speaker and the impressions he creates while speaking *(ethos);* and (4) supplied by the introduction of such aids to argument as documents, witnesses, photographs, and the like. Whether an audience accepts, ignores, or rejects what it is told depends on the weight the hearers give to these classes of proof. While hearing a speech, the listener consciously or unconsciously reacts to the seeming reliability of the logic offered and accordingly tends to accept or reject these reasonings as justifications for belief; he allows the interests, *attitudes,* and feelings aroused by the speech to tell him whether accepting what he hears will bring him any personal gratification or pain; he judges the speaker to be a reliable or unreliable adviser and accordingly allows his impression of the messenger to color his impression of the message; and he is impressed or unimpressed by whatever documentation the speaker may exhibit and accordingly favors or deprecates the speaker's case. Of course, listeners do not respond as deliberately as this description suggests, but each of the four kinds of reaction to proofs contributes in some measure to the disapproval indifference, or enthusiasm with which an audience finally responds to a speech. "The Method of Scientific Investigation," pp. 264-269, relies heavily on close reasoning; "The Inner City—Our Shame," pp. 216-218, seeks to arouse the emotion of sympathy as a proof; the speaker's *ethos* is especially important as proof in "On the Federal Constitution," pp. 272-276.

Propaganda Propaganda is variously defined: as communication that disrespects facts, overlooks facts, withholds facts; as communication systematically designed to propagate the judgment of a few by circumventing reason; as synonymous with *persuasion;* as any doctrine or principle systematically disseminated and argued for. In general use the term is an extraordinarily ambiguous epithet usually expressing disapproval. To understand its further meanings, if any, the listener or reader must inquire into the user's personal definition of "propaganda."

Proposition A statement, usually in the form of a simple declarative sentence, expressing a point to be discussed. In the design of an *argument* the proposition states what the *evidence* proves; in the design of an *exposition* the proposition states what the *amplification* clarifies or reveals; in the design of a *description* the proposition characterizes the relationships to be set forth. The *central idea,* each *main heading,* and each *subheading* of persuasive, expository, or descriptive discourse should be capable of expression as propositions, even though they may or may not be uttered in this form when the message is actually delivered or written. The resolutions commonly used in debate are also propositions, despite the parliamentary or judicial form in which they are sometimes phrased; hence, one finds the term "proposition" occasionally used to refer exclusively to the statement of a point for debate. For central idea as proposition see "The Man with the Muck-Rake," p. 102, par. 5; for main heading as proposition see "Address to the Russian People," p. 243, par. 19; for subheading as proposition see "The Challenge of Abundance," pp. 197-198, par. 9. See also *Assertion, Premise.*

Proverb A wise saying or useful idea expressed in a brief, ingenious fashion ("A penny saved is a penny earned"). See "Address to the Russian People," p. 243, par. 17. See also *Epigram.*

Provincialisms Colloquial terms or pronunciations peculiar to a certain district of a country. Although generally to be employed with caution, such expressions as "you-all" or "nor'easter," for example, may be justified by the locale in which speaking takes place. See *Barbarism, Jargon.*

Purpose See *Specific Purpose.*

q

Quality Sometimes called "tone." The overall impression created by a speaker's voice: pleasant, resonant, harsh, breathy, hoarse, nasal, etc. The basic quality of a speaker's voice is determined by the size, shape, and state of health of his vocal mechanism, but optimum quality for any individual is simply the most pleasing balance of voicing-resonating patterns he can attain. Such a quality generally results when vowels are accurately pronounced and supported by a steady and sufficient column of air but without strain or excess tension in the muscles of the neck and throat.

Quotation See *Authority.*

Rebuttal Literally, a repulsing or driving back. In a speech, the rebuilding of an argument after it has been attacked.

Rebuttal may take the form of (1) a demonstration that the attack leveled against an argument is irrelevant, inadequate, or unfair; (2) the introduction of additional evidence or reasoning to support an argument; or (3) an attack upon an alternative or counterargument advanced by an opponent. Not to be confused with *refutation,* which is an attempt to neutralize or destroy an argument. See "The Challenge of Abundance," p. 200, par. 23; "The City—A Cause for Statesmanship," pp. 221-222, par. 26.

Reflective Thinking This term refers to the process of inquiry that follows the stages of problem solving outlined by John Dewey (see *Patterns of Organization, Reflective order*). Reflective thinking is disciplined, logically ordered thinking about any problem for which a solution is needed. Its opposite is impulsive or emotional decision

making. Reflective thinking, thus, is a method of intellectual attack; good speakers use it constantly in research and in planning speeches. A speaker intending to speak on "Crime and Punishment" would (1) need to find out what to say about the subject and what to disregard. If he (2) tried to delimit and describe his problem, he might discover he must know two kinds of things about his subject: (a) the facts about crime and punishment today and (b) what his audience will already know about the subject. His reflection can now move forward another step to (3) review the ways (solutions) by which he can acquire the two kinds of information he needs: reading, interviewing, speculating, visiting penal institutions, making audience surveys, etc. From among these options he may (4) choose what seem to be the most promising courses of action and (5) verify the wisdom of his choices by trying them out. By the same intellectual method speakers explore what *propositions* deserve *proof* and *amplification,* what will be the ideal kind of *evidence,* and many other problems of speech planning and composition. And if it seems best to urge an audience to explore a problem for itself, the reflective order may prove the best available *pattern of organization.* See also *Exploration.*

Refutation An attempt to neutralize or destroy an argument with which one disagrees. To be distinguished from *rebuttal,* which is the process of rebuilding an argument after it has been attacked.

A speaker may refute an argument (1) by showing that the evidence upon which it rests is insufficient, irrelevant, comes from an unreliable or biased source, or has been unfairly reported; (2) by showing that the conclusion drawn from the evidence is unwarranted; (3) by using one or more of the so-called "special methods of refutation"—*dilemma,* elimination, reduction to absurdity, or *turning the tables.*

The destruction of opposing arguments through refutation lends only indirect support to the speaker's own case. In order to establish his own contentions, he must also introduce argumentation to support them. A speaker cannot prove that he is right merely by proving that his opponent is wrong. See "The Scarcity of Ideas," p. 201, par. 8; "What Can We Prove About God?" pp. 187-189, pars. 2-10.

Repetition The act of saying again. To say anything more than once increases the likelihood that the statement will be perceived and remembered by a listener, but unless repetition is accompanied by *variety,* as in restatement, its power to command *attention* begins to diminish after the third or fourth utterance. "Repetition accompanied by sufficient variety to lend interest but with sufficient uniformity to acquire a constant meaning, produces a genuine cumulative effect" (H. L. Hollingworth, *The Psychology of the Audience* [New York: American Book Company, 1935], p. 144). In this sense repetition becomes a form of *supporting material,* even though it adds no new content or *proof.* For examples of repetition in language for emphasis and clarification, see "The Philosophy of Social Justice Through Social Action," pp. 137-138, par. 25, and p. 139, par. 47; "Coatesville," p. 164, par. 9, "cruel." For examples of repetitions of refrains in order to establish *parallel constructions,* see "I Have a Dream," pp. 154-156, especially pars. 3, 5, 9, 12-18, 19, 20-27.

Reputation The qualities of character and intelligence imputed to any person. See also *Ethos, Prestige.*

Rhetoric As used in this book, "rhetoric" refers to the principles and processes by which listeners or readers are influenced in predetermined directions through spoken prose. During the twenty-five centuries that rhetoric has figured as a branch of knowledge and formal study in Western civilization, definitions of what rhetoric is have varied greatly; contemporary definitions are similarly varied. The definition adopted here is essentially that used by writers on the art of rhetoric in the classical areas of Greece and Rome. When most narrowly defined, rhetoric has usually been described as the study and use of *figures of speech*. When most broadly defined, rhetoric tends to become synonymous with *communication*.

Rhetorical Question A question asked for its effect on the audience and not because the speaker wants or needs an answer. It is often used to introduce a speech or a new topic or to emphasize a point. To be effective, a rhetorical question must be asked so that the answer is uncomplicated, obvious, and the same for almost everyone in the audience. "Isn't it clear, therefore, that we should all vote Democratic next Tuesday?" would not be an effective rhetorical question in an audience of Democrats and Republicans, but might be a successful one at a Democratic rally. See "The Philosophy of Social Justice Through Social Action," pp. 136-137, pars. 7, 9-10, 13, 15; "Inaugural Address," p. 227, par. 23; "What Can We Prove About God?" p. 189, par. 10; "Rout the Forces of Hate," p. 159, par. 22; "Apathy," pp. 165-166, pars. 6, 9, 11, 12, 15. Observe that the questions in "The City—A Cause for Statesmanship," p. 223, par. 38, are not rhetorical questions but express topics for further study.

Rhythm The movement of a speech in terms of sound, accent, tempo, and pauses. All speeches have rhythm, though in some it may be so irregular and jagged as to be hardly worthy of the name; in others it becomes so regular that the speech approaches free verse. Rhythm in speaking is not something to work for directly. An appealing rhythm is one of the happy consequences of correct syntax, variety in sentence structure and beginnings, coherence, and emphasis. It should be added that an appealing rhythm is also one that suits the subject. The rhythm of a call to arms is hardly appropriate for a funeral oration. Examine especially the rhythmic qualities of "I Have a Dream," pp. 154-156.

Ridicule Discourse designed to make fun of somebody or something. Ridicule ranges broadly from good-humored spoofing to the bitterest kind of jeering. To ridicule, one may, for example, mimic, mock, tease, scoff, deride, taunt, or jeer. Any kind of ridicule in a prepared speech, however, must be used with a deft touch, for applied too heavily it tends to make the speaker rather than the object of his ridicule look silly. See "The Philosophy of Social Justice Through Social Action," p. 138, par. 28.

S

Sarcasm Biting denunciation. Sarcasm may be ironical (that is, it may say one thing while obviously meaning another), or it may be direct. To be effective, sarcasm should be used sparingly. ("What a brilliant diplomat he would make: he thinks the Canary Islands are a bird sanctuary!") See "Crime and Criminals," p. 143, par. 11; "Press Conference," p. 252, par. 29, "This is what. . . ." See also *Irony*.

Satire Discourse that by other than logical means attempts to influence thought and conduct by exposing human frailties. Based on firm conviction, satire finds its targets in men's pretensions, follies, and vices. Its object is not amusement but indignation and reform. Its chief means are *humor, ridicule, irony, sarcasm,* and *invective*.

Burlesque is light satire which by distortion makes fun of a class or genre, such as college freshman, political speeches, or TV westerns. Aiming at men's pretensions rather than their vices, the burlesquer is usually as much interested in providing amusement as he is in affecting thorught and conduct.

Parody is light satire on a particular work, such as Poe's "Raven" or Lincoln's "Gettysburg Address." Parody is primarily for amusement

and does not necessarily imply any lack of respect for the target of the spoofing.

Travesty is a burlesque in which a lofty subject is treated trivially.

Mock-epic is a burlesque in which a trivial subject is treated in a lofty style.

Semantics The study of the meanings of words and other linguistic forms; still more generally, the study of how any set of signs or symbols is related to "meaning." For a discussion of semantics and of General Semantics, see "Four Ways of Looking at a Speech," pp. 13-18.

Sentence Movement The tempo and flow of a sentence as determined by its structural pattern. The most common movement is that of the basic English sentence containing a subject, verb, and object in that order—though not necessarily contiguous. ("I hope the subject of my talk will not annoy you.") There are, of course, other movements with an infinite number of modifications of each. The loose (as contrasted with the periodic) movement, for example, is one that continues after the main subject and verb have been given. ("We have assembled here to get to know one another, to work together, to test out our ideas—I hope we shall have some ideas—and happily to write a report that will prove helpful to our entire association.") A parallel or balanced movement is one in which two or more elements are given the same, or parallel, construction. This movement is especially common in formal addresses presented to large audiences. American "spread-eagle" oratory was famous for its use of the balanced movement. ("Senator Bullfinch is not only a great Westerner, but also a great American.") An inverted movement (one in which the subject is not first) is a less common type, and therefore can be used effectively for variety and emphasis. ("Now comes the surprise I promised you.") In an interrupted movement, a lengthy modification or a digression appears between main sentence elements. ("What I am about to say here is that—and I want to emphasize that I say it in the friendliest of spirits—this is the most prejudiced group I have spoken to in a long while.")

Any continued use of the same sentence movement will inevitably lead to monotony. The task of the effective speaker is to vary movements not only to keep the audience generally attentive but to make them especially aware of the crucial points. Well handled, moreover, sentence movement can provide esthetic pleasure that enhances the total effect of the speech. Note the sentence movement in "Coatesville," pp. 163-164. Compare the sentence movement in "I Have a Dream," pp. 154-156.

Set The somewhat ambiguous psychological concept of "set" is increasingly used in discussing the conditions under which listeners respond to speech. Traditionally, it has been said that the listener's knowledge, his *attitudes* toward speaker and subject, and the conditions of the occasion are the chief factors determining how he will perceive and respond to what he hears. A number of psychologists, however, recently have pointed out that "readiness" to react in any situation is the product of more complex psychic conditions. Consequently, increasing numbers of writers on speech suggest that the "readiness" or "expectations" of listeners will be more accurately understood if thought of as a "set" which results from any or all of such forces as: motives, past and present social conditioning, established habits and attitudes, and the tasks which listeners think they are confronted with when listening to speech. So used, the concept of "set" includes each of the traditionally discussed determinants of listeners' responses but is a reminder that still other forces are at work on any listener.

Sign, Argument from That form of *argument* in which a speaker claims that some outward mark or symptom is indicative of an inner state or condition. ("X country maintains an army, navy, and air force much larger than it needs for its own defense. This indicates [is a sign] that it has aggressive intentions against its neighbors.")

Signs may be classified as infallible or fallible, depending upon the degree of conclusiveness with which they indicate a state or condition. ("This metal is glowing red; therefore, it is hot." [Infallible] "He drives a large car and owns a yacht; therefore, he is wealthy." [Fallible]) See "Coatesville," p. 163, par. 1, "The failure of the prosecution. . . ." See also *Cause to Effect, Effect to Cause.*

Simile See *Figures of Speech.*

Slogan A brief, striking phrase ordinarily used to epitomize and make memorable the central idea of a persuasive speech ("Millions for defense, but not one cent for tribute." "Fifty-four forty or fight." "We have nothing to fear but fear itself.") In "The Philosophy of Social Justice Through Social Action," pp. 135-140, note how the title phrase is repeated at many points throughout the speech. In "I Have a Dream," p. 154, par. 5, the reiterated phrase "Now is the time" may be regarded as a slogan. See *Epigram.*

Spatial Order See *Patterns of Organization.*

Specific Purpose The name given by various writers to two somewhat different kinds of purpose statements. As used by some, the term refers to a statement expressing both the *end of speaking* and the *central idea* of a speech. Under this interpretation, "I intend to persuade my audience that the officials of this city do not oppose organized crime with vigor" would be designated a statement of the speaker's specific purpose. Others apply the term to a statement expressing the general response expected from the audience. "I intend to persuade my audience that organized crime still threatens us" would be called a specific purpose statement under the second usage. Those who use the term in this narrower sense assume that the ideas by which the purpose is to be achieved will be epitomized in a second statement designated the subject sentence or central idea. Note that both interpretations presuppose that every speaker must have an exact awareness of his aim and of his major *proposition* if he is to speak with *clarity.* See "Changing Concepts of Public Service," p. 208, par. 3.

Statistics Numbers which express relationships among phenomena or summarize or interpret bodies of data. The forms of statistical information most commonly employed by speakers in explaining or supporting their ideas include means, modes, averages, parts or percentages of a whole, increases, decreases, and concomitant variations. See "Newspapers of the U. S. A.," pp. 107-108, pars. 7-14; "Pan-Africanism, the Communists and the West," p. 256, par. 7.

Stereotype Literally, anything undistinguished by individual marks. A term applied and popularized by Walter Lippmann as a name for the incomplete "systems of thought" and "pictures in our heads" that represent our simplified interpretations of the things about us. We may, for example, simplify a complex system like capitalism into a less complete system which we think of as "competition"; often we also associate visual images with such conceptions—the image of a wealthy tycoon may represent capitalism. These stereotypes, like any other images or systems of thought, evoke favorable or unfavorable *attitudes* and *emotions* whenever they are raised to the level of consciousness. When this happens, we behave as though our stereotypes were true and complete systems or pictures. Speakers can scarcely hope to influence others persuasively unless they deal respectfully with their audiences' stereotypes and attitudes. Neither can be changed swiftly, so the wise persuader associates his cause with his listeners' stereotypes whenever he can and avoids those he would have to contradict were he to deal with them openly. Note the cautious indirection with which Jonathan Smith treats his listeners' stereotypes

of lawyers, "moneyed men," and "learned men" in "On the Federal Constitution," pp. 274 and 275. See also *Concept, Suggestion.*

Stimulate, Stimulation The end or purpose of speaking when one seeks either through his speech as a whole or through some segment of it to inspire, arouse enthusiasm, deepen feeling, or otherwise reinforce beliefs or emotions an audience already possesses. See also *Ends of Speaking, Epideictic Speaking, Impressiveness.*

Stipulation, Definition by See *Definition.*

Stratagems Tricks of argument which make weak proofs appear valid or which hide the fact that no proofs are present. See *Fallacies.*

Striking Phrase or Statement An expression which because of its unusual stylistic qualities or novel juxtaposition of ideas makes a strong and lasting impression upon a listener. See "The Haven of the Defeated," p. 149, par. 2, "havens of defeat"; "Inaugural Address," p. 226, par. 14, "Let us . . . to negotiate," and p. 227, par. 25; "The Writer's Duty," pp. 52-53. See *Epigram, Slogan.*

Structure See *Patterns of Organization.*

Style The distinctive manner of a speech or a speaker. Style is a loosely used word and very hard to define. The expression "a speaker's style" may refer to his appearance, delivery, language, and voice; or it may refer to his language and delivery; or it may simply refer to his language. Whatever its scope, "style" is usually employed to designate the special characteristics of manner, as apart from content, that distinguish one speaker from another. When applied to the use of language, style is employed most specifically to designate the selection and arrangement of words. While there are as many styles as speakers, styles can roughly be divided into two groups: the simple (sometimes called the Attic) style, in which the speaker uses clear, simple words and uncomplicated sentence structure, and (2) the ornate (sometimes called the baroque or Hebraic or Isocratic or Ciceronian, depending on the nature of the ornateness), in which the speaker makes substantial use of *parallel constructions, antitheses,* long and frequent *periodic sentences, figures of speech, alliteration,* and other structural and sound devices. The only thing that can be said arbitrarily about style is that there is no such thing as a good style in any absolute sense. The best style for a speech is the one that permits the speaker to communicate his ideas to a particular audience in the most effective manner possible. For an example of very simple style see "The World of Jazz," pp. 66-76. A more ornate style is illustrated by "What Is Truth?" pp. 180-183; a highly emotional style by "I Have a Dream," p. 154-156. Note the contrasting styles used by the same speaker to express interpretations of facts and aspirations for the future in "The City—A Cause for Statesmanship," p. 223, par. 43, and p. 224, pars. 50-51.

Subheadings The *propositions* that state a point to be proved or clarified in support of a *main heading.* Like a main heading, the subheading gets its name from the position given it in an outline or brief—in this case a subordinate position. The subheadings under a main heading should, together, form a complete and sufficient justification of the main heading. See also *Analysis, Subordination.*

Subject The topic with which a speech deals; what the speech is about.

In selecting a subject, the speaker should ask: (1) Does it "fit" me as an individual? Is it something I already know a good deal about and concerning which I want to learn more? (2) Does it "fit" the audience? Will they be interested in it and be able to understand it? (3) Does it "fit" the occasion? Can it be dealt with in the time allotted? Is it suitable in tenor and mood?

A common fault is the selection of a subject too broad to be covered in a speech of reasonable length. The best speech subjects usually result when the subject that first occurred to the speaker is carefully narrowed or when a certain segment of it is selected for presentation.

Subject Sentence See *Central Idea.*

Subordination The process of arranging under each of the *main headings* of a speech those ideas or arguments that explain and support it. Proper subordination requires that subsidiary ideas or *subheadings* be narrower in scope and of less importance than the main heading, and that they directly support the main heading under which they are placed. If subheads vary among themselves in scope or importance, they should be arranged according to the two rules just stated. In ''Moppet Manipulation,'' p. 124, the ideas expressed in par. 9 are plainly subordinated to the one in par. 8. See also ''The Haven of the Defeated,'' p. 150, par. 13.

Suggestion The effect that occurs when a person responds to an idea uncritically or without reflection. The term may also refer to the practice of evoking such responses. Suggestion invites the listener to react automatically rather than to weigh supporting facts and arrive at a reasoned judgment.

Most authorities recognize two basic types of suggestion: direct and indirect. Direct suggestion consists of employing symbols (words, actions, visual effects, etc.) which, because of the previous conditioning of the listeners, tend to arouse predetermined responses the speaker wants. If a speaker repeatedly calls his proposal ''patriotic,'' ''economical,'' or ''democratic,'' his listeners may accept these words at face value and view the proposal favorably; reference to an opposing proposal as ''disloyal,'' ''wasteful,'' or ''muddle-headed'' may tend to discredit it. Or a speaker may directly suggest that his listeners ''Consider the cost in taxes'' to change their focus of attention. Indirect suggestion is the process of establishing an idea without open reference to it, by arousing habitual responses to ideas consciously or unconsciously associated with it in listeners' minds. Without directly mentioning taxes, a speaker may call attention to them by saying, ''My opponent's plan would increase the costs of government.'' If the listeners commonly associate governmental costs with taxes, their thoughts will automatically turn to that subject. Similarly, ''Moon Glow'' might be a good name for a face powder; though it has little meaning, it indirectly suggests beauty and romance. ''Scritch,'' on the other hand, would be a poor choice; indirectly it may arouse the unfavorable responses associated with ''scratch'' and ''itch.''

A second important distinction is between positive and negative suggestion. Positive suggestion affirms an idea (''Candidate X is a business expert and is highly respected in Washington''); negative suggestion aims to reject an idea (''Ignore any rumors you hear that Candidate X bribed Congressmen to secure government contracts. They are malicious and untrue''). The danger in negative suggestion is that it draws attention to the very ideas the speaker hopes to dispel.

Because the speaker who deliberately uses suggestion attempts to short-circuit the *reflective thinking* process, the ethics of responsible public address demand that the end he seeks be above reproach and that logical arguments and evidence be combined with suggestion.

See ''The Philosophy of Social Justice Through Social Action,'' p. 139, par. 48. Note the dependence on positive, indirect suggestion in ''The City—A Cause for Statesmanship,'' p. 222, par. 33; see also marginal notes to ''On the Federal Constitution,'' pp. 270-276; ''Rout the Forces of Hate,'' p. 158, par. 20, ''rabble-rousers''; p. 159, par. 22, ''claghorns,'' etc.

Summary A review or reiteration, generally condensed, of facts and ideas previously presented. In addition to a final summary at the conclusion of his speech, a speaker may employ an ''initial summary'' or *partitioning* in which, as part of his introduction, he announces the points he will cover; and one or more ''internal summaries,'' in which he reviews the ideas and arguments presented up to that point.

In oral discourse the pace is set by the speaker; the listener is given no opportunity to review for himself what has been said earlier. Carefully drawn summaries are, therefore, important aids to comprehension and memory. Internal summaries occur in ''Crime and Criminals,'' p. 143, par. 10; ''Changing Concepts of Public Service,'' p. 213, par. 47; ''Address to the Russian People,'' p. 245, par. 49; ''Images of the Consumer's Changing Mind on and off Madison Avenue,'' p. 118, par. 16. See also the final summary in ''What Can We Prove About God?'' p. 189, pars. 10-12; ''Pan-Africanism, the Communists and the West,'' p. 259, pars. 24-26.

Supporting Material The subject matter or content used to justify or clarify any *proposition* that is a *main heading* or *subheading* in a speech. The kinds of content available to the speaker for this purpose are variously named and classified. In this glossary these materials are identified and explained under the following designations: *analogy, audio-visual aids, authority, definition, evidence, example, opinion, quotation, repetition,* and *statistics.*

Syllogism A form or scheme in *logic* by which *deductions* may be so expressed as to test their reliability. The syllogistic form tests whether anything must necessarily follow from two premises assumed to be true, and it permits exploration of the necessary relationship between three and only three ''terms'' or concepts within a single syllogism. Two of several possible variations in syllogistic reasoning are demonstrated by the following syllogisms. All animals have bodies, All men are animals, Therefore all men have bodies (All A have B, All C are A, Therefore all C have B); Every person here speaks English, Some people here are French citizens, Therefore some French citizens speak English (All A have B, Some A are C, Therefore some C have B). In each case the form used allows us to demonstrate that the conclusion is necessarily true if the premises are true. Syllogisms occur rather infrequently in speaking because the things talked about are often so familiar that uttering the three-stage syllogism would seem pedantic and because the deductions we can make about human affairs are so fraught with uncertainties that their conclusions are at best probable, seldom necessary or certain. For these and other reasons, the deductions that occur in speeches are likely to be expressed so that either a premise or the conclusion is omitted but understood. Such rhetorical syllogisms or enthymemes can usually be reconstructed to fit the standard syllogistic form, but they may still demonstrate no necessary conclusions. The following rhetorical syllogisms can be fitted to the same syllogistic structures as the formal syllogisms illustrated above. ''We of the Poets' Guild may share with poets everywhere the assurance that we have experienced insights not known to men in other pursuits''; ''We are Americans, so, of course, we understand the history of our land.'' In each example the first premise is unstated; but even if it were stated and the syllogistic form observed, the conclusion of neither would be necessarily true. One can know only that many poets experience unique insights; it is probable that only some members of the Poets' Guild are true poets. The conclusion is probably true that all Americans understand something about their own history, but their understandings are so varied that the conclusion can be highly reliable or highly unreliable, depending on our interpretation of ''understand.'' Still, this argument can be cast into a technically reliable syllogism. As Aristotle first said, we will find in rhetoric a kind of reasoning that is the ''counterpart'' of the syllogism but seldom a genuine syllogism. This formally incomplete syllogism Aristotle called an enthymeme; others prefer to call it a rhetorical syllogism. See ''Address to the Russian People,'' p. 244, par. 39; ''The

City—A Cause for Statesmanship," p. 222, par. 34. See also *Inclusion-Exclusion.*

Symbol An image or concrete detail that conveys meanings beyond the literal meaning. Thus "night" is used frequently to represent death as well as that period when the sun is down; the cross represents Christianity, the hammer and sickle Communism, green the Irish, and so on. Since these symbols are widely accepted, they are known as conventional symbols. Such symbols are occasionally useful in a speech because they catch attention, make communication easy, are often rich in connotations, and are easily remembered. Sometimes a speaker may use what we might call a private symbol. Such a symbol is one that he invents to help the audience understand and remember his point. Thus a speaker might suggest that an appropriate symbol for his class or club is an armadillo, since the group has such a hard shell that it is impervious to the shafts of truth. (It should be noted that in the broadest sense every word is a symbol; here, however, we are concerned with the symbolism of the images communicated by certain words rather than by words themselves.) Note how Bernstein uses Ivy League clothes, crew cuts,• and horn-rimmed glasses as symbols of the well-bred intellectual in "The World of Jazz," p. 76, par. 43.

Synonym, Definition by See *Definition.*

t

Testimony See *Authority, Credibility, Evidence.*

Topic See *Subject.*

Transition A passage in a speech by means of which two ideas or headings are related so that the listener can move from one to the other easily and without confusion. A transition may vary in length from a few words to entire paragraphs. Note the transitional elements at the beginnings of each paragraph in "Science, Technology, and World Development," pp. 83-87. See also "Apathy," pp. 165, 166, pars. 10, 15; "The Haven of the Defeated," p. 149, par. 8. In "The City—A Cause for Statesmanship," pp. 222-223, pars. 36-38 are transitional, connecting one main heading (need for funds) with the next (need for collaborative planning). In "The Minds of the Non-Western World," pp. 236-240, pars. 10, 13, 26, 34, etc., rhetorical questions are frequently used as transitions between the major ideas. In "Pan-Africanism, the Communists and the West," p. 257, par. 16, a needed transition is lacking.

Triteness See *Cliché.*

Turning the Tables One of the special methods of refutation. Accepting an opponent's premise, but drawing the opposite conclusion. ("You say that since our nation needs many highly trained scientists, we should make it possible for more young people to go to college. I admit we need scientists, but I say that is the very reason why we should severely restrict college attendance, accepting only those students showing the most promise.") See "The Scarcity of Ideas," p. 202, par. 14; "The Novel and the Fairy Tale," p. 55, par. 8. See also *Dilemma.*

u

Understatement A statement that makes less of the truth than the facts will allow. Whereas *overstatement* or exaggeration was especially appealing to Americans in the nineteenth century, understatement is preferred now. *Humor,* especially, is more effective today if it is based on understatement. ("A good speaker must have poise, a pleasing voice, and a forceful delivery. It is also helpful if he has an idea or two.") See "The Scarcity of Ideas," p. 203, par. 24, and p. 204, par. 32. See *Overstatement.*

Unity The cardinal virtue which results from including only those matters in a speech which support its *specific purpose.* Any disregard of the principle of unity—that is, any inclusion of material that does not support the specific purpose—confuses the listener, and thus limits the effectiveness of the speech. "On the Federal Constitution," pp. 272-276, is probably the most tightly unified address in this volume. See *Contiguity.*

v

Variety The cardinal virtue that comes from a vigorous and natural way of speaking. No speaker should work for variety simply for its own sake. The problem is to see that each idea is handled in the most effective way possible. Attention to this principle will automatically result in variety, since ideas normally require different kinds of support, different kinds of sentence structure, different kinds of words, and different kinds of delivery. Monotony not only destroys attention to what is said; it falsifies the material of a speech. While variety as such should not be a direct objective, the worst aspects of monotony can be overcome by conscious effort. Any good speech textbook, or just good common sense, will indicate some of the means by which this can be done.

Vividness The color and brightness a speech acquires as a result of emphasis on such matters as *concreteness* in details and *connotation* in language. See *Animation, Liveliness.*

Vulgarism Broadly, any word or phrase not used in standard English, though the term most frequently is applied to coarse or crude expressions.

y

Yes Response Proceeding through a series of related points and winning agreement upon each in turn to gain the acceptance of some more basic *proposition* which these successive admissions imply. ("Do you want to have the respect of your classmates and instructors? Yes. Do you want to merit the hopes and sacrifices of your parents in sending you to college? Yes. Do you want to get a good job after you have graduated from college? Yes. Then you must study hard day after day.")

This device is most often employed as the approach step or introduction of a persuasive speech to an apathetic or hostile audience, but it is also useful in other rhetorical situations where persuasion must be effected. See also *Common Ground, Induction, Suggestion.*

DATE DUE			
RESERVE Speech - 11-10-66			
Off - Mary - 2-9-67			
OCT 4 73 APR 29 69			
FEB 1 6 1976			
APR 2 9 1988			
AUG 2 6 1996			
JUL 1 6 2001			